PENGUIN

THE NEW INTRODUCING SOCIOLOGY

After war service in East Africa and India, Peter Worsley began his academic career as an anthropologist. He graduated from Cambridge in 1947 and, after working as an educationalist in Africa, took an M.A. (Econ.) at the University of Manchester. He then did fieldwork with Australian Aborigines, for which he received his Ph.D. at the Australian National University in 1954.

He taught sociology for eight years at Hull University and in 1964 became the first Professor of Sociology at the University of Manchester. Since 1982, he has been Professor Emeritus of that University.

Peter Worsley is the author of *The Trumpet Shall Sound* (1957), *The Third World* (1964), *Inside China* (1975), *Marx and Marxism* (1982) and *The Three Worlds* (1984), and has edited and contributed articles and chapters to many other books and journals. The first two editions of *Introducing Sociology* (1970 and 1977) became standard texts and best-sellers.

He was awarded the Curl Bequest Prize of the Royal Anthropological Institute in 1955, and has twice been President of the British Sociological Association. He has lectured and taught at many universities in South and North America.

D0263869

Frank Bechhofer is Director of the [illegible] burgh's Research Centre for the Social S[illegible] of the team that produced the classic *Afflu[illegible]* 1968–9 and has since carried out further s[illegible] of occupations and has written widely on the [illegible] social sciences. He is a past Chairperson of the Bri[illegible]al Association.

Richard Brown is Professor of Sociology at the University of Durham, a past President of the British Sociological Association, and joint author of *The Sociology of Industry* and many other works.

Margot Jefferys is Emeritus Professor of Medical Sociology at the University of London. She is joint author of *Rethinking General Practice* (1983).

Mary McIntosh is Senior Lecturer in Sociology at the University of Essex and a member of the editorial collective of *Feminist Review*. She is author of *The Organization of Crime* (1975) and co-author of *The Anti-Social Family* (1982).

Howard Newby is Professor of Sociology at the University of Essex and Chairman of the Economic and Social Research Council. He is the author of many books and articles on rural and community studies, including *The Deferential Worker* (1977), and was a member of the Essex team which produced *Social Class in Modern Britain* (1989).

John Rex is Research Professor and Associate Director of the Economic and Social Research Council's Centre for Research in Ethnic Relations. His numerous books and articles include *Key Problems of Sociological Theory* (1961) and *Race, Community and Conflict* (1976).

Wesley Sharrock is Reader in Sociology at the University of Manchester and co-author of *Applied Perspectives in Sociology* (1984) and *The Ethnomethodologists* (1985).

Jock Young is Professor of Sociology and Head of the Centre for Criminology at Middlesex University. He is author of *The Drug-Takers* (1971), and co-author of *The New Criminology* (1973) and *What is to be Done About Law and Order?* (1984), and author of the Islington Crime Survey.

Michael Young is Senior Lecturer in Sociology and Coordinator of the Post-16 Education Centre at the University of London's Institute of Education and editor of *Knowledge and Control* (1971).

Peter Worsley

The New Introducing Sociology

FRANK BECHHOFER
RICHARD BROWN
MARGOT JEFFERYS
MARY MCINTOSH
HOWARD NEWBY
JOHN REX
WESLEY SHARROCK
JOCK YOUNG
MICHAEL YOUNG

PENGUIN BOOKS

PENGUIN BOOKS

Published by the Penguin Group
Penguin Books Ltd, 27 Wrights Lane, London W8 5TZ, England
Penguin Books USA Inc., 375 Hudson Street, New York, New York 10014, USA
Penguin Books Australia Ltd, Ringwood, Victoria, Australia
Penguin Books Canada Ltd, 10 Alcorn Avenue, Toronto, Ontario, Canada M4V 3B2
Penguin Books (NZ) Ltd, 182–190 Wairau Road, Auckland 10, New Zealand

Penguin Books Ltd, Registered Offices: Harmondsworth, Middlesex, England

First published as *Introducing Sociology* 1970
Second edition 1977
Third edition, published as *The New Introducing Sociology*, 1987
Revised edition 1992
10 9 8 7 6 5 4 3

The graph on p. 192 and table on p. 193 are Crown copyright (1989 and 1990). They are
reproduced with the permission of the Controller of Her Majesty's Stationery Office.
Thanks are due to Henry Neuburger for locating data used in making the map on pp. 42–3.

Printed in England by Clays Ltd, St Ives plc
Set in Lasercomp Ehrhardt

Contents

Preface

This 1992 edition of *The New Introducing Sociology* has necessitated major revisions of parts of the text first published in 1987. This itself was a completely new and different text from the original *Introducing Sociology* of 1970, which was written by a team of colleagues in the University of Manchester Department of Sociology. We primarily wrote it for our own students, because we were so dissatisfied with the few textbooks that then existed. But Penguin brought it to a much wider audience: within a short time it had become a best-seller and was being used in more than half the universities and colleges teaching degree-level sociology. More surprisingly, we discovered — after only a year — that our students were arriving at university having already used the book at school.

Since then, most of the original team have moved on and are working in other places; several no longer specialize in the subjects they originally wrote about. Society has changed, and so has sociology. New theories have emerged, sometimes taking on almost a 'cult' status, and so fast that one writer has described the rise and fall of new theories as a 'panic culture'. At the same time, a solid body of empirical studies has been built up about the massive social changes of the last two decades.

So for the third edition we assembled a new team of leading authorities in each field. We also expanded the range of issues we deal with to reflect changes and debates on the world around us, within the sociological profession and more widely. We introduced new chapters on sex and gender, race and ethnicity, and crime and deviance. But all the other chapters, too, were completely written anew.

Chapter 1 (Introduction) and Chapter 2 on 'Development' were written by Peter Worsley; Chapter 3, on 'The Research Process', by

Frank Bechhofer; Chapter 4, on 'Sex, Gender and the Family', by
Mary McIntosh; Chapter 5, on 'Education', by Michael Young;
Chapter 6, on 'Health, Illness and Medicine', by Margot Jefferys;
Chapter 7, on 'Community and Urban Life', by Howard Newby;
Chapter 8, on 'Work, Industry and Organizations', by Richard
Brown; Chapter 9, on 'Ethnicity and Race', by John Rex; Chapter
10, on 'Class', by Peter Worsley; Chapter 11, on 'Deviance', by Jock
Young; and Chapter 12, on 'Theoretical Schools', by Wesley
Sharrock.

We have not attempted to emulate the American 'blockbuster'
type of textbook, which covers everything from behaviour within the
womb to the afterlife, nor have we written a textbook which is solely
designed to get people through school examinations. We do address
issues which constitute the bulk of the questions which find their
way into examination papers, but our major purpose has been to
write a book, in clear language, using material that is readily accessible whenever possible, in order to discuss the major issues that
anyone living in a decade when the year 2001 already looms on the
horizon has to confront intellectually since these issues affect the
everyday lives of all of us.

This edition of *The New Introducing Sociology* contains many
changes to the 1987 edition. All the statements about social trends,
including tables, figures and diagrams, have been updated throughout
(especially in Chapter 6, 'Health, Illness and Medicine') wherever
information is available. We have also taken new publications into
account. Only a few of the more theoretical chapters, which discuss
schools of thought which are relatively 'timeless', remain unchanged.
In Chapter 2 there is a new section on 'The New International
Division of Labour'.

PETER WORSLEY
Hackney, 1991

1   Introduction

Sociology is a very new subject. Thirty years ago there were only 400 members of the British Sociological Association. Today, there are four times that number. In 1950, only six universities offered sociology degrees and there was only one large centre, the London School of Economics. Today, nearly a quarter of a million people have passed their Advanced level sociology exams; since 1989, the number of students specializing in sociology at university has increased by a third, and in polytechnics one and a half times. In England, where 30,000 people took sociology at 'A' level in 1989, it is the second most popular 'A' level subject after English. In the USA, 15,000 people teach the subject in universities and colleges, five times the number of thirty years ago, and a further 4,000 graduates are employed in professional capacities outside such institutions.

Yet this success story does not mean that sociology is universally popular. In the late 1960s, it was blamed for causing student unrest. It was thought to attract radical teachers and students: people like the villain of the popular novel and TV serial *The History Man*, with a built-in drive to destructive criticism of social institutions rather than any interest in making them work. The hostility was often extreme: sociology, the Director of a London polytechnic observed, 'is in about the condition chemistry was in when it was called alchemy' (*Guardian*, 30.8.75). Open University courses, it was alleged, exhibited Marxist bias. By 1981, a *Daily Telegraph* editorial was arguing that 'a 10 per cent cut would concentrate the minds of sociologists wonderfully' and that 'the expansion of the universities in the past twenty-five years was mostly a mistake' (Eldridge, 1981, p. 5). What was needed, instead, were disciplines which would directly contribute to raising GNP. With the economic crisis of the late 1970s, these criticisms were converted into political practice.

The major source of social science research funding, the Social Science Research Council, was renamed the Economic and Social Research Council: economics now had precedence. The social sciences, many argued, were not 'sciences', only 'studies'. The new ESRC was no longer organized by disciplines but according to areas of public policy: today, Human Behaviour and Development; Industry, Economy and Environment; Society and Politics; and the Research Resources Advisory Group.

This reorganization is based on the assumption that the social sciences, sociology included, are valuable in the formulation of public policy. Radical critics, indeed, have argued that sociology is too much a tool of the ruling class, as the title of one work, *Marxism versus Sociology* implies (Shaw, 1974).

Social science, in fact, has never been simply classifiable as either Left or Right 'in itself'. It has served different interests, and will no doubt continue to do so. It is, however, intrinsically a critical activity to the extent that it involves asking questions about the state of society, about the forces that keep particular institutions going and which preserve the social order as a whole, about the causes of change, and about the ways people try to make sense of the world they live in.

For ordinary citizens and not only specialists are concerned with the ways in which their lives are affected by what is happening in society generally. Often, what starts them thinking is some particular personal problem – losing one's job, divorce, leaving school to enter unemployment. But these are things that obviously happen to millions of others, too. So they now begin to see that their private troubles are also public issues; they develop what C. Wright Mills called the 'sociological imagination' (Mills, 1959).

Popular thinking about society is thus informed by theory: theories about human nature, about justice, about the roles of men and women, about the need for change or about the impossibility of radical change, even about what happens after death:

Although often uncomfortable with their role, men certainly see themselves as 'top dog', and most want to keep it that way. This was justified more often than not by the theory that nature has made man the strong one, the hunter, the fighter and protector, and any change in this system would overthrow a natural and desirable balance. Many men were fixed on the idea that women are different because they have periods and babies. So, as there was no changing that, there was no point in trying to change anything else, either (Ford, 1985, p. 285).

But people do not invent these bodies of theory themselves: they find them ready-made in the culture in which they are brought up. Some of these ideas are acquired via formal *education* in special institutions – schools and colleges – where they are taught by people who specialize in teaching. But this is only one part of the much wider process of *socialization* through which we acquire ideas and values through our involvement with other people in institutions that are not specifically educational in purpose at all. We learn about life in factories, in disco clubs and in pubs, on holiday and on the street, as well as in churches and schools. The behaviour we learn outside school, too, may be quite at odds with what we are taught inside it. Many pupils regard the knowledge they are presented with in school as useless and reject the teachers' values as well.

In all of this sociology has only a limited importance. Indeed, the world got on without social science altogether for most of recorded history (just as it got on without chemistry and biology). The specialists who supplied ideas about society and the meaning of human existence were mainly philosophers and theologians, the former working from basic principles of reasoning, the latter from divine revelation. But the idea of actually going out to look at how people lived in reality, and at what they thought, and to do so in the light of some systematic theory which could be tested, did not take hold until the nineteenth century. These principles – of empirical research and of systematic theorizing – were borrowed from the natural sciences, which had themselves encountered their strongest opposition precisely where they touched on matters relating to the human species and to human society, in the form of religious opposition to Darwin's theory of evolution (Bock, 1979).

Science triumphed in the end, not only in theoretical battles, but because of its spectacular practical achievements in engineering and in harnessing power to human purposes. These triumphs, however, left millions of people in poverty and ignorance. So what was needed to overcome them, it seemed, was the application of scientific method, now, to the study of society.

Founding Fathers

The Frenchman who coined the term 'sociology', Auguste Comte (1798–1857), was, significantly, no radical. (He called the great liberal thinkers of the Enlightenment who had inspired the French Revolution *docteurs en guillotine*.) His own general philosophy he called 'positivism': the use of scientific knowledge in order to predict the likely results of different policies so that we would be able to choose the best one – *savoir pour prévoir, prévoir pour pouvoir*, as he put it. And what he chose was not progress in the sense of constant innovation, but order and authority, with intellectuals like himself as the high priests (Nisbet, 1979).

His contemporary Frederick Le Play (1806–82), though equally conservative, tried to provide a more solid factual basis for his theories with a massive study of the lives of workers and their families in different European countries (in which he pioneered the use of family budgets). In Britain, the first detailed study of the lives of ordinary people was written by a journalist, Henry Mayhew (1812–87), not about workers in factories, but about the far more wretched hundreds of thousands who made their living on the streets of London selling food, pets, needles, coal, toys, their bodies, and a thousand and one other things; the street entertainers; or the boys who collected night-soil, horse-dung, cigar-butts and household refuse (Mayhew, 1949), in some cases competing with the rats in the sewers.

Though Mayhew was a great quantifier (he carefully worked out the volume of horse-dung and of cigar-butts found in the street), most of his writing was almost pure description, or 'ethnography', using only the very simplest of classifications of all those innumerable occupations into street-sellers, street-buyers, street-finders, performers, artisans and pedlars, and labourers. When he did draw more general conclusions, it was not by way of more sophisticated analysis, but by crusading on behalf of this neglected 'underclass'.

But there was another strand, too, in early British sociology, namely, the transformation of Darwin's theory about the successive stages of development and about progress in general in Nature into 'Social' Darwinism: the doctrine popularly known as the 'survival of the fittest' – that if the poor were poor, it was due to their own shortcomings, since Nature had endowed them with poor physique or weak intelligence. A slightly more social version emphasized their lack of energy, of will-power, of mental acuity, or the lack of rational scientific attitudes or of religious 'ethics' which would stimulate the individual to work hard, to innovate and to be enterprising. What was needed, extremists like the 'eugenicists' advocated, was to encourage only the better-equipped to reproduce themselves and to discourage the poor from breeding.

Liberals could not stomach such views. Poor physique, they argued, was the result of poor food and poor housing. Under such depressing conditions, it was not surprising that people lacked drive, and as long as they remained illiterate they would have no chance of better jobs, however hard-working or bright they might be.

Some liberal theorists developed these arguments in the privacy of their own studies. Others, notably philanthropic men of business, more familiar with the world of work and dissatisfied with abstract argument, concluded that what was needed was 'social arithmetic': the accumulation of masses of data specially collected through large-scale surveys and presented in quantitative form, notably Charles Booth's massive study of the poor in London at the turn of the century and B. S. Rowntree's similar study in York.

What was at issue, then as now, was not just the extent of poverty, but its causes. It was therefore not just a question of what the facts were, but a moral debate about causes and about the *meaning* of the facts, liberals and radicals tending to blame social conditions, conservatives the shortcomings of the individual.

In his study, Rowntree concluded that a third of the population was living in poverty, most of which was due to an absolute shortage of the means of life, but part ('secondary' poverty) to the bad management of what little resources the poor did have.

Similar schools and similar debates emerged in the USA at the same period: Social Darwinists like W. G. Sumner (1840–1910) argued that nothing should be done to interfere with natural processes through which the strong and the industrious would come out on top; while reformers like Lester Ward (1841–1913) argued that analogies with animal society were misleading since human society was different in kind, a *higher* form of life than animal society and therefore not subject to natural laws, because it was an artificial creation, under human control and direction. The key difference was that human beings were endowed with the capacity to reason.

This had been, of course, a classical theme of pre-Revolutionary Enlightenment writers in France. That Revolution, and subsequent revolutions and counter-revolutions in France, concentrated the attention of later thinkers on to the question of *solidarity*: what was it that held society together? In his earlier writings, Emile Durkheim (1858–1917) tended to emphasize that the decisive 'social facts' were objective factors: the size or the density of the population. But in his later work, it was the ideas people carried round inside their heads: the basic values and the norms, the social rules they followed, that seemed far more important. Society, however, was a collectivity, not just a heap of individuals: it was a *system*, whose component parts were *institutions*. Where the parts failed to mesh together, or where common values (the 'collective consciousness') were not strong enough to override divisions, society broke down: it became 'pathological'.

These themes, re-labelled 'functionalism' (though mixed with ideas taken from other theorists), were given their most powerful expression in the sociology of Talcott Parsons (1902–79), which dominated American theoretical sociology in the decades before and after the Second World War. The anthropological functionalism of A. R. Radcliffe-Brown (1881–1955) and Bronislaw Malinowski (1884–1942) drew more directly from Durkheim, and swept all before it. Hitherto, anthropologists had explained customs like the mother-in-law taboo (dimly reflected in our own mother-in-law jokes) in evolutionist terms, as survivals from earlier times (in which, some even believed, women had dominated society). Now, they were explained in terms of their *contemporary* 'function'. Mothers-in-law were of special importance because they were the closest female relative of one's spouse in the parental generation of the social group a person married into – and yet, given the assumed social inferiority of women, were of ambiguous status: important, but not as important as males were. So impressive seemed the functionalist achievement in showing that these customs were not irrational, and that societies some thought to be mere savagery and others chaotic were in fact highly regulated societies with complex and coherent systems of ideas, that many years were to pass before some anthropologists began to protest that even in the simplest societies individuals and groups bent the rules to suit their own interests or appealed to different rules. In more complex societies, researchers found strict functionalist theory more obviously questionable. In Europe, theorists from Machiavelli (1469–1527) to Karl Marx (1818–83) had long recognized that the power of ruling classes did not depend solely on force of arms but on the exercise of ideological 'hegemony' too: on persuasion. But exploited classes had their own counter-ideologies. In the case of the major exploited class under capitalism, the working class, this was socialism, together with institutions created in order to resist the power of the ruling class: trade unions, cooperatives, and political parties. Progress consisted, not in using social science in order to paper over the deep divisions of class society, but in using it to destroy class society and to replace it by a society in which everybody could participate in making decisions in every area of life.

Modern Times

Marx's ideas took root among both the working class and the intelligentsia in Germany, and later in the Third World. But not in Britain, or in the USA, where functionalism emerged as the main academic theory of society as a whole. The alternatives to functionalism that emerged in the USA were much less *societal*, less concerned with society as a totality and more with the individual and the local community. One line of thought grew out of the philosophy of George Herbert Mead (1863–1931), who argued that what we usually think of as the individual person is better thought of as a complex Self, because we are all highly skilled actors who play many different roles in life: we behave differently towards the people who are important to us – the people he called 'significant others' – in different ways in different situations. We try to size them up, to interpret their behaviour and their likely behaviour, and we try to estimate the effects of our behaviour on them. Our own behaviour itself is an object of scrutiny, a Me, to the I which does the scrutinizing. The Self, then, is both plural and social (Strauss, 1964). It was a theme which had been emphasized in the sociology of Max Weber (1864–1920) that had grown out of German idealist philosophy, and which now influenced many pioneer American social scientists. To understand human behaviour, Mead insisted, we had to understand what later American sociologists called 'the meaning of the action to the actor'. Sociology, that is, could not be purely objective, because human behaviour was always informed by subjective things: ideas, values, beliefs, purposes, etc. Ideas, as W. I. Thomas (1863–1947) later remarked, were as 'real in their consequences' as wage-packets or malnutrition, for it was people's ideas about whether their wages were 'reasonable' or not that determined their social responses – militancy, passivity or contentment. In social life, then, there was always a dialectic, an interplay, between the objective and the subjective. Ideas, in this sense, are quite as objective as bullets or crankshafts, though they are not material. Hence social changes which can even come about independently of individual awareness of them – such as the consequences of a growing population or of technological innovation, the effects of smaller families or of concentrating large numbers of workers in factories – do obtrude upon our consciousness eventually so that we have to come to terms with them. The interpretations we make – the ways in which we construct versions of reality for ourselves – may be accurate or they may be total fantasies, but they all influence the way we act. Thus prophecies that the world is going to come to an end actually induce people to throw all their money away – the prophecy is a 'self-fulfilling' one (Worsley, 1968).

Because of this subjective component, Weber preferred the term 'social action' to 'behaviour', which sounded rather biological. We are, he recognized, animals, and we behave as animals do: a loud explosion startles us, so we jump out of our skins. But in the front line there are officers present to make sure we don't give in to our instinctive reflexes and run away. Ideals of bravery instilled into us also induce us to try to control our panic. In less threatening situations, like competing for the favours of a girlfriend, men try to look tough and confident, even when they don't feel it, not because there's an officer standing over them with a pistol in his hand, but because that's the macho norm they've been socialized into.

To play all our different roles we do not learn a part written out like the text of a play: instead we learn a set of rules which range from very general principles (values) to the quite specific norms of behaviour expected of a parent, a student, a patient in a hospital, or whatever. The kind of language we use, the dress we wear, the way we behave at work or at parties, are all symbolic statements of the kind of person we see ourselves as being and of the kind of groups we identify with, say as young rebels or sober citizens. On ritual occasions, more formal and coherent symbolic statements are made about society in general through public rituals like a coronation and on private occasions such as birthdays and funerals. All these codes of manners, taken together, constitute the way of life, in ideal form at least, the *culture* of an entire society. Without such symbols, the world would be too complicated and chaotic for us to know how to behave and what other people's behaviour means.

Whereas functionalists had assumed that social life was ordered according to shared ideals and ideas, the more radical Chicago sociologists who developed this newer approach and who called themselves 'symbolic interactionists' concentrated on the values and behaviour of particular social groups, not society as a whole. They used these theoretical insights to make sense of the kaleidoscopic variety of a city that had grown, like Third World cities today, from a mere 30,000 in 1850 to over $1\frac{1}{2}$ million only fifty years later. Many of these people were recent immigrants from Italy, Russia, Scandinavia, Ireland and from the eastern seaboard or Blacks from the rural South. Just how they lived nobody except themselves really knew. To Robert Park, reporter turned sociologist, this was a goldmine, a natural laboratory. In a magnificent series of studies, he and his disciples launched into areas academics had never previously penetrated: into slums and dance-halls, where they studied youth-gangs, as well as studying the life of the rich in the more salubrious parts of the city.

One outstanding feature of Chicago as a city was its segmentation into ethnic areas. So where European sociologists had been obsessed with class, Chicago sociologists had to deal with people who were poor, but who were also living in 'ghettos', where they had only minimal contact with people from other ethnic groups and where vast numbers didn't even speak the national language.

They saw the relevant unit of analysis, therefore, not as the society as a whole, but the local community and the small groups of many kinds of which it was composed. Some of these groups – youth-gangs or outcast communities of tramps – were regarded by respectable society as constituting an 'underworld', a disorganized jungle inhabited by people lacking in social consciousness. But the sociologists found instead that these groups were highly cohesive, with distinctive codes of loyalty and elaborate patterns of mutual aid. Though respectable society wrote them off as 'deviant', they rewarded behaviour that conformed to their own ideals and punished those who deviated from them.

So it was not the institution of the orthodox WASP (White Anglo-Saxon Protestant) 'American' nuclear family of two parents and their offspring, with its ideals of achievement through individual effort and Puritan self-control, that they encountered so much as the use by immigrants of any kinship connections they had to help them find jobs, housing and recreation, to develop friendships or to find marriage partners. Some of them had no family or kin. But they came from cultures in which the family had always been an 'extended', multi-generational family, including, often under one roof, in-laws, the widowed and the dependent, and with elaborate local networks of kinship between families. Many of the immigrants' new institutions, from benevolent associations to criminal organizations like the Mafia, therefore used the idiom of family and kinship, too, as everyone who has seen the film *The Godfather* knows, and developed an elaborate code of honour based on Sicilian family ideals for new, illegal purposes.

The concepts developed in these studies – of group identity and group membership built up through face-to-face interaction; of subculture; of behaviour as guided by norms acquired through group membership – were then extended to the study of all kinds of small groups from jazz musicians to hospital patients. Victims of serious illnesses, for instance, find themselves transformed into 'patients', and have then to pass through a series of stages before they are permitted to resume their normal social identity and activities (Roth, 1963). Goffman's description of institutions like hospitals – where 'all aspects of life are conducted in the same place and under the same single authority . . . in the company of a large batch of others . . . at prearranged times' and coordinated by a hierarchy of officials – as 'total' institutions seemed illuminating (Goffman, 1961). So did his comparison of hospitals with ships. But his further comparison of hospital life with life in prisons and even concentration camps was intended to shock, and did.

Such analogies, and the use of the same analytical categories in studying these very different institutions, tended to break down the comfortable assumption that there is an absolute difference *in kind* between normal and deviant behaviour, between respectable behaviour and that of people like Howard Becker's marijuana-users

(Becker, 1963). It was the process of *becoming* a marijuana-user that Becker focused on, since for the majority this was not a sub-cultural community they were born into, but a set of behaviours they had learned as adults. So deviance, every bit as much as accountancy or being processed through a hospital, could be seen as a 'career', with defined stages.

Far from being naturally inclined to unorthodoxy, let alone criminality, deviants were usually initially little different from most people, who, though largely conforming, do commit some acts – sometimes on odd occasions, sometimes more regularly – which are frowned upon by conventional society or even punishable by law. Most of these acts go unobserved and unpunished, but where they are brought to public attention, the deviant is now openly stigmatized as a deviant. The probability of being pushed into closer interaction with habitual breakers of the law is thereby increased, since people seek or are offered support and protection from other rule-breakers; in the extreme, they are forced into their company in prisons, where they are intensively educated through exposure to a whole variety of deviant sub-cultures. In this milieu, deviance gets 'amplified'; the deviant has now reached the second stage in his or her career and become part of an established deviant sub-cultural world: the opposite of what was intended by those who punish deviations from orthodoxy.

This kind of deviancy theory clearly contains a radical critique of both public policy towards law-breakers and of the kinds of explanation hitherto offered by traditional criminology. But it was pushed in even more radical directions by those who questioned the very labels 'crime' and 'punishment'. Much of what gets defined as crime, 'labelling' theorists argued, changes over time. We no longer hang, maim or exile people for stealing a loaf of bread or a sheep. But offences against property still constitute a large part of all cases brought before the courts. Offences involving relatively minor amounts of property arouse great indignation, even on the part of the poor, since they are the usual victims, especially where physical violence is used or threatened. Crimes which affect vast numbers of people, but which are committed by the rich and the powerful, on the other hand – financial malpractices, income tax evasion, the marketing of dangerous substances, accidents due to unsafe working conditions are either 'invisible' or defined by many as not being 'real' crime at all. Thus speeding is regarded as almost a sporting activity (recently, a member of the Royal Family has been 'caught') by many drivers, even though thousands of people are killed and many more maimed every year. Behaviour which does not involve property or violence, however, can provoke equally furious outrage where conflicting ideas about what constitutes acceptable behaviour are concerned, notably the rage generated by different 'presentations of the Self', such as the styles of dress, of hairdo and of music enjoyed by some of the young, such as punk enthusiasts. It can even provoke what Stan Cohen, in a study of the Mods and Rockers riots of the early 1960s, called 'moral panics' (Cohen, 1972), since the very identities of Mod and Rocker were largely built up, and the extent of their activities exaggerated out of all proportion by the media.

Running through all these studies is a general philosophical theme: that behaviour that is acceptable or even required in some social circles may horrify outsiders. Hence it has been said that deviancy is 'not a quality inherent in certain acts', not anti-social *in itself*. It only becomes so when people define it as such, in the light of social values they hold dear. Killing can be rewarded with medals if you kill the right people at the right time, while behaviour that many of us would think offensive, even as grounded in 'human nature' or in biology, is required behaviour in certain cultures and situations. Thus in some cultures cannibalism – eating part of the corpse of a dead relative – is a profoundly religious and compassionate act. Equally, it might seem natural to seek to avoid pain and search for pleasure, but masochists find their pleasures in pain, as do religious ascetics who express their commitment to God by mortifying the flesh. More trivially, people who would be scandalized were anyone to see them with no clothes on in a hotel corridor will strip everything off on fashionable nude bathing beaches.

Some radical theorists therefore argue that labelling any behaviour as deviant is simply imposing outsiders' categories on the behaviour of members of sub-cultures to whom respectable behaviour is just as unacceptable: 'square' behaviour. Pushed to its logical conclusion, this argument leads to complete relativism: the view that good and bad are not so much arbitrary categories, but that they merely reflect the outlook of one sectional, usually powerful, interest-group or another. It is a view which conflates mildly deviant behaviour which evokes no great public opposition, like pot-smoking, with such serious acts as murder. Few are convinced by this logic.

It was an approach very far removed from older conceptions of the ways in which society determines behaviour. To Durkheim, for instance, the three main characteristics of 'social facts', from formal codes of law to informal codes of etiquette, were that they were *external* to the individual, not something individuals chose or invented themselves; secondly, they were *collective* – they applied to the behaviour of whole sets of people, sometimes to the behaviour of everyone in a given society; thirdly, they were *coercive*: they constrained people; conformity was backed by positive sanctions, rewards; non-conformity (deviance) by negative sanctions, punishments.

Now the accent had shifted to the other term in the phrase 'social action': to 'action'. Where Durkheim had seen individual behaviour as being determined by inflexible norms, usually at the level of society-as-a-whole, symbolic interactionists showed individuals rejecting norms, selecting from various possibilities, some choosing deviant forms of behaviour, with the small group and the sub-culture as the main sources of models of how to behave rather than society at large. If the values of these groups were often at variance with those of official, respectable society, in reality even these latter were only a part of society, a sub-culture themselves, however much they might claim to speak for society as a whole. Since society was composed in reality of many such component sub-cultures, people often found they had to choose which model of behaviour they would conform to. But it was still conformity – even revolutionaries chose 'alternative' forms of personal as well as political life precisely because they were the opposite of the established order. They were not absolutely free.

For symbolic interactionists, people were not as determined by their social origins or upbringing as early role-theorists had believed them to be. To think of social roles simply as equivalents of roles in a play is misleading, despite the parallels. The role of Hamlet is written down, once and for all, in words on paper, even if Olivier does interpret the part differently from Gielgud. But social roles are much more open-ended. In addition to being able to interpret them differently, we have to meet very different expectations from different significant others. Like stage-actors, we can sometimes reject roles, refuse to play them. But, unlike stage actors, we can also create new ones: we can innovate or rebel. Even where the range of options is limited, and even where we conform more closely to what is available, considerable degrees of latitude are possible. Even in the simplest society, there are people who are bad parents, poor providers and unfaithful spouses; there are deviants, even rebels, who are sceptical about even the most sacred religious ideas and practices; there are entrepreneurs like the 'big men' of Melanesia who have no hereditary authority, as chiefs do, but who build up political followings by mobilizing kinsmen, neighbours, etc, through elaborate exchanges of goods and services.

In modern society, there is far less consensus about what it means to be a 'good' parent, since the conventional nuclear family, with the father as its head and breadwinner is now only a minority phenomenon, as we will see in Chapter 4. There is even less agreement about the best way of bringing up children. So since roles have become more ambiguous, everyone is forced to think critically about them and to choose.

Because of this open-endedness, by the 1970s a new school of researchers who called themselves ethnomethodologists were arguing that sociologists were engaged in a scientifically indefensible activity: imposing their own interpretations of people's motives, or simply ignoring them altogether, or assigning 'causes' to behaviour that were not present in the consciousness of the actors themselves (such as arguing that attitudes towards Blacks or towards higher education were attributable to one's social class background). If we really want to know why people behave as they do, they argued, we should find out what specific ideas were actually in their heads when, say, they chose to leave school as early as possible or to live with a partner rather than get married. People did not simply get swept along by social currents, like plankton in a social sea, they argued: they act in the ways they do because they have certain purposes, ends and values, in the light of which they act one way or another. Statistical generalizations about populations pay no attention to this variety of ideas; they merely examine the end-product – behaviour – as so many acts, with no consideration of what actually moved each of the actors. To find that out requires a new kind of precise and detailed in-depth research: observing people in the very process of thinking-and-acting, often using new techniques – video cameras or tape-recordings of real-life situations, from conversations to court proceedings – instead of artificial interviews controlled by sociologists or collecting information about people's backgrounds rather than observing the process of action. And to them, symbolic interactionists had merely replaced the tyranny of Society with a capital S by the tyranny of the small group and the sub-culture.

The emphasis had now shifted from the small group to the situation, and from group norms to the individual's manipulation of norms and situations.

At this point, howls of frustration arose from those they criticized. Social behaviour, it was objected, *does* exhibit regularities; it is not purely random and individual, though where the nineteenth century talked of 'laws' of social life as if they always applied absolutely and determined the behaviour of every individual (rather as if individuals were mindless atoms), in modern conceptions of scientific laws, even in the natural sciences, they are thought of as statistical probabilities rather than as absolutes. Behaviour is not random, indeed, even for the individual except in cases of psychiatric breakdown. And these regularities are associated with yet other regularities: older people do tend to become more conservative, women to be more religious than men, and so on. These things need explaining, and cannot be explained solely in terms of situations or of the internal dynamics of small groups. Larger social units such as nations, societies, cultures, institutions from marriage-rules to trade unions, simply seemed to be missing from this kind of analysis. And though there is indeed always some room for individual manoeuvre, manipulation, and choice – you can even choose to throw yourself on the electrified wire in a concentration camp – the range of options is sometimes very narrow indeed and all of them equally unattractive. The constraints we all experience in everyday life are the results of decisions taken by people who have power which affects large numbers of people with the same social characteristics – as women or men, as members of the less-privileged social classes, ethnic groups or religious communities. Most choices, too, even the most individualistic ones, are between alternatives which are themselves well-established cultural conventions – long hair, skinhead crops, bald pates, Mohican hairdos, are recognized forms of challenge to short-back-and-sides. Individualism itself is in any case a cultural value, for many cultures do not think the expression of individual personality all that important, or even to be a bad thing, whereas in the USA what has been called the 'Me society' and what Lasch calls the 'culture of narcissism' pervades everything, from the respectable accumulation of private wealth and symbols of personal status to the deviant individualism of the *avant-garde*, the Bohemian, the trendy, the arty, the maverick, the hippie, and the ego-tripper (Lasch, 1980).

Ethnomethodologists, who have done some of the best work exposing the unspoken conventions which govern the taking of turns in conversations, have now been accused of failing to examine how those rules are generated in the first place and how they are institutionalized, learned and passed on.

To defenders of older theories, both symbolic interactionists and ethnomethodologists were equally devoid of any theory of society as a whole. For functionalists, society was a system between whose parts there had to be some degree of fit. Thus Davis and Moore, writing in the 1940s, had argued that the function of the educational system was to select a talented minority for positions of authority in business and public office. The untalented majority did not require such extended education and could be allowed to leave full-time education earlier. In order to induce the talented minority to 'defer gratifications' – to put up with low student grants or parental allowances or loans to work their way through college, while their peers were earning more at work and could afford to get married – they had to be compensated retrospectively by paying them higher salaries when they finally did enter the labour-market (Davis and Moore, 1969).

Radical critics often had no objection to the notion that selection and inequality were inevitable in modern society. But the rest of the argument, they said, was simply a defence of privilege. The reason why middle- and upper-class children took most of the places, even in open competition, in prestigious universities, was not that they were naturally more talented, but that they came from homes where they were strongly encouraged to work and pass examinations by parents who themselves knew how to jump the hurdles of the educational competitive race, who could afford to pay for better teaching and to provide good conditions for study and for the general stimulation of intellectual curiosity. And the amount they would earn in their subsequent careers was far in excess of anything that could have been earned by their working-class peers during the brief time they were in college (Tumin, 1969). Were they given equality of opportunity, the natural talents of children from under-privileged homes would flourish also.

This kind of radical critique seemed feeble to socialists, who saw capitalist society as inherently inegalitarian not just because it was loaded against the working class, but as inegalitarian *whoever* came out top in the rat race, a state of affairs that could only be partly changed by reforming the educational system. Children from underprivileged homes – such as those in which English was not spoken – needed compensatory education, *extra* assistance, not merely equal access to the same lessons. Blacks in the USA and feminists demanded 'affirmative action': the reservation of valued jobs for disadvantaged minorities, and, in the event of equal qualification, preference for members of such minorities. Otherwise, the great majority would get beaten in open competition.

Marxists went further. People would only be able to compete on equal terms when they were socially equal; when there were no rich and no poor. Sociologists in socialist Poland raised the question as to why jobs which were inherently interesting should be even further privileged by giving those who do them high status and high income (Weselowski and Krauze, 1981). For these things need not go together. People who do dirty, boring, hard, repetitive, even danger-ous work could be given higher wages and greater social honours for doing such jobs; interesting managerial or academic posts and posi-tions of power were rewarding in ways which made it unnecessary to give people high salaries in order to attract people into them.

Marxists have been equally critical of deviance theory. Where people talk about some acts getting labelled as right and proper and others as improper, Marxists insist that much more is involved than purely verbal, intellectual or moral definitions, for we are talking about *power*: the power to prescribe some kinds of behaviour and to proscribe others, about forbidding and rewarding. So we should study how power is actually exercised by the specialists – the legislators, policemen, judges, lawyers, probation officers, warders – who theoretically act on behalf of the community, for these 'gatekeep-ers', in reality, have a great deal of latitude, as to whether to proceed with a prosecution or not, for instance. And from there, the critics argue, we need to go on to trace out the connections between the law and the class structure of society – the social origins and connections of MPs and judges, and the values they hold, the social distribution of crime, and the kinds of interests the law protects. Marxism today, however, has gone far beyond the narrow 'economic determinism' of the 1930s, which concentrated mainly on political and economic structures. Today, as we will see, though Marxism became a distorted State ideology in Eastern Europe, Marxists have made important contributions to the study of literature and aesthetics, social welfare, urban policy, the family, deviance theory, the study of the mass media, indeed, most major areas of social life, while its social importance as the major revolutionary ideology of the twentieth century is far greater than its importance as a mode of sociological theorizing.

Doing Sociology

By now, we have come a long way from social arithmetic and poverty surveys, and we have only discussed some of the major schools of sociology. All of these traditions, however, are still alive and kicking. Sociology, that is, has no single dominant orthodoxy or intellectual 'paradigm', or even style of research.

Survey research, for instance, has taken on a new lease of life with the advent of the computer which makes possible the processing and even the mathematical analysis of vast masses of data in ways which have hitherto been too costly or technically impossible. Instead of displacing older theories, however, new schools exist side by side with them. Some of these schools are associated with particular areas of social life: Marxists tend to concentrate on society-wide economic and political institutions; symbolic interactionists on deviance and small-group studies. Each, therefore, has its strengths and weaknesses, though partisans of these various schools assert that theirs is the only coherent or valid way of looking at things and pour scorn on their rivals. Most sociologists, like most people in everyday life, take whatever bits from these systems they find useful. But they do try to weld them together to form a coherent body of theory. If they did not, they would rightly be accused of being eclectic, lacking in intellectual rigour. They also refuse to take for granted the common sense which is regarded by most people as self-evident and unproblematic (even though the patent contradictions of folk wisdom are embodied in people's ability to argue – at the same time – that 'absence makes the heart grow fonder', but 'out of sight' means 'out of mind').

Many critics of sociology have probably never read serious work by modern researchers and most are certainly ignorant of the wide diversity of kinds of sociology we have discussed. Those who accuse it of being unscientific usually have a rather rigid and limited conception of what constitutes science, usually drawn from laboratory-based experimental research in the natural sciences (a model which excludes, for instance, much natural science from astronomy to medicine and even work such as Darwin's). Sociologists are rarely able to artificially contrive experimental situations; we cannot make people change their jobs just to see what happens – though in one study students were sent home and told to behave like strangers towards their parents, who suffered severely because deeply held but rarely questioned assumptions about the ways children should normally behave were disrupted (Garfinkel, 1967, pp. 49–53).

The aim of research, despite these limitations, is still to explain how society works and how, despite differences of interest and outlook between various social groups, order comes about or is achieved. These issues can be tackled in a variety of ways, using very different methods and techniques discussed in Chapter 3, ranging from statistical correlations involving resemblances and differences – between persons with similar social characteristics but who differ in another attribute, or comparisons between people in different situations or in different societies – to in-depth techniques such as the life-history, the extended interview, or the case study. The characteristics chosen or the individuals selected in a sample survey, however, will be determined by the nature of the questions the sociologist is trying to answer and the framework of analysis adopted; they are not something that simply exists 'out there', 'in the facts', in the particular piece of social reality being examined. Some social facts are selected, others excluded, in scientific analysis. Reports based on casual talking to the people one simply runs across may be vivid but we have no way of knowing whether these people are typical of some wider category or not.

Sociologists, further, are perfectly willing to accept that there are indeed fundamental differences involved in studying human beings as against studying rocks, amoebae or gorillas. Indeed, these differences mark off the social from the natural sciences. Firstly, rocks do not possess consciousness: do not feel, think, make judgements or choices. For human beings, rocks may have no meaning at all if they are irrelevant to our purposes: we may see them, but we do not necessarily perceive them as significant; they do not become part of our consciousness. If they do, it is because they are relevant to our interests. Yet different people have different kinds of interests. The positivistic conception of research as the gathering and marshalling of facts which 'speak for themselves' is still a popular one – though most people will take what the papers say with a pinch of salt, since different newspapers use the same facts to draw different conclusions, or use entirely different sets of facts. But the facts themselves do not speak: people interpret them, using frameworks within which facts are slotted to make sense of certain kinds of facts only – which they have decided in advance are likely to be the relevant ones. They therefore select these out of the welter of reality for special attention. For this reason, it has been said that instead of talking of 'data' – literally things 'given' to our observation – we should use the term 'capta' – things we take out of reality.

What we see, then, is a function of our interests and values in the first place. To a farmer, rocks in a field are a nuisance; they need removing because they get in the way of the tractor. But an artist will see them as a pattern of tonal values; a geologist as evidence of the process of evolution; a religious person as evidence of God's handiwork. Human behaviour, then, cannot be adequately understood without reference to the ideas – the beliefs, norms, values, concepts, purposes – that inform it. Secondly, though each person is a distinct individual and no two persons are exactly alike, these differences of personality are by no means solely attributable to differences in our physical genetic endowment – the way our hormones work or the adrenalin we secrete and release. We are also individuals because no two people are ever exposed to exactly the same set of social experiences. Even identical twins lead different lives: marry different partners, do different jobs, etc. Thirdly, human society is not exclusively or even predominantly determined by the inherited instincts that drive birds to build nests or ants to play specialized parts in an elaborate division of labour. Our social roles are guided by norms of behaviour built into our culture rather than our genes, and they have to be learned. The idea, in any case, that we can clearly distinguish the biological element in behaviour from the culturally determined is an illusion. The effects of society begin not with the emergence of the child from the womb, but while the mother is still carrying it. Your sex may be determined by your genes, then, but gender is a social product. As Simone de Beauvoir provocatively put it: 'One is not born, but rather becomes a woman' (de Beauvoir, 1972, p. 9). Fourthly, human society takes many different forms, and societies change over time, often rapidly, not because our biology has changed, but because our culture changes. We are capable of inventing and learning new forms of behaviour.

Cultures change because human beings have the capacity, both as individuals and by pooling their resources, to think about Nature, to reflect on themselves and their social institutions, even to think about the way they think, and because these changes of ideas get translated into new ways of organizing our relations with one another.

Criticality is therefore not something that is monopolized by social scientists. People use their intelligence in their relations with others every minute of the day, and they use it, too, when other people do social research on them, from Press and TV reporters and market-researchers and opinion-poll testers to sociological interviewers. Of course, they can be wrong, too, and not all theories are equal:

People . . . have ideas of their own about how and why other people in general behave. They thus have a standard rejoinder with which they can confront any proposition advanced by a sociologist: if they agree with it, it is obvious; if they disagree with it, it is wrong. [In his Second World War study] of *The American Soldier*, Lazarsfeld lists a number of conclusions which . . . most people would dismiss as obvious . . . : that better educated men showed more psychoneurotic symptoms during training, that Southerners stood up better to tropical climate than Northerners, and that white private soldiers were more eager for promotion than Negroes. All these conclusions could have been directly deduced from current platitudes about neurotic intellectuals, unambitious Negroes, and so on. But the interesting thing . . . is that they are false (Runciman, 1963, pp. 18–19).

So while we certainly need to understand the ideas people have about society, we need not assume at all that these ideas are accurate pictures of reality. All of us, too, scientists included, hold quite contradictory sets of ideas in our heads without even being aware of it often. It is perfectly possible for scientists to be religious – something nineteenth-century secularists thought logically impossible – because scientists, outside the laboratory, are simply people: fathers, workers, supporters of Tottenham Hotspur, or whatever.

Even as scientists they are not entirely free from erroneous theory and inconsistency. But they do try to control these things, which they regard as lapses from high standards. Both the standards, and the ways of controlling for bias and inaccuracy, are not left entirely to the researcher, however. They are shared and institutionalized, passed on from generation to generation and improved by a community of scholars, so that when people make false inferences or fail to document their assertions they will be exposed by colleagues around the world because their analyses are published in journals and books and are therefore open to inspection and criticism.

The kind of criticality entailed in scientific research differs from the way people use their intelligence in everyday life in only two, but two quite critical respects (Garfinkel, 1967, ch. 8): explanations are consciously formulated in a coherent manner with the aim not of 'proving a theory', but as *hypotheses*, which may or may not be substantiated as a result of research findings. The effort is as much to *dis*prove, or falsify, the theory, and this is not the way we normally think and act in conducting our everyday affairs. Were we to regard everything as an open question – from social codes about how close we should sit next to a stranger of the opposite sex in a bar (Cavan, 1966) to unspoken rules about queuing – we would quickly find ourselves in all sorts of trouble, ranging from a slap on the face to being imprisoned for causing a breach of the peace. If we didn't systematically take many such conventions for granted, and *fail* to be critical about whether these customs were rational, or justified, or not, we would be regarded as socially or even mentally abnormal.

Scientists, too, accept a lot of knowledge as 'established', and sometimes show the greatest resistance to new theories, not just because of mental conservatism, but because the scientific community, in the shape of learned societies and professional organizations, can deal very seriously with unorthodox heretics, as deviant innovators from Galileo to Darwin and Freud found to their cost (Kuhn, 1962). But scientific criticality does also involve criticizing one's own assumptions *in principle*. If they prove invalid, we start looking for a more powerful explanation. The actual sequence or form in which these operations are performed, though, are often very different from methods used in laboratory testing or as recommended in manuals of methodology. Hunches may be as important as carefully worked out hypotheses, and may occur at any point in the investigation, while the systematic pulling together of theory and evidence may occur at the end rather than being built into an explicit hypothesis tested via a tidy sequence of steps in a research design worked out in advance.

Using Sociology

The ideal of the 'open' scientific community is not, alas, the whole of the story, not just because that community does not always live up to that ideal, but because science, too, exists in society. Just as the institution of the patent has long restricted the commercial use of scientific inventions, so social taboos and powerful institutions made it impossible for centuries to even discuss some kinds of social behaviour, notably in the areas of religion and sex, whereas today there is no shortage of volunteers willing even to copulate under observation (Masters and Johnson, 1980).

Social control over science, however, is by no means simply something that occurred only in the unenlightened past. Where the Church was once the principal force controlling social inquiry, today it is the secular State, armed now not only with the power to repress knowledge, but, by using the new technical power of the modern mass media, to actually create and shape public opinion.

The deliberate restriction of inquiry ranges negatively, from the closing down of whole countries, institutions or areas to would-be researchers to the positive steering of research into officially approved channels. The exercise of indirect influences over research is equally effective. Thus funds are difficult to obtain for research that does not promise some kind of tangible 'pay-off' in the short run either in terms of believed economic benefits or of utility to governments. Basic research – into general theory, into exotic cultures, or into topics like kinship – is often dismissed as a dispensable luxury.

Even, or especially, in the natural sciences, then, the free pursuit of knowledge is an ideal rather than the norm. We need not be unduly cynical: it is still a factor, but only one among others. But in chemistry, it has been argued, whole fields of theory have been neglected, while others, because of their known or assumed immediate utility, have been carefully tilled by armies of researchers working for large corporations or on government funded research (Pateman, 1972). Natural scientists working to develop commodities which are marketed under brand names, or working in defence research, find themselves involved in a contradiction between the institutional interest of those who employ them in *restricting* access to research information and the scientist's commitment to the ideals of freedom of inquiry and of publication, as well as of a collegiality which extends beyond national boundaries. Social scientists encounter similar kinds of ethical dilemma. Physicians, who take the Hippocratic oath to use their medical skills for the benefit of whoever needs them, without social distinction, find it impossible to honour that principle in practice when medicines and medical services, and even food, have to be rationed or paid for by the patient. If the creation and dissemination of weapons of mass destruction imposes ethical dilemmas upon natural scientists, other dilemmas are encountered by social scientists who deal directly with people as clients or customers or who can only get the information they need from people who trust them not to use it against their interests: by, say, divulging information to a third party such as the police or to social security 'snoopers' (Becker, 1967).

The crude distinction between 'pure' and 'applied' research, in any case, is about as problematic as the notion of 'secrecy' in science. The distinction is often only one of time-scale: some kinds of empirical findings can be kept secret for a short time at least, but, as in the case of Soviet atomic research, scientists using general principles can soon replicate even the most sophisticated kinds of knowledge. Further, the status of knowledge can change from 'pure' to 'applied'. Thus the early highly esoteric and purely theoretical mathematical research of Albert Einstein laid the basis for the manufacture and use of atomic bombs in 1945. 'Had I known,' he later ruefully remarked, 'I would rather have been a watchmaker.' Conversely, knowledge generated for quite practical purposes can be codified into theoretical categories and propositions. Thus in the ancient Near East, algebraic formulae were invented by officials who needed to calculate the yield of a given land area for tax purposes.

Sociological research is rarely as fateful as Einstein's. But genealogical research revealing Jewish ancestry was likely to prove a sentence of death in Nazi Germany, while ethnic and national identity (as defined by officials) are grounds for being refused entry into most countries today. The idea that kinship studies are useless soon dissolves even further under the most elementary scrutiny in an epoch when patterns of marriage and of parenthood, even of gender, are undergoing the kinds of changes discussed in Chapter 4; when definitions of what constitutes 'living together' or responsibility for dependent children or relatives – especially the aged or those without other close kin to support them – become, in a highly mobile society, of the greatest practical importance to those charged with administering welfare benefits and to the clients and claimants themselves; when calculations of income and of liability to taxes upon income depend upon definitions of what constitutes a 'household' both as a social and an economic unit. Kinship, furthermore, is fundamental to the capitalist economic system: it is the major mechanism by which property is handed on from generation to generation, while the home is the place where the next generation of workers is both produced and prepared for their future roles in society. Finally, debate about these changes generates deep passions, some seeing them as evidence of growing emancipation, others as signs of moral breakdown. Apparently technical issues become part of this public debate: when sociologists assign women to social classes on the basis of their husbands' occupation, feminists object that this ignores the fact that the majority of women work outside the home and denies women the right to be treated as persons in their own right (Stanworth, 1984; Goldthorpe and Payne, 1986).

Research thus engenders both political and moral debate. Hence justification for policy decisions has to be produced, in democratic societies at least. Social research has therefore become a necessity for decision-makers at every level of society. Parish records of births, deaths and marriages, largely kept for religious reasons, are completely inadequate in societies numbered in millions, even tens and hundreds of millions; undergoing cycles of economic expansion and recession; where one in five of the population changes residence every year; and where whole continents, like the Americas and Australia have been invaded by millions of immigrants often within living memory.

The increasing intervention of the State in every area of life, in capitalist as well as communist countries, means that vast amounts of information are needed – objective data such as population censuses (which only began in Britain in 1801) and subjective data such as voting intentions – in order to devise policies for the future as well as the present: to call up conscripts for the army; to calculate how many student places will be needed in fifteen years' time; to plan the development of new industries and to close down others.

The sheer size of modern society is not the only reason why so much social research is needed simply in order to find out what is going on. Urban society is difficult to grasp for another reason – it has become highly specialized. In the past, the great majority of townsfolk were producers of material things, from agricultural implements to clothing. Today, in a place like the island of Manhattan, New York, a nerve centre of world trade and communications, work, for millions of people, no longer entails producing material commodities like garments, but processing information – words and numbers. A third major type of industry today specializes in handling people. Service industries like the British National Health Service, private medicine, the pharmaceutical and other firms which produce the drugs and equipment they use, plus the construction firms which build hospitals and nursing homes and the educational institutions where doctors and nurses are trained, give employment to hundreds of thousands, many of whom are not working directly on patient care. There are more people engaged, similarly, in higher education (leaving aside primary and secondary education) as teachers, as students, and in administrative and other jobs than there are working in the mining industry.

But the tremendous demand for information does not only come from central and local government. It comes from all kinds of organizations: from business firms to trade unions, from voluntary associations and pressure groups, churches, political parties, package holiday firms, theatres, slimming clinics, hospitals and cemeteries.

For governments, the threat or the use of force is always one of the main sources of political power. It has therefore been called the 'ultimate' sanction in political theory. But the ultimate, by definition, is not usually resorted to unless all else fails. Governments are often reluctant to use bayonets or tear gas, for they are much more secure themselves when their rule, even their periodic or regular resort to force, is based on a belief that they have a legitimate right to do so: that the King has a divine right to rule or the Prime Minister does so because he or she has been elected by the voters. The use of force as a routine method of ruling, then, is an admission that such consent is not forthcoming, and generates further opposition.

Control over information, and, more generally, over ideas, is thus essential not only to governments but even to collectivities whose interests may be quite different, even opposed to those of government. Indeed, where governments are themselves the cause of many social problems, as they often are, ordinary citizens, as individuals and as collectivities, need knowledge about social trends in order to protect themselves and to press for alternative policies. The myriad groups and institutions that make up 'civil society' as distinct from the State cannot, however, legally resort to force, nor can private individuals use violence in order to resolve their disputes with one another. Hence for them persuasion is the main political tactic available (apart from armed struggle).

Karl Marx saw capitalism as a system in which production was increasingly concentrated in ever-larger enterprises in which, though the means of production – the capital, the machinery, etc – was in private hands, the process of producing was increasingly socialized, since it involved coordinating a whole series of operations, often on the part of tens of thousands of people, from the production of the raw materials to the manufacture of the finished article.

Max Weber extended this idea by pointing out that in modern society all domains of life, not just the economic, are now regulated by complex, hierarchical, large-scale organizations, including the administrative machinery of the State itself. Thus, in pre-modern armies, the soldier would often provide, or acquire, his own weapons – a bow and arrow, a spear – himself. But today, only the State can produce the weapons of modern warfare – tanks, missiles, jet-planes. The production of immaterial knowledge, Weber argued, and not just of material goods, was similarly becoming 'socialized'. It was no longer something that could be carried out by 'lone wolf' scholars in their private libraries. Most modern research is carried out in large corporations and in research institutions. The production of the first atomic bombs, for instance, involved the concentration not only of massive engineering resources, but of large numbers of the world's leading atomic scientists in the Manhattan Project in the USA. Even individual research is mostly impossible without access to large and specialized libraries.

Modern governments, even the most dictatorial, also depend upon the contribution of large numbers of specialists from outside the parties and the Civil Service. Trade unions and business organizations are therefore represented on scores of government committees, as are professional organizations – lawyers, doctors, etc – and pressure groups of all kinds, because all of them possess specialized knowledge which governments need (Finer, 1958). Those groups, in their turn, need access to the kinds of information governments collect, from census data to information about income distribution, divorce statistics or school examination results. This reciprocal inter-dependence means that the non-governmental bodies have to be allowed access to information gathered by the State as a *quid pro quo*, and they have the power, because they themselves control other kinds of vital information and also represent a powerful body of public opinion, to demand of government that they be given this access. In democratic societies, this is further considered to be a right.

What they then do with the information they get, however, may be at variance with government policy. In the nineteenth century, the great Blue Books containing the evidence of exhaustive Royal Commissions into conditions of work, of housing, in prisons and in hospitals, were used by social reformers such as Elizabeth Fry, Ernest Chadwick, Florence Nightingale, and Lord Shaftesbury to press for improvements in those institutions. They were even used by revolutionaries, notably by Karl Marx as ammunition for his *Capital*.

Social research, then, has become a necessity not just for the key decision-makers, but for everybody, since we are all affected by their decisions. Changing them, or resisting them, requires access to existing information or going out to generate it where it does not exist already. The result has been an 'information explosion'. A quarter of a century ago a leading nuclear scientist complained that if the *Physical Review* went on expanding at its then rate, it would come to weigh more than the earth some time during the next century. That problem has now been solved with the advent of the microchip revolution – the use of computers, word-processors and data retrieval-systems. But as we saw above, solving society's prob-lems involves much more than simply collecting facts. It involves making sense of those facts – analysing them. It further involves making choices once we have interpreted the facts. We showed how, even in its beginnings, sociology was divided into different schools of thought using different kinds of research methods and with different ends in view, from the positivists who advocated what later came to be called 'social engineering' – the planning of the whole of social life by technocrats – to the liberal reformers who crusaded against this or that social evil and the radicals who saw all of these separate ills as rooted in a generalized poverty, to the revolutionaries who saw poverty as the inevitable outcome of a society based on private property.

To be informed about society, however, involves much more than knowledge in the factual or purely cognitive sense, what one might call the 'Mastermind' conception of knowledge. It means using that kind of knowledge to arrive at an understanding of the issues involved and to arrive, too, at effective policies. From the beginning, sociology has been a science which, because of its special subject-matter, also inescapably raises political and ethical issues. That it does so frightens people who would prefer that such questions never got asked. Yet sociology is not the only source of such questioning; nor does it produce easy answers. To blame it for *causing* social problems is about as sensible as blaming economists for causing world recession or physicists for causing nuclear arms races, for these matters are not caused, or solved, by the activities of scientists alone, however much they may contribute to all these ills, or to solving them. There are others with far greater power to make their influence felt, while everybody, even the most lowly, has the option, too, of trying to do something about these matters and not leaving them to others. However much effective policies ought, in principle, to be based on social understanding rather than ignorance, neither the powerful nor the ordinary citizen necessarily makes much use of sociology.

Sociology, moreover, is only one of the social sciences. Economics, the most widely used specialism in government and in business, concentrates on one vital aspect of human life – production and consumption – and has developed highly sophisticated, often math-ematical techniques and an elaborate body of theory. Yet economists do not pretend to any expertise outside that area of social relation-ships; when they come to, say, explaining changes in taste or fashion – which affect the demand for clothing, entertainment, food, etc – they leave this to others, usually psychologists and sociologists. They also constantly invoke the *ceteris paribus* clause (other things being equal) by which they mean that their analyses and projections cannot allow for non-economic events such as wars or changes of taste. Psychologists have a very different focus: not upon a particular area of social life, but upon the individual as their unit of analysis. In the process, they have to abstract the individual from the real life matrix of social relationships in which we are all embedded. But some psychologists – social psychologists – do study the actual behaviour of collectivities from the internal dynamics of small groups to the behaviour of football crowds. They can even provide illuminating insights by studying artificial groups, such as discussion groups observed through one-way glass. There is often little difference between this kind of social psychology and what people who call themselves sociologists do, apart from differences in their training, which means that they often use different kinds of theories in interpreting what they observe and different kinds of techniques. These differences, though, derive from the observer; they are not in the nature of what is being observed; indeed, different observers will interpret exactly the same behaviour in accordance with the distinctive traditions of their disciplines.

The different disciplines within the social sciences do not necessarily, then, study some special dimension of human behaviour, as economists do. Sociology has no such specialized domain, like production, though there are those who do specialize in industrial sociology. Rather, it takes in all aspects of behaviour from work to war, at all levels of society from face-to-face relations to the study of the whole world as a single social system. But even those who study the minutiae of interpersonal relationships are concerned either with discovering the general principles which inform such behaviour and/ or the ways in which what goes on in particular situations or between particular kinds of people links up with other situations that bring together quite different kinds of people.

Most sociologists are trained as generalists by being exposed to studies of all the main domains of social life and all the main schools of theory. Yet the discipline itself reflects the processes Max Weber saw as typical of modern life: it has its large-scale institutions, its hierarchies, its orthodoxies, and has developed specialisms of many kinds – the sociology of religion, the sociology of sport, urban sociology, political sociology, to name but a few. There have been sociological studies of dwarfs, polyphonic music, traffic wardens, incest, cooking, even of sleep. Thus the daughters of Japanese samurai warriors were taught never to lose control of their minds and bodies, even in sleep:

Boys might stretch themselves into the character *dai*, carelessly outspread; but girls must curve into the modest, dignified character *kinoji*, which means 'spirit of control' (Richards, 1972, p. 170).

This example of the way cultural norms influence behaviour that some might imagine to be completely free from any social influences – sleep – is actually drawn from a branch of social science, anthropology, which is in some respects much wider in its scope than sociology. From the time of Comte onwards, sociologists have often claimed that because theirs is the most general of the social sciences, it is therefore the 'queen' of the social sciences. Yet the great bulk of their work has in fact been restricted to one kind of society only – industrial society in the last hundred years or so – a very limited phase in the story of human development, however crucial it has been.

Historians, on the other hand, have, between them, studied epochs of all ages, and archaeologists penetrate much further back in time than historians, who confine themselves to the written record. Sociologists, *per contra*, study the world around them. But some of them do study the past, and some modern historians the present, while the thinking of many historians who have also read what their sociological colleagues are writing is informed by a thoroughly sociological imagination. For all these reasons, the differences between them come down to differences of approach, of training and of self-definition as members of different professions rather than differences in the subject-matter itself.

The borderline with anthropology is similarly not absolute. Anthropologists have classically studied cultures other than their own: European anthropologists have gone to live with peoples in Asia, Africa and South America, using direct observation in the field as their major research procedure, an approach made necessary because many of the peoples they studied (though not all) have been non-literate cultures. Yet today, anthropologists have turned the spotlight of the methods of fine-grained, first-hand research developed in the study of that kind of culture on to their own and other urbanized and industrialized societies. Anthropology is thus even wider in its scope, in some respects, than sociology, since it involves trying to understand cultures very dissimilar from our own: to understand the logic of witchcraft, or the functioning of societies in which very complex systems of kinship are the groundrock of social organization in general, with elaborate religious belief-systems, and so on. Anthropology therefore provides the widest comparative dimension of the social sciences, since any theory which purports to make general statements about the bases of social organization can be tested against the wide variety of forms of society that still exist or have existed in the past. Yet anthropologists have mainly focused on the present, in part because they feared that the subject-matter was disappearing and urgently needed to be recorded before it did. Modern functionalist anthropology, too, rejected nineteenth-century explanations which, influenced by Darwinism in the natural sciences, concentrated on the *origins* of customs, on the grounds that to explain how an institution came into being does not tell us what the function of that institution is today. Thus the Magna Carta, widely thought to be the foundation of modern democratic liberties, was in fact only a set of rights wrested by powerful barons from King John and was not intended to apply to the common people at all.

In principle, we can and should think of 'social science' in general. Yet just as society has become complex and specialized, so have the social sciences, so that there are now many different social sciences with quite distinctive traditions, methods and techniques, achievements and shortcomings. Only the more narrow minded entirely ignore what goes on in other disciplines. For it is important to try to keep abreast of at least the general theoretical developments in our sister sciences. Any sociologist studying the dynamics of interaction in the classroom is likely to learn a lot not only from studies of similar situations by educational psychologists, but sometimes find surprising insights, too, from studies of the cities of Ancient Greece, or medieval religious movements, or the economy of the Bushmen of the Kalahari Desert, even of quite abstract philosophical debate, for these are all ways of approaching the diversity of responses human beings in different cultures have made to the problems we all confront at any time.

Other problems are quite specific to certain societies or kinds of society only. There are also new, qualitatively different problems: institutions that never existed in the more remote past: trade unions, multi-national corporations, political parties, collective farms; the growth of worldwide nuclear confrontation between the Superpowers, and probably, before too long, the colonization of other planets. In confronting these new phenomena, general theory and particular insights generated in the study of quite other cultures will prove valuable. But we also need to generate new categories of thought appropriate to new forms of social development.

So far, the social sciences have contributed very little to the study of the most pressing problem of all – the high probability that humanity will destroy itself. Like most of the major problems confronting us, this is a social, not a technical problem. There need be no problem of hunger in the Third World or of persisting poverty in the First World, since the technical know-how for solving these problems exists or could soon be brought into existence were it given the priority that is today given to defence. What is lacking are the social arrangements and the policies that would make possible not only a fairer distribution of the world's riches but new kinds of production too. The major limitations upon the kinds of development we have today require that, more than anything else, we devote vastly more effort to new social inventions than to the development of ever more sophisticated technology: new institutions and strategies that might help find answers to the utilization of the enormous creative potential at present condemned to frustration through unemployment and underemployment. We need, that is, better social theories and better institutions than those that have been developed so far, probably new alternatives even to the industrial, centralized, and in many ways dehumanized societies of both the capitalist and the communist worlds.

Tackling these social problems does not mean that we can afford to neglect institutions which seem to function perfectly well, and which do not therefore get defined as 'social problems' – families which endure, children who enjoy being at school, the lives of those who come out on top. For sociology does not exclusively study breakdown, 'pathology', social problems. It studies sociological problems and develops its insights as much in the study of people who are not generally defined as constituting a problem for the rest of society as in studying those who are. Insights developed in either field of research are applicable to the other. This is not to say that the successful are models for the less successful, for their lives, too, are full of tensions, from the frustrations hidden behind the closed doors of respectable marriage to the wounds the 'workaholic' inflicts upon himself and those around him in his obsessional pursuit of wealth, power and social status.

Developing new ideas about society is not something that will be accomplished by social scientists alone; developing new kinds of social institutions even less. But we are not likely to get very far with either if we do not make use of the methods and the findings that have been developed by what have been, after all, only the first few generations of social scientists.

2   Development

The greatest social problems of all – those which affect every person on earth, in every country – are not problems internal to any particular country: they are international problems, which derive from the fact that all countries, from the largest, virtual continents like the USA, the USSR and China, to the smallest micro-state such as Nauru (population 8,000) or Dominica (population 80,000), are only parts of a world-system of society.

Before the nineteenth century, large parts of the globe had no direct contact with countries other than those on their borders or in the region adjoining. There was, however, indirect contact, often intercontinental, due to the enterprise of missionaries, traders and other intermediaries. So religions like Buddhism, Islam, or Hinduism could spread with great rapidity across large stretches of Asia; in the case of Islam, from Spain to what is now Indonesia. But when Marco Polo took the Silk Road to China in 1271, he was the first European to do so. None of these contacts involved the creation of worldwide institutions such as exist today – banks, shipping lines, a vast network of air traffic, instant information systems such as satellite-telephones, commodity and stock exchanges linked by telex and computer, or the modern networks through which ideas are instantly diffused across what Marshall McLuhan called the 'global village' – TV, radio, films, video, etc – with immediate translation into many languages. International institutions such as the UN, or world organizations – from professional bodies to sports organizations – did not exist at all.

The growth of this modern world-system has occurred over only a very short period of time indeed out of the tens of thousands of years during which recognizably human society can be discerned in the archaeological record. It began with the Industrial Revolution in

Western Europe. So profound was the impact of that Revolution within the countries that first experienced it, not only in economic and political terms but also in terms of its social and cultural effects, that it has been called the 'Great Transformation'. The impact of these newly industrialized powers on the rest of the world proved similarly devastating, culminating in the imperialist epoch during which the entire globe came under the direct political control of a handful of capitalist countries.

The last few decades have seen the final incorporation of even the most remote corners of the Amazon, of New Guinea, of Tibet into the world-system. Within the next decade, for the first time in history, there will be more people living in towns and cities than in the countryside; by the year 2001, the population of the earth will be six billions, more than five times what it was in 1850, and eleven times what it was in 1650.

The basic political unit of which the world-system is made up, formally, is the nation-state, of which there are now over 120, a number increasing year by year. But there is clearly an enormous difference in reality between tiny countries like Nauru or Dominica and very large powers, of which the USA is the largest in terms of political, military and industrial strength, and China in terms of population (for which reason she has been called 'half a Superpower').

Despite the obvious importance of such giant countries as the USA, China or the USSR (whose future, however, is problematic), some 125 states are recognized by international agencies, among them the UN and the World Bank. Although the latter organization only classifies less than 40 as 'low-income' economies, while nearly 60 are said to be 'middle-income' economies, the 'middle' category includes many countries such as Senegal, El Salvador and Thailand, which most of us would have little hesitation in calling poor and under-developed. 'Upper-middle' includes Brazil and Mexico, with large zones of poverty. The World Bank's own data show that GNP per capita in Japan is 23 times that of Senegal; that of the USA 19 times that of El Salvador; and in Sweden, over 15 times that of Thailand (World Bank, 1985). A more realistic sociological classification distinguishes between the better-off poor, the middling poor, the poorer, and the poorest — but they are all poor (Goldthorpe, 1975, ch. 4). Such figures, moreover, do not tell us how national income is actually distributed; they are simple statistical calculations in which global national income is divided by the number of people in the population. But in such countries, as in developed ones, what wealth there is is not evenly distributed in this way. A massive proportion goes to tiny elite groups: the propertied classes, those who control the State, and those who control foreign aid, from capital loans to military assistance. And as we will see, it is not enough simply to rank countries in a 'League table' from 1 to 125, for they belong to different divisions.

The Growth of the World-System

It is natural enough that most of us should be mainly concerned with the country in which we live. We also tend to think of the 'country' – the particular nation-state – we live in as the maximal social unit not only of economic and political life, but also of social organization and culture, the 'way of life' we are part of. The nation-state has such special importance that many of us rarely think beyond it and some of us regard people outside it as different in kind, even inferior.

Though we feel ourselves to be – and are – members of many social groups and categories at different levels of the social structure, even local level community groups such as church congregations are usually part of wider, nationwide and even international organizations, while the categories we see ourselves as belonging to – say, as members of a social class or an ethnic group, as women or as men – transcend any merely local boundaries.

Hence in the last fifteen years a new school of history and social science has grown up which rejects not only history written in mainly national terms, but even history written in regional terms. Thirty years ago, radical sociologists like C. Wright Mills tried to shock people whom they accused of having only a 'middle level' consciousness (because they never thought about society as a whole) by insisting that the only relevant unit of analysis, in modern times, was the nation-state. Today, that view would be regarded not as radical but as archaic by 'world-system' theorists for whom the world, not the nation-state, has to be our starting-point (Wallerstein, 1979). To understand our local and even national problems, they argue, we should start with the world as a whole and work down, not the other way round.

Since the Second World War, another term has come into use which has differences in the component parts of the world-system rather than its overall unity: we talk of the 'Third World', which implies that there is also a First and a Second (though these terms are less often used). By Third World, we mean the contemporary underdeveloped countries of Asia, Africa and Latin America. To historians of the world-system, however, the Third World began in Europe, and its emergence is not a post-Second World War phenomenon, but one which dates back to the sixteenth century (Stavrianos, 1981, ch. 3).

In Western Europe at that time, the export of goods to Eastern Europe, especially cloth, began to increase rapidly, in return for grain and lumber, a trade which had long existed, but in which the value of the imports from Eastern European countries had hitherto been much greater than that of Western Europe's exports. The shortfall in this balance of trade had been made good by the export of gold and silver coins from Western Europe. Now, the terms of trade were to be reversed. Henceforward, Eastern Europe, relatively to Western Europe, was to become increasingly disadvantaged, an 'underdeveloped' zone. The gulf between the two parts of Europe thus long antedates the rise of modern communism.

On top of these differences in terms of product and market-relationships, political, social and cultural institutions also diverged in the two zones. A large and powerful merchant class never developed in Eastern Europe, as it did in cities like Antwerp, Augsburg and London, which were the first centres of the mercantile phase of capitalist growth. By the time England came to celebrate the triumph of industrial capitalism, at the Great Exhibition of 1851, the bulk of the population of Russia not only continued to work on the land, with low productivity, but were still serfs. In Tsarist Russia, the bourgeoisie never came to power, as they did in Western Europe, nor was there any equivalent of the twin cultural revolutions of the West, the Reformation and the Renaissance.

Russia did, however, develop in a different way, by expanding eastwards across Siberia at a rate far faster than the Western advance into North America at the same period. Within half a century, it had become a major empire. The conquest of South America by Spain and Portugal had been equally rapid, though these powers, too, were not as economically developed as the Netherlands, France or

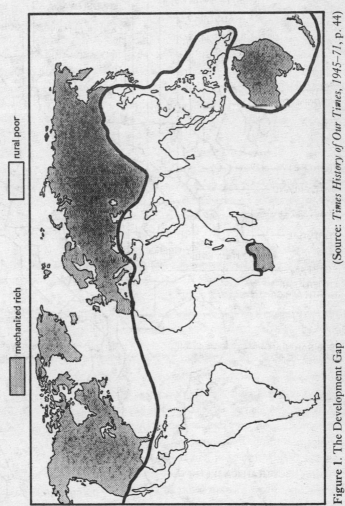

mechanized rich

rural poor

Figure 1. The Development Gap

(Source: *Times History of Our Times, 1945–71*, p. 44)

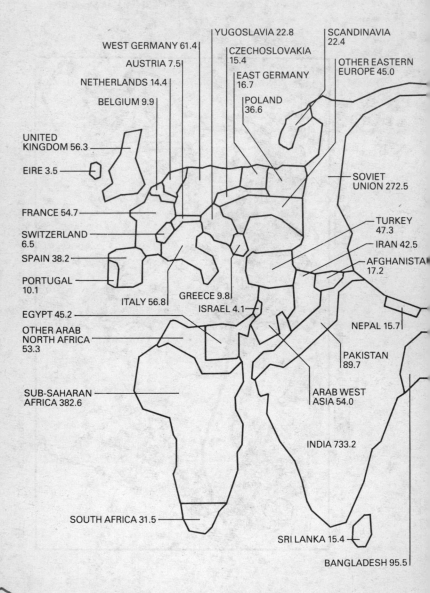

WEST GERMANY 61.4

AUSTRIA 7.5

NETHERLANDS 14.4

BELGIUM 9.9

YUGOSLAVIA 22.8

CZECHOSLOVAKIA 15.4

EAST GERMANY 16.7

POLAND 36.6

SCANDINAVIA 22.4

OTHER EASTERN EUROPE 45.0

UNITED KINGDOM 56.3

EIRE 3.5

SOVIET UNION 272.5

FRANCE 54.7

SWITZERLAND 6.5

SPAIN 38.2

PORTUGAL 10.1

TURKEY 47.3

IRAN 42.5

AFGHANISTAN 17.2

ITALY 56.8

GREECE 9.8

ISRAEL 4.1

EGYPT 45.2

OTHER ARAB NORTH AFRICA 53.3

NEPAL 15.7

PAKISTAN 89.7

SUB-SAHARAN AFRICA 382.6

ARAB WEST ASIA 54.0

INDIA 733.2

SOUTH AFRICA 31.5

SRI LANKA 15.4

BANGLADESH 95.5

(Source: *World Development Report 1985*, Table 1)

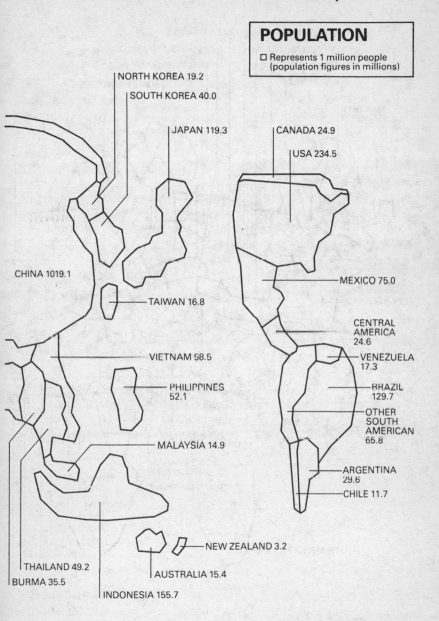

POPULATION

□ Represents 1 million people
(population figures in millions)

NORTH KOREA 19.2

SOUTH KOREA 40.0

JAPAN 119.3

CANADA 24.9

USA 234.5

CHINA 1019.1

MEXICO 75.0

TAIWAN 16.8

CENTRAL
AMERICA
24.6

VIETNAM 58.5

VENEZUELA
17.3

PHILIPPINES
52.1

BRAZIL
129.7

OTHER
SOUTH
AMERICAN
65.8

MALAYSIA 14.9

ARGENTINA
29.6

CHILE 11.7

NEW ZEALAND 3.2

THAILAND 49.2

BURMA 35.5

AUSTRALIA 15.4

INDONESIA 155.7

Figure 2. Population

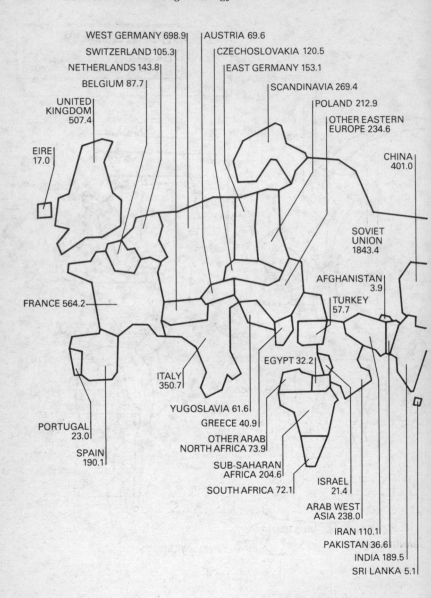

WEST GERMANY 698.9
SWITZERLAND 105.3
NETHERLANDS 143.8
BELGIUM 87.7
UNITED KINGDOM 507.4
EIRE 17.0
FRANCE 564.2
PORTUGAL 23.0
SPAIN 190.1
AUSTRIA 69.6
CZECHOSLOVAKIA 120.5
EAST GERMANY 153.1
SCANDINAVIA 269.4
POLAND 212.9
OTHER EASTERN EUROPE 234.6
CHINA 401.0
SOVIET UNION 1843.4
AFGHANISTAN 3.9
TURKEY 57.7
ITALY 350.7
EGYPT 32.2
YUGOSLAVIA 61.6
GREECE 40.9
OTHER ARAB NORTH AFRICA 73.9
SUB-SAHARAN AFRICA 204.6
SOUTH AFRICA 72.1
ISRAEL 21.4
ARAB WEST ASIA 238.0
IRAN 110.1
PAKISTAN 36.6
INDIA 189.5
SRI LANKA 5.1

(Source: *World Military Expenditure and Arms Transfers,*
US Arms Control and Disarmament Agency, August 1985)

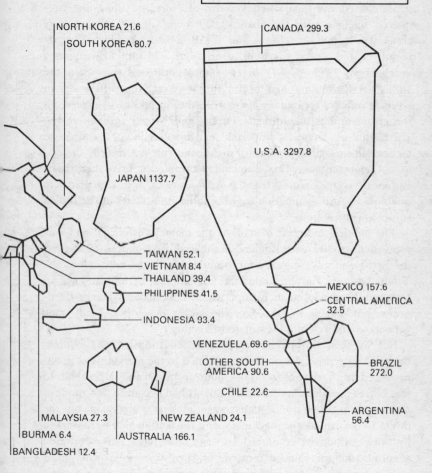

GROSS NATIONAL PRODUCT

☐ Represents $ 10 billion 1983 US dollars (figures in $ billions)

NORTH KOREA 21.6

SOUTH KOREA 80.7

CANADA 299.3

U.S.A. 3297.8

JAPAN 1137.7

TAIWAN 52.1
VIETNAM 8.4
THAILAND 39.4
PHILIPPINES 41.5

MEXICO 157.6
CENTRAL AMERICA 32.5

INDONESIA 93.4

VENEZUELA 69.6
OTHER SOUTH AMERICA 90.6
CHILE 22.6

BRAZIL 272.0

MALAYSIA 27.3

NEW ZEALAND 24.1

ARGENTINA 56.4

BURMA 6.4   AUSTRALIA 166.1

BANGLADESH 12.4

Figure 3. Gross Domestic Product

England, and social transformation had been halted by the Counter-Reformation. The silver from the New World was used to maintain an increasingly archaic social order rather than to modernize the economy along capitalist lines.

European expansion into Asia was far slower and much less definitive. At the time when William of Normandy had just conquered England with less than 30,000 men, China's regular army contained $1\frac{1}{4}$ million soldiers and the Bow and Crossbow Department's central workshops were turning out 3·24 million weapons a year (Elvin, 1973, p. 84). Even eight centuries later, when the Industrial Revolution had begun in the West, the differences in levels of military technology as between the European colonizers and the great empires of Ottoman Turkey and Mogul India were not great. But by virtue of superior maritime technology and naval tactics and the skilful practice of divide and rule policies, by the end of the eighteenth century England was able to drive her major European rival, France, from North America and India and to establish English domination over the indigenous states of the Indian sub-continent as well.

The political conquest of Asia by the major Western powers now proceeded steadily, with England in the lead. Economically, however, the balance of advantage by no means lay with the new colonizers. Trade between Europe and Asia was limited by the absence of commodities produced in Europe which Asia needed. Hence Europeans were unable to take over the highly developed Asian trade networks until well into the nineteenth century.

But by then Europe had undergone its Industrial Revolution: capitalist enterprise was no longer confined to the marketing of goods produced by a variety of forms of labour, from serf and slave labour to that of free peasants and urban artisans. It had become a new mode of *production*, in which the capitalist was no longer a merchant, but the owner of the capital, the machinery, and the land, which were worked by others whom he employed as wage labourers. This revolution of production in Europe created, in turn, a new growing mass market for new kinds of imports from the colonies – sugar, coffee, tea, tobacco, etc – far larger than the much older import-trade in tropical luxuries, especially spices and silks, which had only involved the wealthy classes.

The crucial asset which the colonial powers possessed, however, was non-economic: military and political power. In Latin America, it was used firstly to conquer the continent, then to bring into being a silver-mining industry worked by virtual slave labour; in the Caribbean, a sugar industry worked by actual slave labour. In Asia, likewise, political might was used to transform the economies of the colonies in accordance with the needs of the West. In India, indigenous systems of land-ownership were radically changed to produce a new class of private landlords. The island of Java, an Indian historian has written,

became a plantation of the Dutch United East India Company [in which the Company] was not merely the employer of labour, but also the authority vested with the rights of life and death . . . A whole people was converted by the exercise of sovereignty into a nation of estate coolies, with their natural aristocracy reduced to the position of foremen and superintendents (Panikkar, 1959, p. 88).

The process of colonization, then, was never purely economic; rather, the transformation of the economy took place as a consequence of political domination. The Industrial Revolution in the West stepped up the process of economic transformation in the colonies: plantations and mines were now developed with indentured labourers rather than slaves, or by using forced or migrant labour or by imposing taxes which had to be paid in cash. Indigenous industry, notably Indian textiles and shipbuilding, was destroyed to make way for the manufactures of Lancashire and Birmingham; closed internal markets were forced open to Western goods (in the case of China, to opium); the railways to carry them in and colonial raw materials out were constructed at incredible speed. The outcome was the agriculturalization of the colonies: in 1891, 61 per cent of the population of India worked on the land; by 1921, 73 per cent did.

Africa, the last continent to be divided up, was overwhelmed by the now highly developed economic, military and political strength of the imperialist powers. At Berlin, in 1885, the European powers divided Africa up between them, on paper. Within two decades, despite the capacity of some states – the Ashanti, the Zulu and the Ethiopians – to defeat European armies, those decisions had been effectively carried out. The few countries anywhere in the world that did remain nominally independent – China, Persia, Turkey, Afghanistan, Thailand, most of South America – were effectively 'semi-colonies' controlled economically and politically by the Western powers.

It was this colonized world that was to become known later as the 'Third' World. But that name did not emerge immediately, for the world between the two World Wars was still dominated by the imperialist powers. But once the first of the colonies had gained their independence after 1946, especially India, militant nationalism sprang up everywhere, including armed revolutionary struggles. The defeat of France in Indo-China and violent struggles in Algeria, Kenya and elsewhere persuaded the Western powers that the time had come to relinquish direct political control. During the 'winds of change' which blew in Africa during the 1960s, no less than seventeen newly independent countries came into existence in the first year of that decade alone.

The conquest of the entire world by a handful of industrialized powers had been so rapid and irresistible that it seemed to many, including social theorists, a one-way evolutionary process. The whole world, it appeared, was fated to follow Western models, not only of capitalist economic organization, but the replacement of the entirety of the social institutions and cultural values inherited from the pre-colonial past by Western ones, too.

Yet the victory of Western forms of economic life was not matched in a simple one-to-one way in other spheres. Even in the economic sphere, traditional institutions were not always simply swept aside. Often, the Europeans simply took over and developed for their own benefit trade and production systems that had existed for centuries. In West Africa, for instance, the palm-oil which was the basis of the great Unilever empire was not produced on plantations or on settler estates but by peasants working their own land.

They were not the only people to take advantage of the new opportunities for self-advancement, however restricted these might be and however painful the process. Millions of Chinese fled from the landlords and the social controls of a culture which doomed them to permanent poverty and social inferiority. The more privileged, with a stake in the existing order of society – kings, rajahs, chiefs, aristocrats, priests – sometimes organized initial resistance to Western colonizers where they could, and later revolts against colonial rule, notably the Indian 'Mutiny'. But most of them were either compelled to collaborate with the new colonial power or saw no alternative. Many were rewarded by being given access to new kinds of wealth, power and social status. They also invoked traditional rights and duties – kinship ties, the obligation to help one's fellow villagers or to give labour services to one's lord – as a way of mobilizing labour for new privately owned farms or on hereditary lands producing, now, cash-crops for the new market, or levied taxes and tribute in order to accumulate capital which could be invested in new kinds of urban enterprise.

For their subjects, the new economic order meant mainly hard labour in mines and on plantations owned by white men, or cash-crop production on land they had access to. The more entrepreneurial used the savings they made from selling their labour or their produce to increase the size of their land-holdings (often at the expense of their neighbours) or to move into new economic niches such as shop-keeping.

New economic classes therefore grew up which differed sharply from traditional systems of social ranking. In the cities, the collective experience of working side by side with hundreds, even thousands, of others in factories, and in the mines, led eventually to class and even nationalist organizations, at first of a defensive nature, later oriented to radical social change. Economic bonds were often reinforced by social and cultural ones when people worked or lived alongside others of similar social background – workers recruited from the same rural area or ethnic group – while all of them, whether culturally similar or dissimilar, experienced the common, racially based inferiority of the colour-bar, which excluded them not only from skilled jobs but from political self-expression too.

This political and economic gulf between colonizers and colonized was further reinforced by cultural differences, above all those of religion, though ancient religious traditions themselves had to be adapted in order to make sense of the new world of Western cities and Western power.

The impact of colonialism was therefore not one-way traffic, but a dialectical interplay, in which, however great the West's political and military superiority, pre-colonial forms of social organization and culture persisted, though often combined with new Western elements. Thus new syncretic religions emerged, adapted to the new conditions of colonial life and to the interests of the colonized: Mexican

Indians adopted the Black Virgin of Guadalupe as their patroness; Black South Africans, denied any place in secular life, developed hundreds of separatist churches of their own and believed that they would go to heaven and the Whites to hell; and Melanesians believed that the end of the world foretold in the Bible would occur very soon and would see the wealth of the White man falling into their hands.

Christianity was not the only ideology borrowed from the West, however. The modern secular ideologies of the West – liberalism, nationalism, socialism and Marxism – were the ideologies that were seized upon by the new nationalist movements which were to finally bring the epoch of direct imperialism to an end by the 1960s.

Theories of Development

Histories of Western expansion written in the West have often been simply accounts of the activities of White men and the sources of their success, with minimal attention to the nature of the indigenous societies and cultures they conquered, or the reaction of the conquered to that conquest. Thus South America and Australia were said to have been 'discovered' by explorers from Europe, even though the ancestors of today's American Indians and Australian Aborigines had spread across these continents tens of thousands of years ago and inhabited them ever since. Imperialist historiography, too, often asserted that the indigenous peoples had no history. That view still persists. An Oxford professor could still write, as recently as 1965:

It is fashionable to speak as if European history were devalued; as if historians, in the past, have paid too much attention to it, and as if, nowadays, we should pay less. Undergraduates, seduced, as always, by the breath of journalistic history, demand that they should be taught the history of black Africa. Perhaps, in the future, there will be some African history to teach. But at present, there is none, or very little: there is only the history of the Europeans in Africa. The rest is largely darkness, like the history of pre-European, pre-Columbian America. And darkness is not a subject for history (Trevor-Roper, 1966, p. 9).

Today, our knowledge of the ancient civilizations of the Indus Valley, of ancient Ghana, Mali and Monomotapa; of Egypt and China; and of the Aztec, Mayan and Inca empires is such that European history, even the great cultures of classical antiquity, of

Greece and Rome, now appear as relatively recent, local Mediterranean civilizations rather than, as our Victorian forefathers thought,
the pinnacle of human civilization in general.

More recently, historians from the Third World itself have begun
to write their own versions of Western expansion, usually emphasizing resistance to the colonial invaders; attempts, after conquest, to
eject the conqueror and to restore the past; and the eventual displacement of backwards-looking resistance by a forwards-looking nationalism which included not just the project of expelling the White man
but of replacing the capitalist system he had implanted by a new
socialist one.

Both imperialist and nationalist versions of colonial history are
misleading. The conquest of India, like the conquest of South
America two centuries earlier, was not achieved by a handful of
invincible White men, nor was the technological superiority of the
West as clearcut in the first few centuries of expansion as it became
in the last few decades. It was possible only because they enlisted
powerful indigenous allies and their armies to divide and eventually
rule a fragmented opposition, a fact which nationalist mythologies
of resistance often underplay. The notion of 'Indian' or 'Mexican'
resistance, moreover, is not meaningful when applied to epochs
when India or Mexico as we know them did not exist.

More academic theories of imperialism are usually couched in
terms of political economy alone, often in the form of a simple
binary opposition: a model of the encounter between Western imperialism and the rest of the world which does not adequately take
account of the rivalry between different colonial powers over centuries or the extraordinary variety of societies and cultures they
encountered. Anthropologists, naturally, since they study the latter,
accuse world-system theorists of using a single category – 'pre-
colonial', 'non-European', 'pre-capitalist', etc – which does not tell
us what they were so much as what they were *not* (*non*-European,
pre-capitalist), thereby lumping together hunting-and-collecting societies, world religions like Islam and Buddhism, theocracies, bureaucratic empires, societies based on kinship and societies based on
caste, to name but a few major types.

Debate as to the causes of Western success usually consists in
arguments between the partisans of one set of factors, such as those
who emphasize technology – sea-power or fire-power – as against

those who emphasize superiority of economic strength and of social, including military, organization. Within each of these schools there is debate about the relative importance of one or the other factor (e.g. the debate between those theorists of 'plural society' (discussed in Chapter 9) who argued that colonial society was held together primarily via the economic mechanisms of the marketplace as against those who emphasized the political power of the colonial State).

In the heyday of imperialism, the nineteenth century, the superiority of the West was commonly seen as a totality, not as due to one or the other of these factors: the economic superiority of Lancashire and the Rhineland and the technological and political superiority embodied in armies went hand in hand, and were believed to derive from a general superiority of intellect and culture. Though different writers emphasized different aspects of this ideology – some, such as the Social Darwinists, emphasizing racial superiority, others divine favour – and though there were liberals and others who rejected these racist and imperialist ideas, by and large the notion that Western culture was the most highly developed stage of human evolution prevailed.

That notion is by no means dead. It flourishes in forms which range from crude and still very popular racism to more sophisticated conceptions of development as a unilinear process: in one direction only, that direction being represented by the most highly industrialized countries of the West.

By and large, writers in this century, unlike their nineteenth-century predecessors, have paid little attention to stages of evolutionary development earlier than capitalism, and hardly at all to pre-human biological evolution. But they have retained a basically evolutionist view of progress as something that occurs in definite stages, each marked by the emergence and subsequent predominance of increasingly complex forms of social organization. In the 1960s, W. W. Rostow, an American economist, in a very influential book, distinguished five stages of economic growth through which every society had to pass in the transition to 'modernity'. In the first stage, they were still pre-modern, 'traditional'; in the second, the 'preconditions' of modernization were brought into being, from financial and educational institutions to infrastructures of communications; in the third, the 'take-off' to modernization begins; stage four witnesses the 'drive to maturity'; and by stage five, high consumption has become a mass phenomenon (Rostow, 1960).

Though Rostow was an economist, his was not an 'economistic' theory, one which isolates economic forces and treats them as causally more important than others. Economic development for him required not only appropriate economic, technological and demographic conditions, but also appropriate social institutions and value-systems. It also followed classic nineteenth-century evolutionism insofar as it retained an optimistic view of progress: even the rapid transformation of the USSR, though a perverted form of development, was part of the overall process of development. And like his nineteenth-century predecessors, he remained hopeful that democracy would spread in the world and that countries other than the Superpowers would become more influential.

Most theories of development operate with a much simpler distinction between developed and underdeveloped societies. They also usually confine themselves to economic institutions – markets, production-systems, etc and rarely go much further back than the last century in their search for explanations of development. (By contrast, Condorcet, during the French Revolution, distinguished no less than ten stages through which human society had passed.)

Rostow's theory was more than a mere taxonomy, however, a classification of stages of development, or an optimistic philosophy. It also identified what needed to be *done* to bring about development. Different groups within the 'modernization' school, as it came to be called, might differ about which particular factor or set of factors was crucial to development – for engineers, it might be the harnessing of new sources of energy; for educationalists, inculcating scientific attitudes in children; for biologists and medicos raising standards of health and nutrition. But for all of them, Western standards and methods were the models to be imitated, and the supply of the needed factors – machinery, seeds, textbooks, medicines – would have to come from the West.

Sociologists who began to study development within this general framework, in the 1960s, naturally drew upon the most influential general theory of the time – the functionalism of Talcott Parsons. For him, the basic components of any society were roles. But roles are not just discrete bits of standardized behaviour. They cluster together to form institutions, whole systematic patterns of roles which govern whole areas of life: the institution of the family, the economy, the political system, and so on. All roles, moreover, are informed by differing kinds of cultural values which can be theoretically classified, in his view, by making five pairs of contrasts: between roles based on achievement, as against 'ascribed' roles (those individuals are born into or to which they are allotted); roles which are functionally specific (which involve only one particular field of activities – at work, say, but not in leisure-time situations), as against diffuse roles (like one's position in a kinship system in tribal societies, which determines the whole of one's behaviour in all spheres of life); between particularistic roles which involve relations with certain people only, as against 'universalistic' ones which govern one's behaviour towards everybody: to mention only some of the paired contrasts.

The kinds of roles actually found in most societies, though, usually fall somewhere between these theoretical extremes. And since individuals are socialized into the roles typical of their culture, these value-orientations become part of their individual personality, too; of their way of thinking, the judgements they make, and even the ways they respond emotionally to situations and people.

Applying all this to the study of development, theorists like Bert Hoselitz concluded that there was a broad difference in kind as between developed and underdeveloped societies; that there were clusters of pattern-variables, not just random mixes peculiar to this society or that. Underdeveloped societies, which they called 'traditional', were typically particularistic, ascriptive, and functionally diffuse; developed societies were universalistic, achievement-oriented and functionally specific. Ascriptive, diffuse roles, such as those of kinship, therefore, were unsuited to modern situations calling for personal responsibility and clear-cut, objective managerial decisions.

To bring about development, therefore, 'modern' values needed to be implanted, especially in the young. Government officials should *not* favour their relatives (particularistic behaviour), but treat all their clients alike (universalistically). People would need to be trained for specific jobs in a technically complex division of labour, instead of diffusely, as 'generalists' such as peasants whose work (and non-work) relations entail many different kinds of activity with a wide range of people. The ambitious should be given their chance to achieve, and not be restricted to a limited range of ascribed roles governed, say, by their sex, age or their social rank.

The replacement of ascribed roles of this last kind by roles individuals carved out for themselves was singled out as the most important element of all by David McClelland. What was needed, he argued, was not specific technical skills in, say, maths or biology, but a forced-draught programme to implant achievement-orientation as an attitude and practice in general in the minds of young people, whatever they were engaged in.

These orientations were not seen as relevant to underdeveloped societies alone. They were also necessary if developed societies were to keep on developing. They will therefore be familiar enough today in Britain, the USA and other Western countries since they are the central messages of the new conservative 'conviction politics' which has been so effective in recent years: a philosophy of individualism, competition, and enterprise.

Hence modernization theorists found Max Weber's classic analysis of the connection between the emergence of historic capitalism in the West and the emergence of Protestantism highly relevant for contemporary development strategies in the Third World. For Weber, it was not (as many think he thought) that the Protestant religion *caused* the growth of capitalism; nor was it the converse, that Protestantism was simply a 'reflection' of capitalism. They had grown up independently of, but side by side with each other. Not everything in Protestantism had been of importance in the growth of capitalism, either. It was the 'ethic' of Protestantism, the code of conduct built into it (and more particularly into one denomination, Calvinism), not the theological beliefs about the nature of the universe or the afterlife that mattered: an ethic which prescribed the virtues of dedication to one's calling, the ascetic husbanding of wealth rather than its consumption, and the application of rational thought and organization so as to achieve one's ends with minimum cost. In practical terms, this encouraged saving, hard work, and efficiency (Weber, 1976). Those who worked according to these principles best would be most likely to come out on top.

These values, modernization theorists argued, are still valid today. But though they had originally grown up in the West, even there they had become detached from specifically religious philosophies and institutions and increasingly expressed in quite secular terms in such 'bourgeois' doctrines as Samuel Smiles' 'self-help' which celebrated the virtues of hard work, thrift, ambition, and so forth.

Others were aware that entrepreneurial values similar to those of

the Protestant Ethic could also be found in non-European philosophies and religions: in Hindu and Muslim beliefs which Indian
trading-castes had brought with them to East Africa at the turn of
the century; among the Zoroastrian business community in Bombay;
or in the rational and worldly elements of Chinese thought which,
given appropriate conditions, became predominant over the more
mystical, other-worldly elements in Chinese religions, notably when
poverty-stricken peasants emigrated into the Pacific in the late
nineteenth century, where, initially as small traders and middlemen,
they laid the basis for world business centres such as Hong Kong
and Singapore.

For such values to flourish, social scientists argued, more was
required than education alone. Capitalism required an open market
not only in commodities, but the institutionalization of a liberal
social order under which those with the most initiative, intelligence
and critical judgement could compete and the best come out victors.

In practical terms, however, success stories of capitalist industrialization outside the West were few in number, the major instance
being that of Japan, and this took place in a way far removed from
liberal *laissez-faire* theory. Even in the West, indeed, the triumph of
the bourgeoisie had not been simply an economic victory in the
marketplace. They had had to win political power, in revolutions,
from the English Civil War to the French Revolution. In the
process, beginning long before those turning-points and completed
only long after them, the whole social order, not just the economy,
had to be reconstructed: parliamentary government, and eventually
mass democracy; the centralization and expansion of the State; mass
education; the displacement of religion by science; the transformation
of the family; the introduction, eventually, of the Welfare State, and
so on.

Nationalists in countries like Japan therefore looked at Western
theory and practice – which, in any case, had taken many different
forms over the centuries – critically and selectively. They were
embarking upon capitalist modernization in a world already dominated, not by the old companies which had pioneered the colonial
expansion of the mercantile period of capitalism, but by large-scale
Western corporations. Drawn from traditional aristocratic and military elites, they had little taste for liberal democracy, except insofar
as a skilled labour force was necessary to a modern economy and

concessions to some degree of popular self-expression and organization were needed in order to foster a spirit of mass involvement in the new national project. But older values and social forms could also be harnessed to new ends: loyalty to the State in the form of a deified Emperor, and the celebration of samurai military values; while concepts of the individual as a member of family, kinship and other traditional groupings, to which he owed obligations, rather than Western notions of the freedom of the individual, could be used as models for new ideologies of working for the good of the corporate enterprise and of loyalty to those in charge of it: management. Even the Welfare State could be replaced by the Welfare Corporation, providing schools, medical services, and pensions for its employees, who stayed with it for life, and for their families.

Cultural anthropologists had long criticized their more extreme functionalist colleagues for assuming that coherence of structure and culture were always to be found. Societies and cultures were complex phenomena, subject to varied pressures to change, both internal and external, over time, and at different rates. Parts of the social system might change relatively little; others overnight. There could therefore be contradictions between different institutions, values and classes.

One version of modernization theory saw incompatibilities of this kind as most severe under post-independence conditions, where Western institutions and values clashed with pre-colonial ones. The real problem, they argued, was that societies like these did not function as coherent wholes. For that to happen, a much more thoroughgoing diffusion of Western values would have to take place, and the displacement, too, of traditional elites and institutions In the colonial and post-colonial period, theorists like Edward Shils argued, the problem had become compounded because new elites, made up of intellectuals from varied social backgrounds and educated in the West, were trying to direct social change along lines they had learned about in London and Chicago (including, sometimes, socialist lines) but which were unacceptable, or not even understood by the traditionalist masses (Shils, 1972), and had often generated incoherent mishmashes of old and new ideas. To many, therefore, Japan seemed the exception rather than the rule, because it possessed a strong State, controlled by a coherent ruling class, and had never been subjected to Western colonial control. But most countries *had* become colonies, and for them the State was controlled by foreigners who transformed the economy to the advantage of the mother-country. The central assumption of modernization theory, it seemed, was therefore invalid: that the main barrier to modernization was the persistence of 'traditional' institutions, such as religions inimical to innovation, or rulers interested only in preserving, not changing the social order.

The victory of Christianity in Latin America, four centuries earlier, and the more recent triumph of science, had not resulted in the industrialization of those societies, however. Nor had the removal of pre-Conquest rulers, while in the newer colonies traditional ruling elites such as India's princes, rajahs and maharajahs were retained and maintained by the British to give their rule a certain legitimacy and as a counterweight to rising nationalism.

Dependency and World-System Theory

The challenge to modernization theory, not surprisingly, came from that part of the Third World that had been colonized longest: South America. The critics saw it as a predominantly pro-Western theory, and their response was always nationalistic but not necessarily socially radical.

As nationals of countries which had achieved their political independence over a century ago, during the struggles that brought independence to the USA, Haiti and to South America, they, and those who studied that continent, were aware of the shortcomings of theories which explained the subsequent failure of South America to develop along European or North American lines either in terms of the persistence of pre-colonial institutions and values (for the Spaniards and Portuguese had devastated indigenous cultures and installed their own), or – as nationalists in other continents struggling in the period after the Second World War for their independence were to argue – that the major barrier to development was direct colonial political control.

For the countries of South America, despite having been politically independent since the beginning of the nineteenth century, were still economically underdeveloped. The blame for this, they believed, had to be laid at the door of the major imperialist powers – Britain in the nineteenth century and the USA today. It was also a common condition affecting all of them. Hence though one could argue that economic backwardness was the result of cultural deficiencies in Latin America as a whole, to most Latin Americans it was not due to internal factors, either within any particular country or in Latin America as a whole, but to something external to all of them: indirect economic control exerted via the world-market – *neo*-colonialism, rather than old-fashioned, direct political colonialism, with the aid, however, of local elites who did what the West wanted because they benefited from it.

The most influential critique of modernization theory came from an economist with a wide knowledge of anthropology and sociology and of South America, André Gunder Frank. Modernization theory was open to criticism, he argued, on three counts: in terms of its theoretical assumptions; in terms of its empirical accuracy; and in terms of the patent failure of policies based on it.

Theoretically, he observed, roles are of different kinds, and some are more important than others. The most important of all are economic and political roles. It is therefore illegitimate to lump together as, say, 'universalistic', the very different roles of a patriarchal father and a Prime Minister, for they exercise authority within very different social units, at different levels of the social structure, and with very different consequences for those they control. Further, by firstly abstracting different kinds of roles in this way, and then classifying them in terms of the values typical of them, roles and values, rather than social units, are highlighted. This procedure also obscures the fact that the highest level of modern society is not the 'society', but the world as a single global system within which all societies exist.

Today, countries are determined by their place in this world-system – say, as exporters of cocoa or of high technology. They can no more be thought of as self-contained entities than the tribes anthropologists study, for both have long become incorporated into and dominated by wider states of which they now form merely a part. Though they might retain cultural distinctiveness, they are now only 'part-societies'.

It was not the case, either, Frank insisted, that developed societies were characterized by the values modernization theorists had claimed to be typical of them: universalism, achievement-orientation, and functional specificity, or that underdeveloped societies were particularistic, ascriptive, and functionally diffuse. The directors of modern industrial corporations were not functionally specific: they often occupied a whole set of important positions not only in corporations but in other powerful public bodies such as government committees. They often acquired these positions because of ascription, as the sons of rich and powerful fathers, rather than via achievement. Different social groups and categories are treated quite 'particularistically' (the respectable middle classes, poor immigrants, women) and not 'universalistically', even in developed countries.

Conversely, dictators and oligarchies in the Third World exercise 'universalistic' power over all activities in society; most of them have seized power (achievement), while other social roles are quite universalistic (as when military personnel behave in the same authoritarian way to civilians, whatever the social characteristics of the latter as clergymen, women, educated or uneducated, and so on).

Finally, in policy terms, Frank argues, the 'mix' of values supposed to be conducive to development simply has not proved to be effective, while 'role-ascription and diffuseness in business, government and military circles in the United States has not so far turned that country into an underdeveloped one' (Frank, 1969, p. 38).

Development planning, for modernization theorists, then, consisted in constructing indices for developed societies (the number of telephones per head, rates of infant mortality, etc) – as the World Bank, for instance, does – and subtracting measures of the same items in underdeveloped countries from these: 'the remainder is your development programme', the necessary inputs for which have to come, overwhelmingly, from the developed countries in the form of investment or aid.

In reality, the critics of modernization theory observed, the flow has been the other way – the funnelling back of wealth created in underdeveloped countries to the developed world, not only in the form of capital, but of human capital: the vast exodus of millions to the labour-markets of the 'centre', including the 'brain drain' of people whose education had been funded by their home countries but who now worked for the benefit of the advanced countries where they lived. The theory of diffusion failed to recognize, too, that in the colonial era some liberal institutions – parliamentary democracy and parties – had not been diffused at all, but rigorously repressed, while today, economic controls had replaced these older political controls, since the developed countries kept the most advanced kinds of high technology in their hands while leaving older industries such as textiles to be taken over by the Third World.

As far as Rostow's stages of development are concerned, the stage of traditionalism was, Frank said, 'a category which denies all history to . . . underdeveloped countries' since it included Africa, where the slave trade had transformed society long before colonialism; countries such as Peru and Mexico where indigenous social systems had been wiped out; countries where virtually the entire population had been exterminated and re-settled by white immigrants (the USA, Argentina, Australia, Brazil); yet others where plantation slavery had been established, and so on. The second stage, supposedly one in which the conditions for economic growth would become established, had not led to development, but to underdevelopment, even in those countries which had first experienced colonization 400 years ago and which had been independent for nearly two centuries. Stages three and four (take-off and maturity) had simply not occurred, even less high mass consumption.

And more important than these negative criticisms was the absence in modernization theory of any conception of the world as a whole. To dependency theorists, the underdevelopment of part of the world was due to the exploitation of that part by the developed countries. Both, however, were only parts of a single social system in which the colonized and now the neo-colonial countries – the 'periphery' – were not simply 'underdeveloped', but had *been* underdeveloped by other countries which together constituted the 'centre' of this world-system – a process expressed in the title of a book by a Third World historian, *How Europe Underdeveloped Africa* (Rodney, 1972). Looking for the causes of underdevelopment within any particular country or in the underdeveloped countries as a whole was therefore methodologically wrong, for the cause was to be found in the centre, not the periphery. The only significant development that had taken place in Latin America, Frank wrote, had occurred when the power of the West had been temporarily interrupted, notably during the Depression of the 1930s and during the Second World War. But there would be no *permanent* development in the periphery until the stranglehold of the centre was broken.

Dependency theory evoked a positive response in Latin America because it seemed to explain the phenomenon of underdevelopment despite lengthy independence. To Marxists, it looked like the long-needed updating of Lenin's classic theory of imperialism, which had explained the drive to the final parcelling up of the world, in the late nineteenth century, as the result of a crisis internal to the industrialized capitalist countries themselves, since the poverty of the workers meant that they were unable to buy the goods industry increasingly produced, and where finance-capitalism had become more powerful than industrial capitalism. Since the return on capital invested was declining, capitalists had to look for new areas where 'super profits' could be made – the colonies – because of the very low wages paid there, and which also generated cheap raw materials for Western industry. It also allowed a part of the working class in Europe, what Lenin called the 'labour aristocracy', to share in the benefits of this super-exploitation of workers in the colonies, via higher wages, via the conceding of the right to organize trade unions, and, eventually, via welfare benefits. Other theorists emphasized the advantage to Western capitalism of the opening up of the vast new markets of the colonies to the products of Europe and North America.

Marx himself had seen capitalist colonization as a contradictory phenomenon. Like capitalism in its heartlands, it had been a politically ruthless, but economically modernizing process. In India, the activity of 'British tax-gatherers and the British soldier . . . English steam and English free trade' had been 'brutal' and 'sickening', but had unleashed 'the only social revolution ever heard of in Asia': not only the removal of traditional elites and the dissolution of the caste-system, but the growth of the proletariat, the political unification of the sub-continent, the introduction of a free Press, the modernization of agriculture and of communications, and the beginnings of modern industry (Marx and Engels, 1972, pp. 40, 86).

Capitalism was therefore socially as well as economically progressive; it was also being implanted as a mode of *production*. But radical Marxists followed Lenin rather than Marx in insisting that imperialism had only resulted in and could only lead to a condition of permanent underdevelopment. For this reason, they not only found dependency theory acceptable, but saw in it a rationale for armed revolution. More orthodox communists emphasized the persistence of internal 'feudal' and pre-capitalist elements, especially land-owning oligarchies, which need to be replaced by a progressive, modernizing industrial capitalist class.

Dependency theory therefore evoked a positive response from that class, too: from the 'national' capitalists who found themselves struggling against the giant transnational corporations (TNCs) and who could therefore represent themselves as patriots. In alliance with Labour and peasant movements, they strove to gain control of the State so that investment, both public and private, could be channelled towards national firms instead of importing foreign manufactures from the 'centre' or relying on branch plants of the TNCs set up in the periphery. In countries like Argentina under Perón, and for a time in Brazil, populist alliances of this kind actually came to power. This combination of the masses and national capital frightened the middle classes and foreign capital, who therefore welcomed the Army's seizure of power and the subsequent crushing of popular organizations.

During the populist phase, a wave of revolutionary enthusiasm had swept the Third World following the victory of the revolution in Cuba and the defeat of France and then of the USA in Vietnam. In Latin America, many of this generation had little patience with any kind of collaboration with capitalism, national or foreign, and pointed out that the foreign TNCs, not national capital, had increased their dominance even during the populist phase. With the replacement of populist governments by military dictatorships, a new wave of expansion, guided by a military technocracy, began using the power of the State to encourage foreign investment and bringing prosperity to the greatly expanded middle classes, though not to a working class and peasantry now left defenceless because of the smashing of their parties and trade unions.

Dependency theory therefore appealed for a time to a wide range of opinion, from revolutionaries to nationalist technocratic planners, mostly economists, whose language often therefore sounded quite Marxist though their social vision was in fact quite conservative. Their main preoccupation was to stem the flow of capital abroad, whether in the traditional form of the repatriation of profits or in more modern forms: reinvestment within the country; payment for the use of patents and management services; 'transfer' payments for goods imported from the parent firm back home, often at inflated prices, and so on.

Yet the original version of dependency theory became increasingly less and less tenable, for plainly development had been taking place in many countries. In countries like Mexico, where major industry

was overwhelmingly US-owned, manufacturing industry nearly quad-
rupled and the workforce doubled in the 1950s and 1960s; in Brazil
by the late 1970s there were 830,000 production workers of all
grades of skill, mostly employed in giant plants owned by Volks-
wagen, Scania, Mercedes-Benz, etc, and earning, on average, six
times the minimum wage, the most skilled amongst them getting
twenty, fifty, even a hundred times the poorest paid in the labour
force as a whole. Many even of the auto workers lived, however, in
shanty-towns side by side with the new immigrants from the countryside, people called 'marginals'. Yet they were still relative 'aristocrats'
in a labour force in which a sixth worked less than forty hours a week
and where rural workers, half the entire labour force, were chronically
under-nourished. Industrial expansion had left huge segments of the
population in poverty, as it had done in nineteenth-century Britain.

Whole countries, from city-states like Hong Kong and Singapore
to sub-continents like India, were now being redesignated as 'newly
industrializing' countries in international statistics, even if many of
them, like Brazil, had a large and poor rural sector, and in others,
like India, peasants still outnumbered the rest of the population.

The simple assertion that development was not possible under
neo-colonialism was patently at variance with the facts, at least for
large parts of the globe. Criticism of Lenin's theory of imperialism
now came even from Marxists. Some reminded their audience of
Marx's earlier view of the dynamic, 'progressive' effects of capitalism.
Capitalism, they argued, was not in its dying phase, as Lenin had
asserted, but still expanding, and especially so in the Third World.
They also rejected Lenin's economic historical analysis: the capital
that had fuelled the original Industrial Revolution had been accumulated more in the West itself than out of enterprise in the colonies,
while increases in trade with the colonies had not followed the ups
and downs of Western trade-cycles Lenin had outlined. But the
crucial criticisms related to politics and society. Some revolutionary
Third World theorists, like Frantz Fanon (Fanon, 1983), argued that
the entire population of the West, including the working class, and
not just a privileged segment of it, had become de-revolutionized
because they benefited, too, from the neo-colonial connection (a view
which others rejected on the grounds that workers in the West, not
the East, produced more surplus value and were therefore more
exploited). Others believed that the process of incorporation of the

working class – through rising living standards and the gradual extension of civic rights – would spell the end of revolution in the Third World (Warren, 1980), a view which did not impress dependency theorists, who now conceded that development was indeed taking place in some countries, but a *dependent* development. This primarily benefited the TNCs, and confined the Third World to outdated economic sectors or to a role as suppliers of raw materials, especially oil, to the West; a traditional role which today, however, might well involve high technology and, in a few cases – notably Canada, Australia and New Zealand – was even compatible with a high standard of living. But labour in the Third World was still grossly exploited, and revolutions against repressive regimes were still occurring. Further, growth in the First World took place at the expense of despoliation of the natural resources of the Third World.

Modes of Production

The beginnings of modern capitalism go back half a millennium. Obviously, capitalism has changed greatly as an economic system during that time, from a largely trading enterprise confined to towns and cities that were only islands in a peasant sea, through the factory system of the Industrial Revolution, to the giant TNCs of today. These successive forms have been compatible with very varied political and social structures, from the absolutist monarchies of early modern Europe to parliamentary mass democracy in recent times. Yet beneath all these changes, certain principles have persisted, by virtue of which most writers designate all these different forms of social (and not merely economic) organization 'capitalist' or 'bourgeois'.

In recent decades, the rise of dependency theory has made categories once restricted to Marxist circles more widespread. To Marxists, capitalism is the most important mode of production today, even if it is only one of many that have existed in the past. For most of them, too, the economy is the 'base' of any social system. There is, however, much debate about just how and to what extent this 'base' determines the nature of the non-economic institutions in society, while non-Marxists (and even many Marxists) reject the notion that the economy determines the rest of social life. There is debate, too, as to what modes of production have existed in the past, and, even more fundamentally, about what constitutes a mode of production in the first place. To some, it means little more than a system of technology or work-relations; to others, production for profit on the market; to yet others, relationships wider than the marketplace or the workplace which arise from the way production is organized under capitalism, the key institution being that of private property in the means of production (machinery, land, etc). Labour, conversely, is performed by those who own no such means and who therefore have to earn a living by working for the property-owning class. (For hunters and collectors, conversely, the idea of anyone *owning* the earth is incomprehensible; anyone can make tools; and there is only a minimum of personal property of any kind.)

Within any particular economy, however, there are several different modes of production. Thus slave plantations existed side by side with free peasants working their own land and with miners working for wages. One of these, however, will be more dominant than the others in the economy as a whole.

Over the decades, different writers have distinguished a variety of modes of production. Here we can only mention a few of the main ones, especially capitalism and its immediate major predecessors. Before capitalism, it is commonly believed, society was feudal. But research now shows that the feudal mode of production, in which peasants were obliged to pay rent, either in the form of produce from their small plots, or in the form of work for their lords, or in money, was hardly to be found outside Europe. In the rest of the world, most of the major states were bureaucratic empires (in Turkey, Persia, Central America and the Andes, etc) where the peasant's dues did not take the form of rent paid to his local lord, but of taxes paid to the central State, a system generally known as the 'Asiatic' mode of production.

Wolf has argued, however, that both Western European feudalism and the 'Oriental despotism' that is the political aspect of the Asiatic mode of production are simply variants of one single mode of production, which, following the Egyptian economist, Samir Amin, he calls the 'tributary' mode of production. Here economic surpluses are extracted from the producer, the peasant, through the exercise of political power, not, as under capitalism, via the operation of the market, in which employers, theoretically at least, are free to buy labour-power like any other commodity, and workers, likewise, are free to sell it to the highest bidder. Both the feudal and the Asiatic modes, Wolf argues, are simply variants of the tributary system: in the feudal variant, 'power is held largely by local overlords and the rule at the apex is weak'; in the Asiatic version, 'power is concentrated strongly in the hands of a ruling elite standing at the apex of the power system' (Wolf, 1982, p. 80). These models, of course, are intended to explain the very different paths of development in the East and the West respectively, especially the emergence of strong centralized states of a non-capitalist kind in the USSR and China. The only other major mode that Wolf uses in his sweeping study of world history is the one he calls 'kin-ordered', which is found on the peripheries of powerful tributary and capitalist states, e.g. in tribal societies. He calls these 'kin-ordered' because it is through kinship relations of various kinds that resources (access to land and labour, including rights over women and offspring) are allocated to certain categories of kin and denied to others.

Wolf, however, extends the term 'production' to include the *re*production of *any* social ties necessary for the integration of the social order and its persistence from generation to generation. Hence almost anything (religious cults, marriage-systems, residential groupings, etc) becomes part of the mode of production, a definition far removed from older definitions which restricted the term 'production' to relationships strictly entailed in the process of producing crops or ball bearings.

The World-System and the Three Worlds

In Wolf's comparative study of world history, the unit of analysis is the mode of production. In Wallerstein's earlier influential work, which concentrates primarily upon the capitalist epoch, the unit of analysis is, rather, the country, though all countries are then classified according to their position in the world-system as belonging, respectively, to either the centre, the periphery, or the 'semi-peripheral' countries (Wallerstein, 1979).

Wallerstein did not, therefore, make use of the common division of the world into a First (developed capitalist) world; a Second (communist) world; and a Third (underdeveloped) world. For him, communist countries are only units within a single world-system, either part of the centre, the periphery, or semi-peripheral. Other writers, however, argued that capitalist and communist societies were fundamentally different not only in terms of economic and political organization, but in terms of social structures and culture, too, so that to classify Cuba and Sri Lanka together as 'peripheral' (because they are poor and agrarian), or the USA and the USSR as the 'centre' of a single world-system (because they are powerful and industrialized) obscures the massive differences between them.

Although the USSR maintained a rigorous control over Eastern Europe for decades after 1945, that control was challenged by Yugoslavia in Europe, and, more importantly, by China, which broke with the USSR in the early 1960s. Communist states, then, have not, collectively, constituted a coherent 'world' for a long time; some, like China and Vietnam, have even been at war with one another.

The Third World is an equally problematic concept. In its origins, in the 1950s and 1960s, it was a political grouping of former African and Asian colonies, determined to avoid being sucked into new Cold War alignments and dedicated to decolonization everywhere. Yet most of them have been economically very much part of the Western market-system, albeit a disadvantaged part. The Non-Aligned organization has even been joined by Latin American states which – since they had been independent for well over a century – did not initially share the political concerns of the new African and Asian states. Today, too, though the original purposes of the organization scarcely exist since the Cold War has ended and there are few colonies left, paradoxically, the Non-Aligned movement now includes virtually all the underdeveloped countries and even the 'NICs' – the 'newly industrializing' countries of Asia and South America. What holds them together is their common weakness as suppliers of raw materials in a world-market dominated by Western corporations and financial institutions, and the consequent debt burden which afflicts NICs such as Brazil and Mexico as well as the very poor states which have to spend half their income from foreign trade on paying their oil-bills.

As a result, the meanings people give to the term 'Third World' are widely varied and change a great deal over time. To some, it connotes primarily levels of economic development: they distinguish between rich and poor states, whatever their political colouring or cultural differences. From this perspective, China, for instance,

		ECONOMIC		
		DEVELOPED	UNDERDEVELOPED	
POLITICAL	USA	EEC and rest of Western Europe; Japan; Australia; S. Africa	Rest of capitalist world	WEST
	USSR	Eastern Europe; N. Korea	China Vietnam; Cuba	EAST
		NORTH	SOUTH	

(main or typical countries only)

Figure 4.

despite her communist regime and the power which her sheer size gives her, is still a 'Third World' country – because she is poor. To others, 'Third World' is a political term, emphasizing non-alignment. Yet most Third World states are, and have long been, aligned with the West. (China, too, does not even belong to 'Non-Aligned' institutions.)

We can all think of other important exceptions and difficulties with the notion that there are three distinct 'worlds'. The oil-exporting countries, for instance, are very rich in terms of GNP but are not industrialized. The World Bank therefore rightly treats them as a separate category. More fundamental difficulties arise because we are actually dealing with two polarities: a political distinction between capitalist and communist states, and an economic distinction between developed and underdeveloped. Logically, this results in four, not three, 'worlds': developed and underdeveloped capitalist countries, and developed and underdeveloped communist countries. The first of these is popularly called the 'West' (though 'East' has disappeared with the end of the Soviet bloc). 'North' and 'South', however, are increasingly used to distinguish the industrialized northern hemisphere from the predominantly agrarian southern one – despite the rise of the NICs. Some (but by no means all) of these contradictions are captured in Figure 4.

The New International Division of Labour

In the 1980s, attention switched to the TNC (transnational corporation) as the major force operating at a global level (Froebel *et al.*,

1980). The industries upon which the Industrial Revolution had been founded, it was argued, and which had also made possible the spread of modern imperialism across the globe, were by now obsolete, displaced by modern communications and information technologies based on the microchip and the computer. These new high-tech industries were characterized not by the concentration of production in the advanced countries, as in the past, but by the breaking down of different segments of the production process which were then located in different countries; the advanced operations, however, were reserved for the home base of the TNCs. The obsolete industries, typically textiles, which tended to use unskilled, low-paid, usually young and female, non-union labour, were now relocated in the Third World.

Economic change in the Third World has occurred not only within industry. Agriculture, too, has been completely transformed. The prices peasants get for their goods, increasingly produced for the world-market rather than for household consumption or local sale, are determined by competition on the part of producer countries to meet the enormous demand from Western industry for raw materials and from Western consumers for both basic foodstuffs and luxury commodities. In a number of Third World countries the State has intervened, in order to increase both foreign earnings and the supply of food for the internal market, by backing the 'Green Revolution': new genetic strains, notably of rice and wheat, have been created in research institutes and then put into mass production in countries like Mexico and India. Modern inputs – tractors (and the fuel they use), chemical fertilizers, pesticides and new forms of irrigation – are the main components of what constitutes a new technical 'package'. Despite bank loans, it has been the richer peasants who have benefited from these new programmes. Agriculture, in any case, is no longer necessarily the sphere of the small producer. Ever since the epoch of slavery in the Caribbean, large-scale, centralized, capital-intensive, high-tech management, in the shape of the plantation, has been applied to agricultural production: modern factory organization and the methods used to organize labour, it is argued, were first pioneered on the sugar plantations of the West Indies (Blackburn, 1988).

In the sphere of industry, the prosperity of the 'newly industrializing' countries – such as the 'four little tigers' (or 'dragons') of East

Asia (Hong Kong, South Korea, Taiwan and Singapore) – largely began with the older type of industry. Thus the capitalists who fled Shanghai as the communists rolled southwards through China in 1949 took their capital to Hong Kong, where they invested it predominantly in textiles (Wong, 1988). But although the industry they developed used cheap labour, technologically it rapidly became one of the most modern textile industries in the world. The second wave of growth, however, was very different: the implanting of high-tech industries, notably those based on microchips, by transnational corporations, mostly US and Japanese.

Much global-system theory assumes that decisions to locate production branches in a particular country lie solely with the external transnational corporation. But capital was *attracted* to Hong Kong as a result of internal decision-making by the local State. Although labour was cheap, it was not starvation labour: the diet of the working class was subsidized by the State to the extent of 50 per cent of its real cost. Workers were also provided with public housing. Over time, a modern health service and a cheap, modern and efficient public transport system were developed. Mass primary education was succeeded by mass secondary education and then by a large tertiary education sector, out of which a supply of technicians and engineers, scientists and managers flowed. The development of an infrastructure of communications, banking, insurance and shipping, with favourable taxation policies, was also attractive to foreign capital. Hence, more recently, a new division of labour has grown up: fabricated microchip wafers are shipped from the USA or Europe to assembly plants in Malaysia or the Philippines, but are tested in Hong Kong instead of being flown back to the home-base country. Hong Kong and Singapore, for example, no longer cheap labour countries, have thus become centres of a regional division of labour (Henderson, 1989).

These economic changes have had truly massive effects on all parts of the globe. Although the TNC has been the major organizational force in the sphere of production itself, as we have seen, economic transformation has involved political initiatives which were taken not by the TNCs themselves but by the State. The power of the corporations operating on a global scale does not explain the readiness of some states to welcome foreign investment, and of others to resist it. Nor does the acceptance of Western capitalism as an economic system entail the acceptance of the whole range of Western social institutions and cultural values, from Westminster parliamentarism to Christianity. Ruling classes and elites, too, have responded to the new global capitalism in very different ways from those they govern, and the social changes set in motion have had political consequences which governments had not intended. Thus the early phases of industrialization in countries like South Korea and Taiwan took place under conditions of rigorous political and social control – military or authoritarian rule, the absence of legal opposition and the repression of trade unions. So many and varied were the army, security and police forces used to eliminate opposition and enforce conformity that these societies were described by one commentator as 'semi-militarized societies'.

But industrialization brought into existence new social forces which were no longer prepared to put up with the absence of democratic self-expression. Hong Kong is, of course, still a colony (due to revert to China in 1997), but the growth of an economically crucial skilled labour force has led to pressure for democratic rights both within the colony and in China itself, albeit cut short by the Tiananmen massacre of 1989. Repressive authoritarian as well as military regimes still persist in the Third World. Yet in other newly industrializing countries such as South Korea and Taiwan they have given way to parliamentary systems with legal oppositions. In South America, democracy has been restored in the two major industrialized countries of the southern cone, Brazil and Argentina. In an age of global communications, the dismantling of State communism in Eastern Europe has inspired movements for the ending of one-party rule in Black Africa.

These developments have proved to be at variance with the kind of dependency theory that became popular in the late 1960s. Frank, for instance, divided the world up into 'core' countries and 'peripheral' ones, and, under the influence of the successful revolution in Cuba, saw only two possibilities for the latter: 'underdevelopment or revolution' (Frank, 1969). Yet subsequent decades have seen the eclipse of revolution in South America, signalled by the death of Che Guevara in Bolivia, and elsewhere by the 'destabilization' of revolutionary regimes in Angola, Mozambique and Nicaragua. Organizational structures developed to fight revolutionary wars proved inadequate when it came to coping with post-war economic development in North Korea, Vietnam and China, at a time when capitalist states from Mexico to Taiwan were making rapid strides in industrialization and agricultural modernization – at whatever social cost.

The emergence of the NICs in South America and South-East Asia therefore entailed modification of world-system theory to take account of them: Wallerstein's 'semi-peripheral' state, intermediate between 'core' and 'periphery'. Some writers went much further, optimistically concluding that the rise of industrialism in the NICs marks the beginning of a general evolutionary process that is either already happening or will eventually triumph in all presently under-developed countries. In its train will come both the Welfare State and parliamentary democracy (Warren, 1980). But industrialization on this scale has not occurred everywhere, and even countries with developed industrial sectors, such as Brazil or Mexico, share the fate of the less developed majority of Third World states: chronic in-debtedness to the banks, and consequent chronic social unrest and political instability or repression. Industrialization and repressive political institutions have gone hand in hand for decades, while popular dissatisfaction, far from taking the form of demands for Western-style democracy, has often expressed itself in terms of blam-ing the introduction of Western institutions and cultural forms for the troubles ordinary people, uprooted in their millions from the countryside, experience as the victims of these immense transforma-tions.

Many of the middle-level NICs like Mexico and Brazil (and even countries like Australia and Canada) still remain dependent upon the sale of primary commodities such as foodstuffs and minerals on the world-market. The income from those foreign earnings goes towards paying off not the capital they owe – that they can never do – but the interest charges on that capital. Black Africa in particular has experienced a serious deterioration in its economic relations with the outside world.

It is on this part of the globe that popular conceptions of the Third World are based: the image projected by humanitarian aid organizations, for instance, of a skeletal African child holding out its hands for food. That is, indeed, a horrific part of the reality of the Third World, and is – reasonably – used to appeal to the conscience of the affluent West. Yet famine in the Sahel, for example, is by no means solely attributable to the failure of the rains or population growth: the pressure, compounded by the government, to earn money through cash-cropping has pushed peasants into farming on quite marginal land that was hitherto used mainly by pastoralists – adversely affecting the soil and the economy of the pastoralists – while Ethiopia's national resources have been squandered on the purchase of expensive high-tech military equipment required in the attempt to crush movements of self-determination.

A few countries in the South, however, control crucial resources on which the rest of the world, including the developed West, depends, notably the oil-producing states. This wealth has enabled tiny elites to enjoy spectacularly luxurious lifestyles and the small indigenous populations to live well while cheap labour from poorer Third World countries does the hard work. At the level of the State, the wealth in the hands of the new elites has been used, internally, to strengthen their political control by introducing new techniques of repression, from instruments of torture to riot-control forces; abroad their new high-tech military forces, which include weapons of mass destruction – and in some cases nuclear potential – are employed in nationalist adventures against neighbouring countries (e.g. the Iran–Iraq War) rather than in confronting the developed world. Their wealth has not been spent on relieving the poverty of their peoples or on developing the economies of other Third World states.

The numerical advantage of the more than 125 states of the Non-Aligned grouping in terms of population and votes in international bodies has at times enabled these countries to exercise considerable power in world politics, even in the face of Great Power and Superpower opposition. The USA's frustration at this situation has led to its withdrawal of financial support for the UN itself and from membership of its specialized agencies such as the ILO and UNESCO. Yet the Non-Aligned movement is now rarely an effective *political* organization. It has been successful in pressing for the independence of the remaining colonial territories – the greatest success being the independence of Namibia in 1990 – but such territories are now few. On other political issues, it is neither powerful nor independent of the major blocs. The Arab world, for instance, was split down the middle over Western intervention in the Gulf, when more than half the Arab governments lined up with the USA because of their economic dependence upon the West as the principal market for their oil and the political and military dependence of unrepresentative elites upon foreign protection for their continued existence. Whatever the ideological cast of their governments and their cultural values, most Third World states have been unable to offer a serious challenge to the domination of the First World: Saudi Arabia, founded by the puritanical Wahabi religious movement, has had to shelter behind US military forces right in its hitherto insulated heartland; one after the other, communist states have been forced to introduce market competition and private ownership.

The persistence of ideological diversity further divides the Third World. Unanimity of ideology or policy can scarcely be expected from an organization that includes both the oil-state run by the richest man in the world, the Sultan of Brunei, and Fidel Castro's embattled Cuba. What common policy there is today among Third World states is therefore principally over economic rather than political issues. The 'Third World' of the 1960s has become the 'South' of the 1980s and the 'Non-Aligned' movement, its organizational expression, a predominantly economic pressure-group primarily concerned, despite its name, not with political 'positive neutralism', but with trying to use its power at the UN (beginning with the 'Group of 77' and the UNCTAD meetings of the 1960s) to induce the developed world to create a New International Economic Order. World poverty, and persisting inequalities between North and South, are thus the main forces keeping the Third World in existence both as concept and organization.

Those who insist, on the other hand, that the world is moving closer to one single world-system usually base their analyses upon the economistic assumption that the transnational corporation is the decisive force in international relations. Economically, this is becoming truer every day, while the cultural hegemony exercised over the population of the South by the most industrially developed states, especially the USA, is also growing; it has been vastly increased by satellite and other modern communications technology, which make possible the networking and syndication of TV and radio programmes across the globe (Sklair, 1991). So, whereas thirty years ago, Marshall McLuhan argued that printing – the 'Gutenberg revolution' – had converted the entire world into a 'global village', within only the last generation there has been a succession of technological innovations – transistor radios, television, tape-recorders and videos – which do not require literacy and which integrate even the most remote societies with the rest of the world. Today, Amazonian Indians and New Guinea Highlanders carry portable transistors, and the slum-dwellers described by economists and others as 'marginals' watch the same soap operas as those seen by millions of people in the First World. Here the analytical distinction between 'culture' and 'economy' breaks down, for the new global culture is itself a massive and profitable industry: five multinational corporations based in the USA and Western Europe dominate the world music industry. Yet their profits also come from the increasing production of non-Western forms of culture and of forms of Black music from the New World, ranging from jazz to reggae and soca, and now from Africa and Asia, which have been labelled 'world music'.

Economic globalism, however, by no means brings cultural homogeneity in its train. Ancient religions like Hinduism or Buddhism are not only very much alive but are undergoing renewal and expansion. Economic power, even where it includes the ownership of the culture industries, does not necessarily translate directly or simply into political power; in fact, the giant corporations often steer clear of involvement in politics. Politically, the world is still divided into nation-states which pursue their own interests (or those of the elites who run them) with varying degrees of success, while membership of international organizations is still also based on the nation-state. Even world-system theory, paradoxically, despite its insistence upon the global market, still takes the state as its basic unit of analysis within the world-system. Moreover, the nation is a cultural concept, and at the very time when the autonomy of the nation-state has been eroded by the growth of transnational corporations, nationalism has flourished. It has been a stronger force, indeed, in the twentieth century, than ideologies which purport to unite believers across national boundaries but which have notoriously failed to do so. Thus Marxism, which celebrates 'proletarian internationalism', has in fact produced fiercely nationalist forms of State communism: China has broken with the Soviet Union, and Vietnam has been at war with China; even small communist states like Cuba and North Korea have their own independent and distinctive styles of national communism. Similarly, 'fundamentalist' Islamic states and movements – which are actually highly innovative and quite un-traditional – have waged war on other Islamic states and movements (Zubaida, 1989). They have been equally un-traditional in making use of modern communications techniques to promote their ideologies. In Iran cassette tape-recordings of the exiled Ayatollah Khomeini's messages were a major means of communicating his ideas to the mass of the population.

Many of the new post-colonial states were only recent creations: constructs of the imperialist epoch. There was no such entity as 'Kenya' or 'Nigeria' before well into the last century. Hence when these countries achieved their independence in the 1960s, they gave 'nation building' top priority: the creation of a new, national identity in states whose boundaries included dozens, sometimes even hundreds, of different ethnic groups. The new elites who came to power denounced any attempt to assert these older identities as backwards-looking 'tribalism' or as foreign, 'neo-colonial' intervention and manipulation, and crushed attempts at secession, as in Katanga (Zaïre) or Biafra (Nigeria).

But the official nationalism of the State is bound to be continually challenged by movements which assert national and ethnic identities the State denies, since, in the words of the anthropologist Priscilla Reining, there are '10,000 societies inhabiting only 160 nation-states'. Some of these cultures are large 'nations without states' like the Kurds or the Palestinians; others, small tribal and other micro-nationalist communities (sometimes collectively called the 'Fourth World') encompassed within the boundaries of larger nation-states.

Today, moreover, the majority of the world's population live in the cities. Moving from the countryside necessarily entails not only the abandonment of familiar social institutions and values, but also involvement in new kinds of relationships and institutions, which carry with them new kinds of identity, especially those of ethnicity, nationalism and class. In the cities, political parties base their appeal to the masses on class.

Those who rule the new states have generally tried to eliminate any kind of opposition, whether ethnic/nationalist or class based, by establishing one-party states or via the seizure of power by the military. Populist governments preached 'African' socialism, arguing that class had not existed in pre-colonial Africa, but was introduced by European colonialism. Class-based, Leftist parties were therefore inappropriate to Africa. Despite this, urbanization and the growth of cash-crop agriculture and of 'agri-business' have generated new classes, providing a basis for radical parties and movements, sometimes local, sometimes nationwide, focused on programmes of social justice and the redistribution of wealth.

Nationalism, then, is only one form of cultural identity. Some identities – such as tribal ones – are narrower than the nation-state; others – some religious, like Islam or Christianity, some secular, such as nationalism or Marxism – profess to transcend national boundaries and to link those who belong to them to people in other countries and, internally, to cut across the horizontal divisions of class or caste.

The growing global power of the TNCs does not eliminate but often rather exacerbates economic inequalities between and within states, as well as sharpening political tension and reinforcing older cultural divisions. The world, that is, is far from being a unitary system; hence the notion of the 'end of the Third World' (Harris, 1987) appears over simplified.

As we have seen, the Non-Aligned movement as an organization has little political unanimity, so there is little likelihood of a repetition of OPEC's dramatic attempt, in 1973–4 to exert control over the world price of one crucial commodity, oil. Subsequent attempts to imitate OPEC were unsuccessful: a cartel of banana-producers, for example, failed because rich countries could live without bananas, or could produce them themselves, or could find Third World countries willing to break ranks in the hope of high profits. Other Third World raw materials could be replaced by man-made ones. And though OPEC shook even the economies of the West, the rise in the world price of oil damaged the economies of Third World non-oil states even more severely: in some cases, over half their foreign earnings went to pay the oil-bill.

The majority of the poor countries, even many of the NICs, have experienced a downturn in their economic development during the 1980s. The notion of the 'trickle-down effect' – that increased production would mean wealth to go round – has been falsified, because that wealth has been appropriated by elites for their own ends. Most has gone to pay off international debt. A Japanese writer has noted that 'the average rich world cat consumes around $500 worth of food a year – more than the GNP per capita of the seven poorest nations on earth – Chad, Bangladesh, Ethiopia, Nepal, Mali,

Burma, or Zaïre' (Ichiyo, 1984). We live in a world in which the wealth that exists in many poor countries is largely seized and squandered by elites on high living or on grandiose projects such as building the largest cathedral in the world in the Ivory Coast. Even the more fortunate states, however, share a common life-situation of chronic indebtedness and of helplessness in the face of the power of the transnational corporations and of volatile and deteriorating prices for their exports, while the prices of manufactured exports from the developed world remain high. The inhabitants of the South are politically at the mercy of their ruling classes and elites; economically, both rulers and ruled are victims of a world-market system controlled by financial institutions and commodity-exchanges in the First World – though even here the system as a whole is not under anyone's effective control.

3   The Research Process

Sociology, like any other form of systematic study, has to concern itself with methodology and methods. Methodology deals with the philosophy and logic of social inquiry, and its relationship to sociological theory. Methods and techniques are the nuts and bolts of doing research; the sets of techniques appropriate to the kind of study we are doing. Yet if this were an introduction to physics instead of sociology, there would almost certainly not be a chapter like this. The way in which physics is taught, and the way in which physicists think about their subject, mean that methods and techniques are built in with the bricks. They are an intrinsic part of acquiring understanding. Natural scientists in general do not worry much about methodology.

What is it then about sociology which generates this concern with methodology which some observers see as almost an obsession? Part of the answer is that studying social phenomena is difficult – much more difficult, in certain respects, than studying the physical world. In particular, the consciousness, inventiveness, and imagination of the subject-matter – human beings and their institutions – makes human behaviour far more unpredictable than that of physical objects. And although the problem of the impact of the investigator on what is being investigated is encountered in physics, in the form of the Heisenberg Principle, it can be safely ignored for many purposes. The effect on humans of being studied by other humans is an unavoidable and serious problem in much sociological inquiry. But the debate about methodology does not derive only from the nature of the subject-matter, for there are also genuine and deep philosophical differences between people who recognize each other as sociologists, and considerable disagreement about what doing sociology entails and about how it should be done. There is no single paradigm for inquiry in the discipline (for an excellent discussion of the concept of a paradigm, see Barnes, 1982).

One point must be made at the outset. It is often said that there is a close relationship between theory and method, that certain theories entail using certain methods and selecting and collecting certain kinds of data. In a crude sense this is obviously true; social interactionists make little use of census statistics or of mail questionnaires, for instance. But further reflection reveals that the fit is in fact rather loose. In particular, the common claim that there is a connection between functionalist theory and the use of survey methods holds up poorly under closer scrutiny (Platt, 1986). Indeed, theorists of *all* persuasions, despite their differences, have more in common, when it comes to empirical inquiry, than is often believed. So while it would be foolish to deny the philosophical and theoretical differences which divide sociologists, it is equally foolish to exaggerate them.

Here we are concerned only with *empirical inquiry*. Those forms of sociology which can be conducted entirely from the armchair are another matter.

Before plunging into the topic itself, a word on textbooks is in order. Firstly, there is no one single adequate textbook. Massive as they often are, they tend to be written from the point of view of a particular practitioner and to omit whole areas of research activity. Thus the standard text from an interactionist viewpoint (Denzin, 1970) is weak on problems of measurement and statistical techniques of analysis. Other authors (for instance, Blalock, 1970) might leave the beginning student with the impression that causal modelling and explanation are all that sociology is about, for participant observation figures little and whole areas of modern sociology go unmentioned. Secondly, both these and other such texts are *resource-books* – things to be *used* – to be consulted and dipped into as needed, not riveting 'reads' to be consumed at one sitting. Thirdly, and most importantly, all such texts, on the whole, present an *unreal and idealized* account of research.

The best way to learn about research methods, apart from conducting research under supervision, is also, alas, the one requiring most effort. Most students (and indeed if the truth be told, many professional sociologists) reading a book or article pay *most* attention to the theories or concepts used and the overall argument, *some* attention to the actual substantive findings, and very *little* heed to the methods

used. This is particularly so if the results are statistical or presented
in tabular form. Yet simply paying more attention to how a study
was done, what the substantive results were, and assessing whether
they support the conclusions, will teach more than reading a dozen
texts. One author (Rose, 1982) has looked systematically at this
process of evaluating research reports. Careful examination of this
kind into how the research was actually done reveals two things.
Firstly, good research is not easy in sociology, and even those who
come new to it can often see flaws and think of ways in which the
study could be improved. Secondly, even these accounts of research
– though they are closer to what is really done than the texts which
are the outcomes of the research – are still somewhat idealized, and
convey little of the cut and thrust, hand-dirtying nature of real
research. For that, we have to turn to accounts of their own work in
which sociologists have told all, or nearly all, and these – not just
ideal recipes of how to go about things – are an essential part of the
study of methods (see for instance, Bell and Encel, 1978; Bell and
Newby, 1977; Hammond, 1964; Platt, 1976; Vidich *et al.*, 1964).

Concepts and Theories

One thing that stands out in these accounts is that research must be
understood as itself a social process. Sociological understanding is
something that has to be struggled for in a series of interactions with
other persons, be these the subjects of the inquiry or colleagues. The
reality is far from textbook models. Thus, some texts suggest that
research should be largely carried out from the top down, that is to
say that research is supposed to start with a *theory*. A theory in this
sense is seen as a set of logically interlocked propositions involving
concepts and the relationships between these propositions (Denzin,
1970, ch. 2). The next step is *deduction*. By a strictly *logical* process
of reasoning, moving from general propositions and applying them
to the particular problem in hand, an *hypothesis* – a tentative
explanation – is formulated. The next step is to decide how the
hypothesis can be related to empirically observable events. An
experiment or other research design is therefore set up in order to
test the hypothesis. If the hypothesis is not disproved, then confidence in the theory increases somewhat. If the hypothesis is disproved, then, paradoxically, the research may have advanced the

subject more than in the previous case, because it is now necessary to improve the theory so that it can take account both of previous findings and of the new results. The process then continues as before.

This is often called the scientific method, though it is more precisely described as the 'hypothetico-deductive' model. On the face of it, the model fits quite well what is in fact published in many areas of the natural sciences and even of social science. But a closer study of what scientists actually do suggests that, to some extent, this is a matter, not of procedure, but of presentation! The work and the results are often written up so as to conform to the procedures of 'correct' scientific research which the ideal model of 'scientific' method calls for. Contrary to the model, results which do not fit the hypothesis by no means always lead to revision of the theory. Because the research method is itself complex, discrepant results can be explained away as failures of research design, or as various kinds of error rather than as weaknesses of theory. Good theories frequently survive a very long time indeed, despite contradictory evidence, until they eventually become untenable because they are at odds not with one or two results but with many (Kuhn, 1970). This, Kuhn argues, is because science itself is a social activity, involving vested interests, both in theory – in 'pet' theories or in such 'self-evident' observations as that the sun goes round the earth – and in institutions (schools, professorships, research programmes) based on these theories.

Before looking at the sociological research process in more detail, another model is worth attention, not 'top–down' research, but the strategy of doing research from the ground up. Research, this model asserts, starts with observation, with data gathering and analysis, the two often taking place together. The aim is to build up an understanding of what is going on, to conceptualize the empirical phenomena, and perhaps to develop theory. Rather than *deducing* an hypothesis from a theory, the researcher is *inducing* a conceptual structure – developing concepts – as a result of thinking about the empirical regularities observed. To be sure, induction does play a part in the hypothetico-deductive model described above, for if an hypothesis is disproved, the theory has to be modified inductively in the light of the evidence discovered. Inductive processes, however, play a larger part than this in the natural sciences and certainly so in sociology.

In some forms of sociological inquiry the processes of induction and deduction are closely intertwined. Thus in participant observation, theoretical insights are constantly being thrown up by the fieldwork and are almost immediately checked against further observations. Indeed this 'interplay of data and conceptualization' is often held to be a major feature of the approach (Bulmer, 1979). Other procedures, such as simulation or modelling, frequently preclude direct testing or falsification and are heavily dependent on induction. This diversity of strategies, in particular the 'top–down'/'bottom–up' dichotomy, has generated a lot of debate among sociologists.

In the 1960s, Glaser and Strauss (1964), for instance, argued powerfully that research would advance faster if sociologists concentrated on theory-generation rather than theory-testing and that view still has force today, for much sociological theory does not lend itself to the deduction of testable hypotheses. Despite pleas (Merton, 1957, pp. 9, 85–120; Merton, 1968, ch. 2; Marshall, 1963) for middle-range theories – theories which are less comprehensive than explanations of social life in general or the pattern of a whole society, but wider than minor hypotheses about a particular kind of behaviour – theories are generally couched at an extremely abstract and high level. Concepts are often insufficiently 'grounded' in data which have been obtained by empirical research. Other so-called theories are really only empirical generalizations, not a logical structure of propositions.

The claim that induction and deduction both play a major role in sociological inquiry leads us to a related, but much wider and more complex issue. This is the question of the aims or, as Winch (1958) put it, the 'idea' of a social science. Is the goal of sociology to *explain* or to *interpret* reality? According to the 'interpretative' view, knowledge and understanding arise from the process of living in the world. Knowledge is an emergent property of inquiry and concepts only act to sensitize us to what is going on. Thus, it is not a scientific method that we learn and then apply to a world that exists utterly apart from our perceptions of it. Rather, authentic knowledge is generated out of our immediate experience of the world, so that the way the researcher acquires an understanding of the world is basically similar to the way we all find out what is going on and who is who in everyday life – something we do without using scientific method. In contrast to the model of a physical world which we get to know via external, experimental and often quantifiable methods, the social world, in the 'interpretative' view, can only be understood 'from within', introspectively. In the extreme, some hold that empirical inquiry, in the sense of acquiring facts about an 'objective' world outside us, is not possible, because we cannot perceive that world except by using subjective ideas, concepts, theories, etc.

We cannot, however, simply gather data accumulated in random ways and then hope to see what it all means later. Consider a sociologist observing what goes on at a railway station. First of all it is not possible to observe everything that goes on. Only some things will be seen, partly because it is physically impossible to notice everything but more crucially because some things will be *perceived* rather than others. Also, different observers will perceive different things. The data which are gathered in this situation would depend on what our concerns are – what interests us in the first place – and in the case of the sociologist, this will be some implicitly held theory about the way the world works. Making that theory or, to put it less grandly, set of concepts and ideas *ex*plicit does not necessarily alter what is seen but it does make it easier for others to assess the observations which are made and conclusions drawn from them. It also makes it possible to search for counter-examples. If data are gathered in a mindlessly empiricist way, enormous difficulties then arise at the analytic stage. Crucial data may be lacking so that it is impossible to mould the material into a coherent whole. If a great deal of data has been collected, then without some conceptual framework there are simply too many alternative ways of structuring the data; too many inferences which can be drawn from a given set of data. Even though a great deal of sociological research takes place in areas where very little is known, even there sociologists start with a general sociological orientation to the world which provides a framework within which to start work.

Bearing this in mind, how do sociologists arrive at researchable problems? The process of generating ideas is somewhat mysterious and not easily analysed, and some people seem to be better at the task than others. Undoubtedly part of the story is the development of an attitude of mind. Thus, a good general knowledge of the sociological literature plays an important part; some of what is involved in research is the re-arrangement of old ideas in a new way. Just as many sociologists do not pay enough attention to the methodology used in a study, others do not approach the literature with th right questions. Could one investigate this and could one test that? Is this or that statement really right and how do we know? There are three main sources of ideas: sociologists who constantly interrogate their *reading* in these ways are likely to be overwhelmed with researchable ideas as well as a great deal of dross! Secondly, *everyday experience* is a major source of ideas. Of course one cannot generalize on the basis of personal experience, but once the trick is learned of seeing the world through sociological eyes, research-generation becomes a great deal easier. Despite the paucity of genuinely deductively derived hypotheses, *theory* is clearly the third great generator of research ideas; in particular, the ability to see the applicability of a set of ideas or concepts generated in one situation to a quite different situation.

Much good research questions the taken-for-granted aspects of the world. A moment's reflection reveals why this should be so. Sociologists are well aware that many social processes persist and recur simply because they are not questioned: they form part of the taken-for-granted world. To identify and inquire into just what these processes are brings us quickly to fundamental questions of societal structure. Similarly good research often results from asking a question in a different way. Thus for instance Burns, instead of seeking the social *causes* of the student unrest in 1968, asked why it was that different social groups offered different *explanations* of the revolts (Burns, 1969a). The questions most sociologists and commentators were asking were 'Why have students started behaving in this way?' or 'Why does such behaviour ever occur?'. But by changing the perspective to ask why there were so many different explanations, Burns opened up a different and more imaginative approach to the sociological issues involved. This issue of the nature of sociological explanation, and especially the critical function of sociological inquiry is further developed in his inaugural lecture (Burns, 1967).

Thus, by the exercise of the 'sociological imagination', to borrow the title of what is still the best account of the sociologist's craft (Mills, 1959), and not simply by mechanically applying an invariable 'scientific method', the researcher arrives at a sociological problem. In the present state of the discipline, this often takes the form of an ethnographic (or sociographic) problem. The researcher decides that for theoretical or conceptual reasons it would be valuable to construct an account of what happens in a particular situation. At one time research of this kind was characterized pejoratively as mere 'description'. As sociologists have come more and more to realize that all observation and description is theory-laden; as anthropologists, who specialize usually in 'field-research' based on 'participant observation', have increasingly turned their attention to industrial societies; and above all, as it has become recognized that fieldwork can be as rigorous as other techniques (and more suitable for many kinds of inquiry), ethnography has developed rapidly in sociology. Most descriptive research, in any event, also involves explanation: the distinction is far from rigid. The research-problem, especially in well-developed areas of sociology, may however be more explicitly one of explanation, involving the generation or testing of theory or, in some kinds of quantitative research especially, the development of elaborate causal models based on complex statistical techniques. Sociologists have also become increasingly involved in a rather different style of research: evaluation (for an introductory account, see Weiss, 1972; for more detail see *Evaluation Studies Review Annual*, 1976–). Here sociological techniques, concepts and ideas are used to assess the outcomes and degree of success of educational or social policy, for instance, urban housing or health education programmes. Evaluation may involve not only formidable problems of research design and methodology, but also difficult ethical and political questions.

Methods

Sociology and sociological research are of course not as distinct from other disciplines as this general overview of the research process, up to now, might seem to suggest. In recent years, historians, for instance, have come to use sociological methods, especially quantitative techniques, more and more, while sociologists have belatedly realized that the present cannot be neatly divided from the past and that the research skills of the historian have much to offer (Tilly, 1981; Stinchcombe, 1978). Oral history, where the disciplines most clearly overlap, has become almost a subject in its own right (Thompson, 1978). Sociologists have also borrowed statistical and other techniques from economists, and some economists in turn have begun to make more use of case-studies and surveys. Geographers have developed graphical methods to a high level, and some of these applications are of use to sociologists. The close relationship between sociology and anthropology ranges from a shared use of fieldwork methods and techniques to modern network analysis.

It therefore makes sense to talk of social science methods, particularly so in the case of two very different tools: statistics and computing. The first is almost self-evident. At least an elementary understanding of statistics is a basic requirement for a sociologist. Practically everyone uses descriptive statistics from time to time. Even those who work primarily with qualitative materials have to read and assess more quantitative work.

The actual and potential impact of the computer on research is less well appreciated. The computer is not just an extremely powerful and swift number-cruncher although this is its best-known application. Survey practice has been transformed in the last fifteen years as the machines have increased vastly in power, and as survey packages have been written which are versatile and easy to use. It is now simple to produce tables neatly labelled and percentaged, to perform complex statistical calculations quickly, and to manipulate large quantities of data in exploratory and imaginative ways. Researchers can analyse surveys sitting at their desks (or in their homes), using a terminal linked to a large computer and obtaining rapid responses interactively. It is already possible to handle small surveys on many of these machines and, in the foreseeable future, survey analysis will not depend on the availability of a large mainframe machine.

The speed with which the computer can calculate makes possible elegant techniques of analysis such as log-linear analysis or multi-dimensional scaling which are quite easy to understand and interpret, and make less stringent demands on the data than many conventional statistical techniques (although the mathematics required for a complete understanding are difficult) (Gilbert, 1981; Coxon, 1982). Many researchers are now using computers to help with analysis of interview transcripts and field-notes. For those social scientists who largely deal in words, the word-processor has made the time-consuming business of writing up research a great deal easier and quicker: this chapter is being written, using a simple programme, on a relatively cheap machine. The development of graphics programmes which are easily used and extremely flexible encourages the use of graphical techniques of analysis which have been underused by sociologists. The computer, too, has made possible the archiving (for instance in Britain by the ESRC Data Archive at Essex University) of vast amounts of data now available for analysis by people who did not collect it. An especially useful source of data is the government. Britain has always had one of the finest collections of official statistics in the world and the computer has now vastly increased the potential for their use. Thus, for example, the small area statistics of the Censuses for 1971 and 1981, each 'small area' referring to Enumeration Districts of around 100 households, are now available on computer file. So are the data for the General Household Survey and the Family Expenditure Survey. Very exciting possibilities for research will be opened up after the 1991 Census by the making available to researchers of a sample of the individual responses from the Census made anonymous in a way which will ensure confidentiality. The cost of collecting survey data is extremely high. At the time of writing, a large survey carried out by one of the good commercial organizations could cost around £60 for each interview of an hour or so. The use of archived data makes relatively cheap research possible and, although it is often not easy to find exactly the material the researcher requires, the potential is very great.

An interesting example illustrates three of these developments: the way the computer has opened up research which was simply not possible before; the potential of an archive; and the close relationship between sociology and history. Some years ago, Michael Anderson embarked on an ambitious project, putting a large sample drawn from the 1851 Census on computer. For the Census of 1851, the enumerators' books, showing the entries made for each household, are available in the original manuscript form. The form in which the data were entered on the machine is also an example of the flexibility and power which can be achieved. The decision was made to keep the data in its original, literal form rather than coding it first. The computing problems were formidable, quite apart from the enormous clerical labour involved, but keeping the data as close to their original form as possible enables subsequent researchers to make many of the basic decisions about how the material is to be classified and coded; analysis has been predetermined very little in the process. Using these data, it has been possible to carry out a wide range of analyses on the population of 1851, the structure of households, and the occupations held by their members (Anderson, 1988, 1990). Studies of this kind were to all intents and purposes not possible at all without the computer. The other major gain, however, is that the enormous labour of compiling the data set only had to be done once. Now it is available in the archive and other scholars can use it.

Some of the techniques used in the analysis of these data from the 1851 Census schedules are very different from the number crunching applications with which many people are familiar. Although survey packages can be used to create tables and carry out statistical analyses, other techniques have been devised, for instance for the analysis of lists of names, of occupations, of relationships. Another historian, Robert Morris, has built up a comprehensive picture of the middle class in Leeds between 1820 and 1850 by matching data from a wide range of sources such as trade directories, lists of members of voluntary associations, and so on (Morris, 1983).

So far, we have briefly discussed the nature of social research and the sources of researchable ideas, and indicated some of the kinds of research it is possible to do, including the new possibilities opened up by the computer – possibilities which are changing and developing at such a speed that any account is out of date before it is finished. Before turning to the question of research design, one point will bear repetition: that sociological research is wondrously varied! It cannot be said too often that empirical sociology is *not* equivalent to survey research. At one time, even some sociologists seemed to believe that this was the case, and that the survey was the main form of research (Bechhofer, 1967). But though the situation has changed radically – and for the better – since then, the general public remains unaware of the wide range of methods used and topics studied by sociologists. The scale of modern studies ranges from those which draw on data about the entire population, using Census material, to very small groups. The groups of people may be chosen randomly from the population or from a particular section of it (women, the elderly, schoolteachers, patients in a hospital), or may be highly and non-randomly selected (jazz musicians, drug addicts, lorry drivers). The methods used range from the distant and impersonal (the mail questionnaire) to detailed and repeated interviews with a small group or unstructured close observation. The subject of study may be people as such, their institutions or organizations, social movements such as CND or the New Right, or even entire countries, as in comparative studies of strike rates, or Durkheim's classic study of suicide rates.

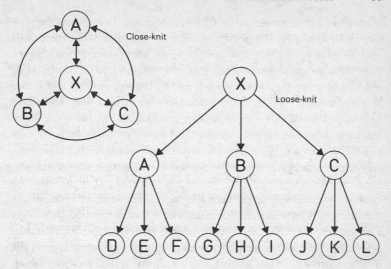

Figure 5. Two extreme cases of networks

The tendency to equate sociological research with surveys is probably also responsible for the belief that research only deals with *variables*. A great deal of research does do this. For instance, age is a variable, a continuous variable which can take any value between 0 and, for practical purposes, say 110. Very often we construct scaled variables, for instance scales of occupational prestige, where a high value denotes high prestige and vice versa (Reiss, 1961; and, for a critique and different approach, Goldthorpe and Hope, 1974). Most survey research deals with variables, using packages which analyse survey data on the computer, such as SPSS, which are designed to make handling variables easy and efficient. The statistics we normally learn, too, is essentially about variables.

A little thought, however, shows that the study of variables like these is only a limited part of modern sociology. A great deal of subjective experience cannot be reduced to variables, though techniques such as attitude-scaling (for a simple account, see Oppenheim, 1966) obviously go some way in this direction. Secondly, the structure of relationships can to some extent be measured, as in network research. Suppose we ask someone (X) who are the three people he or she sees most often, and are given the names of A, B and C. Now suppose we go to see these three people and repeat the process.

There are two extreme cases which can occur. In the first case, A names B, C and X; B names A, C and X, and finally, C names A, B and X. This is very tidy and neat, the four people clearly form a very close-knit network. At the other extreme, when we go to inquire of A, we may be given the names of D, E and F; B gives us G, H and I; and C gives us J, K and L (Figure 5). Here we have a very loose-knit indirect network. Most networks in practice would fall somewhere between these 'ideal type' extremes and we may wish to measure how close-knit they are. We might also wish to introduce further complexities which reflect real life more closely. For instance, we can try and measure the *strength* of each tie in the network. It would also be useful if we could compare networks in various ways, and techniques for doing this have existed for many years, first developed, in a fairly elementary way, in studies of friendship patterns (see, for example, Moreno, 1960), and in graph theoretic methods developed later in the 1960s (Flament, 1963), leading to very sophisticated methods which have been developed in the last fifteen years. The crucial point is that it is *relationships* between variables, rather than the variables themselves – patterns rather than magnitudes – that are being studied.

Research then may be variable- (or attribute-) centred, or, alternatively, structure-centred. Yet a third kind of approach focuses on meaning. Two traditions can be distinguished here. 'Content-analysis' has been part of sociology for a long time, especially among those who are interested in the media (for a useful example, see the work of the Glasgow University Media Group, 1976, 1980, 1982). Techniques, again, range from the fairly elementary to the highly sophisticated (see, for instance, Holsti, 1969; Gerbner *et al.*, 1969), but the intention is to analyse systematically the content of text or pictures. The other line of approach derives from ethnomethodological emphasis on the *accounts* people give of their activities, and the meanings they ascribe to their experiences. Ethnomethodologists have developed their own approaches to studying these, including the use of video cassettes as well as tape-recorders, and their radical critique of other schools of sociology has stimulated even those sociologists who reject their approach to pay more attention to meaning. Techniques for analysing accounts are certainly not widely in use in sociology, as opposed to linguistics, but once again computers have made possible new ways of analysing language, and some sociologists are deeply interested in linguistics and computer-aided analysis of content.

Experimental Design

To all intents and purposes, sociology is not an experimental science, and experimental design as it is understood in psychology or biological science is simply out of the question. We cannot alter people's social circumstances at will – make them suddenly rich, or poor, or marry them off to someone we choose – no matter how illuminating the results might be. It is still well worthwhile making the effort required to obtain a working understanding of the *principles* of experimental design, however, because the whole point of these procedures is to overcome the problems of drawing reasonable inferences from data. Sociologists confront the same problems as researchers in the natural sciences: they cannot solve them in the same ways, but they do not simply go away. Studying the principles of experimental design, then, alerts the sociologist to the difficulties involved in empirical research, and these can be formidable (for an excellent account of experimental design, see Campbell and Stanley, 1966. For a simpler account with which to start, see Blalock, 1970; or Helmstadter, 1970).

The essence of classical experimental design is that one compares a situation in which some variable is known to be operating with one in which it is not. The question is whether differences between the two situations can be 'explained' in terms of this variable or not. The idea of experimental design is to rule out the possibility that the differences are due to something else; a really good design systematically excludes other alternatives.

What this involves can be illustrated by a silly but entertaining example. If parts of Europe with a high density of storks are compared with areas with a low density of storks, it will be observed that the birth rate is higher in the former than the latter. The hypothesis that the storks 'explain' the higher birth rate is possible but unlikely; the alternative explanation – that more storks and a higher birth rate are to be found in deeply rural areas – is, intuitively at least, more convincing. But for that intuition to be rigorously tested, we would have to identify and control the numbers of variables involved, and eliminate other factors. Thus, in the more serious example of procedures used in drug trials, if we wish to be absolutely certain that a particular drug has a certain effect, then we have to carry out complex trials involving two sets of patients: one set which receives the drug, and a second set which does not. Because the mind plays a role in these matters, we may wish to have three groups: one receiving the drug; one receiving a placebo, that is an inert 'drug' that has no chemical effects, but where the patients *believe* they are receiving an active drug; and one receiving neither. Immense ethical difficulties arise in such experiments (which, after all, involve, for instance, deceiving willing subjects). Clearly, too, someone has to observe the effects of the drugs on the patients, and they may well conduct their analyses in ways that result in conclusions that were in their minds when they started. They may wish to believe the drug is effective and, assessment in some cases being difficult, come to this conclusion. It may therefore be necessary to ensure that the observers do not know which patients received the drug and which did not. This is only one problem, however, because many other factors can affect this kind of experiment. Suffice it to say that a good design, as far as possible, rules them out of court.

Comparison and control

The procedures of experimental design involve four fundamental ideas. Two of them have already been introduced into the discussion: comparison and control. Comparison is perhaps the most basic notion in research; control is the process by which we rule out alternative explanations, something which is done experimentally by appropriate manipulation of the design and by randomization. The essence of a random design is that subjects are assigned randomly to one treatment or another; thus patients would be assigned at random to the drug or to the placebo, to take our earlier example. The problems which arise in sociology are illustrated from the other example. One cannot allocate storks randomly to one place or another! The other two fundamental notions – those of external and internal validity – we shall return to shortly.

But before we do, comparison calls for a little more thought. The whole idea is deeply ingrained in everyday thinking and is so much part and parcel of sociological thought that it requires an effort to realize what it involves. Very often when we give what is called a descriptive account of something, we are implicitly comparing it with something else, for it is much easier and more common to think of something in comparative rather than absolute terms. In physical science, a lot of effort has gone into establishing absolutes, but this is even more difficult in social sciences. Thus, for instance, in political sociology it is possible to think of ways of classifying some groups or individuals as being more Right-wing than others, by use of various indicators, or one part of a city may be judged to be more deprived than another, or the control of a company or a school or a university may be said to involve more or less participation by its employees. It is, however, almost absurd to think of an *absolute* measure of Right-wing views or behaviour, or of deprivation or of employee participation. This is not to say that one cannot measure these things at all, because of course it is possible, and sometimes desirable, to construct scales which measure such concepts. But though measurement helps us to compare one group with another, it does not supply an absolute measure. Even where some approximation to an absolute measure may be possible, relative measures may be more sociologically relevant. Thus, early attempts at absolute measures of poverty (Rowntree, 1901) gave way to relative measures (Townsend, 1979), while Runciman (1966) got a lot of mileage out of the deceptively simple idea of relative deprivation. The sociological classics of Marx, Durkheim and Weber involve comparing situations, groups and, especially, whole societies.

We saw earlier how Glaser and Strauss advocated theory-generation rather than theory-testing. The essence of their approach is that the discovery of some 'grounded' empirical relationship should not lead us to seek to repeatedly confirm it (the process of replication), but to proceed more imaginatively, either by looking for a contrasting empirical situation – in which the posited cause is absent – or a situation which is *conceptually* similar or contrasting. This latter process they term 'theoretical sampling' and it lies at the heart of their approach: the search for conceptually analogous or contrasting situations which are, however, empirically apparently quite different; almost, one might say, the attempt to apply concepts in unlikely but sociologically revealing places. Thus, they themselves point out that 'while fire departments and emergency wards are substantially dissimilar, their conceptual comparability is still readily apparent' (Glaser and Strauss, 1964, p. 54).

Internal and external validity

Comparison, then, is fundamental in many ways. Control enables us to draw the appropriate conclusions from our comparison. What then of the other two important elements of experimental design, internal and external validity? An experiment is internally valid if we can say with a reasonable degree of certainty that the experimental stimulus was indeed responsible for the differences found. It is externally valid if the results can be generalized beyond that particular design, place and time. Control is thus the process whereby we achieve internal and external validity.

In sociological research, however, it is extremely difficult to achieve high levels of control. So we need to be aware of the principles which alert the researcher to the advantages and disadvantages of different ways of going about research. For instance, a few but influential studies have started by taking a large sample at one point in time and then following them up at regular intervals, sometimes for very long periods indeed. Britain is unique in having three nationally representative studies of this kind. They all started as studies of perinatal mortality (death very early in life) and have collected data at intervals throughout the lives of the sample. The most comprehensive of these studies is the National Child Development Study, which took all children born in the United Kingdom in the week 3 to 9 March 1958. They and their parents were followed up at the ages of seven, eleven and sixteen, the cohort members alone at twenty-three and a further sweep of the survey took place in 1991 at the age of thirty-three (see, for instance, Kellmer Pringle *et al.*, 1966; Davie *et al.*, 1972; Fogelman, 1976, 1983). These 'panel studies', as they are known, are extremely expensive, time-consuming and difficult to carry out, and the business of repeated interviewing or contact carries with it a number of methodological disadvantages. On balance, however, such studies are immensely productive, as they enable sociologists to obtain a much better sense of process and change over time. What is often less appreciated, however, is that inferences drawn from them are more valid than from many other research designs.

Campbell and Stanley provide an excellent and thought-provoking account of what they call 'factors jeopardizing internal and external validity'. A good grasp of their discussion helps the sociologist to see problems in non-experimental research designs and provokes an attempt to overcome them. One of these was mentioned earlier; that observing or measuring, in sociological research, affects what is being measured. This problem, of so-called *reactivity* is a serious one and although very ingenious non-reactive measures have been devised and used in some research (see, for instance, Webb *et al.*, 1966) they are not very widely applicable. Some designs are better at coping with reactivity than others. Where different observers are used, for instance, or where there are changes in the observers themselves, problems of comparability and reliability arise and are therefore sources of invalidity.

Sampling

So far, we have mainly discussed general problems, which arise both when we study parts of a population, such as samples or small groups, and when we study entire populations, that is, *all* examples of the subject of study. The latter type of study is often quite feasible, for instance by using a national Census which covers the entire population of the country. Exhaustive studies of other, smaller populations, can also be made. If we could obtain access, for example, we could study the entire Cabinet, or all Members of Parliament, because the numbers involved are small. It is more common, however, to study a *sample*, that is a sub-set of a wider population, and the question then arises as to whether we can generalize to the whole population: is the design externally valid? In some cases we can use well-established statistical techniques to generate a sample, and anyone wishing to do sociological research requires at least a basic grasp of what is involved in sampling procedures. Sampling is especially important in survey work and specialist advice is often necessary.

Trickier problems arise, however, where sampling is not relevant. For instance, a sociologist studying an organization – a factory or a school, for instance – faces the question of whether the findings are applicable to other schools or factories, or indeed all organizations. Sampling does not help a lot here as a rule. In theory, we could draw up a complete list or a sampling-frame of all the schools in the country (say), draw a random sample, and then study them. But for most purposes this would mean studying a large number of schools, and this is seldom practicable. Here, we can only make some basic points as to how to tackle such problems. Firstly, we will have more confidence in our findings if the research stems from a good theoretical base and the findings relate clearly to that base. Secondly, comparison rears its head again. To the extent that our findings depend on comparisons *within* the school – say, between classes, between male and female pupils, or between teachers – the small sample may matter less. But if we want to make statements about the organization as a whole, they would be more convincing if explicit comparison were made with some other school or schools (though usually such comparison is almost certainly being made implicitly). Further, research which casts light on the social processes underlying the observed phenomena is more likely to be generalizable than research which only concerns itself with description or association between variables. Thus, for instance, a study of a school may show that one particular teaching style is more successful than another. This might be a generalizable finding or it might depend on other factors peculiar to that school, to that town or to those pupils. If, however, the researcher is able to explain *why* one style is more successful – that is to analyse the underlying processes – then confidence in the finding is increased. Finally, there is the question of replication. It is standard procedure in the natural sciences to repeat a study in various places and at various times, something which is rarely done in the social sciences although broadly compatible results arising from such replications would again increase our confidence in them. But with so much of the social world uncharted, social scientists cannot perhaps be blamed for following the strategy advocated by Glaser and Strauss (1964), among others, of generating theory rather than repeatedly testing it by replication.

Measurement

This important topic is also often disregarded by sociologists, even by those who pay considerable attention to data collection and analysis. Understanding the basic principles involved will help us see what the strengths and weaknesses of the various data-collection techniques are and show us that the issues are often not as simple as they might seem. We are trying to move from our concepts to the empirical occurrences which represent them in the world. Concepts cannot be observed directly; we therefore study the phenomena which serve as 'indicators' of our concepts. We cannot observe 'status', but we can observe 'indicators' which lead us to infer that one person has higher status than another. The essential point is that, as we said in the Introduction, 'data' are in fact badly named; there is nothing 'given' about them (which is what the Latin word *data* means). Rather, the world which we observe is full of masses of information which we can only extract from it by making assumptions. By and large, the more extensive (and possibly unrealistic) our assumptions, the more exact and powerful the measurement techniques we can use. It is usual to speak of *levels of measurement*. The simplest level is that of categorization or classification which is so straightforward that even many researchers hardly realize that it in fact constitutes a form of measurement. Here, the assumptions made are easily met: simply, that the objects being classified have sufficient in common (and are sufficiently different from other objects lacking these attributes) to enable us to count them, and say that 'Five people did such and such' or 'There were eight strikes in one region, and four in another'. This level of measurement is the *nominal* level. But suppose that we want to *rank* occurrences, objects or people. We need, then, to be able to say that this group is more militant than that, or that one occupation has higher prestige than another, or that a particular religious sect is more orthodox than another. Here we introduce, by making slightly more complex assumptions, the idea of *ordinal* measurement: of ranking things at different levels and this calls for the use of more powerful arithmetic or statistical tools. Words such as 'bigger', 'better', 'higher', 'stronger', all imply ordinality. Suppose we have come to the conclusion that miners are more militant than schoolteachers and that schoolteachers are more militant than catering workers. We still cannot say whether the gap in militancy between miners and teachers is greater or less than that between teachers and catering workers. To do that, we have to move up to an *interval* level of measurement, and we can only develop the additional manipulative power this will give us by making yet further assumptions and using suitable measurement techniques. In attitude-measurement, for instance, questions are often asked which require the respondents to agree or disagree, with varying degrees of firmness. They might be offered a statement such as 'It is never right to go on strike', and asked whether they agreed very strongly, or strongly, were indifferent, or disagreed strongly or very strongly. These five positions can be scored from 1 to 5. Then respondents are asked how much they agree with another statement, also held to be tapping 'militancy', such as 'Employers and workers basically have interests in common'. Clearly very militant workers might be expected to disagree very strongly with both these statements and 'score' five on each. If we have a number of such 'items', as they are called, in a questionnaire, we can, if we are prepared to make certain assumptions, add up the scores obtained. The higher the score, the greater the 'militancy'; we have produced a 'scale' – a Likert scale – which, if there are six items, runs from a minimum of 6 to a maximum of 30. Now, to return to the question of levels of measurement, such a procedure certainly produces an ordinal level of measurement. Someone scoring 22 may be taken as more militant than someone scoring 21 and less so than someone scoring 23. Sometimes such a scale is treated as an interval scale, where the *increase* in militancy in going from 21 to 22 is the same as going from 22 to 23: the intervals are taken as all having the same size. Treating a Likert scale in this way requires more stringent and rather unrealistic assumptions; other techniques, such as Thurstone scaling, are actually designed to produce interval scales.

A still higher level of measurement produces a 'ratio' scale. Here a score of 20 would mean that the person was twice as 'militant' as someone with a score of 10. Such a scale is actually an interval scale with one crucial added assumption: a score of zero must be non-arbitrary. Such a zero point is relatively straightforward sometimes. For instance, it is not difficult to see the meaning of zero in a scale of length or weight. But zero 'militancy', 'power', or 'alienation' is quite another matter. It follows that in practice we cannot easily say that one group is twice as militant as another, or has one third of the power.

Measurement can be approached in two ways. We can *assume* that a particular phenomenon can be measured in a particular way and then use the obtained result; or we can *test* whether such measurement is appropriate or not. Researchers often ask people to rank things in order of attractiveness, importance or whatever; they *force* an ordinal view of the world on the people they are interviewing. In the Affluent Worker study (Goldthorpe *et al.*, 1968, 1969) respondents were asked to rank six hypothetical people, such as a 'grocer with his own shop, making £20 a week', and a 'bank clerk, making £15 a week' in order of 'their standing in the community'. Respondents certainly were prepared to and able to carry out this task. If, however, the people had been presented to them in *pairs* we know that the results might have been different. There are fifteen different pairs which can be formed and when the results of such an exercise are examined, apparent inconsistencies will be found in the results. The issue now is whether to regard these inconsistencies as *error* or as *information* about the way the respondent sees the world – telling us that she or he does not see 'social standing in the community' as forming a single ranked dimension. If, for instance, 'social standing' is seen instead as a space formed by two (or more) dimensions, then there are techniques which enable us to place the 'grocer', and the other five people offered to respondents, in that space in a way which eliminates as far as possible what previously appeared to be 'inconsistencies'. We have a choice between *forcing* a scale on respondents, or treating apparent inconsistencies as data and using appropriate, if often more complex techniques of measurement and analysis. As Coombs, an authority on measurement theory, once put it, do we know what we want or do we want to know! If we know what we want, we force respondents to give us a one-dimensional ordinal scale; if we want to know, we approach the data in a more flexible way. For some purposes, it makes more sense to ask respondents simply to scale the data. In other cases, it would be better to use the 'pairs' technique, or even more elaborate approaches can be tried such as presenting the statements to our respondents in threes, and asking them which two are closer. Approaching data in different ways, and under different assumptions, can lead to quite different inferences. Measurement and data, then, are just as theory-laden as observation and data-collection, and the kind of measurement-theory we use affects our eventual analysis.

Data-Gathering

We are now in a position to turn to the business of obtaining data for use in sociological research. First, data-collecting is often the most extended, difficult and exciting part of the research process. A mass of expertise and literature surrounds each part of the process, for instance, interviewing techniques. Interviewing is not, as commonly assumed, merely a matter of practice. The uncomfortable truth is that though you can learn *about* research from books or articles, you cannot learn how to *do* research. This applies with particular force to data-collection and, as we shall see, to analysis. There is thus a kind of dialectical process between the actual conduct of research and the literature on methods. For instance, though some textbook understanding of the interviewing process is useful before attempting to interview, it must be complemented by some initial practice in carrying out interviews, preferably under the supervision of an experienced researcher, before returning to the literature and especially to the more advanced and specialized writings.

In what follows then, we shall discuss the various sources of data, and the way they are used, in the context of ideas we have already developed in this chapter. Looking at data-collection in an idealized way, it seems to sit in the middle of the research process; we can look both forward and back. Backwards to the stage in which we were determining the kind of data we require to answer the questions we had set ourselves, and backwards, too, so as to relate the data-collection process to the original research design, and the concepts, the hunches or hypotheses we developed and are using. Forwards, because it is no use collecting data which we cannot analyse or which, while amenable to analysis in principle, cannot be handled within the time-scale or resources available. Fairly unstructured, free-flowing interviews, for example, are often used in research. The researcher takes care to think in advance about various issues such as whether the interview should be recorded, and often devotes a great deal of thought to whether respondents will be happy in the presence of a tape-recorder; whether note-taking might be adequate instead; whether various technical problems can be overcome; whether the subtlety of response that is wanted may even require a video recording. But what is often *not* considered is the brutal truth about recorded interviews: they have to be analysed. To do this they have either to be transcribed, which can take several hours for each hour of interview, or at the very least, listened to once, which requires an hour's listening for an hour's interview! So the sheer volume of work entailed in analysis must always be considered *before* data are collected, and many a researcher has regretted not following that simple rule. In some kinds of research, on the other hand, such as participant observation, the processes of data-collection and analysis proceed to a considerable extent hand in hand. Thus, Donald Roy (1952, 1953, 1955) observed patterns of behaviour on the shop floor and developed the analytic categories he was to use and his explanations of what was going on as he went along. He did not simply note down what he saw and then later carry out the analysis. Inferences are drawn from what is seen, and these inferences are checked and refined as the fieldwork goes on.

Reliability and Validity

Next we must come to grips with the ideas of the reliability and the validity of data. Reliability is best thought of in terms of repeatability, that is the extent to which another researcher using the same method would collect the same data, or the extent to which the same data would be collected at a different time or place using the same method. Validity is the extent to which the data really represent what they are supposed to represent. Of the two, reliability is undoubtedly the more easily understood. The nuts and bolts of research technique are often aimed at increasing reliability, and most researchers aim at producing data which are not idiosyncratic. In some areas, that of attitude-scaling for instance, there are rigorous methods for assessing reliability. Researchers doing fieldwork go to considerable lengths to cross-check data. Occasionally a piece of fieldwork can be replicated, sometimes by the same fieldworker, more often by another, as when a different researcher returns to the same locale or informants. In one celebrated example, the anthropologist Oscar Lewis studied a Mexican village, Tepoztlán, which had been first studied by Robert Redfield seventeen years earlier. Lewis obtained very different results from Redfield indeed: whereas Redfield had characterized the village, in functionalist terms, as homogeneous in structure and culture, free from internal frictions and isolated from external forces of change, Lewis described the villagers as individualistic, competitive and mistrustful of each other, and emphasized their poverty, the presence of endemic illnesses, and violence (matters skated over in Redfield's account) (Redfield, 1930; Lewis, 1951). The issue that then arose was 'Had the place actually changed, or was the startling difference in the two accounts due to the unreliability of the research of one or both of them?' Another interesting and more recent example was a re-study carried out unintentionally, when Michael Burawoy studied a factory in the United States and only late in his fieldwork discovered it had been the location of the celebrated work by Donald Roy over twenty years before to which we have already referred (see Burawoy, 1979). In this latter case, in contrast to the Tepoztlán studies, the reliability seems to have been high. Problems of validity, on the other hand, go to the heart of the relationship between theory and concept, and between concept and its indicator, which we discussed above. Although there are situations in which validity can be tested by the use of techniques found in most standard textbooks (see, for instance, Helmstadter, 1970) and in specialized articles (for an old but still interesting account, see Campbell and Fiske, 1959), the concept of validity is perhaps of most use, normally, simply in sensitizing researchers to what is going on.

Primary and Secondary Data

One crude but useful distinction is that between sources of ready-made data (sometimes called secondary) and those which involve the researcher in collecting the material from scratch (primary data). It is sometimes said that the use of ready-made data reduces the problem of reactivity and sometimes this is indeed so. For instance, if analysis is carried out on television news broadcasts (Glasgow University Media Group, 1976, 1980, 1982), or on letters and diaries not collected specially for the research, then we do not have to worry about the impact of the researcher on the data. It does not, of course, follow that the data are reliable. The analysis of material such as diaries and letters is fraught with difficulties because the intentions of the authors have continually to be taken into account. Historical materials are a wonderfully rich source of data, much of it relatively accessible at low cost. But historians are very aware that the materials they use are full of pitfalls, for what they are using are the historical traces left by various events and people. The passage of time erodes some data and leaves others; some people leave a trace behind, others none. This presents immense problems of control for in many cases we are left with a sample of data and cannot be certain of the population from which it came. Only its incompleteness is certain! So just as we can learn from specialists in experimental design, the study of the ways in which historians use historical materials is helpful in sociology. Though sociologists do study past epochs, in the main they study the world around them. That world, however, is changing, so that, to that extent, sociology is the history of the present. The present, too, is the outcome of past events, ideas, etc, and is also conditioned by people's actions insofar as they are oriented to the future. The borderline between sociology and history is therefore by no means obvious; problems of change over time simply become greater the further back you go.

Although the problem of reactivity does disappear where we are using some kinds of secondary data, in most cases it is still there in a less obvious form. To be sure, the researcher cannot affect the material, but the data *were* collected by somebody for some purpose in the first place, so the question of reactivity is simply pushed further back. The collection of data is always a process. Consider official statistics. Many, for instance the Decennial Censuses of Population, are reliable, indeed extremely so. But we have always to remember the process by which statistics are obtained. The 'social construction' of crime statistics, in particular, has been the subject of many studies which emphasize that official statistics about people convicted of various offences are only the end of a long chain which begins with, say, victims' decisions to report crimes (they may or may not); varying police practices when they are reported; varying rates of detection; varying rates of conviction of people brought to trial, involving lawyers, judges and others; the categories recognized in the law; and so on (Box, 1971; Cicourel, 1976; Kitsuse and Cicourel, 1963).

In addition to official statistics and other public data, such as reports in the media, private archive material can be used. It is extremely varied, ranging from personal letters and diaries to business records and laundry lists, bills, photographs and so on (Gottschalk *et al.*, 1945; Platt, 1981a, b). And a new, rich major source of data available for secondary analysis, as mentioned earlier, are the data collected by other researchers, and now available through organizations such as the ESRC Survey Archive.

If the sociologist decides not to use existing data but to collect them, which is indeed still the more common situation, there are a large number of ways of gathering data, each of which produces different *kinds* of data. The sources of data are more limited perhaps: people, institutions and organizations. The range of potential research situations is enormous but, in practice, one's choices are more limited. Firstly, there is the question of resources. Large-scale research is becoming extremely expensive, and it is undeniable that problems are sometimes tackled not by using the best approach, but the one which can be financed. And money is not the only scarce resource, for some projects are simply too time-consuming. Secondly, there is the question of access to and sensitivity of information. Some research situations are more easily entered than others, although this should not be exaggerated. Despite popular beliefs to the contrary, it is surprisingly possible to interview elite groups (Seldon and Pappworth, 1983; Dexter, 1976), to obtain what may appear on the face of it sensitive information (see, for instance, Ditton, 1977), or to enter unusual research situations (see, for instance, Humphreys, 1970; Wallis, 1976). Nevertheless, there are limits, and they place constraints on research. Thirdly, there is the question of appropriateness, both for the problem in hand and for the particular researcher. It is fairly obvious that some methods will not yield the right kind of data for a particular study. The subtleties of parental behaviour cannot be tapped by a survey but can be approached with repeated, intensive interviews (Backett, 1982). Similarly, it is always necessary to make difficult decisions about sample sizes. The more intensive the fieldwork technique used, the smaller the number of cases which can be studied with given resources. In some kinds of research we may be more interested in the insights we can gain from depth, rather than the statistical advantages and ability to generalize we may achieve from using larger numbers.

Although one can learn how to interview or to observe, or how to carry out statistical analysis, the sociologist who is equally happy with all techniques is a rare and fortunate bird. The ability to extract novel and sociologically insightful information from the Census requires a certain flair which not everyone possesses, just as some sociologists find participant observation extraordinarily difficult. We can all learn to understand what is involved and to evaluate other people's research, but a leaning towards one approach rather than another does partially determine the kind of research done and the data collected.

Fieldwork

A classical and still useful fieldwork typology is that of Gold (1958). Essentially, he suggests that fieldwork roles vary according to the degree of the researcher's involvement in the situation. Thus, at one end of the continuum one has pure or complete observation; and at the other, complete participation. He identifies two other intermediate states which he refers to as observer-as-participant and participant-as-observer. Examples of the first would be most interview situations, and of the latter most fieldwork situations. The pure observer role is self-explanatory, though seldom encountered in sociology. The pure participant role involves some difficult ethical questions about the propriety of studying people without their knowledge and indeed by pretending to be 'one of them'. But examples do exist in the literature (such as Festinger *et al.*, 1956; Humphreys, 1970; Wallis, 1976) and there are indeed extensive discussions of the ethical problems involved in this kind of research and in research in general (Barnes, 1979; Bulmer, 1982). Most fieldwork, however, falls between these extremes and it should be stressed that a single technique such as the interview may vary a great deal, involving more or less participation and involvement in different situations. Thus, the formal and structured interview (see below) is normally associated with surveys, and the observer-as-participant role, rather than with fieldwork. Yet sociologists carrying out fieldwork in schools, factories, communities or elsewhere, may use interview techniques, sometimes even fairly formal ones, though at other times the researcher may simply be observing. (There is a large literature on fieldwork. See, for instance, Burgess, 1982, 1984; Hammersley and Atkinson, 1983; Lofland, 1971; McCall and Simmons, 1969; Schatzman and Strauss, 1973; Spradley, 1979, 1980.)

Movement towards the participant end of the continuum involves identification and involvement and not just participation. Reactivity obviously increases as we move from one end of the observer–participant continuum to the other. The behaviour of those who are being watched but are unaware of the presence of the observer is the most non-reactive (though such research, in many people's eyes, is unethical). If subjects are aware of being observed, some degree of reactivity exists, although experience suggests that it diminishes after a while. But the problem increases as the researcher becomes more actively involved in the situation. A nice example is provided by Whyte (1955) in a classic study of a street corner gang. He reports that when he went bowling with the gang, his presence influenced the outcomes and, being an excellent fieldworker, he managed to incorporate this 'distortion' into the analysis. The more the observer becomes involved – becomes more participant – the more he or she will influence what goes on. But the gain is the enhanced capacity to get at the meanings behind people's actions. This is sometimes expressed as a 'trade-off': buying validity in exchange for reliability. Participation may also bring problems of identification and commitment; it is difficult to associate with a group for long periods without to some extent identifying with their goals and values, or at least being assumed to do so. Again, Whyte provides a dramatic example when he was asked to assist the people he was studying by illegally voting in several different voting precincts!

The interview is found in many kinds of research and can take many forms. Once again we have a continuum. At one extreme is that kind of interview where the schedule is completely specified; the order and form of questions is fixed, the questions themselves either call for a precise answer (for instance, the respondent's sex, vote at last election, membership of a trade union) or offer closed alternatives to questions (as for instance, in the Likert-scaling example given earlier). At the other extreme, we have the totally unstructured interview, built flexibly around a few general issues which the sociologist wishes to examine. Most schedules fall between these extremes. The more unstructured the interview, the less the control, the lower the reliability – but, generally, the richer the data. Analysis becomes more complex, time-consuming and expensive, as does the interview itself. Large sample studies using professional survey agencies are therefore usually tightly structured. As Pahl (1984) remarks: 'given the constraints of survey methodology, open-ended questions had to be reduced to a minimum'. Exploratory studies of small samples, however, requiring a sensitive and probing interview technique, tend to be more unstructured.

One kind of survey which deserves mention, because it employs highly structured schedules, is the mail questionnaire. Very large numbers of respondents can be contacted for a given cost but response rates are often extremely low and considerable demands are made on the respondent's literacy, comprehension, interest, honesty and so on (for a fuller discussion, see Scott, 1961; Erdos, 1970; and the general survey literature, such as Moser and Kalton, 1971; Warwick and Lininger, 1975; Hoinville and Jowell, 1978). In sociological research, on the other hand, interview-schedules are seldom so completely closed, and interviewers are encouraged to 'probe' where answers seem incomplete, evasive or difficult to comprehend without additional information.

Interviews are sometimes conducted by telephone and this practice is becoming more common. Until quite recently the technique was only appropriate for a small number of studies as it obviously excludes those without a telephone, and they tend to fall into particular social groups. As telephones become more and more widespread, the technique offers a relatively cheap and efficient way of carrying out fairly straightforward interviews (Frey, 1989). In computer-aided telephone interviewing (CATI), the interviewer is guided through the interview by the computer and responses can be entered into the database on the spot. This approach can also now be used in face-to-face interviewing with the aid of laptop machines. Interviews are used in many forms of research other than the survey, however. Indeed, they are perhaps the commonest form of data-collection in any kind of research, though rarely the only technique used, observation being the other major technique. Sometimes, only key informants, such as elite figures, will be interviewed, rather than whole populations.

The interview situation, we noted above, is itself a sociological interaction, about which there is now a sizeable literature, even if little of it is particularly theoretical (see, for instance, Gorden, 1980; Kahn and Cannell, 1957; Richardson et al., 1965; Spradley, 1979). There are several specialized forms of the interview. The *focused* interview, for instance, selects respondents known to have experienced a particular event, perhaps a disaster such as an earthquake. Although the interview itself may or may not be highly structured, it is tightly focused on the events thought to have occurred and reactions to them. The event experienced is analysed from other sources – for example, the media – in order to develop an interview guide, and this is then used to study how the respondent defines and experiences the situation (Merton and Kendall, 1946; Merton et al., 1956). The non-directive interview, which has much in common with some kinds of clinical interview, deliberately allows the interviewee free rein, as far as possible basing questions only on what the respondent has already said. In the 1960s, several studies tried to investigate images of class in this way, asking just one non-leading question and then building on what was said (for instance, Goldthorpe et al., 1969). Not all interviews follow the usual pattern of one interviewer and one respondent: there are group interviews (Banks, 1957; Chandler, 1954; Hoinville and Jowell, 1978, pp. 9–26) and interviews using more than one interviewer (Bechhofer *et al.*, 1984; Braithwaite, 1985).

In recent times, there has been a revival of interest in life-histories, first discussed by Dollard years ago (1935), and a number of extremely interesting studies based on this technique have resulted (for an overview, see Bertaux, 1981; Plummer, 1983; Oral History Society, 1985–). The life-history is the core, in particular, of the burgeoning specialism of oral history (Thompson, 1978), which overlaps with sociological research since it involves obtaining information about change over time directly from respondents.

Another way of trying to capture process, change over time, is by a panel-study in which the same group of people are repeatedly interviewed over a period of time (Wall and Williams, 1970). A fairly short time-span may be involved, as in Backett's fascinating study of decision-making in families referred to earlier (Backett, 1982), or a period of years or even decades, as in those studies where infants have been followed from birth. Such long-term studies are inevitably very expensive but provide some of the richest data available. The Censuses of Population offer great potential for following a very large sample over time, although the methodological and computing problems are formidable. In 1971 the Office of Population Censuses and Surveys started a project which succeeded in linking the data obtained from a 1 per cent sample in the 1971 Census to the information gathered from those individuals surviving in 1981. It is intended to repeat the process with the 1991 Census. Although the information in the Census itself is limited, it has been augmented by another complex exercise in data linkage using information obtained from the Registrar of Births and Deaths. The data-set offers exciting opportunities to researchers interested in change over the decade and such topics as migration, factors affecting demographic processes, household structure and so on.

All interviews involve asking questions. The design of the interview schedule is therefore of crucial importance and an exacting and skilled task. The ways in which questions are worded, and the order in which they are asked, greatly affect the answers you get (Payne, 1980; Sudman and Bradburn, 1982). A question such as 'Do you think Britain should remain a member of NATO and maintain a nuclear deterrent?' could be faulted on several counts. First, two questions are in fact being asked, one about NATO and one about nuclear deterrence. Secondly, deterrence is itself a loaded term. Thirdly, the question assumes an understanding of the acronym NATO. Some of the key issues in question design are precision, lack of ambiguity, a focus on one issue or topic at a time, comprehensibility, and the need neither to 'lead' nor to threaten or embarrass the respondent.

Most schedules are a mixture of factual material (such as age, marital status, education, religion and so on, sometimes referred to as 'facesheet' information) and the central, substantive part of the questionnaire where questions are asked arising directly from the interests of the investigator, some of which will be factual and some attitudinal. Obviously, in an inquiry concerned with education, questions on this topic form the main part of the schedule; in another inquiry, a person's educational history would be merely 'background' data, covered in one or two facesheet questions. Even apparently simple facesheet questions, though, can hold pitfalls. Asking someone's age can produce errors as some people round up and some down, and some give approximate answers! A more precise question, such as 'What is your age next birthday?', may be necessary. Questions asked earlier in the interview can bias or contaminate those asked later, effectively they put ideas into people's heads. Thus, a general question about social services such as, 'Do you think that, on the whole, welfare services are best provided privately or by the State?' should not follow a series of questions asking specifically about one of these services, such as the National Health Service.

Although analysis largely takes place after the data have been collected, issues of method have often to be resolved before data-collection begins. Thus, if it is going to be necessary to construct a scale, for instance to measure attitudes to trade unions, this is generally done in advance, and the questions comprising the completed scale form part of the questionnaire at an appropriate point during the interview. Similarly, questionnaires require piloting, that is administering to a 'guinea-pig' group of people who are similar to those to be studied but are in fact different people. Care is usually taken to carry out the pilot among a group suitably removed from the research population so that 'contamination' – knowledge of the questions and time to think about 'appropriate' answers to them, or knowledge about the ways other people have already replied – will not occur. The pilot will also reveal questions which are ambiguous or which do not elicit analysable answers; are regularly misunderstood or too difficult; or come at the wrong point in the questionnaire, and so on. The schedule may also prove to be too long; some parts may cause unnecessary embarrassment, and so on. Two pilot stages, not one, are normally required before all these problems are solved.

A problem which all surveys have in common with other kinds of fieldwork is that of entry and disengagement; in other words, it is necessary first to obtain access and subsequently to leave the interview or the field situation in as non-reactive and non-damaging a way as possible. Most sociological research involves some invasion of people's privacy and interferes, however slightly, with their normal life-course. It is important to keep a sense of proportion here; the fact is that many people seem to enjoy being interviewed and it is not difficult to see why this should be. Although the interview is a social interaction and should always be thought of in these terms, it is a somewhat unusual one. Most important of all, the expectations which participants have of each other affect the interview: people respond differently to different kinds of interviewers (young/old; male/female; middle class/working class and so on) according to their own age/sex/class or other social attributes and their own perceptions of these attributes in the interviewer. The interview is a rather special, if not peculiar, situation, too, in that it is an opportunity to converse with someone who is interested in what you tell them; who does not criticize or appear disapproving; and, above all, is not supposed to argue or answer back! The interviewer is placed in a special social category, that of a 'stranger' (Simmel, 1950), who is likely to go away, or as a 'professional' to whom a certain amount of trust can be given, so that, either way, paradoxically, you can talk with more confidence than you would to people closer to you. Hence, people seldom respond with hostility even to questions on sensitive topics. The interview situation thus has parallels with other situations in which people will tell all kinds of intimate and personal details to total strangers, almost always in situations where they never expect to meet again.

The fact that people usually seem to enjoy being interviewed, though, does not remove the problem of obtaining access in the first place, nor the responsibilities of disengagement in the end. Quite small details, such as the tone and precise wording of a letter sent in advance of the interview, or the interviewer's appearance, or attempting to obtain an interview during a particularly popular TV programme, may determine the whole subsequent response of a person being interviewed, while the way in which an interview is ended may have considerable consequences for further interviews in the same area. Such problems become much more acute in extended fieldwork, especially within a small community or institution. Access to an organization such as the BBC (see Burns, 1977) or a factory, may require careful planning and skilled fieldwork, and it is always advisable to make it very clear what will be done with the results, both in terms of publication and in terms of policy uses.

Analysis of Quantitative Data

As we have seen, then, data-collection and analysis may go hand in hand, and the collection of data is always undertaken in the light of the theoretical and conceptual interests of the sociologist, *with analysis in mind*. But the range of analytical techniques is very considerable indeed. In order to get some idea of the variety, it is worthwhile looking at issues of sociological journals which publish different kinds of work, say, *Sociology, Sociological Review,* and *American Sociological Review*. Probably the first thing one would notice is that quite a lot of these analyses employ various kinds of statistical techniques. While it is true that sociologists who lean towards interpretative approaches may never use any statistics at all in their work, any sociologist who wishes to read reasonably widely will have to acquire a basic grasp of statistical techniques. As soon as the researcher decides to count anything at all, even if all that is required is a straightforward description, we are in the world of statistical analysis.

There is no need to be nervous about approaching statistics; at an advanced level, it is indeed demanding and difficult and requires some mathematical training and probably aptitude, but descriptive statistics and basic analytic techniques are well within the grasp of anyone who makes the effort. Descriptive statistics enable us to summarize large amounts of material in a brief form. If, for example, we take the ages of everyone in an organization, say all the miners at a particular colliery, then most people are familiar with the idea of an *average* or a mean as it is known. The mean age summarizes a whole set of ages, possibly several hundred. We could compare the

Table 1. Sex of respondent and belief in God

	Believe in God	Do not believe in God	Total
Males	35	40	75
Females	55	30	85
Total	90	70	160

mean age of two sub-groups, say faceworkers and others, and this would enable us to make a statement comparing these two groups; probably the faceworkers would be younger. But we may also want to be able to compare the *spread* of the ages as well, and once again there are simple statistical techniques that help us to do this. Descriptive statistics then tell us about the size and shape of a particular set of figures, and various techniques also exist for showing these data graphically, in such familiar forms as the bar-diagram (histogram) or the 'pie' divided into segments.

More problematic is the problem of inference. Usually we have data on a sample, drawn from a larger group . . . the population. The question we want to answer is whether our observations really tell us something meaningful about the population or whether they could arise by chance. Thus, if we took ten miners at random from the colliery and their mean (average) age was 27, we might by bad luck have chosen ten rather young miners (say) from a colliery where the average age was actually 34. Inferential statistics permit us to assess how likely this is.

Other statistical techniques allow us to summarize and express quantitatively the *strength* of relationships. Thus, if we know the age and income of a group of one hundred individuals, and we believe that older people are likely to have higher incomes, and vice versa, we can measure the strength of the relationship between income and age – the extent to which they 'fit' together.

Data relating to attributes of samples drawn from different groups within a wider population may be presented in tabular form, with, say, males and females on one axis and a 'Yes'/'No' answer about their belief in God on the other, producing what is called a two-by-two table. In the fictional example given, it looks as if women tend to believe in God more than men. A numerical measure of association, as it is called, can be calculated to give us an idea of the strength of this relationship between the two variables. Cross-tabular analysis, as in the two–by–two example we have just considered, can be approached in various ways, may become quite complex and is fundamental to the analysis of variable–centred data (Davis, 1971; Hellevik, 1984; Marsh, 1988).

As the number of variables increases, however, and as the relationships between them in which we are interested become more complicated, we require more and more sophisticated statistical tools to tease out the relationships.

Analysis of Qualitative Data

Yet the journals of sociology are not entirely filled with thickets of figures. There will also be descriptive accounts, and analyses of more qualitative data gathered through various kinds of fieldwork. Although these articles are often more easy to read, it would be wrong to imagine that they are the product of less taxing and time-consuming analysis. The careful classification, organizing and combining of field–notes requires patient checking and cross–checking and the application of systematic techniques; 'systematic' does not necessarily imply numerical, although numerical methods are sometimes applied to field–data too. The task of drawing valid and reliable inferences from qualitative field–data too is as problematic, and therefore much discussed in the literature, as that of drawing inferences from numerical data (see, for instance, Burgess, 1982, 1984; Lofland, 1971; Spradley, 1979, 1980).

Another noticeable feature of the more qualitative studies is the use they make of often quite extended quotations from respondents. In this kind of study, such illustrations play a rather different role than do illustrative quotations in more quantitative research. In the latter case, the data are usually presented *first*, in summary statistical form, and the quotations simply provide a vivid or typical illustration of the generalized statements that have already been made on the basis of the numerical, tabular material. But where the quoted speech is intended to actually *provide the evidence* with which the reader is expected to assess the author's interpretation – rather than merely illustrate – the burden placed on it is correspondingly greater. It requires care, experience, and a good deal of honesty and judgement, to present material in a balanced way, and places a great responsibility on the researcher.

Postscript

Most sociologists have come to realize that research is at its best when it does not depend on one method alone, or indeed possibly on sociology alone. More and more, then, a single study involves using several methods. It cannot be said too often that *there is no one best method*. For *any* one particular problem *can* be approached in several ways; all methods have their strengths and their weaknesses, and no single method can reveal all aspects of reality. Strategies of combining several techniques together have been described, in one interesting theoretical discussion, as multiple 'triangulation' (Denzin, 1970), on the grounds that we can have the greatest confidence in our findings when dissimilar methods, preferably three or more, are brought to bear on the same unit of analysis, or a particular method is applied to several units.

One point remains to be made: about the way in which research is finally presented. While we can all read an article and form an opinion of the validity of the argument on the evidence presented, the finished product conceals almost as much as it reveals! A lot has to be taken on trust, for no research report, however lengthy, can fully describe and reproduce the lengthy and complicated procedures followed. This applies just as much to the coding procedures of a survey as to the interpretation of hundreds of pages of fieldwork notes. Of course, simple deceit and cooking the books are not unknown in research in any discipline, and indeed it would be a poor sociologist who did not realize that the same pressures and motives which lead to forgery, embezzlement and confidence trickery in the wider world can also lead to doubtful behaviour in academic life. Far more common, however, are weaknesses in the data and analysis arising from biases built into the research design, small methodological flaws, short cuts enforced by lack of resources, failure to supervise interviewers or coders adequately, computing errors, the human capacity for self-deception and so on. The crucial point is that, because the reader cannot easily detect such things, the researcher has to meet high standards of training, dedication, professional ethics and honesty. There is usually a tidiness and order to written research accounts – a sanitized quality which fails to reproduce the messy reality of the research-process even in the hands of the most experienced and rigorous exponent – that should paradoxically remind us of what research is *really* like.

For research *is* a process, not a series of precise and separate steps which can be neatly dissected and analysed. At every point decisions have to be made and these decisions are seldom if ever perfect. Compromises have continually to be accepted. In the last resort, the sociologist is in the business of making the best sense possible of an extremely complex reality and this has to be done by the best means available. A good grasp of methodology provides an understanding of those means; it equips the sociologist with a varied bag of tools and the basic training with which to use them. The skill and talent which is required to produce a good piece of research, like a really well-made piece of furniture, is another matter altogether.

4   Sex, Gender and the Family

Introduction

I cannot be just to books which treat of woman as woman . . . My idea is
that all of us, men as well as women, should be regarded as human beings
(Dorothy Parker, quoted by Simone de Beauvoir, 1972, p. 14).

A noble ideal, but the world, it seems, is otherwise. Women have
had the vote in Britain for over half a century, yet only 3.5 per cent
of Members of Parliament are women. Women have access to almost
every trade and profession and constitute 42 per cent of the labour
force, yet fewer than 1 per cent of members of the Institution of
Mechanical Engineers are women. More girls than boys leave school
with two or more 'A' levels, yet women have barely half of polytechnic degree places, 43 per cent of university undergraduate places and
39 per cent of university graduate places.

Everyday life and our common culture are pervaded with images
and assumptions about the differences between women and men. It
starts at the moment of birth, when a baby boy is spoken of as
bouncy and strong and a baby girl as pretty and sweet. Then in
childhood, girls are given dolls, boys are given toy trucks and even
story books and comics are sex divided. Even if parents try to be
non-sexist, no nine-year-old child can be unaware of a clear set of
normative differences between girls and boys – though many a nine-
year-old resists following the norms in one way or another. By the
teenage years, the focus often shifts to the specifically sexual arena,
with boys defined as macho and sexually predatory and viewing girls
in terms of their sexual attractiveness and availability and with girls
treading a tightrope between being labelled as a 'whore' or a 'slag'
and rejected as a sexless 'drag' (Cowie and Lees, 1981; Wood, 1984).
In adulthood we are surrounded by words and images that depend

for their very meaning on a shared understanding of male and female, masculine and feminine. We could not 'read' most advertisements or most plays, novels, paintings and films if we did not understand the language of sexual difference: what sense would we make of the plot of *Don Giovanni*? Or of the latest television commercial for convenience food?

In everyday life, we take this language for granted, so that it usually seems quite natural to us. It was only the advent of the women's liberation movement in the early 1970s that made it problematic once again. In fact feminism has always raised this question as to whether the differences between women and men are natural or social. Writing over a hundred years ago, John Stuart Mill argued that we can never know what, if any, the natural differences may be, because the social ones are so great:

I deny that anyone knows, or can know, the nature of the two sexes as long as they have only been seen in their present relation to one another. If men had ever been found in society without women, or women without men, or if there had been a society of men and women in which the women were not under the control of the men, something might have been positively known about the mental and moral differences which may be inherent in the nature of each. What is now called the nature of women is an eminently artificial thing – the result of forced repression in some directions, unnatural stimulation in others. It may be asserted without scruple, that no other class of dependants have had their character so entirely distorted from its natural proportions by their relation with their masters ... (Mill, 1869, pp. 38–9).

Modern feminists would want to add that men's characters have been equally distorted by their position of mastery, and would problematize the 'nature' of masculinity as much as that of femininity.

Robert Stoller (1968) used a distinction between 'sex' and 'gender' as a way of separating the natural from the cultural components. But for him – as for many modern feminists – the only natural differences are the biological ones of sex: 'chromosomes, external genitalia, internal genitalia, gonads, hormonal states, and secondary sex characteristics'. These determine whether a person is male or female – or, in extremely rare cases, not classifiable as either. Stoller refers to all differences that are psychological and cultural – to 'masculinity' and 'femininity' – as 'gender', a word that has become the standard term for those differences between men and women that are socially constructed and depend upon the individual being socially identified, and having a self-identity, as a man or a woman.

It is easy enough to state, as a matter of definition, that gender is different from sex. What most of us find much harder is to actually *believe* that most of what we think of as sex-difference is in fact gender-difference. Our own gender-identity is central to us as individuals and we are formed within a culture that posits gender difference as natural, *not* social. In support of this apparent common sense there are the widely popular pseudo-scientific theories of sociobiology, claiming that male dominance and women's specialization in reproduction and childcare are rooted in the evolution of the human species and hence are inherent genetically. (For a useful critique of sociobiology in this context, see Sayers, 1982.)

To challenge this formidable alliance of common sense and pseudo-science, we need to step outside our own culture and examine the various forms that gender difference and the relations between the sexes have taken in different societies. This will not answer Mill's question about 'the *nature* of the two sexes' – perhaps that is a question that has no answer, since it is in the nature of human beings to transcend nature. But it will at least demonstrate that 'what is now called the nature of women' – and of men – in our society is by no means entirely natural.

The Cultural Variability of Gender and Family

Division of labour

All societies appear to have some kind of division of labour between the sexes. In foraging societies – which are the simplest of all societies, in terms of their technology and in terms of their social structure – men have the primary responsibility for hunting large animals or for dangerous fishing and women the primary responsibility for gathering plant foods, such as roots and berries, and small animals. There are variations from one foraging society to another, but in general men are the hunters and women the gatherers. The reason for this is not the simple fact of differential strength (for there is much overlap between men's and women's strength and the differences are probably as much a product of differences in lifestyle as a cause of them). In any case, in such societies women's work of gathering involves much walking and bending, while carrying heavy burdens of vegetable foods and also carrying any of their children who are too young to walk far. It is generally accepted that the reasons relate to the fact that women bear and nurse children in infancy. In a society where the expectation of life is low, the reproduction of the group depends on how many mature women it has, so their lives cannot be put at risk as readily as men's. In a society where the major food sources are crude and indigestible, children may have to be breast-fed for the first four or five years of life. Factors such as this – peculiar to these foraging societies – are sufficient to explain the hunter/gatherer sexual division of labour.

Sociobiologists often extrapolate from foraging societies to all more elaborated forms of society, drawing analogies between a man's role as hunter and his role as worker in industrial society, or between a woman's role as gatherer and as child-bearer and feeder and her role as housewife and mother in industrial society. The analogy is rather poor, since in many such societies the hunters are not really 'providers' in the way that a male wage-earner is for his family: they often contribute only a small proportion, albeit an important and welcome one, of the foraging group's diet. It is also an analogy that cannot be applied to many societies that have existed. Among horticultural people, who have domesticated plants and animals, there are far more varieties of sexual division of labour. Clearing new land for cultivation is nearly always men's work. But the often heavy work of planting, weeding, harvesting and transporting of crops is divided differently between men and women in different societies: sometimes women do it all, sometimes men, and sometimes both do it, either together or, more commonly, specializing in different crops.

Masculinity and femininity

Turning to the question of 'masculine' and 'feminine' personality, cross-cultural studies again reveal considerable variety. The first variation is in the extent to which gender difference is a salient organizing feature of the culture. Even cultures as close as the Mediterranean and the northern European are different in this respect: Mediterranean culture has highly complex and explicit views on the nature of gender, and many spheres of life – religion, work, leisure – are organized in terms of these; while in northern Europe questions of gender and sexuality are more muted and less elaborated.

In different societies (and in different periods of history) masculinity and femininity are differently defined. The classic study of this is Margaret Mead's (1935) description of three contrasting New Guinea tribes. Her first two tribes had little gender differentiation. Among the Arapesh, the ideal and expected personality of both men and women approximated to our feminine ideal: gentle, caring, passive. Among the Mandugumor, on the other hand, the ideal for both was similar to our masculine model: vigorous, assertive, independent, sexually aggressive. Most strikingly, Mead describes the third tribe, the Tchambuli, as having gender differentiation in the opposite direction to the modern Western pattern: women were practical, competent, assertive and plainly dressed; men were petty, vain, gossiping, ornamented.

Mead's study has been much criticized, and she perhaps exaggerated the divergence from Western patterns. But it, together with more recent anthropological evidence, reveals much greater cultural variety in ideas about masculinity and femininity than we would expect, living, as we do, within one culture.

Some anthropologists have suggested that there is a universal tendency in all cultures to associate women with 'nature' and men with 'culture' (Ortner, 1972). Others express a similar idea in somewhat different terms, seeing men as associated with the 'social good' and women with 'self-interest' (Strathern, 1981) or men with the 'public domain' and women with the domestic domain (Rosaldo, 1974). It is important to remember, however, that even if such associations are found in all societies, this does not mean that women *are* closer to nature or more governed by biology, or that men have a monopoly of culture and the advancement of social interests. Such a view is a male-centred one. As Simone de Beauvoir put it:

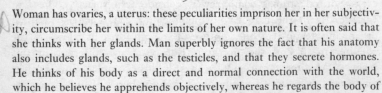

Woman has ovaries, a uterus: these peculiarities imprison her in her subjectivity, circumscribe her within the limits of her own nature. It is often said that she thinks with her glands. Man superbly ignores the fact that his anatomy also includes glands, such as the testicles, and that they secrete hormones. He thinks of his body as a direct and normal connection with the world, which he believes he apprehends objectively, whereas he regards the body of woman as a hindrance, a prison, weighed down by everything peculiar to it (de Beauvoir, 1972, p. 15).

Insofar as there is anything universal about cultural definitions of gender, it seems, they are the definitions of a male perspective. Possibly this means nothing more substantial than that male European anthropologists have only listened to what men have to say (MacCormack, 1980). But it is more likely that a male-centred culture *is* universally the dominant one.

Male domination

There has probably never been a society in which women were dominant, or even politically equal to men. It is sometimes thought that matrilineal societies, in which inheritance of social position is in the female line and children belong to their mother's rather than their father's clan, are matriarchal. But this is not so: matrilineality simply means that a *man* is in a line of inheritance from his mother's brother and to his sisters' sons. It is also sometimes thought that in societies where there is no private property there is no structured inequality of power. Friedrich Engels (1884) started from this position when he argued that the development of privately owned property – land and cattle – saw 'the world historical defeat of the female sex', because men owned the property and subordinated women as wives in order to ensure inheritance. Later anthropologists (especially Ernestine Friedl, 1975) have suggested that, even without private property, a sexual division of labour is frequently associated with men having greater rights to distribute and exchange valued goods and services to people outside their immediate domestic unit and so gain power and prestige within the society. Yet, as Michelle Rosaldo put it: 'male domination, though apparently universal, does not in actual behavioural terms assume a universal content or a universal shape' (Rosaldo, 1980).

In some societies male domination is enforced through the institutionalized use of force as in the ritualized punishment of women by gang-rape on behalf of men as the dominant group. In others, such collective use of force is unnecessary – and indeed impossible – since women are confined as daughters and wives to a private sphere where they never offend men as a whole, but are subordinated to their fathers and husbands. Because of this wide variation in the form that male domination takes, it seems unwise to give it all a single label, 'patriarchy', since this obscures the very different consequences for women (Young and Harris, 1976). It is better to reserve the term patriarchy for those situations where men control 'their' women through the personal relations of the age and sex structure of the family.

Mothers and fathers

Even aspects of human relations that we think of as unproblematically biological and natural sometimes turn out on closer inspection to be cultural constructs. Even parenthood and family disappear as human universals in the light of cross-cultural study. For instance, the Trobriand Islanders, studied by Bronislaw Malinowski (1922), believed that intercourse merely 'opened the passage' for a spirit child to enter the womb and that further intercourse 'moulded' the child. So the child was not related by blood to the father but only to the mother and her kin. Fatherhood was a socially intimate relationship and intercourse with the child's mother would even produce physical likeness, but it was not a blood relationship as motherhood was.

On the other hand, among the Lakher of Burma the mother is only a vessel for carrying a child which the father implants there, so that children of the same mother are not considered to be related unless they have the same father (Keesing, 1976, cited in Edholm, 1982). As Felicity Edholm writes,

'Natural' and 'biological' relations are not necessarily those which organize human relations at a very fundamental level, since what is understood as 'biological' is socially defined and therefore is expressed in different ways (Edholm, 1982, p. 169).

Edholm goes on to argue that the mother–child tie is not a universal elementary relationship, and cites as evidence the widespread practice of adoption:

In many societies, children do not live with their 'real' parents, but often stay with their mothers until some time after they have been weaned, when as they say in N. Ghana, they have 'gained sense' (at about six). However, throughout Melanesia and Polynesia, children are adopted just after weaning or, in some instances, well before – a phenomenon which is considered as absolutely acceptable (Edholm, 1982, p. 170).

Family and household

If the 'biological' concepts of kinship and parenthood are problematic, so too is the concept of family. Western anthropologists have tended to take a modern Western idea of the family and, in effect, imposed it on other cultures. Many languages have no word to identify the unit for which we most commonly use the term family: co-residing parents and children. Many cultures are not concerned to distinguish this grouping from other people around it. Yet traditional anthropology claimed to see such units in all societies; and the modern orthodoxy has only modified this to the extent of recognizing that fathers are frequently not present and that a mother and her children may be the basic unit.

Even the Western European concept of the family is a fairly recent one. Up to the late eighteenth century 'family', if used at all, meant either an aristocratic lineage or else a household, including servants and any dependants who lived in it. Only the emergent bourgeoisie established an orderly and exclusive domestic life organized around the rearing of the next generation to inherit the father's status and property.

The present state of cross-cultural evidence is not adequate to explain either the universals or the variations in gender and 'family'. It does, however, enable us to see clearly that the familiar forms of modern industrial societies are far from being natural or inevitable and that they need explanation in terms of the society of which they are a part, rather than in biological or evolutionary terms.

Employment and the Sexual Division of Labour

The emergence of the modern pattern

There has always been a division of labour between men and women, but in industrial societies it takes on new and specific forms. Only here do we find male stockbrokers, managers, lathe-operators and motor mechanics, and female cleaners, clerks and nurses, because only here do we find these jobs at all. And only here do we find such a clear distinction between the work that is carried on in the home – cleaning, washing, cooking, all for domestic use – and the work that is carried on outside in shops, offices and factories. In pre-industrial societies, housework cannot be distinguished from any other kind of productive work. Consider the following injunction to a sixteenth-century farmer's wife, in Sir Anthony Fitzherbert's *Boke of Husbandry*:

When thou are up and ready, then first sweep thy house, dress up thy dishboard, and set all things in good order within thy house, milk the cows, suckle thy calves, strain up thy milk, take up thy children and dress them and provide for thy husband's breakfast, dinner and supper and for thy children and servants and take thy part with them. And to send corn and malt to the mill, to bake and brew withall when need is . . . make butter and cheese when thou may serve thy swine both morning and evening and give thy chickens food in the morning . . . (quoted in Clark, 1919, pp. 47–8).

In the towns, too, many trades were conducted in the home, and women as well as journeymen, apprentices and children, played a part alongside their husbands. Though women worked in all these ways, they were not recognized as workers and rarely accepted into craft guilds, and then usually only as a result of inheriting their trade from a husband or father who had died. When the first factories were set up, men, women and children found work in them, and there was public concern at the resulting impoverishment of home life. During the course of the nineteenth century, children, and later many women too, were excluded from the factories, and the emerging trade unions were frequently all-male organizations. Women often worked as servants or as needlewomen, though the ideal of the wife who stayed at home and as her husband's dependant was a growing one.

The second half of the twentieth century has seen a reversal of the nineteenth-century trend. Today, more married women go out to work, and most of them stay at home with young children for a shorter time than in the past before returning to the labour-market. Forty-four per cent of employed women work part-time, most of them either women with children or else older married women.

'Industrial Apartheid'

Women now constitute 43 per cent of the workforce (Central Statistical Office, 1990 (1988 figures), p. 67), but this does not mean that

Table 2. Current economic activity by marital status: all women except full-time students

Economic activity	Marital status				All women except full-time students
	Married/ cohabiting	Widowed/ divorced/ separated	Single	All non-married women	
	%	%	%	%	%
Working full-time	27	40	79	64	35
Working part-time	33	23	3	11	28
Total working	60	63	82	75	63
'Unemployed'	5	7	10	9	6
Total economically active	65	70	92	84	69
Economically inactive	35	30	8	16	31
	100	100	100	100	100
Base	4,060	469	766	1,235	5,295

(*Source:* Martin and Roberts, 1984, p. 12.)

they are working alongside men in a position of equality. For one thing, women tend to be more concentrated in the service sector of the economy, especially in health, education and welfare, in shops, hotels and catering and in financial services, while men predominate in manufacturing, farming, mining and so on. But even more conspicuously, women tend to be in 'women's jobs' within each sector: very few women are skilled manual workers, but very few men are secretaries or typists, sewing-machinists or canteen assistants. This segregation into different kinds of work amounts to an 'industrial apartheid between men and women' (Wainwright, 1978).

Along with this goes inequality in earnings. Obviously, women tend to earn less each week when they work part-time, but even when they have full-time jobs they are less likely to get overtime work or bonus rates. If we take hourly rates of pay, women only earn three-quarters of what men do. In 1988 men's average hourly pay (excluding overtime) was £5.73 while women's was only £4.29. 'Equal pay' for men and women doing the same work only produces equal pay overall if men and women *are* doing the same work. If women are concentrated into the low-paid jobs in the unorganized sectors of the economy then their earnings suffer accordingly.

Some common explanations

(*a*) *Skills and aptitudes.* How can this 'industrial apartheid' be explained? It is a fact of everyday life and as such is often given everyday explanations, many of them quite unfounded. For instance, it is said that men are stronger than women and better suited to heavy work. This may indeed explain why some jobs are reserved for men, yet many men (the best-rewarded ones) do sedentary work and many women do exhausting physical work like canteen cooking, waitressing or geriatric nursing – even looking after small children involves lifting heavy weights that often scream and struggle! On the other hand – extending the argument that 'it's only natural' – it is often said that women have particular skills: that they are better at caring for people, at being charming, at dull repetitive tasks or at intricate work needing dexterity. Again there may be an element of truth. Women are more often socialized into these 'feminine skills' which are, after all, the skills of women's domestic roles. Indeed it is remarkable how many of the so-called 'women's jobs' are social forms of housework, such as nursing, childminding, infant teaching, cooking, waitressing, cleaning, garment-making. A secretary has been likened to an 'office wife' and a receptionist is, in a sense, an office hostess. Perhaps the most interesting aspect of this is that these skills are not rewarded as such in job evaluation schemes, but treated as natural abilities of women. If anything they serve to downgrade the jobs that women do rather than class them as skilful or demanding.

(*b*) *Discrimination.* Another common explanation for 'industrial apartheid' is that employers discriminate against women: they do not appoint them to 'men's jobs' (or men to 'women's jobs'), and favour men rather than women for promotion. This continues to be true in many spheres, despite legislation in the 1970s against sex discrimination. But, in itself, it cannot explain very much, since we need to ask: *why* do employers behave in this way? In part it may be due to prejudice, to false preconceptions about women's abilities. But it seems unlikely that capitalist employers, as economically rational beings, would operate for long in the labour-market with completely false conceptions unless it were indirectly to their advantage. So we need to see prejudice and discrimination not simply as due to the outcome of acts and decisions, but built into structures of economy and society.

(c) *Women's home responsibilities.*   A final, common explanation is that men have a greater commitment to the labour-market because they are breadwinners for a family, whereas women have home responsibilities that prevent them from working such long hours, committing themselves to a career, or undertaking training for a skill they will practise all their lives. Furthermore, a woman has a husband to support her, so she does not need to be concerned about pay so much. Women, it is said, do not expect or need to get the same out of work as men do; they are less highly motivated and less ambitious. This argument makes the unwarranted assumption that all women workers are married with children, while all men workers have a family to support and no other domestic responsibilities to distract them. Yet single women, women without children and women whose children have long since left home are as much disadvantaged in the labour-market as any others. Nevertheless it is true that the women who have part-time jobs tend to be those with young children or other family members to look after, and many women do leave the labour-market for periods because of family responsibilities, so that the whole question of whether to take a job, and for what hours, is a subject of family negotiation for married women in a way that it is not for men.

Structural explanations

For a sociologist, however, all of these common explanations are unsatisfactory, and not just because they are wrong or only partially true. The problem lies in the model of explanation that they offer, which basically involves accounting for each individual's place in the world of work in terms of individual or innate abilities, experiences or motivation, and seeing the overall outcome as simply the sum of all these differences between men and women. The model emphasizes *differences* (whether innate or social) between men and women which tend to lead them to occupy different positions, rather than the *structure* of 'industrial apartheid'. Sociologists, on the other hand, focus first upon structural arrangements in society and how they relate to one another. The question they ask about the relation between the domestic sphere and the sphere of employment, for instance, is not 'How does the individual's position in one sphere affect her or his position in other spheres?' but 'How do these two *spheres* fit together or contradict one another?'

The main theory that has been put forward to answer this question, that of the 'dual labour-market', starts from 'industrial apartheid': from the observation that the occupational structure is segregated into 'men's jobs' and 'women's jobs'; that the vast majority of employed women occupy the low-paid positions and that the lowest paying jobs tend to be occupied by women. But it then goes on to note that segmentation in the job-market is not confined to segmentation by gender. Dual labour-markets are those in which:

1. There is a more or less pronounced division into higher paying and lower paying sectors;
2. Mobility across the boundary of these sectors is restricted;
3. Higher paying jobs are tied into promotional or career ladders, while lower paid jobs offer few opportunities for vertical movement;
4. Higher paying jobs are relatively stable, while lower paid jobs are unstable (Barron and Norris, 1976, p. 49).

This dual structure is partly the result of changes in the economics of production – in particular the historical tendency for many jobs, both manual and non-manual, to become de-skilled (see Chapter 8), leading to a secondary status for a section of the workforce. This is partly due to the logic of the labour-market – in particular the fact that in order to attract and retain the stable workers in the higher-paid job sector, employers have not only to pay high wages for some jobs but must also develop a promotional structure or incremental pay-scales relating to length of service. Other, more radical writers have pointed out that a dual structure enables employers to gain control over their workforce both as a technique of 'divide and rule' between higher-paid and lower-paid sectors, and as a consequence of competition for promotion (Gordon, 1972). Such divisions within the workforce, and competition between segments of the workforce, in this model, are not to be explained in terms of gender at all.

Why is it that men occupy the primary sector and women the

secondary sector? According to Barron and Norris (1976) this is because women (and particularly married women) have characteristics that match the (non-gender) distinguishing features of the secondary labour-market. They tend to change jobs more often and readily accept the loss of a job; they are a socially distinct category, which appears to legitimate different treatment; they display little interest in acquiring training; they are less concerned than men about the economic rewards for their work; and they are less effectively organized into trade unions. But this only leads us to ask a further question: why do women and men workers have these different characteristics in the first place? Barron and Norris's answer is two-fold. 'These attributes,' they say,

are the *product* of the social relationships between employer and worker, and not something which an individual possesses independently of that relationship. At the same time, they are qualities which are to some extent shaped elsewhere in the social structure and brought *to* the employment market (Barron and Norris, 1976, p.53).

Workers in the secondary sector thus tend to take on characteristics appropriate to that sector. Hence if they expect to be excluded from primary sector jobs, they will not bother to qualify themselves for them, even at school. But all this tells us is how the patterning of the dual labour-market, including the sex patterning, is reproduced over time and over the generations, not what its origins are. But the second part of this explanation leads us beyond the sphere of employment altogether, for in this model, the labour-market produces *ungendered* boxes, which then get filled by gendered individuals because of the operation of factors extraneous to the economy. Heidi Hartmann has expressed a similar point of view:

Marx's theory of the development of capitalism is a theory of 'empty places' . . . Just as capital creates these places, indifferent to the individuals who fill them, the categories of Marxist analysis, 'class', 'reserve army of labor', 'wage-laborer', do not explain why particular people fill particular places . . . Marx's categories, like capital itself, are sex-blind . . . (pp. 7–8). Capitalist development creates the places for a hierarchy of workers . . . Gender and racial hierarchies determine who fills the empty places (Hartmann, 1979, p. 13).

But as we shall see when we look at racial inequalities in Chapter 9, racial hierarchies and racial categorization itself do not originate completely outside the relations of wage labour. And on the other hand, the form of the hierarchy of places in the labour-market may depend upon the availability of appropriate social categories of workers (for instance, mechanization may be postponed if there is a ready supply of cheap migrant labour; conversely, domestic servants may be replaced by washing-machines and vacuum-cleaners when the price of their labour becomes too high). Similarly, the form that gender takes originates partly within the sphere of employment (if only in the shape of women's partial exclusion from much employment); while the structure of the labour-market (even the location of factories and offices) is adapted to the existence of a pool of married women workers, made available in the first place for low-paid, part-time, insecure, local work by a sexual division of labour within the household. There is thus a dialectical interplay between the domestic division of labour and the structure of paid employment outside the home.

Hence in industrial society, where employment, or the lack of it, is an important aspect of everyone's identity, the imagery of gender derives from the world of paid work as well as from the world of the family. Even the practice of motherhood is now strongly influenced by books written by specialists which tell mothers how to bring up their children. The modern mother is now an amateur unpaid nurse and infant teacher in a way that an early nineteenth-century mother was not. Conversely, masculinity is associated with an affinity for vehicles and machinery, and with the idea of earning 'good money': with the spheres of work to which men in our culture aspire.

The historical development of the division of labour in employment has thus not just been the unfolding of a 'sex-blind' capitalist logic. And although the dual labour-market was indeed developed partly as an employer's strategy to 'exploit race, ethnic and sex antagonisms in order to undermine unions and break strikes' (Edwards *et al.*, 1975, p. xiv), as Jill Rubery has firmly argued, organized labour has played its part, too, in accepting and institutionalizing these divisions (Rubery, 1978).

An example: male dominance and technological change in printing. Many of these points about gender and employment are vividly illustrated in Cynthia Cockburn's book *Brothers* (1983), a study of printers carried out in the late 1970s and early 1980s. Computerized photo-composition has transformed the composing-rooms of most major London newspapers – the first major technological change since the introduction of linotype machines in the 1890s. The compositors are a long-established elite body of men, strongly committed to traditional practices. They had a long apprenticeship, effective local union organization, and considerable control over their own work. The new technology required them to learn new skills – type-setting on a typewriter style keyboard instead of the ninety-key linotype keyboard, and pasting up paper copy on layout boards instead of assembling galleys of metal type into a printing form. In the newspapers, the National Graphical Association (NGA) has managed to retain control over these new processes of composition. But the new work, though hard to learn, is experienced as being less skilled, since it has become sub-divided into separate tasks, which can now be performed by so-called less skilled workers, including women. For instance, after Rupert Murdoch bought Times Newspapers Ltd he farmed out the composing of the three *Times* supplements to a trade type-setting house where women workers are employed. As a woman told Cynthia Cockburn:

Some of these houses advertised for typists, rather than compositors . . . When women are taken on that way, they apply to the NGA for a Temporary Working Card. This provisional membership is taken away if the individual leaves that particular job before two years is up. In this way, many women go back to being ordinary non-unionized typists after a while (Cockburn, 1983, p. 168).

So the craftsmen's monopoly position is under threat. Many other old and relatively privileged primary sector jobs are slipping into the secondary sector of a dual labour-market, too.

How far this process will go is not determined solely by the technological and economic considerations of management, for the trade unions contest policies that they see as furthering the interests of management, but not their own interests. The attitudes of the skilled craftsmen, trying to come to terms with a world that is changing around them, however, are complex and ambivalent today as they were when earlier technological changes were introduced. In the first decade of this century, for example, the Scottish Typographical Association waged a successful 'crusade' against women compositors. In the process, an association between ideas of 'masculinity' and 'solidarity' was established that is not a necessary or a logical one, but has become built into British craft trade unionism, an association which Cockburn interprets as an intersection between the contradictions of capitalism and those of patriarchy.

Reserve army of labour?

Another way of explaining gender patterns and employment – that of the 'reserve army of labour' – emphasizes the role of the employers' interests. This derives from Marx's analysis in volume one of *Capital* where he states that as capitalism develops it has varying requirements for labour, caused by changes in the incidence of mechanization and by the expansion or contraction of different kinds of production. Capitalism therefore always requires a reserve army of labour waiting in the wings – not fully part of the proletariat but ready to be drawn into it.

Modern writers in this tradition have asked whether such a reserve army exists today. Many argue that male and female migrant workers, and White women (especially married women) are especially appropriate categories of 'reserve labour' since they are able to survive on the margins of the wage-economy, or, if it disappears altogether, can be sent home – women back into dependence on their husbands; migrant labourers to the countries they came from. Indeed such women do not usually even appear in official statistics of unemployment and are often reluctant to see themselves as having *left* work, or as redundant or 'unemployed', but regard themselves as having *returned* to a role that was always there for them: that of 'housewife'. A slightly less rosy view would be to say that married women are always vulnerable to periods of 'voluntary' unemployment because of their responsibilities for caring for children and for sick and disabled relatives, and that some groups, like single mothers and Black women, are so disadvantaged that they are forced to take whatever marginal work they can get.

But while women may seem particularly suited to the industrial reserve army, occupational segregation – the 'industrial apartheid' we discussed earlier – means that they cannot constitute an all-purpose reserve pool of labour. At times of decline in heavy industry, for instance, more men than women will be thrown out of work; but where expansion is under way, they will benefit when specifically 'men's' jobs are being produced. Nevertheless, in periods of decline, women's job losses are greater than men's and the loss of part-time jobs is greater than losses in full-time employment (Bruegel, 1979). For employers, the population of women in the labour-market thus provides some welcome flexibility.

Conclusion

The division of labour between women and men today is clearly not just the unfolding in modern conditions of a 'natural' sexual division of labour – an updated version of the man hunting animals and the woman gathering roots and berries. Neither is it an inevitable part of capitalist industrial society, determined by ineluctable imperatives. It is, rather, the product of a complex and specific history and considerable changes have already taken place during the industrial capitalist period. The most important of these has been the increase in the number of married women in paid employment. The causes of this do not lie in the economy alone, but involve changes in the whole social order: in the educational system, in the home, and in women's changing expectations and demands. These generate political movements at the structural level, and interpersonal tensions too. To understand these more fully we need to examine the family.

Family and Gender in Industrial Capitalism

The modern pattern of the family: two functionalist theories

The largest and richest tradition in the sociology of the family is functionalist. In its simplest form, functionalism asserts that the family exists in all societies and performs certain basic functions that are essential to social life. G. P. Murdock, for instance, specified four basic functions sexual, economic, reproductive and educational – each essential to the carrying on of everyday life and to the transmission of culture from generation to generation (Murdock, 1949). The 'many-sided utility' of the family, Murdock says, meant that it was an indispensable and inevitable feature of *any* society. But he did not in fact explore very carefully whether these social needs could be or sometimes actually were fulfilled by other institutions, or whether there was much real similarity between, say, the economic or the educational functions (or even sexual functions) in simple foraging societies and in complex industrial societies.

Other writers in the same vein have added another item to
Murdock's list of basic functions: social placement. By this they
mean the way in which a person's social position is determined by
the family they were born into. In some societies, individuals are
born into a particular lineage group, or a particular caste group, or
are born a lord or a peasant, and this completely determines their
future place in society, their major relations with others and the kind
of life they will lead. In others, your family of origin has a considerable but not so all-determining effect on your future (as we shall see
when we look at Britain in the next section).

Other sociologists, notably Talcott Parsons (Parsons and Bales,
1955), offered a much more elaborated version of the way in which
the family performs its function of socialization (which Murdock
called 'education'). Primary socialization, they argued, especially in
the pre-school years, structures the child's personality not just in
general terms, but according to the particular culture of its society.
Drawing on psychoanalytic theories, Parsons argued that in order to
carry out this 'primary' socialization effectively, the family needed to
have the roles of mother and father clearly differentiated, with the
mother providing a context for warmth and emotionality within the
home, while the father, as a breadwinner, saw to its economic
security by his activities, especially economic, in the world outside
the home. Having been reared in such families, people have a need
to live in them again as adults, in order to 'stabilize their personalities'. This, according to Parsons, is the second major function of the
family in modern industrial societies.

Others, however, have pointed out the historical tendency for new
specialized institutions, often associated with the State, to take over
what were previously the much more generalized functions of the
family – leaving it with only the four or five basic functions. Thus
MacIver and Page (1950, p. 264) represented the emergence of the
modern family as shown in Figure 6.

Today, this kind of argument usually emphasizes that the Welfare
State has taken over some of the non-productive economic functions
of the family, as well as the provision of a safety net of financial
support and of care for those in need, an argument we will consider
later on.

In addition to the Welfare State, the education system is another
State agency which replaces the family in providing for a key

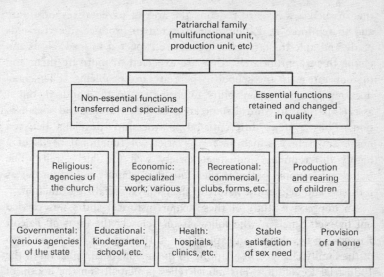

Figure 6. Emergence of the modern family type

(*Source:* MacIver and Page, 1950, *Society: An Introductory Analysis*, p. 264.)

functional need in society. Universal education was only provided by the State from 1870 onwards, although the introduction of schooling for working-class children had begun on a piecemeal basis much earlier. Before that, families had been responsible for bringing up children. Children got such socialization and training as they did receive either in the parental home or in someone else's home, as a servant or a farm-servant or as an apprentice. So the emergent education system took over part of what had been a function of the family. In the process, the way that function was performed was divided up: the family became responsible for socializing the child in its early years and training it in basic social skills and in obedient habits; the school became responsible for more specific training in skills relating to work and public life.

It is often argued that the State-supported system of schooling serves to bridge the gap between home and work because it performs the function, for society, of differentiating school-leavers within a hierarchy of qualifications matching the different levels of the hierarchical structure of occupations. At the same time, the schools did this in such a way as to redefine the area of parental responsibility and to reinforce it, Parents are expected to produce five-year-olds ready and able to start school; they are expected to feed, clean and clothe them appropriately; they are expected to motivate them and to cooperate with the school if there are any problems. The school does not assume responsibility for bringing up the children, but it asserts its right to control some areas of their training and socialization. Thus a new, differentiated 'partnership' develops between home and school which serves a variety of functional needs of a highly differentiated industrial society well (or fairly well). The State's educational policy is therefore also a family policy insofar as it directs and defines the nature of the family's socializing function.

An impressive study of these major historical shifts was carried out by Neil Smelser, who followed very closely the ideas of Talcott Parsons, in developing an explanation of the ways in which the form of the family changed in adapting to the major social upheaval of the Industrial Revolution. His model relies principally on the notion of the operation of blind evolutionary mechanisms. But he does also see State legislation as playing an important part in establishing the new institutional form of the family. In his book, *Social Change in the Industrial Revolution* (1959), Smelser does not question the universality of the family, but he does see it as changing in *form*, as the development of the factory system of production displaced the earlier cottage industry where the family formed a productive unit.

Writing of the Lancashire cotton industry between 1770 and 1840, he shows how at first all the members of the family, including children, went to work in the factories and describes the strains that this put on the working-class family and in particular on its ability to perform its functions of socializing children and of handling adults' tensions. This involved functional 'adaptation': a new differentiation between the sphere of production, on the one hand, and the sphere of the family on the other, with the family becoming a more specialized, *non*-productive unit. At the same time, there developed a new kind of differentiation of occupational roles within the family: instead of all working together within the home, men became the chief factory workers, young children ceased productive work, and women tended to stay at home, engaged on 'domestic' work rather than working alongside their husbands. This historical process, according to Smelser, was not simply a smooth adaptation, but involved protests, struggles, campaigns and attempts to implement various kinds of solutions to the problems experienced by the people involved and as they were interpreted by different social groups in the light of the culture and expectations of the day. But Smelser sees legislation – and particularly the factory legislation that restricted the hours of women's and children's work and eventually excluded children from the factories altogether – as a central part of the process by which men's and women's involvement in production, and hence roles in the family, became differentiated.

In Smelser's model, social change produces stresses in existing social arrangements. In the process of overcoming these, institutions like the family gradually become adapted and a new functionally integrated equilibrium is established.

Functionalist (and evolutionary) accounts of historical change thus assume that, whatever the struggles and false trails along the way, the social pattern finally arrived at will be the one *best adapted* to the new social situation.

Alongside this theme – of the family moving from a multi-functional to a more specialized institution in modern industrial societies – is another major theme: that the nuclear family becomes more structurally isolated. According to Talcott Parsons, in most societies, especially in societies with a simple social structure overall, the nuclear family exists within an extended family household. In modern America, each new nuclear family formed on marriage tends to establish a new household and to become relatively isolated from the families of origin of each of the couple. This 'isolated conjugal family' is, he says, the 'normal household unit' (Parsons, 1964, p. 183). By relating the organization of the family to other institutions in advanced industrial societies, Parsons produces an overall functionalist analysis. Since the occupational system emphasizes the qualifications and abilities an individual has achieved, rather than social connections – 'who you know' or the kinship ties one is born with – social and geographical mobility replace permanence of residence and occupation. These factors weaken the bonds of kinship, but they do not weaken the nuclear family or the conjugal bond. Indeed they make it all the more important as a haven from the impersonality of the world of work.

Since Parsons first put forward these views in 1943, they have generated much research and lengthy debate. What has emerged is that, on the one hand, wider kin ties may not have been of such great importance as the 'Merrie England' myth of pre-industrial society suggests; on the other, that they remain of considerable importance in modern America and Britain.

David Morgan summarized the main findings relating to kinship in urban society as follows:

1. The term 'isolated nuclear family' is misleading and inaccurate in relation to the modern urban family. A more appropriate term is the 'modified extended family'.
2. This modified extended family is not confined to working-class, rural or upper-class sections of society but is found among the mobile, urban middle class, the grouping most likely to exhibit isolation according to the Parsonian formulation . . . indeed, perhaps *because* of the impersonality of urban life people are *more* likely to turn to kin – even kin some distance away – for help and for social relations.
3. The use of the term 'modified extended family' reminds us that we are not dealing with a bounded system. Out of the total possible number of persons in a kin universe only a few are 'selected' for more intimate relationships. This selection process is influenced by degree of relationship, geographical distance and personal choice, usually in that order of importance.
4. Within the category of degree of relationship the order of preference (for a married ego) is normally parents, siblings and others. A large element of this modified system, therefore, revolves around generational relationships.
5. In the maintenance of kinship ties and the handling of flows of aid, information and resources, women play the most important part (Morgan, 1975, pp. 65–6).

More recently, it has been observed that not only are kin ties significant for many people, but also that, at any given time, about half of the population are not living in a nuclear family household at all – if the nuclear family is defined as a married couple with their dependent children. So Parsons's 'normal household unit' is not in fact the statistical majority.

There is a curious parallel between the theories of Talcott Parsons and his fellow functionalist sociologists and certain recent Marxist analyses of the family. The parallel is curious because sociological functionalism is usually seen as conservative in its implications, defending the status quo on the grounds that it is inevitable because it is functionally necessary. Marxism, on the other hand, is usually seen as premised on the possibility of social change and as involving a critique of the existing institutions of capitalist society. In fact, it is not incompatible with functional analysis, as is often supposed.

In the 1970s, for instance, there was a lot of interest among Marxist feminists about the ways in which the family was central to the *social* reproduction of capitalism. In particular it was argued that women's domestic labour – especially housework and childcare – serves the function of reproducing a vital element of capitalist production, namely labour-power, by servicing, refreshing and training both today's workers and the workers of the next generation. In other types of society, people's ability to engage in productive work is also reproduced in the family. But because production does not take place separated from the home, but usually within the household and other kinship-based units, the reproduction of the labour force does not occur in a separate location, nor does it require a family exclusively devoted to care and consumption. Similarly, in societies where production is not organized around the wage-system (where people's subsistence depends upon having a cash income in return for their work), it never occurs to anyone that housework is peculiar in that it is unpaid. To be unpaid only becomes significant in a wage based society.

Insofar as women's domestic responsibilities go along with a marginal and intermittent involvement in employment and with low wages, the unpaid nature of housework has further consequences, in that it involves partial or complete dependence on someone who does have a wage – the husband. So there is a neat functional fit between a division of labour at home, in which men are breadwinners and women homemakers, and a division of labour in paid work, in which men have the best and most secure jobs, commanding a family wage, and women have the poorer jobs that enable them to contribute only a subsidiary income to the household. The same division of labour within the home also fits neatly with the role of women as a reserve army of labour. This functional fit helps to reproduce and maintain the social relations of a capitalist mode of production. The analysis, then, is a classically functionalist one, although there are many disputes as to whether unpaid domestic labour is really an essential and inevitable part of capitalist society or merely a highly convenient arrangement.

Another functional analysis of the family derives from the Marxist

Louis Althusser's identification of the family as an 'ideological state apparatus': that the family, together with institutions like education and the media, contributes to the reproduction of the relations of capitalist production. In particular, individual self-supporting families provide an important ideology, and motivate their members to work hard, especially the men, who have the responsibility for breadwinning. In addition to child-rearing practices that are based on gender differences, the family helps to produce individualistic personalities appropriate to life in capitalist society. Some add that paternal authority within the family provides the model for state authority, and that the experience of childhood submission establishes the basis for obedient adult citizens. Others emphasize the way in which the elaboration of privatized family life, especially in the form of consumerism, serves to divert the working class from a concern with exploitation at work and reduces the need for a more overtly repressive State. Again, these are classically functionalist analyses, which show how the form of the family fits in with the specific society in which it is located.

The parallel between the Parsonian style of functionalism and the Marxist one is only partial and disappears when it comes to substantive questions. For one thing, the implications of traditional sociological functionalism are very different from those of Marxist 'reproduction' theory. Whereas the sociological functionalists see society as a set of functionally interrelated institutions, all contributing in their different ways to the integration and stability of the whole, Marxist functionalists explore the ways in which different social patterns and institutions contribute to the reproduction of the conditions of capitalist production in a way that emphasizes contradiction, not integration. Thus apparently progressive institutions like education, social welfare, medical care and collective bargaining are shown to have their dark or contradictory side in that they serve to reproduce the conditions of capitalism and, most importantly, help to overcome or dampen the effects of the deep-seated contradictions that are inherent in the capitalist system. Furthermore, for Marxists, this is not an accident or the result of the action of blind evolutionary forces, but is to some degree orchestrated by the purposive action of a State which acts on behalf of the class that benefits from the continuance of the capitalist system.

So although some Marxists and some functionalist sociologists may share the general view that the family and the welfare system, for instance, perform complementary functions, and although they may even agree in general terms about what those functions are and how the functional contributions of the family and welfare are related, nevertheless it is important to recognize that the overall theoretical perspective of the two is very different. Parsons and other functionalist sociologists, as we have seen, tend to concentrate on functions that are seen as common to all societies. They emphasize what they see as the universality of the family and how it serves needs that are found in all societies. In their view, the form of the family changes as other aspects of society change, but in such a way that it can continue to perform its core functions. Marxists, on the other hand, see each era of history (such as feudalism, capitalism and the communism of the future) as having a fundamentally different social system. They emphasize the specific features of the family and the functions they serve for a specific social system, not universal attributes and functions.

Social placement in Britain: a neglected function of the family

Sociologists have long been so concerned with the study of social mobility, that they have often forgotten to stress the other side of the medal – the extent to which people's social class position is fixed by inheritance. For the main way in which social classes reproduce themselves over time is by bearing and rearing children (see Chapter 10). Most boys will live out their lives in the same class they were born into, and even in the same section of it; most girls will marry a man in a situation very similar to their own fathers. During the course of the twentieth century, there has been an expansion of the 'new middle class' of bureaucrats, clerks, technologists and managers, largely achieved by recruitment from below, and engendering a large amount of social mobility. Though this expansion is now slowing down, the experience of social fluidity has left its mark on popular as well as sociological consciousness. The career of the grammar school boy and the success of the working man's son at a redbrick university have become celebrated images, evidence that the old class destinies were broken and that there was 'room at the top'.

This question of social mobility was a dominant concern of the sociology of education during the 1950s and 1960s (see Chapter 11).

With the growth of new ambitions for social mobility after the Second World War, the selective system of secondary modern and grammar schools was found wanting. Children from working-class homes, and especially from 'lower working-class' homes were severely disadvantaged. Those who did do well at school tended to have unusual families in some way: the mother was better educated than average, or the parents were interested in reading. Unfortunately, there were no parallel studies of the ways in which parents with professional and managerial jobs generally contrived to ensure that their children did do well at school and not suffer *downward* mobility. If there had been, a more balanced and structural interpretation might have been achieved – one in which inequalities of opportunity can be seen as a feature of the family's functions *as an institution*, rather than placing the credit or blame for an individual's success or failure with the child's home and especially with its mother.

If, instead of studying upward social mobility, we look at the overall picture, we find that most men follow their fathers. A large-scale survey conducted in the 1970s by John Goldthorpe and his colleagues found that 62 per cent of the sons of men who had been in Class I and Class II occupations (professionals, administrators, managers, supervisors, higher-grade technicians, etc) were themselves in jobs in the same classes. Only 13 per cent of them had manual jobs. A similar pattern of fathers passing on social position to their sons is found at the other end of the scale, where 58 per cent of the sons of men who were in manual jobs themselves had manual jobs, and only 18 per cent had Class I and II jobs (Goldthorpe *et al.*, 1980, pp. 70, 75).

The picture for women is somewhat different, with families proving less effective in passing on the father's job status to their daughters. Women often marry 'up' or 'down'. Anthony Heath reports that

the typical father from Class I is more likely to see his daughter downwardly mobile than his son, or, to be more precise, to have a son-in-law of a lower social class than his son. Conversely, the girl from Classes VI or VII is more likely to be upwardly socially mobile than her brother (Heath, 1981, p. 113).

A woman's own occupation, too, is less determined by her father's than is a man's. (Unfortunately, the reports of this study do not tell us to what extent women follow in their *mothers'* footsteps, rather than their fathers'.)

Criticisms of functionalism

Functionalism has been subjected to so much criticism that it is often considered to be dead and buried. Yet, as far as the study of the family is concerned, it would be more accurate to say that 'it's dead but it won't lie down'. We can now summarize, and evaluate, these criticisms.

(*a*) *Functionalism confuses function with cause or with explanation.* While it is true that some functionalists have thought an analysis of the functional interrelations between the parts of a society was all that was required of the sociologist, most have seen functional analysis as one aspect of a total study, recognizing that no item, however functionally useful, is irreplaceable or indispensable.

(*b*) *Functionalism is conservative.* As we have seen, functionalism can come in radical as well as conservative guises.

(*c*) *Functionalism ignores social conflict, cannot analyse power, cannot analyse human action or meaning.* The criticisms are accurate. They are the main reason why functional analysis can only ever be partial, which is why we turn to the study of conflict, power and social meanings below.

(*d*) *Functionalism tends to reify the institutions it analyses.* We have seen how much of the debate about Parsons's theory of the isolated nuclear family revolves around the question of whether he was falsely stereotyping the modern family. Similarly, Marxist 'reproduction' theories need to be challenged in the same way. Insofar as they assume a population divided neatly into nuclear families, each with a breadwinning husband, a dependent housewife and dependent children, they may be false.

Myths and realities of modern families

The stereotype of the modern family is of a married couple living with their dependent children. Yet in fact, though this is an important stage that most people pass through and though most children spend at least their early years in such a setting, such nuclear families are not the dominant form of household. An examination of statistics

144   The New Introducing Sociology

Table 3. Households and people in households: 1987

Type of household	% of households	% of people
One person	25	10
Married couple	27	21
Married couple with dependent children	28	44
Married couple with independent children	9	12
Lone parent with dependent children	4	5
Other	7	8

(*Source:* Central Statistical Office, 1990, pp. 36, 37.)

An examination of statistics
from British official sources reveals a very different picture from the
stereotyped one. As Table 3 shows, well under half the British
population live in such households and only 28 per cent of all
households take this form. (The difference arises because so many
people live in smaller, one-or-two-person, households.)

Individuals are economically and socially dependent for the first
sixteen-to-twenty years of their lives and may have dependent children of their own for a further sixteen-to-twenty years. So even
those who become parents and remain married throughout spend
little more than half their lives in a classic nuclear family household.
There is nothing very new about this. Though it is true that smaller
family sizes and the prolongation of life in old age have changed the
actual figures, nevertheless the principles of family-building and
decay remain the same. Yet this *stage*, that most people and most
households pass through, has become *the* image of 'the family', in
functionalist theories as well as in popular imagination and public
policy-making.

A further aspect of this image is that of the man as the breadwinner. This idea, as we have seen, is commonly used to explain and
justify the advantages that men have in pay and opportunities in the
labour-market – 'They've got families to support, after all'. In
reality, since only about half of married mothers are not employed
outside the home, only 11 per cent of all households consist of the
stereotypical family made up of a breadwinning husband, a full-time
housewife and their children. Even more startling is the fact that
only 39 per cent of the male labour force are married men with
dependent children, and as more than two-thirds of their wives are

Table 4. Employed women's reasons for working

	Main reason			
Reasons for working	*All women*	*Married women*	*Non-married women*	*Non-married with dependent child(ren)*
	%	%	%	%
Need money for basic essentials such as food, rent or mortgage	35	30	48	78
To earn money to buy extras	20	26	3	8
Enjoy working	14	16	11	4
Other reasons	31	28	38	10

(*Source:* Martin and Roberts, 1984, p. 69.)

also employed, only 15 per cent of these men 'support their families' in the full sense. So some of the supposed justification and (perhaps more importantly for our purposes) the supposed explanation for differentiation in the labour-market begin to look rather thin.

If men are seldom breadwinners, in the stereotyped sense, women are seldom dependants either. Many women have others depending upon them, whether as single parents, as wives of men who are unemployed or not working, or as relatives of elderly and disabled people. Among couples where both are in full-time employment, one in seven wives actually earn more than their husbands (EOC, 1984, p. 92). Women are spending an increasing proportion of their lives in paid work although, as we have seen, their participation tends to be more intermittent than men's, for domestic reasons. Fifty-eight per cent of wives are employed at any one time.

In the main these changes have come about because women now tend to return to work sooner after having had a baby than in the past – on average, now, three and a half years after their latest baby, and they quite often return to work in between births (Martin and Roberts, 1984, p. 130). Their reasons for working are largely economic; as Table 4 shows, they are seldom working simply for 'pin money'. Even where women are not earning, and are living with husbands who are, feminist writers have pointed out that they may not

be able to 'depend' very much on their husbands. Often their support comes in the form of 'housekeeping money' which may involve
a very unequal and arbitrary internal distribution of the household's
resources controlled by the husband. In extreme cases, they may be
given support in kind, but no money to spend at all (Pahl, 1980).

The rising divorce rate makes the situation of those women who
are dependent more problematic. Projections based on current divorce rates suggest that one in three marriages may be expected to
end in divorce. In many cases (about one in three) this occurs before
the couple have children and therefore often before the wife has
become her husband's dependant. But many divorced and separated
women have great financial difficulties. Present trends in divorce law
are towards a 'clean break', where the husband's obligation to
support his wife ceases soon after divorce (on the grounds that the
assumption of dependency is incompatible with sexual equality).
Even when husbands have been expected to provide financial support,
court maintenance orders have been notoriously hard to enforce.

It is often said that the high divorce rate is not a social problem
because it is accompanied by a high rate of remarriage. It is
estimated that something like 80 per cent of those divorcing under
the age of thirty will remarry within five years (Rimmer, 1981,
p. 44). But meanwhile, many of these people will form one-parent
families. In fact, divorced women are the largest group of lone
parents and make up 5.4 per cent of all families with dependent
children (lone parents altogether are 14.3 per cent of all such
families) (OPCS, 1988, p. 17). One-parent families are also much
more likely to be in poverty than others.

Even if they have no children, women who have been out of the
labour-market for a while, or only working part-time and who have
not built up pension rights or savings because they assumed they
would continue to be supported by their husband, will find great
difficulty in managing financially. Furthermore, remarriage often
cannot solve divorced women's problems, since the second husband
may himself have a first wife and children he contributes to and
anyway may be reluctant to take on the support of children he thinks
are another man's responsibility. So a high divorce rate, even with a
high remarriage rate, makes it difficult for women to expect to be
dependent on their husband for life.

There is one aspect of the stereotype of the family that does seem to be accurate: the idea of the woman as a housewife. The fact that more married women go out to paid work has modified but not fundamentally challenged this pattern. In 1973, Michael Young and Peter Willmott published a book called *The Symmetrical Family*, in which they argued that the emergent family form is a symmetrical one, in the sense that increasingly both husband and wife work outside the home and men are becoming more home-centred, so that both men and women have two roles, in paid work and in the domestic sphere. The new pattern, they said, had started at the top of the class structure and was now trickling its way down to the working class. Unfortunately, their own evidence contradicts them to some extent, for their study of how much time a sample of 350 people spent working at household tasks showed that men did under 10 hours, while women who had full-time jobs did over 23 hours; women with part-time jobs did over 35 hours and full-time house-wives did over 45 hours (Young and Willmott, 1973, p. 113). These were people aged between 30 and 50 years old, so there were not many couples in their sample with very young children or with sick or elderly dependants — for whom the housework hours, especially for the women, would be considerably higher. Other studies covering the full age-range, have, on the whole, found lower housework figures for men and higher figures for women. It is true that husbands help more in the home than they did in the past, but the emphasis should usually be on the word 'help'. The wife is usually the one with primary responsibility for the work, and a study in the United States even found that the husband's help often did not relieve the wife of much work: for instance, when he helped in getting the meals she was saved only about half the time that he spent (Leibowitz, 1975, p. 239). In relation to childcare, mothers tend to do the routine daily physical care while fathers take on the more interesting activities of supervising or joining in play or outings. As Hilary Land has put it, 'We do not need research to establish that in most households it is still the women who do most of the domestic work (or if they do not actually do it themselves they are responsible for seeing that it is done and . . . probably pay for substitute help, which is almost certain to be female)' (Land, 1980, p. 18).

Recent research has demonstrated that women's work as house-wives is not just one side of an egalitarian 'differentiation of roles' as writers like Talcott Parsons suggest, for there is a very unequal division of labour within most homes. Women tend to define their housework as *real* work, but on the whole do not enjoy it or at best feel ambivalent about it. In her detailed interviews with forty London housewives, Ann Oakley (1974) found that their main sources of dissatisfaction were the monotony, repetitiveness and fragmentation of the tasks. They often found caring for children and cooking fairly satisfying, but many other tasks that were not. Keeping a house clean and tidy and caring for children who constantly make messes contradict one another. The hours they worked were long (she found an average of seventy-seven (1974, p. 92) hours per week – much higher than Young and Willmott) and the pace was often pressured. The work was isolated and low in status, appreciation from others in the household often taking the form of absence of complaints.

So although women are increasingly to be found in the sphere of paid work, they are still primarily responsible for unpaid work in the home. There is a real sense in which the separation of spheres into public and private, men's worlds and women's worlds, still exists. The privacy and pleasantness of home life has been celebrated by many writers, and many feminists as well as others contrast the personal values of intimacy, caring, commitment and harmony with the impersonal 'masculine' values of formality, toughness, rationality, competition and striving. Yet this image of the qualities of domestic life is in many ways also a myth. The belief in the privacy of the family, combined with the inequalities in power within it, make domestic despotism as probable as domestic bliss. Indeed, for the last decade or so, the women's movement has cast a searchlight on very dark aspects of family life indeed: such things as child-beating, incest, wife-beating, marital rape, and women's mental illness.

'Wife-beating' has long been a recognized aspect of marriage, and women are usually loath to report it because they fear it will only get worse, or because they obscurely believe that *they* are to blame, and because 'outsiders' are very reluctant to believe them or to interfere in a private matter. Even so, assaults by men on their wives account for as much as a quarter of all *reported* crimes of violence (Dobash and Dobash, 1977–8). Much the same reluctance to report applies to domestic rapes, and yet rape crisis centres find that among women coming to them a very large proportion have been raped by men who know their victims well: husbands, boyfriends, fathers and uncles. In British law, despite feminist protests, rape by a husband still does not count as the criminal offence of rape – which means effectively that it is tolerated by the State. What all of this suggests is that family life is often far from being a haven of peace.

Studies of gender differences in mental illness, too, suggest that marriage and family often put particular strains on women. Officially recorded rates of mental illness are notoriously hard to interpret, since the definitions involved are so much a question of what social categories to 'label' behaviour, which in turn affect a person's readiness to seek medical help or hospitalization for what may be regarded as a 'mental' problem (Busfield, 1983), as we will see in Chapter 6.

Nevertheless, there are fairly consistent figures showing that married women are more likely to become mental patients than men. Single men have higher rates than single women (and than married men), but married women have higher rates than both single women and married men. One possible explanation is that fewer mentally ill men and more mentally ill women get married. But it is more probable that marriage fosters the mental health of husbands and undermines that of wives (Gove, 1972). Women are particularly prone to the neuroses, especially depression, whereas men are more prone than women to psychopathy and to drug and alcohol dependence. One famous study by George Brown and his colleagues (1978) found that, among married women, having more than three children under the age of fourteen at home, and having no outside job, were among the factors making women more vulnerable to depression.

Even a brief look at some of the evidence about the realities of households and families, then, lends support to criticism of the functionalist approaches:

Firstly, and most obviously, it shows up the dangers of an analysis that is based on a stereotype. It is all very well to show that a nuclear family household with a male breadwinner and a dependent housewife is functional to modern industrial society, or to capitalism. But what is the value of such an analysis when this household form is so far from being universal? It certainly cannot be argued that functionalist analyses straightforwardly explain the existing family form. What can be said, perhaps, is that the functionalist analyses may explain why that particular family form is so much privileged in ideology and in social policy. Its functionality cannot make it universal, but can explain why it is favoured, nurtured and supported and other household forms marginalized, discouraged and even penalized.

Secondly, the sort of evidence that we have reviewed makes more sense in terms of power-relations between men and women rather than in functionalist terms. Functionalism tends to see what goes on in the family as a subordinate part of the whole society. An approach emphasizing conflict and power would tend to see family relationships and organization as much more variable outcomes of the totality of relations between men and women, both those within the family itself and outside it.

The Future of Family and Gender?

This chapter started with the proposition that gender is socially constructed and then discussed the specific ways in which it is constructed in employment and in the domestic sphere in contemporary Britain. The critique of functionalism suggests that there is nothing necessary about the current forms of gender and family and that, though functional relations may set some limits, they may change in the future. Are there, then, any pointers to the likely direction of such changes?

Debates in this field usually focus around two questions:

1. Is 'the family' in decline, and if so, what next?
2. Can feminism be successful as a movement for social change?

Is 'the family' in decline?

The discussion in the last section makes it clear that the answer to this question depends on what you mean by 'the family'. In the current debates, too, it is impossible to separate questions of definition from questions of value. For instance, one of the classic positions is that stated by Ronald Fletcher in his widely read book *The Family and Marriage in Britain* (1966). For him, the family has benefited from shedding burdensome peripheral functions and from better access to divorce. It has become more popular, more stable, less oppressive to women and children and altogether a more satisfying and egalitarian means of providing people with warm affective relationships and a comfortable home. Fletcher, then, defines 'the family' in terms of those personal relationships and sees – from the high rate of remarriage, among other things – that it is alive and well.

On the other hand, there are some who would reject this as liberal complacency, Christopher Lasch, for instance:

> In fact, the so-called functions of the family form an integrated system. It is inaccurate to speak of a variety of functions, some of which decline while others take on added importance. The only function of the family that matters is socialization; and when protection, work and instruction in work have all been removed from the home, the child no longer identifies with his parents or internalizes their authority in the same way as before, if indeed he internalizes their authority at all (Lasch, 1977, p. 130).

Lasch, then, defines 'the family' in terms of authority relations between parents and children (and also between husband and wife) and comes to a much more gloomy conclusion than Fletcher.

Another theme in the debate about the family is the relation between State and family. But here again, values do not correspond neatly to definitions. Feminist writers like Hilary Land (Land, 1978; McIntosh, 1978; Wilson, 1977) have argued that the State in a sense constructs the family through its welfare policies. These define wives and children as dependent on men, and women as responsible for housework and caring for others. Implicit in this position is a view of 'the family' as an ideological construct rather than a given entity, and such writers point to the fact that dependence is to some extent a myth and caring problematic. On the other hand, there are writers such as Jacques Donzelot (1980) who share the 'deconstructive' view of 'the family' but see State agents – such as social workers, juvenile courts, teachers, doctors and psychiatrists – as intruding upon relations between husband and wife, in the interests of supervising the way in which children are reared. The deplorable result, according to Donzelot, is that wives have been co-opted by these professions as agents of their policies within the family – as petty authorities on health, childcare, diet, psychology – while men have become marginalized and lost their authority.

There are also views of the State/family relation that accept 'the family' as a pre-given institution, constituted by the relations established by its members, rather than by practices outside of it. These tend to see the State and the family as opposed to one another, locked in a struggle between a State that seeks to extend its domain and a family that resists its intrusion. Some believe that with the rise of the 'interventionist state', and especially the Welfare State, the private sphere is in decline; for instance, that people no longer feel responsible for family members or even for their own old age because they rely upon the State to provide. On the other hand, it can be argued that the Welfare State is based on the assumption that basic provision will be made through private family ties and that State provision is only needed where these are unable to cope: wives and children should depend upon husbands and fathers; the disabled and mentally ill should live with relatives, and so on. If that is so, the Welfare State has the effect of reconstituting, rather than destroying, the sphere of the private, by redefining family responsibilities.

Assessments of the future of the family seem to be as various as definitions of what it is and value-positions about what it should be. But it is certain that, whatever may be happening to families and households, the *idea* of the family is widely popular and the language of the family – 'brotherhood', 'fatherly', 'she's like a mother to me', 'my son' – seems the best language we have for our most valued, deep and caring relationships. Given that actual family ties often do not live up to these cultural expectations, it is perhaps a pity that the family continues to claim a monopoly on warmth and intimacy and makes it so hard to have a fulfilling personal life in non-familial terms.

Can feminism be successful?

In the early 1970s, there was a great deal of optimism about improving women's position, ending male privilege and reducing gender divisions and even gender difference. Equal opportunities legislation was enacted in many countries and the voice of the women's movement was heard criticizing sexism in every sphere from the Stock Exchange to strip-shows. Now it is clear that legislation can make only a marginal difference to entrenched patterns of job segregation and inequality. The voices of feminism too, are varied: some demanding equality with men – albeit on the basis that men will change, take more part in childcare and domestic life and give up their domination of the public sphere – while others pursue the revaluation of women's skills and 'womanly' virtues and the replacement of 'male' aggression and competitiveness with 'female' nurturance, caring and interdependence.

Though the women's movement itself may lack coherence, its dynamism is undoubted; hence its ideas continue to grow and spread. The most unlikely women can be heard saying, 'I'm no women's libber but . . . I'm not going to let men do this or that to me'. The new thrust for independence and self-assurance is reflected even in mass market women's magazines. Women, even if only a few, have broken into many bastions of male privilege like Oxbridge colleges and building sites. More women are choosing employment, rather than a life exclusively devoted to domesticity, and more women want to do well out of their jobs and are joining trade unions and undertaking training to improve their pay and their conditions of work. The high divorce rate and the increasing number of single and lesbian women who are choosing to have children outside of marriage are changing the family as well.

All of these changes are putting a strain on the old taken-for-granted patterns. Of course there is a backlash and much talk of re-establishing Victorian values and putting women back in the home, but it is unlikely that these important trends will be reversed entirely. Even in a period of economic recession when public expenditure cuts have increased domestic burdens and women's poverty, women are increasingly insisting on their right to live independent lives, their right to a job and to a place in the public world.

5   Education

The sociology of education has frequently been at the centre of political and social controversy. Education is a subject of intense public debate: hence the sociology of education has never been just an academic discipline, with no relation to policy and practice. In the 1950s and 1960s, controversy raged highest about equality of opportunity, about who got into privileged schools, and into colleges and universities. By the 1970s, sociological analysis and critique had shifted to the conventional academic school curriculum. This questioning of what most people in education took as given was described in one pamphlet as 'softening up the minds of teachers for the marxist takeover' (ISC, 1977). Other less political but equally alarmed writers responded with reviews and articles with titles like 'Knowledge out of control' and 'The abyss of relativism', which expressed deep disturbance because the status of universities as unquestioned 'gatekeepers of knowledge' was being questioned. This had at least potential implications not only for academics, at the top of the educational system's hierarchy, but for everyone. The idea that the knowledge which is communicated in school or university is only a particular selection of all available knowledge, organized in a particular way, and that there might be very different ways of selecting and organizing knowledge, seemed to touch deeply held beliefs and values, especially the notion that there is a unitary body of Knowledge with a capital K which everybody accepts.

The sociology of education has thus been characterized by continuing disputes about its very nature, expressed in repeated claims and counter-claims to be offering 'new directions'. Furthermore, it has always been a field for radicals – whether of the Right or the Left – who have either wanted to use educational institutions to transform society or who have tried to transform educational institutions themselves. The sociology of education – as against more traditional educational research – generates strong reactions because it, too, seeks to show how even the most technical disputes, about, for example, a new mode of assessment (Broadfoot, 1984), are expressions of much wider conflicts about the nature of our society and its priorities.

Two issues have dominated research in the sociology of education, at least in Britain. These have been the origin and persistence of educational inequalities, and the relation between education and the economy; and, at a more fundamental level, the question as to whether formal education (or schooling) is really educational at all, except for a few. Illich (1971) and Reimer (1971), for example, argue that the failures of schooling are intrinsic to school systems as such, while others, such as Gintis (1972), see the school system as doing little more than mirroring the inequities of a capitalist society and 'reproducing' them.

In this chapter we shall trace these themes by looking mainly at developments in the sociology of education in the UK, though similar processes can be found in most industrialized Western countries. Changes in sociological ideas and in the kinds of questions that have been asked about education do not take place in a social vacuum: they occur because of wider political and economic changes in society which affect all communities and institutions, including educational institutions. Recent political and economic developments, in particular the persistence of high unemployment and the contraction of manufacturing industry, common to all Western industrial societies, have forced questions of the content and purposes of education onto the agenda of public debate. Sociological questions about education are thus an important part of wider public debate both about the kind of society we live in now and about its possible future development. Views of the relationship of the educational system to the economy have shifted in important ways since the Second World War. From the 1950s to the mid-1970s, education was treated as a *contributor* to economic growth, a view often associated with 'human capital' theory (Karabel and Halsey, 1977). This was an influential economic theory of the time which saw education, whether from the point of view of the State or the individual, as an investment. Individuals in whom education had been invested would, at a later date, yield 'profits' in the form of higher earnings. It was not an uncontested view, for older, elitist theories did not accept that everybody had capacities which could be developed through education. For these theories, only a minority possessed talents which could be harnessed for the benefit of the economy and the society as a whole. In contrast, 'human capital' theory provided a justification for a new policy of educational expansion, as against the more traditional view that 'more means worse'.

A typical education system can be thought of as a pyramid, in which most school-children never get beyond the lowest levels and are 'selected out' at various stages. Others continue long after the compulsory school-leaving age and climb into the higher, 'tertiary' levels of the educational system. Such an inherently unequal system creates an obvious bottleneck on opportunity at these higher levels. Hence, to the followers of 'human capital' theory, priority had to be given to increasing the number of places in higher education, and reducing the pressure of selection lower down. By the 1960s, such ideas had become dominant and were the basis of a new expansion of tertiary education that was most powerfully advocated in the Robbins Report of 1963, discussed below. From the mid-1970s, however, successive governments became disillusioned with such ideas and the expansionist educational policies associated with them, partly because of changing economic and political circumstances, and partly because no direct correlation between exposure to schooling and subsequent income, let alone national growth and productivity, could be demonstrated (Berg, 1973). Rather, as sociologists such as Collins (1981) and Dore (1976) suggested, expansion had merely led to 'credential inflation': this tendency, with the expansion of schooling, for those in control of employment to raise their entrance requirements, is paralleled by occupational groupings who try to use schooling as a way of enhancing their position *vis-à-vis* other groups. Thus a number of professions, for instance accountants and lawyers, have, over the last twenty years, gone over almost entirely to graduate recruitment.

By the late 1970s, therefore, governments were beginning to see publicly provided education not as contributing to economic growth, but as a *cost*, and even an inhibiting factor. It is not the purpose of this chapter to explain these wider changes, however, so much as to relate them to the kinds of questions generated by research in the sociology of education. It is possible to distinguish three dominant themes that, albeit with some overlap, largely succeeded each other in time. The first, the dominant ideas of the 1950s and 1960s, we shall refer to as *access and opportunity*. The second, which emerged in the late 1960s, is *curriculum and content*. The third, which has been dominant since the mid-1970s, has centred on questions of *social and cultural reproduction*: these are the problems which face any society of how to ensure its continuity from one generation to the next. The main question we will focus on is the role of formal education in this process, and the extent to which any changes in the educational system merely 'reproduce' the status quo in society or may be in contradiction to it.

Access and Opportunity

In France, the sociology of education was established by Durkheim (1961) as long ago as the beginning of the century. In the USA, a classic study, by Waller, appeared in the 1930s (Waller, 1932). In Britain, its history has been much briefer. Karl Mannheim, a refugee from Nazi Germany, was the first Professor of the Sociology of Education for one year – 1946 – a position not filled again until 1967, by Basil Bernstein. Through the 1950s and early 1960s there was only a small body of researchers, ten at most, of whom the most well known are Banks (1956), Bernstein (1971), Douglas (1964), Floud, Halsey and Martin (1956) and Glass (1954). Yet this small group of researchers, together with others such as the historian Brian Simon, were able to have a considerable influence on policy. Government Reports, such as *Early Learning* (Department of Education, 1954) – which arose from a concern with the shortage of skilled manpower – had already documented the tendency of a considerable proportion of pupils with high measured intelligence to leave school without any qualifications. What the sociological research showed was that this denial of access to even a complete secondary education was a *social class* phenomenon.

The research concentrated primarily on the selection process at the age of eleven. The overt intention of the 11 + test (as it was called) was to select the 'most able' for grammar school education, regardless of background. Yet what the research disclosed was that in the group selected for grammar school, children with high IQ from working-class backgrounds were under-represented and children of average IQ from middle-class backgrounds were over-represented (Floud *et al.*, 1956). Low educational achievement, the research demonstrated conclusively, was not primarily an outcome of lack of individual ability, but of lack of opportunity.

For governments wanting to improve the educational quality of the labour force, then, there were two obvious strategies. The first, the expansion of higher education, was accelerated from the early 1960s. This was followed, with the advent of a Labour government in 1964, by Circular 10/65, which tried, by persuasion rather than legislation, to abolish selection at 11+ and to establish comprehensive secondary schools. This has still not been achieved in some parts of the country. Despite these changes, the middle-class bias of the education system continued to flourish, primarily because of the existence of a private sector – the fee-paying 'public schools' – which continue to be powerful mechanisms for transmitting privilege. In 1970, 80 per cent of judges, 83 per cent of ambassadors, and 86 per cent of generals had been educated in such schools (Boyd, 1973).

The major concept used in the sociology of education at that time was that of *educability*. This referred to the discrepancy between the expected educational achievement of pupils of different social classes (in terms of measured ability) and their actual achievement. This discrepancy pointed in two directions, with implications both for theory and for policy. On the one hand, it suggested that differences in educational achievement might be the outcome of the different cultures and social conditions that children of different social classes experienced outside school. On the other hand, it raised questions about the social and cultural assumptions of the schools themselves. To educational policy-makers and to researchers it seemed relatively unproblematic to identify and to change those aspects of lower-class culture that (it was believed) inhibited educational achievement. This policy – of trying to make the attitudes and behaviour of working-class families fit the demands of schools – became known as 'compensatory' education. It was given considerable public credibility by the publication of the Plowden Report on primary schools (Department of Education, 1967), a report which drew on extensive research to argue that parental attitudes to school were a major factor in promoting or inhibiting educational achievement. It proposed the establishment of 'educational priority areas', which would be granted extra resources. However, the actual amounts subsequently made available represented a minute proportion of the total educational budget.

The early work of Basil Bernstein on the ways different social classes used language linked together the two elements of the concept of educability – class cultures outside the school and the dominant cultural assumptions and practices within the school. The very originality of this research resulted in its also being some of the least well understood work to have emerged in British sociology of education and the subject of intense and continuing debate. Bernstein's research at this time is usually thought of in terms of the distinction he drew between 'elaborated' and 'restricted' codes. The distinction was developed to explain how different social class experiences were expressed in different patterns of language use.

However, Bernstein's work had a much wider significance than a description of linguistic differences. He was arguing that in a society that was divided into social classes, these divisions would manifest themselves in a cultural discontinuity, for working-class pupils, between home and school. For middle-class pupils, the expectations that teachers had, their values, and the ways in which they related to others were not so different from their experiences at home. However, this was not the case for working-class pupils. It was as if, Bernstein pointed out, working-class pupils had to leave their identity at the school gate.

The emphasis on access and on expansion of educational opportunity was part of a much broader sociological concern with social inequalities. With hindsight, it is all too easy to point out its weaknesses, even within its own terms. For example, although the statistics of the time demonstrated that the extremes of educational inequality were experienced by working-class *girls* (Little and Westergaard, 1964), the gender aspect of educational inequality was not taken up. Nor was there any attempt to incorporate an analysis of the private sector of fee-paying schools, and in particular the disproportionately high number of those leaving them who gained entry to Oxford and Cambridge universities. More generally, it was assumed, along with most sociology in Britain at that time, that inequalities could be significantly reduced by social and educational policies that did not involve any fundamental changes in the overall distribution of power and wealth.

The research nevertheless provided a vital empirical base from which later work was able to develop, in particular in its use of survey analysis and statistical data. A more recent study (Halsey *et al.*, 1980), which set out to replicate earlier research by Glass in 1954, was able to show that despite forty years of educational expansion there has been no overall redistribution of educational opportunity between social classes. They argued, from their evidence, that it is only when a higher social class can gain no special advantages from educational expansion that the proportion of a lower class at a particular level of education begins to rise. But what was significant in 1980 was that this study, though meticulously researched, had no impact on government thinking or policy, whereas the earlier work of Halsey and others in the 1950s and 1960s did.

The 1960s was a time of dramatic expansion of higher education in most industrialized countries. In Britain this was largely based on the recommendations of the Robbins Committee on Higher Education (Department of Education, 1963). Within a very few years, eight new universities were created, eight colleges were upgraded into universities, and all existing universities were encouraged to expand. Thirty polytechnics, all concentrating on degree level work, were established out of existing technical colleges, and the teacher training colleges, renamed colleges of education, were allowed to offer four-year honours' degrees for the first time.

As important as these quantitative changes were several aspects of the Robbins Committee's philosophy. Firstly, they proposed that some form of higher education should be regarded as a *right* for anyone reaching a certain minimum standard. Their evolutionary educational philosophy envisaged a higher and higher proportion of the population gaining higher education over time. Further, in place of the older pattern of the monopolization of the highest level of education by the universities, they envisaged that more and more higher educational institutions would gradually achieve university status (a policy which is now being implemented, with some polytechnics becoming universities).

A third aspect was that the direction of expansion should be shaped by student demand rather than by government policy. One consequence of this, in the climate of the 1960s, was that virtually every university and polytechnic was to offer undergraduate courses in sociology. As part of this 'efflorescence' of sociology, the sociology of education was rapidly transformed from a specialist research field with very few students to a major teaching subject with undergraduate, postgraduate and research programmes of its own. Two institutions created in this period symbolized the widely held belief that sociological study and research could contribute to improving education: the Open University and the Social Science Research Council. By far the largest group of OU students in its early years were teachers, and the majority of them took courses in the Sociology of Education. But the Open University's influence also drew in to higher education many who had no such previous experience, and often no previous formal qualifications. The OU's low-priced collections of well-designed readings and other course textbooks were also available to students in a whole variety of smaller institutions. The creation of the SSRC, in 1964, provided an institutional basis, for the first time, for the financing of research in the social sciences (among them sociology). This had previously been limited mainly to disciplines like economics, thought to be of practical relevance, with little support available, apart from a few private foundations, for other disciplines.

The Curriculum and the Content of Education

The expansion of sociology and of the sociology of education as a special field of study led to changes of focus in terms of the issues researched and the way they were researched from the end of the 1960s onwards. In addition to the emergence of new forms of sociological analysis, there was a shift in the attitudes of sociologists of education towards more practical educational politics. The earlier sociologists had seen themselves as researchers in the 'political arithmetic' tradition, providing empirical evidence with which to influence policy-makers. Though this policy role continued, it was now complemented by a more local level involvement with groups of teachers who were experimenting with school-based forms of assessment and curriculum innovations, and producing grass-roots radical journals such as *Teaching London Kids*. These and some of the 'free school' projects of the time were all examples of practical attempts to change or at least challenge existing educational practice (see, for example, the account by the White Lion Free School in Whitty and Young, 1976).

But little of this sociological work, even the newer developments, paid close attention to processes internal to the school. There had been only a small number of studies of teacher–pupil interaction (for example, Becker, 1952; Cicourel and Kitsuse, 1963), largely in the USA, but there was little, even in the American sociology of education, which concentrated on the curriculum. Such a topic was perfectly appropriate for sociological investigation, but until the late 1960s research had concentrated almost exclusively on the distribution of success and failure in school rather than on what it was that pupils succeeded and failed at doing in the school itself.

The shift towards processes internal to the school reflected a number of influences. One was the changing institutional base of the sociology of education, as a result of which researchers in the field were brought more closely in contact with practising teachers. There had also been pioneering studies of the form and content of education, in the work of Olive Banks (1956), for example, and in Bernstein's work as early as 1969 (Bernstein, 1969), and these now began to bear fruit. Furthermore, doubts were already growing about whether the expansion of education would lead in itself to greater equality. At a more theoretical level, an increasing number of criticisms of accounts of educational under-achievement had found it necessary to break new theoretical ground, by going beyond the concepts of cultural deficit and cultural deprivation as explanations of working-class educational failure (Keddie, 1973).

Changes of theoretical focus and of research did not come about simply as a consequence of intellectual developments within the discipline, however. The end of the 1960s saw the emergence of much wider political and intellectual movements, within the universities and beyond, in which questions about the role of education were central to a critique not only of educational institutions themselves but also of their role in society. What was taught itself became the subject of intense debate. Sit-ins and student occupations became increasingly common in universities in practically every Western country; demands were made for student access to confidential records, for student participation in every level of university government and even for a say in the content of courses. The theme that ran through these differing forms of protest was a questioning of academic hierarchies, and ultimately the power of teachers over students. This challenge was expressed in the titles of books like

Student Power (Cockburn and Blackburn, 1968), *Counter-Course* (Pateman, 1972), *The Dissenting Academy* (Roszak, 1969), *The Great Training Robbery* (Paton, 1970) and *Warwick University Ltd* (Thompson, E. P., 1970).

Each of these books questioned what had till then been the almost divine right of academics to be the 'gatekeepers of knowledge', and sought to show the kinds of knowledge which were excluded from university courses. This questioning of intellectual hierarchies was sustained by the emergence of a whole range of radical journals, such as *Radical Philosophy*, *Radical Science* and *Red Rat* (*Radical Psychology*), each of which set out to break down the barriers between conventional academic disciplines.

Sociology, at least in England, had only recently been established as a degree subject in most universities. It had been strongly influenced by US sociology; particularly by structural-functionalist theory and positivist methodology, though these aroused criticism, too (Lockwood, 1956). The former assumed consensus about the goals of society; the latter, that social phenomena were objectively measurable in much the same way as natural phenomena. The first English textbooks in the sociology of education (Banks, 1968; Musgrave, 1970) reflected this particular combination of theory and methodology, supported by and reinforcing the belief that education was an unquestionable value, like happiness, or progress. The basic ideas implicitly guiding research in the sociology of education at this time were decribed by Wexler as 'progressivism' – 'the belief that schools should be used to improve society and foster social equality'; a belief in 'efficiency' – '[that] *organization* could counteract . . . the waste of private privilege'; and a faith in science. This, Wexler argued, 'was reflected in the way sociologists studied how knowledge is transmitted [but neglected] the nature of knowledge itself' (Wexler, 1976, italics added).

It was to question this set of ideas, and to make explicit what they left out, that a new framework was developed which came to be called the 'New Sociology of Education' (Whitty, 1985). The starting-point, the idea that education was a *social* phenomenon, produced both in direct interaction between teachers and pupils, and in society as a whole, was not new. It had been stated long ago by Durkheim. But in its new formulation, a set of diverse and novel theoretical ideas were introduced into educational research and debate (Young, 1971).

These drew upon two traditions in social theory: phenomenology and structuralism. The former had important methodological implications as to what the sociology of education should study and how it should be studied. It argued that the starting-point of any sociological analysis of education had to be the meanings, language and knowledge that teachers and pupils used in their everyday activities. This *was* the social reality of education, according to this theory. In England, the most influential and widely quoted piece of research in this tradition was Nell Keddie's *Classroom Knowledge* (1971). Keddie analysed the way teachers categorized pupils in terms of their social class background and school grouping. She described how these categorizations influenced the way they selected curricular materials as appropriate to different kinds of pupils, and the ways in which they interpreted pupil responses.

Structuralist analysis, which focuses on how the basic categories of a society's division of labour are expressed in its educational arrangements, made an equally powerful impression via the work of Bourdieu and Passeron (1977) and in the later work of Bernstein (1977). In a series of papers which linked his earlier research on educability to a more general sociological analysis of the curriculum, Bernstein showed how the curriculum, pedagogy and evaluation were related to the degree to which social categories are insulated from each other (Bernstein, 1977). In the case of the curriculum, these categories involved the separation of educational knowledge into 'subjects' that were taught quite independently of each other, and the separation of school knowledge that was required to pass examinations and to achieve 'good marks' from the common sense knowledge that pupils bring to school and use in their day-to-day activities.

Both phenomenological and structuralist analyses, then, in very different ways, highlighted the persistence of perhaps the most pervasive feature of secondary schooling – at least in England – the 'subject'-based curriculum. This was not just a matter which concerned academics alone, because at the time there was considerable pressure for a move away from a subject-based curriculum towards programmes in which the humanities and the sciences were combined. What sociological analysis was able to point out was that these 'subjects' were not just features of purely *educational* organization that could be changed at will, but represented practices and forms of thought which were part of the consciousness not only of teachers, but of society as a whole, and which were used to exercise control over the thinking of pupils, too. Analyses such as Keddie's, which were based on classroom observation, emphasized how the categories and meanings which made the curriculum a reality were also crucial to the teacher's conceptions of their own identity as professionals and as 'specialists'. Such analyses, however, lacked a framework for understanding how these meanings originated. 'Subjects' seemed self-evident logical divisions, which, therefore, could not be readily changed. Structural analyses of education, on the other hand, started from a model which argued that the forms and organization of educational knowledge mirrored the structure of society itself. But because these analyses were conducted at a somewhat abstract level, their implications for educational practice were not obvious.

This tension – between a focus on agency or actors (teachers, pupils, etc) in particular situations such as the classroom, as against those wider structures of society which constrain those interactions – is part of a much wider debate in sociological theory. One influential study which attempted to bring them together was Sharp and Green's (1975) account of the infant classes of a primary school. How to keep children occupied has become of increasing importance to teachers, they pointed out, because flexible timetables and open-plan architecture have removed traditional restrictions on the planning of pupil activities. They set out to show that it is constraints *out* of school, not the priorities of the teachers themselves, that lead teachers to label pupils in particular ways: 'through a subtle process of sponsorship . . . opportunity is being offered to some and closed off to others' (Sharp and Green, 1975, p. 218).

The Hidden Curriculum

The emphasis in the sociology of education on the internal processes of schooling was not restricted to the *overt* curriculum content. It is a commonplace of educational thought, widely shared by parents especially, that education is about far more than passing exams. It is not necessary to have studied sociology to recognize that the overt curriculum – the organization and distribution of subjects on the timetable – is only a part of what is learnt in school.

Hence the concept of the 'hidden curriculum' refers to those values and patterns of behaviour that are often not formally taught, but are an integral part of schooling as we know it. As originally coined by Jackson, it referred to the ways in which pupils learn to accept 'the denial, delay and interruption of their personal desires and wishes' (Jackson, 1968, p. 18).

School is only a part of the wider process of socialization through which young people become adults in a particular society and culture. Much of this socialization takes place through the processes which the concept 'hidden curriculum' describes. A pupil who wants to learn physics, history, or some other subject on the timetabled curriculum has to defer, firstly, to the authority of the teacher, without question, and to the selection of what is presented as knowledge in the textbook that the teacher has chosen, or, in some countries, which is prescribed by central educational authorities. Pupils therefore have to learn to defer to authority, and are dependent on texts as reliable sources of expertise. They are also encouraged to give priority to their own individual work, which is recorded in separate books, while sharing with others, except in strictly limited contexts, is defined – and punished – as 'cheating'! Achievement is assessed competitively, in relation to other pupils, rather than via collective diagnosis of errors and verification of ideas and ways of arriving at findings.

These values – of deference to authority, of individual achievement and of competition rather than cooperation – appear at first so obvious as to hardly warrant discussion. But it is by no means self-evident that learning actually *needs* to be organized in this way. In an autobiographical novel about his experiences as a high school teacher in the USA, Herndon describes his totally unsuccessful attempts to teach maths to a group who call themselves the 'dumb class'. But when he found that one of these 'dumb' pupils was keeping a running score in a bowling alley for three simultaneous games in the local league, the idea came to him of basing his maths classes on bowling alley calculations. The result of this 'curriculum innovation' was dramatic: 'All the kids immediately rushed me yelling "Is this right?" "I don't know how to do it!" "What's the answer?" . . . "What's my grade?". The brilliant bowling alley scorer couldn't decide whether two strikes and a third frame of eight amounted to 18 or 28 or whether it was one hundred and eight and a half' (Herndon, 1976).

The problem, Herndon recognized, was not just the overt curriculum content of his maths lessons, and its lack of relevance to the interests of pupils outside school hours, but the passivity expected of them as 'learners' within the formal organization of the school. The result is that the hidden curriculum, through which a minority becomes motivated to achieve, actually *de*motivates the majority, particularly working–class pupils.

From Content to Context – the Consequences of Economic Recession

As we emphasized at the beginning of this chapter, sociological research in education has not developed independently of other changes in society. The focus on the internal processes of curricular and school organization in the first half of the 1970s reflected a period of expansion, in which innovations were possible because they did not challenge any existing interests, directly at least. Sociology, for example, was able to expand as a teaching subject in both secondary schools and universities alongside, rather than in competition with, existing subjects.

This period, however, was short-lived, partly as a result of economic pressures on public expenditure generally and partly through the emergence of Right-wing political reactions among professional educators (Cox and Dyson, 1969, 1971). In a series of influential Black Papers, Cox and Dyson argued in favour of a return to academic standards and traditional disciplines and asserted that the 'progressive' moves in curriculum and teaching methods were neither popular nor effective. The effects of this campaign were not confined, however, to conservative circles. In a speech in 1976, the Labour Prime Minister, James Callaghan, suggested that the education system was not giving enough concern to the needs of industry and that it should be made more accountable to popular wishes and desires. This questioning of the popularity of the educational reforms of the 1960s and early 1970s also came from those further to the Left though with a different emphasis. In an influential study, the Birmingham-based Centre for Contemporary Cultural Studies argued that all educational reform up till then had been imposed, and in that sense was *unpopular* (CCCS, 1981). These arguments were given support by the much publicized case of William Tyndale

School, in which a group of progressive Left-wing teachers were dismissed and the school was closed. It was a substantial group of *working-class* parents who had expressed strong opposition to the teachers' attempts to give pupils a wider say in the curriculum. These parents felt that their children were being denied the basic skills which it was the job of schools to teach them.

Within the sociology of education, doubts were expressed about some of the newer trends in primary education in the research of Sharp and Green (1975) already referred to, and in a paper by Bernstein (1977). Bernstein argued that as there had been no change in the distribution of power and wealth in society, moves towards a more child-centred pedagogy (which placed more reliance on the cultural resources that children bring to school) could actually work to the disadvantage of working-class pupils.

By this time, the orthodox consensus which, up till then, had assumed that the only problems with the State provision of education were that there was not enough of it, was becoming increasingly questioned. A so-called 'great debate' about the future of educational policy was initiated by the then Labour government (Department of Education and Science, 1977), which was followed by the slowing down of the expansion of education (Donald, 1981). In addition, various measures were taken to increase the control of central government over educational policy (Lawton, 1980); the dominant view which hitherto had allowed the nature of the education to be determined by individual choice within the existing framework was now rejected. Public expenditure on education, it was argued, now had to be justified in terms of its direct contribution to productivity and economic growth.

The questions that had begun to be raised through analyses of the overt and hidden curriculum were now displaced in favour of an increasingly urgent search for a theory of the relations *between* school and society – a theory that could provide both understanding and relevant strategies in the face of new forms of government intervention which were transforming the nature of teachers' work. This was the social and political context in which new concepts – of *correspondence*, and of *social* and *cultural reproduction* – now began to be formulated in the work of Bowles and Gintis (1976), Althusser (1971), Bourdieu and Passeron (1977) and Bernstein (1977), and soon came to dominate sociological analyses of education.

Correspondence, Reproduction and Resistance

The work of these researchers shifted the framework of analysis once more from the internal processes of schooling to the role of education in the wider structure of power in society. To Althusser and Bowles and Gintis the distinguishing feature of Western industrial societies is the domination by a small group of property-owners of the majority who receive wages for their work.

In their study *Schooling in Capitalist America* (1976), Bowles and Gintis start by asking why liberal educational reforms designed to increase opportunities never seem to have worked. Using previously available statistics, they documented the extent of class, gender and race inequalities and argued that American schools were pervaded by hierarchical social relations and subservient attitudes to authority. None of these characteristics, they pointed out, was consistent with the explicit aims of educational policy-makers or with the ideals of a democratic society. Their own explanation of this apparent contradiction is that though these patterns may not correspond with the ideals of educational policy, they do *correspond* with the requirements of an economic system which is based on wage-labour for the majority. In other words, in school pupils learn deference to authority and an acceptance of powerlessness because these will be the principal features of their future employment. They also learn that those who succeed do so on the basis of individual merit, not because of any advantages of social position.

Louis Althusser, the French philosopher (Althusser, 1971), addresses similar issues from a rather different perspective. The school system, for him, is part of what he calls the 'ideological apparatuses of the State' (ISAs). These include the family, churches, welfare institutions, and the media, all of which have a key role in persuading people that the capitalist economic order is inevitable and unchangeable. Their function explains why, despite the systematic inequalities of capitalist societies, those who rule these societies so rarely have to resort to the use of force. The school, he argues, has displaced the church as *the* key ISA. For Althusser, it is their structural position in a capitalist society that explains the nature of schooling, not the purposes or intentions of teachers. Althusser does not argue, as Bowles and Gintis do, that there is a *direct* relationship between the school and capitalist economic needs. But he does see economic requirements as *ultimately* determining what happens in education. Indeed, it is because education is perceived as neutral in relation to conflicts between workers and employers that, according to Althusser, it is able to do its ideological work so effectively.

These theories have been widely criticized. They depict capitalism as a consistent and coherent whole, whose overall requirements determine what goes on in any of its parts, such as the educational system. Hence they omit human activity: the history, in particular, of how ordinary people have had to *struggle for* education. They also lack any sense of conflict about the very purposes of schooling, or of how many of those who work in education have constantly explored alternatives to its existing structure and content. Despite these short-comings, these theories became influential and widely discussed at a time in which expanding unemployment, and in particular youth unemployment, was being presented by politicians and industrialists as the result of an inadequate educational system. They provided an important counter to these arguments because they laid the blame on the economy rather than the educational system as the source of youth unemployment. They also challenged the still widely held assumption, particularly among educationalists, that education in its existing form was in some unquestioned way beneficial to all.

Although Bourdieu and Bernstein were also both concerned with how schools are involved in reproducing social class relations, their emphases were very different. They were less concerned with capitalist economic relations than with how schooling *legitimizes* overall patterns of class power and domination. Unlike Althusser and Bowles and Gintis, they therefore pay attention to specifically educational issues such as the curriculum and examinations. So despite the rather abstract way in which their theories were expressed, they opened up new kinds of empirical investigations into the relations between changes in educational institutions and wider social changes.

The most radical questions about education from the perspective of social and cultural reproduction were raised by Willis's influential and much-quoted research. His book *Learning to Labour* (1977) was widely used in challenges to over-deterministic, passive models of pupil response that were built into earlier concepts of social and cultural reproduction (Apple, 1983; Giroux, 1983). Willis's study was based on a year of fieldwork in a secondary school and in pupils' homes. It set out to demonstrate, in a most vivid and graphic way, that the attempt to impose schooling on working-class pupils fails because they themselves actively oppose it by creating their own counter-culture of resistance. Willis argues that the 'lads' attempt, within this counter-culture, to take control of school classes, to impose their own timetables, and to control their own life in school. This, he argues, mirrors the attempts of their fathers, within what he calls the shop-floor culture, to control *their* own workplace. Through their resistance to and consequent failure at school, then, the 'lads' prepare themselves for a future bounded by low-paid, unskilled work. Willis's research points to the need to investigate not only the reproduction of class relations but also resistance within schooling, and to distinguish further between those forms of resistance which can be seen as part of wider social transformations and those which simply sustain the status quo. It is a continuation, in many ways, of earlier research which tried to demonstrate how class divisions are mediated through educational institutions (Hargreaves, 1968; Lacey, 1970). It also accepts the familiar two-class model of middle-class schools against working-class pupils. But it pays only passing attention to those working-class pupils – those he calls the 'ear 'oles' – who conform rather than resist. It can be argued that this two-class model may be more specific to the industrial Midlands area in which he based his research than Willis admits. His emphasis on social class relationships, too, may have led to the underemphasis on conflicts between teachers and pupils that are peculiar to the hierarchy of power in schools, and which are probably also more characteristic of male attitudes and relationships than he acknowledges (McRobbie, 1980). However, this and other such empirical studies (Anyon, 1981: Werthman, 1963; Corrigan, 1980) do raise serious doubts about the adequacy of the more schematic global conceptualizations of education as simply 'reproducing' class relations. Similarly in sociology in general, an emphasis on the common interests of capital was being replaced by a view of the capitalist class as divided into 'fractions' (finance capital as against manufacturing capital, for example) which might make for conflicting demands on education. The growing volume of research on gender and race inequalities was also beginning to question any unitary view of social classes. Likewise, the reproductionist insistence on a view of education primarily as part of an overall social system had led again to the neglect by sociologists of what was specific to the education system: questions of curriculum, teaching and learning. The irony of this neglect was that, in England at least, the 1980s proved to be a time of massive restructuring of the content of education by central government.

By the mid-1980s, many of the developments that facilitated the growth of the sociology of education in the early 1970s were reversed. This has been both a quantitative process (the closing of departments, cuts in student numbers and research grants) and a qualitative one, as lecturers appointed to teach the sociology of education found themselves diverted into developing courses in management and evaluation.

The Influence of Other Disciplines

So far we have looked at the way in which research in the sociology of education has to be seen against the background of a much wider movement of ideas generated by changes in society as a whole. That approach, though fundamental to the sociology of education, is not generally typical of education as a discipline overall, which tends to concentrate on rather narrow and technical issues and rarely to address itself to issues concerning the relationship of education to society. The sociology of education, on the other hand, is part of the broader study of society and is therefore always concerned with both developments in social policy and in public social and political controversies. The sociology of education therefore investigates the ways in which educational arrangements, from national policy to classroom encounter, express values, priorities and struggles in society as a whole.

Such questions have of course often been raised first outside the discipline of sociology itself and were often raised, too, long before there was a sociology of education. In recent times, the transformation of the study of literature into a critical examination of the nature of culture, and developments in social history and cultural anthropology, have also stimulated new thinking about education. The debates about culture from Matthew Arnold in the nineteenth century to Leavis in the twentieth have always been indirectly about education, for this is a major way in which culture is transmitted. Yet it was not until the work of Raymond Williams, in his *The Long Revolution* (Williams, 1961), that the connection was made theoretically explicit. There he showed how the ruling class in Britain has dominated both the education they wanted for their own sons (and to a much lesser extent their daughters) and the education they thought should be provided for the sons of those they ruled. Williams shows how and why particular forms of knowledge were included and excluded at particular times, invariably as a process of conflict between those who saw education as *preserving* the culture and those, the 'industrial trainers', who wanted it to be geared to industrial needs. His work was extended by Layton (1973), who investigated the way in which natural science first became part of the secondary school curriculum in the late nineteenth century. What he showed was how a more practical and socially relevant approach to school science (the 'science of common things') had been displaced by one modelled on the detached literary mode of learning that was thought appropriate for those receiving secondary schooling at the time.

A similar approach was also adopted in Johnson's study of early nineteenth-century popular educational movements (Johnson, 1979). In considering the early history of mass State schooling, Johnson shows how this was seen by the Chartists and others as a form of cultural invasion of the working class which had to be resisted. They wanted a quite different kind of education: under local control, and teaching 'really useful knowledge' which reflected the true needs and social conditions of working people at that time. Free schooling became compulsory for all children up to eleven by 1870 but was not made compulsory for those up to sixteen until 1973. However, from the start it took a very different form from that argued for by the Chartists. Both Williams and Johnson have argued that those in power have always managed to ensure that each phase of expansion expresses certain dominant notions of what education should be and what is worthwhile to be studied.

One key debate, throughout the history of mass education, has been the controversy over the relationship between intelligence and achievement. The major issue has been about whether intelligence is a matter of genetic endowment or the outcome of social conditions – the 'Nature versus nurture' controversy. A related issue has been the controversy as to whether measures of intelligence do in fact measure innate capacities. It was anthropologists, in studies of cultures very different from our own, rather than sociologists, who raised radical questions about assumptions involved in intelligence testing. Studies of the kinds of knowledge possessed in very different cultures thus began to influence the sociology of education in the early 1970s. In Gladwin's studies of Micronesian islanders, for example, he tried to explain why Micronesians who were able to navigate across several hundred miles of ocean using the stars and no instruments were quite unable to score anything on intelligence tests (Gladwin, 1970). In another piece of research, in West Africa, Gay and Cole (1967) compared the local people and some Peace Corps volunteers in their ability to complete certain numerical tasks. When the task involved classifying cards with different signs, colours and numbers, the Peace Corps volunteers did markedly better. When the task was estimating the relative volume of containers containing rice, the local tribesmen were much superior. These studies raise issues which go beyond traditional debates about whether intelligence is inherited or nurtured. One major question that arises is to ask why it is that in our culture – unlike others – such high priority is given to classifying its members according to measures of intelligence and why it is that this is, after all, a relatively recent phenomenon (Dexter, 1964). Secondly, what is it precisely that leads people from different social classes to respond to tests so differently? Part of an answer to the latter question is suggested by the research of Mehan (1979). In investigating the practice of setting and doing tests, he shows that children often bring quite different cultural understandings to answering questions to those assumed to be natural, normal or appropriate by testers. Thus an English child whose answer to the question 'Belfast is in . . . ?' was not that Belfast was in Northern Ireland but in Devon, did so because his father had been stationed at the army camp at Okehampton (in Devon), which was known as 'Belfast' because that was invariably the soldiers' next posting.

Sociology of Education and Social Movements

The influence not only of other academic disciplines, but of broader social and political movements, is most apparent in the relatively recent emergence in the sociology of education of issues of sex and race inequalities. Acker (1981) has documented how sex inequalities have been neglected in the sociology of education. As she puts it, 'mainstream sociology of education and feminist work on education are like the proverbial ships that pass in the night' (p. 94). This is all the more surprising when the dramatic extent of even the most superficial empirical evidence is considered. Let us give two examples. First, the distribution of secondary pupils in terms of exam entries:

Table 5. Certificate in secondary education entries

	1967 (000s)		1972 (000s)	
	Boys	Girls	Boys	Girls
Metal- and woodwork	35.	.054	63.	.213
Domestic subjects	.36	31.	1.9	66.
Technical drawing	34.	.227	55.	.59

(*Source:* Byrne, 1978, p. 124.)

The pattern of inequality is also apparent in the distribution of men and women within the hierarchy of positions in the teaching profession (see Table 6).

The impact of recent feminist critiques and pressure from the small but growing group of feminist sociologists have nevertheless placed the reproduction of gender relations firmly on the agenda of the sociology of education. MacDonald, for example, argues that schools transmit a gender code through which the power relations of male–female hierarchy are sustained (MacDonald, 1981). Similarly, the combined pressure of radicals from the Black community and of the few Black sociologists has moved from the more obvious earlier documentation of race inequalities to attempts to develop a theory as to how racist hierarchies are expressed even in policies such as multicultural education which are designed to overcome them (CCCS, 1982; Mullard, 1981).

Today, then, the ways in which gender and race divisions are sustained by educational practices can no longer be treated as marginal issues as they were, as recently as 1981, in an otherwise outstanding textbook in the field (Robinson, 1981) in which neither was mentioned.

These new issues also reveal the inadequacy of a unitary model of conflict between social classes. Different ethnic groups, for instance, make radically different demands on the educational system, e.g. over the questions of religious instruction and separate education for

Table 6. Headship of schools, by sex

	1965 (%)		1974 (%)	
	Male	*Female*	*Male*	*Female*
Primary				
All	26	74	22	77
Heads	49	50	57	43
Secondary				
All	58	41	56	43
Heads	76	23	81	19

(*Source:* Byrne, 1978, p. 218.)

girls. One consequence of these educational movements within the Black community is that much more localized alternatives to existing State provision are developing. It is these rather than alternative national educational policies which could well become the basis both of struggles for resources and of future debates about curricula and pedagogy. Likewise, the impact of feminism is likely to go far beyond studies of sex-differentiation within the curriculum to a much more all-encompassing critique. A sexist educational system, it has been argued, is not only negative for women. A 'man-made sociology of education', Acker writes, 'is not merely neglectful but seriously debilitated . . . We cannot legitimately claim even to understand the experiences of men and boys if we have excluded or distorted the experiences of women and ignored the interactions and inequalities between the sexes' (Acker, 1981, p. 80).

Future Directions

By the mid-1980s new kinds of debate about education had been generated which were quite different from the debates that characterized the sociology of education a decade earlier. The changes in both economic conditions and educational policy that underlie these debates have been common in varying degrees to all Western industrialized societies. As we have seen, the traditional view of education as a contributor to economic growth has given way to one in which education is seen as a cost, something to be curtailed where possible.

The implications of this have been both a quantitative reduction in public expenditure on education and qualitative changes which have led to a more fundamental questioning as to the nature and purpose of education. The earlier struggle between those Raymond Williams called the 'industrial trainers' and the 'liberal elitists' has reappeared, with the political dice now loaded firmly in favour of the former (and with expressions of genuinely popular will as disenfranchized from decision-making as 100 years before). The academic curriculum is no longer seen, even by those in positions of economic and political power, as the only or unquestioned standard from which to judge educational performance. It is now viewed as having two related and negative outcomes, both of which must be opposed in the interests of making the country more competitive and more productive. The traditional subject-based curriculum is seen as encouraging the academically successful away from courses geared to manufacture, marketing and the development of technical innovations, towards the humanities or 'pure' sciences. At the same time, it denies the majority any sense of demonstrating their own competence and skills while at school, and throws them on the labour-market with nothing to offer their future employers. Clear policy trends are emerging in relation to each group in most Western countries. These are a rigorous and technology inspired curriculum for the academically successful and a combination of work experience and assessment on the basis of practical skills for the majority.

From a sociological point of view, therefore, new rigidities in the division between mental and manual labour are being created through the curriculum. Moreover, all these policies represent an attempt to use the educational system to deal with problems – notably high unemployment and lack of competitiveness – which have their roots not in the education system but in the mode of production and investment of Western societies. Sociological research, on the other hand, is increasingly focused on developing strategies which see educational innovation as involving more than shifts in the balance of the curriculum. Recent studies thus question both traditional elitist academic schooling and the newer emphasis on what has been called the 'new vocationalism' (Cohen, 1984), and argue that neither of these is a natural or unproblematic way of organizing learning. Rather they represent, as one writer puts it, 'the outcomes of particular struggles for cultural authority, for the intellectual, moral and ethical leadership of society' (Donald and Grealy, 1983, p. 94).

The notion of cultural authority expressed here draws on the ideas of the Italian Marxist, Antonio Gramsci (1971). Through the concept of hegemony (or dominant influence), Gramsci wanted to show how intellectuals 'organic' to the ruling class did not simply act as a transmission belt for ruling-class ideas. They also acted as a mediating force through which such ideas were brought into relationship with popular thought and thereby made comprehensible. Popular thinking was thus *incorporated* into a 'common sense' which sustained the social order far more effectively than an imposed, one-way orthodoxy. Ideas about education, and about the standards by which successful education should be judged, are part of this common sense. From a Gramscian perspective, there are two roles for sociologists. They can, through their research and teaching, sustain the view that things will get better and that no radical changes are necessary; the alternative is that they can try to develop their research and teaching in a way that takes people's common sense understandings seriously, but goes beyond them – to establish a *counter*-hegemonic culture. Existing ways of organizing education are themselves only the outcomes of the history of past and current social divisions of class, gender and race. They have been consolidated in social institutions and in the form of the intellectual categories of the curriculum. If these divisions are to be overcome, it is their history and institutionalization that has to be understood.

The idea that curriculum divisions represent struggles for cultural authority (or hegemony) therefore involves rejecting the notion that those who fail in the educational competition are 'less able' or 'non-academic'. The curriculum, indeed, has changed massively over the last century. At the turn of the century, new subject divisions and hierarchies were established which replaced the older curriculum in which Latin and Greek had a privileged place. This new subject-based curriculum was pioneered, moreover, as part of a radical transformation of the education provided by the 'public schools' for children of the upper classes. Thus the Association for Science Education which now embraces 17,000 science teachers in virtually every secondary school in the country – was founded in 1900 by four masters at Eton as the Association of Public School Science Masters (Layton, 1984). Other school 'subjects' (English, Geography and History) were literally invented around the same time and each quickly formed a professional association to define and defend its boundaries. These subject innovations quickly became transformed into new orthodoxies, which were then imposed as the almost unchallengeable criteria of a good education, upon the selective schools of the State sector designed for the masses. The forms of State-provided schooling, however, were not accepted passively. In the 'elementary' schools, there were pupil strikes and other forms of militant resistance (Humphries, 1981). Sociological research has largely concentrated on the process by which educational innovations have been successfully imposed from above. It has paid less attention, however, to resistance to such changes or to grass-roots innovation and experiment. A Gramscian approach involves looking at the two together, and would try to show how the form the academic curriculum takes also sets the terms of the educational debate and of popular responses and resistance. But 'hegemonic' ideas have sunk deep roots; most people, for instance, accept the idea that intellectual activity is the special province of those with educational qualifications rather than something for which everyone has the capacity.

The issues we have focused on are only some of the more important ones in the sociology of education. Other writers have put more emphasis on the role of the State, the stresses and conflicts of teaching as an occupation (Grace, 1978), or on the relationship between families and schools (David, 1980). We have chosen to focus on questions of curriculum and content and how they manifest wider social conflicts and divisions and have taken most of our examples from secondary education. There are also large and important areas which remain all too little researched: primary education, where debate centres on the tension between what are called child-centred and subject-based curricula (Alexander, 1984). There is an interesting contrast between State schooling from the ages of five to eleven which has been considerably influenced by educational ideas which give priority to play and other child-initiated modes of learning, and private preparatory schools for pupils in the same age range, where the curricula closely resemble the subject divisions of the academic secondary school. But because of pressures which are perceived as emanating from economic necessity, primary schools in England are also being encouraged to place greater emphasis on 'subject skills' in mathematics and science. The traditional concentration of sociology on secondary schooling is therefore becoming increasingly indefensible. It is not only courses for school-leavers that are experiencing pressures to think about employment-related skills. Sociologists will need to examine this process as a whole, from the content of degree courses in higher education to the way pupil choices are guided in the early years of secondary schooling.

The sociology of education has also paid little attention to historical and cross-cultural studies of education prior to the nineteenth century and even less to educational systems in non-Western civilizations. Earlier educational systems are simply assumed to be outdated, irrelevant and inferior to those that have replaced them. Even if we agree that, for all their faults, the mass State-provided education systems of Western societies do contain important progressive elements, at least in relation to what they replaced, this narrowing of perspective has its dangers. For example, we take for granted that education is an activity largely carried out with children in specialized institutions by experts who have specific kinds of qualifications, and that it will stop at some point in early adult life. Once they have passed adolescence, those without formal qualifications are rarely able to resume education. But there is nothing inevitable, natural or rational in such cultural practices, and some of these tendencies are being reversed in many parts of the world. In New Zealand some schools have become community colleges where as many as half of the pupils in some classes are adults returning for further education. 'Work experience', in which education does not take place in a classroom as something that a teacher provides to pupils, is now being presented as a substitute for the disappearing tradition of apprenticeship.

These examples, often presented as highly original and innovative, are nothing of the sort. Age-specific education is itself a recent phenomenon, which began only with the provision of education by the State in the nineteenth century. Before 1870, when schooling became legally compulsory for young children, the majority of them began work from the age of six or seven. For them, 'work experience' was the major form of education.

A more general, and increasingly important question, is the relevance of Western educational practices to less developed countries. Third World countries are usually thought of as 'catching up' with the educational systems developed in and for Western countries. But radical educationalists such as Ivan Illich and Paolo Freire have argued forcibly that orthodox Western methods are completely inapplicable; that basic education is what is required for the mass of the population, and that people are best motivated to learn when they can see the connections between what they are being taught, by people who understand their conditions of life; and where they feel that learning is likely to lead to significant, even radical improvement in their lives (Freire, 1971; Illich, 1971). Third World countries have quite different problems from Western ones, and see the educational system as performing different social purposes than it is expected to fulfil in the West. One of these, for instance, is the use of education as part of nation-building. Third World countries also have cultural legacies of their own, often superior to Western forms of knowledge, as the recent upsurge of interest in Chinese herbal medicine and acupuncture in the West indicates. Again, Japanese education involves a blend of competition and cooperation, which in the West are invariably viewed as in opposition. All such developments therefore involve combinations of Western and non-Western values as well as forms of knowledge. Rapidly developing countries such as Japan, Singapore and South Korea, moreover, spend far higher proportions of their national budgets on education in comparison with the countries of Western Europe. Many of them have also developed policies for low-cost programmes to bring basic skills, such as literacy, to as many people as possible, including the adult population. All these developments suggest that the way education is valued in the West, the expenditure of the bulk of our educational budgets upon a small proportion of the population who stay on into higher education is only one way of using educational resources, not a strategy which has universal validity. In exploring alternative modes of education for our own society, we can therefore learn a great deal, not necessarily by imitating other countries, but by examining the very different strategies they are adopting to solve their own social and cultural problems.

6   Health, Illness and Medicine

The Social Distribution of Life and Death

All of us are born and all of us will die; but there is infinite variety in the nature and circumstances of these two events themselves and in what happens to our bodies and our minds in between. Some individuals, for example, are born without difficulty and grow uninterruptedly during childhood and adolescence, suffering at worst only minor infectious diseases and accidents. As adults, they reproduce their kind. They age gradually while retaining their physical and mental capacity until, in extreme old age, their bodies cease to reproduce the cells needed to sustain life, and they die peacefully without pain or discomfort.

This is an idealized picture of how we would like life to be, rather than the reality that most people experience. Death comes to many of us, not when we are old, but during or before birth, in infancy, in adolescence, in early adulthood or in middle age. And life may have been endured rather than enjoyed through some or all of these stages.

The notion that sociology has a part to play in explaining these differences in basic human experiences – in the length of human lives, and in the amount of physical and mental distress individuals suffer – however, is not immediately obvious. Rather, we assume that our understanding of such matters has grown as a result of the work of natural scientists – physiologists, biochemists, pathologists, physicians and others. Their work has indeed been central in throwing light on the functioning of the human body and on the various micro-organisms, parasites or chemical substances which can invade and destroy or undermine its finely tuned interacting parts. But whether or not individuals become ill, and then whether they recover, die or are left with residual handicaps, does not depend only on their genetic, inborn make-up and on their subsequent exposure to various kinds of disease agents; for health and illness are also determined by the social, economic and cultural characteristics of the society in which people live and their position in it. Sociologists therefore have a role to play. Epidemiology – the study of the incidence or prevalence of specific diseases and of mortality in different social groups – has long been accepted as a major contribution of social science to explaining the reasons for different collective and individual experiences in health and illness because of its historical successes in identifying the causes of particular epidemics, such as the tracing of the cholera epidemic of 1850 to the water supply, or the wider statistical evidence of links between illness and poverty.

Shifting patterns of disease

Not only has the incidence of disease changed over time; so have the kinds of disease from which people have suffered. When human beings were mainly nomadic hunters and food-gatherers, they were most likely to die from exposure, from accidents, from injuries inflicted in inter-tribal conflicts, or from starvation at times of drought or other natural disasters (Powles, 1973). But when people began to live in settled communities, and to grow crops and to domesticate animals in order to eat them or to use them for transport purposes or to plough the land, infectious and parasitic diseases of various kinds emerged as the major causes of ill-health and death. On a world scale, the main endemic scourges for many centuries were probably tuberculosis and malaria; but, periodically, there were massive epidemics of diseases like the plague, which was spread by fleas which lived on rats, which in turn, passed the micro-organisms on to the humans whose habitations they invaded. In mid-nineteenth-century Britain there were several severe epidemics of cholera, a bacterial water-borne disease; it was finally brought under control in London by the removal of the handle from the pump in Broad Street, near present-day Carnaby Street, which supplied the water to the poor local inhabitants. They were dying like flies despite the prayers offered for their deliverance. Today, a pub in the vicinity is called the John Snow after the medical doctor who took the step for which he was much criticized at the time. Children, especially those who were chronically malnourished, were very likely to succumb to diseases like measles, smallpox and diphtheria, against which there was then no artificial protection. Periodically, drought, poor harvests and devastating wars could put whole communities at risk of starvation, leading to mass deaths from malnutrition and deficiency diseases. Despite our increasing knowledge of how to prevent such disasters, they are unfortunately not a thing of the past, as recent experiences in Ethiopia, Sudan, Mozambique and other parts of Africa have shown.

Demographers believe that, until the middle of the eighteenth century, deaths about equalled births overall, despite fluctuations from year to year. Consequently, the population of the world only grew very slowly for many centuries. With increasing trade in raw materials and manufactured goods some settlements grew and others declined. But the great expansion in world population only came later, from the nineteenth century onwards (Laslett, 1971).

With the development of capitalism in Europe from the eighteenth century, patterns of disease again altered radically. For the first time in world history, live births began greatly to exceed deaths (Burnet, 1971). There is still controversy as to why, in Britain, the economic and social changes which have been called the Industrial Revolution should have been accompanied by an unprecedented increase in population. One epidemiologist has claimed that, however dreadful the working conditions in the new factories were, and however appalling the squalor and the insanitary conditions of the new industrial towns, increased production of food from the newly en-closed farms worked by wage-labour resulted in all-round better nutritional standards (McKeown, 1976). This, in turn, increased fertility and survival in the first years of life. Others have argued that the increase can be largely accounted for, not by a better nourished population, but by a lowering of the age of child-bearing which, in turn, was due to the removal of some of the customary constraints on early sexual intercourse characteristic of stable rural communities which were disrupted by enclosures and enforced mobility (Laslett, 1971). Still others believe that the changes were due in part to the production of a successful prophylactic against smallpox – vaccination – and in part to a change in the virulence of the micro-organism involved in the plague (Razzell, 1965).

In nineteenth-century Britain, in Western Europe generally and in North America, the predominant diseases were still the infections, and their victims still infants, children and young adults. However, as death certification became general and better records were kept by hospitals, Poor Law and sanitary authorities, it became clear that, although no class was immune from infectious diseases of childhood and early adult life, death was most likely to occur among the poor (Flinn, 1970). They were the most at risk because they were the least well nourished and the most likely to live in the filth and squalor of back-to-back houses or tenement buildings where food was easily contaminated and air, water, and gut-borne bacteria were rife. It was not hard for contemporary analysts and reformers, such as Chadwick, in 1842, and Engels, in 1845, to recognize that poverty and illness were two sides of the same coin (see Chadwick, 1965, and Engels, 1984).

The poor, crowded into the insanitary dwellings of the rapidly expanding industrial towns, were the most vulnerable. Public health reformers, like Chadwick and, later, Simon (Lambert, 1963), were able to argue that the ill-health of the poor, particularly during epidemics of cholera and typhoid – carried through contaminated water and food – constituted a threat to the rest of society as well. Firstly, there was the direct danger of contagion, since the poor could not be confined to ghettos. Their labour was needed in the factories and workshops. Secondly, sick men, women and children meant an inefficient labour force, which became increasingly important in the last decades of the century when Britain began to face competition in manufactured goods from Europe and North America. At the end of the century, when Britain fought the Boers of Dutch descent for territorial control of the rich spoils of Southern Africa, the poor health of the volunteers was used by public health reformers to urge preventive health services for women and children. The First and Second World Wars led to similar widespread demands for better health services for the poorest sections of the community.

During the twentieth century, the predominant disease pattern changed once again. As nutritional status and environmental conditions improved, the infectious diseases of childhood and of early adult life gradually became less common and less lethal. Some credit for the decline is rightly given to the discovery and use of effective measures to prevent diphtheria, measles, whooping cough,

Table 7. Expectation of additional years of life for males and females at birth, aged 20 and aged 60 in 1901 and 1986

Year	At birth		At aged 20		At aged 60	
	Males	*Females*	*Males*	*Females*	*Males*	*Females*
1901	48.0	51.6	42.7	45.2	13.4	14.9
1986	71.9	77.6	53.1	58.6	16.8	21.2

(*Source: Population Trends: winter 1990*, No. 62, p. 50.)

tuberculosis and poliomyelitis. But a downward trend had already begun by the turn of the century, and changes in social and economic life – notably improvements in nutrition and sanitation – played an even greater part in the decline of these diseases (McKeown, 1980). The pressures exerted by trade unions and by social movements of various kinds to improve living and working conditions little by little began to pay off in reduced mortality. As long as such improvements did not threaten profits or the institution of private property, employers were willing to go along with them or even support them (Navarro, 1978).

Contemporary patterns of illness and death in men and women

The decline in mortality in children and young adults has changed the age-structure of the populations of advanced technological societies and, with it, the pattern of disease and mortality. With increasing numbers of middle-aged and elderly people, the morbid conditions to which they are most prone now dominate the health profile of such societies. Among men, the most common cause of death is coronary artery (heart) disease, followed by cancer, strokes and other respiratory diseases. They are still more likely to die at every age up to 100 years old than are women (Central Statistical Office, 1984). For women, cancer is the most common cause of death, followed by strokes, respiratory and heart disease.

These and other differences in morbidity and mortality rates for men and women raise important theoretical questions for the sociology of health and illness, because differences between the sexes are found not only in industrialized societies, but in all societies where adequate records are kept. Some, for instance, have argued that females are biologically programmed for longer survival than men, that is that biological differences ('nature') rather than social factors ('nurture') are involved – an argument that runs counter to the functionalist argument of sociobiologists, who claim that contribution to the perpetuation of the species (in this case *homo sapiens*) is an important reason for the survival of some individuals and not others (Wilson, 1975). For males remain reproductively potent from puberty to the end of their lives, whereas females lose their capacity to reproduce after the menopause in mid-life.

Examination of the incidence of conditions which cause death or chronic disability but which affect men and women differentially suggests that differences in the lives men and women lead account for some at least of these differences in mortality rates. For example, until recently, males were more likely than females to take hazardous jobs and to engage in dangerous sports. Even in early childhood, boys are encouraged to take risks while girls are urged to caution (Sharpe, 1976). Such deep-seated social attitudes to appropriate sex roles, reinforced by employment patterns, may account for the substantial differences in mortality from violent deaths, accidents and similar causes and comparable differences in the gender frequency of certain kinds of illness (Wadsworth *et al.*, 1983). Until recently, too, male deaths from lung cancer greatly exceeded female deaths from this cause, and this can be satisfactorily explained by differences in their smoking habits, since smoking is the single most important cause of this form of cancer (Royal College of Physicians, 1977). In recent years, however, girls have been as likely to start smoking as boys and men more likely than women to stop, so that the gender differences in both smoking habits and mortality from tobacco-related causes are diminishing (OPCS, 1990). These trends in smoking habits are indications if any were needed that social rather than – or in addition to – biological factors can alter the different health experiences of men and women. Men are also more likely both to contract alcohol-related illnesses and to die from them. This difference, too, can be attributed to differences in the typical lifestyles of men and women and in normative values which *pro*scribe the habit for the one sex and *pre*scribe it for the other (Robinson, 1976).

Although men are more likely to commit suicide than women, women are more likely to attempt it and very much more likely to be diagnosed by general practitioners and psychiatrists as mentally depressed or over-anxious. Once again, the explanation for this finding is unlikely to be a purely biological one (Gove, 1972). It is much more likely to have multiple causes. For example, it may be that the division of labour – which tends to confine women to the home or give them only subordinate, poorly paid jobs in industry, commerce and personal services – is itself responsible for depressing women's emotional state by restricting the social recognition they receive – which, in turn, affects adversely their self-esteem (Brown and Harris, 1978). It has also been alleged that males, under stress of whatever kind, are likely to resort to alcohol rather than appeal for help to doctors, which they commonly think will be interpreted as a sign of weakness, which men in our culture do not like to admit to. Women on the other hand do not suffer so much social stigma if they accept the label 'the weaker sex'.

Differences in the *reported* incidence of mental illness may then reflect a difference in the willingness of the sexes to declare their need for help. But they may also involve differences in the diagnostic practices of doctors when confronted with a man or with a woman. The analysis of possible reasons for reported sex-differences in the prevalence of mental illness thus illustrates the significant part which social, economic and cultural factors all play in the onset of illness and in its treatment. It emphasizes the need for sociological investigation of phenomena which, at first sight, appear to have a purely physical explanation.

Class differences in mortality and morbidity

The need to think sociologically is even greater when we examine the persistence, throughout the twentieth century, of substantial differences in the morbidity and mortality of men and women in different social classes. In mid-century, when it seemed that the major killer diseases associated with gross poverty were in the process of being overcome, an end to such social class differences was confidently predicted. Indeed, the emerging disease pattern – in which more and more deaths were from heart disease, strokes, cancer and respiratory illness, mainly in middle age – was thought to

Table 8. Mortality of men[1] by social class 1911–85 (all causes)

Period covered	Social class						
	I	*II*	*III*[2]			*IV*	*V*
			All	*N*	*M*		
1910–12	88	94	96			93	142
1930–32	90	94	97			102	111
1970–72	77	81		99	106	114	137
1981–5	58	77		93	98	107	130

1. Aged 14–65 in 1910–12, 15–64 in 1930–32 and 1970–72, and 16–64 in 1981–5.
2. The figures for 1910–12 and 1930–32 include all men in Class III; those for 1970–72 and 1981–5 are divided into non-manual (N) and manual (M) workers.

(*Source:* Office of Population Censuses and Surveys, 1978, *Occupational Mortality, England & Wales, 1970–72*, HMSO, p. 174, and Goldblatt, 1989.)

be associated with economic affluence: the victims of this new disease pattern were more likely to be the affluent, and especially the new rich rather than the poor. It was the well-to-do who had the money to over-indulge themselves by smoking, drinking and driving fast cars. It was they, so the belief ran, who had to carry the stressful burdens of decision-making in industry and commerce, burdens likely to give them raised blood pressure and leave them peculiarly vulnerable to heart attack or stroke. Perhaps, for the first time in human history, it seemed that the first would come last and the last first.

It came as something of a shock to those who accepted these popular notions uncritically to find that the reality was very different. In fact, the relative class differences in overall mortality remained virtually unchanged from 1911 to 1971 (Table 8) and since then appears, to the surprise of many, to have increased rather than diminished (Wilkinson, 1986). This is as true for the so-called diseases of affluence, such as heart disease, as it is for the infectious diseases long associated with poverty (Marmot and McDowall, 1986).

Most of the data which enable us to reach this conclusion come from comparing the number recorded in each occupational group in

Table 9. Social class and mortality in Great Britain

Social class	Stillbirth[1]	Infant mortality[2]	Mortality aged 1–15[3]	SMR[4]
Males[5]				
I	4.8	8.7	25.2	58
II	5.6	9.6	24.1	77
III N[6]	5.6	10.1	26.3	93
III M[7]	7.2	11.5	32.5	98
IV	8.5	15.1	38.3	107
V	9.2	18.1	56.8	130
Females[8]				
I	4.2	6.8	20.2	59
II	5.3	7.6	18.7	72
III N[6]	6.0	8.2	20.1	81
III M[7]	6.7	9.0	23.5	98
IV	8.1	11.7	26.6	103
V	8.1	13.1	39.6	179

1. Per 1,000 legitimate total births (1982–3).
2. Per 1,000 live births (1982–3).
3. Per 1,000 in age group (1982–3).
4. Standardized Mortality Ratio. All classes each sex = 100 (1979–80).
5. Aged 15–64.
6. Non-manual workers.
7. Manual workers.
8. Married women only, by husband's social class (1976–81).

(*Source: PopulationTrends: summer 1990*, No. 56, p. 8, and Goldblatt *et al.*, 1990.)

Table 10. Standardized mortality ratios (SMRs) of manual and non-manual males (aged 20–64), Great Britain

(SMR for all men in 1979–83 = 100)

Mortality from	1970–72			1979–83		
	Non-manual	Manual	Ratio of non-manual to manual	Non-manual	Manual	Ratio of non-manual to manual
All causes	99	129	1.30	80	116	1.45
Lung cancer	87	150	1.72	65	129	1.98
Heart disease	102	113	1.08	87	114	1.31
Stroke	118	148	1.25	76	120	1.58

(*Source:* Marmot and McDowall, 1986.)

the decennial Census with the number of death certificates issued for men in the same occupational group in the same year, as well as in the year before and after it. Because the age-structure of occupations differs, this has to be taken into account by a statistical process called age standardization. Once this has been done, it is possible to compare the death likelihood of different occupational groups which are then themselves grouped into 'social classes'. The mortality figures of each of these social classes are then expressed as ratios of the national death rate (SMRs), which is taken as 100. Social classes with mortality ratios of less than 100 are less likely to die; those with ratios over 100 more likely.

The Office of Population Censuses and Surveys, which compiles these statistics, analyses deaths for all occupied men aged sixteen to sixty-four by cause of death, as well as death in general. Married women are assigned to the same social class as their husbands, on the grounds, not always adequately tested, that they have comparable living conditions and lifestyles. Infants, too, are classified on the basis of their father's occupation on their birth and death certificates. Single women have so far been omitted from the resultant class analyses of deaths, because it is held to be misleading to equate the class statuses of the work they habitually undertake with those of men. Criticisms can be made of the classification, of the comprehensiveness of the coverage, and of the accuracy and reliability with which individuals' occupations are recorded on Census forms and death certificates. Allowing for these, however, Table 9 shows the social class distribution of stillbirths, infant, childhood and adult mortality for males and females, in the years 1982–3 (the last date for which national figures are available). In Table 10 the mortality differences between non-manual and manual workers for three of the major causes of death are shown, and Figure 7 shows that social class differences are also present in childhood deaths from all causes, and noticeably so from diseases of the respiratory system and from external causes such as accidents and poisoning. The evidence for inequalities in the *incidence* or *prevalence* of diseases and disabilities, which do not necessarily lead to death but are incapacitating (Table 11), also shows a similar social class gradient (OPCS, 1990).

What accounts for this consistently poorer health record of unskilled labourers, their wives and children, who constitute 'Social Class V' in official records, compared with that of higher executive,

ALL CAUSES

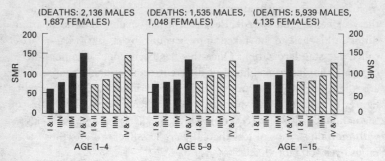

DISEASES OF THE RESPIRATORY SYSTEM (ICD 9 460-519)

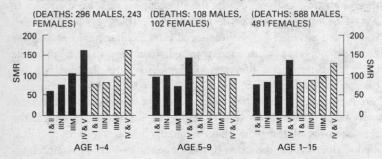

EXTERNAL CAUSES OF INJURY AND POISONING (ICD 9 E800-E999)

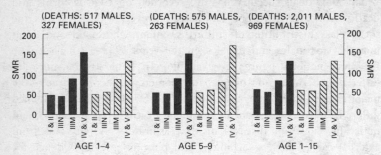

Figure 7. Mortality of children aged 1–15: Standardized Mortality Ratios (SMRs) by age, sex and cause of death in 1979–80 and 1982–3

(*Source:* Office of Population Censuses and Surveys, 1989, *Childhood Mortality 1979–80, 1982–3*, HMSO, pp. 46–8.)

Table 11. Chronic sickness by socio-economic group in 1985 (rate per 1,000 persons aged 16 or over)

Condition group	Professional	Employers and Managers	Intermediate and junior non-manual	Skilled manual and own account non-professional	Semi-skilled manual and personal service	Unskilled manual	Total[1]
Musculoskeletal system	98	132	141	163	187	235	154
Heart and circulatory system	67	90	77	95	117	134	93
Respiratory system	56	58	64	71	80	102	69
Digestive system	30	34	32	42	53	70	40
Nervous system	19	27	27	27	32	42	29
Eye complaints	11	23	29	19	29	53	26
Ear complaints	16	17	21	21	29	29	22
Average number of condition groups reported by those with a long-standing illness	1.27	1.34	1.37	1.39	1.49	1.56	1.40
Base = all persons 16 or over	1,098	3,722	4,089	5,926	3,121	978	19,654

1. Married women whose husbands were in the household are classified according to their husband's occupation. Members of the Armed Forces, persons in inadequately described occupations and all persons who have never worked are not shown as separate categories but are included in the figures for all persons.

(*Source*: Office of Population Censuses and Surveys, 1990, *General Household Survey 1988*, HMSO, p. 75.)

business and professional men and their dependants who make up Social Class I? And what accounts for the gradients in the tables and graphs which indicate that non-manual workers generally and those in professional work in particular have lower death rates and are less likely to have chronic, incapacitating illness than manual workers, including those with considerable skills?

There have been various attempts to explain these differences, and it is indeed probable that there are several reasons for them. Some analysts, for example, have argued that ill-health itself or accidents may lead men and women to leave better-paid, more prestigious jobs for less exacting, and hence less skilled ones. This certainly occurs in industries as different from one another as coalmining and the Civil Service. In the former case, skilled face-workers are often moved to unskilled work on the surface when they are no longer fit. As a result unskilled surface-workers in Social Class V have higher mortality rates than skilled face-workers (Social Class III Manual), although face-work is more dangerous and likely to cause illness than surface-work. In the Civil Service, many unskilled, Social Class V classified jobs, such as messenger, are taken by partially disabled ex-servicemen or others from occupations which they held while younger and which required more skill and training.

Such downward occupational mobility seems to account, at least in part, for the finding in Chicago in 1938 (Farris and Dunham, 1938), and confirmed in this country since (Goldberg and Morrison, 1963), that schizophrenia, a particularly debilitating and intractable form of mental illness, is more prevalent in the lower than the higher social classes. There is also evidence that of those born into lower social class families, those with the best physique are the most likely to be recruited into higher social classes, by marriage for women and by educational achievement or success in the entertainment industry for men (Illsley, 1955). Upward or downward social mobility thus affects health measurement, and accounts in part for the stability, over time, of inter-class ratios, in mortality and in the incidence of some illnesses.

Yet another theory tries to account for social class differences in health on cultural grounds. In an extreme form, for example, it has been argued that there is a 'culture of poverty', which distinguishes an underclass from other working-class people (Lewis, 1968). Those who belong in this culture are supposed not to share the same values as the rest of society. They are isolated from it, except insofar as they are parasitic upon it. They do not take advantage of the education and welfare benefits provided by the modern State: they are fatalistic and unwilling to postpone immediate gratification for the sake of future gains. They live dangerously and cut themselves off deliberately from the services offered by those who could help them to improve their health. They are often small peasant farmers in exhausted agricultural areas or immigrants from such areas or from impoverished Third World countries to the more prosperous West.

One of the troubles with this explanation (and there are others) is that it is not just the unskilled and the 'underclass' whose health records are inferior, but manual workers as a whole, who constitute more than half the total population in modern, capitalist societies and who have higher death rates for most diseases than do the middle and upper classes.

Politicians and others in occupations which enjoy the best health records are apt to explain class differences by pointing to the greater prevalence of cigarette smoking and alcohol consumption among working-class people when compared with professional people. Since such habits are often considered to be under the control of the individual – no one forces you to smoke or drink and everyone knows the dangers of excess – they see nothing wrong in 'blaming the victim'. Other sections of the community cannot be held responsible, especially if steps have been taken to inform everyone of the dangers involved.

Sociologists, however, are not satisfied with this stance, which is often used as an excuse for acceptance of an unsatisfactory state of affairs. They argue that, because social differentiation based upon class considerations is still such a feature of every aspect of daily life in capitalist society, it is hardly surprising that differentiation extends into the field of physical and mental health. For example, children born into working-class homes in the failing manufacturing centres of northern Britain will, from birth, look at the world and their own place in it through very different spectacles than will children born to professional people, living in the comparatively prosperous commuter belt outside London. The two sets of children and their parents will have entirely different experiences in the job-market and in private and public life generally.

Well-substantiated empirical evidence to support this contention is at present partial and incomplete but is gradually increasing. For example, unemployment and irregularity of income are more likely to be experienced by manual than by non-manual workers, and are known to affect physical and mental health in the families involved (Fagin and Little, 1984; Moser *et al.*, 1984; Marmot and McDowall, 1986). Among those in work, manual workers are the most likely to face poor and dangerous working conditions, including those known to be associated with cancer (Townsend and Davidson, 1982). Health is also related to housing: working-class families are less likely to be owner-occupiers, who have better health records than those living in local authority owned or privately rented accommodation (Fox and Goldblatt, 1982). Widening income differentials between manual and non-manual workers since 1970–72 may also have contributed to the increasing differences in their patterns of mortality.

In addition, there is growing evidence that working-class wives with young children are more likely than their middle-class counterparts to become mentally distressed. It seems that this is because they are more likely to face chronic social difficulties and life-events involving loss, such as the death of a near relative. And given the more marked gender division of roles in family life, they are also less likely than middle-class women to have a confiding relationship with their husband or boyfriend, which helps to overcome crises and to prevent depression (Brown and Harris, 1978).

Enough has been said to show that there are many and complex reasons why, despite overall reductions in death rates and in the incidence of diseases which used to kill, the relative differences between social classes in advanced technological societies remain virtually unaltered.

Ethnic differences in mortality and morbidity

Social class differences are not the only systematic ones found in the health field. Most Western industrialized societies today, especially those with an imperialist past, have substantial ethnic minorities on which their economies depend. These are often distinguished from the host population by skin colour, by family and community organization, by culture, by beliefs, and by health behaviour. Since members of these ethnic minorities are usually forced into the least well paid jobs, it is not surprising that their mortality and morbidity rates frequently resemble those of the most disadvantaged of the host population.

At any given occupational level, however, ethnic minority status may create either a double jeopardy to health or, more rarely, provide greater protection against disease than that enjoyed by those who constitute the ethnic majority. For example, it has been argued that the extended family system and beliefs of immigrants from the Indian sub-continent and their descendants in Britain are safeguards against the depressive mental illnesses experienced more commonly by native born white people. On the other hand, women from the sub-continent are more likely to have lower birth weight babies than those of European descent. This could be due to maladaptation to the new climatic, nutritional and social conditions of Britain, and the absence of sufficient female kin support.

Recent migration is in itself a health hazard; but data from a report of the United States Department of Health and Human Services (1985) suggests that the disparities in the health record of the Black minority and the White majority are of long standing. They show few signs of changing. The Report estimated that 'more than 60,000 deaths could be avoided each year if mortality rates for Blacks and members of other minority groups were as low as the rates for non-Hispanic whites' (*New York Times*, 17.10.85) – enough to fill a large sports stadium.

Health and Illness Behaviour and the Sick Role

We still have to ask, however, whether the perpetuation of differences in health is due in any part to class or racial discrimination in the way that health services operate. Before we can answer this question, we need to consider a number of other issues. Firstly, we cannot say, for example, whether doctors are likely to be more successful in treating upper-class than working-class patients unless we know whether all those who suffer from the diseases in question are equally likely to consult a doctor. Furthermore, if we find that this is not the case, we need to know the reasons why, and the possible effect of medical treatment on the health of those patients who do consult doctors.

Much sociological work, particularly in the United States, has been devoted to studying and explaining the ways in which people act when feeling unwell: 'illness behaviour'. Talcott Parsons (1951) argued that the stability and cohesion of any social system was threatened by ill-health, because those who experienced it were unable to fulfil their normal social obligations in their family and work settings. It was in the general interest of society, therefore, to ensure that those who became ill should feel obliged to seek expert help to enable them to recover as quickly as possible and resume their usual social roles. In modern, industrial societies, seeking expert help implied consulting the qualified medical doctor or physician. While they remained ill, they occupied a new role – that of a sick person (Americans use the word 'sick' where the British normally say 'ill'), which itself attracted certain rights and obligations.

Parsons implied that, although in most instances individuals seeking to rid themselves of the pain or discomfort of their illness would willingly obey their doctor's orders, some might see advantages in prolonging the sick role if they could thereby avoid onerous social obligations. In this he drew upon psychoanalytic theories which purported to explain hypochondria as a state in which individuals claim to be ill when experts can find no abnormality to explain the pain or the behaviour.

Parsons's theoretical model seemed to make good sense: but how far does the actual behaviour of individuals faced with pain or other distressing symptoms confirm his view of the sick role? A number of studies, undertaken since he wrote, tended to show that his model was too simple. Responses to illness, in practice, were much more complicated and they varied, depending upon the socio-cultural milieu in which they occurred.

The illness 'iceberg'

Several studies have shown that distressing symptoms, which might or might not be precursors of life-threatening illness, are very widespread in the population at any point in time (Dunnell and Cartwright, 1972; Wadsworth et al., 1971). Indeed, those who were entirely symptom-free were a minority – only about sixteen in every 100. Furthermore, most of those with symptoms either did nothing about them or took only self-prescribed remedies. Only a small minority consulted a doctor and even fewer were seen in hospital. From these findings, therefore, it is reasonable to conclude that unpleasant symptoms, such as headaches, backaches, constipation, skin rashes, coughs and colds are widespread and that most people put up with them and do not define themselves as ill if they have them. Indeed, most people who admit to such symptoms in health surveys nevertheless describe themselves as in good health. We must also conclude, therefore, that doctors do not by any means see all the ill-health that exists in a community at any given time because many sufferers do not consult them. There is, in fact, what has been called an 'iceberg' of disease (Last, 1963). Only a small proportion of the illness experienced is above the surface, in the sense that it comes to the notice of authorized health service personnel.

Consultation triggers

The next question then is what is it that induces the minority to consult a doctor. Once again, there are no simple, common sense answers. Zola (1973) found that there was a general pattern behind the decisions people took to consult or not. He identified a number of situations which he called 'triggers to consultation'. An increase in the pain or discomfort caused by the condition was obviously one of these; so too was previous experience of the condition. Those with chronic conditions which flared up episodically were particularly knowledgeable about whether they needed to obtain a doctor's prescription or not. Equally important was whether or not the complaint or symptom began to interfere with work performance or valued leisure activities. The decision to consult, moreover, was frequently not solely that of the individual alone. Close relatives and friends – what Zola and others have called the 'lay referral system' – (Freidson, 1970) were often consulted; it was often at their instigation that the sufferer would take the plunge. Here is evidence, if it were needed, that matters of health and illness are of significance to a social group and not merely to individuals and their personal doctors.

Social differences in illness behaviour

Zola's work and that of another American sociologist (Zborowski, 1969) were also important in showing that different socio-cultural groups had different expectations of the consultation. Both research-ers found that members of different ethnic groups in New York and in Boston, Massachusetts, tended to present their problems in different ways and to want different things from the doctors they saw. Broadly speaking, Irish Americans were the most likely to deny pain, to be fatalistic and to accept the doctor's diagnosis and treatment proposals without demur. Italian and Jewish patients were the most likely to emphasize the amount of pain they were suffering; the Italians, however, were usually interested only in relief, while the Jewish patients were more likely to want explanations of the cause of the pain and advice on how to avoid further episodes. WASPs – White Anglo-Saxon Protestants – were the most likely to behave in ways which the doctors themselves considered rational and likely to facilitate treatment; that is, they were less emotional in their self-presentation than the Italians or Jews, but more likely to ask appropriate questions and to carry out prescribed regimens than the Irish.

There have not been comparable studies in Great Britain, but we do know that there are social class, age and sex differences in the reasons for consulting general practitioners. Not surprisingly, working-class men are more likely than middle-class men to consult, because the former are more likely to need a doctor's certificate to authenticate their claim to national insurance sickness benefits (Townsend and Davidson, 1982). Middle-class women are more likely to take their children to the doctor for immunizations and health check-ups than working-class women (Cartwright and O'Brien, 1976). This could be due in part to the fact that the latter more often find it difficult to come to the doctor's surgery because of their work or domestic circumstances; but it could also be that middle-class women are less fatalistic about health matters and more convinced of the value of immunization. They may also possess greater self-esteem than working-class women and feel less intimidated in situations in which they may feel that their competence as mothers is being tested.

The finding that working-class men consult more frequently than middle-class men, however, is not entirely accounted for by their need for certification. They and their wives also consult more frequently for other reasons, according to data from the General Household Survey (OPCS, 1990). Is it because they experience more ill-health and are therefore in greater need of medical help, or is it that they are less able or willing to care for themselves? The question is not easily answered, and different researchers have come up with different answers.

One analyst, using General Household Survey data, calculated that, if self-reported illness was taken into account as an indicator of need for medical advice, unskilled workers actually consulted *less* than professional men (Brotherston, 1976). On the other hand, other researchers, using the same survey data but for another year, claimed that among chronically ill and disabled people there were no significant social class differences in consultation-rates; but, when illness was transient and acute, they reckoned that working-class men were more likely to consult than middle-class men (Collins and Klein, 1980). They argued, therefore, that there was no sign that working-class people received less than their fair share of general practitioner services. Critics of this research, however, have suggested that it takes no account of the severity of *acute* illness, which is likely to be greater among working-class people (Townsend and Davidson, 1982). Other commentators have noted, too, that, if the findings are correct, they may merely reflect the fact that many working-class people have dull, routinized or hard, manual work to do, and so may need relief from it to a greater extent than professional people, whose work is more likely to be congenial, psychologically rewarding and physically less arduous, and who are therefore less likely to want some respite from it if they feel off-colour.

As far as age is concerned, it is not surprising that old people and very young children (through their parents) are the most frequent consulters. At both ends of the age spectrum, people are more vulnerable to disease and death than are schoolchildren or adults of working age. Among the latter, women consult more than men for a variety of reasons. Fertility control, pregnancy and childbirth – although not in themselves pathological – have come more and more under medical control and management. Part of the greater tendency for women to consult is thus easily accounted for. They are under great social pressure to behave responsibly in their role of child-bearer, and a regular consultation with a doctor is considered to be responsible behaviour. Furthermore, the major methods of female-controlled contraception – the pill and the intra-uterine coil – have to be obtained from a doctor. Feminist sociologists have questioned how far this induced dependence on medicine is really essential to safeguard the health of women and children (Oakley, 1979). It illustrates, in yet another context, how practices which at first sight appear to be merely technical matters are really determined in large part by social rules.

Three things are clear from these studies. First, few people are free from some form of distressing symptom. Ill-health is common and more the norm than perfect health. Most of it is treated, not by the medical services, but by the individuals who experience it. Second, doctors are consulted for many reasons other than illness. Third, there are differences between social groups, both in what they regard as requiring professional advice or treatment, and in the expectations they have of their doctors when they do consult.

The doctor–patient relationship

We can now go on to consider the relationships which are established between doctors and patients in the consultation situation. Once again Parsons (1951) was a pioneer in this field, suggesting a theoretical model of the doctor–patient relationship based on structural–functionalist assumptions. Given the social importance of restoring sick individuals to health, he argued, doctors and patients were expected to enter into a pact. For the duration of the illness, patients agreed to surrender some of their normal autonomy to the doctor, while the doctors, for their part, agreed not to use their authority to exploit the dependency of the patients. Thus, for example, patients had to permit doctors to examine them physically and ask detailed questions about their intimate daily habits. Patients would only do so, Parsons postulated, if they were confident not only of the doctor's technical knowledge and skills, but also of his discretion and objectivity and his personal disinterestedness and commitment to their well-being. In this way, Parsons drew up a profile, or patterning of the requirements of the doctor's role in the relationship, which could be compared and contrasted with the patterning of other so-called professional roles and with that of a businessman.

No sooner was this model of the doctor–patient relationship expounded than its limitations as a reflection of real relationships began to be demonstrated. Szasz and Hollender (1956) argued that the extent of asymmetry in the relationship was not always as it had been painted by Parsons. Two other kinds of doctor–patient relationship were common. In one, there *could* be no patient cooperation in getting well, i.e. when the patient was anaesthetized or suffering from delusions. In the other, the patient might be as knowledgeable about the condition as the doctor, as in the case of diabetes, a chronic condition where there is much medical uncertainty, and therefore much more mutual participation and less asymmetry in the doctor–patient relationship.

Szasz and Hollender in essence did no more than modify Parsons's model; they did not challenge it. A more fundamental criticism of the model, however, came from Freidson (1970). He argued that the underlying assumption of mutual consensus and cooperation in the relationship could not be sustained. The relationship was as often characterized by conflict as it was by consensus: conflicts about objectives and conflicts about different beliefs about cure and cause. Again, doctors might try to limit their involvement with the patient, but it was in the patient's interest to enlist their unconditional, 'particularist' support as much as possible. Tension could also arise because doctors could not always fulfil patients' expectations of cure or pain relief. In addition, of course, there were times when the doctors' commitment to confidentiality might be sorely tried, especially if the patient had committed a crime or was likely to endanger the health or safety of others.

Confirmation that conflict is often experienced in the doctor–patient relationship comes from studies which have been undertaken of both doctors and patients. Many doctors acknowledge their own sense of frustration when patients do not conform to the Parsons ideal (Jefferys and Sachs, 1983). Some of them admit to difficulties they habitually face in remaining detached and scientific when they dislike or disapprove of a patient's conduct. Patients, too, although usually appreciative of the services they receive from their doctors (Cartwright and Anderson, 1981), will, when pressed, often admit that they are dissatisfied with many aspects of the consultation. They do not always obtain the advice or the consideration and sympathy they look for (Stimson and Webb, 1975).

Is conflict in the doctor–patient relationship more common when the patients are working class than when they are middle class? If so, it could be argued that the former were less likely to obtain as good a service from their doctors as the latter. This, in turn, might help to account in part for the greater prevalence of chronic disability among manual workers.

Some sociologists have, indeed, assumed that the social relationship between doctors and working-class patients makes communication and empathy more difficult than when the patients are middle class. There is some evidence of a limited kind which certainly suggests that even well-motivated, socially astute doctors give longer consultations to their middle-class than to their working-class patients. Cartwright and O'Brien (1976), in a study involving sixteen doctors and a sample of their patients aged sixty and over, found that the doctors gave their middle-class patients more information and asked them more friendly questions about their everyday lives. They knew more about their personal circumstances.

This small but impeccably conducted study was not able to show, however, that the outcome of the consultations was better for the middle-class patients. Indeed, evidence about the effect of the quality of the doctor–patient relationship on the patient's health is not easy to obtain. Furthermore, survey after survey shows that middle-class men and women are more likely than working-class people to criticize the services they receive (Cartwright and Anderson, 1981). This is almost certainly not due to the fact that working-class people receive better quality services (Hart, 1971). Rather, it is likely to mean that they have lower expectations of their doctors in the first place, or are less articulate in expressing their views.

The experience of illness and disability

So far in this chapter we have talked about disease and illness mainly in general terms. Yet obviously different kinds of disease or illness have different kinds of social consequences both for those who suffer from them and for their relatives. In particular, when an illness or handicap is believed to be due in part to moral turpitude of some kind, the sufferers, and even those associated with them, are likely to be subjected to some form of social stigma.

Explanations for the onset of specific diseases and social attitudes towards them have changed over the centuries in Western societies and there is still great variation in the explanations given in the contemporary world (Helman, 1984).

Every society has its own cultural ways of thinking about the human body and of explaining the multitude of ills which can befall it (McKeown, 1971). In some societies, for example, certain kinds of illness and even accidents are thought to have occurred because those involved have failed to fulfil their obligations to living kin or to dead ancestors (Evans-Pritchard, 1937). In some Christian communities, past and present, many kinds of illness have been attributed to sins committed against God and/or one's fellows (Skultans, 1975). In some contemporary societies, and in much of Europe before the eighteenth century, many diseases were attributed to witchcraft or to evil, demonic spirits which literally possessed the victims. Men, women and children fell ill because others wished to harm them and did so by casting spells or the evil eye on them.

While such systems of quasi-religious or magical beliefs about the causes of illness persist in twentieth-century Western societies they have largely been replaced by another system of belief based on the theoretical precepts and empirical methods of the natural sciences that have evolved in the last two hundred years (Armstrong, 1983). Although progress in the natural sciences has been uneven and limited where health is concerned, most people see them as providing more valid explanations for the ways in which our bodies work than the explanations which they replaced.

The dominant, scientific model of disease causation today draws attention to the part played by invasive micro-organisms, pollutants and inherited traits (Dubos, 1959). As a result, many older assumptions that illnesses were due to moral lapses on the part of the individual sufferer are no longer so common. Decline in religious belief in general in the twentieth century has also lessened other beliefs which attributed almost any illness to sinful behaviour.

Stigma

Nevertheless, older ideas still persist, and social stigma attaches to certain illnesses (Goffman, 1968). Indeed, the discovery — beyond much doubt — that the social behaviour of individuals is a major contributory factor in some conditions has meant the development of a new form of stigma assignment, 'blaming the victim': it can be applied to those suffering from many forms of illness, including sexually transmitted diseases, AIDS, alcoholism, lung cancer and heart disease. The sufferers are accused of bringing on or perpetuating the condition by indulgence in such disapproved kinds of behaviour as promiscuous sex, smoking, over-eating or over-drinking even when such behaviour is not the sole cause of the condition. In the eyes of others, the sufferers have to some extent brought their fate upon themselves and therefore are less deserving of sympathy than other patients. Thus women requesting abortions, or people who have attempted suicide often arouse condemnatory if not punitive feelings from the doctors and nurses they encounter (Doyal, 1979). Such condemnation is, however, often misplaced. It may, for example, be the sexual conduct of the partners of people who are infected with sexually transmitted diseases, or the morality of those who pressurize women to have abortions that are more blameworthy than the behaviour of the sufferer.

Even when individuals patently cannot be blamed for their illness or disability, certain kinds of illness commonly result in social rejection to a greater or lesser degree. Mental illness and severe mental handicap are conditions where such rejection is particularly strong (Edgerton, 1967). Attempts to reduce the stigma of mental illness often use the analogy of physical illnesses, which generally evoke sympathy and not condemnation. Legislative measures, too, have reduced the power of the courts to decide the fate of patients with severe mental illness or handicap. Those with less severe problems are now more likely to be treated in the wards of general hospitals and not in asylums (Martin, 1984). Nevertheless, because the behaviour or the speech of some mentally ill or handicapped individuals may appear bizarre, they often still face avoidance or ridicule. Moreover, those with a known past history of disturbance may find it difficult to find jobs which they are quite capable of doing. Their near relatives – parents, brothers and sisters, spouses and children – may also experience the stigma: guilt by association (Voysey, 1975).

But mental illness and handicap are not the only conditions which invite rejection. Similar social difficulties are faced by those with a variety of chronic conditions such as epilepsy and insulin-dependent diabetes. In both these instances, the condition can be controlled by modern drugs and there is no medical reason why individual sufferers cannot lead a normal life (Scambler, 1985). Nevertheless, they and others, for example those with facial skin blemishes, the blind and the deaf, people who are obese or severely malformed, and those who depend upon crutches or a wheelchair, often find that one single, but very much despised characteristic leads other people to behave towards them in a patronizing manner, or to avoid contact with them altogether (Blaxter, 1976). All their other characteristics are ignored. So the kinds of reciprocal friendships which develop between able-bodied people are difficult to establish and maintain and in addition to the physical pain and the practical problems inherent in many forms of chronic illness and disability, social penalties are often exacted.

Healing and Caring

Theories and therapies

We have already discussed the doctor–patient relationship in general terms. Sociologists have also studied the specific ways in which doctors and other health workers treat patients and the reasons they give for their treatment methods.

The methods used to diagnose and treat illness, in any society, tend to follow logically from the dominant beliefs held by the expert healers in that society about the causes of disease. Thus, for example, if it is believed that illness is due to sins committed against the society's gods or ancestors, the appropriate treatment will be to induce repentance and restitution for the supposed injuries inflicted. The responsibility of the diagnostician or healer is to identify the kind of misdemeanour which has been committed, perhaps unwittingly, and then to prescribe the form of expiation and penance which is appropriate to it (Lewis, 1979). Even if such measures do not achieve their purpose and the sufferer dies, his surviving relatives are likely to feel reassured that at least they cannot be blamed for the death, which they might have been had they failed to take the prescribed steps. It is usual, indeed, in all societies, for surviving relatives to want reassurance that they 'did the right thing'. What changes are ideas about what the right thing is.

In much of Europe before the eighteenth century, many diseases were attributed to witchcraft or to evil spirits. This is still the case in many contemporary cultures. The correct behaviour, in such circumstances, is to seek help in discovering the reasons for an individual's illness from an expert diagnostician, who also possesses powerful remedies to counteract the malign forces undermining the sufferer's health and well-being. The diagnosticians, often called 'witch-doctors' or some such name by outsiders, rely on techniques of divination handed down from father to son or from mother to daughter, or involving lengthy apprenticeship. Their remedies generally involve not merely treating the individual who is ill, but rituals which involve whole families, and are designed to exorcise evil, possessive spirits, or to propitiate angry gods or destroy the power of those who were practising the witchcraft which was harming the victim (Marwick, 1970).

Traditional healers also administer herbal remedies with pharmaco-logical properties capable of destroying invasive micro-organisms, of altering moods, or of promoting the natural healing resources of the body (Horton, 1967).

The placebo effect

Research workers in the Western scientific tradition now accept that many of the herbal remedies used by traditional healers throughout the world are indeed chemically potent and effective in treating some conditions, and the World Health Organization regards the involve-ment of traditional healers as essential if the medical needs of the populations of the Third World are to be met. Some, indeed, regard non-Western medical systems as superior in their appreciation that illness is often of social derivation. The traditional Western scientific attitude to such systems, however, is still usually one of rejection: most of the remedies of traditional healers, other than those which demonstrate chemical properties, are dismissed as ineffectual mumbo-jumbo, contributing nothing to the cure or even making the victim worse. At best, they are placebos, substances or procedures which have no intrinsic healing properties but which nevertheless effect positive changes.

The capacity of inert substances – for example, coloured pills composed of chalk – to reduce physical pain or remove other symptoms has been demonstrated many times in clinical-controlled trials of new drugs, showing that healing is not brought about solely by the action of modern therapeutic drugs. Many doctors now acknowledge that the quality of their relationship with their patients may be as effective in promoting an improvement in health as any drug (Balint, 1964).

Sufferers can be helped in many situations by the demonstration of social support. It is such a factor which accounts for much of the effec-tiveness of traditional healing in Third World societies today. Modern medicine, for all its highly developed theory and technical resources, sadly often ignores the social dimensions of illness experience.

The 'medical model'

In modern Western societies, although certain religious or magical beliefs about the causes of illness and appropriate treatment still persist, the close connection between organized religion and healing which often resulted in the dual role of doctor–priest, has been largely broken. The doctor has perhaps acquired some of the mantle of the priest; but the priest, by and large, has lost any healing function he might once have had. Doctors look to the disciplines of biochemistry, physics, microbiology and pathology, not to theology, to explain why individuals become ill. As aids to diagnosis they use laboratory tests, not divination procedures involving oracles. They use pharmacology and surgery to treat disorders, not prayers or incantations.

This way of explaining, diagnosing and treating illness has come to be called 'the medical model'. Many medical practitioners are so impressed with its explanatory powers and its success as a guide to action that they tend to see illness in purely physical terms. Nevertheless, although this biophysical, reductionist model of illness is very strong and still dominates the practices of most doctors and the expectations of most of their patients too, general practitioners, in particular, have found that they often cannot discover any signs of illness in those who consult them (Balint, 1964). When faced with such patients, or by patients with chronic conditions for which there are no validated medical cures, some doctors merely complain that the patients are 'hypochondriacs' suffering from imaginary complaints. Others, however, have turned to the relatively new disciplines of psychology and sociology to gain greater insights into patient behaviour and their own response to it (Jefferys and Sachs, 1983), and, in the process, have begun to re-evaluate their own medical training as inadequate, insofar as it was predominantly based on a mind–body dualism. This involves the conception of the human body modelled on that of a machine; a conception of illness as due to the presence of germs and viruses; and a conception of treatment based on negating these. Today, orthodox doctors, trained to accept the medical model, are increasingly prepared to listen to the alternative theories of illness held by other healers, such as homoeopaths or acupuncturists, and adopt some of their therapies (Inglis, 1964). Many now adopt the view that too much emphasis has been given to their 'curing' role and not enough to 'caring' – which is specified as a duty under the Hippocratic oath they take when qualifying, but which is in actuality a less valued aspect of the doctor's role.

Alternative medicine

The inability of the medical model to deal with the consequences of chronic diseases or of emotional states has led many of those who suffer from them to seek alternative treatments from those with other explanations and therapies to offer (Robinson and Henry, 1977). Some of the alternative practitioners use remedies which have an age-long history. Acupuncture, for example, has been practised for many centuries in China but, until recently, was rejected by most orthodox practitioners of Western medicine until increasing knowledge of its effectiveness, even in major surgery, became more general. Naturopaths make use of many ancient herbal preparations, which, as the name implies, they believe to be superior to the laboratory-produced drugs of modern medicine. The latter are usually dangerous as well as effective and may undermine the natural resistance of the body to infections. Osteopaths, whose claims to treat effectively have been accepted in most states in the USA but rejected by the British medical profession, believe that many diseases can be dealt with best by anatomical manipulation designed to relieve pain and remove tension, which they see as one of the main reasons why people succumb to disease. Many Christians and members of other faiths, too, believe that prayer or meditation can bring about the alleviation of suffering.

Orthodox Western doctors often argue that there is no statistical empirical evidence that any of the medical systems of alternative healers are effective. They criticize the practitioners involved for not permitting clinical control trials, such as those now required for new drugs, even though many of the procedures they themselves use have also not been subject to a rigorous testing of their efficacy (Cochrane, 1972). For example, the practice of tonsillectomy (removal of tonsils) as a method of preventing further throat infections has never been evaluated scientifically, but the procedure is still carried out extensively. Alternative healers can, of course, exploit the credulous; but their very existence, and the increase in recent years in the numbers who consult them, suggest that, for many people, they supply what Western medicine does not. It is likely, indeed, that medicine of any kind is effective in alleviating suffering when both practitioner and patient have a shared faith in it.

Healers and Carers

The modern doctor

Those who perform the role of doctor or physician in modern society, as individuals, exercise considerable power over those who consult them, and as a collectivity occupy a commanding position in the modern State (Johnson, 1972).

In advanced technological societies, those who become doctors have to be able to master adequately the natural sciences as applied to medicine and some technical skills. They are therefore recruited at the end of secondary education or, as in the USA, after under-graduate work, from those with good preliminary qualifications in the sciences. They are by no means, however, a random selection of young adults with such capacities.

In Britain, and elsewhere in the West, doctors are more likely to be men rather than women, and to have come from professional and upper-class backgrounds, including medical families, than would occur by chance (Simpson, 1972). Individuals with these characteristics are more likely than those without them to apply for admission to medical schools. Girls and working class boys, who could certainly manage the course and qualify, are often discouraged from applying by their parents and schoolteachers. The latter frequently believe that, to be successful, applicants must possess an upper-class accent and have an authoritative manner (Elston, 1977). University selectors also look for such qualities and are most likely to find them from those applying from a public (fee-paying) school. In both Britain and the USA, since the 1970s, however, there has been a substantial increase in the proportion of women admitted. The class selection, on the other hand, does not appear to have changed, despite the professed intention of medical schools to make the profession more socially representative (Atkinson, 1981).

It is not surprising that there should be many more candidates wanting to enter medicine than there are training places available for them. In the USA, where the medical system is predominantly private, doctors receive very high incomes; so much so, that the high cost of the training, which is long and expensive, can be counted a good initial investment. In Britain, where training costs are met, for the most part, by the State, and where average earnings are much lower, the profession is still better remunerated than most others which recruit from the same pool of potential applicants. Moreover, the material rewards are not the only attraction of the profession. Public opinion polls show that medicine enjoys a higher social standing than all the other professions and higher than business jobs, which carry higher incomes (Coxon and Jones, 1974).

The medical profession, however, is not a homogeneous one. Within it, some branches – or 'specialties' as they are called – enjoy more prestige than others and offer those who reach the top greater opportunities to make very high earnings. In Britain, until the 1960s, general practice tended to be the Cinderella branch of the profession, with lower prestige, lower peer group esteem and lower earnings than most hospital-based specialties. Since that time, general practitioners in the National Health Service have increased their income relative to other specialties, and changes in their training and conditions of work have given them more opportunities for professionally rewarding work, all of which increases the respect accorded them by their own reference-group – the hospital-based consultants (Jefferys and Sachs, 1983). Among the latter, surgeons, perhaps as a result of their dramatic life-prolonging procedures as well as their opportunities for lucrative private practice, tend to enjoy the highest prestige. Hence, surgery is the most sought-after specialty for young, aspiring doctors. Psychiatry and the treatment of mental deficiency are the least popular, along with public health medicine, which is now largely concerned either with epidemiological research or with the administration of health services.

Popular interest in matters of life and death, and therefore in medicine, is so great that doctors are often made into folk heroes, especially by television. Serials such as *Casualty* are viewed weekly by millions. The doctors are always the heroes, performing superhuman feats of rescue from the jaws of death, while displaying the utmost modesty and small eccentric weaknesses, which demonstrate that they are still human and approachable. The nurses in the soap operas, on the other hand, although competent and dedicated, are depicted as the adoring helpmeets of the authoritative doctor. Documentary programmes relating to medical matters attract huge audiences.

The nurses

Indeed, health services are not only staffed by doctors. In most modern systems, they constitute only about one in six of those working in them. The single largest occupational group is made up of nurses.

The social contrast in their position with that of the doctors could not be greater. Over 90 per cent of nurses in Britain, and even more in most other developed countries, are women. In popular imagery, they are usually portrayed as doctors' hand-maidens, while social scientists and feminists have pointed to resemblances between the doctor–nurse and the father–mother relationship, since similar roles are assigned, in both cases, on the basis of gender. Thus, the decision-making authority and instrumental requirements of both the doctor's role and that of father are contrasted with the subordinate, affective and domestic management requirements of the roles of nurse and of mother. These, of course are 'ideal' typifications: in practice, there are many variations in the way in which roles are played, depending upon the specific context in which they are set and on the personalities of the performers (Garmarnikow, 1978). Moreover, such social institutions as the family and the hospital are not static. Their composition, their functions and their culture change. Women, in both institutions, have been less willing in the last two decades to accept the roles assigned to them. In the hospital, for example, they now undertake many technical procedures in wards and in operating theatres which were once exclusively done by doctors. Some of these changes have come about because the tasks themselves can now be performed more routinely than before, or because they are not very congenial and doctors are therefore glad to be rid of them. Nevertheless, nurses are demanding more involvement in decision-making with regard to patient care which, they believe, will bring with it greater equality of professional status (Carpenter, 1977). They are certainly able to make more detailed observations of the patients' physical and mental states than are the doctors who have to rely on the nurses for this, since their own presence on the wards is only episodic.

Other health workers

One of the consequences of this growing complexity of medical technology and the need to operate and service it has been a proliferation of specialized occupations within the health services. Some of these are concerned primarily with diagnostic tests, others with treatment procedures. Those who work in them are said to belong to the professions 'supplementary to medicine'. The nomenclature itself is significant; it reflects the determination of the medical profession, which is dependent on their specialist knowledge and skills, to maintain control over their activities, and ensure that they are carried out only under its auspices (Larkin, 1983). The exclusive possession of knowledge gives a powerful weapon to any occupational group which will try to wield it to determine its own conditions of work, and possibly, to encroach on the 'territory' of adjacent groups (Freidson, 1970). The medical profession, like any other, practises 'boundary-maintenance': it seeks to maintain a monopoly of the knowledge and skills its members acquire during their training while trying to prevent other groups from exploiting to the full the value of the knowledge they possess.

In the health services, clinical psychologists, non-medically qualified pathologists, radiographers, physiotherapists, ophthalmic opticians, chiropodists and others have all tried to become more independent of the social controls exercised over them by the medical profession. They have not been very successful either at the individual or collective level, probably for two reasons. First, doctors have been able to prevent these occupational groups from having direct access to patients. They can only diagnose or treat patients referred to them by doctors and are under an obligation to report back to the doctor. Patients belong to doctors! Those opticians, chiropodists and pharmacists who wish to be more independent of the doctors have had to work outside the official health services, in the commercial sector, and in so doing have acquired a 'tradesman' status, rather than the coveted 'professional' status. A second reason for the success of the medical profession in preventing encroachment on its preserves is the support which it has been able to secure from the State, a theme to which we will return.

Besides the various occupational groups directly involved in patient care, diagnosis and treatment, the modern hospital employs many domestic and other maintenance workers (Manson, 1977). This is primarily so because hospitals have to provide specialized, hotel-like facilities for their in-patients. Workers who undertake the necessary functions of cleaning the wards and providing food are among the lowest paid workers in the economy. Until comparatively recently they were not organized into trade unions. In the twenty years following the Second World War in Europe, rates of pay were often so low that native-born Europeans were unwilling to fill the posts so that there was considerable recruitment from Third World countries. Their initial lack of militancy and unwillingness to take strike action may have reflected not only their ambiguous, alien status; it may also have been due to the vicarious prestige which association with hospitals, doctors and healing gave them and their native-born colleagues. Over time, such subordinate occupations became less willing to accept the low valuation placed on their vital work (Miliband, 1978). By the 1980s, however, high unemployment throughout the economy had tended to dampen down this militancy once more.

Informal carers

It is sometimes forgotten that, although formally organized health services now employ relatively more people than ever before, and more than any other industry, most of the burden of caring for sick, handicapped and frail old people still falls on relatives within the context of the informal, unpaid, domestic economy (Stacey, 1988).

Despite the growth of hospital-based medicine, the care of the very old and of the dying is provided mainly by kin. The idea that we have become callous towards the old and the chronically sick, whereas our forefathers shouldered their responsibilities is, however, a myth based on two fallacies. Firstly, historical demographic work has shown that the three-generation, extended family household was unusual, even in pre-industrial Britain, except among the well-to-do aristocracy and landed gentry (Laslett, 1971). Until the twentieth century, very few people survived into their sixties or seventies, let alone into their eighties or nineties – which is not uncommon today. Secondly, a higher proportion of those who did survive so long were likely to die in Poor Law institutions and workhouses than the proportion of old people today who die in residential institutions or in the long-stay wards of hospitals. Today, death is less likely than it was to occur at home but most likely to occur after only a short stay in an acute hospital ward.

The smaller, twentieth-century family does support older, disabled kin: 95 per cent of those aged sixty-five or more in Britain are not institutionalized: they live in their own homes. But the burden of caring for them when they become frail and need care falls mainly on women and especially on unmarried daughters. It is women who look after not only their own parents, aunts and uncles but also their spouses' relatives and who often sacrifice their own opportunities for paid work and for some leisure after having brought up their own children. If they were given more financial help and more community-based nursing and social support services, they might be able to prevent some of the institutionalization of the old and chronically sick which does occur. A wider provision of sheltered housing, too, appropriate to the needs of frail people, would further relieve women of much unpaid work and allow the old and feeble to retain their independence of both relatives and institutions for longer – an ambition shared by most retired people.

Starting in the 1960s in Britain, and now more widespread throughout the English-speaking world, there is now a facility, called a hospice, where dying people can obtain pain relief and social support in their last days (Taylor, 1983). The hospice movement reflects a reaction against the clinically cold regimens of the modern hospital, where life-prolonging procedures are often imposed at the cost of patient dignity or comfort (Parkes, 1972). It is apparent, however, that many of those who are terminally ill, as well as their relatives, now wish for the expected death to take place in the dying person's own home, and hospices are responding by developing 'Hospice at Home' services where relatives are helped by trained nurses to take the necessary steps to ensure a peaceful, pain-free, dignified death. Older formal hospital procedures, including those which forbade junior nurses and domestic workers from developing sympathetic communication with patients – resulting often in a conspiracy of silence – are increasingly seen as making it more, not less, difficult for all concerned to come to terms with death. Too often, social death preceded biological death, and it still can (Sudnow, 1972a).

The Role of the State in the Provision of Health Care

Health services, and particularly the hospitals, are complex work organizations. In order to understand how they function, and how the various occupation groups employed in them relate to each other and to their chief product – that is, the people they 'process' – we need to use sociological tools and perspectives first developed in studies of other kinds of complex institutions, from large-scale industrial firms and the 'professions' to studies of small formally organized work groups. All of these help to throw light on the hierarchical division of labour in health service units, on decision-making processes, and on the tensions which constantly threaten existing power relations. Because the raw material to be worked on in the health services consists of people and not of inanimate objects, or of information coded in writing or in numerical form, there are also analogies to be drawn between medical institutions and other 'people processing' institutions, such as educational establishments, legal institutions and the police (McKinlay, 1975). We can also learn much about them by applying conceptions of bureaucratic control which stem from Weber's work (Albrow, 1970).

An even wider sociological approach is provided by those who emphasize the part played by organized medicine in the maintenance of the overall social order in the developed world (Navarro, 1979).

Marxist sociologists have thus argued that the social classes which control the organs of the State – by dominating the executive offices of government, the mass media and the commanding heights of the economy, the banks, the City, the insurance companies and the big corporations – have an interest in maintaining the class structure from which they benefit and therefore the health of employed workers (Elling, 1979). For the State to meet in full or in part, directly or indirectly, the cost of medical services to some or indeed all of its citizens can be regarded, therefore, as a necessary investment which helps to stabilize the social order.

The economic advantages of measures to safeguard the health of workers and of central or local government provision of treatment facilities were not initially recognized, however, by more than a few of the powerful new class of industrialists in the early nineteenth century. Most entrepreneurs were reluctant to spend money on the poor. It needed, therefore, the combined and continued pressure of liberal reformers, trade unions and, in the early twentieth century, new political parties representing the workers, to bring about most of the legislation which, little by little, extended the scope of health service provision. Even by the outbreak of the First World War, Britain had only embryonic maternity, child health and school health services, where the emphasis was on prevention; a primitive system of national health insurance which gave workers access to the services of general practitioners and cash benefits when ill, and a network of fever hospitals and asylums for the care of lunatics and idiots (as the mentally ill and the mentally handicapped respectively were then called). These measures supplemented existing hospitals provided by the Poor Law authorities or by charitable organizations.

During the inter-war years, services were extended sparingly and with an eye to economy, though more workers were covered by compulsory health insurance. It was not until the Second World War, however, that varied studies of existing health services, making proposals for radically improving them, were undertaken, and not until 1948 that central government in Britain took on the responsibility of providing comprehensive health services for the whole population from the cradle to the grave, and irrespective of their capacity to pay.

In the event, the Labour government which brought in the legislation feared that, if its socialist proposals for the NHS were too revolutionary, it would lose the support of the organized medical profession, whose willingness to work within the proposed service was necessary. Hence, whereas the government did not need to consult the nurses or other occupational groups about the shape which the NHS should take – since those groups did not possess the power to undermine any government plan – it had to make many concessions to secure the cooperation of the organized medical profession. Hospital consultants, for example, were permitted to practise privately (and lucratively) in NHS hospitals; and teaching hospitals, where the elite of the profession had posts, obtained direct access to the Minister of Health, and were not subject to the authority of the new Regional Boards, which administered all the other hospitals. General practitioners, too, won some important concessions. They were able to maintain the status of independent contractor, which they felt was necessary to ensure their freedom from government control over their clinical practices, and plans for a salaried general practitioner service were abandoned.

The degree to which the State directly owns health service facilities such as hospitals and clinics, and controls or finances access to them, differs throughout the developed world; but in all 'mixed' capitalist economies throughout the last century, it has increased its involvement in health services. In all of them the State has been able to secure the support of the organized medical profession despite initial reluctance, but in order to do so has usually had to make concessions to it.

Medicine as an institution of social control

The power that organized medicine exercises over patients and other health occupations has led some sociologists to argue that it has become a major institution of social control in modern society (Zola, 1975). The boundaries of its work, according to Zola, have been steadily expanding as it claims competence in dealing with more and more aspects of human behaviour. Conduct or states of mind which used to be considered the province of the priest, the lawyer, the policeman or the teacher are now regarded as medical matters. Metaphors drawn from the practice of medicine, increasingly used in everyday speech and in political and economic analysis, indicate the increasing power of its practitioners in our society. How often is the economy said to be 'ailing' or to need 'an injection of fresh blood'? Politicians are prone to claim that they have 'taken the nation's pulse'; in the home and workplace we do 'what the doctor ordered', or 'take our medicine like a man'.

There is little doubt that the number and variety of tasks of social significance assigned to the medical profession have increased during this century. But there is controversy as to why this has happened. Some authors write as though the impetus to aggrandizement has come from the profession itself. The prime motive, according to them, is the profession's self-interest, not the health of the population (Illich, 1977). Illich, for example, claims that increasing medical hegemony (predominance) has decreased the capacity of ordinary people to look after themselves and made them more and more dependent on medicine. He suggests that it is the evil force of industrial technology, controlled in this instance by the doctors, which has enabled them to usurp so much of the freedom and autonomy which individuals once possessed. He argues that what is needed is to return to less complex health procedures and to revive self-help in place of reliance on doctors.

Other social scientists, most notably the Marxist analyst of health, Navarro (1979), argue that, insofar as doctors do undermine the autonomy of their patients, they do so, not for their own benefit but as agents of the ruling class. In providing health services in the way they do, doctors help to persuade workers that the State has their interests at heart and thus reconcile them to their own unsatisfactory lives and subordinate position in capitalist society. Yet, given the increasing contradiction of that society, the professional status, the aspirations and the independence of the doctors themselves are also undermined. They, too, are increasingly subject to bureaucratic rules and to the business interests of drug and medical equipment companies rather than acting in accordance with the scientific and humanitarian values they formally espouse. Their interests, he argues, therefore become increasingly parallel to those of the working class. Furthermore, the development of specialties in their ranks, representing different and sometimes conflicting interests, jeopardizes their unity as 'professionals' and hence their bargaining power in their relationship with the State. It is not only Marxists, however, who have suggested that the role of commercial interests and especially of drug companies, is as often marked by self-interest as it is by humanitarian objectives. Paradoxically, many of their products can be dangerous as well as effective, and some of their sales-promotion techniques and experimental work during the developmental stage of new drug production, above all in poor Third World countries, have been strongly criticized (Lichtman, 1971).

Conclusions

The issues we have discussed are only some of the many kinds of research carried out by sociologists of medicine. Enough has been said, however, to show that sociology has already a great deal to offer health workers and to those who use their services; and provides a deeper understanding of everyday health behaviour as well as of the less frequent episodes of ill-health which involve consultations with doctors or admission to hospitals.

The field of health care also poses many problems for which both theoretical thought and hard research are needed, for continuing inequalities in health, and the variety of ways in which social structures and social processes relate to biological structures and processes are complex and often subtle issues (MacIntyre, 1980). The sociology of medicine was once considered something of a 'poor relation', unimportant as compared with such fields as political or industrial sociology. Women were more likely to be found in it – in part because it was an undervalued field, in part because they were subjected to the usual stereotypes which view 'caring' as appropriate primarily to women. The sociology of medicine is now the largest single branch of the discipline and as theoretically challenging as any other.

7   Community and Urban Life

A strong case can be made that sociology itself emerged as a distinctive discipline during the first half of the nineteenth century out of fear that contemporary Western society was experiencing a 'loss of community' and that unfortunate social consequences were bound to ensue. These feelings are not entirely absent today. The yearning for 'community' often represents not so much a carefully weighed assessment of current social developments as a gut feeling that the quality of life in the contemporary world leaves much to be desired. In other words, the desire for community has come to represent a deeply felt dissatisfaction with modern life and therefore an oblique critique of modern society. Frequently these concerns are tainted by nostalgia. A somewhat idyllic past is portrayed in which everyone was integrated into a stable and harmonious community of kin, friends and neighbours, whereas in the present people often feel insecure and rootless, buffeted by social changes and by impersonal and alien social forces.

The longing for community thus symbolizes a desire for security and certainty in our lives, together with a demand for a greater sense of personal identity and authenticity.

Unfortunately, however, it is not always clear precisely what is meant by community and whether, in what ways and how, it has been lost. There has been an unfortunate tendency to confuse what *is* with what *ought to be*. Sociologists, no less than other people, have tended to regard community as an unmitigated good thing, without being too precise in defining what it is. The attraction of community, indeed, has always rested as much on an emotional appeal as upon a rational analysis. The concept of community has therefore proved capable of encompassing any number of contradictory values which different writers have seen fit to include in it. Much of the confused state of writing on community thus derives from the failure to distinguish clearly facts from values. This, in turn, has led to a bewildering multiplicity of definitions. It is important, then, at the outset to define the terms we will use in this chapter.

Definitional Problems

A paper written by an American sociologist in the 1950s (Hillery, 1955) concluded, on the basis of ninety-four definitions of community uncovered in the literature, that the only common factor was that they all dealt with people! They can all, however, be reduced to three broad types:

1. *Community as locality* – that is, as a geographical expression, denoting *a human settlement located within a fixed and bounded local territory*. This is not really a sociological usage of community because, apart from the observation that they are all living together in a particular place, there is no consideration of the inhabitants at all, nor of how or, indeed, whether they interact with one another. However, this usage of community does raise the issue of whether there is any *inherent* link between geographical location and social life.

2. *Community as a local social system* – that is, as *a set of social relationships* which take place wholly, or mostly, *within* a locality (Stacey, 1969). This is a more sociological usage of community since attention is now focused upon a particular pattern of social relationships rather than geographical location. Thus a community in this sense may be said to exist when a network of inter-relationships is established between those people living in the same locality (for example, where everyone knows everyone else). It should be noted, however, that nothing is being implied here about the *content* of these relationships, merely the fact that a pattern of relationship does exist. In particular it does not imply that these relationships are harmonious: the community may be riven by conflict, but as long as the relationships are there and we are dealing with more than a collection of isolated individuals, then we have established the presence of a local social system, and thus a community, in this sense of the term.

3. *Community as a type of relationship* – more particularly, community is frequently portrayed as *a sense of shared identity*. This

corresponds most closely to the colloquial use of the term – a community 'feeling' or 'spirit' of community. Two points should be noted about this definition of community as a sense of shared identity. First, it need have no local, geographical basis at all. Those who share particular kinds of common identity may be widely scattered geographically – for example, the Jewish community, the 'scientific community' and so on. Secondly, not only does community in this sense not refer to locality, it may even exist among a group of people who have never actually met one another. In principle, at least, therefore, this meaning of community can be separated from the previous two. As such it is perhaps best called *communion*, since this word more clearly conveys what is involved. Most references to a loss of community in the modern world are in fact references to a loss of communion: a loss of meaningful identity with other people and an absence of the shared experiences which often accompany such identification.

Unfortunately sociological writing in the past tended to run all three of these definitions together. One influential, but largely unexamined, assumption has been that life in a particular locality promotes a certain structure of relationships which results in the presence or absence of communion. For example, rural villages were often assumed to consist of closely knit inhabitants living in happy communion, while in cities there are only isolated, lonely individuals lacking any sense of mutual identity. These assumptions, which purport to identify a unity between locality, local social system and communion, reflect little more than prevailing cultural myths and/or the values of the sociological observer.

Cutting across all these definitions is the distinction between *empirical descriptions* of local social systems – that is, studies of communities as they actually are, and *normative prescriptions* – that is, an expression of values about what community life *should* be like. Because the desire for community often symbolizes a desire for personal and social fulfilment, community often signifies the good life, a utopia. What this utopia actually consists of will vary, of course, from one individual to another, according to their personal aspirations and scale of values. But as long as the desire for community expresses, however minimally, a gap between life as it is actually experienced and life as we would like it to be, the concept of community will always be laden with normative overtones. It is important, then, to try to separate out normative prescription from empirical description.

Community as a Critique of Urban Industrialism

As an example of how normative prescription can influence empirical description let us begin with a significant historical example: the way in which, in the nineteenth and early twentieth centuries, the concept of community was used as a means of expressing a deeply felt anti-urbanism and anti-industrialism in the industrializing nations of northern Europe and North America, and, later in the twentieth century, came to infiltrate sociological theory on community and urban life.

During the nineteenth century, the concept of community was used as a contrast to the new urban, industrial and capitalist society which was then emerging. A wide spectrum of intellectual, middle- and upper-class opinion regarded this new form of society as the very antithesis of community – as impersonal and de-humanizing, rather than harmonious and humane. These judgements grew out of the eighteenth-century mood of Romanticism, which stressed the unity of the human and the natural world, and opposed emotions, values and tradition to Reason. The scientific and technological advances of the new age, it was held, involved spiritual and emotional impoverishment, the loss of community being one major consequence. Community signified a more humane and intimate existence, more stable, more traditional, and less tainted by the rational pursuit of self-interest. Writers like Cobbett and Coleridge summoned up an image of a past Golden Age in which the inhabitants of Arcadian 'organic communities' lived in happy harmony until they were destroyed by rapid industrialization and urbanization.

The destruction of community meant not merely the replacement of villages and agricultural estates by cities and factories. It also implied a change in the *quality* of human relationships. The Romantic version of rural life defined it as more profound and fulfilling as well as more harmonious and virtuous. Cities, on the other hand, were 'unnatural'. They separated their inhabitants from Nature, provoked social conflict and dislocation, and promoted a more superficial and alienating way of life. Such a distinction came to dominate large areas of Anglo-Saxon thought: in aesthetics, in literary criticism, in architecture and planning and, eventually, in social science.

These preconceptions about community and about urban, industrial society were imported into sociology through the writing of the German theorist Ferdinand Tönnies. Tönnies was convinced that the rise of urban industrialism represented a fundamental transformation in the *quality* of life, so that the present had to be viewed as a complete contrast with the past, rather than a continuation of it. In order to describe this contrast Tönnies coined the terms *Gemeinschaft* and *Gesellschaft* in his book with this title which was first published in 1887.

Tönnies was writing about types of *relationships*, not settlement patterns: not with urbanization as a geographical phenomenon, but with what this process was doing to patterns of human relationships. *Gemeinschaftlich* relationships were intimate, enduring and based upon a clear understanding of each individual's position in society. Personalized relationships were paramount, so that an individual's status was estimated according to *who* that person was rather than *what* that person had done. There was also very little mobility, either geographically or socially. This can be expressed sociologically by stating that Tönnies believed that in the pre-industrial world, based on *Gemeinschaft*, the status of an individual was *ascribed* (that is, relatively fixed, given at birth) rather than *achieved* (based on merit or performance). The culture of such societies was also relatively homogeneous, enforced by well-recognized moral custodians, particularly the Church and the family. Kinship was, indeed, one of the fundamental building blocks of *gemeinschaftlich* societies, so that a 'community of blood' coincided with a 'community of place' (territory) and a 'community of mind' (shared culture) to produce a greater emotional cohesion, a greater depth of sentiment, a greater continuity and therefore a more meaningful way of life.

Opposed to *Gemeinschaft* was *Gesellschaft* – usually translated as 'association'. This was everything which community was not. *Gesellschaft* refers to the large-scale, impersonal, calculative and contractual relationships which were, according to Tönnies, on the increase in the industrial world at the expense of *Gemeinschaft*. Tönnies believed that both industrialism and urbanism involved an increase in the scale and, therefore, the impersonality of society. Because of the impersonality of modern society, social relationships were predominantly regulated by contract, so that *gesellschaftlich* relationships were more calculative and more specific – more 'rational', insofar as they were 'restricted to a definite end and a definite means of obtaining it' (Tönnies, 1957, p. 192). The virtues and morality of community were therefore lost under the process of urban industrialization.

Tönnies' greatest legacy was this pair of contrasting concepts, *Gemeinschaft* and *Gesellschaft*. In order to criticize the evolving new form of society he presented them as two antithetical models of human relationships and used them to make sense of the changes sweeping across nineteenth-century Europe. His general tone was one of pessimism. He feared the breakdown of social order which the new social forces might engender, whereas *Gemeinschaft* was a source of stability in society. These ideas are very much alive today, 'loss of community' being one of the commonest complaints about modern life. Subsequent writers, however, have distorted Tönnies' original emphasis upon *Gemeinschaft* and *Gesellschaft* as types of human *relationships* by using the terms to refer to different kinds of geographical *localities* (for example, rural localities as against urban ones). And they have shifted from an emphasis on social relationships *within* society to using the two concepts as a way of classifying different kinds of total communities.

The first person to apply the concepts of *Gemeinschaft* and *Gesellschaft* to specific *localities* was Tönnies' German contemporary Georg Simmel. In his essay published in 1903 entitled 'The Metropolis and Mental Life', Simmel applied some of Tönnies' insights to modern society which, like most others in the nineteenth-century Romantic tradition, he viewed with thinly veiled hostility. Simmel set out to investigate the effects of urbanization on the culture and personality – the 'mental life' – of its inhabitants. Like Tönnies, he regarded urban society as more rational – that is, impersonal and calculative, rather than personalized and traditional – than its rural counterpart. The rationality of urban society was a result of the increased tempo of life, which is in turn brought about by the increasing division of labour. He saw the city as kaleidoscopic, an ever-changing pattern of social relationships and shifting stimuli. He also saw the city as the seat of the money economy, encouraging a purely matter-of-fact treatment of people and things so that social relationships became more impersonal and standardized. The crucial intervening factor here is the market: '. . . the interests of each party acquire an unmerciful matter-of-factness; and the intellectually calculating economic egoisms of both parties need not fear any deflection because of the imponderables of personal relationships' (Simmel, 1950, pp. 411–12). The urban mind thus becomes much more calculating. It also leads to a 'blasé' outlook – an inability to distinguish the individuality of people and things. This begins as a degree of impersonality in everyday social relationships, but develops into a demeanour of formality and reserve, and eventually culminates in concealed aversion, estrangement and alienation.

Simmel, then, presents a catalogue of urban social evils which have since passed into the prevailing assumptions which many people hold about the city. Impersonal, isolating, alienating, urban life is viewed as a temporary and unfortunate necessity from which its inhabitants will seek to escape to the comforting womb of *Gemeinschaft* at every available opportunity. It was a common reaction to the apparently dehumanizing aspects of a vast and impersonal urban culture which he summed up in a memorable metaphor:

The individual has become a cog in an enormous organization of things and powers which tear from his hands all progress, spirituality and value in order to transform them from their subjective form into the form of purely objective life . . . The metropolis is the genuine arena of this culture which outgrows all personal life (Simmel, 1950, p. 422).

Simmel, then, like Tönnies, feared the loss of community in modern life, but unlike Tönnies he related this process simply and solely to the growth of the city as a form of social organization peculiar to modern society.

This approach to urbanism reached its apotheosis thirty-five years later in a classic paper by the Chicago sociologist, Louis Wirth, entitled 'Urbanism as a Way of Life', published in the *American Journal of Sociology* in 1938. For Wirth modern society *was* urban society. Urbanism was the dominant feature of contemporary life, rather than, say, industrialism, capitalism, liberal democracy or the bureaucratic state. Because cities were the centres of progress and innovation in modern civilization, urban culture had spread out to envelop all of the population – even those physically resident in rural areas. The most remote parts of the entire world had long since been drawn into the urban 'orbit', inducing 'profound changes in virtually every phase of social life' (Wirth, 1938, p. 2). He was disturbed by this prospect. The growth of cities had brought about a fundamental break with what he termed (in a typically Romantic fashion) society's 'natural' situation: 'Nowhere has mankind been further removed from organic nature than under the conditions of life characteristic of great cities' (pp. 1–2). Three major factors underlay this fundamental break: population size, population density and the heterogeneity of the population: demographic factors that were the basis of his search for an 'ordered and coherent framework of theory' which would account for a distinctively urban way of life.

Size of population

Here Wirth largely follows the analysis of Simmel in 'The Metropolis and Mental Life'. Wirth, like Simmel, emphasizes that the increased size of population in the city promotes social differentiation – which results in the formation of separate neighbourhoods defined by class, ethnicity, etc. Wirth also agrees with Simmel that in the city 'personal mutual acquaintanceship is lacking' and that human relationships become compartmentalized or 'segmented'. This produces what Wirth calls a 'schizoid' urban mentality. Yet

this is not to say that the urban inhabitants have fewer acquaintances than rural inhabitants, for the reverse may actually be true; it means rather that in relation to the number of people whom they see and with whom they rub elbows in the course of daily life, they know a smaller proportion and of these they have less intensive knowledge (Wirth, 1938, p. 12).

Thus while social contacts in the city may indeed still be face to face, they are 'impersonal, superficial, transitory and segmented'. One consequence of this is that all urban relationships tend to be reduced to utilitarian ones – that is, people enter into relationships only for what they can get from them in pursuing their own ends. For Wirth the superficiality, the anonymity and the transitory character of urban relationships made this inevitable. One of the central paradoxes of urbanism was its tendency to create feelings of individual loneliness in the midst of huge crowds. While the city might emancipate the individual from the crushing conformities of *Gemeinschaft*, it also left the individual rootless and unintegrated into anything resembling a 'real community'.

Density

Wirth argues that the increasing concentration of people in a limited space also has a number of consequences. Some of these are environmental, such as overcrowding, pollution, etc. Others are more sociological. For example, differences between rich and poor become more visible – even though they may not be any greater than elsewhere – because of the greater numbers in each category and their geographical proximity. Wirth also argues that increasing density encourages increasing competition for scarce resources. Drawing on Darwinian notions of the 'survival of the fittest', he notes that the city seems to encourage a competitive spirit, personal aggrandizement and mutual exploitation. There are echoes here of the familiar portrayal of city life as a 'rat race' and a 'jungle'. Indeed Wirth draws upon analogies with biological ecosystems in order to emphasize the frictions and pathologies which ensue when organisms are crowded together in an enclosed and densely populated habitat.

Heterogeneity

The city is characterized by an increasingly diverse and occupationally specialized population caused by the expanding division of labour. This produces a more complex but also a less rigid social structure. A more mobile (geographically and socially), fluid urban society is the result. Within this 'fluid mass', as Wirth termed it, the individual is relatively powerless to influence the pattern of urban life and so there is a tendency for political activity to be expressed via mass movements and organized pressure groups – the *gesellschaftlich* organizations which Tönnies regarded as characteristic of modern society.

Urbanism as a way of life, in this model, then, involves three interrelated perspectives:

(a) a physical structure, comprising a population base, a technology and an ecological order;
(b) a system of social organization, that is, a social structure, a set of institutions and a typical pattern of social relationships;
(c) a set of attitudes and ideas and a constellation of personality

types who engage in distinctive forms of collective behaviour and subject to characteristic mechanisms of social control.

Thus Wirth, like Simmel before him, was suggesting that *where* we live has a profound effect on *how* we live – that geographical location influences ways of life. Thus the countryside can be contrasted with the city, not merely in a physical and environmental sense, but because they support entirely different, indeed contrasting, patterns of behaviour.

The kind of portrayal of urban life set out by Simmel and Wirth remains a powerful influence over prevailing cultural perceptions of the city. Given the belief that geographical location influences the character of human communities, it should then be possible to create a classification of communities, based upon observed differences between rural and urban ways of life and of various gradations between them. Such a classification was indeed developed in the 1930s and was known as 'the rural–urban continuum'.

The Rise and Fall of the Rural–Urban Continuum

Both Simmel and Wirth offer an approach to urban communities which is implicitly (and not so implicitly) critical of the dehumanizing aspects of urbanization and urbanism. As with Tönnies, this critique implied its opposite: an idealization of rural life. The explicit statement of this position, however, was only worked out in 1947, in the form of Robert Redfield's 'The Folk Society' (Redfield, 1947). Redfield based his conception on studies of rural communities which he had carried out in Mexico in the 1930s. Like Wirth, he was trying to develop a general, theoretical appraisal of the 'rural way of life' which would summarize existing findings from individual community studies. Redfield's notion of 'the folk society' turned out to be very reminiscent of Tönnies' *Gemeinschaft*: an emphasis upon tradition, kinship, shared culture and stable personal social relations – in other words, the very opposite of Wirth's view of urbanism. Both Redfield and Wirth shared the belief, however, that ways of life were intimately connected with geographical locations (an idea which was not, of course, a 'discovery' of theirs, but a common cultural assumption).

As early as 1929, Sorokin and Zimmerman's text, *Principles of Rural–Urban Sociology*, had attempted to organize a great deal of empirical material about American life around what they called a 'rural–urban continuum'. This lengthy passage sums up their key ideas:

Up to recent times, at least for the bulk of the city population, the city environment, as such, has been much less natural and has given much less opportunity for the satisfaction of basic human needs and fundamental impulses than the rural environment. For a clarification of this idea, let us consider the situation of the urban proletariat, its work, its occupational environment, and the essentials of its mode of living. This group works in a closed factory or shop, which has been, especially in the past, often unhygienic, ugly, unaesthetical, and unattractive to eyes, or ears, or to the organs of smell or other perceptions. They are surrounded by the kingdom of dead machinery, steel, iron, coal and oil. Enormous noises, clangs, grinds, knocks, raps, clatters and taps of machinery and tools fill their ears. Dirt, summer heat, and winter cold assail them. Such has been and still is their occupational environment to a considerable degree. The work itself is also tiresome, monotonous, mechanical, half automatic. It furnishes little, if any, creative or interesting outlet for them. It goes on monotonously day in day out, for months and years . . . Can such a city environment and manner of living satisfy these fundamental impulses and habits developed in quite a different situation and adapted to a quite different environment? The answer is no. Neither the impulses for creative activity, nor for orientation, curiosity, and novelty; nor the lust for variety and adventure; nor the physiological necessity for being in touch with nature, nor to enjoy with eyes the greenishness of the meadow, the beauties of the forest, the clear rivers, the waves of golden wheat in the fields; nor to hear the birds singing, the thunderstorm, or the mysterious calm of an evening amidst nature; these and thousands of similar phenomena have been taken from the urban man . . . In spite of the enormous improvement of the conditions of the urban labour classes in these respects, the city has a great deal of these elements of 'unnaturality' and through that stimulates dissatisfaction and disorders.

The farmer–peasant environment, on the contrary, has been much more 'natural' and much more identical with that to which man has been trained by thousands of years of preceding history. The basic impulses of man, as they have been shaped by the past, are to be satisfied much easier in the environment and by the occupational activity of the farmer. There is neither the lack of nature, nor the killing monotony of work, nor extreme specialization, nor one-sidedness. His standard of living may be as low as that of a proletarian; his house or lodging may be as bad; and yet the whole character of his structure of living is quite different and healthier and more natural (Sorokin and Zimmerman, 1929, pp. 466–7).

Using these criteria, we could not only locate any particular community on such a continuum but would also be able to read off its degree of community 'health' or pathology. By the 1950s, the urban–rural continuum had become a generally accepted way of categorizing communities and an important organizing principle in both urban and rural sociology (Frankenberg, 1965). The belief that there was something *intrinsically* different about urban and rural communities and ways of life was rarely challenged, probably because it corresponded so well to commonly held assumptions in society at large. The tendency to identify settlement types with 'ways of life' and with the presence or absence of 'community' remained a strong one.

Gradually, however, the rural–urban continuum came under attack, at first through evidence emerging from empirical studies and only later via theoretical criticism. The notion that ways of life could be linked to settlement patterns was first undermined by the American anthropologist Oscar Lewis, in his 1949 account of *Life in a Mexican Village*. The village in question, Tepoztlán, had originally been studied in the 1930s by Redfield, and had led him to formulate the concept of the 'folk society'. As we saw in Chapter 3, whereas Redfield described a homogeneous, smoothly functioning, well-integrated, contented, stable and harmonious community, Lewis found an underlying individualism, lack of cooperation and mutual suspicion, and fear, envy and distrust among the inhabitants. Such startling differences in observation were due in part to the differing preconceptions which Redfield and Lewis took with them into the field (see Bell and Newby, 1971, pp. 42–53, 75–8). For Redfield, the concept of the rural–urban continuum had influenced his expectations and affected the emphasis of his ethnographic account; Lewis had been dedicated to improving the material standards of life in Tepoztlán, and was therefore less inclined to accept a 'noble savage' view of its inhabitants; he found poverty, cruelty, disease and suffering. The Redfield/Lewis debate became something of a *cause célèbre*, and still stands today as a cautionary tale of how theory, methods and 'findings' may become intertwined in community studies. What was clear, however, was that, whatever the reality of Tepoztlán, it fell far short of ideal *Gemeinschaft* and that the conception of a rural–urban continuum had misled Redfield in many ways. It was Lewis's view of rural society which found support in subsequent studies which questioned the 'misplaced polarities' of the rural–urban continuum (for example, Gusfield, 1967; Avila, 1969).

Meanwhile doubts were emerging about 'urbanism as a way of life', too. During the 1950s, a number of community studies had established the existence of indubitably urban neighbourhoods which bore all the characteristics of settlements which ought to have been at the rural end of the continuum. In Britain, the most famous of these were the studies of Bethnal Green in East London, most notably Michael Young and Peter Willmott's *Family and Kinship in East London*, published in 1957. Here, in the heart of one of the largest cities in the world, they found, not the dehumanizing anonymity which many might have expected, but what was later to be termed an 'urban village'. Instead of a 'fluid mass', Young and Willmott found Bethnal Green to be remarkably stable and homogeneous, and kinship, they discovered, was a very important aspect of life:

Here the family does more than anything else to make local society a familiar society, filled with people who are not strangers ... Bethnal Greeners are not lonely people: whenever they go for a walk in a street, for a drink in the pub or for a row on the lake in Victoria Park, they know the faces in the crowd (Young and Willmott, 1957, p. 116).

A similar portrayal of life in Hunslet, a working-class area of Leeds, was also given by Richard Hoggart in his book, *The Uses of Literacy* (1957). In the United States, similar findings emerged from Herbert Gans's study of an Italian neighbourhood in Boston, *The Urban Villagers* (1962a). Ironically, Gans's study bore many of the hallmarks of studies carried out in Chicago by Wirth and his colleagues in the 1920s and 1930s. As one who wrote about 'the ghetto', Wirth could hardly have been unaware of the existence of 'urban villages', yet this did not sit well with the theory of 'urbanism as a way of life', nor with the notion of a rural–urban continuum. The implication of these studies of urban villages appeared to be that, as Peter Mayer put it: 'While some are born "urban" and others achieve urbanization, none can be said to have urbanization thrust upon them' (1962, p. 521).

If urban villages were difficult to square with the rural–urban continuum, so were their obverse in the countryside – the commuter villages of northern Europe and North America, which, by the

1960s, were filling up quickly with an ex-urban, 'adventitious', rural population. In Britain, for example, R. E. Pahl's study of Hertford-shire, *Urbs in Rure* (1965), showed the difficulties of fitting such settlements into the rural–urban continuum. People who *lived* in the countryside but *worked* in towns, just didn't fit at all. And even studies of wholly agricultural communities (e.g. Littlejohn, 1962; Williams, 1964) demonstrated that business rationality, endemic geographical mobility, loneliness, anonymity, class conflict, etc, were by no means absent from rural British society. Rural *Gesellschaft* combined with urban *Gemeinschaft* to undermine the cultural presup-positions and theoretical statements on which the rural–urban con-tinuum had been founded.

Thus by the mid-1960s neither the rural nor the urban end of the continuum was proving to be typical of the way of life expected of it. The desire to identify ways of life with particular localities neverthe-less remained strong. Nowhere was this more apparent than in the so-called 'myth of suburbia' which accompanied steady suburban development during the affluent 1950s and 1960s. In his book, *The Organization Man* (1957) – long before the term 'Yuppie' had been coined – William H. Whyte had portrayed American suburbia as a vast transit camp for upwardly mobile, middle-class executives and bureaucrats, concerned only with the conspicuous consumption of consumer durables, keeping up appearances with like-minded neigh-bours and hyperactively pursuing the membership of local societies and voluntary associations. Whyte also emphasized the homogeneity of suburban life: the serried ranks of identical houses, each containing a respectable family relentlessly engaging in lifestyles of crushing conformity. Such dull conformism merely reflected the tendencies of modern bureaucracy – these organization men commuted back and forth between the arid routines of the office and the bogus neighbour-liness of the housing estate. In Britain a similar stereotype was commonplace: that all suburbanites were commuters, devoted to 'keeping up with the Joneses', cleaning the family car and mowing the lawn on Sunday mornings. Wirth's isolated, anonymous urban man, it seemed, was alive and well and living in a three-bedroomed 'semi'.

How far does this stereotype conform to more systematically observed findings, and how far does suburbia in some way induce particular 'suburban' lifestyles? The 'myth of suburbia' was subjected to a thoroughgoing critique by Herbert Gans in his second community study, *The Levittowners* (1967). Gans had earlier worked with Whyte, and was concerned by the growth of an over-simplified and exaggerated conception of 'suburbanism as a way of life'. *The Levittowners* was the study of a new 'dormitory' suburb outside New York. Gans found that life there was far more varied than the myth of suburban conformity would suggest. There was little evidence of overt conformism, or of deliberately changed behaviour in order to be more like the perceived behaviour of neighbours. Instead Gans emphasized the diversity and heterogeneity of Levittown. What shaped and moulded life there

was not the *pre-occupancy* aspirations of the residents but rather a complex process of external initiatives and *subsequent* internal transformation that produced organizations and institutions which reflected the backgrounds and interests of the majority of the population (Gans, 1967, p. 141, italics added).

Gans's findings were broadly confirmed by Bennett Berger in his study of suburban Detroit, *Working-Class Suburb* (1969). Berger showed that large numbers of unquestionably working-class people had migrated to the suburbs in the United States and that although suburbia may appear from the *outside* to be uniformly middle class, close inspection soon reveals that this is by no means the case. More recent work by Samuel Kaplan in his book, *The Dream Deferred* (1977), has revealed the extent to which American suburbia hides quite surprising degrees of poverty, unemployment and multiple deprivation.

In Britain, suburban community studies have been relatively few and far between, but again the evidence supports the view that there is no necessary causal connection between a shift in the location of residence to suburbia and the adoption of a particular lifestyle. Willmott and Young, for example, in the 'sequel' to their Bethnal Green study, found that close-knit social networks of the kind which they had found in Bethnal Green could be maintained *after* the move to suburban Woodford via telephone calls and regular visits in the family car (Willmott and Young, 1960). Colin Bell, in his study of a middle-class housing estate in Swansea, *Middle Class Families* (1968), also demonstrated how these ties could be maintained over very long distances indeed. In both cases these studies showed how extensive geographical, and even social, mobility did not necessarily involve the dissolution of *Gemeinschaft*-like social relations, even though it did, of course, often attenuate their *local* bases. Community, in other words, was becoming dissociated from locality.

Community Theory Reconsidered

Findings such as these, from a whole range of urban, suburban and rural community studies, tended to leave the study of community in something of a state of turmoil. It was clear that the rural–urban continuum simply did not fit the empirical data. Moreover, it was less than clear precisely *what* it was that was being studied. Some studies took localities as their object of study, and described all aspects of the local society and economy; others were concerned with local social systems, but where close-knit ties were not the whole of social life; others were less concerned with locality than with the quality of social relationships – with 'communion', whether or not this had a local basis. The major problem was that the rural–urban continuum simply ran all three aspects together. It *assumed* that a particular kind of locality fostered particular kinds of social relationships, and that 'communion' was a distinctively *rural* characteristic. Normative assumptions had influenced empirical description.

These assumptions, however, remain very common among the population at large. Those who sought to dismantle the rural–urban continuum therefore faced an uphill task in taking on 'common sense' evaluations of community. They were also faced with the difficult task of replacing the rural–urban continuum with something more adequate. For whatever the now manifest inadequacies of the rural–urban continuum, it possessed an intuitive appeal to many people which rendered it extraordinarily difficult to dislodge. No one would wish to suggest that there are *no* differences between, say, the rural and urban populations. The difficulty was how to explain these differences without sliding back into a way of thinking which flew in the face of all the evidence.

In the search for a new theory of community, two seminal contributions were Gans's paper entitled, 'Urbanism and Suburbanism as Ways of Life' (1962b), and Pahl's 'The Rural–Urban Continuum' (1966). Both took up the question as to how far locality (*where* one lives) influences ways of life (*how* one lives). Gans's paper is a critique of both Wirth and Whyte in the light of more recent studies, including his own. He argues that lifestyles are not determined by locality, but by two other variables – *social class* and *stage in the family cycle*. Gans finds social class (which he interprets in terms of income levels) the best predictor of what induces an individual to *choose* where (and how) to live. Other things being equal, the higher the social class of an individual, the greater the degree of choice over housing, and therefore *where* to live. Stage in the family cycle is also important because it is the best indicator of the area of choice which is most likely *within* any given social class. For example, middle-class families may possess the income to join the ranks of owner-occupiers. But young couples with small children may lack the capital to purchase anything other than a new house on a modern estate because that is the type of housing for which they can raise the largest proportion of the price. The housing market therefore acts like a series of sieves through which families with appropriate resources fall to their appropriate place in the urban or suburban structure (see the comments on housing classes below).

Thus observed similarities between residents of the same geographical area are not *caused* merely by living in the same locality. They are caused by the actions of the housing market, which tends to allocate individuals from a similar social class at a similar stage in the family cycle to similar types of housing in certain districts. It is not 'locality' which causes this; rather, it is the *outcome of a series of constraints on choice* of where to live which differs for different individuals. As Pahl puts it in his paper:

Whether we call the process acting on the local community 'urbanization', 'differentiation', 'modernization', 'mass society' or whatever, it is clear that it is not so much *communities* that are acted upon as groups and individuals at particular places in the social structure. Any attempt to tie patterns of social relationship to specific geographical milieux is a singularly fruitless exercise (Pahl, 1966, p. 238).

Of much greater importance, to Pahl, is the impact of *national* changes upon *local* areas: '. . . the basic situation of conflict or stress that can be observed from the most highly urbanized metropolitan region to the most remote and isolated peasant village' (1970, p. 286). This approach was eventually to produce a change in perspectives on the sociology of community, although, for reasons outlined below, this took some time to occur.

Relating community to constraints on choice of housing did, however, provide insights into urban processes which began to influence urban studies in the late 1960s and 1970s. For example, John Rex and Robert Moore, in their book, *Race, Community and Conflict* (1967), explained the growth of quasi-ghetto concentrations of coloured immigrants in inner city areas by emphasizing competition for scarce and desired types of housing. Rex devised a number of what he called 'housing classes' in order to explain the formation of socially distinctive urban neighbourhoods and communities and in order to explain how the social structure of urban society is related to the spatial structure of the city. The pros and cons of the concept of housing classes have subsequently been quite hotly debated (for a summary, see Saunders, 1983), since they raised issues not only of academic analysis, but of public policy.

Once Gans and Pahl had demonstrated how constraints on choice of housing successfully explained the links between locality and lifestyle, there was little left of the concept of community. It was difficult to see how the study of any locality, then, could be worthwhile for its own sake. But, in retrospect, Pahl's statement can be seen to be something of an over-statement. For geographical milieux *may* help to influence social relationships because they, too, constrain people's access to one another and to scarce material resources – a point which Pahl himself was later to develop in writing about urban inequality (Pahl, 1970), and which he vividly demonstrated in a more recent study of the Isle of Sheppey (Pahl, 1984). The Sheppey study shows that certain social relationships and institutions are constrained in such a way as to render them locality-based: that there may indeed be a 'local social system' – a predominantly self-contained community where spatial factors may have some effect on social relations – although whether this is so or not, and to what extent, are matters that need to be investigated empirically. In Sheppey, high rates of unemployment and consequent constraints on material resources meant that many of the inhabitants could not escape from the spatial constraints imposed upon them. But it is important to note here that Pahl does not attempt to classify Sheppey as 'rural' or 'urban' or to deduce its characteristics from such a judgement. He merely notes that the relatively deprived are trapped in a locality which then sets limits upon the social and economic resources available to them.

A similar approach to the study of communities had been taken by Margaret Stacey as early as 1969. If institutions were locality-based *and* interrelated, she argued, there might well be a *local social system* that could be studied sociologically; in particular it would be possible to examine systematically:

(i) the establishment and maintenance of a local social system; (ii) local conditions where no such system can be expected; (iii) some circumstances under which an existing system might be modified or destroyed; (iv) certain interrelations between systems and their parts; (v) the interaction of local and national systems (Stacey, 1969, p. 139).

Stacey is thus questioning rather than assuming the extent to which locality still remains an important principle of organization in modern society: in other words, do localities matter? To what extent are local social systems self-sustaining and autonomous? Or have all such local social systems been swallowed up in the national level changes to which Pahl directed our attention?

The initial response was to concede that perhaps communities did no longer matter, at least not to the extent that they once did. During the 1970s community studies thus went out of fashion, leaving a theoretical vacuum left by the dismantling of the rural–urban continuum. The lengthy and often tedious attempts to define 'community' too, had had some effect; why bother to study something which could not be defined? There was mounting impatience, too, with the non-cumulative and sometimes downright idiosyncratic nature of many community studies – communities were either simply different from each other, it seemed, or, as in the case of the Redfield/Lewis debate, merely the projection of the preconceptions of different researchers on to their 'findings'. But more than anything else there was the suspicion that local communities were not worth studying because the factors which determined people's lives were no longer to be found locally. The decisions governing our everyday lives had, it seemed, now shifted decisively to the national, or even the international, level. Community studies simply appeared less *relevant*.

In stressing the need to relate the national to the local, Pahl had been trying to bolster the study of localities. But the effect turned out to be almost the opposite. The work on 'housing classes' had similar unintended consequences. Rex and Moore's attempt to

understand social relations, especially ethnic relations, in a particular
locality (Sparkbrook in Birmingham), through the study of housing
allocation, was extraordinarily successful: *Race, Community and Conflict* not only became a sociological classic but had some influence on
race relations legislation in the late 1960s. It was clear from their
study, however, that in order to understand fully changes in Sparkbrook it was necessary to look at the system of housing allocation
across the city of Birmingham as a whole. The character of Sparkbrook, Handsworth and other areas with high Black and Asian
populations had to be related to other areas like, say, Solihull and
Sutton Coldfield with very different ethnic and class composition
populations. The housing market and the system of council housing
allocation (among other things) was producing both Sparkbrook and
Solihull. The next step, therefore, was to look at the forces and
agents involved in housing distribution as a whole: also the planners,
the council officials and politicians, the building society managers,
private landlords, and developers who between them 'managed' the
allocation of housing resources. The study of 'housing classes' thus
led to the study of city-wide 'urban managerialism' (Pahl, 1970;
Dennis, 1970, 1972; Davies, 1972). From this it was only a further
short step to look at the constraints upon these 'urban managers'
themselves, especially the encompassing role of the State (Cockburn,
1978). A theory of the State was therefore needed (Castells, 1976).
Very soon, the logic of this kind of argument drove some to insist
that an examination of the political economy of the capitalist State
was necessary before it was possible to investigate, say, the lifestyles
of the inhabitants of a particular suburban housing estate! But since
there is no generally accepted macro-theory of the relationship
between State and society available in sociology, such abstract debates
could not be resolved as a prelude to empirical research. The result:
the demise of community studies and a decline in empirical research
in this field.

As early as 1964 the American sociologist Maurice Stein had
hinted at these problems in his book, *The Eclipse of Community*
(though not the eclipse of community *studies*). Stein's book was a
synthesis of over thirty years of American community studies, from
which he deduced a decline in local autonomy as a result of three
interrelated processes – urbanization, industrialization and bureauc-
ratization:

Community ties become increasingly dependent upon centralized authorities and agencies in all areas of life. On the other hand, personal loyalties decrease their range with the successive weakening of national ties, regional ties, family ties and finally ties to a coherent image of one's self (Stein, 1964, p. 329).

Stein suggested then that a set of vertical ties to centralized decision-making bodies are replacing the 'horizontal ties' of local autonomy (cf. Vidich and Bensman, 1958; Warren, 1963).

If the character of any given locality is indissolubly linked to the character of society as a whole, defining the latter is a necessary step to understanding the former. But it was nearly a decade before a soundly based appreciation of the role of community studies re-emerged. Much of the basic thinking was made by writers working within a Marxist tradition, particularly David Harvey and Manuel Castells. Their insistence on the primacy of national (and even international) determinants of life in local communities is well captured in this comment by Castells:

The fundamental point is this: everything described by Wirth as 'urbanism' is in fact the cultural expression of capitalist industrialization, the emergence of the market economy and the process of rationalization of modern society (Castells, 1968, p. 38).

For Castells, the economic forces of advanced capitalist society destroy the autonomy of local communities, rendering the closely knit urban villages of Bethnal Green and elsewhere 'vague recollections'. Hence it is necessary to penetrate beyond the visible structure of urban communities and investigate the economic factors upon which they are dependent. Harvey's approach is very similar:

Many investigators, after a ritualistic bow to the notion of totality which asserts that cities are not just statistical aggregates of things and activities, quickly reduce their problem (in the name of competence or tractability) to the analysis of things and activities. The insights gained from such investigations are not to be dismissed – in fact they are invaluable raw material out of which we may fashion a conception of urbanism. But their net import is that we learn to deal . . . with problems *in* the city rather than *of* the city.

Urbanism has to be regarded as a set of social relationships which reflects the relationships established throughout society as a whole. Further, these relationships have to express the laws whereby urban phenomena are structured, regulated and constructed (Harvey, 1973, pp. 303–4).

Harvey, then, is arguing that problems familiarly regarded as 'urban' (for example, slums, poverty, crime, etc) are not peculiarly urban at all, but general social problems made more manifest in an urban setting because the numbers involved are so much greater. It follows from this that both Harvey and Castells seek to bring together two hitherto separate lines of theoretical analysis into one: a theory of social development (which they, as Marxists, would both locate in the capitalist mode of production) and a theory of the social production and organization of space. Harvey's book, *Social Justice and the City* (1973), attempted to do this by investigating the allocative mechanisms of land use and their consequences in terms of distributional justice for the various sections of the urban population. In addition, both Harvey and Castells see a connection between the allocation of space in the city, the formation of homogeneous urban neighbourhoods, and the formation of urban social movements which compete for the distribution of scarce resources.

They were thus critically questioning something which the rural–urban continuum had taken for granted: that there was such a thing as a sociologically meaningful definition of 'urban'. (One of Castells's most celebrated papers was even entitled, 'Is there an urban sociology?' (Castells, 1968). They were sceptical of the view that it was possible to delineate a specifically 'urban' theory of social life (and, by extension, a 'rural' theory – see Newby, 1980). Instead, it was necessary to generate broadly based theories of socio-economic development; to demonstrate how such development influenced the spatial form of society; and to observe the political consequences that ensued in the shape of urban social movements. 'Urbanism' was thus viewed as an *effect* rather than a *cause* of the living conditions of urban inhabitants. The causes had to be sought elsewhere – in the more general (economic) processes affecting society as a whole (see also Pickvance, 1976; Dear and Scott, 1981; Friedland, 1965).

There were parallels here with the general development of more abstract levels of theorizing we saw above when discussing housing classes and urban managerialism. Many of the urban social movements constituting what David Donnison (1973) was to call 'the micro-politics of the city' – tenants associations, squatters movements, environmental protection groups, etc – sprang up, indeed, in direct opposition to the intervention of the state and the manipulations of 'urban managers'. They also provoked – and were provoked by – a sense of 'communion' (see Cowley *et al.*, 1977). Although often somewhat ephemeral, it provided a dynamic of local protest movements and an antidote to political apathy and fatalism, which became known as 'community action'. It did not, however, leave an enduring residue of political organization which could counter the persisting territorial injustices of urban economic development (cf., for instance, Hindess, 1971; Bell and Newby, 1976; Saunders, 1978; and Harrison, 1984).

The rural–urban continuum had thus been an attempt to classify communities as discrete entities and to describe them as *objects of study* in their own right so as to provide a catalogue of the lifestyles of particular localities. But this approach simply seemed a less meaningful level of analysis by the 1970s, as the new urban sociology that followed the work of Harvey and Castells argued. A much more fruitful approach has been to look at community studies as a *method* for the study of social change. Localities are studied, not for their own sake, but as a method of obtaining data on those processes of social change for which the locality is the *appropriate* level of analysis, and a complete understanding of these processes may take the analyst far beyond the confines of a particular locality. Thus more recent community studies have attempted to perform the tricky task of simultaneously paying attention to broader processes of change and development, while investigating their specific local effects in detail. The next section takes three specific examples of this approach.

Over-urbanization, Under-urbanization and De-urbanization

The studies we will examine are not selected simply because they are detailed descriptions of particular localities and communities. The intention, rather, is not merely to say something about the localities themselves, but also about wider processes of social and economic development. The community study is used to look at society in *microcosm*, to look at major social changes at the grass roots, as it were.

Over-urbanization in the Third World

At the beginning of this chapter it was argued that the growth of concern for 'community' arose out of the new industrial capitalism of nineteenth-century Europe. This produced rapid urbanization, and a recognition among most observers that a qualitative change was occurring in the fundamental character of society. During the twentieth century, the rate of urbanization has slowed down considerably in all the major industrialized societies and, in many cases, has gone into reverse. In the Third World, however, the rate of urbanization has been very rapid indeed and shows few signs of abating. This raises the question of whether the Third World today is merely experiencing the same kinds of development which occurred in Europe and North America over a century ago. Can, therefore, the ideas of Tönnies, Simmel and Wirth be applied to contemporary Calcutta, Mexico City or Lagos?

Certain superficial comparisons can be drawn:

Two visions haunt the intellectuals who view the urbanization process in the Third World. In the first vision the cities are seen as 'enclaves' surrounded by a hostile peasantry. In these enclaves foppish elites play luxurious games with the power and wealth they have inherited or created since Independence. In the other vision the cities are seen as 'beach-heads', centres of modernization which act as the catalysts for economic growth, the centres from which the benefits of modernization flow outwards to revitalize the stagnating agricultural sector (McGee, 1971, p. 5).

McGee believes that both visions overstate their case because they are based on unreal assumptions about Third World urbanization. The rate of urbanization is, indeed, phenomenal, but it is also very varied, particularly in Latin America where, in many countries, between a third and a half of the entire population live in one metropolitan centre. Mexico City is now generally regarded as the largest city in the world.

Researchers entering the *barrios* and *bidonvilles* of Third World cities evinced the same intrepid spirit which characterized Victorian social reformers in the East End of London a century ago. Both sets of investigators assumed that they were observing 'modernization' and that 'urban villages' with their own distinctive sub-cultures were in the process of being created. The way of life of these new city-dwellers soon became labelled, by Oscar Lewis, a 'culture of poverty' (Lewis, 1961). The culture of the shanty towns, he asserted, inhibited the adoption of 'modern' values, particularly the kind of enterprising spirit which was needed if the poor were to improve their deprived living conditions, as they had eventually done in the West.

During the late 1960s, however, the view that Third World development consisted of merely following a path already blazed by the industrial economies became increasingly untenable. The process of urbanization was seen not as an index of 'modernization' but as a symbol of Third World *dependency* inherent in 'neo-colonial' trade with the West. In the most celebrated attack on modernization theory – that of Frank (1967, 1969) – metropolitan growth in Third World countries is the result of their invasion by foreign capital, which has produced and sustains today a situation of economic and political dependence which hinders indigenous development. The urban centres of the Third World therefore represent a form of capitalist development, but one which is 'clientelist' – dependent upon the dominant external power of the developed world. These urban centres in turn exploit their rural hinterlands: local elites in urban centres establish dominance over the surrounding rural areas, and are themselves dependent upon the industrial nations for their privileged economic position and their political power. Manufacturing industry remains relatively underdeveloped, while an overblown service sector becomes the basis of the 'modern', urban economy. The end product is urbanization *without* industrialization. In contrast to nineteenth-century Europe, many Third World countries therefore appear *over-urbanized*: they appear to support a much larger urban population than either their level of industrialization, or their provision of infrastructure, would warrant. The Third World shanty town has thus become a potent symbol of this distorted form of development.

Recent research into the urbanization process in the Third World suggests that it is much more complex than Frank's model allows for. The huge urban-based service sector, for instance, is highly dependent on a rural, agrarian base, but the penetration of capitalist social relations into agriculture in turn displaces the peasantry in vast numbers and propels them to the cities, contributing to the process of over-urbanization (Goodman and Redclift, 1981). The result is a polarization of the urban population between a 'modern', relatively affluent section and an underemployed 'lumpenproletariat'. Studies of the shanty towns have shown the consequences of this process (Roberts, B., 1978) and emphasize the qualities of enterprise and inventiveness which are required in order to survive in such a society. Networks of kin and neighbours devise complex strategies of survival which involve a complex fitting together of component incomes gained from both the 'formal' and the 'informal' sectors of the economy: evidence not of a fatalistic 'culture of poverty' but of an enterprising capacity to adapt to rapidly changing economic circumstances (Lomnitz, 1977).

Under-urbanization in Eastern Europe

In Eastern Europe, planned industrial development has forced sociologists to address issues at the macro-social level, even when studying a particular locality. In state socialist countries, therefore, theoretical issues raised at the end of the last section have long been on the agenda. Recent work on regional inequalities, especially in Hungary and Czechoslovakia, has drawn attention to *under-urbanization* as a characteristic feature of these and other Eastern European societies. Konrad and Szelenyi, for example (two Hungarian writers), have drawn a number of contrasts between this situation and the over-urbanization typical of many Third World societies:

Over-urbanization in developing countries is produced by the low level of industrial development and an insufficiency of employment. Under-urbanization in Eastern Europe, on the other hand, is the result of excessive industrialization at the expense of the infrastructure. The high rate of industrial investment could only be assured by central planning which made the growth of the infrastructure dependent upon economic policy rather than demand, and withdrew infrastructure products in short supply from the market, distributing them as administrative rewards, independent of wages ... Since housing and the products of the infrastructure were not considered commodities, wages and salaries could be fixed at a much lower level than in countries at a similar stage of economic growth. On principle, wages did not include the price of infrastructural products and services, since the State provided these for all wage-earners as an additional allowance. The proportion of industrial investment was too high, that in investment goods too low; relatively little housing was built out of State resources. Most of those finding new employment could therefore not be allotted dwellings through administrative channels, and their income was too small to allow them to obtain their own housing on the limited open market (Konrad and Szelenyi, 1974, p. 207).

This unbalanced form of industrial development does not allow workers to decide for themselves whether they will move closer to their new industrial employment or remain in the countryside and travel daily into the towns and cities: in practice, since they have little option other than to reconcile themselves to the latter, the journey to work, Konrad and Szelenyi argue, remains a major cause of social tensions (see also Szelenyi, 1984).

The strategy of industrial development adopted in Eastern European societies necessarily results in a conflict with demands for investment in the urban infrastructure (especially housing) which the process of urbanization demands. The result is a form of 'pseudo-urbanization', as regional planners seek to curb urban growth so that scarce investment funds will not be diverted from industry. Urban housing then becomes much sought after, and the higher social strata possess a much better chance of obtaining it:

The categories of vertical or hierarchical social stratification can [therefore] be applied in order to differentiate between village and urban society. Families of a lower social status live in villages and those of a higher social status in towns; the bulk of those in villages work with their hands . . . The slope of the urbanization curve in industrializing Hungarian society therefore corresponds to that of social stratification (Konrad and Szelenyi, 1977, p. 161)

Under-urbanization therefore produces an uneven distribution of the burden of industrialization, and does so in a manner which is generally socially regressive — despite the egalitarian principles on which regional planning policy is supposed to be based.

The disadvantaged rural dwellers seek to redress their deprivation by supplementing their earnings from urban employment through the cultivation of domestic smallholdings. A micro-agriculture therefore emerges alongside the large-scale state farms:

It is a characteristic of under-urbanization that the growth in industrial employment exceeds the growth in the capacity of towns to absorb population. Thus an increasing number are forced to have their domicile in villages, though they are employed in industry . . . Commuters are mainly peasants who are restratified for eight hours a day. These mainly semi-skilled and unskilled workers make up the 'new working class' . . . Following eight hours' work and long hours spent waiting and travelling, they are often met at the station by their wives, carrying two hoes, and they go off for another four or five hours' work on land allotted to them as share-croppers by the cooperative or to their own household plots, which in the course of the years have been turned into extremely intensively cultivated smallhold-ings (Konrad and Szelenyi, 1977, p. 161).

In this sense the worker-peasant forms a kind of 'transitional class' (Kolankiewicz, 1980) which lives in two economic systems simul-taneously. This kind of commuter population does not fit into the rural–urban continuum at all easily. Through policies of giving priority to industrial investment, under-urbanization on a massive scale has been created in Eastern Europe.

De-urbanization in Britain

Our third example is one which might be labelled 'work in progress'. Since the late 1970s, British sociologists and geographers have become increasingly concerned with the economic and spatial restruc-turing which has become intensified under the impact of economic recession (see, for example, Massey, 1984; Gregory and Urry, 1985). At the demographic level, there is a growing 'population turnaround' in British society: the continuing outflow of the population from major urban centres and their movement to small towns and rural areas (Fothergill and Gudgin, 1982). But these population move-ments are part of a more fundamental process of technological change and economic restructuring. Urry (1984), for example, argues that the spatial restructuring of capitalist production and of civil society has given *local* systems of social stratification a new impor-tance and that in rural areas these local systems cannot be seen in terms of the older encounter between a new middle class and an old established (agrarian) rural class structure. He goes on to argue that the stratification structure of any locality (whether formally urban or rural) is the 'inter-dependent effect of [several] mutually modifying forms of structural determination', but especially of the complex overlap between diverse spatial divisions of labour (Urry, 1984, p. 45). One important process of contemporary change is 'ruraliza-tion' of industrial/urban relations. This process reinforces others; together, they fragment and decompose established industrial classes and set in train other economic and social changes.

Earlier versions of this restructuring thesis employed a rather unfortunate geological metaphor. In 1978, Massey, for instance, wrote that we take as starting-point the historically dominant processes of production, and define the uneven geographical distribution of the conditions for accumulation in relation to those processes. In general terms, this means beginning with those elements of accumulation which both have an effect on the rate of profit and are unevenly spatially distributed . . .

One schematic way of approaching this as a historical process is to conceive it as a series of rounds of new investment, in each of which a new spatial division of labour is evolved. In fact, of course, the process of change is much more diversified and incremental, though certainly there are periods of radical re-direction. In general, however, any new form of spatial division of labour will typify only the more advanced sectors of production, and may well vary between each sector. Between rounds, in other words, conditions will change . . .

This new distribution of economic activity, produced by the evolution of a new division of labour, will be overlaid on, and combined with, the pattern produced in previous periods by different forms of spatial division. The combination of successive layers will produce effects which themselves vary over space, contributing to a new form and geographical distribution of inequality in the conditions of production, as a basis for the next round of investment. A spatial division of labour is suggested, on the contrary, in which the social and economic structure of any given local area will be a complex result of the combination of that area's succession of roles within the series of wider, national and international, spatial divisions of labour (Massey, 1978, pp. 115–16).

The present emerging spatial division of labour, then, does not characterize every branch of production: it arises from the interaction of new and advanced sectors of production with an inherited, and different, spatial division of labour. From this articulation springs a series of effects which can be empirically researched. To that extent, her use of a geological metaphor is valid: it is, however, simply a metaphor, not a theoretical construct or a necessary part of her analysis. Like all metaphors, however, it is restrictive as well as illuminating. The 'laying down' and subsequent transformations of successive phases of productive relations and the emergence of distinctive local and regional cultures as a result of the interaction of all of these over time obviously helps to illuminate much of the complex and bewildering diversity of local social structures 'on the ground'. Such an approach also draws attention to the links between a particular locality and broader regional, national and international contexts, in contra-distinction to earlier locality studies which tended to take particular localities as isolated units.

The problem is that such research can still leave us with a set of studies of particular localities rather than an analysis which is focused on the general processes which underlie all these local instances of evolution and development.

Many recent empirical studies of localities are aware of these dangers (see, for example, Murgatroyd *et al.*, 1984), and emphasize the ways in which 'the spatial unevenness of productive relations coalesces with the local particularities of other dimensions of the social structure to generate characteristic forms of political expressions in such communities' (Rees, 1985, p. 5). The revival of locality studies is long overdue. But it will now have to be much more sophisticated than the 'community studies' of the 1950s and 1960s were, for today – in conditions of economic recession and large-scale industrial restructuring – it is plainly inadequate to treat local responses to these national and international changes simply as 'community' phenomena: as *local* political movements, or as changes within an abstracted community. The general processes informing all these diverse responses can no longer be taken as a mere 'background'.

Conclusion

Despite the fact that community has been one of sociology's core ideas, the history of writing on the subject has been marked more by confusion than by conceptual clarity. Community as 'normative prescription' has all too often distorted 'empirical description', with the result that no general sociology of community is yet available. It has taken a long time to disentangle ideas about community from prejudices about particular settlement patterns, and although the concept of community has been considerably clarified as a result, the work, in many ways, has only just begun. There is no tidy classification, for example, with which to replace the rural–urban continuum, only a number of lines of inquiry on the relationship, if any, between locality, social relationships and a sense of identity.

Yet the nature of community continues to be of both a practical and ideological importance to most of us. No study has yet demonstrated the absence of *any* local relationship from most people's lives. Modern media of communication and transport have *not* rendered local ties completely obsolete, and we have a long way to go before we are all absorbed into an amorphous 'global village'. There still remains, therefore, an empirical basis to the local community which is worthy of sociological attention. Moreover, it should be apparent that studying the community enables us to examine major processes of social change: not only the structural effects of macro-social changes upon particular localities, but even the gap that often exists between our ideals and aspirations and the real world.

The constraints of locality have been gradually eroded, but the ideology of community remains strong and the desire to realize an idealized notion of community continues to inspire visions of a better life in the future. Often, though, these dreams divert attention from more pressing and more significant social issues – our preoccupation with the intimacy of community often distracts attention away from the wider societal forces which shape our lives. In a provocative book, the American writer Richard Sennett queries this preoccupation with community. Our attempts to establish 'real' communities, he argues, represent what he calls 'destructive *Gemeinschaft*' and a 'tyranny of intimacy'.

The refusal to deal with, absorb, and exploit reality outside the parochial scale is in one sense a universal human desire, being a simple fear of the unknown. Community feeling formed by the sharing of impulses has the special role of reinforcing the fear of the unknown, converting claustrophobia into an ethical principle.

The term *Gemeinschaft* meant, originally, the full disclosure of feeling to others; historically it has come at the same time to mean a community of people. These two taken together make *Gemeinschaft* a special social group in which open emotional relations are possible as opposed to groups in which partial, mechanical, or emotionally indifferent ones prevail . . . This is the peculiar sectarianism of a secular society. It is the result of converting the immediate experience of sharing with others into a social principle.

Unfortunately, large-scale forces in society may psychologically be kept at a distance, but do not therefore go away (Sennett, 1977, pp. 310–11).

Our concern for community, therefore, actually prevents us developing a better understanding of macro-social forces which are shaping modern society:

Localism and local autonomy are becoming widespread political creeds, as though the experience of power relations will have more human meaning the more intimate the scale – even though the actual structures of power grow ever more into an international system. Community becomes a weapon against society, whose great vice is now seen to be its impersonality. But a community of power can only be an illusion in a society like that of the industrial West, one in which stability has been achieved by a progressive extension to the international scale of structures of economic control. In sum, the belief in direct human relations on an intimate scale has seduced us from converting our understanding of the realities of power into guides for our own political behaviour. The result is that the forces of domination or inequity remain unchallenged (Sennett, 1977, p. 339).

The long tradition of sociological writing has always used the concept of community to say something, however indirectly, about the human condition in the modern world. It has always emphasized the relationship between community and society. Now we need to become more aware of the ways in which our apparently 'private' lives within the small circle of the family and the locality in which we live are themselves shaped by wider structural forces and by cultural values which derive from the public spheres of our society and affect all who live in it.

8   Work, Industry and Organizations

Work and Employment

Work is central in our culture. When someone asks us 'What do you do?', they really mean 'What work do you do?' When a woman is asked 'Do you work?', what is meant is 'Are you doing a paid job?' Yet many people without a paid job work at other kinds of productive activities. Women, notably, perform an unpaid 'double shift' in the home as housekeepers and mothers. To confine the term 'work' to paid employment therefore restricts it far too narrowly. There are many other kinds of work, some of which can take more time and energy than we put into our paid employment: from voluntary work to working in the garden or repairs to the house or the car.

In other cultures, work is not as highly valued as this. Some peoples value leisure more, and work only as much as they need to in order to provide basic necessities. 'Why should we work', Kalahari Bushmen say, 'when God has provided so many mongongo nuts?' (Lee, 1979).

'Work' can refer to any physical and mental activities which transform materials into a more useful form, provide or distribute goods or services to others, and extend human knowledge and understanding. We cannot, however, distinguish work from its various opposites – 'leisure', 'idleness', 'play' – solely by reference to activities. Almost any activity *can* be work, and many of them, if performed for their own sake, are considered to be recreation, play or leisure – the antithesis of work. Some people play games, for example, to earn an income for themselves and to provide entertainment for others. Others play the same games – football, cricket, tennis, darts, snooker and so on simply for pleasure and recreation.

So, in industrial society work activities are instrumental activities directed either towards meeting one's own needs or those of one's family, household, or community, and/or towards securing the means by which such needs can be met. Work, in our society, involves providing goods or services for others for which others are willing to *pay*, and providing goods and services for which payment would otherwise have to be made. 'Any action on nature, people or ideas intended to increase their value for future use can be defined as work. The opposite of work thus defined, is not leisure, but consumption, when we use up value by doing things for their intrinsic satisfaction' (Roberts, K., *et al.*, 1984, p. 241).

These distinctions still leave us with uncertainties as to whether we should classify some activities as 'work' or non-work. One major source of such difficulties is the fact that, for some people – artists and musicians, for example, sportsmen and women, craftworkers, or scientists and scholars – their paid work, their job, provides great intrinsic rewards, sometimes so great that they would be glad to do the work for its own sake even if no remuneration was involved. Similarly work in the garden or 'do-it-yourself' jobs in the house may be enjoyed: they are seen as a 'hobby'. Indeed, almost all jobs, even the most repetitive and apparently unrewarding, can provide some satisfactions for those who do them.

Thus Baldamus has described the 'traction' associated with many repetitive jobs, the 'relative satisfaction . . . of being pulled along by the inertia inherent in a particular activity. The experience is pleasant and may therefore function as a relief from the tedium. It usually appears to be associated, though not always, with a feeling of reduced effort, relative to actual or imagined situations where it is difficult to maintain continuity of performance' (Baldamus, 1961, p. 59). Similarly, in recounting his own experience of highly repetitive work in a small group, Roy described how though no satisfaction could be found in the tasks themselves, they could be made more tolerable by developing games which broke up the monotonous and unending sequence of tasks (Roy, 1960).

The same sorts of definitional problems, and variations in the subjective significance of what are objectively the same tasks, occur outside paid employment. Cooking a meal for one's friends involves work-tasks, for example, but may be experienced as pleasure both in relation to the activities themselves and because of the anticipation of an enjoyable social and gastronomic occasion to follow. Such satisfactions are more likely to occur if the tasks involved have been freely undertaken and if they represent a change from normal patterns of work. In contrast, the regular provision of meals for a household, a normal recurrent domestic task, is characterized by constraint and repetitiveness, and is much more unambiguously 'work'. The boundaries between work and non-work, therefore, whether that is seen as leisure, play, idleness or consumption, may sometimes be difficult if not impossible to establish.

The term 'work' is ambiguous, too, in everyday language, sometimes referring to a paid job, sometimes, more widely, to a range of activities and contexts which may not be sharply demarcated from leisure or play. It is the more general meaning which will be emphasized here. In advanced industrial societies *employment*, including self-employment, is the most important context within which work takes place. It is the most significant economically; whatever the social value placed on work for which no pay is received (domestic work, for example; or do-it-yourself activities), paid work is the source of the major part of the Gross National Product. (Unpaid work within the household, however, adds some 35–40 per cent to the GNP.) Paid work is also crucially important socially, because so much else – people's life-chances, their lifestyles, their world-views – all tend to be related to occupation.

The Social Organization of Work

Comparisons across societies, historical periods and cultures, and in particular comparisons with pre-industrial traditional societies, demonstrate that work can be socially organized in very different ways from those with which we are familiar and that employment can be a relatively unimportant context for work, if indeed it can be found at all. In many societies work is, or was, inextricably interwoven with many other aspects of life – family, kinship and household activities and relations, magical and religious ceremonies and rituals, political and military relationships and actions. Thus, for example, Malinowski has described how the cultivation of vegetables by the Trobriand Islanders was regulated at each stage by the *towosi* (magician), whose authority ensured the coordination of the various tasks and the maintenance of adequate standards in matters like the fencing of plots. The distribution of agricultural production similarly was not a question of market forces but determined by two sorts of obligations, those 'imposed by rules of kinship and relationship-in-law, and the dues and tributes paid to the chief'. The activities of fishing, the building of houses or canoes, or big trading expeditions were similarly 'dependent upon the social power of the chief and the influence of the respective magicians. In all of them the quantity of the produce, the nature of the work and the manner in which it is carried out . . . are highly modified by the social organization of the tribe and by their magical belief' (Malinowski, 1985, p. 18). Work in such a society was not something clearly demarcated from other activities and relationships, to be undertaken for a set number of hours in a special place, as employment tends to be in highly industrialized societies.

The peasant household, the crucial institution in many societies, illustrates further the way in which work could scarcely be separated from every other aspect of life. In French peasant families, the allocation of work reflected positions within the family: the contributions of husband and wife, together with any help available from grandparents, children, other single relatives, and possibly servants, were necessary for the carrying out of daily tasks; certain activities could require reciprocal help between households; while a more extended family grouping might be involved on important social occasions. In such settings it is not possible to draw a sharp line between domestic work and agricultural work, nor to demarcate production for use from production for sale (Segalen, 1985; see also Littler, 1985, and Pahl, 1984).

In contrast to such traditional rural settings, one of the major transformations involved in the process of industrialization was the creation of a labour force of *employees*. The status of employee is markedly different to that of a peasant or an independent artisan, or of a worker in domestic industry. Factory organization involves the concentration of workers in one place, separated from their homes; the close supervision of work activities; and, increasingly, the use of power machinery. As a result, workers have lost much of whatever autonomy on the job they had previously enjoyed. They are required to work set hours and with a regular and continuous intensity of effort. Their productive efforts are directed by and for the benefit of others so that their prime attachment to work is through the wage packet. They also have to submit themselves to the authority of an employer, or of an employer's agents – managers and supervisors.

This organization of work activities under supervision on a systematic and regular basis – quite apart from the long hours of work commonly demanded in the early stages of industrialization in Britain and elsewhere – represented a marked break from customary and traditional patterns of working. Work oriented to the demands of the *task* frequently allows for periods of rest interspersed with periods of intense activity. Such irregular work-rhythms, on a daily, weekly or seasonal basis, appear to have been common wherever workers were not otherwise constrained and are probably the natural rhythms for work. In agriculture, for example, hectic activity during harvesting, or working day and night during lambing were, and to some extent still are, combined with periods of time when the pace of work can be much more relaxed. Before the Industrial Revolution in Britain workers used to fail to work on 'Saint Monday' (and even 'Saint Tuesday' as well) often after a weekend's heavy drinking, and crowded the required quota of work into the final days of the week.

In contrast, factory work, shop work, work in commercial offices and work as a wage-labourer in capitalist agriculture are oriented to the demands of *time*. Employers discipline their employees to keep to regular hours on each working day and to fill those hours with continuous labour. Learning to work by the clock was an integral part of the development of industrial capitalism. Both the availability of clocks and watches, and the emphasis on time-keeping, spending time and saving time increased greatly in the late eighteenth and early nineteenth centuries. Eventually this discipline was not only imposed from outside but *internalized* by workers themselves (Thompson, E. P., 1967).

This internalized ethic of work performance for factory type organization of production

involves a number of variables. Workers must be willing to do the work assigned with a degree of steady intensity. They must have a positive interest in accuracy and exercise reasonable care in the treatment of tools and machinery. And they must be willing to comply with general rules as well as with specific orders in a manner which strikes some reasonable balance between the extremes of blind obedience and capricious unpredictability . . . It is probable that in England this ethic of work performance developed among the masses of workers out of the combined legacies of craftsmanship, the Puritan ethic, and the rising ideology of individual striving and success (Bendix, 1963, pp. 204–5).

The precise relationship between the development of Protestant, and especially Calvinist, religion and the rise of modern capitalism suggested by Weber is still controversial however. The main focus of his thesis was on the growth of a spirit of capitalism which influenced the behaviour of entrepreneurs. But the same argument can be applied to those who became their employees. Protestant beliefs, and later those of Methodists, can be said to favour regular and diligent patterns of working and acceptance of an employer's authority, and thus to provide important normative support to the relations of employment and the new social organization of work which developed during the Industrial Revolution.

The transformation of work in this way was neither instantaneous nor complete. In many industries where the workplace became separated from the home, workers continued to exploit the labour of their own wives and children. The frequent use of sub-contractors as a means of organizing a larger labour force, and of piece-rates as a means of payment, permitted some elements of autonomy on the job to continue; until well into the nineteenth century workers in some of the metal trades in the West Midlands, for example, would go home when they had completed their day's quota, not stay until the official end of the working day. The process of rationalizing and organizing work has continued to the present day, as occupations which enjoyed at least some autonomy and variation of work-load and pace characteristic of the pre-industrial modes of working have found themselves increasingly subject to the same criteria of efficiency and productivity, and to control from above.

These transformations of work which involve performing most of it within relations of employment have been welcomed and defended because they have made possible the higher material standards of living we currently enjoy. Yet such an easy assumption of the superiority of contemporary patterns of working is both criticized and opposed because higher output has also demanded more intensive physical and mental effort from the worker – social costs, in the form of 'alienating' work, which need to be put against increased levels of material consumption in assessing the overall quality of life.

The origin and success of the factory lay not in technological superiority, but in the substitution of the capitalist's for the worker's control of the work process and the quantity of output, in the change in the workman's choice from one of how much to work and produce, based on his relative preference for leisure and goods to one of whether or not to work at all, which of course is hardly much of a choice (Marglin, 1974, p. 62).

By contrast, work in hunting and gathering economies, such as those of the Kalahari Bushmen and Australian Aborigines, is not alienating. One anthropologist, indeed, has described *them* as 'the original affluent society . . . one in which all the people's material wants are easily satisfied' (Sahlins, 1972, p. 1). The material standards of living of such peoples were clearly far lower than our own, but their cultures did not institutionalize scarcity as the market-industrial system of the modern world does, where there is a forever unbridgeable gap between unlimited wants and limited, even if expanding, means of meeting them. Among hunters and collectors, by contrast, Sahlins argues, 'human material wants [were] finite and few, and technical means unchanging but on the whole adequate'. Men commonly worked three to five hours a day on average, women perhaps slightly longer. As a result:

A good case can be made that hunters and gatherers work less hard than we do; and, rather than a continuous travail, the food quest is intermittent, leisure abundant, and there is a greater amount of sleep in the daytime *per capita* per year than in any other condition of society (Sahlins, 1972, p. 14).

As far as property is concerned most hunting and gathering peoples needed to be highly mobile: as soon as one area's food supply was diminished they had to move to another area. Material possessions which could not easily be carried were therefore of limited value, and the same applied to individuals, particularly the very old and the very young, who hindered the movement of family and camp. On the other hand they could expect to find adequate food and to renew the minimal stock of other possessions without great difficulty by moving elsewhere.

In industrial societies work and employment in the 'formal' economy based on wage-labour are not the whole of the economy: there is also an 'informal' economy outside officially recognized and statistically recorded employment and self-employment. Indeed Gershuny and Pahl have distinguished three different areas within the 'informal' economy:

1. *Household economy*: production, not for money, by members of a household and predominantly for members of that household, of goods or services for which approximate substitutes might otherwise be purchased for money.
2. *Underground, hidden or black economy*: production, wholly or partly for money or barter, which should be declared to some official taxation or regulatory authority, but which is wholly or partly concealed.
3. *Communal economy*: production, not for money or barter, by an individual or group, of a commodity that might otherwise be purchasable, and of which the producers are not the principal consumers (Gershuny and Pahl, 1985, p. 248).

Much work is done outside the social relations of employment. Certain sorts of economic activity, too, have moved between the formal economy and one of these areas of the informal economy and sometimes back again. Washing clothes, for example, 'moved from the wash house at home into the laundry, and then back into the home with the technological help of the washing machine' (Gershuny and Pahl, 1985, p. 250); similarly, changing levels of unemployment, and the desire to avoid paying taxes, often leads to car repairs being undertaken in any of the three areas of the informal economy (by the car owner, by a mechanic working for 'cash on the side', or by a friend or neighbour, unpaid but compensated eventually by reciprocal services of some kind) rather than by a 'proper' garage in the formal economy. But these are not to be seen as separate sectors of the economy: rather they refer to different strategies which households use in order to get work done, and which different members of households adopt at different stages in the family life-cycle, according to the availability of paid work and the demands of other, dependent, household members. Levels of income from employment, in turn, affect the ways in which other needs are met. Repairs to a roof, for example, may be undertaken by a member of the household (domestic self-provisioning); by friends, neighbours or relatives (informal/communal sources of labour); or by a firm of builders (formal provision of services). Pahl argues that concentrating on employment in the formal economy leads to a neglect of other kinds of work essential to a household's survival (Pahl, 1984, pp. 114–40).

Pahl's work provides a partial corrective to the picture of industrial capitalism other writers have provided. In an important critique of modern capitalism, Braverman, for example, has argued that 'the capitalist mode of production takes over the totality of individual, family and social needs and, in subordinating them to the market, also reshapes them to serve the needs of capital'. As a result it transforms 'all society into a gigantic marketplace' (Braverman, 1974, p. 271). Historically, the disappearance of possibilities of 'self-provisioning' as a result of urbanization, for example, has increased dependence on the market, simultaneously creating a demand for the products of capitalist industry and the labour force with which to produce them. Men and women are compelled to seek work outside the home to earn an income to purchase what they can no longer provide for themselves. Today their 'needs' are further continually increased by advertising and marketing. This 'commodification' of social life, and the creation of what Braverman terms 'a universal market' has clearly been very pervasive:

Even where the effort is made by one or another section of the population to find a way to nature, sport or art through personal activity and amateur or 'underground' innovation, these activities are rapidly incorporated into the market so far as is possible (Braverman, 1974, p. 279).

Almost everything can be made into a profitable commodity: commercial publishers, for example, including the publishers of this book, have very successfully marketed books by Marx and others which advocate the overthrow of capitalism! Nevertheless, Pahl is right to warn against regarding these processes as total and has shown how there are still contrary processes in action.

Wage-Labour

So far we have considered employment mainly in comparison with situations in which workers are largely autonomous, or constrained only by material factors and by custom and traditions − tribal economies, peasant families, and households in industrial societies. Employment for wages in modern societies also differs fundamentally from two modes of organizing which have been of great importance: slavery and serfdom. In the former, the workers are personal property, compelled to work for their owner as directed for fear of physical punishment, or worse. In the extreme, the slave has no right to any income or rewards for work at all, but slave-owners clearly have an interest in maintaining the value of their property and in having a physically efficient workforce. Hence the physical needs of slaves for food, clothing and shelter are likely to be met at some minimal level.

Systems of serfdom have varied considerably, but they typically involve the performance of labour services on the lord's land for certain periods of time in return for the serf's right to work their own plots of land to secure subsistence for themselves and their families. Serfs are therefore responsible for their own maintenance and have some areas of autonomous work; but they remain in varying degrees unfree, unable to move geographically, and limited as to the forms of productive activity in which they may engage, and they have no or very limited involvement in the cash economy.

Legal and/or physical coercion, or forced labour, are by no means entirely absent in modern economies based on employment; nevertheless, as both Marx and Weber emphasized in their rather different accounts of the development of modern capitalism, a crucially significant characteristic of such a system of production is that the worker is formally and legally free. This freedom is double-edged: workers are not compelled to work, but neither can they expect others to provide for them. Typically they do not possess their own means of production which would enable them to be economically independent; in the British case, for example, enclosures, and the cheaper products from the new factories, destroyed the bases for economic independence in agriculture and in handicrafts and created a potential wage-labour force. Such free wage-labourers have to look for employment: they have to sell their capacity to work to an employer in order to secure their means of subsistence. In contrast to the more diffuse social relations between slave-owner and slave, or between lord and serf, the obligations of employer to employee need not extend beyond the limited exchange involved in the employment contract: the employer paying a wage or salary for so many hours of the worker's labour. This contract, freely entered into, Weber argued, was an essential presupposition for modern capitalism:

Persons must be present who are not only legally in the position, but are also economically compelled, to sell their labour on the market without restriction. It is in contradiction to the essence of capitalism, and the development of capitalism is impossible, if such a propertyless stratum is absent, a class compelled to sell its labour services to live; and it is likewise impossible if only unfree labour is at hand. Rational capitalistic calculation is possible only on the basis of free labour; only where in consequence of the existence of workers who in the formal sense voluntarily, but actually under the compulsion of the whip of hunger, offer themselves, the costs of production may be unambiguously determined by agreement in advance (Weber, 1961, pp. 208–9).

As we shall see, the determination of costs of production on the basis of wage-labour is more difficult than Weber suggested. The employment contract regulates an exchange of pay (and possibly other rewards) for work. Unlike most contracts regulating buying and selling, however, this exchange cannot be instantaneous. Except in certain pieceworking or sub-contracting situations, what the employer secures by the offer of a wage or salary is the employee's *capacity* to work. This capacity can only be realized over a period of time, and will only be realized effectively from the employer's point of view if the employee's activities are directed and controlled. Continuing relations of superordination and subordination are therefore an inherent part of the social relations of employment.

Marx's writings provide a classic account of the relations between capital and labour (Marx, 1959a, b). Though they cannot be applied without modifications to all contemporary relations of employment, they still accurately describe many central characteristics of employment in advanced industrial societies. For Marx, a crucial characteristic of capitalist production is that workers create 'surplus value' by producing more than is necessary to maintain and eventually replace the raw materials and means of production (machines, etc) and to maintain and reproduce the workforce itself. In the capitalist mode of production the materials and instruments of production are owned by one class, the capitalists or bourgeoisie, while work on and with them is performed by members of another, the workers or proletariat. In order for capitalists to utilize and benefit from their ownership of the means of production they have to employ workers. What they obtain, however, is not *labour* but the worker's potential ability to work, their *labour power*. This potential can only be realized within the workplace itself. Capitalist employers, or their agents, must therefore control their employees' activities at work to ensure that the work that the workers have been hired to do is in fact done at the required pace, to the required quality standards and so on.

The payment workers receive in wages or salaries for their labour, in Marx's analysis, tends over time to be no more than the socially necessary costs of the maintenance of themselves and their families, and their eventual replacement by a new generation of workers. The surplus labour they provide and the surplus value they produce over and above this are appropriated by the employer; they provide the capitalist's profit. Both these elements are contained (and hidden) within the single payment, wages. This hidden expropriation of the surplus is very different from that under serfdom, for example, where it is quite apparent how much time the serf spends working on the lord's land as against growing food to support himself and his family.

Since they operate in competitive markets, capitalist employers are under pressure to reduce labour costs and to increase the productivity of labour. This can be achieved in various ways: by making workers work longer hours for the same pay (creating what Marx termed *absolute surplus value*); by making them work more intensively (creating *relative surplus value*); and by cheapening the cost of labour. To make workers work more intensively demands greater control by employers or their agents. This control is rendered easier by two changes in the organization of work: the introduction and development of a detailed division of labour within the workplace, so that each individual performs a smaller and more easily monitored proportion of the total task; and the introduction and development of machinery, which both increases labour productivity and makes it possible to control the pace of work more easily. Both these developments allow less skilled workers to be employed – for example, unskilled labourers, immigrants or women and children – thereby cheapening the cost of labour.

These ways of organizing work depend upon other social arrangements outside the factory or office. The labour force has to be maintained from day to day and reproduced from generation to generation. These contributions to the economy are made by the family and household. (Of course, where labour is brought in from outside, as with immigrant labour, the process of producing workers takes place in another society.) Furthermore, production in capitalist enterprises functions more smoothly if the social relations involved are seen as legitimate, and if workers consent to the terms and conditions of their employment. Thus provision has to be made for their socialization and education, not only in order to instil appropriate attitudes to work but also so that there will be ideological acceptance of the overall pattern of social relations. In this the State plays a crucial role: providing and enforcing an appropriate legal framework (one which protects private property rights, for example) and controlling the labour force.

In certain of his writings Marx also stressed the ways in which 'the capitalist mode of production' separated the workers from the means of production, from the products of their labour, from each other and from their own 'real' selves. A great deal of attention has subsequently been devoted to this notion of 'alienation', much of it emphasizing the subjective implications of the coercive and instrumental nature of work and the absence from work of any personal fulfilment or self-development for the worker. But 'alienation' is more than just 'job dissatisfaction'; it implies a particular pattern of social relations.

There is a clear conflict of interests between capital and labour over the size of the share in the earned income of the enterprise that goes to profits and wages respectively. These conflicts of interest are structural, since they are not merely the result of individual greed but are inherent in the logic of the capitalist economy. However, in modern capitalism, it has been argued, there are now powerful restrictions on the capitalist's ability to do what he likes, above all the trade unions. Similarly, while Marxists have usually emphasized the repressive, controlling activities of the State, others stress its welfare and redistributive activities, for example in protecting health and safety at work, and regulating the hours of labour. To the latter, the State is not an instrument of repression, but a 'balance wheel', even a benevolent force, restraining the power of both capital and labour.

It has also been argued that in the large corporations which dominate advanced capitalist societies, ownership and control are now exercised by quite different sets of people. Some have concluded, therefore, that there are no longer any capitalists, only directors and managers, themselves employees. Ownership, today, is dispersed among thousands of shareholders, many of them 'institutions' (pension funds, unit trusts, etc) which, it is argued, exercise pressure on the corporations to run their businesses in ways which take the interests of employees and customers into account, and not only those of shareholders. Though this 'separation' has been exaggerated, transnational and other large corporations are clearly very different from small family businesses, and social relations within the enterprise and its business strategies reflect this. Day-to-day control of these large enterprises is exercised by managers, whose function, however, is still to optimize their company's capacity to compete and to make profits.

In the public sector, the interests of private shareholders are not directly relevant; industries may be expected to meet public policy objectives, like keeping prices low, maintaining employment, or providing 'infrastructural' services such as transport or power essential to the (largely private capitalist) economy as a whole; and in some cases there is no competition from rival firms. Nevertheless, conflicts of interests between management and labour still persist. Early hopes that public ownership would usher in a new era of industrial relations in industries like coalmining were not fulfilled.

Employment in local and national government and in parts of the public sector, like the police force, health and education, which provide services rather than producing goods, are governed by yet other considerations. They provide the *social* conditions – law and order, a fit and educated workforce – without which industry cannot operate; but on the whole they are not subject to the competitive market pressures which underlie the conflicting interests of employer and employee in private industry. Though these are missing, as the public sector has grown in size and its total cost risen, it has become increasingly subject to demands that it operate with the same efficiency as private industry. Government employment, the education authorities, the National Health Service and so on have to operate within budgets which constrain the amounts payable in wages and salaries, and to account for their expenditure and output, and are under increasing pressure to cut labour costs and to achieve the provision of the same level of services with relatively smaller workforces.

Even in the public sector, then, two aspects of Marx's analysis remain valid: the recognition of an inherent conflict of interests between employer and employee; and the necessity for employers to exercise control over their employees if the labour power they purchase with wages or salaries is to be effectively used.

Indeed there is evidence that, at least until recently, this has been the case in the 'State socialist' societies of Eastern Europe where most of the economy – not just a sector of it – has been State-owned and State-run. In such societies the market has played a very much smaller part in regulating economic activity, yet even in this context the pattern of social relations between employer and employee has often appeared to be basically similar to that in the 'capitalist' West. In a vivid account of work in a Hungarian tractor factory, for example, Miklos Haraszti (1977) described the problems experienced by workers in trying to manipulate incentive schemes to their own advantage, and the conflicts with inspectors, foremen and managers comparable to those in factories in Britain or the United States. Though there were no 'profits', managers of State enterprises were under pressure to accumulate a surplus for further investment and for government expenditure, which had the same consequences so far as wage-earners were concerned. Yet such conflicts of interest could not be openly expressed when the official ideology stressed united endeavour by everyone working together to build socialism. As we saw in the case of Solidarity in Poland, any independent trade union movement which pursued its members' economic interests outside the bounds of what was officially allowed therefore represented a political challenge to the existing order – a challenge which eventually led to a change in that order.

Employment Relations

We have already seen that what the employer secures through the employment contract is the employee's *capacity* to work over a certain period of time, as directed by the employer, manager or foreman. With few exceptions, contracts of employment do not specify in any detailed and unambiguous way the work which the employee is being hired to do. Partly this is because it is not in the employer's interest to specify it too precisely – it would reduce flexibility in the use of labour; partly because of the inherent difficulties of specifying the content and intensity of work. Thus, except in strict piecework or sub-contract situations, the contribution which the employee provides in return for pay is left within basic limits to be worked out in the day-to-day interactions between workers and their superiors. Three aspects of work are sources of constant management–worker negotiation: effort, skill and responsibility.

The application of physical and mental effort to the task is a major element in all work, particularly for manual workers (Baldamus,

1961). The experience of effort, what it 'costs' the employee to work, is something which is only fully known subjectively by the worker, which cannot be measured and which, in any case, can be highly unstable – the same task may be experienced as easier one day, or at one time on a shift, than another. It is, however, a cost which employees will wish to limit, while employers are constrained to maximize effort as far as possible. The determination of the actual levels of effort in relation to pay is therefore subject to on-going negotiations on the job. It is important to note that this 'effort bargain' is concerned with both sides of the relationship: with the rate for the job – as in negotiations about incentive payments – and with the intensity of work demanded – as in negotiations over the speed of the assembly line or the level of manning on a particular job.

One study of manual work (excluding jobs that required an apprenticeship) in one local labour-market (Peterborough) suggested that 85 per cent of the unqualified manual workers could do 95 per cent of the jobs; and that 87 per cent of them exercised less skill at work than was needed in driving to work (Blackburn and Mann, 1979, p. 250). Nevertheless even 'unqualified' workers acquire some skills and experience which they can contribute in employment, and many employees, of course, are hired because they possess considerable skills. As with effort, however, establishing a relationship between pay and skill can be a highly contentious business. Both the skills needed to fill a particular occupational role, and the pay differential due to someone who has troubled to acquire qualifications or experience, cannot be determined in any objective way; they too are subject to negotiation between employers and employees, or their representatives.

Managers are also concerned about the responsibility, stability and trustworthiness of the workers they select for employment or for promotion. Even the most routine job usually leaves some room for the exercise of discretion by the worker, and such scope for judgement and for taking responsibility clearly increases as one moves up job hierarchies. How much responsibility is required and being carried, and what level of compensation would be appropriate for a given level of responsibility, represent a third aspect of the employment contract where employer and employee are likely to have differing interests and where such differences can only be resolved through on-going negotiations. The notion of a 'fair day's work for a fair day's pay', far from being obvious and consensual, is in fact subjective and complex. What may be seen as constituting 'fairness' is in reality that which emerges after lengthy and conflictful negotiations.

Managements are also under continuous pressure to reorganize work, to make it more efficient, to reduce labour costs and to secure greater control and predictability. These pressures come partly from technical changes, which themselves occur because of the need to compete with market rivals. Braverman (1974) has argued that the overall trend of these changes is towards a general and universal 'degradation' of labour, arising from the more and more widespread adoption of the methods of 'scientific management' as *the* means of managerial control over work. The key features of scientific management are that all knowledge about the process of production should be gathered together by management, systematized and developed; that this knowledge should become the exclusive preserve of management; and that their monopoly of this knowledge should be used to plan and control each step in the production process. Combined with increased use of machinery, and a further fragmentation of work, this strategy, involving a sharp separation of mental from manual labour and of conception from execution, results in the employment of a workforce which is less skilled and more easily controlled. Such 'de-skilling' involves eliminating not only most of the skill but also the responsibility and any room for the exercise of discretion from the majority of jobs.

There has been considerable debate about the accuracy of Braverman's characterization of these trends (Wood, 1989; Thompson, 1989). Many industrial workers were never very skilled. Much of the work of those who were has disappeared, or can now be undertaken on a machine operated by an unskilled worker (or even automatically), but new, highly skilled work roles (e.g. electronic engineer, computer programmer) have also been created. There have also been some contrary trends: the realization of the dehumanizing and 'alienating' nature of many people's jobs, and the costs to the employer of their dissatisfaction with them has led to attempts to introduce programmes of 'job enrichment' and 'job enlargement'. Some of these programmes have restored some real skill; others have clearly only been cosmetic. As a chemical process worker said to

Nichols and Beynon (1977, p.16): 'You move from one boring, dirty, monotonous job to another boring, dirty, monotonous job. And then to another boring, dirty, monotonous job. And somehow you're supposed to come out of it all enriched. But I never feel enriched – I just feel knackered.'

Perhaps the most important criticism of Braverman's thesis, however, is that it explicitly takes no account of, indeed discounts, the resistance which employees can offer to these attempts to remove skill and discretion from their jobs and to control them more closely – an argument which leads us to the whole question of the manifestations and consequences of industrial conflict.

Industrial Conflict

In the discussion of the conflicts surrounding employment the emphasis so far has been on the inherent conflicts of interest between employer and employee which arise from their respective positions as buyer and seller in the markets for labour, and from the exercise of authority by the employer over employees within the work situation. To this important extent, fellow-workers share common interests, as against those of their employer, in securing the best rate of pay possible for their work and the least burdensome exercise of managerial authority; but such a picture ignores or obscures a number of other lines of division of major importance.

In the first place employees, and even more so those seeking work, are competitors for whatever opportunities for employment are available. Sometimes this competition is made very visibly apparent, for example among labourers seeking work on the docks, before such work was decasualized; or when the unemployed or immigrants are brought in as 'blackleg' labour to take over strikers' jobs and break a strike; or when the threat of redundancy leads to competition to secure one of the 'safe' jobs. In addition to these vivid instances, however, conflicts between worker and worker are manifest in other ways: in demarcation disputes in industries like shipbuilding, for example, and in the attempts, often by skilled workers, to establish exclusive rights to certain areas of work and to prevent dilution. In the first case, the insecure nature of employment in shipbuilding led each group of skilled craftsmen in this industry to try to maximize their job prospects by claiming that only they could use certain tools or carry out certain processes. The defence of skill, and of the need for qualifications and credentials, is not peculiar to manual workers: it can be observed, for instance, among professionals like doctors and lawyers. Such tactics of 'closure' can increase the job security, and the earnings, of those able to exercise them, but at the expense of those workers who are excluded. The defence of 'job property rights' may lead to conflicts with other workers as well as with management.

Secondly, employer and employee do have some interests in common, even though these are weaker than the issues which divide them. Production, the provision of goods and services, involves cooperation, and this may well dominate the daily experience of employment. Employer and employee share, too, an interest in the prosperity of 'their' enterprise in competition with other enterprises, because the profits of one and the wages of the other depend upon it. This has been and still is used by many employers as the basis for denying any real conflicts of interest with their employees and for creating an image of the firm as 'one big family', or as a cooperative endeavour from the success of which all will benefit. Such 'paternalism', whether in the form of the traditional family firm or of modern and sophisticated managerial 'employee relations', may lead to the adoption of a style of consultative management and of policies designed to increase the welfare of employees, an approach sometimes described as 'smothering the workers with chocolate'. So long as the firm is commercially successful such policies can persist for a long time. But where it is necessary to cut costs by reducing the workforce and making employees redundant, or where decisions are taken to close a plant or to relocate production in the Third World, where labour costs less, the commodity status of labour, and the very different interests of employer and employee, once more come to the fore. It is significant that the large Japanese enterprises which have pursued such policies most successfully have done so because they have guaranteed lifetime employment for their core workforces; temporary workers, on the other hand, are employed on inferior terms of employment, to meet fluctuations in demand (Dore, 1973).

Thirdly, just as employees do not share exactly the same situations in the labour-market, neither do they share the same work situation, even when working for the same employer. A substantial minority of employees even play a part in the exercise of authority, not only managers and supervisors but also technical and clerical and even some skilled manual workers. Such employees, who have more 'responsible' jobs, can be offered preferential terms and conditions of employment with the expectation that they will identify with their employer. Their differentiation from other, lower-status employees is often reflected in lower levels of union membership or none at all, or in membership of separate white-collar unions and staff associations (Lockwood, 1958). The patterns of social relations between employer and employees, between managers, supervisors and workers, and between worker and worker, are therefore likely to be very complex, reflecting the firm's position in the market and the history of its growth.

Industrial conflict may be apparent in a whole variety of different ways, or may exist but not be reflected in behaviour at all. The most obvious expressions of conflicting interests, such as strikes, are by no means the only ones. Before striking becomes a possible option certain preconditions are typically necessary, especially a degree of organization among employees without which they will be unable to act collectively. Strikes are only likely to occur if they are accepted as legally and politically legitimate; if there are the economic resources necessary to sustain strikers and their families in the absence of wages, and so on. Where such conditions do not exist, and even where they do, employees may use a variety of other forms of action to try to control, or modify, permanently or temporarily, their conditions of employment. Some of these may involve collective action – go-slow, working to rule; some, individual action – absenteeism, sabotage or quitting work altogether.

In some situations there may be no overt manifestations of conflict at all. This can be because the disparities of power are so great that no possibilities of protest are open to those in subordinate positions. Indeed, such power can be used to make the existing state of affairs appear inevitable and unchangeable. More rarely, certain occupational groups, for example, printers, have used their key role in the production process to secure highly preferential terms of employment, and only occasionally need to threaten action to maintain their privileges. Yet in both types of situation conflicts may well be latent.

Further, it is a mistake to assume that 'conflict is something that only workers engage in; managerial behaviour, be it strategy in strikes, an attempt to increase effort levels, or the enforcement of discipline on the shop floor', is equally important (Edwards and Scullion, 1982, p. 256). Employers often have the power, however, to define their own actions as legitimate and rational, and to deny the legitimacy and rationality of the actions of their employees.

Edwards and Scullion have differentiated three 'levels' and four 'categories' of conflict, based on a study of seven factories. At the 'behavioural' level there is 'overt' conflict – 'where a conflict is recognized by participants and where action is taken to express it' – and 'non-directed' conflict, where the behaviour, such as absenteeism, is not overtly conflictual but nevertheless has significance for management–worker relations. At the 'institutional' level conflict may be recognized in 'a formal agreement, a customary rule, or even a traditionally accepted practice' which may prevent or make unnecessary the behavioural expression of conflict. At the 'structural' level conflict is implicit; 'there is a recognizable clash of interests' but 'specific reasons can be adduced to explain why this clash does not lead to an observable expression' (Edwards and Scullion, 1982, pp. 10–14).

In earlier investigations of the forms of industrial conflict, notably one in coalmining by Scott and his colleagues (1963), it was suggested that there was a clear *inverse relationship* between 'organized' and 'unorganized' conflict. The higher status and more powerful underground face-workers took collective action to pursue their interests through the disputes machinery; the lower status, and more dissatisfied, surface-workers, who had few resources to deploy, grumbled and went absent. Edwards and Scullion found a much greater variety of relationships between collective and individual manifestations of conflict. 'Patterns of behaviour', they claimed, 'reflect patterns of control, and . . . actions gain their significance as forms of conflict within particular structures of control' (1982, p. 282). Thus, for example, where management had tight control of the systems of production and payment, and where workers treated this as natural and inevitable and lacked resources and opportunities for collective action, high levels of individual absence, and labour turnover, were the typical responses; where there was a considerable worker shop-floor organization and weak managerial controls, considerable 'unrecorded' absence – informal rotas for time off – reflected well-organized collective custom and practice not 'individualistic' behaviour.

Even well-established shop-floor trade union organization, and well-developed traditions of custom and practice, however, prove ineffective against managerial challenges such as the threat of plant closure. Beynon (1984), for example, has described the difficulties for workers trying to counter the production and industrial relations strategies of large transnational firms like Ford:

. . . to work in the factory is to work on management's terms. Where management finds that its right to manage is being challenged within a factory, it is involved in a political struggle. Often this struggle takes the form of skirmishes on the shop floor, and at this level shop steward organization can be extremely effective, and shop stewards can amass a considerable amount of political influence and personal prestige. Where the challenge to managerial authority seriously affects the profitability of the Company, however, the response of management is likely to be firmer. To lay men off or to close plants down permanently ultimately involves political decisions, and it is at this level of struggle that the conflict between capital and labour becomes obviously biased against the worker. Capital is inherently flexible, machines can be written off, investment switched from one part of the world to another. Against the might of capital the power of the shop stewards' committee is negligible unless backed by a strong international organization (Beynon, 1984, p. 372).

Employer–employee relations, and conflicts, thus extend beyond individual workplaces and form part of a 'system' of industrial relations.

One of the most important manifestations of the conflicting interests of employer and employee is the way in which such conflicts have been institutionalized, expressed and contained within organizations and procedures which regulate the ways in which they should be managed. These vary from industry to industry within a country, and even more so internationally, but the basic elements are more or less universal. These are the organization of the parties to the conflicts – trade unions and other employee associations on one side, and employers' associations on the other; procedural rules and less formal understandings as to how disputes should be handled, providing a normative framework within which relationships between the parties are regulated; mechanisms for the discussion and resolution of conflicts – collective bargaining procedures, quasi-legal arbitration procedures, etc; and in many cases, arrangements for the intervention of third parties, possibly including the State, as mediators or arbitrators, should there be a failure to agree at an earlier stage. In most highly industrialized societies the institutionalization of procedures for resolving industrial conflict has become highly developed and of great importance in limiting more overt expressions of conflicting interest, such as strikes.

Before industrial conflict can be institutionalized, however, there has to be an acceptance on the part of those involved of the *legitimacy* of the interests of both parties. On the employers' side this was far from universal in the nineteenth century and even now there are employers who take a 'unitary' view of the enterprise; that it is their property, with which they should be able to do whatever they wish, and their employees, who have 'freely' entered employment in it, have no legitimate interests as a collectivity incompatible with the good of the organization as a whole (Fox, 1973). Trade unions will not be recognized by such employers, who will only be prepared to negotiate with employees on an individual basis. Such a 'unitary' view is much less common in large corporations and in the public sector, though it can be found even there, as for instance in the British government's withdrawal of trade union rights and recognition from employees at the intelligence communications centre, GCHQ, in 1984 because they were seen as potentially threatening to the national interest.

Most large employers, private and public sector, now accept a 'pluralist' view of the enterprise, according to which it is right and proper for different interest groupings to be organized, and to seek, and get, the right to make representations regarding policies and decisions which affect them. Such a view of the enterprise acts both ways, of course; it implies that employees accept – with whatever qualifications – 'management's right to manage'. Participation in the making of decisions through consultation, collective bargaining or some other mechanism, even limited, involves entering into some commitment to and acceptance of those decisions once they are made. It can therefore contribute considerably to the stability of social relations within the organization, which is why many employers have welcomed and encouraged it. It does so because in part it pre-empts the possibility of a more 'radical' challenge from below, one which might question the legitimacy of managerial authority altogether and demand a fully 'democratic' constitution for the firm or organization. Institutionalizing industrial conflict in this manner stabilizes and contains it in ways which leave existing distributions of power and resources largely unchallenged.

Industrial Organizations

In early industrial organizations control was exercised directly by employers, or by their managers and supervisors, and in some cases through the payments system. Such direct control is still typical of many smaller organizations today. As the machinery and systems of production became more complex, more integrated and, often, more automatic, this technology could also be used to establish control over workers' activities, avoiding much of the need for personal intervention by superiors. As enterprises grew in size and complexity, control over the activities of supervisors, managers and technical and clerical staff also became necessary and was increasingly secured through the organization itself (Edwards, 1979).

The classic analysis of bureaucracy by Max Weber identified several different ways in which the exercise of power can be legitimated. One of these was the justification of domination of one group of people by others on 'rational grounds – resting on a belief in the legality of enacted rules and the right of those elevated to authority under such rules to issue commands'. This he termed 'legal-rational' authority (Weber, 1968, p. 215). When authority was legitimated in this way (rather than on the basis of tradition or on the personal charisma of a leader), bureaucratic organization was the most common and important system of administration. Bureaucratic organizations have the following characteristics: (a) the tasks of the organization are divided between functionally distinct 'offices' or departments, the personnel of which have specified duties and spheres of competence, and appropriate, limited authority and sanctions; (b) offices are organized hierarchically so that each is under the control of a higher one – and so on up the pyramid; (c) the conduct of work is governed by a system of rules – both technical requirements and behavioural norms; (d) rules, activities and decisions within the organization are recorded in writing and filed; (e) the staff of such an organization are appointed by contract and do not own, and cannot appropriate, their position, though they are subject to the impersonal order of the organization only in their official capacity; (f) they are selected on the basis of qualifications, rewarded by salaries and (generally) pensions, and have the possibility of a career, with promotion on the basis of seniority and/or merit, as judged by their superiors.

There is no doubt that Weber's ideal type captures important aspects of modern organization, not only in industry, but also in government, in the churches, in voluntary bodies and so on. The modern world *is* more 'bureaucratic' than were pre-industrial societies. The growth of bureaucracy within industry itself can be seen as a response to increasing size and technical complexity, and to demands from others – the State, trade unions, shareholders, etc –for control, predictability and accountability. Personal and particularistic control is no longer adequate. To Weber, bureaucratic organization was *technically* superior to other forms of organization: 'the fully developed bureaucratic apparatus compares with other organizations exactly as does the machine with non-mechanical modes of production' (Weber, 1968, pp. 973–4), since it ensured both control over the activities of its subordinate members – through the system of rules and the authority hierarchy – yet it provided incentives which induced them to act in ways which met organizational requirements, via the salary system, pension, job security and prospects of promotion.

This 'ideal type' model of bureaucracy is *meant* to be one-sided, even exaggerated. It is not surprising, therefore, that empirical studies of organizations reveal patterns of action which differ from Weber's ideal type. Bureaucratic strategies of control have unintended consequences. In a theoretical critique Merton argued that pressures on the 'bureaucrat' to conform to prescribed patterns of action lead to the rules becoming regarded as ends in themselves rather than as a means to an end. The resulting *over*-conformity can lead to rigidity and to an inability to adapt to circumstances not necessarily envisaged when the rules are formulated: to what is often referred to as 'red tape' (Merton, 1957, pp. 195–206).

In a classic empirical study, Gouldner showed that in practice many of the functions (or consequences) of bureaucratic rules are unintended, and that such unintended consequences could well feed back in such a way as to perpetuate the use of bureaucratic solutions to problems. Thus, in an American gypsum plant which he studied, management's perception that the workers were not working hard enough and meeting performance targets led to a more stringent interpretation of the rules governing behaviour in the plant. This did indeed lead to greater control over the workers' behaviour, but it also increased the tension between management and workers, and indicated to workers the minimum acceptable level of performance. Their 'working to rule' confirmed management's perception of workers' performance and of the need for rules. At the same time emphasis on enforcing the rules made the exercise of authority more impersonal and justified the imposition of penalties. These unanticipated consequences counteracted the tension between management and worker arising from the more stringent enforcement of rules; but the original problem, and management's ineffective strategy of dealing with it, still persisted (Gouldner, 1955).

These and other deviations from Weber's ideal type of bureaucracy have led some writers to argue that Weber's notion was only applicable to the 'formal' aspects of an organization, whereas in reality there were always 'informal' social relations and patterns of action as well. In a study of two public sector organizations in the USA, for example, Blau suggested that informal behaviour could in fact increase the effectiveness of the organizations. In one, a Federal law-enforcement agency, staff who had a problem in dealing with a case were required by the rules to consult their supervisor. To do that implied incompetence, and adversely affected their chances of promotion. Instead (and contrary to the rules) there was a great deal of consultation among colleagues. Blau argued that this contributed to the effective operation of the agency and had beneficial consequences for the social cohesion of the workers involved. Thus, in contrast to the bureaucratic norm of impersonality, Blau argued that 'congenial informal relations between co-workers, and not completely detached ones, are a prerequisite for efficient bureaucratic operations' (Blau, 1963, p. 177).

Clearly, unanticipated consequences arise when bureaucratic solutions are used in dealing with the problems of controlling employees in large organizations, and the ideal type formulation of bureaucracy is inadequate as a description of such organizations. But the notion of 'informal' patterns of action and social relations also has its limitations. If the distinction is limited to one between those actions and social relations which are officially prescribed and those which are not, it is useful enough. Formal rules and arrangements intended to secure the achievement of organizational goals may not do so, however, while the opposite can be true of informal activities. More generally, it is by no means necessarily possible to specify in advance how goals can best be achieved, nor do the leaders of the organizations necessarily have the power to do so. Relying on rules and controls, too, may lead to the neglect of efforts to bring about commitment by employees to the overall goals of the organization and willingness to innovate in order to secure them.

Burns and Stalker's study of firms in the electrical engineering and electronics industries in England and Scotland demonstrates this clearly. Where there was stability with regard to technology, products and markets, it was both possible and effective for firms to operate bureaucratically – as Burns and Stalker term it, 'mechanistically'. The head of the concern could realistically expect to foresee what needed to be done and was therefore able to plan all necessary activities by allocating duties and powers to subordinates, who could then get on with their tasks without concerning themselves about the enterprise as a whole. Coordination of all these activities rested with the head of the concern, who was at the top of a clear hierarchy of control and communication, with instructions going down and information flowing up.

In conditions of uncertainty, however, as when there were innovations in technology or markets, it was not possible to determine in advance what needed to be done nor to allocate all necessary tasks to specialist departments with specific commitments. In these circumstances, the authors argued, what was needed was an 'organic' system of management:

Organic systems are adapted to unstable conditions, when problems and requirements for action arise which cannot be broken down and distributed among specialist roles within a clearly defined hierarchy. Individuals have to perform their special tasks in the light of their knowledge of the tasks of the firm as a whole. Jobs lose much of their formal definition in terms of methods, duties and powers, which have to be redefined continually by interaction with others participating in a task. Interaction runs laterally as much as vertically. Communication between people of different ranks tends to resemble lateral consultation rather than vertical command. Omniscience can no longer be imputed to the head of the concern (Burns and Stalker, 1961, p. 5).

In appropriate circumstances an organic system of management is just as rational as the mechanistic (or bureaucratic) pattern is in conditions of relative stability. In situations of greater uncertainty a much more open-ended commitment is required of employees: they are expected to behave more like professionals than bureaucrats. The organization remains stratified, but in terms of greater or lesser expertise rather than of position in the official hierarchy. In such a structure, too, it 'becomes far less feasible to distinguish informal from formal organization' (Burns and Stalker, 1961, p. 122).

Burns and Stalker discovered that management frequently failed to adapt to changed circumstances. Entering conditions of greater uncertainty, for example, firms often failed to adopt organic systems, so that attempts to develop and produce new products, or to open up new markets – while still operating mechanistically – usually failed. One major cause of failure was that in any firm there is always not only a 'working organization' but also a 'political system' and a 'status structure'. For employees were not only concerned with the actual tasks they did. They were also concerned with the *distribution* of the resources of the organization (space, money, manpower, equipment) between the various departments and sections into which it is divided, and with the degree of control exercised over that distribution and over the direction of the enterprise – its 'political system'; and with the distribution of rights and privileges, duties and obligations, amongst the members of the organization – its 'status structure'.

Changing from a mechanistic system to an organic one (or in the other direction) inevitably disturbs existing distributions of power and resources, and existing status structures, and is likely therefore to be resisted. Such resistance can only be overcome if there is a forceful lead from the head of the concern, and when employees are successfully persuaded that the overall goals of the enterprise are more important than their sectional and personal preoccupations. But the change over to an organic system can also threaten the power and status of the chief executive, making such a lead less likely to be given.

At much the same time as Weber was writing – at the turn of the century – pioneers of management theory were also stressing that there was 'one best way' to organize a business. Such theories remained dominant until after the Second World War, when work such as that of Burns and Stalker reached the conclusion that such a quest was mistaken: 'the beginning of administrative wisdom', they wrote, 'is the awareness that there is no one optimum type of management system' (1961, p. 125).

Similar conclusions were reached in studies which concentrated on the nature of the production system or the technology with which the various plants and factories were working. In a study of a hundred manufacturing organizations in south-east Essex, Woodward argued that the objectives of an enterprise, and the methods and processes necessary to achieve these objectives (its technology), were the most important, though not the only determinant of its organizational structure. Different production systems could be classified in general according to increasing technical complexity – in terms of 'the extent to which the production process is controllable and its results predictable' (Woodward, 1958, p. 12). This gives rise to three main patterns of production: those where goods are produced singly or in small batches to meet customer orders (shipbuilding, bespoke tailoring); those produced in large batches or by mass production (standardized products in large quantities such as consumer durables or motor cars); and process production (continuous flows of liquids, gases and/or solids such as detergents or pharmaceuticals).

Some organizational characteristics varied directly with increasing technical complexity; for example, the number of levels in the management hierarchy and the ratios of managerial and supervisory staff to other personnel both increased. Other organizational characteristics, for example, 'human relations', were claimed to be more similar at the extremes than in the middle. In unit production, little attempt was or could be made to control the physical limitations of production, and people were subjected to relatively little pressure; it was traditional, for example, that engineers engaged on the development of a complicated piece of equipment 'were unwilling to work well with a gun at their backs' (Woodward, 1958, p. 29). Pressure on people was at a minimum also at the process production end of the scale, because production was genuinely under mechanical control and predictable: 'people were hard pressed only when things went wrong'. Pressure was greatest in large batch and mass production where the capacity of the production system was calculable in theory (e.g. as in assembly-line production), but where output still depended on the amount of effort operators were prepared to put into the job.

Similar conclusions were reached at about the same time by an American sociologist, Robert Blauner, who compared four industries and argued that the experience of work was greatly influenced by technology (Blauner, 1964). Work was much less 'alienating' in printing (a craft industry) and in chemicals (process production), than in textiles (machine-minding) and, especially, on car-assembly lines. Later studies contested both Woodward's and Blauner's conclusions, for it can be shown that not all mass production plants are characterized by poor human relations (Turner *et al.*, 1967), while research in both a unit production industry (shipbuilding) (Brown *et al.*, 1972), and in process production (chemicals) (Nichols and Beynon, 1977) have undermined any general claim that human relations in such industries are more harmonious.

Despite such criticisms, Burns and Stalker's, and Woodward's work have remained influential examples of what subsequently was called 'contingency theory'. This approach recognizes that different organizations can be structured in different ways, and tries to explain these variations by reference to the different contexts within which such organizations operate. This means that rather than thinking in terms of one ideal type – bureaucracy – as characteristic of all industrial organizations in modern societies, one should expect there to be a range of different types. In a particularly ambitious comparative study, designed to establish a comprehensive typology, Pugh and his colleagues investigated fifty-two work organizations in the West Midlands in the 1960s and took into account not only technology but factors such as origin and history, size, location, and interdependence with other organizations (Pugh and Hickson, 1976).

In 'contingency theory' very little weight is given to *choices* made by organizational members in explaining the variations in the forms which organizations take and in behaviour within them. Thus, for example, although Pugh and his colleagues found that variations in technology were of less importance, they argued that an organization's size, and its dependence on other organizations, largely determined aspects of its structure.

This sort of theoretical position has rightly been criticized. In the first place, Child (1972) has argued that, even in competitive market conditions, industrial organizations may have a degree of slack with regard to their performance so that there *are* possibilities of choice as to what structural arrangements can be adopted. Indeed, environmental constraints themselves are perceived and evaluated by members of the organization. Thus the key managers will have ideas about how the organization operates, and should operate, and will put these ideas into practice. They – the 'dominant coalition' – make 'strategic choices' about the goals the organization will pursue, the setting within which it will pursue them, the level of performance to be regarded as satisfactory, and the organizational arrangements to be adopted.

Secondly, studies in coalmining in Britain, and of a textile firm in India, moreover, demonstrated that even *within* the confines of the same technological arrangements there was room for significant 'organizational choice'. The use of particular machines and layout in cutting coal, or of automatic looms in a weaving shed, did not necessarily predetermine the work-roles and relationships of those employed (Trist *et al.*, 1963; Rice, 1958). Thirdly, work-roles, however closely prescribed, do not determine the attitudes and behaviour of those who occupy them in some straightforward way. Rather, employees respond to the situations in which they find themselves in terms of their own perceptions of the situation and their own expectations and priorities.

A quite different approach to the analysis of industrial organizations treats the 'structures' of organizations, and organizations themselves, not as 'things' which can be observed, measured and discussed without difficulty, but as arrangements which, in their nature are transient outcomes of the actions and interactions of individuals and groups pursuing their own ends with whatever resources are available to them. In such a view, the very process of identifying and measuring various dimensions of an organization gives 'structure' a spurious solidarity and permanence which is quite unjustified. It also implies that there is only one model of the characteristics of the organization and its environment rather than the possibility, indeed the likelihood, of several competing interpretations (Silverman, 1968, 1970).

Since industrial firms can be considered as comprising a political system and a status structure as well as a working organization, it is important to recognize the competition, conflict, negotiation and compromise within organizations. In their study of psychiatric hospitals, for example, Strauss and his colleagues argued that the organization should be seen as a 'negotiated order':

. . . order is something at which members of any society, any organization must work. For the shared agreements, the binding contracts – which constitute the grounds for an expectable, non-surprising, taken-for-granted, even ruled orderliness – are not binding and shared for all time . . . the bases

of concerted action (social order) must be reconstituted continually; or . . .
worked at. [Hence we] emphasize the importance of negotiation – the
processes of give and take, of diplomacy, of bargaining – which characterizes
organizational life (Strauss *et al.*, 1971, pp. 103–4).

They therefore described the extent to which what happens within
hospitals cannot be seen as simply determined by sets of rules
(which always have to be interpreted) or by an established hierarchy
of authority and division of labour (for staff can differ in their
interpretations both of what these are and of what they should be).
Instead they saw the hospital as:

a locale where personnel . . . are enmeshed in a complex negotiative process
in order both to accomplish their individual purposes and to work – in an
established division of labor – towards clearly as well as vaguely phrased
institutional objectives. We have sought to show how differential professional
training, ideology, career, and hierarchical position all affect the negotiation
(Strauss *et al.*, 1971, p. 121).

Though hospitals and industrial organizations are both settings
within which people work as employees, there are clearly important
differences between them. But Strauss and his colleagues are justified
in arguing that their approach would be equally fruitful in studying
industry. What needs to be added to it, however, is a more explicit
recognition that negotiation within organizations does not necessarily,
or even normally, take place between parties with equal power and
resources; nor does it take place in isolation from the wider society
which affects political processes within an institution. The emphasis
on the organization as a 'negotiated order', like that on 'strategic
choice', is an important corrective to deterministic views; but even
though members of organizations do have significant choices as to
the courses of action they will pursue, there are always limits upon
their freedom of action.

Social Action

All analyses of social relations in employment make certain assumptions about how individuals will respond and act, and this is so
whether or not these assumptions are made explicit. Some of the
earliest social research in industry implicitly adopted the assumptions
that economists usually make: that employees will act rationally to

maximize their material rewards from working, so that, for example, if they are offered higher pay for producing more work they will work harder. Very soon, however, social researchers were questioning such assumptions and arguing that the evidence suggested that other considerations could be equally or more important. Such a view, emphasizing that employees wanted more from their work than just pay, was given considerable support by the results of the 'Hawthorne Experiments' in the Chicago works of the Western Electric Company as early as the late 1920s. The study showed how one group of women workers increased their output in response, apparently, to the increased attention they were receiving from supervisors – and even from the social researchers – and to the opportunities they were given to participate in decisions about their conditions of work. A group of men were found to be deliberately 'restricting' their output – so that they lost pay under an incentive scheme – because they wished to conform to group norms about appropriate workplace behaviour – not to be seen as 'rate-busters' who worked too hard – and so preserve the social cohesion of the work group (Rose, 1975, Part 3).

The 'human relations' tradition in industrial sociology which developed from this and other work became extremely influential in the United States and in Britain in the period after the Second World War, and still remains so, especially in management teaching. It emphasizes 'social' rather than 'economic' motives, and in more recent versions has stressed that employees have a more or less standard hierarchy of needs, of which material needs are only the first and the most easily met. A contented and cooperative workforce could therefore be created, they argue, by appropriate managerial leadership, which respects workers as individuals, and so organizes their work that it provides them with opportunities for satisfying social relations on the job and for individual participation, creativity and self-development at work. Investigators like Woodward and Blauner operated with similar assumptions about workers' needs, though they argued that under certain technologies it might be impossible to meet them.

Criticism of the 'human relations' tradition was not new, especially of its assertion of a potential harmony of interests between employer and employee; but the arguments developed by Goldthorpe and his colleagues, arising from their research into 'affluent' manual workers in three factories in Luton in the early 1960s, provided the most influential alternative to this assumption of a fixed hierarchy of human needs. That assumption, they found, could not account for a whole range of findings: satisfaction with jobs which paid relatively high wages, despite the unsatisfying nature of the tasks involved; a lack of interest in opportunities for social relations with fellow workers on the job, or in their supervisors' behaviour (so long as they did not interfere too much), and so on. The researchers argued that the crucial determinant of these workers' attitudes and behaviour was their 'orientation to work': the priorities and expectations which had governed their choice of a job in the first place (under conditions of full employment), and which continued to influence their behaviour on the job. In contrast to the assumptions of the 'human relations' school they argued that 'wants and expectations are culturally determined *variables*, not psychological constants' (Goldthorpe *et al.*, 1968, p. 178).

These men, they argued, displayed an 'instrumental' orientation to their work, which had originally influenced their choice of employment, and was unaffected by their experiences on the job. Goldthorpe and his colleagues argued that this orientation was a product primarily of the men's social situations *outside* work: the great majority of them had at least one dependent child, their stage in the family life-cycle was that of maximum financial pressure; their recent geographical mobility meant that they were not well integrated into the local community but had a very home- and family-centred lifestyle; experience of downward occupational mobility led to them placing little value on the work they did but a high value on seeking as high an income as possible to support their desired standard of living.

This, though, was only one possible orientation to work (though one which Goldthorpe and his colleagues regarded as likely to become increasingly common as older industries and settled communities declined). At least three other orientations to work were identifiable: a 'solidaristic' orientation – where work was valued as a group activity; a 'bureaucratic' orientation – where the emphasis was on 'service' within an organization as part of a 'career'; and a 'professional' orientation, which emphasized membership of a particular skilled occupational group (Goldthorpe *et al.*, 1968, pp. 38–41). All these different orientations were greatly influenced by the experiences outside work, especially those coming from community life (Lock-wood, 1966).

Goldthorpe and his colleagues were among the first to outline a 'social action' approach to the analysis of social relations at work. Orientations to work were seen as largely independent of the work situation and as an important factor in explaining what happened there. Critics of their approach agreed that one could not assume that all workers had the same hierarchy of needs, but they differed in their views about the origins, clarity, stability and consequences of these *varying* orientations to work. The experience of past work frequently influences attitudes to the work you are doing now. The Luton workers had no affective involvement in their work at all, but this is unusual. They were unusual, too, in having a very clear set of priorities: many employees expect their work to meet several needs, not only to provide good pay but also interesting work, opportunities for advancement, job-security, friendly workmates, and so on. Thus the *context* of workers' behaviour and in which they express opinions must be taken into account. Daniel, for example, argued that in the petrochemical industry there was 'strong evidence to the effect that factors that attract a person to a job are very different from those that determine his satisfactions, performance and behaviour on the job. These in their turn are often very different from those that predispose him to leave the job' (Daniel, 1969, p. 367). Pay, security and physical working conditions attracted people to the job and kept them in it, but the opportunity to use their mental abilities and to learn and their experience in solving problems were the main sources of satisfaction on the job, while lack of promotion opportunities was the main reason which caused a few of them to leave.

Even where there are fairly clear and stable sets of priorities and expectations about employment, there are important limitations on their usefulness in explaining people's behaviour. For example, Goldthorpe and his colleagues attached considerable importance to the fact that the 'affluent' workers in Luton had *chosen* relatively high-paying jobs, and sacrificed other possible rewards, such as autonomy on the job, interesting tasks or satisfying social relations with workmates or supervisors. Each of the three factories was therefore made up of largely 'self-selected' workforces with similar orientations to work. The possibility of making choices about what job you do depends on a condition of full employment, however, and on information about alternative possible jobs, or the possibility of obtaining such information by trying jobs out and moving on if they do not fulfil expectations. High rates of unemployment since that time make relatively free choice impossible; while as Blackburn and Mann show, in their study of the Peterborough labour-market, adequate information about jobs for manual workers is not readily available and is costly to obtain. Shopping around to try out possible jobs, too, is likely to reduce the worker's chances of getting better rewarded work because employers look for employees who are stable and reliable, and length of service with a previous employer is seen as a major indicator of such qualities.

So explanations of differing orientations to work often fail to recognize that choice is severely constrained by the conditions under which individuals and groups have to act. They may well be faced with no, or very restricted, choice; especially those with the fewest resources, such as the poor and less skilled. Nor are attitudes to work simply individual matters: the dominant values and beliefs in a society are internalized during early socialization, are reinforced through the mass media and through other social pressures through-out life, and form part of unquestioned attitudes for most people. These values include the 'work ethic', a strongly internalized obligation to earn one's living, accepting the deprivations this may involve; and an equally important 'obligation to consume' – acceptance of the desirability and the importance of constantly seeking a higher stand-ard of living.

Women and Work

The importance of both these issues – of constraints on action, and cultural values – is especially visible when we look at women's employment and the attitudes of women towards work. As we saw in Chapter 4, women's participation in paid employment has increased steadily since the Second World War. In 1989 53 per cent of all women aged sixteen and over were employed or seeking paid work (as compared with 37 per cent in 1951 of those aged fifteen and over). Women comprised 44 per cent of the occupied population in 1989 as compared to 31 per cent in 1951. Most of the increase has been due to the increased employment of married women, and much of it has been in part-time jobs (Brown, 1984; Lonsdale, 1985;

Central Statistical Office, 1991). Despite this increased participation, and despite official commitments to equal opportunity and equal pay reflected in the Equal Pay Act of 1970 and the Sex Discrimination Act of 1975, women remain largely occupationally segregated from men. They are segregated 'horizontally' in that most women are concentrated in jobs such as clerical and sales work and catering, while three-quarters of all occupations are dominated by men. Women are also segregated 'vertically' in that few of them reach higher status and better paid managerial, administrative and professional jobs, or are in skilled manual work (Hakim, 1979). Not surprisingly, in view of this occupational distribution, women's earnings and rates of pay remain substantially lower than men's: women's hourly pay in 1990 was 76·6 per cent of men's, as compared with 63·1 per cent in 1970. Their average weekly earnings were even lower: 68·2 per cent of men's for all employees (Department of Employment, 1990).

The changed position of women, and especially of married women, reflects and reinforces changed attitudes to women's employment. With very few exceptions it is illegal to exclude women from any occupation or to discriminate in recruitment on grounds of sex; the bar to the employment of married women which operated at least until the Second World War in many areas of the Civil Service, banking, some kinds of factory work, etc, has been removed. The assertion that a 'woman's place is in the home' is less frequently heard, and likely to be justified by reference to caring for children, while the standard of living of many families – their ability, for example, to buy their own homes, run a car or take holidays abroad – is dependent on two incomes. In one important respect, however, traditional attitudes and values have not changed significantly. It is expected that wives and mothers will take the prime, if not the sole, responsibility for childcare and domestic work. This expectation has crucial implications for women's employment.

Clearly the mother must interrupt her employment for the birth of a child and provision for maternity leave is now statutorily enforced in many, though not all, areas of employment. But such an interruption can be relatively short, perhaps a matter of months. With some exceptions most mothers, if they can afford to do so, stay at home for some years while their children are young, though the average period out of paid work has shortened since 1950 (Martin and Roberts, 1984, pp. 128–32). Such an interrupted employment record means that in comparison with men many women are less likely to gain the skills, experience and opportunities for promotion which give them a chance of obtaining better rewards and more responsible jobs. Indeed, employers may in effect not bother to provide training or promotion opportunities for *any* women simply because they expect *some* to leave work when they start a family. As a result, men in general have higher-paid jobs than their wives, and, if the question of who should interrupt employment to care for children ever arises, can argue that it makes economic sense for them to continue working and for their wives to stay at home. This perpetuates the conditions which apparently justify that division of labour in the first place, though because they are badly paid and underemployed, not because of biology.

The inferior position of women in terms of employment is sometimes explained as being due to, and justified by, the subordinate place which paid work has in women's priorities. Evidence of apparently lower levels of ambition, of more ready acceptance of repetitive tasks and of inferior conditions of employment, and of lower levels of trade union membership and activity, is used to support the argument that women's interests are centred on the home and family so that their employment is of marginal importance to them. This view is inadequate in several respects. In the first place, it regards women as a homogeneous category so far as their orientations to work are concerned, yet these vary, as do men's, in accordance with their position in the family life-cycle, and other considerations; employment has a different significance for young single women, for women with dependent children, and for older women without dependants, to take only the three most obvious groupings (Brown, 1976; Martin and Roberts, 1984, pp. 60–78). Secondly, there is an increasing body of evidence that work has much the same meanings for many women as it has for many men – as a source of economic independence and status in society, for example; and it cannot be assumed that women's earnings are somehow of secondary importance or that they are less severely affected by the experience of losing their job through redundancy (Coyle, 1984). Further, insofar as it can be argued that 'women accept pay and conditions which the majority of men would not work for', this does not itself support the stereotyped view of 'passive women workers' (Purcell, 1979). The meaning of work for women, as for men, is or may be affected by their experiences of the labour-market and of employment, not just by factors in the home.

Female employment is concentrated in industries and occupations (like distribution, private sector services, and clerical work) where union membership and militancy are *generally* at relatively low levels, not because of the high proportions of women employed but because these are areas of employment characterized by small establishments (factories, offices, shops, etc) with low levels of unionization regardless of the sex of the workers (Bain, 1970). Some of the industries employing large numbers of women, like clothing and footwear, operate in unstable product markets, and both men and women in such conditions, who may well know their 'boss' as an individual, are likely to see industrial action as inappropriate and likely to be ineffective; on the other hand, levels of absence and labour turnover are often high (e.g. Lupton, 1963). The organization and procedures of trade unions can also inhibit women's active involvement in union affairs; it is more difficult for them to attend branch meetings in the evenings or weekend conferences (Purcell, 1979). Low levels of union membership and activity among women can then become self-perpetuating: male trade unionists see women as uninterested, do not try to recruit them, and give little attention to women's problems. Women come to see the union as 'the men's affair' (Beynon and Blackburn, 1972, pp. 115–17). Yet in the 1960s, when the National Union of Bank Employees pursued claims for shorter hours (Saturday closing) and equal pay, issues which were important to women, female membership of the Union increased rapidly and women members actively supported the strike action which gained the Union recognition from the employers and success in securing its demands (Heritage, 1983).

Thus the structure and operation of the labour-market leads to women being concentrated in certain industries and occupations; women's attitudes and actions represent a response to these specific work situations, mediated by their orientations to work. Their actions are constrained by what is realistically possible, and their orientations reflect and incorporate past experience in employment and in the labour-market. Attitudes and behaviour cannot be explained by reference to fixed 'orientations to work' on their own; they are constrained by the expectations and actions of others and by the experience of work itself.

Comparisons between Organizations

Most, though not all, organizations have employees: many organizations also contain other kinds of members who are not under contract of employment: clients, conscripts, inmates, patients, prisoners, pupils, residents and other categories of rank-and-file member. In many organizations, including some with large numbers of employees, the relationship between the organization, or more strictly its leadership, and these other participants may be more important than employer–employee relations for understanding the way it is structured and operates.

Etzioni has developed a typology of organizations based on an analysis of the different ways in which they control the behaviour of their 'lower participants'. This typology focuses on the *compliance* relationship – 'the power employed by superiors to control subordinates and the orientation of the subordinates to this power' (Etzioni, 1961, p. xv). Etzioni suggested that there are three types of power based upon the use of different ways of making subordinates comply: *coercive* (physical force), *remunerative* (material rewards) and *normative* (symbolic, and social, rewards and deprivations) respectively. These different strategies of exercising power generate three different types of orientation to the organization: negative (*'alienation'* – rejection of the aims of the organization); neutral (*'calculative'* involvement); and positive (*moral* identification with the organization's aims). Etzioni argues that the three congruent types are most frequently found where the kinds of power used match the kinds of involvement lower participants are likely to have. These he labels *coercive*, *utilitarian* and *normative* respectively, each being the most appropriate for the achievement of different kinds of goal.

Prisons, concentration camps and custodial mental hospitals, for example, pursue 'order' goals (controlling members of society perceived as deviant) using coercive means because their inmates are alienated from the institution's goals. Industrial and commercial organizations pursue economic goals (producing and providing goods and services), and use material rewards to secure the cooperation of their employees, who tend to be calculative in their orientation to the organization which employs them. Religious bodies, hospitals, schools, colleges and universities, ideological political organizations, professional organizations and voluntary associations, on the other hand, pursue cultural and social goals (the creation, preservation, transmission and application of symbolic objects, and securing commitment to them) and use persuasion, influence and social pressure to evoke the positive and relatively intense commitment expected of lower participants (Etzioni, 1961, esp. pp. 4–6, 9–14, 66–77).

Organizations outside these 'congruent' types tend to be less effective: forced labour has been found to be less efficient than wage-labour in industry; a degree of commitment is needed if students in educational institutions are to learn and internalize what they have been taught; it is difficult to use therapeutic methods in custodial mental hospitals, and so on. Organizations with mixed compliance structures tend to pursue policies which reflect an uneasy compromise between partly incompatible patterns: many trade unions, for example, can be seen as 'utilitarian-normative'; utilitarian insofar as they win their members' support by offering material rewards – whether directly as in sick benefits and pension schemes, or indirectly by negotiating pay-increases – but also normative because they rely upon ideological persuasion and social pressure from fellow-members.

Yet the typology is an oversimplification of reality. A 'mix' of modes of ensuring compliance is both normal and effective. As we have seen, employment for many has been and to some degree still is 'coerced', because of the absence, or even the deliberate destruction, of alternative means of satisfying material needs; while a great many industrial and commercial organizations do attempt to secure the positive commitment of their employees by paternalist policies. The purely utilitarian organization is probably as rare as the purely instrumentally oriented worker. The typology also depends on rather arbitrary decisions as to which category of person is taken to be the crucial 'lower participant'; hospitals, for example, may have as many staff as patients, while department stores have more customers than staff. There are other ways of looking at social relations within organizations apart from dividing people simply into leaders and 'lower participants'. Organizations which process people, for example (prisons, hospitals, schools, etc), reveal both common features and differences in their ways of handling them.

Many can be described as 'total institutions', to use the term introduced by Goffman. Whereas normal social life involves sleeping, playing and working in different places, with different co-participants, under different authorities and with no overall plan, in total institutions all these activities occur in the same organization. In prisons, hospitals, monasteries, military camps and boarding schools, and in some work organizations, all activities take place in the same location and under the same authority and in the company of the same batch of others, all of whom are treated alike. The day's activities are tightly scheduled, imposed from above and form part of a single rational plan designed to fulfil the official purposes of the organization (Goffman, 1961, pp. 5–6).

Some total institutions exist to carry out a work-task and it is the nature of that task, and the way it is organized, which causes one set of social relations to pervade all areas of life, at least for a time, for example on ships at sea, in mining camps or, to a lesser extent, in a company town. The total institutions which interested Goffman most, however, are those which are designed to change the ways in which people perceive themselves – prisons, mental hospitals, military training establishments, boarding schools, monasteries which take in novitiates, and so on. In such contexts, Goffman argues, there is a basic split between staff and inmates, and inmates typically follow a clear 'moral career', whose features are broadly common despite the different ideologies and purposes of these various kinds of organization. On admission, new entrants are deprived of all the symbols of their former identity (e.g. clothing and personal possessions) and are systematically degraded. By judicious use of privileges and punishments it then becomes possible for the staff not only to secure the inmates' conformity to a particular regime but also to create a new, and from the authorities' point of view, a more acceptable identity for them. Such processes are not necessarily completely successful, of course, and there are various modes of adaptation to life in a total institution which reduce its impact on the individual, notably various forms of resistance or withdrawal. But because the organization controls the whole life of the inmate, its influence can be very hard to escape.

In total institutions there is an almost completely one-sided distribution of power within the organization as between staff and inmates. At the other end of the continuum are those organizations which attempt to establish and operate democratic control of the policy and direction of the organization by its members, such as many voluntary associations, some religious and political organizations, retail and producers' cooperatives, and trade unions. Yet a common feature of all such organizations is that democracy, in the sense of effective control by ordinary members, is often very imperfect and an elite emerges which exercises the real power. Attempts to establish workers' control or workers' management, for example, have to confront the twin problems of the need for expertise (e.g. in operating technically complex processes, compiling and interpreting financial accounts, and exploring potential markets) and the need for an authority structure in order to ensure efficient coordination of work-tasks. It then becomes increasingly difficult for 'ordinary' workers to control technically qualified staff in positions of authority (Brannen, 1983).

The question of democratic control of organizations by their members has attracted particular attention in relation to trade unions. Such organizations typically have constitutions which are formally highly democratic and ideologies which place considerable emphasis on membership participation in and control of the affairs of the union. Yet many commentators have endorsed the claim made before the First World War by Michels, in relation to Left-wing political parties, that there is an 'iron law of oligarchy' (Michels, 1959, p. 401). Bodies like trade unions need leaders to administer them and to represent them in relations with employers, the government and so on. Such leaders tend to become very powerful: they control the means of communication in the union and develop an expertise denied to ordinary members. They also develop the motivation to retain their union position because it offers status, and generally an income they could not obtain elsewhere. On the other hand, union members tend to be 'apathetic'; they have neither the time, the ability nor the interest to participate actively and continuously in union affairs. As a result, for psychological and technical reasons, the members are unable to exert effective control over union leaders, whose policies may diverge increasingly from members' wishes and interests. Indeed, attempts to oppose or criticize the leadership may be treated as disloyal and illegitimate on the grounds that internal disunity threatens the union's position in conflict with employers.

One means of controlling leaders is what Hemingway (1978) has labelled 'control through opposition', when union government is like parliamentary government, with contested elections and the alternation of two or more parties in power. It is actually more common for there to be factions within unions presenting alternative policies and trying to influence the leadership, though even here such competition between two cliques can still leave the majority indifferent. 'Control through participation' in branch and workplace meetings to influence union policy and the actions of their leaders does not necessarily involve challenging them for office. Levels of participation in union government outside the workplace are usually very low in fact, and often remain unresponsive to such pressures. Finally, there is 'control through satisfaction', where members, like customers, can 'vote with their feet' if the union fails to offer what they want. But members often do not know what policies the leadership are pursuing and what alternative policies might be pursued, nor can they leave and find an alternative union to join: the closed shop may effectively prevent them leaving, and in Britain agreements about membership recruitment often prevent them joining another union, while break-away unions find it very difficult to secure recognition.

'Control through conflict', Hemingway suggests, would be more effective since different types of resources can be deployed in different situations. Thus, a 'persuasive' strategy involves using institutional resources (motions, resolutions, etc, through the union's governmental machinery). If this is unsuccessful, the parties may form alliances (cliques, factions, ginger groups) to try to manipulate leaders and policy; finally, direct action (forming a breakaway union, expelling dissidents, legal action) can be resorted to in order to coerce others to follow a particular line. None of these possibilities, though, guarantees union democracy, nor does the predominance of any one form of behaviour constitute unambiguous evidence as to whether members' control of their organization is effective or not. An apparently apathetic and inactive membership, for example, might indicate – variously – satisfaction with current leaders and policies, ignorance of policies and alternatives, or a fatalistic acceptance of their powerlessness to change policies and leaders members dislike or to leave the organization altogether. Legislation to secure the election and re-election of union leaders, and the balloting of members about decisions to take strike action, could contribute to union democracy, but whether it did so or not would depend on the existing constitution and practice of the union. Such measures on their own cannot guarantee control, and membership control could exist without them.

Work and the Future

At the time of writing, unemployment in Britain stands officially at over two million, nearly 8 per cent of the labour force, and in reality there are probably a further million people who are either on a government scheme or have no job and would like paid work. Though some 'frictional' unemployment is unavoidable as people change jobs, unemployment on this scale is mainly of a 'cyclical' and 'structural' nature. A worldwide recession has increased cyclical unemployment – a downward spiral of demand for the products of our own and other countries. Structural changes include not only the decline of many of the traditional, relatively labour-intensive manufacturing industries – shipbuilding, engineering, textiles and so on – but also the first effects of the introduction of micro-electronic technology into many areas of employment, including white-collar and office work.

Some argue that, as in the case of similar major innovations in the past, there may be dislocation, structural unemployment and hardship for a time, but that in the longer term the productivity and wealth creation made possible by the new technology will generate increased demands for goods and services which will lead in turn to the creation of new jobs. Others suggest that the changes are qualitatively different from any in the past and there is no possibility of generating enough jobs to replace those lost. The new technology is not labour-intensive and it will be used to produce the new products and services. Existing or even rising levels of demand, therefore, can be met with very much lower levels of employment, and of human effort, so that average standards of living can be maintained or increased. At this point in the argument views divide again. Some optimistically envisage a future where everyone can spend a much smaller proportion of their day, their week, or their lifetime in paid work, and consequently can have greatly increased leisure *and* the means to enjoy it. Others fear that the necessary changes in the social organization of work and the redistribution of incomes will not take place; instead a proportion of the population may have well-paid jobs requiring education and skills, a proportion low-paid jobs which cannot be automated, and the remainder, possibly even a majority, would be more or less permanently unemployed and without the resources, either material or cultural, to utilize their 'leisure'. In such a divided society there are clearly prospects of considerable social conflict and disorder, and of authoritarian solutions being adopted to deal with them (Watts, 1983).

It is impossible to be certain which of these or other possibilities is more likely to be realized. It is important, too, to acknowledge that in the contemporary world it is the choices and actions of governments and of large multi-national corporations which may well prove of decisive importance. Nevertheless, the nature of work in advanced capitalist societies is changing, and patterns of employment and of unpaid work are becoming more varied, sometimes of necessity but also by choice. The Protestant work ethic is being challenged as it has not been for 200 years or more, and the proper place and significance of work in men's and women's lives is being questioned. In such a context there are opportunities to create new and more satisfactory relationships between work, education and leisure, and to seek to enlarge the scope for individual choice and freedom. An understanding of the sociology of work, industry and occupations can make a vital contribution to the debates and decisions which face us all.

9 Ethnicity and Race

It is surprising that the main traditions of sociological theory have paid little attention to racial and ethnic divisions and conflict. This is not because they avoid discussion of conflict altogether, for industrial and class conflict play an important role not only in the Marxist but also in the Weberian tradition. Yet they have not been able successfully to conceptualize the notions of race and ethnicity, nor have they given them the central place in theory that their importance in contemporary politics warrants.

Contrary to Marxist expectations, it is not the divisions and conflicts which derive from differential relations to the means of production which have been most evident in national and international politics in the last fifty years, but rather those based upon race. A major feature of the rise of Nazism, for instance, was the attempt to exterminate a large ethnic minority. In the post-war world, newly independent post-colonial states have found themselves divided on racial and ethnic lines. South Africa is a society deliberately based upon the principle of excluding the majority of its population from the exercise of political power on the grounds of race. Those who are excluded seem to unite on a racial rather than on a class basis for the overthrow of the system. In the United States, a major political change has been a growing recognition of the civil rights of Blacks and the development of a policy of 'affirmative action' to bring the Black population into the mainstream of American life. And throughout the world, nationalism provides a more significant rallying banner for revolutionary movements than class struggle.

The same issues, moreover, have become important not only in the colonial periphery but in the metropolis itself, where, with technological change, native-born working-class people with increasingly high status aspirations generated by the educational system, have moved into better jobs, leaving the hard, dirty and de-skilled jobs to be done by immigrants. Racial conflicts now occur not merely in distant ex-colonies but on the streets of British and other European cities.

These conflicts, it will be argued here, cannot be divorced from conflicts which arise from the differential relationship of groups of men and women to the means of production. But that relationship is mediated in complex ways by racial and ethnic factors, and some of the potential for conflict arises from sources other than those which have to do with production. In this chapter, therefore, we will first tackle the conceptualization of race and ethnicity and then consider the consequences of racial and ethnic divisions and how these relate to and intermesh with conflicts based upon class.

The first possibility we have to consider is a very simple one. It is that human beings are drawn to those who share their own characteristics and naturally oppose those who do not. This was a very common notion in early American sociology, usually going under some such label as 'consciousness of kind' (Giddings, 1898). It has been revived recently by sociologists whose work has been based on social biology. Van den Berghe (1983), for example, argues that human beings, like other members of the animal kingdom, have a genetically based tendency towards what he calls nepotism, though this tendency is extended beyond literal 'nephews' to wider groups recognizable as having similar characteristics because of such 'markers' as phenotype (observable physical characteristics) and cultural behaviour.

There are a number of difficulties with this theory. Firstly, even if we were to accept that such a tendency towards nepotism exists, no explanation is given as to why it should be extended to wider groups and to certain kinds of wider groups only. Van den Berghe therefore has to introduce subsidiary hypotheses in order to deal with these issues, but nepotism plays a minimum role in these subsidiary arguments. Moreover, he is neither a fatalist nor a racist: the main importance of his work is that, once we have recognized how nasty human beings can be, it becomes more possible and more urgent for sociologists to address themselves to the moral and political task of creating a common humanity.

There is a residue of the theory of 'consciousness of kind', and of modern socio-biology, in much of the sociology of race and ethnic relations. This is the notion that perceived differences in physical and cultural characteristics do actually present a problem of social organization. Thus, it is commonly assumed in most sociological as well as in political discussions that we respond to people with different physical or cultural characteristics with at least a certain wariness, if not actual hostility, rather than finding such differences attractive because they offer complementarity or enlarge our experience.

There is no need to reject this idea outright. It is quite possible that the 'consciousness of kind' school may be right: that people do naturally seek security in living close to others with similar characteristics, though the enjoyment of complementarity and differences probably depends on tastes or even moral ideas we have in the first place. But the key question is whether 'consciousness of kind' in *itself* provides a sufficient basis for a sociology of race and ethnic relations, or whether it contains only a trivial truth, a starting-point which does not take us very far.

Racial Differences and Ethnic Differences

Before we go on to consider these other factors, we should note one important difference within the 'consciousness of kind' school: between those who emphasize the importance of perceived *physical* or *racial* differences and those who emphasize *cultural* or *ethnic* differences.

The emphasis upon perceived racial and physical differences as a source of conflict has been considerably discredited since the defeat of Nazism in 1945. Most biologists (Hiernaux, 1965) appear to agree that socially perceived physical differences are by no means the same as the actual differences scientists record, and that what actual differences do exist do not themselves provide an adequate explanation of racial conflict. We have therefore to explain these false perceptions. But since there are also real physical differences between races or populations, others argue that the study of the relations between physically different groups is what sociology should concentrate on. Some, indeed, insist that there can be no such thing as a sociology of race relations at all without such research, a view, however, rejected by yet others who argue that even if such a special field as the study of physical differences exists, it cannot be very important.

In the classic case of anti-Semitism, for example, the Jews who were the victims of anti-Semitism in various cultures and societies were usually not systematically distinguishable in physical terms from the majority population. Dark-skinned Yemeni Jews, for instance, look like their non-Jewish neighbours; Jews in Germany physically resemble other Germans. The real and undeniable differences were cultural. Sociologists who emphasized the importance of physical differences were therefore seen to be lending their authority and support to political 'racists' who suggested that the behaviour of groups resulted from their physical endowment. The liberal reaction to racist theory, therefore, was to insist that social science should see conflicts such as those between Jews and Gentiles as based upon cultural or ethnic rather than racial differences. Even in cases where there were broad differences of physical characteristics between groups – as between Black and White in South Africa – the important differences between the groups, the liberals said, were ethnic rather than racial.

Such a view seemed to be commended both by its moral humanism and by its scientific truth. The physical differences between, say, Negroids and Caucasoids were insignificant as compared to the common attribute both shared as varieties of *homo sapiens* and as members of human cultures, and could not possibly justify differences in political rights. The central issues were therefore cultural ones, and it was these that sociologists should address.

What such a view left out, however, were *inequalities* between them, as opposed simply to the *differences*. Ethnicity tended to be thought of as a benign phenomenon, not necessarily involving any sort of oppression, coercion or exploitation. Hence the strategy for resolving ethnic conflict was seen to be in the fostering of mutual comprehension and the amendment of cultural practices. Such an approach was reasonable enough where there was benign interaction between ethnic groups, but, in focusing on problems of cultural differences, attention was diverted from the problems of oppression, exploitation and conflict which are so often associated with both racial and ethnic situations.

Conflict and Race Relations Situations

In reaction to this, many sociologists (including the present writer (Rex, 1983)) were inclined to leave the study of ethnic relations to those who were interested in the limited field of benign ethnicity. They, on the other hand, concentrated on situations of conflict, oppression and exploitation, under the title of 'race relations'. The term 'race' was used here in a special sense – not because the authors concerned considered that it was actual, as distinct from perceived, racial characteristics which gave rise to this kind of conflict, but because racist theories were in reality more often than not used to justify situations in which one group (whether an ethnically or a racially distinct group) oppressed or exploited another.

A 'race relations situation', it was argued (Rex, 1983, p. 183), contained separate elements:

(1) a situation of peculiarly severe competition, conflict, exploitation or oppression, beyond what was normal in peaceful labour-markets;
(2) competition, conflict, exploitation or oppression between groups, rather than individuals, to the extent that it was not possible for an individual in a subordinate position to leave his or her group and 'join the other side';
(3) a situation justified by the superior group in terms of some sort of deterministic theory, usually, though not always, of a genetic or biological sort.

This attempt to demarcate a field of study met with much criticism. Firstly, it did not seem to distinguish race relations situations either from ethnic situations or from class situations. Thus, many people found it misleading to call a situation like that in Northern Ireland a '*race* relations situation'. Secondly, the distinction between class and race situations seemed untenable, since both severe conflicts and a low degree of mobility from one group to another were often present even in class situations in a free-labour-market.

Powerful as these criticisms seem, the central insight of this conception of race relations should be retained, for the situations commonly designated as race relations situations are almost always marked by severe inequality and oppression. But that insight does need to be combined with those conceptions of race relations which emphasize the criteria, physical and/or cultural, by which people are distinguished.

There would thus appear to be four possible theoretical boxes:

	Situations of relative inequality and oppression	Situations of relative equality and harmony
	A	B
Phenotypical distinction between individuals	Race relations situations such as in South Africa	Contact between elites from different racial groups
	C	D
Cultural distinction between individuals	Situation of ethnic conflict (as in Northern Ireland)	Situation where two ethnic groups or some of their members live in harmony (e.g. Switzerland)

Figure 8. Types of racial and ethnic situation

The examples given in Figure 8 are extreme or 'ideal' types, in Max Weber's sense of the word 'ideal'. Quite clearly there are numerous instances which would have to be placed in box A even where the inequality and oppression that exists is not so extreme as in South Africa, including that which continues to exist in the United States despite Affirmative Action programmes; that of most post-colonial plural societies (e.g. Malaysia, Guyana); and that in many situations of immigration by racially distinct minorities into metropolitan societies such as Great Britain. Again the situation in Northern Ireland (box C) is an extreme case insofar as ethnic conflict has reached the stage of armed conflict, but even short of such a resort to violence ethnic groups are often to be found living in situations of competition and peaceful conflict, e.g. Walloons and Flemish in Belgium.

It is the situations in boxes A and C, however, that we defined as situations of 'race and/or ethnic relations'. This is why it has been said that there are *no* 'good race relations': because if they were good we would not be talking about them. The bulk of race relations theory, therefore, and a good part of the study of ethnic relations is part of the sociology of conflict.

Much anthropological theory about inter-ethnic contact falls within the two right-hand boxes. Thus, Barth and other anthropologists (Barth, 1969) have concentrated on studying the ways in which individuals distinguish between their own in-group and other out-groups in terms of subjective meaning. The emphasis, in these studies, is not upon inequality, but on perceptions of differences and of identities. Barth and his pupils have shown, for instance, how the idea that ethnic boundaries are important can be sustained in people's minds even when there is in fact considerable traffic between one group and another. Since such 'folk' theories of ethnicity influence people's behaviour, they have to be taken into account even in analyses by social scientists who emphasize social conflict, since the bonding of social groups may rest upon or at least be strengthened by feelings of belonging together based on ethnic and cultural criteria (language, religion, etc), and not only on the basis of shared interest. In Marxist language the capacity of a class-in-itself to become a class-for-itself is likely to be greatly enhanced where the members of that class also share an older ethnic identity.

Class, Conflict and Race

Our four-fold table above, some sociologists would argue, fails to distinguish between racial and ethnic situations, on the one hand, and class situations on the other. A more complete table, they would say, would require six boxes (see Fig. 9).

This classification, however, separates racial and ethnic conflict from class conflict, as if phenotypical and cultural differences fully accounted for ethnic and racial conflict in themselves. Yet even if we accept with 'consciousness-of-kind' theorists and the social biologists that some small part of the conflict may be due to hostility to the unlike, it clearly cannot explain the whole of it. A much more convincing position is that race and ethnic conflict are activated when they operate in conjunction with conflicts arising from other sources, most notably in the economic and political spheres.

This leads us to what is probably the more fundamental proposition in this chapter: that racial and cultural differences are *not* in themselves the major structuring factors in the development of societies. The development of the social division of labour and the structural conflicts it gives rise to have to be explained in terms of class, status and power. Phenotypical and cultural differences are 'markers' which are used to assign individuals to roles within the division of labour or the system of social conflict. This is the value of Banton's suggestion that 'race' should be treated as a 'role-sign' (Banton, 1967).

	Unequal or oppressive situation	Situation of relative equality and harmony
Phenotypical distinction	Race conflict	Inter-racial equality and cooperation
Cultural distinction	Ethnic conflict	Inter-ethnic equality and collaboration
Class distinction	Class conflict	Class cooperation

Figure 9. Possible classification of race, ethnic and class situations

But racial or cultural differences can only be used as role-signs assigning individuals to unequal roles where some kind of social hierarchy already exists. Such hierarchies have their roots deep in history, usually in the history of conquest. But it is as a result of contemporary or more recent economic processes that racial and ethnic groups are brought into interaction with each other.

The notion of racial and cultural differences as role-signs is shared both by functionalist sociologists who see society as based upon some kind of consensus and by conflict theorists. But whereas the former see race and culture as resources of the social system which can make it work efficiently, conflict theorists see them as lines of structured conflict. The most important sources of structural conflict derive from class and status differences and differences in the distribution of power (that goes with them but sometimes derives from control of political institutions alone).

A theory of race and ethnic relations has therefore to show the different ways in which phenotypical and cultural markers are used in relation to the major different kinds of stratification systems: class-systems, status systems and estate-systems. In the last of these – such as the 'Western medieval' feudal system – inequalities between groups rest upon differences in political and legal rights. Membership of one estate or another is determined by birth.

The term social class has both a wider and a narrower meaning. In its widest sense it refers to *all* forms of group differentiation. In its much narrower sense, it refers to the relationships between groups which arise in market situations and especially in labour-markets. Weber defined classes or categories of people having the same *market* situation, e.g. as sellers or buyers of various kinds of goods, including labour. To Marx, private property in the means of *production* was the starting-point, not the market: the formally 'free' market concealed the reality of a capitalism in which a property-owning minority had the power to employ those without property.

Class relations in this second sense appear at first sight to be incompatible with differentiation based upon race and culture, for a free market implies competition among suppliers, competition amongst buyers and bargaining between them. For Weber, formally free labour is one of the distinguishing features of this kind of modern rational capitalism in the West (Weber, 1968). And although Marx saw the notion of a free-labour-market as an ideological 'mystification', for him, too, the ideological peculiarity of capitalism still lay in the institution of free wage-labour rather than the justification of the social order on the basis of birth or ancestry.

Hence the ordering of class-systems in accordance with the racial or cultural divisions of society represents a deviation from both Weber's 'rational' market situation and Marx's notion of a society in which labour had become a commodity, freely bought and sold like any other.

There are three different kinds of class components in the growth of modern capitalism: first, there are those forms of stratification which already exist in the societies where capitalism grows up; second, there are the new institutions and forms of exploitation which capitalism itself establishes; and, third, there are situations in which the free-labour-market sometimes breaks down (as in fascist societies).

On the first point, it is unusual to find free-labour-markets and exploitation through the labour-market in pre-capitalist societies. Far more common is the direct exploitation of slaves, or exploitation through the institution of the feudal manor or the more centralized form of exploitation via the State referred to by Marx as the 'Asiatic' mode of production. Exploitation, in such societies, is not 'mystified' by the notion of a market. It is direct, often based on force, and, if it is justified at all, is justified in terms other than market ones, such as the accepted superiority of one group over another.

The penetration of such systems by expanding capitalism raises new problems. Sometimes the new institutions which are established look very like 'feudal' institutions, e.g. the *haciendas* established by

Spanish conquerors in America in which settlers from what were fast
becoming capitalist societies set themselves up as the proprietors of
manors. But though they looked like feudal manors, they developed
in a capitalist way within a capitalist market. So though Weber saw
capitalism as incompatible in principle with unfree labour, in practice
the capitalist entrepreneur has often resorted to political and military
power rather than depending on 'rational-calculation' alone, exploiting the labour of slaves, of helots or of serfs in productive enterprises
which were 'oriented' to capitalist market-opportunities but which
were not worked by capitalist wage-labour.

It is in situations like this that racist justifications of inter-group
exploitation flourish. Whereas pre-colonial forms of exploitation may
be justified in traditional terms by referring, for instance, to the
divine qualities of the emperor or the aristocracy, newly arrived
colonizers cannot appeal to that kind of justification. For them, the
easiest justification is in terms of the superiority of their own race
and culture. In colonial countries, racist legitimation and racial
stratification become integral to the working of capitalism.

So far we have only discussed class differences. We now have to
turn to the question of status. Marx hardly dealt with this question
except to think of differences of rank or title, say, merely as feudal
survivals. But Weber is probably right in suggesting that it represents
a separate dimension in the ordering of social relations. Whatever
their position in terms of the market, people also rank each other and
form groups on the basis of the differential 'apportionment of
honour' (Weber, 1961).

Ideals of honour and of how it should be legitimately pursued,
Weber noted, were *socially* regulated. However individual its pursuit,
the 'honour' sought after was embodied in certain styles of life and
members of superior status groups tried hard to ensure that their
style of life was available only to a privileged few. Such status groups
were communities and were quite as capable of collective political
action as social classes based on economic differences. Even groups
like the bourgeoisie, which acquired their original power through
their control over the market, consolidated that power by making
themselves into a socially exclusive status group by restricting entry
to only a few would-be entrants who conformed to their distinctive
style of life.

Clearly, in a situation of 'closure' such as this, where a status group is marked off by a special 'culture', there seems to be a similarity between status systems and ethnic systems, such as those in box C in Figure 8. Where, however, a ruling-status group succeeds in getting itself recognized as superior even though it is of the same ethnic identity as the rest of the population, and via competition rather than conquest of a foreign people, it belongs in box D, because it involves the *collaboration* of culturally differentiated groups. As in the case of economic exploitation, the resort to the political domination of another group marked by 'ethnic' *difference* is most likely where the relation between two groups arises out of new contact (such as conquest) rather than through internal differentiation.

We have already distinguished domination by class and domination by status groups from estate-systems, where groups are distinguished not simply in terms of styles of life and cultural traits but by differential access to the law. There are also systems in which individuals are given respect when they achieve a certain style of life which conforms to values which are shared in common, but where closed-off groups as such are not necessarily formed at all.

The American sociologist W. Lloyd Warner (Lloyd Warner, 1936; Lloyd Warner and Lunt, 1941) showed, in his perceptive study of the status system of 'Yankee City', how despite a great deal of social mobility, and even though the amusingly described attempts of the higher status groups to achieve closure were not very effective, the status order was still preserved. Yet while relationships between White Americans (whether native-born or immigrant) tended to be based on class (by which Warner really meant status), he argued, relations between Black and White were like those in a caste-system.

Warner's work on both levels was criticized by a Black American Marxist, Oliver Cromwell Cox (Cox, 1948), who argued that relations between Blacks and Whites in the United States could not be compared to those of the Hindu caste-system. Whereas the caste-system was based upon a good deal of assent, relations between American Whites and Blacks were based on economic exploitation. Race relations in the United States were a matter of class, not of status.

Cox accepts Warner's conception of *social* class as a system in which differentiation is not so much structural as conceptual – where there is so much social mobility that individuals are not seeking to enter a distinctive group but rather seeking to place themselves and others high up in a continuous cultural scale.

This kind of open, 'conceptual' status system (misleadingly called 'social class' by both Warner and Cox) is not all that open. It is closed on the basis of phenotype and race. So Warner was right in insisting that racial features constituted a barrier to entry into the status order at all, even though for some social purposes the definition of 'White' was often couched in terms of 'style of life' associated with 'White' people rather than with physical features. If a Black person achieved a high social status, that is, he was treated as being that much 'whiter'.

Earlier on, we distinguished status groups from both this kind of 'open', conceptually continuous status system and from estate-systems. We now need to return to the latter because they are not only typical of bygone societies of medieval Europe or of the pre-colonial world but because the conception of society as a system of estates can be used to analyse modern colonial societies and race-relations systems.

We have seen that Warner's description of racial division in the USA as a caste-like one failed to recognize that there was nothing like the same degree of consent in the American situation as there was between Hindu castes. Cox, on the other hand, did not distinguish sufficiently the differences between the situation of Black slaves and of Black workers and between both of them and the White working class.

Slave plantations, the key institutions on which Black–White relations in the Americas rested, were either manorial-type institutions at one extreme or capitalist enterprises at the other. In either case, however, they depended upon the exploitation of unfree labour, and the existence of such unfree labour presupposed differential legal rights as between master and slave. Such a relationship cannot properly be called one of caste, since it involves no religious justifica-tion. It was a purely secular distinction between legal estates. True, this distinction coincided with a racial and colour distinction, and Blacks had originally been enslaved by means of force. But slavery, now, was a legal condition. The use which White slave-owners made of this differential legal status as between themselves and their Black slaves was, of course, for productive purposes, so it is arguable that the social distinction between Whites and Blacks was really one of class rather than of estate. If we use the term 'class' in a narrow sense to refer to the relations between employers and labour in a formally free-labour-market, however, then it cannot be applied to slaves in a plantation system. There is, in fact, no agreement amongst sociologists on what is the appropriate terminology here, for relations between employers and labour on slave plantations combine class-like economic exploitation with estate-like legal unfreedom.

Still focusing attention on plantation societies in America, there were also groups which, although not in the same situation of economic exploitation in the labour-market as slaves, were differentiated in terms of the legal rights which they possessed. Thus, freed slaves, poor Whites, 'Coloureds', small traders and free settlers, all had a different legal situation from either masters or slaves, as did the clergy and the military, usually (Rex, 1983).

In many respects a system like this is reminiscent of the estate-system of medieval Europe. In both cases there is a division of labour or of social function and a differentiation of the legal rights of the groups which exercise these functions. What is missing is the highly developed religious ideology in terms of which social relations are justified. That ideology, however, was connected more with feudal society as a whole than simply with the estate-system, so that it appears to be more accurate to call slave plantation societies an estate-system rather than a feudal one. Cox is therefore quite right in insisting that capitalist operations are at the heart of the system. Colonial societies, too, like the *haciendas* mentioned above, may involve estate-systems without being feudal.

Unlike feudal society, too, the different estates in the kinds of societies we have been discussing were ethnically and racially differentiated. For the most part, each social function was performed by a distinct ethnic or racial group, so race and ethnicity clearly did function as role-signs allocating individuals to one group or the other, each group having quite different sets of legal rights. There are also differences *within* ethnic and racial groups, between different groups of Whites, for instance, or, as in Mexico, between different communities lumped together as 'Indians'. Overall, however, it was differences between estates, not within them, that were accentuated by differences of ethnicity.

The emancipation of the slaves in the Southern USA, land reform, and the liberalization of trade during the period of Reconstruction, all served to undermine the older estate-system, and should, indeed, have led to its total disappearance. But at this point race and ethnicity took on a new significance, now as role-signs. They no longer indicated differences in formal legal rights (since in theory all were now equal before the law), but they remained as indicators of custom, which might be enforced by informal sanctions, including those of the most severe kind, such as lynching.

The main kinds of racial differentiation found in the modern world are of this type. One hundred and fifty years after slave emancipation, full equality of opportunity in practice, as distinct from formal legal equality, is still far from being achieved in many post-colonial societies. Even in the United States, where there has been a serious commitment by government to a Civil Rights programme since the 1960s, racial discrimination still exists and may take decades to overcome. The struggle against *de facto* inequalities going under the name of the 'Civil Rights' movement is therefore still central to the politics of societies in which slavery has long been abolished, and makes political struggle in these countries very different from the ordinary process of class struggle under capitalism.

Plantation societies, in which there are White masters and Black slaves, are only one type of colonial society. In economic terms, the plantation is not the only type of productive enterprise and slavery is not the only form of labour organization under colonialism. Indentured labour may be used both in plantations and mines. Agriculture may be organized in terms of latifundia (large-scale farms which use 'squatter' labour – the labour of those who originally owned the land and who still live there) – but allow labourers a little land or part of the crop, as tenants or share-croppers. Peasants may be exploited, too, not only directly by those who employ them, but also by marketing organizations, by quasi-governmental organizations, and via taxes, rents and other dues rather than the profits made out of employing wage-labour.

The plantation society of the Americas we have described above is actually only a very simple form of colonial system. Perhaps the extreme in complexity is the combination of class, estate and ethnic relations which was generated by the formation of the British Empire in India – too complex to be dealt with adequately here – for even before the penetration of the East India Companies, a complex system of exploitation already existed, based upon the exaction of tribute from the peasantry (Habib, 1963). It was a system that involved marked class differences, that is to say, differences determined by relationships to the means of production, but these differences were overlaid by differences of caste and of ethnicity. On top of all this, White English and other conquerors moved in to take over the business of tax-gathering, using military force.

Slave plantation colonies were artificial constructs that could be designed from the start as such. But such a complicated social system as that of India could not be reduced to a simple relationship between English as a whole and Indians as a whole. True, the English formed a closed ruling elite, and developed their own superior style of life, treating all Indians with arrogance. But there were bound to be differences in their relations with some social classes as compared with others. With some of the ruling groups they entered into collusion, and members of these groups sought to associate themselves with upper-class English lifestyles. But the vast peasant masses and other economic and social groups had their own interests in the system to defend, and had to be dealt with differently. Hence one finds great complexity in the attitudes of the English towards Indians. On the one hand there were attitudes typical of the arrogance of conquerors, shared by working-class Englishmen who often served as the foot-soldiers who enforced exploitation and imperial rule. On the other hand were the attitudes which grew out of contacts with Indians who had their own vested interests in the system and who, even if they were not treated as equals, were not powerless in defending their own interests and were needed by the British.

Many colonial societies lie somewhere between these two extreme, 'ideal type' situations – the plantation colonies and the Indian Empire – and their subsequent history does not necessarily follow the same path as either of these. In the United States, the plantation colonies of the South had to come to terms with the settler society based upon European immigration which grew up in the northern states (Ringer, 1984). In South Africa, after an initial period of slavery, a considerable minority of White settlers had the military and technical means available to put the conquered Black nations to work, usually as indentured labourers in the mines and cities or as squatters on the farms. And there were many cases in which colonies existed without White settlement on any scale, but with sufficient military force available to make possible the creation and persistence of a system based on the exploitation of the Black majority, or, in modern times, via unequal trade with the outside world.

The most naked forms of racial and ethnic domination occurred in places like South Africa, where settlers were both sufficiently numerous and possessed enough military strength to establish what Van den Berghe has called the *herrenvolk* state (Van den Berghe, 1967). The structure of political domination and economic exploitation in the world colonial system as a whole involved many different ethnic groups as well as classes, each with its own distinctive relationship to the economic and/or political apparatus. Just as relations between the descendants of masters and slaves continued to be affected by the heritage of slavery even after emancipation, so other, even more complex, relations between colonialists and colonized survived the legal, political and economic relations which gave them birth, not merely in the ex-colonial states themselves, but where groups and individuals from these states migrated to the metropolis. Hence the race relations situation in Britain today is not simply a Black–White, two-fold relationship, but involves relations between native British, on the one hand, and a whole range of people of other ethnic backgrounds – Irish, Cypriot, West Indians, Sikhs, of different nationalities, different class backgrounds, from peasants to businessmen, and with different positions, now, in the British class-structure.

Sociological Theory and Colonial Society

Before we leave the study of the structure of colonial societies to consider race relations in metropolitan countries, however, we need to look at attempts by sociologists to formulate general theories of colonial societies, because these have important consequences for the theory of race relations in general. In particular, we will look at the work of plural society theorists and that of Marxist writers seeking to understand colonial forms of production.

The theory of the plural society was not developed by a sociologist but by a British colonial administrator, J. S. Furnivall, in his two books *Netherlands India* and *Colonial Policy and Practice* (Furnivall, 1939, 1948). In the former, he starts from the observation of the Dutch economist, J. H. Boeke, that in the case of colonial capitalism:

there is materialism, rationalism and individualism and a concentration on economic ends far more complete and absolute than in homogeneous Western lands; total absorption in the Exchange and Market; a capitalist structure with the business concern as subject, *far more typical of capitalism than one can imagine in the so-called capitalist countries which have grown slowly out of the past and are still bound to it by a hundred roots* (Furnivall, 1939, p. 452, italics added).

What both Boeke and Furnivall are suggesting here is that there is a sharp difference between established European capitalism and capitalism of a colonial sort. Boeke seems to suggest that the former is characterized by market processes, but that these come truly into their own in the colonial case. This may seem to contradict what we argued above – that the free market was characteristic of European capitalism, whereas there was more direct resort to force in the colonial economy. But both Boeke's theory and our own assume that under colonial conditions capitalism involves more brutal processes.

Furnivall, on the other hand, is less concerned with the absence of a 'social will' in the case of colonial capitalism. He is more concerned with its consequences, especially with the fact that the various 'peoples' are not bound together in a single unit by any kind of normative bond. As he puts it in his later book,

in Burma, as in Java, probably the first thing that strikes the visitor is the medley of peoples – European, Chinese, Indian and native. It is in the strictest sense a medley for they mix, but do not combine. Each group holds by its own religion, its own culture, its own ideas and ways. As individuals they meet, but only in the market place, in buying and selling. There is a plural society, with different sections of the community living side by side but separately within the same political unit. Even in the economic sphere there is a division of labour on racial lines (Furnivall, 1948, p. 304).

According to him, then, a plural society is a situation in which separate peoples or ethnic groups organize their own separate communities, each held together by a distinctive religion and culture. The society as a whole, however, is one which is only held together by the operation of the market, unconstrained by moral considerations, such as a shared ideal of justice, as functionalist theory postulates. Moreover, all this is not just a matter of relations between buyer and seller. It also affects the whole social division of labour.

The 'villain' of Furnivall's piece is 'the market'. He does not draw attention to the fact that the 'economic' relations of the colonial marketplace are often based on the colonial power's ability to resort to the use of force if necessary, i.e. that political as well as economic power is involved. Nor does he recognize that social relations in production itself, in colonial circumstances, are always based upon force and the use of unfree labour.

In these respects, the work of M. G. Smith (Smith, 1965) seems at first more helpful in that Smith lays primary emphasis upon the political order as the means of holding colonial society together. He develops his version of the plural society in the process of explaining Caribbean society, and begins by giving an anthropologist's account of the divisions between the various ethnic segments. He makes no attempt, though, to give an account of the economy which brings these various ethnic segments together. Possibly he simply takes this to be obvious, but the result is that cultural differentiation appears in his work simply as an historical given, unrelated to economic differentiation. What he does go on to contribute, however, is a description of the differences between the various cultural groups and the relationship between them. To do so, he uses a conception of culture as an institutional system derived from the anthropologist Malinowski.

According to Malinowski (Malinowski, 1944), any society has a set of institutional arrangements through which it meets its basic and derived needs. These are such matters as family life, education, law, religion and economic organization. It is the sharing of all these institutional arrangements taken together which normally unites people into a society. But Smith departs from Malinowski in arguing that an anthropologist trying to make sense of the Caribbean has to recognize that *there is no single society in this sense at all*, only a number of separate societies each with its own complete set of institutions.

Like Furnivall, he then develops a theory of how the various ethnic segments are held together. For Furnivall, the key was to be found in a somewhat brutalized marketplace. For Smith, unity is achieved through the one institution which covers all the groups. This is the political institution of the state. The colonial state, however, is not simply some sort of steering mechanism through which shared values are realized. It is divorced from the values of the separate groups or at least of those who are the underdogs. What it serves to do, therefore, is to impose the will of one group on the others.

But there is an absence of any reference to the economy or to what Marxists call the 'mode of production' in all this. Political processes are seen as both historically and theoretically prior to economic ones. It is because political domination by one group has occurred, usually through military conquest, that the various ethnic segments occupy the positions which they do. The key notion, therefore, developed in a later work (Smith, 1974), is that of 'differential incorporation'. So whereas Furnivall fails to emphasize the influence of political forces on the market, Smith goes to the other extreme: political incorporation appears to take place *in vacuo*, divorced from the economic purposes which originally brought the various ethnic segments together.

One writer who tries to bring the two elements of economic and political relations together is Smith's collaborator Leo Kuper, whose view of race relations in plural societies has been summarized by Banton as follows:

1. Societies composed of status groups or estates that are phenotypically distinguished, have different positions in the economic order, and are differentially incorporated into the political structure, are to be called plural societies and distinguished from class societies. In plural societies political relations influence relations to the means of production more than any influence in the reverse direction.
2. When conflicts develop in plural societies they follow the lines of racial cleavage more closely than those of class.
3. Racial categories in plural societies are historically conditioned: they are shaped by inter-group competition and conflict (Banton, 1983).

Kuper's conception of estates which occupy different positions in the economic order and are differentially incorporated into the political structure clearly comes close to our own theory of colonial society. But there is no justification for regarding racial conflict as *transcending* class conflict. Conflicts between ethnic and racial groups become converted into conflicts between estates when the groups are both legally unequal and have a different relationship to the means of production. In a literal sense, this is a matter of political economy.

Marxists start from precisely the area – economic relationships – that plural society theorists underemphasize, though their theories have other shortcomings. For them, the starting-point in analysing any society is the mode of production. For a long time, the dominant

Marxist view of colonial social systems was that they were pre-capitalist or 'feudal' (Hilton, 1976). This view, however, came to be criticized by a new generation of Marxist writers dealing with the political economy of developing societies and influenced by the work of writers like A. G. Frank (Frank, 1967, 1969). To them, the whole colonial system has to be seen as integral to the development of capitalism. Underdevelopment in the colonial periphery, it was argued, was the other side of the coin to capitalist development at the centre.

This view, however, itself came in for criticism from other Marxists. World-systems theory, notably as developed by Immanuel Wallerstein (Wallerstein, 1974), defined capitalist social relations in terms of market-relations rather than in terms of capitalist (and other) modes of production and the social relations they entailed (Brenner, 1978).

There are difficulties, however, in applying the term 'mode of production' to colonial societies. Since the position of groups in the division of labour was originally established via conquest, and since labour-market processes in subsequent colonial societies continued to be based upon the use or threat of force, the relationship of individuals and groups to the political structure must be as important or more so than that of relationship to the means of production. As against those who described colonial society *simply* as an estate-system, the Marxists' insistence that some of the central conflicts in these societies were the consequence of differential relationships to the means of production was correct, but, in the process, the concept of mode of *production* had to be enlarged to include the political structure of the society as a whole. Indeed, Marxist writers went on to argue that the determining feature in the social structure of colonialism was not the structure of production internal to any given society but rather the imperialist system as a whole, including the contemporary world-system in which exploitation is not the result of direct political control of colonies, but of 'unequal exchange' on world-markets.

There are three key elements, then, in the debate between Furnivall, Smith and the Marxists about the structure of colonial societies; to which the three different authors give different weight. These are the relative importance, as factors of cohesion in colonial society, of the binding together of ethnic groups as a result of market forces, by political domination, and by the 'mode of production' respectively.

The view argued here is that *all* of these elements must enter into the analysis of colonial society, that rather than an 'economic' explanation or a 'political' one, we need an explanation in terms of *political economy* – and, more than that, one which takes history and cultural differences into account, too. It is true, as Furnivall suggests, that relations in the marketplace are crude and brutal and less restrained by any common will. This is even more so so far as the employment of labour is concerned. Weber saw these features as characteristic of the institutions of what he called 'booty capitalism' (Weber, 1961). The use of force and violence is especially clear in the very early phase of colonialism. The *capacity* to use force, or the threat that it could be used, continues to be central long after the period of 'booty capitalism' and conquest, however rarely it may be resorted to. But it is there, institutionalized as the guarantee of a social order in which the different social groups are differentially incorporated.

In colonial society then, it is difficult to distinguish between 'pure' market forces and a purely economic mode of production, on the one hand, and political and legal structures on the other. But what, it may be asked, is the relevance of all this theorizing about colonial society for the analysis of race and ethnic relations? The answer is a three-fold one.

1. Whereas the notion of a free, peaceful labour-market excludes racial and ethnic domination by definition, the organization of employment in colonial societies does not.

2. The existence of legally unequal estates has been highly conducive to the development of such domination and continues to have an effect even after colonies have become independent states.

3. Historically, the groups which are differentially incorporated have been in fact distinguished by their ethnicity and culture and often by their racial characteristics, and still are.

The overall question is whether conflicts between ethnic and racial groups derive from perceptions of physical and cultural differences which one group sees in another, or whether they rest upon the fact that there are conflicts of *interest* generated by the political and economic structure, without which the cultural differences would exist – and be noted – but would not give rise to inter-ethnic or inter-racial conflict. Obviously there can be no convincing experimental proof of which is the prime determinant. Two observations may, however, be made about likely developments. These are (1) that even insofar as race and ethnicity *are* potentially important sources of in-group unity and intra-group division, that potential does require a structural context if it is to become activated. Hence even the sociology of race relations and ethnic relations must take account of conflicts which are *non*-racial and *non*-ethnic, especially those which derive from political and economic inequalities; and (2) that while the unity of interest groups, and the divisions between opposed interest groups posited in any kind of conflict sociology (including Marxist sociology) are normally difficult to achieve in practice solely on the basis of the rational perception of these common and opposed interests, such unity will be much easier to achieve when the groups concerned are united and divided by bonds of ethnicity and race.

Race and Ethnic Relations in Free Market Economies

So far in this chapter we have confined ourselves to a discussion of colonial societies and have suggested that they are easily distinguishable structurally from metropolitan societies which were assumed to be characterized by free-labour-markets. This is a considerable oversimplification. A comprehensive theory of race and ethnic relations has to be based upon an analysis of the initial colonial situation in which racism emerges, but must also be capable of explaining the subsequent connections between colonial and metropolitan labour-markets.

All market processes, and especially labour-market processes, are inherently unstable. The free market process can go on only so long as the only sanction used by bargainers is the threat to turn to another supplier or buyer. But both buyers and sellers can collude among themselves to create conditions of monopoly. Where a monopoly is established by one side only, that side will be able to dictate terms to the other side, which is still subject to competition. More importantly, when *both* sides form monopolies market bargaining becomes replaced by collective bargaining.

Classical economics and exchange theory in sociology rest upon an optimistic assumption: that market processes will continue to mutually benefit both participants. Conflict theory is based upon the recognition that once you have monopolies economic or market processes become superseded by political ones: market bargaining is replaced by collective bargaining, and this is an inherently *political* process.

Free markets therefore only prevail for relatively short historical periods. Market bargaining is then replaced by collective bargaining, which is based upon the threat of the lockout and the strike, and the possibility of even more severe sanctions. Thus the employers' side may resort to the use of state violence to establish authoritarian relations in industry.

A development of this kind is commonly described, rather loosely, as 'fascist'. It does not, however, entail the development of a racist theory. It simply establishes some kind of leadership principle or some notion that certain individuals have a natural capacity as rulers. Since very often this leadership lacks any kind of traditional social superiority, such as aristocratic descent, its ideology has to allow for social mobility from the ranks into the leadership, which is incompatible with any sort of biological racist theory.

Fascism in Europe, however, did become associated with racism, in a rather special way. It entered the field of politicized collective bargaining with a theory that an ethnic minority, the Jews, both as members of the working class and as employees, had interests of their own which were incompatible both with working-class solidarity and with national capitalism. The process of class struggle was, therefore, diverted into anti-Semitism. All that was necessary was a group, clearly distinguishable by its ethnicity and culture, which could serve as a scapegoat for the problems of the societies concerned. This is a possibility which readily recurs in capitalist societies such as Britain where Black and, more especially, Asian workers may face a destiny similar to that visited upon the Jews. Immigrant groups and racial minorities may become scapegoats, however, in any society where free market processes break down.

Yet basic race relations situations – situations of ethnic domination – occur either before a free-labour-market is established or in colonial circumstances where one group has conquered another. Thus at the beginning of the Industrial Revolution in Britain, before the working class became organized, the workers, far from being able to choose their employers and negotiate their wages, were threatened with the workhouse if they did not accept the wages on offer. In such circumstances, the workers were often seen by their masters as biologically inferior, a view expressed by Disraeli's complaint that

England was becoming two nations 'bred by a different breeding, fed by a different food'.

But we should not exaggerate the extent to which class domination in metropolitan countries developed the characteristics of racial or ethnic domination. Disraeli's two nations did to some extent become one, and there is at least some truth in T. H. Marshall's contention (Marshall, 1964) that, in twentieth-century Britain, citizenship had become a more important focus of identity than social class. But where nations have to be constructed after the conquest of one group by another it is rare that the two nations ever become one.

We have already described the way in which the exploitation of labour occurs within the overall framework of an estate-system. Now we have to consider the situation in which colonial social systems confront free market economies, either through the establishment of a free settler society within a colony, or through the juxtaposition of a free settler and a colonial society or through the migration of colonial workers to the metropolis. South Africa provides us with an example of the first; the United States of America of the second; and post-war Britain of the third.

White Settler Domination in South Africa

No incident characterizes the social structure of South Africa more clearly than the declaration of independence by the two small towns of Swellendam and Graff-Rienet in 1789 (De Kiewiet, 1941). The settlers there saw themselves as subscribing to the ideals of the French Revolution. They too believed in liberty, equality and fraternity – but in liberty, equality and fraternity amongst White men only. There was never any intention that these ideals should be applied to the conquered Blacks or to former servants.

The subsequent history of White South Africa is marked by class struggle between farmers and workers on the one hand and capitalist employers on the other. The Nationalist movement, which was the victor in this struggle, was and still is based in the first place upon the organized working class, especially in the gold mines, and upon farmers who want the best prices for their products and the right to get labour at the lowest possible cost. True, once the Nationalists established their control over the State, they too entered the field as capitalists, with the aid of their various secret societies; but this should not conceal from us the fact that White politics in South Africa have to a considerable extent been based upon class struggle.

The White worker in South Africa comes to enjoy all the benefits of his peers in Europe: the right to free collective bargaining; the availability of a generous welfare system; and the protection provided by minimum wages legislation. So well developed are these rights that South Africa remains to the present day an attractive alternative for European workers who have migrated there in large numbers.

None of this, however, applies to the four-fifths of the population who are Black. South African society rests upon an estate-system, the core of which is a system of rural 'reserves', from which an unfree population migrates to the towns in search of work. The existence of these 'reserves' is itself the result of conquest and of the occupation by settlers of the bulk of agricultural land, but it makes available a labour force whose absence of political rights ensures that they can be employed on quite different terms to those offered to White workers.

Complementary to the institution of the native reserve are those of the labour compound and the urban location (Rex, 1974). The labour compound is the means of exploiting Black male labour without incurring the social costs of supporting the worker's family or supporting him in his old age. What Weber saw as the irrationality of slavery – the need to support a worker when his product could not be sold at a profit in the market – did not hold here. The obligation to feed the worker was for nine months only, so that the compound labour system enjoyed all the advantages of the disciplines of slavery without suffering any of its disadvantages.

The so-called 'locations' involved a somewhat weaker extension of the principle of the labour compound. In the location the worker could live with his family, but these families were kept segregated from the rest of urban society, received little in the way of a redistributive subsidy from the urban population at large,* and were continually harassed by municipal police so that their tenure was extremely insecure.

Living in such circumstances, the estate of Black migrant workers

* For many years social services for the urban locations were paid for from the profits of the beer-halls which were provided by the Municipalities which successfully maintained a monopoly of the right to brew and sell so-called 'Kaffir beer'.

was available for a degree and kind of exploitation far beyond that suffered by the White working class. Moreover, whereas the White worker could use his vote to protect himself, Black workers were increasingly deprived of the limited voting rights a minority of them had.

The South African situation has been considerably challenged by a combination of outside intervention and of resistance by the Black population itself. Both sociologists and politicians, however, are divided about the nature of the Black Nationalist movement. Some see it as part of a class struggle which will necessarily involve alliance with White workers on a non-racial basis. Some, at the other extreme, maintain that Black nationalism is not a form of class struggle but rather of resistance to White political domination. And there are, of course, many positions in between these, involving varying emphases on race and class (Wolpe, 1970, 1976; Johnstone, 1976; Leftwich, 1974; Legassick, 1976; Wright, 1977; Bonacich, 1972).

To sum up the South African race relations situation:

1. South Africa is a highly developed capitalist society.

2. South Africa is a society with a large free settler minority exercising political domination over the indigenous population.

3. The so-called native 'reserves' are not an alternative mode of production, but are an integral part of the South African capitalist system of labour exploitation.

4. Capitalism as a social and economic system is capable of simultaneously exploiting labour both through a free-labour-market and through the use of force. The existence of separate estates makes the coexistence of such systems not merely possible but inevitable.

5. South Africa as a result has not one working class but two. As Frederick Johnstone has put it, the employers established a wages colour-bar; the White workers then defended themselves against possible undercutting by establishing a jobs colour-bar (Johnstone, 1976).

6. There is a considerable degree of overlap between the struggle between Black and White and the three-sided class struggle between White employers, free White workers and unfree Black migrant workers. White employers and White workers, it is true, engage in class struggle among themselves but unite in maintaining the subordination of the Black workers through a politically directed estate-system.

A subsidiary set of problems not dealt with here concerns the position of Cape Coloureds and Asians – racial groups which, as a result of their differential incorporation into South African society, have become separate estates intermediate between Black and White. For a long period they have been confined to certain niches in the division of labour. Their numbers, their power and their skills are such that both Whites and Blacks may seek to form alliances with them in the future.

The future of South African society is not just a local issue: it is very much at the top of the world's political agenda today. It is seen as a moral issue akin in importance to the question of slavery, which was resolved more than a hundred years ago. But it is also important as a polar case in the sociology of race and ethnic relations: as an extreme instance in the modern world of a situation in which groups clearly marked both by racial and ethnic characteristics enter a labour-market with unequal rights, and in which the group exercising political power is able to maintain a system of racial domination even though it is a minority. The question then arises as to whether such a system might not possibly become established in other situations where there is a split labour-market and in which the group exercising political power is in the majority. With this in mind, we turn now to the cases of the United States and Great Britain.

Race Relations in the United States

In North America, as Benjamin Ringer (Ringer, 1984) has pointed out, two distinct types of colonial society were established. One was the plantation colony using slave-labour; the other was a settler society welcoming as free workers in a capitalist industrial society the 'huddled masses' of Europe's poor. These two distinct types of society were united in the War of Independence (or at least the Southern Whites were united with Northern Whites) but split apart in the Civil War seventy years later. United again after the defeat of the South, they still continued their separate ways until the period after 1945 when an attempt was made to extend the Northern concept of Civil Rights to all states.

The plantation colonies were similar to other plantation colonies established in the New World. For a long time there was academic argument (see, for example, Elkins, 1959) about whether North

American slavery was 'better' or 'worse' than that in the Caribbean or Latin America. Probably there was less manumission and less inter-marriage (as distinct from concubinage), as well as a sharper colour distinction in North rather than in South America. But basically the institution of slavery was the same, sometimes producing intensively for the market, sometimes developing its own manorial lifestyle, but always employing Black slave-labour. Around this basic system of masters and slaves there developed other estates which, taken together, made up what came to be called the 'Deep South', together with a set of practices – known as 'Jim Crow' – which provided meticulously for the prevention of social contact of any kind between Black and White which might be taken to imply the recognition of equality between them.

The colonies of the Northern States were based upon industrial enterprises rather than on plantations, and employed free labour. But whereas in Europe the capitalist industrial system led to the emergence of a trade union movement to bargain on behalf of the workers and to represent them politically, the availability of an apparently endless supply of new migrants prevented a similar development in North America. The result of this was the emergence of an open and individualist society in which workers looked to the possibility of upward social mobility in an expanding economy for their welfare, rather than to the protection of collective bargaining. Insofar as such protection was needed at the outset it was likely to be provided as much by immigrant associations as by trade unions.

Two very different social types and therefore two very different patterns of race relations emerged. In the South, Blacks lived in a separate and subordinate society. Bound to their masters for purposes of earning their livelihood, they had no vote and were forced to establish their own separate institutions in other spheres. If anything, racial distinctions became stronger after slave emancipation, since without legal distinctions being available customary racialist practices became the principal means whereby the subordination of the Blacks was maintained. At the same time the society was a unitary one to the extent that the way of life of Whites was unthinkable without Blacks and that of Blacks unthinkable without Whites. Some writers (Van den Berghe, 1967) have referred to this system as 'paternalistic', a term that may perhaps be accepted provided that it is not taken to imply that the Whites were necessarily virtuous fathers.

Those Blacks who migrated to the North found a very different world. The most obvious difference was the absence of Jim Crow practices, and for many Blacks that in itself involved a considerable liberation. Yet Blacks could not enter fully into the new open and competitive society. In the job-market, in the housing market and in education they were confronted by discriminatory practices, so that although the whole society was often described as a 'melting-pot', Blacks were left out. They did *not* melt or disappear into the mainstream. While Irish, Italians, Germans and Poles came in and found their way upwards, Blacks stayed at the bottom of the status system and in the lowest occupational positions. Even those few Blacks who did grow rich or enter middle-class jobs found that they were not socially acceptable. This was the basis of Lloyd Warner's famous contrast between the open-class system within the White group (and to some extent within the Black group), and the caste-like barrier between the two groups.

Since 1945, for a number of reasons – including the role played by Black Americans in the army; Black resistance; and the sheer logic of a legal system which was set up to guarantee individual rights the racial practices of both South and North have come under attack. Though it is all too easy to be taken in by what may be simple legal 'tokenism', it has now to be admitted that the United States has moved from being, along with South Africa, a '*herrenvolk* society', to one in which processes have been set in motion which are designed to allow Blacks full participation in an open and individualistic society, with a realistic prospect of the opportunity of advancing to the highest positions.

Civil Rights programmes have a different aim and a different significance, and have in some ways been more successful in the South than the North. It was a relatively simple matter to make segregationist practices no longer legal, and to make it possible for Blacks to claim rights they had hitherto been denied both by law and by social practice. It was much less easy to change the open society free market system of the North, where – though no individual could be blamed or held to account – the 'system' seemed to produce a result which left Blacks at the bottom.

To rectify the situation in the North, Civil Rights activists concluded the 'system' would have to be confronted with an alternative system: not that of the free market, but one which demanded that Civil Rights be given overriding priority. What was proposed therefore was that Blacks' achievements should be monitored; where it was evident that they were achieving less than their due, there should be 'positive discrimination' on their behalf. Thus it was no longer accepted that Blacks should have bad schooling just because they lived in particular neighbourhoods. They could be bussed. It was no longer accepted that employers and educators should have unfettered freedom in the choice of their workers or students. They had to show that they were employing or admitting appropriate numbers of Blacks even if they did not have the necessary qualifications. The whole system came to be called 'affirmative action'.

Inevitably Positive Discrimination and Affirmative Action have run into opposition. They are resented by Whites whose own chances are inevitably reduced by the accelerated promotion of Blacks, and it is sometimes claimed that those promoted are not only unqualified for but incompetent in their jobs. But, given that such opposition was inevitable, the remarkable thing is that concepts like Affirmative Action, Positive Discrimination and Civil Rights have become part of the American ideology. So also has the notion of giving training in 'ethnic awareness' (i.e. awareness of their own racist tendencies) to those who serve the public. Those who resent these programmes (and they may be a very large minority) still grumble resentfully about them, but the most they have been able to do is to slow them down, not to stop them altogether.

A sceptical view of the limitations of even these programmes, however, is offered by W. J. Wilson, an important Black sociologist, in his book *The Declining Significance of Race* (Wilson, 1978). Wilson argues that while Affirmative Action has undeniably helped some Blacks into middle-class jobs it has still left behind in the ghetto the vast majority who are both Black and poor. Insofar as Wilson is only saying that the issue facing America is one of poverty, the response to him might be that Affirmative Action was never expected to cure poverty as such. But, even as far as Black poverty alone is concerned Affirmative Action has its limitations. Wilson, in fact, has drawn attention to *the* crucial issue: that a settler society still pushes the vast majority of Blacks into a hopeless and despairing situation which

Gunnar Myrdal (Myrdal, 1944) labelled as that of an 'underclass'.*

Despite these limitations, no one can doubt that some change has been achieved in American society. From being one which was characterized by Jim Crow in the South and the ghetto in the North, and in which a Black who attempted to succeed was put down as an 'uppity nigger', America now accepts that Blacks are entitled to perform middle-class roles, both in government and in the private sector.

As a result of these changes, Black politics have become complex and confusing. At one time there was talk of Black Revolution, which expressed itself both in the Black Muslim movement – which proposed to substitute Islam for Christianity among Blacks, since Christianity had been shown to be the religion of the oppressor – and in the Black Panther movement, which showed revolutionary and Marxist tendencies. More commonly it was concerned with improving Black identity through Black Consciousness programmes which stressed that 'Black is beautiful'. Affirmative Action programmes, however, created opportunities for Black intellectuals which did not require any revolutionary transformation of society. Among those who emerged as leaders in these circumstances were many whose Black militancy was an ideology of opportunists seeking to enlarge the area of jobs reserved for Blacks. There is a great deal in the discourse of Black politics today, moreover, which must be seen as Black racism, however much such ideas may be 'excused' as being a reaction to the racism of Whites.

This original race relations situation has been made more complex since the Second World War with the arrival of millions of Hispanics from South America and the Caribbean. Because of the diversity of their origins, however, most of them retain an identification with their country of origin which is national and not only racial or ethnic, there being considerable differences in background between countries in Latin America which have been independent for over 150 years, between Caribbean countries which were colonies up to the Second World War, and a country like Puerto Rico, which is still a 'dependent territory'. A complex economic and social pattern is generated by a lengthy history of colonization by different powers,

---

* A term which is relative to the open society in which it occurs. In American society it is assumed that all individuals are motivated to compete and ultimately to look after themselves. Myrdal sees the tragedy of Black poverty as lying in the fact not only that Blacks do not succeed but cease to be motivated to do so.

which has included slave plantation economies, large *hacienda* estates worked until recently by tied labour, and modern capitalist agriculture and industrial enterprise. Though Hispanics in US society are as restricted to lower-class occupations as Blacks, these differences – which also divide the Hispanic community – mean that the prospect of a 'Rainbow Coalition' uniting Blacks and Hispanics against the dominant Whites does not seem likely in the near future.

Race Relations in Britain

Britain is the country in which industrial capitalism came to birth. It is also the country, *par excellence*, of politics based upon trade unions and class struggle. While this has not led and appears unlikely to lead to the political hegemony of the working class, it has for a limited period at least been able to transform naked capitalism and has produced a series of compromises generally thought of as the Welfare State. These compromises include the recognition of the *right* to free collective bargaining; the development of a mixed economy; economic planning which aims at creating full employment; social insurance to provide minimum income during unemployment and illness; a free health service and free secondary and higher education, as well as other social services. Because these measures were supported by both political parties, T. H. Marshall (Marshall, 1964), in the 1960s, argued that citizenship rather than social class was likely to become the main focus of political loyalty in the future.

One has only to list these compromises to recognize that they have been considerably undermined in the last decade. It is generally agreed that politics in Britain in the 1980s was entirely different from the politics of the three decades that followed the Second World War. Since this has profound importance for race relations, we will return to it later. But it is also true that the process of assimilating dark-skinned immigrants from former colonial territories took place at a time of relative prosperity and social peace in the 1950s and 1960s. Our first task, then, must be to consider the social processes involved at that time.

It is not true, as Sivanandan (Sivanandan, 1976) and others have suggested, that British racism arose because of the onset of recession. It arose, in fact, in times of high prosperity and therefore requires a different kind of explanation: the high-point of racism in politics, signalled by the development of the campaign to control Black immigration and eventually by the popularity of the Powellite movement in 1968 and 1969, came at a time when the economy was prospering and unemployment was low.

The actual volume of immigration of West Indians, South Asians and East African Asians to Britain was small. By 1981 the total number of these immigrants together with their British born children was only 2 million in a population (in England and Wales) of 49 million – less than 4 per cent. There were at least an equal number of White immigrants from Ireland, Europe and the White Commonwealth. Yet it was the three groups of 'Black' immigrants alone who were seen as an 'immigrant problem'. Hence the so-called immigration policies developed in the 1960s were not designed to limit immigration but to Keep Britain White – the slogan of one of the fascist groups which emerged in Britain, but one which was supported in practice by all the major political parties, including the Labour Party, which had originally opposed racist immigration controls, but now argued, in the words of Roy Hattersley, 'without integration, limitation is inexcusable; without limitation, integration is impossible' (Rose *et al.*, 1969). In fact, as two successive studies by the independent research organization, Political and Economic Planning (Daniel, 1968; Smith, 1977) showed, racial discrimination against Black and Asian people was characteristic of both the employment and housing markets. Why then was this the case? If there was a concept of equal rights for all citizens within the Welfare State, why was it not extended to Blacks and what were the likely consequences going to be for British society as a whole?

Most specialist commentators and sociologists agree that in terms of access to jobs, housing and other social benefits Black and Asian immigrants are at a disadvantage. More than this, the disadvantage extends to the children of these immigrants *who are Black but were born British*. Ought they, then, to be considered to have a separate class position? Miles (Miles, 1982), who insists upon a narrowly Marxist definition of what constitutes a class, nonetheless admits that the Black and Asian immigrants are a separate 'class fraction'. Others, including the present writer (Rex and Tomlinson, 1979), have taken over Myrdal's term 'underclass', but have redefined it to suggest not a rotting and despairing mass but rather a group of workers and citizens whose relation to the means of production, to political power and to social rights is different from that of the mainstream working class. To use M. G. Smith's terminology, Black and Asian settlers in Britain in the 1950s and 1960s were 'differentially incorporated', if not strictly legally, at least *de facto*. The British Welfare State, with its ideal of class-balance, now had tacked on to it a separate estate distinguished primarily by skin colour.

But the immigrants who arrived came from different parts of the Empire, and therefore had and claimed different kinds of economic and political rights, as well as the right to membership of the British class-system. They included the underemployed and unemployed from the West Indies; socially mobile middle classes from the same territories and from the Indian subcontinent and East Africa; Jat Sikh farmers from the Punjab; poor Mirpuri and Bangladeshi peasants; entrepreneurs and often prosperous merchants from Gujerat and from East Africa, and many other groups. All of these, despite their very different economic, social and cultural characteristics, suffered discrimination because they were 'Black', since in the eyes of most British natives the differences between these groups were small as compared with the differences between Black and White. At first, they were regarded as not being entitled to the rights of British people. The question soon arose, however, especially as a new British-born generation emerged, as to whether this could continue to be a permanent feature of British society.

Although all these immigrants were labelled simply as 'Black' by many English people, there were in fact great differences between them, and there is a danger that labelling the different groups may give them the appearance of being more coherent internally than they really are. But because they *are* stereotyped together and treated as 'Blacks', these different kinds of immigrants nevertheless experience a common discrimination and seek to develop their own ways of combating or bypassing it.

A very important development in Britain in the late eighties was the intensification of conflict between society and its Muslim immigrants from Pakistan and Bangladesh. These communities have suffered severely from unemployment and other social disadvantages but have been distinguished by their Muslim religion. Many of them feel that their religious identity is under attack in Britain and there has been considerable hostility towards them as Muslims. Protests by British Muslims about the publication of Salman Rushdie's novel, *The*

Satanic Verses, as well as the sympathy felt by many Muslims towards Iraq in the Gulf War, have increased this alienation, and these factors have added a new dimension to the conflict between Pakistani and Bangladeshi immigrants and British society.

A great many Asians have succeeded both educationally and economically despite discrimination. So too have some West Indians. On the other hand there are many Black immigrants and their children who have suffered cumulatively from discrimination and deprivation. The parents are less able to provide a supportive background for their children, who in turn are less able to cope with being treated as inferior and less able to adopt White patterns of achievement. Although the possibility of cumulative deprivation over the generations is often exaggerated (Rutter and Madge, 1976), there is clearly a structural possibility that something of the kind could come about, a process parallel to that in the United States in which some Asians and Blacks would succeed, even without the aid of Affirmative Action, while the majority sank into an underclass position.

Policy towards Black and Asian settlers has varied over the years since 1962 (the date of Commonwealth Immigration Control). First there was a period of racist panic by public authorities, and more or less open racial discrimination. Then token Acts against racial discrimination were passed (in 1965 and 1968). But the characteristic policy posture was to deny that there was any special problem of discrimination and to assert that the hardships suffered by Blacks were part of a more general and non-racial problem of disadvantage. Finally, after a stronger Race Relations Act was passed in 1976, local authorities were specifically enjoined to promote equality of opportunity for minorities. At the time of writing, such equal opportunity policies are still in their infancy and it cannot be said whether they will materially alter the situation of Black people or not. They may, however, help to create a climate of opinion in which the concept of equal opportunity for ethnic minorities becomes part of the normal political consciousness.

The achievement of such a change is by no means impossible, because there are universalistic elements in the ideologies of all political parties (see Rex and Tomlinson, 1979, ch. 2). But it is not helped by the fact that political leaders of all persuasions have regarded race as a political hot potato and have been more inclined to appeal to racist sentiment for support. Thus, while the American

President launched his Civil Rights programme with the words 'We shall overcome', the British Prime Minister in a similar situation merely said 'People feel they are in danger of being swamped'. Such a statement hardly serves to give legitimacy to an equal opportunities programme and the racial and ethnic awareness training which goes with it.

In one respect, however, we should notice that there are ambiguities in those equal opportunities policies which have been developed. In the social services and in education, for example, it is often suggested that the best way of giving minorities equality of opportunity is to give them a special and different service which takes account of their ethnicity. Many White people agree with this, but take it to mean giving a service which is not only different but inferior. The whole debate is strikingly different from that in the United States where, after the Brown versus the Board of Education judgement, it was widely held that that which was deliberately provided differently was likely to be inherently unequal.

Multi-culturalism and multi-racialism were in vogue in Britain in the 1980s and were commonly held to be an egalitarian and anti-racist philosophy. But it may not be so: in addition to justifying differential provision, it may be used to deny that Black people are really British. Although many young Black and Asian people today speak and act like British men and women, this has not yet led to a mental redefinition by others of what it means to be British. The problem of cognitive dissonance presented by the young Black British man or woman is solved by the notion of multi-culturalism. It is possible to be British in a general sense, but not in the narrower sense in which only White men and women are thought of as 'really British'.

One factor which gives strength to the multi-cultural movement is that it gives jobs to Black and Asian people. This is also the case with the Commission for Racial Equality and its associated Community Relations Councils. Some indeed argue that instead of Blacks advancing into the mainstream middle-class jobs, what British race relations policy has achieved is the creation of a specialized middle class working in the 'race relations industry', a form of integration which restricts Blacks' positions in a White-sponsored control apparatus.

There are in fact considerable similarities between West Indian politics in Britain and Black politics in the United States. Both talk in terms of Black Consciousness; both talk the militant language of revolution. In both cases, too, there are jobs available for Black militants and the profession of Black militancy may well be a means by which middle-class Blacks lay claim to jobs. To say this is by no means to cast doubt on the sincerity of Black leaders. It is, however, to say that the role of such Black leaders in a White-sponsored multi-racial society may benefit the sponsors more than the people they represent or who are their clients.

It would be wrong, however, to draw too close a parallel between American and British experience. Both British politics and models of politics derived from India open up possibilities here not available to America's Blacks. Thus Indian immigrants have brought with them political parties and political traditions both of a working-class (often Marxist) and of a middle-class sort which enable them to find a place within the British political system. Such traditions are also to be found amongst West Indians, who are beginning more and more to relate to the Labour movement and who are now demanding Black sections within the Labour Party.

Clearly there has been change. There is now a greater commitment on the part of British Society to giving such settlers and their children equality of opportunity than there used to be. But there is still a racial divide, and most British people recognize it by talking about a multi-cultural or multi-racial society. At the same time, both Asian and Black people have made progress, despite discrimination and without the benefit of Affirmative Action policies. On the other hand, many have been drawn into the White-sponsored 'race relations industry' with the result that their potential for militancy has been bought off.

One important feature of the British situation is the role played by the police. Up till 1981 there was little evidence that the police force had been much affected by the development of anti-racist policies elsewhere. Two kinds of complaint were heard against them. One, emanating from young Blacks, was that the police 'harassed' them. The other, emanating primarily from the Asian community, was that the police did not adequately protect them. It is difficult to provide adequate evidence to sustain or refute these claims mainly because the police are reluctant to give access to the information required. One study, however, carried out by the Policy Studies Institute, suggests that both allegations are justified (Policy

Studies Institute, 1984) though in two different ways: immigrant communities are 'outlawed' by the police, either because they are harassed or because they are not protected. Either way, though, the *de facto* differential incorporation of the minority communities is reinforced. Some objectionable police practices have been abated since the publication of the Scarman inquiry report, but little seems to have been done by way of education to check racist attitudes amongst the police at any level before 1984.

All that we have said so far has assumed the maintenance of relative prosperity, full employment and the Welfare State. Since the late 1970s, however, none of these things can be assumed. The British economy is in a deep crisis with little prospect of an end to massive unemployment.

In such circumstances, two things might have been expected. One was the escalation of formal racist politics, both through the activities of fringe parties and through the adoption of racist policies by the main political parties. The other was the development of spontaneous racist attacks by unemployed Whites on Blacks.

Both of these had been problems in the late 1960s and early 1970s, a period in which the National Front flourished and in which the speeches of Mr Enoch Powell were widely supported by members of all political parties. It was also a period in which young so-called 'Skinheads' made 'Paki-bashing' (beating up Asians) a popular sport. But even though there is still a racist element in all the parties and though racial attacks go on, they have not escalated and, if anything, race has dropped out as a main theme in politics.

The reason for this is the restoration of class war to its place as the main theme of British politics. The government has taken advantage of the recession to weaken the unions by new industrial relations legislation and has been prepared to confront the unions in prolonged industrial disputes. In this way, it has no need for racial scapegoats, for the scapegoats which it blames for the nation's problems are the unions and their leaders.

So far as the ethnic minorities are concerned, their members are to be found on both sides in this renewed class war. The first employer to use the new industrial legislation against the unions was himself an immigrant, albeit one educated at an elite English public school. On the other hand, many of those who resist the government's policies directed at limiting the powers of Left-wing local councils are members of minority groups which benefit from such policies.

The question arises, then, as to whether, contrary to all expectations, the intensification of economic crisis and the pursuit of political conflict on a class basis actually serve to diminish racial conflict as such. Before we draw that conclusion, however, we should note that the potential for renewed and intensified racial conflict is still there. If the government fails to achieve its aims, and is seen to have no policies for dealing with the economic crisis, it is possible that some of its supporters may seek a scapegoat amongst the Blacks. Equally, in the event of a massive defeat for the unions in a major industrial dispute, one might see energies canalized in a racist direction. The racial situation in Britain therefore remains precariously balanced. In such an indeterminate situation, however, the possibility of political action aimed at establishing links between members of racial groups by those opposed to racism is one of several possibilities.

10   Class

Pre-industrial Societies

In all societies some social groups are systematically excluded from access to the most highly valued goods, both material and immaterial: wealth, respect, power. Even societies with only the simplest of technologies and production systems, such as Australian aboriginal tribes – whom many people think of as 'primitive communists' – are not wholly egalitarian: the key political decisions and the solution of disputes are matters for men only, and especially the senior men, even though in economic terms women actually contribute more to the household's food supply. 'Big men' also used women directly, as disposable assets, in what has been called the 'politics of bestowal', to build up political support, while young men were dependent on their elders for marriage partners. Control of women was thus a major political resource. Among the Tiwi, for instance, a really powerful man would have seven or eight wives by his middle forties; a young man would be unlikely to be betrothed before the age of twenty-five and had to wait until he was in his late thirties before his first wife actually took up residence (Hart and Pilling, 1960, pp. 14–18).

Inequality was thus structured on the basis of sex and age, the oldest inequalities. So were production roles, since the economic activities of men, the hunters, and of women, the vegetable- and fruit-gatherers, were determined by sex. But such societies are not divided into rich and poor, for material prosperity is minimal and there is no accumulation of wealth. What wealth there is is used to build up influence, often by giving it away in public competitive exhibitions of conspicuous 'generosity'. Nor is there any private property in the means of production, for every man and woman knows how to make the instruments they need in order to produce: spears, digging-sticks, etc, and everyone has access to the land and its resources. Society, then, is not divided into economic classes.

In our society, on the other hand, class differences pervade every aspect of life: economy and society are based on inequalities of wealth and of economic function which are reproduced from generation to generation. So we tend to think of class as the most important social institution, even as something inevitable. Yet even in Western Europe this has been so only for a few hundred years. Before that, for a very much longer time, one's position in society and one's life chances were determined by birth. In medieval Europe you were born into an *estate*, not a class, as a nobleman, a clergyman or a peasant, and could not move out of that condition.

Such systems of fixed ranking were often the result of conquest of one community by another. At worst, the conquered became the property of their conquerors – slaves. In the ancient world, those captured or, later, born as slaves were regarded as 'an *instrumentum vocale*, a speaking tool, one grade away from the livestock that constituted an *instrumentum semi-vocale*, and two from the implement, which was an *instrumentum mutum*' (Anderson, 1974, pp. 24–5). Slaves and their offspring could be bought and sold; families were split up and women and men even used as breeding-stock to generate still more slaves who would also be their master's property. This system persisted in the British West Indies until some 150 years ago; in the USA until the 1860s, and in Brazil, Cuba and other countries until within living memory.

The other major historic system of closed, hierarchical groups where entry into one or the other caste was determined by birth, was that of Hindu India. But birth itself was believed to be not a natural process so much as one determined by supernatural forces. Caste-membership was the result of one's behaviour in previous lives. Virtuous behaviour could lead to reincarnation in a higher form in the next phase of the cycle of life. But for now, the totality of one's rights and duties was determined by one's caste: the highest, 'twice-born' castes – the priests (Brahmins) and the Warriors (Kshatriyas) – were normally the wealthier and more powerful land-owning castes, while the lower castes worked the land or were craftsmen. Even lower were the 'Outcastes' who performed the most menial tasks, such as the sweepers who disposed of polluting refuse, including human excreta. These economic divisions of wealth and occupation were reinforced by an elaborate and all-pervasive system of social prohibitions which governed every aspect of life, from whom you might eat with to whom you might marry. Lower castes could pollute higher ones by touch, by coming too close, even by letting their shadow fall on their superiors (Srinivas, 1952).

At least, that was the religious orthodoxy. But people rarely follow the religious rule-book strictly and, as in all societies, people of different rank had to interact in everyday life, while energetic, entrepreneurial, innovative, or just plain rebellious or deviant personalities found loopholes or simply flouted the rules and were rewarded for their ingenuity. For even the most rigid social structure needs to make provision for taking advantage of the talents of those who might be of lowly birth, but whose abilities are exceptional and needed. Since they were dependent on their masters, even slaves might be entrusted with the administration of their master's estates, as in ancient Rome, and might become wealthy and powerful in the process. A master might reward a slave for a lifetime's devoted service by giving him his freedom, through manumission, while some slaves even formed savings clubs to buy their freedom. In the Turkish Empire, a slave might even rise to the rank of minister or general because, as slaves, they could never pass on their high office; especially, unlike noblemen, they could never aspire to become king or emperor. Slaves therefore often also formed elite military corps guarding the monarch and, because of their strategic position, sometimes became politically very powerful indeed. But the great majority were doomed to work for their masters for ever and would never shed their slave status.

Hindu society, likewise, was not completely closed and fixed, nor did ritual caste-status always coincide neatly with, or completely determine, one's economic position. At the top, just as Church and State disputed their relative precedence in medieval Europe, the priestly caste might be recognized as the most elevated, theologically, but the Warrior caste which provided the rulers (*rajas*) were 'the real linchpin of the system' (Wolf, 1982, p. 47).

There was a certain ideological contradiction, too, between the doctrine of fixed status and the injunction laid upon everyone to strive to move upwards. Normally, that contradiction was readily resolved, because upwards mobility was conceived of as something that would occur in the next life, not this one, through reincarnation into a higher caste by acquiring merit through following the correct path (*dharma*), i.e. conforming to one's caste position. The aim of life, in any case, was not to accumulate worldly goods but to purify oneself of earthly attachments. For the more impatient and worldly, however, upwards social mobility was possible, for some, as individuals: men could make money through farming or trade despite their low caste-status; women might marry upwards (hypergamy).

The four broad castes (*varna*) of Brahmins, Kshatriyas, Vaisyas (herdsmen, farmers and traders) and Sudras (menials), in any case, were ancient divisions that only corresponded very loosely to modern occupational divisions. The really important unit for everyday purposes, therefore, was not the *varna*, but the *jati* (often translated as 'sub-caste'), the small local group at village level which controls the day-to-day life of its members and their relations with members of other *jatis*. But how the *jatis* fit into the broad system of *varnas* is often problematical and therefore gives rise to disputes. So *jatis*, as groups, try to improve their position in the caste-hierarchy by imitating the behaviour and the symbols of identity of superior castes. Conversely, even Brahmins can be found in humble occupations.

Economic class, then, and caste are not neatly congruent. Hence religion does not necessarily determine one's occupation or class membership. Many specialists, too, argue that much of the inequality (e.g. deferential behaviour, hostility on the part of the lower castes towards the higher) is straightforward class behaviour that could be found anywhere and does not have to be explained in terms of Hinduism (Silverberg, 1978). Though caste is perfectly compatible with modern life – as when workers recruit fellow caste-members to the same factory (Sheth, 1968) – modern industry and urban life make caste divisions, particularly locality-based ones, increasingly difficult to operate, while class becomes more important. In the countryside, too, increasing peasant discontent is controlled more by resort to force and political pressure as religious controls over behaviour become less effective (Berreman, 1979).

Class Societies

All these types of society exhibit structured social inequality. Are they, then, class societies? To the extent that in all of them, whole sets of people occupy different positions in a hierarchical system in which superior groups exploit the labour of others, they are class societies. But the basis of membership of one caste or the other is determined by birth, in such a way that escape from the condition one is born into is unlikely, if not impossible. In contrast, individuals are juridically free and equal in societies like Britain. Yet classes clearly exist and persist, for whatever the volume of social mobility it is individuals who move up or down, whereas the classes they move through remain.

Much mobility, too, is short range, and many will not experience it at all: 'A manual job', an authoritative study of social mobility in Britain concludes, 'is now, more than ever, a life sentence'. But social mobility on a large scale does occur, not only from generation to generation, but within a lifetime, both via competition within the market-economy and via non-economic channels, notably the educational system and politics. Ideological rhetoric about the 'open society' or 'equality of opportunity' – in the USA, the idea that every American has a chance to rise from log-cabin to the Presidency – often evokes only cynical amusement. Yet it is not entirely without significance that a grocer's daughter became the first woman Prime Minister of Britain.

Countries like Britain or the USA are nevertheless extremely inegalitarian societies, with a tiny wealthy minority at one pole, and the vast majority of the population at the other, as wage- or salary-earners who own little more than a house, its contents, and a car, and often not even those. Many people think of society, in consequence, as a pyramid. Others argue that, with increased prosperity for the majority, and the virtual elimination of complete destitution on a mass scale, the shape of the class-system is now diamond-shaped, with few at either extreme and most people concentrated in the middle, neither wealthy nor impoverished. In reality, the distribution, as the diagram of social stratification in the USA (by income and occupation) on pp. 344–5 shows, is pear-shaped.

The situation is similar in the United Kingdom. A Dutch economist has developed the following realistic fantasy. Let us assume that a person's height is determined by their income level. Let us then assume that we ourselves have the average income level for Britain as a whole, and therefore the average height, and are spectators at a grand parade which lasts an hour and in which the entire population of the country passes by. This is what it would look like. First would come the smallest (poorest) people, 'tiny gnomes . . . the size of a matchstick, a cigarette . . . [such as] housewives who have worked for a short time and so have nothing like an annual income . . . It takes five minutes for them to pass.' They are followed, for five or six minutes, by people who are taller than the gnomes but still only three-footers: 'They include some young people . . . old-age pensioners . . . divorced women . . . owners of shops doing poor trade . . . and unemployed'. Next, for fifteen minutes, come ordinary, low-paid workers, 'dustmen, Underground ticket collectors, some miners. The unskilled clerks march in front of the unskilled manual workers . . . We also see a large number of coloured persons.' It takes a quarter of an hour before marchers more than four feet high begin to pass by. We keep seeing dwarfs for another ten minutes. Then come the skilled industrial workers and office workers, still only as high as our collarbones, though. 'Forty-five minutes have gone by before we see people of our own size arriving' – teachers, executive civil servants, clerical workers, shopkeepers, insurance agents, foremen, a few farmers.

In the last six minutes of the parade come the Top Ten Per Cent: at first, mere six-footers: headmasters, young university graduates, farmers, heads of departments, and seamen.

In the last very few minutes come the Giants – moderately successful lawyers eighteen feet high; then some doctors, and the first accountants, seven or eight yards high. In the last minute come 'university professors, nine yards high; senior officers of large concerns, ten yards, a Permanent Secretary thirteen yards tall, and an even higher High Court judge; a few accountants . . . and surgeons of twenty yards or more'. During the last seconds only, 'the scene is dominated by colossal figures: people like tower blocks, [mostly] businessmen, managers of large firms and holders of many directorships' (Donaldson, 1971, pp. 178–80).

The astoundingly wealthy are indeed 'out of sight'. The US chart, for example, only shows incomes up to $60,000, which is a very comfortable income indeed. On the original chart, the $60,000 level is forty inches from the baseline of no income at all. But the incomes of the 5,000 people who declared more than one million dollars in their 1982 tax returns could not be fitted on to a chart

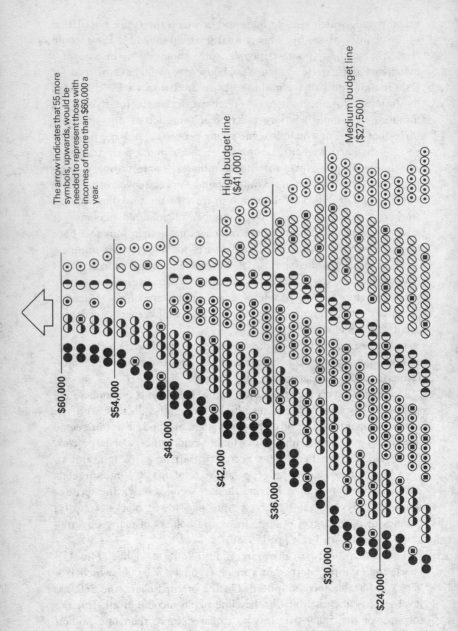

The arrow indicates that 55 more symbols, upwards, would be needed to represent those with incomes of more than $60,000 a year.

$60,000

$54,000

$48,000

$42,000

$36,000

$30,000

$24,000

High budget line
($41,000)

Medium budget line
($27,500)

Figure 10.

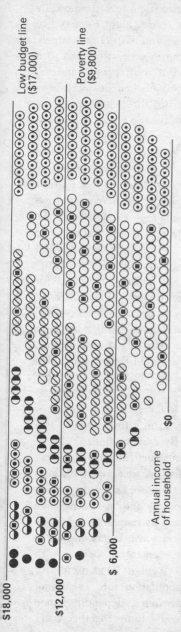

$18,000

$12,000

$6,000

Annual income
of household $0

Low budget line
($17,000)

Poverty line
($9,800)

Social Stratification in the United States (1983)

(1) by annual income-level and occupational group

This diagram represents the population over 18 years of age (omitting children living with parents, elderly people living with their children, and persons in institutions such as the Armed Forces, prisons and mental hospitals). Each symbol (◑ ⊙ etc.) represents 139,000 people, or 1/1000 of the non-dependent population.

The population is divided vertically into annual income-groups (before tax), in $6,000 brackets, from $0–6,000 up to the $54,000–60,000 level. It is also divided into six occupational groups with those outside the paid labour force classified either as 'unemployed/not in the labour-force' or 'retired'.

Married people (including 3.2 million adults who are not married but who live with another adult of the opposite sex) are placed in the income-level group of the combined household.

The positioning of the symbols *within* each income-bracket is merely for convenience of layout.

● **Administrators/Owners**
Salaried managers and self-employed professionals (doctors, lawyers, etc.)

◖ **Professionals**
Salaried professionals (teachers, engineers, technicians, etc.), small business owners, sales representatives

◐ **Skilled blue collar**
Construction workers, craftspeople, machinists, supervisors, firefighters, police, guards, etc.

⊙ **Clerical/Sales**
Secretaries, sales clerks, telephone operators, postal workers, etc.

⊘ **Less skilled blue collar/Service**
Assembly line workers, labourers, drivers, material handlers, janitors, orderlies, food handlers, domestics, etc.

○ **Unemployed/Not in the labour force**
People actively seeking employment/Those not seeking employment (in school, disabled, discouraged, on public assistance, etc.)

⊙ **Retired**

■ **Keeping house**
Married people not in the paid labour force defining themselves as housekeepers. These are included in the occupational and income-level group of their spouse.

(Source: Dennis Livingston, Stephen J. Rose, and Kathryn Shagas, *Social Stratification in the United States*)

drawn to this scale at all – we would have to use a logarithmic scale instead – for otherwise they would be six stories high! Figures like these, and diagrams like those on pp. 344–5 and 370–71, are largely based on information from tax returns about income, combined with information about people's occupations. For most people, indeed, income and occupation do go together: most of their income comes mainly from their wages or their salaries. But three-quarters of the wealth of the top 1 per cent, and half that of the top 5 per cent, comes from inheritance or entrepreneurial fortunes. Isolating inheritance alone, at the very top, 0.1 per cent of the population leave £500,000 (1980 prices) to their heirs (Pond, 1989, p. 71). Income, property and occupation are, then, different aspects of class. So though they are all *economic* questions, 'Who owns what?' is a different question from 'Who gets what?' or 'Who does what?' – even though the answer to the first question affects the answers to the second. The law also exempts many kinds of income – from some expenses and mortgages to 'fringe benefits', such as company cars, private insurance, health care, schooling and loans, and trusts established for close kin and others – from tax, in whole or in part (tax concessions). Illegal failure to report taxable income too (tax evasion) is widespread at all levels from the very rich to the 'black economy' which has been estimated at £45 billion a year (14.5 per cent of national income, nearly a sixth), where goods and services are paid for in cash which never gets reported to the tax authorities for income tax or VAT purposes.

Dividing the population into income brackets in this way thus reveals the *spread* of incomes, but it does so in a linear way – as a continuum from zero income to millions. By drawing lines at chosen intervals, as in the chart, we can then construct 'income brackets': the number of persons or households, for instance, with incomes between £10,000 and £15,000 a year. But these are analytical classes, constructed by specialists for their purposes, and according to a single, economic criterion, wealth or income as measured in money terms. Income brackets, however, are arbitrary constructs, insofar as there is no significant line, in real life, separating people with £11,999 per year from those with £12,000. It might be as useful, for some analytical purposes, to split the population into even finer divisions (say, £1,000 brackets) or cruder ones, depending upon what we are trying to get at. Thus, we could lump together every household below the $12,000 a year line, in the US case, because this is the official 'poverty line'.

Social classes, on the other hand, are not just arbitrary 'observers' constructs' created by researchers or officials. They exist in real life, in the form of institutions and differences in whole ways of life. Nor are they linear: they are discontinuous, qualitatively different categories, rather than merely groupings with more or less of the same thing, money. Being an electrician is a quite different *kind* of occupation from being a teacher, though they might earn the same amount of money, and could therefore be put together in the same income bracket.

Nor do social classes exist 'in themselves'. They are parts of a class-*system*. 'We cannot have two distinct classes', an eminent historian has written, 'each with an independent being, and then bring them *into* relationship with each other':

> We cannot have love without lovers, nor deference without squires and labourers. [Class] is therefore not a structure, nor even . . . a 'category', but . . . something which happens in human relationships . . . Class happens when some men, as a result of common experiences (inherited or shared), feel and articulate the identity of their interests as between themselves, and as against other men whose interests are different from (and usually opposed to) theirs . . . Class is a relationship, not a thing (Thompson, E. P., 1968, pp. 9–10).

That class is a relationship is recognized both by conservative thinkers, when they assert that workers and management both have common (or parallel) interests in the prosperity of the firm, and by socialists when they say that workers are exploited by capitalists. Even at the most naïve level of analysis, workers have to work for *someone*, while owning factories would be very unprofitable without someone to do the work. The system, moreover, is an hierarchical one; not just one of the different yet complementary functions, or even inequality of income, but of inequality based on differential relationships to the means of production and consequential differences in the parts each class plays in the division of labour, since some benefit at the expense of others.

Social classes, though they certainly arise from and reinforce economic divisions, are not confined to directly economic relationships such as work relationships. They condition behaviour in every sphere of life, from the ways in which parents bring up their children to attitudes to religion. Social class is thus wider than mere occupation. Tens of thousands of distinct occupations are all reducible to a few classes, both in official and academic analysis and in popular thinking, because they stand, as Marx put it, in a common 'relationship to the means of production', some as workers, others as owners. Classes, then, are not just observers' constructs, and people who belong to classes are normally conscious of that fact.

Economy and Society

The growth of Marxism in the twentieth century as the main ideological critique of and social alternative to capitalism has resulted in the popularization of a model of society in which the economy is seen as the 'base' of social life, with the rest as a 'superstructure'. Many Marxists themselves now reject this simplistic model. True, without production there would be no social life – we all have to eat, and raw materials have to be converted into bicycles and computers. It is equally obvious that what is produced, how it gets produced, and who gets what at the end of the day depend upon social arrangements and on cultural values which do not arise directly or solely from the way production itself is organized.

Institutions outside the economy do have to be fitted somehow to the requirements of the productive system: the family, as we saw, and even churches, instil attitudes in children and adults alike appropriate to the work ethos of society. But the forms the family takes, or the structure and the value-system of a religion, from Roman Catholic to Protestant, Muslim to Hindu or Buddhist and smaller religions, are not products of capitalism. They came into existence centuries, some, millennia ago. Hence, though they do have to be adapted to the logic of the industrial order, they also contain values which do not fit modern capitalism – notably, the belief in the superiority of the religious life over the pursuit of material gain and in charity as the highest practical virtue. Similarly, the value placed upon obligations to other members of the household, to children and the aged and to wider categories of kin, some argue, conflicts with the strictly individualistic activities each may pursue in the outside world of work and the market.

The triumph of industrial capitalism therefore necessitates

changes, innovations and modifications – not necessarily the total eradication – of other social institutions and changes of values too. We have already seen how difficult it was to get workers new to the factory system to conform to the new disciplines of working by the clock, day after day. In the modern organization, Etzioni has argued, control is exercised in three main different ways which he labels, respectively, coercive, utilitarian and normative (Etzioni, 1964 ch. 6). Early industrialization usually involves drastic measures, which he labels 'coercive', in order to transform those aspects of existing institutions, economic and non-economic, which conflict with the requirements of the new economic system, notably the creation of a labour force, usually by driving peasants off the land, or, in the colonies, by imposing taxes which have to be paid in cash, or by importing unfree slaves, forced or indentured labour (van Onselen, 1976). To bring such changes about, force usually has to be used. In the British Industrial Revolution, the ruling class combination of the new industrial and commercial bourgeoisie and the modernizing land-owners used their control of Parliament to pass Enclosure Acts and to repress trade unions ('combinations') and their monopoly of the central and local apparatus of violence – police, army and militia, plus spies – to overcome resistance. More troops were quartered on the rebellious cotton districts of Lancashire in 1812 than Wellington had under his command to fight Napoleon in the Peninsular War (Thompson, E. P., 1968, p. 617).

One alternative to force, however, is material inducement, which Etzioni labels the 'utilitarian' form of power. Millions thus gravitate towards the factories in the centres of the capitalist world, not because they are driven there at the point of the gun, but because they choose to go, hoping to make a much better living. They therefore become susceptible to the third mode of control Etzioni identifies: 'normative' appeals – to work hard and to improve their skills, not only because it will pay off in terms of wages and 'fringe' benefits (a utilitarian calculus) and not solely in their own interest (an individualist one) but also in the interests of their families. They may also be told – as in Japanese firms today – that work benefits the corporation, even the nation, and is a conscientious duty, a creative contribution one ought to make to the collective good, however alienating it might be for the individual.

Most readers will probably respond to such rhetoric with more than a little cynicism: it is difficult to regard standard operations on a car assembly-line which used to be timed in minutes, but which are now timed in seconds, as satisfying work. Many workers are indeed so alienated from their work that they only do it for the money and find no intrinsic satisfactions in it, and think of home or of the leisure-time pursuits their wages make possible while they are working (Goldthorpe *et al.*, 1968–9). To tens of millions of unemployed, the ideology of 'service', too, rings hollow.

Attitudes to work are not always negative, as we saw in Chapter 8. Work can be a major source of satisfaction and provide a crucial source of social identity. Two-thirds of those interviewed in the Essex University study of social class carried out between 1983 and 1985 saw their job as more than merely a means of earning a living: 82 per cent of them, including 80 per cent of the working class, found it 'rewarding', 'fulfilling','worthwhile', or 'enjoyable'. Four out of every five had friends among those they worked with, and saw them in non-work contexts (Marshall *et al.*, 1989, pp. 215–16).

An earlier classic study of 'affluent' workers, however, discounted the notion that any single orientation to work was predominant (see pp. 285–8 above), and found that while attitudes to work of course depended upon the nature of the work itself, they were not only affected by the ties people developed with others while at work, but were also deeply conditioned by wider cultural attitudes which they brought into the work situation from outside. Attitudes to the economy itself, as well as to the work we do within that economy, are shaped by the families we grow up in, the schools we attend, the neighbourhoods we live in, the media, and so on. Economic institutions and structures, that is, exist *in society* and are sustained by non-economic institutions and values. Thus although critics of social sciences other than economics often seize upon the study of kinship as singularly irrelevant and 'impractical' for any understanding of modern society (however important it might be for pre-industrial societies), capitalism depends fundamentally on the family for the accumulation of capital and on the mechanism of inheritance for the transmission of property. Land has thus been handed down for centuries through the family. Laws restricting inheritance to the senior legitimate male heir were designed, among other things, to prevent the fragmentation of large estates (and therefore any weakening of the power of the big lords). Where there was only a female heir, women became valuable properties as wards or potential marriage partners, while if there were no surviving children at all, the relative who did inherit would often pay tribute to the institutions of family and kinship which had brought him good fortune by adopting the name of the family whose estate he had inherited or married into. Genealogies of ancient families, if looked at carefully, are thus often records of the continuity of the *property* rather than of the family itself.

Industrial capitalism similarly transmits property through the family. Though capital has become both more impersonal and more institutional, since shares are floated on the market and 'institutional' investors such as insurance companies and pension funds are now the largest investors, what is often forgotten – because it is something so deeply (and uncritically) assumed to be part of the natural order of things – is that the institution of private property itself rests on two major cultural (and moral) assumptions: that people have the *right* to own the means of production, such as land (an idea as unthinkable, in some cultures, as the idea of owning the air would be to us), and the notion that owners have the right to dispose of their property as they wish (often to their children). There is, then, a dialectical *interplay* as between the operation of the economy, on the one hand, and other social institutions and cultural values. Social organization cannot be reduced simply to an economic 'base' which determines other social relationships.

Marx on Class

Having criticized simplistic forms of Marxism, let us now look at its strengths. In Germany, Marx's influence has been so great, for so long, that one writer has said that the history of sociology since his day has been one long 'debate with the ghost of Marx'. This has not been so elsewhere. The rich tradition of research into social class in Britain, for instance, from the poverty surveys of Booth and Rowntree to the studies of unemployment between the wars and the post-Second World War researches of Titmuss and his followers, owe much more to liberal and social-democratic ideas than to Marxism. The former looked to the humanization of society by stimulating individual self-help and personal charity; the latter to using the collective resources of society in the form of State welfare to eliminate poverty. Neither, however, envisaged abolishing capitalism or class society.

Marx did. For him, the dynamic of capitalism which had turned Britain into the workshop of the world had also produced and reproduced poverty on a mass scale. As we saw in Chapter 8, he believed that the essential relationship upon which capitalism was based was one of a conflict of interests, not of complementarity, between the capitalist owners of the means of production, on the one hand, and the workers they employed for wages on the other (Worsley, 1982, ch. 2). Fierce as Marx's moral denunciation of exploitation was, it was in the first place an analytical category. It was the worker's labour that produced value. Machines, in the absence of labour, were inert, even if labour had gone into their making and was 'congealed' in them and even if they were, as Marx recognized, increasingly displacing labour long before robots were invented. The central contradiction of capitalism was that workers were not paid the full value of what they produced, but only enough to keep the worker and his family alive and in a fit state to work and bring up a new generation of workers. Rising productivity was putting constantly increasing quantities of goods on the market, but the impoverished mass of the population could not afford to buy them. Hence cyclical crises. The general tendency of capitalism, too, he believed, was to push wages downwards towards minimal levels. Organized pressure from trade unions could interfere with this by counterposing working-class power to the power of capital. New ideas about minimal standards of living, and aspirations towards new possibilities – of a life that would go beyond minimal needs – also constituted a challenge to capitalist pressures towards impoverishment. The holding down of wages and resistance to improvements in working conditions was not just the result of cruelty on the part of the employers. It was necessary to the working of the system, part of its economic logic, for they had not only to strive to maximize their share of the social product as against labour, but to compete with each other by undercutting competitors. The contending classes thus had opposed interests, but competition was the order of the day between firms, too.

Though he often acutely recognized the non-economic dimensions of class, Marx's major theoretical work, *Capital*, concentrated overwhelmingly on economic relationships in the workplace and in the market, and on the objective working of the system (its 'laws'), with little explicit attention to the non-economic dimensions of class or to its social, cultural and subjective dimensions. His discussion of class consciousness, however, did entail some theoretical treatment of these elements. The working class, he argued, finds itself necessarily in opposition to the class which exploits it: workers are obliged to defend themselves if their wages and working conditions are not to deteriorate. Sheer self-defence, however, was only the most elementary beginning of a wider, more militant class consciousness via the gradual maturation of working-class organizations: trade unions, cooperatives, and eventually, political parties. Working-class struggles had begun as localized, defensive resistance to particular owners, managers, or foremen at the 'point of production', in a given factory or workshop within a factory. The idea, let alone the practice, of cooperating with workers in other factories or across whole industries, scarcely existed. The working class, he said, existed 'in itself', in that, *objectively*, they all stood in a similar position *vis-à-vis* the employing class. But *subjectively*, they did not necessarily see themselves as a class, and had therefore not developed their own class organizations. They had not become a 'class-for-itself'.

Over time, workers discovered that localized resistance could be broken by lockouts, importing strike-breakers, etc, or by competition from other firms which kept their wages low and thereby drove high-wage firms out of business. Collective solidarity was needed, therefore, at ever higher levels: the backing of workers in other factories, and eventually in whole industries. In the process, class consciousness would be transformed firstly into what Lenin was later to call 'trade union consciousness' and then into a revolutionary political consciousness.

Society, Marx believed, was becoming polarized. The reserve army of labour grew with every downturn in the regular cycle of boom and slump. In the process, intermediate strata – the self-employed artisans, family-owned farms, small factories and businesses – were driven to the wall or would end up by being swallowed by larger competitors, and the middle strata forced to join the ranks of wage-labour. Eventually, the working class would become sufficiently well organized to become aware that their numbers and organization now made it possible to think in terms, not just of defending their interests, but of replacing capitalism *as a system*.

What would replace it was already visible, for large numbers of workers were now being concentrated in factories where complex products were produced by breaking down operations into separate tasks, some requiring training and technical skills, but the majority being unskilled, repetitive operations. Even such a simple object as a glass bottle, in Marx's day, involved many such operations in its making (Marx, 1976, Part IV, ch. XII). The socialization of production even linked together workers in different countries, including the colonies, from which raw materials were brought thousands of miles to be turned into manufactured goods in Europe. But this increasingly socialized production was in conflict with private ownership, because the owners ran industry for *their* interests, to maximize profits, not in the interests of their workers or of consumers. The solution, Marx believed, was to recognize that modern enterprises and modern capitalism were highly socialized and to run them as such, in the interests of the producers and of society as a whole by abolishing private ownership. The bourgeoisie – the capitalist owners – would resist by every means in their power, from lockouts and the breaking of strikes to the use of State power – Parliament, the courts, the police and the army. The working class would therefore have to organize itself not just for economic, but for political class struggle: to take over the State. After a period of transition, Marx believed, since both productive enterprises and social institutions would be run by the people themselves in their own interests, the repressive machinery of the State would begin to 'wither away'.

The Problem of Order: Explanations

It is commonplace to observe that most of Marx's predictions have not come true; in particular, that no proletarian revolution has taken place in any advanced capitalist country. On the other hand, communist-led revolutions have taken place in backward, agrarian countries, notably in Russia and China, with a third of the world's population between them. The question then arises as to where Marx went wrong.

In part, it was because of erroneous basic assumptions; in part, because he did not devote the same scrupulous attention that he devoted to economic issues – such as the declining rate of profit or the nature of value – to social issues. Had he done so, he might have avoided some of these errors, even in his day. True, most of the social developments that were to prove fateful for his general theory of capitalist development were only incipient when he was alive: the growth of social mobility; the beginnings of better housing and education for the working class and other forms of welfare provision; the political incorporation of the working class. In his day, too, welfare provision and the extension of political rights were being fiercely resisted by powerful sections of the bourgeoisie.

But his analysis can scarcely be dismissed out of hand, even for the contemporary West, given the persistence of massive economic inequality, and the association of these economic inequalities with social inequalities and differences of lifestyle in all spheres of life. Yet his analysis of class was overwhelmingly economic in nature. However perceptive his observations on such matters as the effects of Irish immigration on working-class solidarity or the 'bourgeoisification' of the working class, these were often remarks in letters to friends, not central parts of his analysis.

The sociological problem entailed, however, goes far beyond Marx's theory. In general terms, it is only one particular aspect of the major issue which functionalist sociologists have termed the 'problem of order': why it is, given the massive structured inequality we saw above, that the underprivileged put up with it.

There are several major *kinds* of answer to this question. The first emphasizes the overall capacity of capitalism to keep on expanding, even given booms and slumps. The second emphasizes redistribution, notably the rise of the Welfare State. A third school emphasizes social mobility; a fourth, divisions *within* the working class; a fifth, political rather than economic change (the 'incorporation' of the working class), or part of it, into parties controlled by other classes, and the later 'taming' of Labour; a sixth, ideological rather than economic *or* political factors (the acceptance of ruling class ideas, or, in more modern terms, the influence of the media); a seventh, 'world-system' factors external to the British (or US, or German) economy and society – the existence of a *super*-exploited 'external proletariat' in the Third World and/or of an internal 'reserve army of labour' of Third World origins. Other sociologists regard all these models as inadequate because most of them assume that what matters most is political economy, and rarely look at the much wider phenomenon of *social* class. Yet others point out that in order to explain why even the discontented put up with their lot we have to consider what alternatives they have, if any. Let us look at the empirical evidence relevant to each of these arguments in turn.

Affluence

Most of us, in everyday life, use bits and pieces of all of these types of explanation, and that is quite a sensible way to proceed, for no one of them is adequate in itself to explain why it is that such markedly unequal class-systems do not break down. The term 'affluence' was originally introduced by the economist J. K. Galbraith, not as a celebration of capitalism, but as part of a critique: capitalism, he said, generated 'private affluence' but also 'public squalor'. However, it has come to be used in general parlance as equivalent to 'prosperity'. The argument from affluence is indeed strong, since the capitalism built upon coal and iron has been displaced by ever-changing technologies, among which microchips and genetic engineering are the most important; these technologies have not only transformed production – the kinds of work we do and the things produced – thereby vastly expanding human productive capacity, but have also made possible mass consumption on a scale unimaginable in the nineteenth century.

As we saw in Chapter 2, large parts of the South have not shared in this kind of prosperity. Nevertheless, since 1945, capitalism as a world economic system has succeeded in massively expanding production in its older heartlands of Europe and North America as well as in Japan, in Australia and South Africa, in Hong Kong and Singapore, in Taiwan and South Korea, and in Brazil and Mexico. It has also eclipsed the communist economic system, which had brought the USSR from Tsarist backwardness to number two Superpower in only thirty years.

Not everyone sees this as an unequivocally positive process. 'Green' critics stress the costs of all this mass consumption in terms of another kind of consumption – that of finite resources – and damage to the natural environment. Egalitarians maintain an older critique, directing their fire at persisting massive inequality within the developed world. Conservatives, on the other hand, encourage people to think not in terms of demanding bigger shares of a fixed cake (even less of taking over the bakery), but to devote their energies to helping bake an even bigger one. In more formal language, the economy is not to be seen as a zero-sum game, in which one can only win at the expense of the other. This way, they argue, working-class income will grow in absolute terms but not relatively – at the expense of the bourgeoisie – for, in a growing economy, the income of the latter will also grow vastly. In fact, real incomes for manual workers have tripled in three-quarters of a century and for ten hours' less work per week, with three weeks' paid holiday a year. The average Briton, moreover, now lives thirty years longer. Plainly, capitalism is far from being exhausted (Halsey, 1986, p. 29). Hence, though the major modern study of social mobility in Britain concludes that 'no significant reduction in class inequalities has been achieved' and that 'the general underlying processes of inter-generational class mobility – or immobility – have apparently been little altered, and indeed, have, if anything, tended in certain respects to generate still greater inequalities', 'sustained economic growth' has 'removed the possibilities of any widespread resentment over the extent of inequalities of opportunity' (Goldthorpe *et al.*, 1980, pp. 85, 252, 274). 'Economic expansion', it concludes, 'has made it possible ... for a widespread sense of social achievement to be experienced even where at the same time [there has been] a basic inequality of class position' (p. 272).

Social surveys of this kind are very difficult, time-consuming projects. That one is now over ten years old, and since then the capitalist world has entered a recession. Unemployment, which many thought would be socially unacceptable if it rose much above a million, has, in fact, risen first to two million, then to three and more in real terms, while some fifteen million people – more than a quarter of the population – according to one study live in poverty (Mack and Lansley, 1985, p. 7). By 1984, the poorer half of the population owned only 7 per cent of total marketable wealth (homes, stocks and shares, etc). At the same time, the share of the top 10 per cent increased to nearly a quarter of all after-tax income; that of the super-rich top 1 per cent rose for the first time since 1949 (Mack and Lansley, 1985, p. 5), a rise which began in 1981. By 1986, the most wealthy 1 per cent of the population owned nearly a fifth of the marketable wealth; the richest 10 per cent owned over half. True, the share of wealth owned by the top 1 per cent had been far higher in 1914 – around 70 per cent – and had declined to two-fifths by

1960. But no great democratization was involved: wealth was simply spread among the richest 5 per cent rather than the richest 1 per cent, and they owned twenty times as much as the poorest 20 per cent (Halsey, 1986, pp. 30–31, 37).

At the bottom end of the social hierarchy, the privatization of nationalized industries in Britain led to a sudden increase in the numbers of working-class people who owned shares. Most of these, however,. ended up in the hands of the major financial institutions (including pension funds, whose prosperity affects the retirement incomes of vast numbers of people). Nevertheless,

total disposable incomes in 1986 were 30 per cent higher in real terms than they were ten years earlier; . . . 64 per cent of skilled workers, 46 per cent of semi-skilled workers and 33 per cent of unskilled workers now own their own homes. Two-thirds of households have a car today compared with one-third in 1961. Eighty-six per cent of British homes now own a colour television set, 80 per cent have a telephone, 28 per cent have a video. Thirty-three million people out of a population of fifty-six and a half million took holidays in Britain in 1985 and a further sixteen million went abroad (Saunders, 1990, pp. 105–6).

These are impressive changes, which deeply affect the attitudes of millions towards the society they live in: their ideas about opportunity, their feelings about inequality and their sense of identity, including their political identities and their membership of trade unions.

Information like this, which purports to reflect levels of personal affluence, is still based upon statistical and administrative categories which take the individual as their unit of analysis. They therefore conceal rather than help us to understand some fundamental realities: that three out of four people live in households where more than one person may bring in income, while nearly a million single-parent families (1984), mainly headed by women, live at or near the poverty line, and even women who work full-time earn only two-thirds, on average, of male earnings; that millions, especially the unemployed and their families, may depend exclusively upon meagre State benefits.

A scholar very critical of left/liberal class analysis provides a reasonable summary of these changes in working-class living standards (even allowing for economic recession since these words were written):

In strict sociological terms, the fact that the working class has become more affluent and now owns a range of goods which was out of its reach just a short time ago does nothing to alter its class situation . . . Social class has to do with how people get their incomes, not how they spend them . . . Nevertheless . . . taken together with . . . extensive opportunities for upwards social mobility . . . rising affluence is likely to influence working-class culture and ways of life (Saunders, 1990, pp. 105–6).

Redistribution

The second major explanation commonly offered for the absence of severe class conflict during recession has been the argument from redistribution. Today, there is no counterpart, in advanced capitalist countries, to the tens of millions of urban poor who live on the streets of the Third World (Worsley, 1984, ch. III) as many tens of thousands of people used to live on the streets of nineteenth-century London (see above, pp. 243–6). Today, although poverty is still widespread, our ideas about what constitutes an acceptable minimal standard of living have changed massively. For the three-quarters of the population who were manual workers at the turn of the century, unemployment meant hunger and destitution. Today, working-class aspirations (which are not the same as their more realistic *expectations*, or, even less, what they actually get) include, as a minimum, not only decent heating, an indoor toilet, a bath, and beds for everyone, but, for three-quarters of them, a fridge and carpets on the floor, and for two-thirds, a washing-machine and holidays for a week a year (not with relatives) (Mack and Lansley, 1985, Table 3.1, p. 54).

An expanding rich economy has made it possible for the State to redistribute some of that wealth so as to remove the prospect of death, illness and destitution for the very poor. The three main mechanisms involved are taxation policy; the provision of State social services; and welfare provision tied to occupation. On the first of these, R. M. Titmuss definitively demonstrated a generation ago what subsequent research has confirmed: that welfare is largely paid for by those it benefits, and that overall the middle classes benefit most. In 1974–5, taxation only reduced the share of personal income going to the richest 10 per cent from 26.6 to 23.2 per cent, while 'the poorest 10 per cent took 2.8 per cent before tax . . . [and] 3.1 per cent after tax . . ., scarcely . . . evidence of a hugely distributive "welfare" state'. 'Welfare', Halsey concludes, 'is largely self-financed for the bulk of the population. The activity of the state makes for no dramatic reduction of market inequalities' (1986, p. 33). The quality of life at the end of a lifetime's work depends, for the fortunate, not on a meagre State pension, but on lifetime savings and on pensions related to occupation (1986, pp. 35–6).

Increasing State expenditure on education during this century has primarily benefited the children of the middle classes. The social reproduction of the upper classes has depended on the flourishing private sector in education, notably the much understudied public schools. But the process starts much earlier than the age of compulsory schooling and goes on long after it. Children of Class I parents are twice as likely to go to nursery school as those from Class VI; two out of every three of the former will end up with degrees, but only one in ten of the latter. Yet nearly three-quarters of the top class are not university graduates at all: if you are born into a very wealthy and well-connected family, you can stay where you were born without having to acquire formal educational qualifications. The unequal distribution of wealth can also frustrate the levelling intent of educational reformers. In Finland, a country where private fee-paying secondary schooling was abolished many years ago and where nearly a third of upper working-class males, and *half* the women in that class, now acquire university degrees (Pöntinen, 1983, Table 9.1, p. 112), the effects of social differences in the home – encouragement and help from parents who are themselves highly educated; the intellectually stimulating effects of living in homes where books and informed discussion of public affairs and intellectual issues, plus exposure to 'high' culture, are part of everyday life – are such that children of upper-class parents still do disproportionately well in the educational competition and are more likely than a generation ago to go on to a higher degree. In the UK, one in five of those accepted for university in 1983 came from 'Class I' homes and one in five had attended 'independent' schools; only 563 out of 61,306 came from 'unskilled' backgrounds. Yet despite these large class differences, which have persisited over generations, the educational system as we shall see, has also been one of the most important channels through which large numbers of children have moved upwards through the class structure.

In the field of health, where private and public health care systems exist side by side (and where the middle classes make more use of the NHS), class inequalities similarly persist, as we saw in Chapter 6. In the UK, 'the most important general finding is the lack of improvement, and in some respects deterioration' of the health of the partly skilled and unskilled (a quarter of the economically active population), as compared to the 5 per cent in the Registrar General's Class I (higher professionals, managers, etc) (Townsend and Davidson, 1982, p. 74).

Social mobility

The third type of argument concentrates on mobility. Even before economic slowdown turned into recession, the general conclusion of the Oxford Social Mobility Study of 1972 was that 'no greater degree of openness has been achieved . . . in recent decades' (p. 86), some 15–20 per cent of those in the highest class did, nevertheless, come from working-class backgrounds.

Class I classifies together 'higher professionals, higher administrators and officials in central and local government, and in public and private enterprises (including company directors); managers in large industrial establishments; and large proprietors'. Class II is made up of 'lower-grade professions and higher-grade technicians; lower-grade administrators and officials; managers in small business and industrial establishments and in services; and supervisors of non-manual employees'. These two classes, together, the authors term the 'service class', Class I being 'a class of those exercising power and expertise on behalf of corporate bodies, plus such elements of the classic bourgeoisie (independent businessmen and "free" professionals) as are not yet assimilated into this new formation'; Class II is the 'subaltern or cadet levels of the service class', below Class I, but carrying 'staff status and conditions of employment' (Goldthorpe *et al.*, 1980, pp. 39–40).

At the other end of the scale are Classes VI and VII: skilled manual, and semi-skilled and unskilled workers respectively. Together, they constitute the working class. They exhibit far higher levels of continuity of occupation from generation to generation: three out of four will follow their fathers into manual work. In between come three 'intermediate' classes: routine non-manual (Class

III); workers 'on their own account' (Class IV); and lower-grade technicians and supervisors (Class V), all of whom show considerable intergenerational and intragenerational mobility.

The gulf between manual and non-manual work was once regarded, by the public and by social scientists alike, as the major division within the working class apart from that between skilled workers and others. The extent of the erosion of both economic and social distinctions between manual and non-manual labour, because of successive shifts in office technology, from handwritten bookkeeping to typewriting and adding machines, then to computer-processed data, has resulted in the decline in status of clerical work from a respectable, male occupation in the nineteenth century to a predominantly lower-status female occupation today (Lockwood, 1958). Yet the extent of de-skilling can be exaggerated: job autonomy, income and status are still likely to be higher for those – usually men – who reach the higher grades.

The whole 'intermediate' zone has become one of great fluidity in any case, as people move in and out of these occupations on a large scale. Little more than half stay in the class they were born in, so new arrivals outnumber those born into the middle classes by nearly two to one (Halsey, 1986, pp. 114–16).

There is even some significant inflow into Class I, where some 15–20 per cent come from working-class backgrounds and *each* class contributes at least 10 per cent to the top class. By any reckoning, Class I shows a 'very wide basis of recruitment and a very low degree of homogeneity in its composition' (Goldthorpe *et al.*, 1980, p. 43). On the other hand, the children of those in the service class, including recent arrivals, are likely to stay there, and here non-economic mechanisms such as the educational system come into play, for privileged social classes not only defend their privileges but pass them on to the next generation. Nine out of ten university graduates go into professional and managerial jobs. Today, however, half of them come from state schools. It might seem paradoxical that such large-scale upward mobility into top positions has not taken place at the expense of those already there. This is because of structural changes in the economy, which have generated demand for greatly increased numbers of professionals, administrators and managers. Though there is also considerable *downward* mobility out of Classes I and II, there has indeed been 'room at the top'.

The affluence argument thus does help explain part of the phenomenon of content despite persisting inequality, for many have moved upwards, and not only they but their relatives and friends know it.

We have given some detail about the component occupations of Classes I and II (though not of other classes) for another reason: to illustrate the way in which classes are constructed by social analysts. Like all models of the class system, this particular one involves controversial decisions, and, indeed, has been criticized for blurring over 'vital distinctions between core capitalists, hired managers and bureaucrats' (McLennan, 1984, p. 254) (a criticism Goldthorpe and his colleagues anticipated – and rejected).

So when you read these, or any other statistics about class, or the statement (in a university staff house magazine) that '90 per cent of Japanese are middle class', or the converse conclusion, in one Marxist analysis, that upwards of 90 per cent of the population are working class, you should ask yourself two major questions: what criteria are being used to *define* class in the first place; and what procedures are used to *classify* groups into classes. In our last example, for instance, the definition of 'working class' was 'all those without ownership and control', i.e. not just differences of wealth, but differences in the kind of *authority* exercised at work. The effect of that definition is to leave only a tiny class of top owners and top management, faced by a massive working class. On the other hand, another Marxist writer, Poulantzas, insists on removing from the working class all those who perform 'unproductive' labour, which includes both those who assist the bourgeoisie to subordinate 'productive' workers and technicians and engineers too, because they 'only' perform *mental* labour. The result of *this* definition of 'working class' is that you end up with a tiny (and shrinking) working class, since manual workers are now a bare half of the labour force (Parkin, 1979, pp. 16–19).

So the 'boundary problem' – of what occupations you *choose* to include in a given class – is of immense importance. Two main types of procedure are used to justify including this group and excluding that one: objective and subjective. In the former, the indicator normally used is unambiguous, often even quantifiable, usually wealth or occupation. Yet as we have already seen, there are problems with both: income brackets are not social classes, while occupations can be classified in different ways.

So some turn to subjective criteria in the hope of avoiding these problems; others because they believe that they will be able to reach a deeper, 'lived-in' appreciation of what class means to its members. They may ask people to say what class they think they belong to, or they may present them with a list of classes. Responses to the first kind of 'open-ended' question, however, produce formidable problems of how then to classify extremely diverse answers. How do you deal with the Black cleaning worker, for example, who described herself as 'upper class' because, she said, she 'liked to look on the bright side', or the widespread high prestige accorded by 'upside-downers' who rate doing a hard manual job or a socially valuable one highly, but have a low opinion of the work company directors do? (Young and Willmott, 1957). Where do you put 'deviant' occupations such as gamblers, prostitutes or burglars?

The second strategy generates other problems. If they are offered a simple choice between 'middle' and 'working' class only, people's answers often correspond closely to objective criteria which observers use to place them in a particular social class, especially at the 'extremes': over three-quarters of Class I will see themselves as 'middle class', and a large majority also of the bottom two classes will choose the label 'working class' (Reid, 1989, pp. 35–8). But if they are given more categories to choose from, or different categories, their answers may be different. Thus in one famous study, people avoided calling themselves 'lower' class – so the researchers wrongly concluded that 'America is middle class'. When a similar sample were offered the possible category 'working' class, many more were quite happy to accept that label – so the American middle class suddenly shrank!

To avoid these problems, some have turned to 'experts' in the community, and asked *them* what class so and so belongs to – which still leaves the problem of classification. A second type of subjectivist approach is to rank people according to some hierarchy of social prestige recognized in the community or else constructed by the researcher, such as a 'prestige ranking' of occupations. Others, who argue that occupation is not the only or even the most important aspect of class, either in the analyst's eyes or in the eyes of the people being studied have, like W. L. Warner, in his famous studies of Yankee City, used a mixture of objective and subjective 'factors': income, money, type of housing, 'talent' (sic), etc, which were then rated by 'judges' in the community (Warner, 1936, 1940; Warner and Lunt, 1941). What we end up with, therefore, is not objective at all (and not intended to be): it is an average of the opinions of selected persons from different walks of life about other people. A more satisfactory approach is to analyse the degree of 'congruence' between income or occupation and, say, voting-behaviour.

Divisions within the working class

In technically primitive societies, the total 'role-inventory' does not run to more than a few dozen roles of all kinds, from mother to priest (Nadel, 1957, ch. IV). Modern industry, on the other hand, entails a remarkably complex division of labour: more than 30,000 different occupational titles are used in constructing official British labour statistics. This extraordinary differentiation is in part determined by technology; in part, because all these activities have to be coordinated via elaborate chains of authority, all the way down from the managing director's office to the foreman on the shop-floor and the supervisor in the office.

Given this enormously diversified range of occupations, it would seem that organization and solidarity across the whole working class would be extremely unlikely. But historically this has not been the case. Under conditions of great difficulty, and despite the organized hostility of employers and the State and lack of resources, organizational and educational, new kinds of social organizations, from friendly societies and trade unions to cooperatives and mass political parties of Labour, were created *on a class basis*, because all these diverse occupations saw themselves as sharing a common life situation as people exploited and dominated by the owning and ruling classes. Their culture was an oppositional culture which transcended, therefore, narrower local and occupational boundaries:

There is an assumption that the kind of working-class unity which finds expression in industrial, or more especially in political, action draws its nourishment from the simpler and more intimate loyalties of neighbourhood and kin. Consequently, it is postulated, as the latter are weakened, so the former declines. The assumption is highly questionable. For it implies that the solidarity of class – which is societal in its sweep, and draws no nice distinctions between men of this place and that, this name and that, this dialect and that – is rooted in the kind of parochial solidarity which is its very antithesis . . . Sectional loyalties of region and occupation have contributed in the past to the formation of wider loyalties of class; but the permanence of that contribution has depended upon a transcendence of the original narrow basis of solidarity. Thus the developing labour movement has in many cases drawn special strength from the workers of such locally cohesive, homogeneous communities as the mining valleys of Britain and the timber districts of Scandinavia . . . and the industries in communities of this kind are still characterized by a comparatively high incidence of strike action. Yet, at the political level, especially, the collective force of the labour movement grew precisely as the local isolation of these and other working-class communities declined (Westergaard, 1972, p. 147).

'Particularistic' divisions within the working class, of many kinds, nevertheless still exist. Even within the same industry or plant, sectional 'demarcation disputes' arise as to whether a job rightly falls within this trade or that. The biggest divisions are those where the jurisdiction of different trade unions is involved. Unemployed workers, again, have an interest in schemes to make available some of the jobs held by their more fortunate brethren, such as job-sharing or early retirement, because this would make room, especially, for the young. The established working class, however, not only cling to their jobs, naturally, but also to overtime, which is paid at higher rates. Older divisions – between manual and non-manual occupations, between skilled and less skilled – also persist, and involve distinctions of superiority and inferiority not only on the job, but outside work, too.

In the early phases of industrialization, industry was often located in isolated communities in which son would follow father into the mill or down the pit, and little alternative employment existed. A rigid division of labour also grew up between the sexes, especially where women were entirely confined to the home. The solidarities generated by working together, and reinforced by a consciousness of shared class interests *vis-à-vis* the employers – the counter-culture of work – were consolidated by relationships outside work, from leisure spent in the company of one's workmates in the pub to membership of cohesive Nonconformist chapels. These congruent and mutually reinforcing ties, taken together, resulted in a singularly class-conscious culture of which the mining community is the archetype. (For a classic account of one mining community, see Dennis *et al.*, 1956; for a classic account of life in working-class neighbourhoods in northern cities, see Hoggart, 1957.) There, the most widespread form of culture is not that of the ruling class, not even of working-class *sub*-culture, but working-class *counter*-culture (Worsley, 1984, pp. 41–4, 50–60).

This kind of 'congruent' classness disappears with increased social and geographical mobility and with technological innovation, e.g. the mechanization and then the computerization of the mines, and with competition from newer industries, eliminating the need for a mass of manual labour. The threat and reality of redundancy in that kind of community is likely therefore to evoke specially powerful resistance of whole communities, of which the miners' strike in Britain in 1984–5 is a classic example.

Yet that strike failed, in part because local solidarities *were* so strong; in areas like Nottingham, stronger than loyalties to fellow-workers in other coalfields and to the national union. The solidarity and determination of employers and the State were also equally great, and they disposed of superior force. Confident in their own power, and that support from other unions was either a luxury or would be forthcoming anyhow, the strikers made insufficient effort to *win* that support, while, by refusing to conduct a national ballot on the strike, they lost legitimacy and therefore potential support from both working and middle classes. Grassroots financial support was no substitute for action on the part of organized labour – from other unions and the TUC – who, however, confined themselves to purely verbal expressions of support.

If 'single-industry' communities like these, with a strong tradition of militancy, could not succeed, the chances of mobilizing opposition to the State in other kinds of industry were even less. And pervading the whole industrial scene was an awareness that those who still had jobs were lucky, and that militancy might result not just in individuals being fired, but in the closing down of whole factories, even, in the case of multi-national corporations, their being moved abroad.

The major divisions within the working class which have become of major importance today, however, are no longer only differences of skill or differences between manual and mental labour, but those of gender and ethnicity, to which the traditional White, male working class and its institutions have been unresponsive to any serious extent – some would say sex-blind and colour-blind. These are not class differences, for women do not constitute a class: the place of wives of company directors or of female professionals in the social division of labour is quite different from that of women packers or office-workers. At the same time, women suffer various kinds of social discrimination by virtue of their sex, while the mass of female labour is unambiguously part of the working class, but a special segment of that class – concentrated in routine manual and non-manual occupations as clerks, secretaries and typists, shop assistants, cooks, cleaners and waitresses (Westergaard and Resler, 1976, Table 14, p. 102). As we move down the class-system (see Fig. 11, below) we therefore find more and more households headed by women where incomes are very low indeed.

Women thus constitute a *specially exploited* segment of the working class, and the basis of this exploitation is not just that they have to work for those who own the means of production – men do, too – but that, in addition, they work disproportionately in the least rewarding jobs, in both the financial and psychological senses of 'rewarding'. On top of this special exploitation at work, as we saw in Chapter 4, many women work an unpaid 'double shift' in the home. Even those in better-paid jobs, e.g. the Civil Service or the universities, find themselves in a minority in a male world or in less prestigious branches of professions, professions which are often seen as extensions of maternal roles (teachers, nurses, social workers and other person-oriented and 'caring' professions). Only 3 per cent of full-time non-medical university professors are women (102 of them, out of over 3,300, as at April 1982). Over three-quarters of the lowest grade in the Civil Service, Clerical Assistants, are women, and two-thirds of the next lowest grade, Clerical Officers, but there is not a single woman in the top grade, that of Permanent Secretary.

This special underprivilege, then, cannot be explained simply in terms of economic differences – 'relationship to the means of production' or of wealth and ownership – for these inequalities themselves are based on a *prior*, sex-based social value-system which governs the distribution of resources as between men and women.

The 'primordial' values which thus govern female life-chances also determine those of ethnic minorities. But whereas women are a slight majority of the population, Blacks – a label which covers not only people of West Indian but also those of Pakistani and Indian parentage and others, many of whom are far from physically black – are a numerical minority of the population. In sociological terms, however, they are a minority not because they are fewer than Whites, but because they are a category that is discriminated against (Glass, 1962). Thus in Britain, 'in general terms, the West Indians are being allocated to the most menial working-class jobs, that require little or no training, provide low economic rewards, possess no career structure', with more likelihood of unemployment and a casual working pattern (Allen and Smith, 1974, p. 46). Discrimination, however, is not confined to the workplace; it is practised in all areas of social life. A sociological minority can thus be an actual numerical majority, as in South Africa, where Blacks outnumber Whites by 9 to 1.

In Western Europe and the USA, however, they are a numerical minority: in the USA, a fifth of the population; in Britain, only 4 per cent. Yet, once again, Blacks are over-represented the lower down the social scale we move. Official statistics, though, underestimate both the social salience of the Black population and its symbolic significance. Firstly, they are mainly concentrated in ghetto areas where they form a much higher proportion of the local community. Further, official statistics commonly count as 'Blacks' only those actually born in the 'New Commonwealth' and who subsequently migrated into Britain, on the grounds that their children, born in Britain, are Cockneys and Lancastrians. This admirable liberal sentiment omits, however, the central fact of racism: that people are treated, socially, as 'Blacks' according to their physical appearance or their lifestyle, not according to their place of birth. The social significance of Blacks is, in any case, out of all proportion to their actual numbers, for their presence evokes what Cohen has called a 'moral panic': in the extreme, racist fears that they threaten the 'British way of life'; more generally, that they produce problems of multi-culturalism in a country that has hitherto been culturally homogeneous (though the history of Ireland in particular should remind us that the United Kingdom has been a multi-national State for centuries, with four main nationalities – Irish, Scottish, English and Welsh – and that the relationship between the English and the rest was founded on conquest and colonization).

The working class, then, exhibits both economic and social solidarity *and* internal differentiation. Organized labour would not exist if

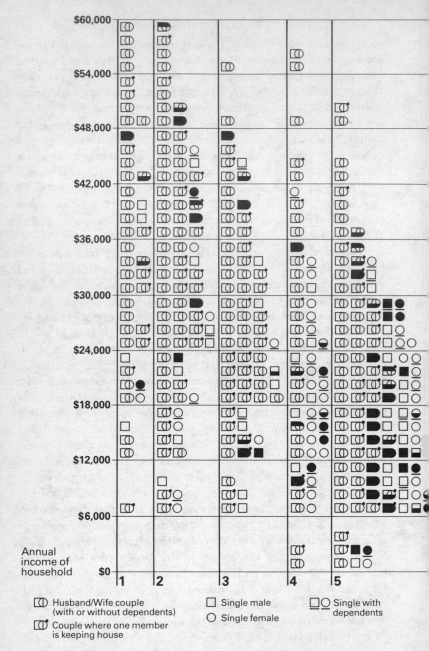

Figure 11.

Social Stratification in the United States (1983)

(2) *by income-level, occupational group, household type, and ethnicity*

This diagram further
• divides households into different types: married couples (*with or without* dependents), indicating whether one member is keeping house; single heads of households (male *or* female) with dependents; and single persons
• shows the racial composition of the households

1 **Administrators/Owners**
Salaried managers and self-employed professionals (doctors, lawyers, etc.)

2 **Professionals**
Salaried professionals (teachers, engineers, technicians, etc.), small business owners, sales representatives

3 **Skilled blue collar**
Construction workers, craftspeople, machinists, supervisors, firefighters, police, guards, etc.

4 **Clerical/Sales**
Secretaries, sales clerks, telephone operators, postal workers, etc.

5 **Less skilled blue collar/Service**
Assembly line workers, labourers, drivers, material handlers, janitors, orderlies, food handlers, domestics, etc.

6 **Retired**

7 **Unemployed/Not in the labour force**
People actively seeking employment/Those not seeking employment (in school, disabled, discouraged, on public assistance, etc.)

6

7

White   Hispanic   Other
Black   (Asian, Native American, and other Non-White)

there were no underlying sense of class identity. But this is often 'communitarian' rather than a political consciousness: a consciousness of having a different way of life and set of values from the middle and upper classes. It does, though, contain a radical ethos for the majority. Thus half of the council house tenants interviewed in one study in London strongly condemned people who owned more than one house; nearly three-quarters approved of sit-ins by workers; and a half believed that workers should have more say in running the factories they worked in – either a 'big say' or as much as the owners (Moorhouse and Chamberlain, 1974). But as we saw in Chapter 2, the interview situation is a special social situation. The answers people give to questions about life-chances put to them by interviewers tell us what they say and do when asked to think about such matters. But they do not spend all of their time thinking about class inequalities.

Most people, Runciman has shown, do not normally compare their lot with that of company directors or stockbrokers. But they do compare themselves with people closer to them in everyday life or, at least, with stereotypes about such groups (Runciman, 1966). So, for married men, their 'reference group' is often young men 'without family responsibilities'; for shift-workers working 'unsocial' hours, those who work '9 to 5'; for manual workers doing hard, dirty, dangerous work, clerks who 'sit on their bottoms, drinking tea all day long'. Women compare themselves with men; workers in one branch of industry or in a particular factory with those in other industries or factories.

Such comparisons take into account not only wages and working conditions, and the comparative, 'market' advantages of different occupations, but also the social status accorded them. Some of the distinctions people use in order to recognize and categorize others are highly visible differences of dress and behaviour and, above all, differences in the way people speak, which are evident even to strangers; others are fine distinctions only visible to those familiar with the community. In popular parlance, they are called 'class distinctions', though sociologists, following Weber, usually reserve the term 'class' to refer to work-related differences, and use the term 'status' to refer to differences of lifestyle and social prestige. Weber did not dismiss class as unimportant. As much as Marx, he considered that property or the lack of it were 'the basic categories of all class situations . . . The factor that creates "class"', he wrote, 'is unambiguously economic interest' (Parkin, 1982, pp. 91–2). But ownership of the means of production, or the lack of ownership, were not the only ways in which people related to the economy. Some class groups monopolized professional or technical skills rather than capital; others used *political* power for economic advantage.

Status differences reflect differences in source and amount of wealth, such as income from land, from investments, from wages, from a profession. But given large-scale rapid mobility, both upwards and downwards, especially in the 'intermediate' levels of class society, the style of life a person acquires in childhood may be disconsonant with their current economic position. All social classes consolidate themselves, and exclude others, by what Parkin, following Weber, calls 'closure': the use of identifiable social or physical attributes to restrict access to rewards and opportunities (Parkin, 1974, p. 3). At the two extremes, privileged groups use these strategies to *exclude* others from membership, and therefore from access to scarce, valued goods; excluded groups respond by building up 'solidarist' organizations which direct pressure upwards in order to claim a larger share of resources at the expense of the privileged strata, even to 'usurp' their privileges.

Over the generations, this results in a coherent upper-class culture in which, in old-established families and circles, there is a strong degree of congruence as between economic position and all other aspects of social behaviour, down to the rituals of everyday social intercourse we call 'etiquette'. But social mobility also produces discord as between economic position and social status: downward mobility, in which the genteel but impoverished dispose of 'more respectability than means'; upward mobility, where the *nouveau riche* is too new to have acquired the requisite social manners: not even elocution lessons will give him the Standard English accent of the social circles to which his wealth now gives him the *entrée*. So he will invest capital not only in his business, but in sending his children to expensive private schools, where they will acquire not just 'correct' accents, but the whole gamut of the cultural tastes of their peers. For the parents, it is too late: there is little they can do except to buy a country house, ride horses, be seen at Ascot, Henley, Wimbledon and Covent Garden, and become public benefactors. They, alas, will always need to be told how to behave by writers who provide a ready-made 'Guide to Excruciatingly Correct Behaviour' (Martin, J., 1983).

Political incorporation

All the foregoing explanations of how and why it is that the working class adapts to structural inequality, some analysts argue, fail to recognize that society is held together not only by economic forces and by social arrangements but by political means: by the exercise of *power*. Politics, they argue, has its own (relative) autonomy, for the ruling classes, unless they rely wholly on force, as in a military dictatorship, must, as theorists from Machiavelli onwards have observed, make some effort to *persuade* the majority – or at least a sizeable segment of them – that their rulers have a *right* to rule. Rulers, and ruling classes, seek legitimacy. In the past, this has taken many forms, from the Divine Right of kings to cosmic destiny embodied in caste-systems. In a modern, 'bourgeois' democracy, the dominant ideology is that of a 'property-owning democracy', in which the private possession of property is seen not simply as compatible with democracy, but as a *condition* of it, without which there can be no liberty and security. This argument conflates various kinds of property which socialist theorists of inequality have tried to distinguish. Thus R. H. Tawney separates 'property for power' – the kind of property which gives the possessor control over the lives of others – from 'property for use': possessions which free a person from control by others (Halsey, 1986, p. 37). Wealth counted in millions and invested in stocks and securities, that is, is different in kind and consequences, not just in quantity, from the modest domestic possessions and the earned income of the majority.

The use of economic resources for political ends is rarely as direct or open today as it was when votes were bought and sold for beer or cash at the hustings and the parson's sermons justified the coexistence of the rich man and the poor man at his gate. Though the first election on a full franchise only took place in Britain in 1931, successive extensions of the vote, in 1832, 1867 and 1884 extended the vote, firstly to the middle classes, then to the 'labour aristocracy' of skilled workers, and, finally, in 1928, to women.

Yet only twice – in 1906 and 1945 – has the Conservative Party been decisively defeated, and this in a country where over two-thirds of the population are defined by most people as 'working class'. The process of co-opting significant sections of the working class – of creating a 'Tory Democracy' – began as soon as adult suffrage was extended to them, not simply by creating overtly political institutions, such as Party branches, but by establishing *social* institutions such as Conservative Working Men's Clubs. Today, despite these efforts, only a third of the working class votes Conservative. But the very size of the working class means that nearly a half of Tory votes do come from the working class, while landslide majorities – in those constituencies where the Labour vote is said to be weighed rather than counted – are 'wasted'. A third of all trade unionists, indeed, have voted Conservative since the Second World War, to go back no further, while the Labour vote has declined from its height reached in 1951 and a new party of the centre has emerged to threaten even further its role as the major alternative to the Conservative Party.

The property-owning classes clearly exert a significant 'hegemonic' influence *within* the working class, an ideology which is diffused downwards. Discussions of working-class ideology often underestimate the effect of constant exposure to a political diet, in the mass media, which is overwhelmingly anti-Labour. The Labour movement, for instance, does not have a national daily newspaper of its own, as is often the case in other countries. The hegemonic ideology, as in all capitalist and indeed class societies, includes not just an economic ideology – in the case of capitalism, that of 'possessive individualism', the legitimacy of private property in the means of production and the right to profit from other people's labour – but a concomitant set of social beliefs which, in some ways, run *counter* to the unbridled power of private capital: formal equality of all before the law and the ballot box, whatever one's economic position, the separation of powers, and the legitimacy of opposition (Worsley, 1984, pp. 308–9). Here we will not go into the counter-values or the institutional bases of liberalism or socialism, since our point is only to note that segments of the working class are attached to the middle and upper classes in a 'vertical' alliance that cuts across their horizontal objective common life situation. Taken together with the segmental divisions within the working class we discussed above, they divide a class so numerous that if all were to vote the same way, there would be a permanent Labour government. This is not to say that Labour cannot win power in the future. In the past, the bedrock of the Labour vote was the manual working class, who are now little over a half of that class. Plainly, a political strategy based on a shrinking population cannot succeed; opposition parties have to attract support from other disadvantaged groups besides the manual working class.

Marxists have often treated working-class conservatism as 'false consciousness'. Sociologists influenced by Weber have argued, however, that clerical workers, for instance, have been justified in the past at least, in regarding themselves as superior to manual workers because not only were their work situation – their working conditions and relationships at work – and their market situation – their position in the labour-market (income, job-security and promotion opportunities) – better than those of manual workers, but their status situation – their social standing – too (Lockwood, 1958). Others emphasize, as we have seen, that the persisting capacity of advanced capitalism, whatever its inequalities and ups and downs, has provided a high and improving standard of living for the majority, not just for non-manual workers.

Sub-societal responses

All the foregoing types of analysis depend upon workers' attitudes towards economic, social and political institutions and values at the societal level. But most people, Runciman has pointed out, do not necessarily spend much time thinking about society as a whole – Society with a capital S – and also do not think about policies except when it impinges upon them or those around them directly, for instance at special times in personal and national life, as during economic crises or elections. Only a minority are consistently interested in, even less engaged in, national politics; they, however, are to be found at opposite ends of the political spectrum.

Within the working class, one thus finds radicals opposed to the existing political and social order at one end; at the other, those who have internalized the idea that the existing social order is fair – whether because those who own industry are believed to have a right to decide how it should be run, or because managers are thought to deserve whatever rewards their labour can command on the market, or because workers or bureaucrats in charge might be worse.

Most people operate with a mix of these and other attitudes, which are evoked in different situations, and therefore fall between the polar extremes of radicalism and conservatism, operating with one or other of a wide variety of attitudes towards life which, taken together, Parkin terms 'accommodative'. Thus many find their satisfactions in interpersonal relationships in the family or the neighbourhood, or with their friends. For others, their leisure-time activities are their 'real' life, not their work. For yet others, the material world is even less important, for they are concerned with the fate of their eternal souls in the life beyond, while others live for a much more materialistic hope of winning the pools, or find fantasy satisfactions in identifying with rock or film stars.

Very different constructions, then, can be put upon exactly the same objective realities of wealth and occupation. A purely 'materialist' theory of class which omits the subjective element is thus incapable of explaining the variability of responses on the part of people who occupy the same objective positions. Purely subjectivist models, which concentrate on self-images and on prestige-rankings and ignore the material realities of power and wealth, are equally inadequate, for class, like all other social phenomena, involves a dialectic of both the objective and the subjective.

The external proletariat

A final type of explanation for working-class toleration of class inequalities looks beyond the boundaries of any particular society to the world-system as a whole. In 1915, Lenin, for example, laid great stress upon imperialist 'super-exploitation' of colonial labour, which meant not only cheap imports of raw materials for British industry, but also the siphoning off of a certain amount of this wealth to a privileged segment of the working class, the 'labour aristocracy'. Half a century later, Third World theorists were arguing that the whole working class, not just a part of it, benefited from imperialism (Fanon, 1983).

But the world is not composed only of capitalist countries. Even after the collapse of communism in Eastern Europe, hundreds of millions of people still live in 'State socialist' societies, including the largest country of all, China, though private ownership and the market economy have also been introduced even there. The introduction into the economy of a capitalist sector means that the classes familiar to us, particularly workers and entrepreneurs, are now coming back. But there are class differences within the still-persisting, and much larger, State sector of the economy, too. That class-system, however, is based not on economic ownership of the means of production, but on political power: the power of the dominant class is based on its control of the State and Party machinery. It has therefore been called the 'New Class' (Djilas, 1957).

Apart from short-lived, though major, experiments such as the 'Cultural Revolution' in China, communist theorists and those who plan the economy have not even claimed to be running the economy on egalitarian principles: that, they say, is something for the future, when 'communism' proper will emerge. The wage-differentials which govern people's lives are based on 'meritocratic' principles: jobs which require higher educational levels or levels of skill and work experience, or which involve creativity, effort, responsibility, and risk are better rewarded. The latter obviously apply primarily to managers and supervisory personnel; the others are rationales for differences as between mental and manual labour and between skilled and less skilled jobs. Socialist egalitarian principles – which might, in the extreme, involve equality of reward, whatever the job, or at least 'positive discrimination' in order to bring the underprivileged up to the level of the rest by giving them superior access to sources of reward, from higher wages to access to universities – seem to be underdeveloped in comparison to meritocratic principles not dissimilar from those of the capitalist world. The egalitarian principle, however, for a long time prevented the range of rewards from becoming too unequal (Weselowski and Krauze, 1981). Nor did the State socialist countries seek to avoid the same kind of 'status crystallization' that occurs in the West: high salaries for jobs that are intrinsically interesting and of high status. Ideally, one could compensate for unattractive work by giving those who do it compensation, whether in the form of high wages or of special privileges or esteem, an option which has not been taken. The converse was the case: access to goods in short supply (especially from the capitalist world) was only available to members of the political and social elites. For the mass of the people, the main channel of upwards social mobility was via the education system, and, for those who aspired to enter the political elite, via Party and trade union (not unlike the West).

These inequalities in socialist societies are also significant for workers outside those countries, for the latter saw the Second World not only as less free than the First, but as living at lower living standards, symbolized by queues for goods. But the persistence of the inequalities in capitalist society discussed in this chapter means that positive support for that kind of social order is also qualified, especially among those classes which benefit least from it.

The widespread view that traditional working-class solidarity in capitalist society has been replaced by sectionalism, egoism and privatism has been challenged by the major recent survey of social mobility, the Essex University study of social class, which argues that the nineteenth-century working class was never as solidary as the myth would have it – but nevertheless produced the modern Labour movement. Today, though class may not be to the forefront of people's consciousness in everyday life, it is still 'by far the most common . . . frame of reference employed in the construction of social identities'. Two-thirds of the sample, too, thought that the main social conflict was between those who run industry and those who work for them, and therefore pursued higher incomes and wanted class organizations to pursue them. But they did not see industrial conflict as part of an explicit 'class struggle', and thought that the two sides of industry shared a number of interests in common. Politically, the majority

endorse . . . such redistributive efforts as were likely to result in a more just society, but judge these unlikely to be forthcoming given existing social, economic, and political arrangements. They do not approve of social injustice, can conceive both of a more just society and the means by which it might be achieved, but nevertheless have judged present arrangements to be largely unassailable, for the foreseeable future at least. People are not generally fatalistic about what governments might achieve given sufficient will and/or competence. However, they do doubt whether these actually exist. Party politics are an object of widespread cynicism . . . [This] is not the fatalism of the naïve . . . but a fatalism informed by an awareness of distributional inequality and social injustice . . . a mood of what might be called 'informed fatalism', some might say simply 'realism' (Marshall et al., 1989, pp. 149–65).

11   Deviance

Behaviour in human societies is governed by rules or norms. There are appropriate and inappropriate ways of acting whether one is talking about a classroom during a lesson, running in a marathon or dancing at a disco. The sociology of deviance focuses upon rule-breaking: it looks at who breaks rules, why they do and what happens to them. Much of sociology, of course, is concerned with how social order occurs, the way in which society manages to hang together. The study of deviance looks at the other side of the coin. Ironically, to study deviance is often a short cut to understanding why people conform. And, of course, the sociology of deviance involves precisely the same theories as those occurring in the rest of sociology, merely approaching the same problems from the reverse direction.

Deviance and crime (that is deviant behaviour which involves law-breaking) are the staple fare of much of our mass media. For example, every evening on British television there is on average five hours of police drama programmes on four channels. Even the Western, of course, is a very stylized study in rule-breaking: of crime, robbery and deceit in a mythical frontier America. The news, too, is full of stories of crime, terrorism and disaster, and tends to highlight *bad* news, the deviant side of events and happenings. The ways in which deviance and deviants are presented, however, are often grossly stereotypical. Part of this is because the media are part of the entertainment business: newspapers have to sell and television channels have to compete. Journalists the world over have discovered that audiences avidly consume news which titillates their sensibilities and confirms their prejudices. It is not difficult for the more discriminating television viewer to realize that the Western he or she is watching is a moral tale and not a depiction of reality. It is considerably more difficult for someone watching a popular television police drama to realize that the story unfolded is in ninety-nine times out of a hundred completely inaccurate in its depiction of crime, of how the police attempt to control crime, and of their likely chances of success. None of this would have much significance if we had direct knowledge of these events. But in the highly complex, socially segregated world we now live in, we have often very little real knowledge of alternative versions to run against mass media stereotypes. Thus far more people have read articles in the newspapers or watched television programmes about heroin addiction than have ever met a heroin addict, and they have no reason to disbelieve the images presented to them. Yet among experts on drugs, there is great controversy as to why people use heroin, and even about how many heroin addicts there are and what addiction means.

The study of crime and deviance, then, is crucial, firstly, because the study of deviance helps us to understand how society works and gives us insights into the policies which might help solve major social problems. Burglary, drug abuse, prostitution, child abuse, wife battering, racist attacks, muggings . . . the list of serious problems in our society is endless. Many seem almost intractable, and the need for rational, well thought out policies is paramount. Yet, secondly, despite this, there is no area which attracts more irrationality than public pronouncements on deviance. This is not new: witches, the archetypal deviants of the Middle Ages, were a prime repository of people's fears, concealed desires and worried projections. Today, the mass media provide us with a daily stream of images, often equally fantastic, with regard to modern deviants. Thus we have a contradiction: the area of human life where rational action is most necessary is also the greatest focus of irrationality.

This is the reason why it is important to be objective and systematic about our study of deviance. In approaching the sociology of deviance, we will take two major perspectives and contrast them with their conceptions of the problem point by point. We have chosen drug use as the deviant activity to illustrate the argument, both because it is a typical issue and because there are well-developed views in this area. But you should hold in mind throughout that these positions are typical of any area of deviant behaviour. So it would be useful, if, when you have completed reading this chapter, you thought how the two perspectives would apply, say, to mugging or rape or child abuse.

Drug use to change one's mental state, referred to as psychoactive drug use, is present in nearly all known human societies and groups. The few social groups who have not used drugs at all, for instance puritanical religious societies such as the Mormons, are historically exceptional. Most societies use drugs, though the drugs they use vary immensely: alcohol and tobacco in advanced industrial countries, marijuana in India and North Africa, opium in the Far East, peyote among some American Indian people, amanita mushrooms among Norse warriors, kava in Polynesia, the henbane and thornapple used by medieval European witches. To this host of naturally occurring psychoactive substances we have now added a series of synthetic compounds, for example heroin, the amphetamines, the barbiturates and LSD.

In contemporary Britain, a wide variety of drugs is used. For every £1 spent on food, 64p is spent on alcohol and tobacco: indeed there are drug supply shops – pubs and tobacconists – on many a street corner. Caffeine in the form of tea is consumed at the rate of four cups per day for every man, woman and child in the country, and this is supplemented by vast quantities of coffee. The National Health Service spends £60 million a year on tranquillizers, stimulants and anti-depressants. No one knows how many people have smoked marijuana, but a reasonable estimate would be in the region of 10 million, and within certain groups, such as Afro-Caribbeans, smoking is a cultural norm. Add to this the increasingly fashionable habit of snorting cocaine, the widespread, more down-market, use of illicit amphetamines, and the spread of heroin abuse in the inner cities, and one can truly talk of a society in which drug use is widespread, various and commonplace. A whole series of questions then arise: why do certain people take particular kinds of drugs? What is the basis of social reactions against drug use? What policy conclusions can we come to as a rational basis of drug control? We will attempt to answer these questions from two different theoretical perspectives.

The positivism which emerged in the nineteenth century, attempted, under the influence of Darwinism, to carry through a radical change in the dominant conception of the place of humankind in nature. Just as Darwin's theories served to replace the conception of the human species as a unique category of divine creation into one which saw *homo sapiens* as only one species within the wider evolutionary context of life on this planet, positivism's tried to show that human *behaviour*, too, was understandable because the same scientific laws governed all living activity. Human behaviour, however, could be guided by rationality, equality and free-will.

Positivism's major postulate, from which all of its major characteristics derive, is its insistence on the unity of the scientific method: that the premises and instruments which had proved so successful in the study of the physical world and of animal biology are of equal validity and promise in the study of society and humans. From this premise, positivists proceeded to propound methods for the quantification of behaviour, so as to claim the objectivity of the scientific export and to assert the determined, law-governed nature of human action.

There have been many varieties of positivism both in criminology and in the social sciences in general. The particular version we will focus on here is by far the most widespread variant, both as a theory and as used in public practice. The theory admits that biological, physiological, psychological and social influences all contribute to the creation of the criminal, but sees the fundamental predisposition to crime or deviancy as situated in the individual. Furthermore, the social order is seen as consensual; crime is therefore the result of the undersocialization of the individual into this consensus. This type of positivism – what might be termed individual positivism – is the focus of our present analysis.

There was little sustained and converted effort to dislodge positivism until the 1980s, when the 'New Deviancy' or 'labelling' theorists criticized the accepted paradigm: the way in which crime and social intransigence had been viewed for a century. They drew, however, upon a very substantial body of theory and research that had been developed over decades by the Chicago School of Sociology, especially the symbolic interactionists (see above, pp. 7–16). The key works were Howard Becker's *Outsiders* (1963) and David Matza's *Becoming Deviant* (1969). Their critique focused directly on the main tenet of positivist criminology: that the criminal or deviant was suffering from a lack of socialization, arising out of either a genetic inability to become fully human or from environmental influences which had impaired his or her social development. The social world was envisaged as a taken-for-granted consensus, where all 'adequate' men and women agreed about the essential fairness and rationality of their society. To steal, to be gay, to smoke marijuana, to engage in acts of violence – all these activities were viewed as indicative of a fundamental malaise on the part of the individual involved. The task of the positivist was then presented as 'progressive', for whereas conservative law and order campaigns called for severer punishment of the offender, the 'scientific' expert advised appropriate diagnosis and treatment in order to deal with the irrational compulsions which had propelled criminals or deviants into their anti-social actions. The view of schizophrenia as the consequence of biochemical disorder; drug treatment programmes inflicted on Californian criminals; the labelling of Soviet dissidents as mentally ill, were all instances of correctional or positivist conceptions of deviance which went largely unchallenged until the 1960s.

The 'new wave' of deviancy theorists trenchantly dismissed such notions. A satisfactory explanation of criminal action, they argued, needed to answer two questions: why did the individual *wish* to commit the crime; and why was the action considered criminal or deviant in the first place? Positivism had mystified both answers: the first by taking from the criminal any sense of human purpose, the second by totally ignoring the problem of social reaction. The reasons for criminality were reduced to non-human, material factors either of the individual's inner physiology or of his or her social environment, which impelled them into crime. On the first point, the new deviancy theorists insisted on using a model of a fully human actor: a person whose choice, whose deviancy was understand-able and comprehensible as part of an overall career in the world of society. On the second issue they accused positivism of having managed to discuss crime for nearly a century without recourse to a theory of the State. That it was the State which punished the criminal or deviant was taken for granted, because all decent-minded men were in agreement as to what constituted social behaviour, and the State simply acted on the basis of that consensus.

At this juncture, the new deviance theorists introduced their most characteristic concept: labelling. Society, they argued, did *not* consist of a monolithic consensus, but rather of a pluralistic array of values. For an action to be termed criminal or deviant demanded two kinds of social activity: one, a group or individual acting in a particular fashion; the other, another group or individual, with different values, labelling the first kind of activity as 'deviant'.

Human beings, acting creatively in the world, constantly generated different systems of values. But only certain groups – variously and vaguely termed 'the powerful', 'the bureaucracy', 'the moral entrepreneurs' – have more power than others and enforce their values upon the less powerful, labelling those who infringed their rules with stereotypical tags. Groups and individuals that develop value-systems and modes of behaviour that conflict with the dominant codes, conversely, are labelled, by the authorities, as 'homosexuals', 'thieves', or 'psychopaths'. Moreover, this very act of labelling, by limiting the future choices of the actor, and by being presented to the actor as the truth about his nature, with all the force of authority, had a self-fulfilling effect. The old adages 'once a thief always a thief', 'once a junkie always a junkie', *became* true, not because, as earlier criminologists had maintained, this was the 'essence' of the people involved, but because the power of labelling transformed and cajoled them into acting and believing as if they possessed no freedom in the world.

These two contrasting ways of approaching the explanation of drug-taking, and these two different world-views, are found throughout the study of deviant behaviour as a whole, not only in the works of sociologists and psychiatrists, but in the commentaries of politicians, journalists, priests, or anyone, in fact, who tries to understand or interpret the social world around him.

Positivists view society as an organic entity, comparable to the human body: each part has its place in an organized division of labour. Over and above individual ends stands the notion of the general social good. New deviancy theorists, on the other hand, contest this, seeing society as a multitude of groups, each with their own ends and interests, who agree and cooperate over certain issues but who conflict, sometimes drastically, over others.

From these initial stances a number of fundamental points of contrast between the two schools can be made, concerning both their explanations of drug-taking and their advice as to what ought to be done in order to ameliorate the problem, though the absolutist approach has almost totally dominated the study of drug-taking. We will take these point by point, illustrating them by quotation.

We start with the two most significant questions we can ask of any interpretation of social behaviour. First of all, what is its conception of social order? How do the writers conceive of the way in which society maintains itself? Secondly, what is their conception of human nature? How do they understand the processes which motivate and determine the behaviour of human beings? For all statements about human activities, whether they are stories about the wayward in the *News of the World* or theoretically sophisticated analyses of human behaviour in psychology or sociology textbooks, must of necessity contain – however implicitly – conceptions of social order and human nature. So the prime questions one must ask, before looking at any detail whatsoever, are the 'global' questions: how does the author see society hanging together, and what, in his or her view, makes human beings tick?

The Basis of Social Order

Society, according to the positivist, is held together by a consensus of values. Coercion is only necessary in a limited number of cases where recalcitrant 'undersocialized' individuals refuse to recognize their problems and are unwilling to be integrated into society. The positivist sees the vast majority of people agreeing as to what is correct behaviour and what is reprehensible; moreover, that there is a large degree of agreement over the ends that people should pursue and little conflict between the interests of different groups. Behaviour, according to this consensus, is seen to be functional to the organic system they envisage society to be, and behaviour which violates this consensus is dysfunctional to society. Legal drug-taking – alcohol, caffeine, amphetamines and barbiturates on prescription – is seen as behaviour in tune with the values of society and as activities which help to keep the system functioning. Illegal drug-taking, on the other hand, is contrary to these values and deleterious to the body politic.

The basic image that 'new deviancy' theorists have of social order is that of a pluralism of values. Individuals live in an overlapping world of normative ghettos. In contrast to absolutism, the notion of a consensus in society is challenged and replaced by the concept of a diversity of values. Consensus is seen as a mystification, an illusion foisted on the public by the powerful. More precisely, it is an attempt by the powerful to foist their own particular value-system on the diversity of groups within society. This is achieved, on the one hand, by their control over the major ideological apparatuses within society (e.g. the mass media, the educational system) and on the other, by their control and use of the repressive apparatus (e.g. the police, the courts). Consensus is thus a human construct, a system of values created by a specific group of people, but it is presented as if it were something outside and above human creation.

New deviancy theorists deny the possibility of speaking *ex cathedra* on behalf of society in general. Different groups, they argue, have different norms as to appropriate drug use. What is deviant or normal, then, cannot be judged in an absolute fashion: one cannot say that to act in a certain way is absolutely deviant or normal; one can only judge the normality or deviancy of a particular item of behaviour relatively, against the standards of the particular group you choose as your moral yardstick. To act in a certain way, then, can be simultaneously deviant *and* normal, depending on whose standards you are applying. In this perspective, the smoking of marijuana may be normal behaviour amongst young people in Notting Hill and deviant to, say, the community of army officers who live in and around Camberley. Similarly, to drink to the point of collapse may be valued behaviour amongst merchant seamen but would be anathema to members of the Temperance League.

New deviancy theorists do not deny that there *can* be consensus: that a majority opinion can exist concerning a particular type of behaviour – for example, the use of heroin – but this is not sufficient to justify embracing an organic image of society. There is a vast difference of opinion in Britain, for example, as to the proper use of alcohol and cigarettes, and there are sizeable populations which take barbiturates, marijuana or amphetamines. Moreover, the relativists would suggest that a consensus, where it exists, is often created by the persuasive manipulation of public opinion through means such as the mass media, by groups possessing sufficient power to propagate their own particular values and notions of appropriate and reprehensible behaviour. In the field of drug use they would point to the activities of the Temperance Movement in the USA before Prohibition.

Drug-taking, then, is not necessarily deviant nor necessarily a social problem; it is deviant to groups who condemn it and a problem to those who wish to eliminate it. To talk of a personified 'Society' which must be protected is to camouflage a simple conflict between two groups: those who wish to pursue a particular activity unmolested and those who feel that this activity threatens their interests or conceptions of proper behaviour.

The Conception of Human Nature

Positivist and new deviancy theorists have basically different perspectives on human nature. To the absolutist, a person's psychic make-up is like a blank sheet of metal on to which are stamped the homogeneous values of society. Human beings are programmed, so to speak, to react in the right way at the right time: to emit appropriate responses to prearranged cues. Here and there, however, the machinery goes wrong: child-rearing is inadequate, social control of adults is weak, or the norms inculcated are unclear, and then imperfections are built into the printed circuits of normality. Individuals, through no fault of their own, are unable to fulfil the 'normal' roles expected of them. Human deviancy is seen as not morally reprehensible, because it is a product of forces which is beyond the control of the individual.

In contrast, the new deviancy theorists' conception of human nature is one which emphasizes free-will and creativity. People create meaning in the world and, in striving towards their various cultural goals, impose a multitude of interpretations on the social and physical world around them. Hence human behaviour has to be understood in the light of the meanings imparted to it by the people involved. Reality is not 'given' or predetermined: it is socially constructed. Human rationality is therefore not universally the same: it varies according to the logic and norms of a particular culture; it is relative rather than absolute. Human nature is then open and in principle boundless. But though human beings are born free, they lose their freedom because of the structures through which society controls their behaviour.

For the new deviancy theorists, human beings are seen as independent of the values and ideas they receive from their surroundings; accepting or rejecting them as they see fit and, more importantly, creating new values in accordance with their interests and values. In this view, culture is seen as a collection of approved solutions to problems occurring amongst members of society. But people experience problems for which there are no suitable available solutions in their culture. Therefore, in certain situations they create new cultural responses and forms in face of the inadequacy of the established social order. The widespread use of drugs in our society suggests that they provide significant solutions to certain widespread problems.

The difference between legal and illegal drug-taking, however, is that, by and large, the taking of illegal drugs involves developing hitherto forbidden solutions to individual or collective problems, while legitimate drugs – alcohol, caffeine, and nicotine – are acceptable.

New deviancy theorists, then, see people as morally responsible for their choices to the extent that fate is not determined, but partly in their own hands. If people have a degree of free choice, then, it is a mystification to regard people who deviate from your own standards as 'ill'; it is better to say candidly that one disapproves of a particular form of behaviour (for example, the use of amphetamines) for moral reasons and will do all in one's power to eradicate such practices, than to hide behind a mask of therapy and a vocabulary of healing. At the same time, the relativist will freely admit that a certain proportion of drug-takers do willingly act as if they were determined creatures, but would argue that such fatalistic lifestyles are initially chosen and internalized; they are not proof that man is intrinsically devoid of free-will.

Why do People Take Drugs? (The Absolutist Case)

The positivists' view of society is that of a vast area of agreement, on the edge of which lie a tiny minority of deviants. These are the diseased cells in the body of society – a pathology not only at the social but at the individual level as well: that is, the individuals who make up the social pathology are personally inadequate. A person is seen as being unable to act 'normally' because, for various reasons, he or she has not inculcated the norms of society. Two major reasons are given for this: either he is undersocialized or he is 'sick'.

The undersocialized drug-taker is seen, to use Freudian terms, as having a weak superego, an inadequate ego and – if a man lacking in proper masculine identification. He is, in short, psychopathic. Because of his lack of norms he has a personality which is immature and infantile.

Most individuals addicted to drugs are considered self-centred and narcissistic and are interested only in satisfaction of their own primitive needs. This is a very infantile form of behaviour; it is acceptable in infancy but not in adults. These individuals have not matured in a healthy way and so do not accept mature roles. They make poor husbands and wives, fathers and mothers; they are poor sexual partners because their social development has been retarded. They experiment with many types of sexuality but usually they cannot accept a mature heterosexual role. They are not interested in giving to anyone; they are interested only in receiving (Rasor, 1968, p. 18).

Thus sexual inadequacy is often seen as a lack of correct masculine identification, an attitude which leading heroin experts Chein *et al.* express in a revealing passage:

An extraordinarily high proportion of adolescent addicts can be seen as 'pretty boys'. They would not appear out of place in a musical comedy chorus. They are vain in their appearance. They spend much time preening. They are preoccupied with clothes, which they wish to be of the finest materials and the latest styles. They spend much time before their mirrors experimenting with their hair, moustaches, and goatees ... Adolescent addicts do not look, behave, or deport themselves as adolescent boys usually do; they do not try to appear manly, rugged, vigorous, energetic, rough-and-ready. These deviations suggest that they have strong feminine identification ... They try to impress the observer with their independence and bravery, with their ability to function well in the most difficult circumstances. They know better than any middle-class professional person what life 'really is'. They boast of their exploits with women, crime, and narcotics, to prove what strong men they are. In one of Shakespeare's telling observations, 'they do protest too much'; the psychologically trained observer cannot help but see through to the problems of masculine identification beneath the veneer of masculinity (Chein *et al.*, 1964, pp. 224–5).

New deviancy theorists, on the other hand, reject the notion of drug use as a pathology; it is simply not possible to regard all the various activities popularly considered as deviant (for example, homosexuality, communism, heavy drinking, marijuana smoking, sexual promiscuity, abortion, prostitution and petty theft) as diseases in the body of society, for if we were to extract all these deviants there would be precious little left of the organism which the absolutists postulate! Rather, they suggest, what is a deviant form of behaviour is a matter of opinion, and opinions vary. The use of the word 'pathology' and organic metaphors are subtle means by which one group (who consider themselves normal) combat the values of those they consider different from themselves.

Further, there is a tendency for the middle-class observer to view social organization aimed at goals which he or she disapproves of, as *dis*organized, normless behaviour. Instead, many drug groups, the relativist would argue, are sub-cultures with finely spun norms, dictating what is appropriate and inappropriate behaviour for the drug-user. The tendency to view alternative values as an *absence* of values is a convenient method of ignoring groups whose existence questions the basis of one's own social world. Nowhere is this practice more prevalent than in descriptions of those drug sub-cultures which espouse values concerned with hedonism and excitement as major goals of life.

Thus D. P. Ausubel writes of the heroin addict:

He fails to conceive of himself as an independent adult and fails to identify with such normal adult goals as financial independence, stable employment, and the establishment of his own home and family. He is passive, dependent, unreliable and unwilling to postpone immediate gratification of pleasurable impulses. He demonstrates no desire to persevere in the face of environmental difficulties or to accept responsibilities which he finds distasteful. His preoccupation with a search for effortless pleasure represents both an inappropriate persistence of childhood motivations which he has not yet outgrown and a regressive form of compensation for his inability to obtain satisfaction from adult goals (Ausubel, 1958, p. 42).

Thus, 55 per cent of addicts at the US Public Health Service Hospital were classified as having 'psychopathic diathesis', which is characterized by nomadism, irregular employment, unstable marital history, and tolerance to all forms of thrill-seeking vice. What is forgotten in these reports is that hedonism, thrill-seeking, lack of employment, unstable formal marriages, are often the 'norms' of the groups from which drug-users emanate. The middle-class social scientist, with his nuclear family, planned life and careful leisure, takes his or her pattern of life as the only possible form of civilized existence, any deviation from this being regarded as profoundly asocial.

Drug use is thus associated, in the minds of such scientists, with both social and personality disorganization. Moreover, the two are easily linked, since it is further argued that the 'weak' family structure associated with socially disorganized areas gives rise to personality inadequacies. Positivists substantiate their thesis by pointing to the groups where the incidence of drug-taking is high, namely the lower working class and Blacks, both groups which, they would argue, have poor child-rearing techniques and are therefore populated by inadequate personalities. Additionally, the high prevalence of adolescent drug-users is attributed to their as yet immature personalities, aggravated by living in areas where social control is weak (e.g., the ghetto or the large university campus).

A few positivist theorists, however, accept that a proportion of drug use occurs in individuals with essentially normal personalities, but see these personalities as having been 'infected' by contact with the 'virus' of addiction. The spread of addiction is thus often seen – especially by medical epidemiologists – as similar to an epidemic, and the victim is regarded as being 'sick'.

New deviancy theorists do not denigrate the notion of undersocialization. But they insist that it is used over-often, and used without reference to the particular group of which the person referred to is a member. If there are many different 'correct' ways of behaving in a society, then there are as many ways of being 'normal'. To suggest that a person with different norms from oneself is psychologically inadequate is merely a way of negating any argument as to the validity of one's own way of life. To new deviancy theorists, however, drug-taking groups are seen as having their own particular norms, against which the non-drug-taker would seem personally inadequate and undersocialized. The teetotaller in an Irish drinking group would soon find that the – in his eyes – 'asocial' gathering had a finely developed set of values and required behaviour, which he would have a hard job living up to. Moreover, if he were to find himself involved in such a group for any length of time, he might himself begin to interpret any lack of social ease on his part as a sign of personal inadequacies. Richard Blum found that regular LSD users have a conception of the 'straight' world as consisting of people who are 'uptight' or – to use the vocabulary of psychoanalysis – of obsessive neurotics pursuing material and social status in an unbalanced manner (Blum, 1965)!

There is, however, a proportion of drug-takers to whom the models of the absolutist theorists *are* appropriate, for some individuals accept the idea that other people have of them of being people with a weak superego, inadequate ego and a lack of masculine identification. This ready-made sick role of the drug-determined individual, unable to make adult choices in terms of sex and occupation, is easily accepted by certain individuals. So a proportion of drug-takers do accept that they have an inadequate personality – an idea they readily pick up in clinics and hospitals manned by doctors who invariably have a positivist perspective on drug dependency. These clinics, then, are institutions where drug-takers are socialized into fitting in with positivist theory.

Now deviancy theorists deny any one-to-one simple connection between social disorganization and personality disorganization, for the apparent social disorganization of slum areas is often really organization which centres around different ends to those of respectable society, and what is perceived as faulty child-rearing practices on the part of individual families is more easily understood as different kinds of socialization practised in different kinds of groups, utilizing different techniques. To grow up as a mature adult in Harlem or Brixton demands the inculcation of different norms, by different means, than those needed to produce a conforming citizen of White, middle-class Manhattan or Hampstead.

The inadequacy of the positivists' stress upon personal inadequacy becomes apparent when one considers that gigantic sections of the entire population, for example, Blacks and the working class, are presumed to be socially inferior. For instance, Hans Eysenck writes that:

there is no reason to assume any differences between social classes with respect to conditionability (i.e genetic difference), but there are very good reasons for assuming considerable differences between them with respect to the degree of socialization to which they are subject (i.e. childrearing differences). Particular attention has been drawn, for instance, by Kinsey in the United States to the different value laid on the repression of overt sexual urges by middle-class and working-class groups. He has shown that where, for middle-class groups, parents put very strict obstacles in the way of overt sexual satisfaction of their growing children, and inculcate a very high degree of 'socialization' in them, working-class parents, on the whole, are much more lax and unconcerned. In working-class groups, for instance, he found premarital intercourse viewed as not only inevitable, but as quite acceptable to the group.

Similarly, with respect to aggression, there is a considerable amount of evidence too from a variety of sociological studies, carried out both in the United States and in Great Britain, to show a tendency for middle-class groups to impose a stricter standard upon their children than the working-class groups. The open expression of aggressiveness which is frowned upon in the middle-class family is often not only accepted but even praised in the working-class group (Eysenck, 1958, p. 294).

That pre-marital sexual intercourse and overt aggression should be considered as essentially asocial is a gross middle-class ethnocentrism which demands that sexuality should be expressed in marriage and that aggression should only be channelled in ways approved by King and Country, if they are to be allowed the designation of truly 'social'. Considering the prejudices which the word 'drug' arouses, it is not surprising that the insinuation of personality defects is automatically affixed to all and sundry who stray beyond the narrow limits of the middle-class behavioural scientist's style of life; including the kinds of psychoactive drugs permissible in that sub-culture.

The Problems of Large-Scale Deviancy: The Role of the Corruptor

Positivist theory then, is especially vulnerable when we are considering deviancy on a large scale for, if deviant drug use is a product of sick individuals, would not large-scale use of, say, heroin, be a product of a sick society? One way of explaining this is the model of the epidemic: that it is a sickness that spreads like an epidemic through the population. Thus the cover of *Newsweek* in July 1971 is emblazoned with THE HEROIN PLAGUE; Melanie Philips, in the *Guardian*, 25 June 1984, talks of 'The White Plague'. Here, there is a transition from seeing heroin addicts as coming from a 'deviant' group to seeing them as coming from 'normal' groups. Thus in the American heroin panic of the early 1970s *Newsweek* wrote:

Ten years ago, heroin was a loser's drug [that] made helpless addicts of thousands of ghetto Negroes, a few jazz musicians and a handful of showbusiness types . . . an aberration afflicting the black and the longhair minorities. Now all that has changed. New heroin users are turning up in . . . the glossiest suburban highschools, on factory assembly lines . . . [Thus] the UCLA psychiatrist Dr J. Thomas Ungerlidier says that since the heroin plague began, 'Nice Jewish boys are coming out of the woodwork – as well as Mormon kids, Japanese-Americans and all the other exemplars of healthy, hardworking, middle-class ideals' (5 July 1971, p. 29).

Similarly, in Britain, an article in the *Sunday Times* by Dr Martin Plant, having noted the widespread use of heroin amongst the young, goes on to discuss the qualitative nature of the problem: 'Heroin is no longer for people with personality problems. The new users are often normal, young working-class and particularly unemployed' (8 April 1984, p. 17).

The image of the 'epidemic', however, is not adequate on its own to explain the spread of its use, for heroin use is not like smallpox, and one needs some linking concepts to explain how it is 'caught' on such a wide scale. The answer, in the present period, is that unemployment is driving young people into heroin abuse. Thus the analysis moves from the level of psychological to a sociological determinism: they are not abnormal people, but people placed in abnormal circumstances. To this another key has to be added – the notion of the 'pusher'. Drug-taking is seen as being facilitated by a small clique of unscrupulous, yet normal (i.e. economically motivated) individuals (the corruptors), manipulating or seducing a majority of innocent or immature bystanders (the corrupted). Thus every heroin smoker is induced to begin the habit because of the activities of a Machiavellian pusher. This is a sub-type of 'corruption theory' in general which sees, for instance, every strike as being engineered by a small group of Marxist agitators, or prostitutes becoming lured into the 'game' by pimps, or every delinquent as being led astray by other people's children. The corollary of this, as far as the social control of drug-taking is concerned, is that the 'corrupted' must be viewed in a humanitarian light and treated leniently, while the 'corruptors' must be dealt with in a severe manner. They are the 'real' intransigent deviants. Thus, typically 'enlightened' opinion distinguishes between the penalties doled out for the possession and supply of drugs. We thus have an epidemic carried, so to speak, by random germs to youngsters who are socially weakened by unemployment. Because of the sickness notion, it is impossible to blame the addict but it is very easy to lay all the blame on the carriers. The theory of the corruptor presumes a body of innocents within society who are corrupted by normal people who are wicked and who seek to gain from their fellows' weakness. This is how the *Daily Mirror* sees the problem, for example:

DRUGS: THE REAL CRIMINALS
The drug pusher – the contemptible creature who peddles poison for profit – deserves no mercy from the law. The criminal who sets out to hook young people on drugs deserves far more implacable retribution than the victim of the evil (*Daily Mirror*, 12 March 1970).

Deviance, in general then, does not ever occur out of volition. It is assumed to be essentially unpleasurable and can only occur either out of sickness or corruption. Given these assumptions, it is possible to discern the intervention of some corrupting agent in every situation of widespread deviance.

The *Daily Express* can thus discuss the wave of industrial disputes and student protest in the early 1970s in precisely these forms: 'The docks, the car industry, mines, major airports, electricity, the building trade, and the students have all been steadily infiltrated in one guise or another until the militants can disrupt the national life at will' (9 December 1970).

In contrast, new deviancy theorists insist that deviance is a response to the social problems and predicaments with which people are confronted. It cannot be explained as the inevitable result of a 'sickness' – whether psychological or sociological – or the result of the Machiavellian wiles of outside agitators. They thus argue that illicit drug-taking is a response to problems faced by individuals, who are not corrupted, but who willingly embrace that kind of solution to their social difficulties. William Burroughs understood this well when he wrote:

If we wish to annihilate the junk pyramid, we must start with the bottom of the pyramid, 'the addict in the street', and stop tilting quixotically for the 'higher ups' so called, all of whom are immediately replaceable. The addict in the street, who must have junk to live, is the one irreplaceable factor in the junk equation. When there are no more addicts to buy junk there will be no junk traffic. As long as junk need exists, someone will service it (Burroughs, 1968, p. 10).

Very few studies of drug-taking have ever shown drug use to be initiated by pushers. In fact, most drugs are bought off low-level dealers who are themselves users. Certainly, the users pursue the dealers and *not* vice versa. The antagonism directed towards 'corruptors' is a mystification which, by scapegoating a few, manages to maintain the illusion that everything would be all right in the social system if only we could eliminate the small minority of saboteurs intent on destroying its organic unity.

Furthermore, modern deviancy theorists are suspicious of the invocation of social determinants – such as unemployment – as inevitably leading to more widespread heroin use. First of all, they point out, the spread of heroin in the 1970s, particularly in the

United States, was ascribed to *affluence*, not unemployment, as ten years later. Secondly, they are suspicious when they find that public concern with heroin only escalates when it is no longer confined to groups who are denigratingly seen as marginal ('Blacks and long-hairs'). Thirdly, though there may be a relationship between unemployment and heroin, it is not a simple one-to-one relationship, because only a small minority of the unemployed take heroin. In fact, it involves *choice* and is only one of a number of possible choices. This is the vital missing factor in positivist analysis, for none of the positivist theorists seem to accept that people take drugs for pleasure, or if they do, they presume that it is only for a short while, until withdrawal symptoms set in, and that from then on they take drugs merely to gain relief from their 'sickness'. The modernists would say that this contradicts the evidence of drug-takers themselves, and takes no account of the context of continuous boredom that long-term unemployment entails. Here again, there is a parallel with discussions of deviancy in other areas. As we saw in the Introduction, the Chicago School in the 1930s broke new ground by stating the obvious: that delinquency could be enjoyable. As David Bordua mockingly remarked about positivist studies of gang delinquency:

I have purposely attempted to convey the distinctive flavour of essentially healthy boys satisfying universal needs in a weakly controlled and highly seductive environment. Compared to the deprived and driven boys of more recent formulations with their status problems . . . or psychopathological ones . . . delinquency and crime were attractive: being a 'good boy' was dull. Fun, profit, glory and freedom is a combination hard to beat, particularly for the inadequate conventional institutions that form the competition (Bordua, 1962, p. 292).

Drugs and Moral Panic

New deviancy theorists not only argue that the way in which drug use is conceived is wrong; they also deny the size of this problem. Images of drug use, they argue, are both qualitatively and quantitatively distorted, both by the mass media and in positivist discussions. This they term 'moral panic': periodic widespread public hysteria about particular social problems which not only blatantly exaggerates their extent and impact, but creates 'folk devils': distorted stereotypes of the how, why and whereabouts of the typical deviant. Examples of this are the 'Black mugger' panic of the early 1980s and the 'Mods and Rockers' panic of the 1960s (Cohen, S., 1972; Cohen and Young, 1981). But drugs are the source of moral panic *par excellence*.

Let us take, as an example, the heroin panic in Britain which started in 1984. If the more sensational reports are to be believed, we are only a short step from Sodom and Gomorrah. In May, the London Borough of Islington produced a well thought out report on the problem of heroin use in their area. They hazarded an estimate that 15 per cent of young males were regular users. This was no doubt an overestimate. It was reported on the BBC news of that day, however, as 30 per cent. Thames Television reported it, in their headlines, as under 40 per cent. In the news story itself, it had escalated to 'nearly half of all young people in Islington'. Tony Moss writing in the *Sunday Times* had already written (8 April) that the majority – i.e. over 50 per cent – of kids in south-east London estates were experimenting with heroin. Dr Martin Plant, 'Scotland's foremost authority on drug addiction', had said that 'heroin is being handed out like Smarties'. The Angel area of Islington, it seemed, had a higher use of heroin than Harlem, and Clapham High Road more street-hustling than the Bronx.

Many kinds of people stand to gain by exaggerating the predicament. Very few, conversely, have reasons to be realistic about it. Journalists find drug scare stories remarkably good copy; social work agencies can lay claim to greater resources in the middle of a panic; the police can claim that special drug squads are necessary; and sociologists can apply for grants to study the phenomenon. Yet the one certainty, in the study of heroin use, is that, as with so many aspects of deviant behaviour, there are simply no hard facts. Thus thoroughgoing analysis of the American 'epidemic' of 1968–74 (a 'fact' which is usually regarded as incontestable) came to this conclusion:

One difficulty with the epidemic hypothesis is that almost all the indicators which have been used, by social scientists as well as the public, to document the 'epidemic' of heroin use are derivative. That is, they are not direct measures of the incidence or prevalence of drug use in the general population, but measures which infer such incidence or prevalence from various data gathered by law enforcement or medical agencies (Lidz and Walker, 1980, pp. 48–9).

They go on to point out that the figures based on the number of arrests rise and fall in proportion to the amount of money spent on policing drugs, as do the figures of the number of people treated in clinics. An important outcome is that moral panics produce what appears to be 'real' rises in all the relevant statistics.

The development of a moral panic typically goes through several stages:

1. Most deviancy, including heroin use, is unknown to official agencies – there is a large 'dark figure' of deviant behaviour.

2. The mass media, perhaps because of a particular individual scandal or a social survey, begin to focus on heroin as a problem.

3. The public and politicians become initially sensitized to heroin abuse.

4. Pressure is put on the police, on customs officers and on social services to tackle the problem.

5. They dig deeper into the dark figure, arresting more heroin users, catching more smugglers, and highlighting heroin abuse as a major issue in social work reports. So the figures rise.

6. The mass media respond to this use by putting more journalists into the field investigating heroin abuse.

7. More articles on heroin confirm to the public, the various agencies and – *very importantly* – to journalists themselves that there is a rapidly increasing problem.

8. More police, customs officers, social workers, politicians and journalists demand more funds for dealing with heroin abuse, which results in more agencies which pick up more heroin users.

9. More parents and social workers realize their kids and clients 'have a problem' and get them to register. More heroin users do likewise. The official figures increase even further.

10. To the mass media, this confirms their panic prognosis, so they pay even more attention to the problem. A vicious circle is set up with positive feedback to stage 2 of the process.

A fantasy crime wave has now been created which need not *necessarily* involve any actual increase in users.

The Effects of Drugs

For positivists, the effects of drugs are a matter for scientific investigation. Their physical effects are charted in the laboratory and their social effects by surveys. The generalizations that emerge, moreover, are believed to have universal validity: such knowledge is also cumulative. So if you want to know the effects of marijuana or heroin use, you simply look them up in the pharmacopoeia.

A central part of positivist thinking is that human behaviour can be studied by the same methods that are used in the natural sciences. Thus in tackling questions like 'Does heroin lead to crime?' or the likelihood of escalation from marijuana to heroin, generalizations obtained from a certain number of cases are assumed – as in the physical sciences – to have a high degree of accuracy, expressed in terms of probabilities, whatever the situation in which the particular drug is used.

Thus Professor G. Joachimoglu, a distinguished member of the United Nations Drug Supervisory Body, writes:

In a paper presented to the International Congress of Criminology in Paris in 1950, Professor C. G. Gardicas mentioned a group of 117 individuals, by no means criminals initially, who became addicts and criminals after smoking hashish and were sentenced for threats, blackmail, murder, offences against property, and other offences. It is not necessary to go into further details. Hashish is a social evil and the International Conventions are of great importance for the protection of society (Joachimoglu, 1965, p. 5).

Thus, because marijuana use correlated with crime in these 117 cases, this connection is assumed to have the same causal status as the observation that the ignition of hydrogen and oxygen together invariably yields water: to invoke universal laws, unrelated to either the desires of the individuals involved or the theoretical aspirations of the investigators. To take another example, newspaper reports about the Sharon Tate murders suggested that the film star and her friends were murdered by Charles Manson and his family 'because' the latter were high on speed. Likewise, the My Lai massacre in Vietnam was thought to have occurred 'because' American troops had been smoking marijuana. From these observations, marijuana and methedrine were linked irrevocably with murder. Strange and unpalatable acts were given instant explanations, while Manson and the GIs were excused responsibility for their behaviour. Less dramatically, invoking the use of drugs has become a routine basis for pleading 'mitigating circumstances' in court. Thus the heroin addict can plead that it was 'smack' that *forced* him to steal two lamb chops from the deep freeze in the local corner shop.

New deviancy theorists oppose such excuses. They argue that whereas it is undoubtedly true that drugs facilitate many forms of behaviour, it is to the strange cults of Hollywood that we must look for an explanation of the murder of popular film stars, and it is in the dehumanizing effect of wars that we will find the reasons for the murder of innocent Vietnamese peasants. Generalizations about drugs, that is, must always be grounded in specific cultures and particular social situations.

Theories evolved by social scientists, moreover, often have 'self-fulfilling' effects on the very drug-users whose behaviour the theories were erected to explain. They may either introject the interpretations others provide of their behaviour and act accordingly, or they may be placed in situations where they have no option but to act in accordance with other people's definition of the situation and other people's ideas about their motivations and predictions as to how they will act.

People also learn the effects of drugs from other drug-users. Thus, H. S. Becker, in his classic article 'Becoming a Marijuana User' (1963), outlines the learning process involved in marijuana use. The novice – the naïve user – does not experience a 'high' at first; he may feel slightly strange, but that is all; and he is unable to interpret the meaning of the physiological sensations he is experiencing. Indeed, the novice may feel that nothing at all has happened to him – he may feel totally cheated by the drug – and it is not until a sophisticated user has indicated to him the likely effects that he realizes that he is in fact being affected by the drug. Moreover, it is not until the beginner learns firstly how to smoke marijuana and then – more importantly – how to interpret his feelings as pleasurable that he experiences a 'high'. Before this the effects of the drug are usually either ambiguous or physically unpleasant. A similar process is noticeable in terms of more powerful drugs like heroin:

The learning process involved in the first trials of the drug is illustrated by incidents related to me by addicts. For example, a man who experimented with opiates in the presence of two addicts reported that he felt nothing except nausea, which occurred about half an hour after injection. It took a number of repetitions and some instruction from his more sophisticated associates before this person learned to notice the euphoric effects. In another instance an individual who claimed that she felt nothing from two closely spaced injections amused her addicted companions by rubbing her nose violently while she made her complaints. A tingling or itching sensation in the nose or other parts of the body is the common effect of a large initial dose (Lindesmith, 1951, pp. 24–5).

Pharmacological generalizations about responses to drugs, moreover (in this case alcohol), are often applicable to particular cultures:

At this point it is necessary to interject a note of caution with reference to various physiological and psychological studies on the effects of alcohol consumption. We should not let ourselves forget that the subjects for these investigations have been drawn from our own culture and that there are very few cross-cultural studies of the physiology and the 'psychology' of alcohol ingestion. Such comparative studies as have been made raise more than fleeting doubts that what often passes for constant 'physiological effects' of alcohol in American research in reality may be manifestations of a variable cultural overlay. Thus, for example, in one study of the function of alcohol in a primitive Mexican culture located in the mountains of Chiapas, few of the more extreme types of behaviour which arise in connection with intoxication in our culture were found to occur. There, in the stage of feeling high, native men could play guitars, or handle a machete with perfect safety. In extreme intoxication there seemed to be less interference with speech than that observable in inebriation in our culture, and even in stuporous states the natives carried through with familiar routines and transacted complicated business of which later they had no memory. There seemed to be very little vomiting after over-indulgence, and there was little evidence of hangovers beyond mild tremors and shakiness. Little fighting arose in drinking parties, and there was no evidence of lowered inhibition in erotic behaviour. These people typically drank for the sense of warmth it induced and as a prelude to sleep (Lemert, 1951, p. 341).

Drug-induced behaviour thus involves an interaction between the physiological effects of the drug and the norms of the group of which the drug-taker is a member. These effects are socially induced and structured. In New York, for instance, the most common opiate addicts (addicted to opium, heroin and morphine) are lower class Black 'junkies' and physicians. One lives on the street, the other high in the wealthy apartment blocks of Manhattan. Although they take the same substances, their lives and social status could scarcely be more different. Figure 12 illustrates these stark differences.

The effects of different social milieux are thus very marked. A New York street addict taking the daily injection that a physician takes would die of overdosing, and despite the total differences in

Morphine/heroin users in New York City	Physician addict	Street junkie
Amount of drug used	Builds up to very large amounts over time	Small
Purity	Pure	Very dilute or unknown dilution level; heavily contaminated; talc, amphetamines, strychnine, etc
Mode of administration	Surgically sterile syringes	Makeshift, often dirty syringes
Motivation	To keep working despite painful illness, as part of a competitive culture	To gain a 'high', as part of a hedonistic culture
Effect	Loss of pain, calmness, ability to work	Immense pleasure
Length of use	Often many years	A few years
Prognosis	Low death-rate; cure in private clinic and return to practice	Early death from overdosing, infection or adulterants

Figure 12.

lifestyle and prognosis, it is the physician who is usually very much more physically addicted.

Why People Take Drugs: The 'New Deviancy' Explanation

Society consists of a large number of groups of people with their own norms and values. Each of these sub-cultures has its own solutions to problems experienced by people in their own part of the social structure; they have approved means of achieving desired ends. Old people, young people, working class, middle class, West Indian, Irish, criminals and doctors all face their own particular set of problems and all evolve cultural ways of solving them. Some of these problems can be solved by using consciousness-altering drugs. As explained earlier, the effects of drugs are also partially controlled by the culture itself. But only partially so; for certain drugs are more pharmacologically suited to aiding certain activities than others.

Amphetamines, for instance, because they are stimulants, are a much more appropriate solution to the problem of a high work-load (for example, in the case of physician or student) than would be a depressant like alcohol. A specific drug is therefore adopted partly because of its availability, partly because of its pharmacological suitability. But its effects are then *re*structured and given meaning by the sub-culture concerned.

Alcohol, nicotine and caffeine are psychoactive drugs that are freely available in our society, together with – to a slightly lesser extent – prescribed barbiturates, amphetamines and tranquillizers. Their widespread use shows that they provide a common solution to the problems of a vast number of individuals. The extent and nature of their use is not, however, uniform but varies with the particular sub-culture involved. To take alcohol, for example, there are wide differences between the drinking habits and rituals of merchant seamen and businessmen, between Italians and Orthodox Jews. Each sub-group in society will have a conception of what is the appropriate situation for a drink; what the permissible and desirable effects of alcohol are; how much it is necessary to drink to achieve this desired state; what meanings are associated with the drunken state (e.g. feelings of masculinity); what is normal and what is deviant drinking behaviour. They will have a definition of the social drinker and a notion, too, of the alcoholic. The phrase 'It's enough to turn a man to drink', for instance, indicates that there are definite theories as to the inception of alcoholism. And there are definite notions, too, of how an alcoholic acts. Thus the social drinker in our society is commonly seen as someone who 'holds his drink' and enjoys himself, while the alcoholic is seen as someone who is sick: he is determined and controlled *by the drug*, alcohol.

We argued above that the effects of drugs are related to the conceptions people have of them. Although alcohol is physiologically addictive; the ease with which one is able to cure oneself of this addiction; the speed at which one becomes addicted; and the type of behaviour displayed during addiction will be at least partly related to the social pressures and beliefs surrounding alcoholism. Both the roles 'social drinker' and 'alcoholic' are culturally defined solutions to particular problems. That is, the person who needs to relax and enjoy himself will find himself attracted to social drinking, while the individual who feels that it would be preferable to induce a state where he is 'out of control' (i.e. where he is determined) will be recruited readily to the role 'alcoholic'.

The definition of the alcoholic as the determined person thus attracts those who wish to opt out of particular social situations. They can then say 'It's not me who is doing this; it's the "booze"'. Similarly, the conceptions a sub-group holds of the typical marijuana smoker or heroin addict will attract certain individuals and repel others. The way we define the type of person who takes a certain drug, then, and its likely effects control to some extent the kinds of people who take specific types of drug. Society, that is, creates a series of psychoactive 'boxes' which certain kinds of people find congenial but others reject. The alcohol molecule itself does not contain a solution to a person's problems. Rather, the culture he belongs to defines the problem, states whether or not alcohol is relevant to its solution, and programmes and structures the administration of alcohol so as to provide an array of possible and permissible effects. In short, the psychoactive 'box' erected around alcohol in the particular sub-culture to which the individual belongs may or may not be capable of handling the problem which he faces.

The problems faced by an individual, of course, may not involve deviance at all. They may well be solved by the normal behaviour suggested by his culture. A man who feels it difficult to relax after work, for example, will find that there is a programmed psychoactive drug, alcohol, available, and that the role of 'social drinker' is a perfectly acceptable one which will solve his problem. But what of those for whom the culture provides no such 'normal' solution? The individual who faces a particular strain has two alternatives: to solve his problem in isolation, or to join with like-suffering others to create a collective solution. To take the individual solution first, a person facing severe strain, but unaware that there are others who feel likewise, will probably interpret his troubles in terms of self-blame and personal inadequacy rather than as a result of stresses commonplace in society. He will take recourse to the pervasive absolutist explanations of deviancy which are commonly held in our society. He will 'individualize' the problem and will fail to see himself — or be seen by others — as someone whose troubles are explicable in terms of the wider social context. The deviant's behaviour is then viewed as a matter of personal pathology, and labelled with a medical metaphor. Thus the isolated housewife using tranquillizers may think that both her dependency on drugs and the anxieties which generated it are her own fault, that she is the only woman in the world who finds being confined to the house frustrates her personal development and sanity.

But isolated individuals may well find that there *are* roles associated with certain types of drug use and effects which are appropriate to them. The main such role, in any society, is that of the isolated alcoholic, but similar conceptions of heroin addicts exist in some deviant sub-cultures. Thus, for the adult middle-class Briton, the social drinker is the normal role. For his son, on the other hand, marijuana-smoking may be a normal psychoactive activity, with heroin use as a deviant one. That is, both 'straight' and 'hip' cultures have distinctive and different conceptions of what constitutes a 'sick' drug-user.

Not all isolated drug-takers view themselves as having pathological personalities. An alternative, and more insidious, analysis would be that although the person is 'normal', the drug to which he has been casually introduced – whether it be alcohol or heroin or tobacco – has such power to addict that it is impossible to resist its use.

Each way, individuals are seen to be sick: they either have a sick personality which has led them to addiction, or they have caught the 'sickness' of drug addiction. Such determined roles are peculiarly attractive to people who find themselves in impossible and irreconcilable situations. They enable them to continue a particular line of action, for example mainlining heroin, while at the same time both to condemn the practice in general, and at the same time to deny responsibility for the behaviour, in their own case, as a necessity.

Thus unemployed men excuse themselves for their inability to perform the 'normal' masculine role of worker, into which they have been socialized, because they have heroin 'sickness'. 'Physical' sickness caused by withdrawal from heroin will be interpreted as a confirmation that he suffers from a 'social' or 'psychological' sickness. His desire to avoid choice has become translated into a notion of himself as being unable to make a choice. Withdrawal symptoms are perceived as chronic and irresistible, so that one is 'forced' into using a greater dose. Physical dependency will then indeed become greater; withdrawal distress will increase; and so on. The addict has entered a spiral of involvement in the sick role.

Giving Deviants Meaning and Taking it Away

Positivists argue that, as experts, they have a superior understanding of deviancy than the deviants themselves. Deviants, they say, because of their lack of cognitive ability and a tendency to conceal the real causes of their troubles, are the *last* people capable of understanding what is happening to them.

The study of social phenomena, positivists argue, should be value-free: social scientists should utilize objective concepts as in the natural sciences. Values merely decide which problems we are interested in; they must not be allowed to distort the evidence we examine.

Blackburn has criticized this position on the grounds that although this view assumes that 'once theories are thoroughly cleansed of all value judgements' 'they will be governed by the wholesome discipline of objective facts, the predictable consequence of this attempted purge of values is to orient theory and research towards certain crude over-abstracted value notions masquerading as scientific concepts' (Blackburn, 1968, p. 205). This 'ideology of objectivity' which pretends to have evolved value-free concepts, in fact reflects middle-class values. 'Psychopathy', 'anomic', 'social disorganization', 'under-socialization', 'weak superego', 'lack of masculine identification', 'retreatism': all are views of one group's behaviour as seen from the perspective of members of the liberal professions, part of the 'enlightened' middle classes. Because of their privileged social position, the views of those at the top are viewed as more 'realistic' than those of the lower echelons of society. As Becker has put it, there is a 'hierarchy of credibility'. The meaning that the individual drug-takers themselves ascribe to their activities is ignored.

Junkies, for instance, are said to be notorious liars. The 'real' causes of their action therefore, can only be discussed by experts who possess 'insight' into the problem. Occurrences in the drug-taker's past are then invoked as the 'real' explanations of present actions. Thus, for instance, a man is said to inject heroin into his veins because his father was a weak and ineffectual figure, or smokes marijuana because he was fixated at the oral stage of his development as a child. The taking of a drug is denuded of any meaning that individuals themselves attribute to it. Their ideas are merely rationalizations for the hidden forces which, unbeknownst to them, impel them to take drugs.

Drug dependency, like all deviant behaviour, tends thus to get explained by reference to events in the distant past which resulted in psychotic or asocial tendencies which became part of the deviant's psychic make-up. Both these approaches are 'essentialist', but in different ways: pharmacological analyses assume that a certain type of behaviour is automatically released in any individual under the influence of a specific drug; psychological explanations insist that the drug merely triggers off inherent repressed tendencies which are part of the essential nature of the individual in question. Both assign a minor role to social factors. These may cause peripheral variations in drug-induced behaviour but are never a major focus of analysis.

By contrast, not only are drug-taking groups regarded as asocial, but drugs themselves are seen to be 'desocializing': drug-induced behaviour is seen as bizarre, meaningless and uninhibited; it represents the release of primitive, instinctual passions. The drug-taker is seen to be temporarily transported 'beyond' the control of society. The study of drug-taking therefore concentrates on the pharmacological properties and effects of the drug in question or on the supposed formation of a personality predisposed to drug use in the early years of life, or acquired in the early stages of addiction.

Thus the addict is often characterized not only as having a weak ego, a defective superego and a lack of masculine identification, but also unrealistic aspirations and an 'irrational' distrust of major social institutions, all of which derive from the addict's family background. 'Realistic' behaviour is thus predicated upon the belief in the rationality of the major social institutions in the governmental agencies which protect our lives, property, and rights. Thus Chein *et al.* note:

This does not prohibit us from regarding particular instances of such institutions with disapproval, anger or cynicism. But, despite such instances, we accept the institutions as a valid and potentially useful social arrangement. We generally trust persons who embody these institutions until they betray this trust; should they deceive us, we criticize them as individuals, though we maintain much of our regard for the institution *per se* (Chein *et al.*, 1964, p. 265).

Normality, then, involves a basic acceptance of society as it stands; distrust, even by the dispossessed or the underprivileged, is regarded as symptomatic of personal and family pathology.

Deviancy theorists acknowledge that events in the biography of the individual drug-taker, are, in general, likely to provide only very partial explanations of present drug use. Dependency, that is, is not caused by impersonal forces which impel the individual on to the road to addiction, but develops because drug-takers respond to the forces which impinge upon them in ways that are socially available – and satisfying – to them. We therefore need to know their interpretation of the situation and assessment of reality. To do so, we need to examine the values and the ideology of the drug-user. This is not to say the drug-taker's perception of the situation is necessarily an accurate one; simply that his or her evaluation of their own situation is a major component governing their behaviour.

Behaviour also has to be located within the context of the wider society. We do not adequately explain human action by assuming that it is the outcome of purely individual propensities (e.g. that a person is violent because he is a 'psychopath'; or that a woman has a large number of sexual partners because she is a 'nymphomaniac'). Rather, individuals can only be understood in terms of the sub-cultures of which they are a part.

As an instance let us look at the phenomenon of the relatively high level of drug addiction amongst physicians. Let us take the case of the doctor who is overworked and who has a painful gastro-intestinal disorder. As a member of the sub-culture of the profession of medicine, he has a considerable knowledge of drugs, in terms of their effects in various quantities. He also has access to them. Secretly, therefore, he prescribes himself daily shots of morphine. He does not think that he will become addicted; his expertise, he believes, will enable him to control its use. He also takes the opiate in order to pursue ends compatible with his profession (i.e. to continue working), rather than for pleasure, as with the lower-class addict. If he does, eventually, become dependent on morphine, the addiction will be shaped, timed, administered and resolved in terms of the sub-culture of medicine to which he belongs.

Now, let us take a type of deviance that does not involve drugs: misbehaviour in the classroom. Positivists often assume that disruptive pupils are 'hyperactive'. They are suffering, that is, from an individual problem, of possibly metabolic origin, which *makes* them inattentive and rebellious in class. In contrast, the outstanding study of classroom misbehaviour dismisses all pathological interpretations, such as 'hyperactivity', and shows instead how the lower stream of the class realize that they are destined for low-skilled jobs where academic achievement is irrelevant. Their structural problem is that they are being asked to compete against middle-class standards for which their own background ill prepares them, in order to achieve academic qualifications irrelevant to their future jobs. They culturally 'solve' the problem by 'playing up' in the classroom, rejecting the teacher's discipline; and by despising 'swots' while at the same time evolving a sub-culture which gives high status to manliness and physical toughness. That is, they begin to evolve a culture which rejects standards which threaten their self-esteem and more relevantly fits their future work as labourers. They turn their misfortune into a virtue.

The Causes and Effect of Social Reaction Against the Drug-user

From the positivist point of view, widespread deviancy is disruptive of social order. What is needed, then, obviously, is expert intervention. The task of the expert is thus not just that of explaining the deviant to the rest of society; he is also expected to reform and treat the rule-breaker. Certain personnel are therefore selected to mediate between society and the deviant. Chief among these – apart from the police and the clergy – are the social worker, the psychiatrist, the psychologist and the criminologist. They perceive themselves as having a primarily therapeutic role: of assimilating the 'poor', the 'maladjusted', those with 'immature personalities', 'the undersocialized', 'the sick', 'the adolescent gone wrong' into the ranks of decent, well-integrated people like themselves. When some of their clients interpret these attempts at therapy as being punitive and coercive, they are said to be lacking in self-insight; while the few who go further and accuse them of being professional ideologues with middle-class values are dismissed as unbalanced.

The expert, who is in a position of power *vis-à-vis* the deviant, will tend to maintain his position by eliciting from the deviant those responses which tend to verify his theories: a procedure which has been described as 'negotiating reality' (Scheff, 1968). If the deviant is cooperative and helpful, and shows insight into his or her problem, the expert will also be cooperative: he will provide material help or obtain an early release, will not give the 'client' shock therapy, but instead give warmth and sympathy and protection from the law. In short, successful therapy involves convincing deviants of the stupidity of their own ideas about their own behaviour and replacing those ideas by those of the therapist's, a process paradoxically called 'self-insight' (Berger and Luckmann, 1967).

But the expert not only has the power to 'negotiate' reality (to determine the sort of information which he is willing to see and hear); he also has the power to *change* reality. The stereotypes that experts hold about deviants therefore have very real consequences both for what happens to them and in terms of the way they perceive themselves. Thus individuals incarcerated in total institutions begin to look, act, and feel like the anomic, under-socialized, psychotic, amoral individuals which the therapeutic personnel portray in their theories of deviancy.

Any protest by the deviants themselves against the treatment which they receive is seen as confirming the theory. Thus Chein *et al.* write of heroin users:

When the hospital staff attempts to impose controls which would be accepted, though not enjoyed, by most adolescents, adolescent addicts perceive this as a threat to their masculinity, so they are regularly involved in such problems as truancy, keeping late hours, refusing to get up in time for breakfast and refusing to turn the lights out at some curfew hour. They will let no one tell them how to conduct themselves, for to do so implies that they are not man enough to know themselves . . . (Chein *et al.*, 1964, p. 226).

The fragmentation of knowledge, the segregated middle-class existence of the expert, his or her power to negotiate reality and ignore protest, the seeming fulfilment of his hypotheses, all combine to ensconce him securely in a positivist position. These tendencies are particularly strong amongst experts on drug dependence, for drug use poses obvious medical and physiological problems, so that physicians and pharmacologists tend to specialize in this field. Their natural-science training makes it unlikely that they will be sensitized to the fundamental differences between physical and social phenomena, while their study of the human body encourages them to see society, too, as an organic system.

To the positivist social scientist, social reactions against certain kinds of deviant behaviour are simply natural. It is not questioned, for example, why society reacts against people who smoke marijuana but not against those who smoke tobacco. In contrast, deviancy theorists regard deviancy, not as a property inherent in certain kinds of activity, but as a label that is put upon some kinds of behaviour. From this point of view, studying what kinds of people condemn drug-taking is quite as important as studying those who take drugs. Hence, they study the power structure of society: the ways in which certain groups are able to proscribe the behaviour of others, and legitimize only the kinds of behaviour they themselves engage in.

Social reaction to drug use, in fact, is often itself irrational. Thus moral panic and public concern about drugs is often out of all proportion to their real incidence and effects, for example in relation to actual mortality rates. Thus in the 1960s there was an enormous media coverage on the dangers of marijuana though there was no authenticated case of anyone ever dying of the drug. Yet around 200 people a day die of the effects of tobacco, and more people die of tobacco in one day than heroin in a year. Again, despite the considerable carnage resulting from adolescent motorbike crashes, newspaper headlines do not portray this as an 'epidemic' of deaths or call for sanctions against motorcycle manufacturers or describe retailers as 'pushers'!

Deviant activities, even though they may have no direct effect on those who merely observe them, are often condemned because they are seen as behaviour which, so to speak, 'dodges the rules'. People who live by codes of conduct which forbid certain pleasures, or demand the deferring of gratifications, react strongly against those they see as taking short cuts. This is a partial explanation of the vigorous repression against what Edwin Schur (1973) calls 'crimes without victims': homosexuality, prostitution, abortion and drug-taking. And drug-taking is, of course, a target *par excellence* for moral indignation. A further common reaction to drug use is that of ambivalence, however, for the 'normal' person simultaneously covets and castigates the 'deviant' action. This, after all, *is* the basis of moral indignation, namely that the wicked are undeservedly realizing the covert desires of the virtuous. Richard Blum captured well this fascination–repulsion relationship to drug use when he wrote:

The amount of public interest in stories about druggies suggests attraction and repulsion in ordinary citizens. 'Fascination' is the better term, since it implies witchcraft and enchantment. People are fascinated by drugs – because they are attracted to the states and conditions drugs are said to produce. The other side to the fear of being disrupted . . . is the desire for release, for escape, for magic, and for ecstatic joys. Drugs represent keys to forbidden kingdoms inside ourselves (Blum, 1969, p. 335).

Moral indignation, then, is based on a conflict between values and desires: hence the remarkable interest in certain drug-using groups, despite their minute size, and the denunciation, in the mass media, of the heroin addict (who presumably is 'enjoying himself') rather than the methylated spirits drinker (who presumably is too miserable to be attractive).

Social reactions against particular forms of drug-taking, in general, are proportional to the degree to which the group involved embraces values which are hedonistic and disdainful of work. Conversely, where drug-taking is linked to productivity, either because it aids work or facilitates relaxation before or after work, it is viewed with much greater favour, if not encouraged. Even the *same* drug, however, can be differentially evaluated according to the group which uses it and the ends which its use facilitates in the following ways:

Amphetamines

Legal use. Seventy-two million tablets were issued to British armed forces during the war to be used to combat exhaustion, astronauts carry stocks in case of emergency; civilians use them, on prescription, to slim and counteract depression.

Tolerated use. By teenagers to stay awake at all-night clubs and parties.

Alcohol

Tolerated use. 'Social' drinking at business functions or to relax after work at approved leisure times.

Condemned use. 'Problem' drinking, the clinical definition of which involves the disruption of work-habits and domestic duties.

Opiates

Legal use. Morphine to alleviate pain amongst the sick (the largest number of most heavily addicted people in Britain is the terminally ill).

Condemnation, but little social reaction. The use of morphine by physician addicts to enable them to continue working, addiction which is only discovered after admission into hospital for a 'cure'. The retrospective reaction of the doctor's community, however, is usually remarkably slight.

Condemnation and harsh reaction. Use of heroin by 'street addicts' for hedonistic reasons. In Britain, however, where addiction is perceived as an unpleasant sickness, the social reaction is less punitive than where the addict is seen as a criminal hedonist.

Tobacco

Probably one of the most universally acceptable drugs in the West, despite the immense health risk smoking involves. It is one of the few drugs which is tolerated during the performance of many occupational roles, since it does not interfere with efficiency and has a reputation for aiding concentration on the job at hand.

The illuminating way of summarizing these reactions to deviancy, sees them as successive phases in a process that has been called *deviancy amplification* (Wilkins, 1965).

The argument starts from the proposition we discussed earlier: that under certain conditions society will define as deviant a group of people who depart from valued norms in particular ways. This negative societal reaction – by driving deviants into each other's company if they are to pursue those kinds of behaviour and by driving them out of 'respectable' society – increases the probability that deviants will act even more deviantly. Societal reaction will then increase at the same pace; more deviancy will be induced; in turn, the reaction escalates further. As a result, a 'deviancy amplification spiral' is entered into, where each increase in social control is matched by a corresponding increase in deviancy.

It should not be thought that the deviant group is, so to speak, a pinball propelled in a deviant direction, or that the agencies of social control will inevitably react in an equally mechanical way to deviancy. The drug-taking group can create its own circumstances in various ways, and reactions on the part of society will also vary in accordance with the kinds of theories which both the society and the drug-using

Diagrammatically:

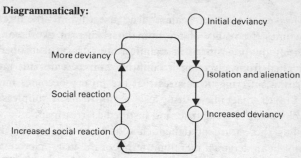

Figure 13.

group evolve in order to explain each other and which they test out in the actual course of events – which range from arrest situations to casual encounters on the street, and from articles in the mass media to discussions among friends.

Overall, however, whatever these variations, it is the definitions imposed by the powerful on the situation that will be most decisive in shaping public policy and social attitudes.

Social Policy

From the positivist position, the causes of drug-taking have to be ascertained by an expert; a diagnosis made; and intervention undertaken in order to treat the individuals involved. The parallel with medicine is explicit: an epidemic has occurred. Hence we must treat the individuals afflicted and control likely carriers. Deviant subcultures must therefore be eliminated.

All of this is anathema to the relativists. To them, the notion of an automatic transmission of drug use, whenever individuals contact drug sub-cultures, is a fallacy. Since people become socialized into drug cultures because they find them attractive in terms of solving problems which they face, to end drug abuse you must find alternative solutions to these problems which do *not* involve the use of drugs. In the meantime, the cultures themselves contain and regulate drug use, so what must be attempted is to feed rational information into those cultures. This may seem to be only an interim palliative, but until we make determined efforts to tackle the root causes of drug-taking, it remains the most likely way of minimizing deleterious physical and psychological effects in the populations at risk.

The social reaction against drug use, despite the rhetoric and sometimes the reality of the humanitarianism it expresses, achieves precisely the opposite of its manifest aims. Instead of liberating the individual from addiction it confirms him as a deviant rather than obviating suffering; it ensures that the misery becomes inescapable. The myth that illicit drug use is intrinsically unpleasurable is thereby made to come true, and justified as 'treatment'.

Thus the nature of dependency and the life of the drug-taker cannot be understood merely in terms of the drug. Heroin addicts in Britain, the United States, Hong Kong and Japan all take the same drug but the pattern of addiction is remarkably different. Different social reaction against the drug-taker, in different cultures, and the various policies designed to control drug-taking, have remarkably different effects on the ways drug-takers behave. For example, in the United States, they are cast as criminals, legally harassed, and forced into crime (thus substantiating the stereotype) in order to find money for the high black market prices. Organized crime grows up as an unintended consequence of narcotics legislation, an exploitative culture is set up which dominates the life of the addict. Since the strength of these adulterated drugs is low, death is not an inevitable consequence of a drug like heroin but a consequence of supply and cost on the market. On top of this, criminal exploitation, police harassment, therapeutic correction, and social stigmatization all give rise to a culture which defends itself against these very agencies.

If we wish to reduce the extent of drug-taking we therefore have to:

1. Eliminate the problems which are the underlying causes. This involves much wider areas of social life than the drug-taking sub-culture alone. Combating heroin use amongst youth, for instance, would involve fundamental alterations in the economy and in levels of unemployment. Above all, social problems must not be reduced to medical problems; they demand social solutions.

2. Look for viable alternatives to the use of drugs (some of which might also arouse social antagonism), including alternative drugs or safer methods of using existing ones.

3. Avoid, wherever possible, the onset of deviancy amplification. At the most immediate level, this involves changing the absolutist stereotypes held by many agencies of drug control (e.g., the police and the drug clinics). On a wider level, it involves a change in public attitudes, including those of parents and citizens.

4. At the level of the individual, the actor, too, has to realize that his or her problems are social, and that their solution can be achieved not by fatalistically accepting determined roles (such as the sick addict in the clinic) but involves action on their own part, and on the part of others, to change their social situation and thereby eradicate the root causes of their addiction.

We have used drugs as an example of deviant behaviour because it is a topical and controversial issue. But the same kind of analysis is valid in analysing other forms of deviance. Whereas the positivist will ascribe delinquency to poor family background or even inadequate physical type, and see its concentration among the lower orders as indicative of their poor social norms, child-rearing practices or genetic stock, deviancy theorists observe that while all kids (and adults) commit delinquent acts, it is, however, only lower working-class youngsters who get picked up by the police. The moral panic about youth crime, based on mass media stereotypes and inappropriate social reactions, is a process of deviancy amplification which eventually transforms the delinquent into the hardened criminal.

Absolutism, Relativism and Realism

This chapter is obviously written with considerable sympathy for the 'new deviancy' approach. But there are problems with that approach, too.

It is as fallacious, for example, to depict human beings as being totally free as it is to see them as totally determined. People make real choices but they do so under circumstances which are not of their own choosing. Furthermore, they often make these choices on the basis of misconceptions and with inadequate knowledge, which limits the solutions they attempt and often makes things worse. New deviancy theory tends, then, to assume too much rationality in the drug-taker's behaviour. Resort to alcohol, for example, may make a person less competent and their confidence will then shrink even further.

In rejecting the positivist notion of people as being determined by their individual psychological and genetic past, and in studying the dynamics of the drug-taking community, deviancy theorists often neglect pressures which are built into society as a whole. The unemployed Black in the ghetto has very limited choices; the suburban housewife is stuck at home. Their freedom is limited. Further, by stressing the way in which administrative control of deviancy amplifies the problem, and by emphasizing the injustices of policing and the stereotypes of psychiatrists and social workers, attention is diverted from the injustices. Ghetto addicts are not driven to heroin use simply by false 'labelling', though this certainly exacerbates their problems. They are driven into it because of the circumstances of the ghetto.

New deviancy theory rightly stresses that many of the dominant values of society are not directly in the interests of large numbers of its members and that there is a considerably greater diversity of interpretations of the world than is often recognized. This is not to say, however, that there is no sense at all in the notion of consensus, for it does, in fact, represent the interests and values of the majority. Condemnation of drugs may be based on particular conceptions of 'respectability' and on the desirability of hard work. Yet people *do* have to work, and families do have to bring up children, to keep up decent living standards and ensure that there is a compassionate relationship between people – all of which are threatened by the use of strong drugs. The Temperance Movement of the 1920s and 1930s may well have been based on a prudish and puritanical approach to alcohol, but it was also true that the culture of the drinking saloon and the bar threatened the impoverished family, brutalized many men and led to the domestic abuse of many women. The reaction of 'straight' society to drug use on the part of its more bohemian members often degenerates into mere stereotyping and fantasy – as many a jazz and rock musician has discovered, drug use both enhances and encumbers creativity. To argue against present systems of control is not the same as arguing against control, and however fallacious consensual stereotypes of drug use may be, there is a wide-scale consensus across all social groups that incoherence, impotence and early death are not social goods.

A realistic approach is to accept that there *is* a problem of drug use within society, but that the real problem is caricatured, exaggerated and converted into a moral panic by powerful forces in our society. The mass media take real fears about drugs and inject hysteria into people's minds. But they would not be able to if there were no actual fears to play upon.

Drugs, then, really are a problem. The deleterious effects of many drugs have been grossly exaggerated, but this is not to say that they are innocuous. Heroin, for example, does not itself produce direct physical damage as tobacco and alcohol do, and most deaths are the result of using contaminated, dirty needles and overdosing because the strength of the dose is unknown. All of this, is, of course, largely the consequence of its illegality. But even if all heroin use were legal, it is an extremely strong drug. Even when used in pure form, with clean needles as in medical clinics, there is always a possibility of overdosing, and there is the tendency to go to the edge of one's tolerance-level. Physician addicts can often use large quantities of morphine or heroin over long periods of time without killing themselves, but it is a very different matter in hedonistic junkie sub-cultures. It is precisely *because* drug use and effects vary by sub-culture that there are higher dangers in one culture than another. Different groups use the same drugs with methods ranging from extreme caution to abandon.

Similarly, while it is correct to say that tobacco and alcohol kill far more people than heroin or cocaine, it does not follow that other unpermitted drugs are innocuous. It would probably take $1\frac{1}{2}$ lb of cannabis, for example, to kill you. But the inhalation of any substance into your lungs is not innocuous, and people who are already very unstable may become more unbalanced through constant smoking.

Conventional policies of drug control have lamentably failed. Why, then, many ask, should we continue with policies which manifestly only make things worse, and why should governments have the right to interfere in activities which harm no one but the deviants themselves? Why should we interfere, in any case, with free individuals doing their own thing? The realistic answer is that individuals are not free. It is precisely the structural determinants which they choose to ignore which limit their freedom and the rationality of their choices. Nor is the exercise of power in itself an inherent evil, for power can be used to combat repressive institutions. And though widespread changes in society do undoubtedly evoke opposition from those with interests, material and ideological, in the status quo, radical reforms in minor areas of social life are possible without total transformation of the entire social order.

12   Theoretical Schools

The various topics discussed in earlier chapters are not disconnected from each other. Arguments over, say, the importance of the family are often connected with arguments about how we are to understand deviance, and these in turn to controversies as to whether social stratification is an inescapable necessity, and so on.

Though examining different aspects of society, sociologists, in doing so, are typically arguing about the same issues and about how sociology in general is to be approached. They therefore aim at developing a common frame of reference – a theory – though they have very different views on just what that theory should be.

The first question that arises, however, is whether it is possible at all to arrive at one general framework. Any society is made up of a collection of institutions, some of which – such as the family, the local community, the educational system – we have discussed in earlier chapters. But a society is not just a collection of separate and unrelated institutions. All sociologists agree that the institutions of a given society are related to one another; that there are organized interconnections between them; and that they fit together into an organizational whole. They disagree, however, as to just how institutions fit together so as to make up a whole society, and about how to analyse the institutions themselves.

Some would even argue that there is nothing in sociology really worth calling 'theory' similar to the theories of the natural sciences: an explicit system of logically interrelated propositions from which fairly precise predictions about the behaviour of phenomena can be derived. Such predictions can be tested against the facts, and if things do not occur as predicted then, ideally at least, the theory on which the predictions are based has been falsified, refuted. Thus, for example, Karl Popper has argued that Marxism was not really scientific (Popper, 1947). Marx's original theories were scientific: they entailed the prediction that there would be a working-class revolution in industrial societies. But those predictions proved false, for there has been no revolution, and the theory was therefore refuted. By contrast, Popper thinks, Marx's followers have tried to protect Marx's theories *against any possibility of being falsified* and, in doing so, have only made them vague, ambiguous and incapable of providing a basis for formulating genuine, clear predictions: they do not operate as genuine scientific theories at all.

Few would maintain that sociology has much in the way of theory that would meet the criteria given above. Sociological theories are not usually formulated as systematic, explicit and deductive propositions in the way that those using the word 'theory' in a restricted sense demand. Hence, they are often called 'approaches' or 'perspectives', to indicate that they are rather more diffuse than theories in the strict sense: they are guidelines for thought or programmes for inquiry which suggest general directions in which studies may be fruitfully pursued; they do not tell us very precisely how one thing will be connected with another; and they do not give rise to definite or firm predictions.

Others, though they may agree that there is nothing much of this kind in sociology, do not find this a major objection. Why, they ask, do we have to conceive of theory in terms of a system of deductively related general principles (often thought of as 'laws')? The understanding of human behaviour may call for quite different ways of thinking than those which have proved relevant to understanding inanimate nature.

These debates as to the nature of the sociological enterprise in general are one source of its division into different theoretical schools. The first of these we will consider is Marxism.

Marxism

The first great problem we encounter is to decide exactly what Marx really meant and which of the many interpretations of his thinking since his death most accurately represents his position. For there are now many, often sharply opposed, interpretations of Marxism. What is offered here, then, is one view of Marx's complex and puzzling theories.

Any given social arrangement, Marx believed, is historically transient: it has come into being at a particular phase in history and will eventually pass out of existence (Marx and Engels, n.d.). The most elementary error is to think that any pattern of social behaviour or any particular way of organizing social activities is 'natural' or eternal. If we live in a capitalist society – one which is organized around the private ownership of industrial capital and economic production through hired labour – there is a tendency for us to think that it is natural for economic activity to be organized everywhere in the way it is in our kind of society. We take capitalism for granted, and imagine that people in other cultures must behave as we do. However, the evidence of history and anthropology shows that other societies operate on different principles to ours. As we saw in discussing work, they do not necessarily seek to accumulate wealth endlessly, nor do they value work as an end in itself, as a 'good thing'. A general economic theory cannot be founded simply on the workings of our economic system.

This, thought Marx, was precisely the mistake some of his predecessors had made. In order to correct such tendencies it was necessary to recognize that capitalism was only a late and specific form of economic organization, which had itself arisen out of earlier systems. To understand capitalism, therefore, we need to examine not only what it is like now, but how it came into existence. We cannot understand contemporary capitalism except in an historical context.

Marx's thinking was influenced by his philosophical precursor, G. W. F. Hegel. The latter believed that understanding human life was an essentially historical task, since human history was essentially a process of change, and not just of change, but of development, for there is a direction in human history – towards general and complete freedom (see, e.g., Taylor, C., 1975, ch. 15). This development, for Hegel, took place through the growth of human consciousness, through religious, artistic and philosophical thinking. Once people became fully conscious of their own relationship to history they would become free.

Marx agreed that history was a progress towards comprehensive freedom, but thought that Hegel's own understanding of the actual process of development was basically mistaken, and if anything tended to get things upside down. It was not the development of philosophy which was the culmination of the process of human history, the way in which we think about the world of nature and the place of society in nature. Hegel's own philosophy, Marx observed, had made little actual difference to the legal, political and economic servitude under which most people existed. Important as the growth of human understanding of the world around us is, it is our *control over* the world around us which really matters (Bottomore and Rubel, 1963, pp. 67–91).

Though rejecting Hegel's emphasis on consciousness, Marx agreed with him that the development of history and the achievement of freedom must be a collective matter. Hegel had thought that the decisive force in history was not the activity of individuals, not even the greatest individuals – though these could be important – but the general development of the 'human spirit', the collective creation of ways of thinking and understanding. Marx likewise recognized that the transformation of the world around us could not be achieved by individuals acting alone. Only collectivities – organized groups of human beings – could have the power to achieve this.

To Hegel conflict was not a negative and destructive but a creative and constructive force. The development of history, therefore, was not a smooth, continuous and accumulating progression in which the past was progressively built upon. It was, rather, a seemingly conflictful, disruptive and revolutionary process, in which old forms of life had to be broken up in order to permit the further and full development of new ones. Struggle, division, conflict and violence were, then, not temporary deviations from a desirable and harmonious order of things but were the very essence of history, the driving force of change and development.

For Marx human progress could be achieved only through conflict between social groups. He did not, however, think that any or all groups were equally important to the bringing about of social change. That decisive role in historical struggle he assigned to social classes.

We have already discussed, in Chapter 10, Marx's notion of social class, in which the organization of production and the exploitation of one set of people by another is the crucial division in society. We must now relate those ideas to Marx's general theory of society.

We said just now that it was not human understanding of the world that was decisive but control of the environment; that, for

Marx, the crucial thing was not the development of 'consciousness' but the relationship of human beings to their environment, both the natural and the social one.

The basic relationship between human beings and the world around them, he argued, is constituted by the way they work. Human beings work upon nature and transform it in order to meet their requirements for survival, shelter, sustenance, etc. That relationship is one which must have begun in a very simple way, when human beings had only the most limited resources with which to work on nature: only the most simple technology. However, human beings have creative capacities and can develop and enlarge their capacities to control nature by improving not only their technical equipment but also the social organization of production. The development of technology and social organization go hand in hand, for a given technology involves relations of specialization, cooperation and coordination between people at work. Marx thus gives the development of the organization of economic activity the kind of historical significance Hegel had awarded to consciousness. It was through the continuing expansion of its productive powers that humanity could achieve genuine freedom, and capitalism in particular develops such immense economic potential that it makes possible the transition to a communist, genuinely free, society.

It is not simply a theory that the development of technology brings about the development of society. Certainly, technological change *is* one important kind of social change, and the development of technology involves changes in social relations both at work and outside it, while the relations between social classes generate creative struggles that move history forward and raise economic potential to a higher plane.

The growing complexity of economic activity eventually leads to a crucial watershed in historical development: a separation between those who take part in actual production, who work, and those who do not take part but who benefit from the labour performed by others, because they own the resources which make production possible. Social classes have come into being.

A class is, in the first place, an economic category, defined by relations to the conditions of production. Hence, because the relationship between a dominating class and a subject one is one of exploitation, then there is a conflict of interest between them. The exploiting class improves its own conditions of life by increasing the proportion of production it takes for its own needs and purposes. It improves its position by intensifying the exploitation of the subject class, while the latter can only improve its situation by reducing the exploitation it is subject to. Conflict, then, is built into economic relations wherever a minority is able to exploit the majority of producers by virtue of its private ownership of the means of production.

The relationship between social classes is thus not merely an economic relationship: it involves inequalities of power, political domination, and political conflicts of interest, too. These conflicts are thus not confined to the economic sphere alone: they pervade the whole society, for a class which dominates in the economic sphere dominates in the society at large. Those who meet as master and servant at work will meet as superior and subordinate in other spheres of life too. Those with economic power will convert it into political power to provide favourable conditions for their economic affairs.

Let us take feudal, rather than capitalist, society for example. This is a system based on agricultural production. In return for the granting of land to a serf and giving him military protection the feudal lord is entitled to a share of the produce of that land and the service of the serf in his army. The lord is able to sustain his army because he extracts rent from the peasantry. Those serfs are legally bound to the land and to pay rent. Once they have entered into the contract with the lord they cannot leave the land without his consent.

A capitalist system, by contrast, requires a formally free labour force. The capitalist owns the plant, the raw materials, etc, required in production, but he cannot produce goods – or commodities, as Marx would call them, since they are produced for exchange on a market – on his own. He cannot single-handedly work the equipment required to turn out, say, cars. He requires the assistance of others, perhaps many tens of thousands of people to do the physical work, for which he pays them a wage. A population of serfs, who are bound to their land and to their lord, would not be available for employment in capitalist industry.

The legal and political conditions of a society thus affect the form of economic activity that can be carried on in it. Consequently, a class in power will try to strengthen legal, political and social relationships which help maintain its position and the kind of economic system to which it owes its position. Though classes may be rooted in economic relations, then, conflicts between them take place in all spheres of life and involve struggles for control of the whole society (Bottomore and Rubel, 1963, pp. 67–9).

Yet although a given way of organizing economic activity may prevail for a very long time (as capitalist industrial production has prevailed in Europe for the last couple of centuries) this does not mean that it becomes the sole mode of production overnight. New ways of organizing production grow up side by side with other, existing forms of economic activity and older forms of social organization, too. Thus, industrial production grows up in societies that have hitherto relied mainly on agricultural production. At first, though, the feudal form of production is economically and politically dominant, it coexists with capitalist industrial production within the same economy and society. But as industrial production develops and expands in importance, so there will be increasing conflicts between the two different ways of organizing production.

There are two kinds of political struggle going on: between the lords and their exploited serfs and between the older ruling class, the landed nobility, and the representatives of the new, rising, industrial system of production. The nobility stand in the way of unlimited capitalist expansion, so a struggle for the political control of the central institutions of power over the society as a whole – the State – now becomes inevitable.

The dynamics of capitalism

Though we have drawn our example from feudal society it was the analysis of the capitalist system which provided the main focus of Marx's theoretical thinking (Marx, 1976). Capitalist society, unlike its historical predecessors, had a unique characteristic – the capacity for virtually unlimited economic expansion – for capitalist production involves the repeated revolutionizing of technology and industrial organization. Because this results in ever-rising productivity, capitalism has the capability to free humankind of economic necessity. Yet it cannot realize that capability because it is an anarchic arrangement of production, not directed to the actual satisfaction of the general needs of humanity, but to the individual profit of the capitalist owner and his short-term pursuit of competitive advantage. In consequence, it is a wasteful and chaotic system, characterized by repeated economic crises.

Since capitalists compete with each other for business survival the capitalist class is not unified internally, and it is this competition which makes the capitalist system dynamic and expansive, both via technological innovation and via the search for new market-opportunities. Capitalism tends, therefore, to draw more and more of the world within its orbit: it expands itself across the globe, eventually bringing the entire globe within its influence.

However, capitalism is also an inherently self-destructive system. The capitalists themselves are engaged in mutually destructive rivalry, seeking to further their own position by eliminating their rivals. More importantly, however, capitalism – like other historical systems before it – creates the very class which can accomplish its abolition. As capitalism increases in scale and geographical extension so it creates an increasingly large and international working class. It spreads across the world, bringing the great bulk of humanity within its influence, but making them into members of its dominated and exploited stratum, with the motivation and power to overthrow the capitalist system.

Under capitalism, as compared with feudalism, the mass of the population are freed from legal constraints: they are no longer bound to the land or to the service of a lord. They are free to find whatever kind of employment they want. However, there is a difference between having legal freedom and being free in actuality. Wage-workers in capitalist society are not in fact free to do whatever they like, but are compelled to hire themselves out for employment if they wish to sustain themselves and their dependants.

Despite appearances, too, the capitalist system was no less exploitative than any of its predecessors. The difference lay in the way the exploitation was achieved, and the manner in which it was concealed from view. In slavery, the fact of exploitation is visible enough: the slave is literally owned by the master and the products of his labour belong to that master. Under feudalism, the peasant hands over a portion of the product to his lord. In a capitalist society, however, relations are carried on through money. The worker is paid in money, and this obscures the reality of exploitation. The key to exploitation under capitalism is that the worker is capable of producing, within the length of a working day, more wealth than is

428   **The New Introducing Sociology**

required for his own and his dependants' sustenance. The extra product accrues to the capitalist as 'surplus value'.

Despite this concealed exploitation, Marx anticipated that in time it would become clear to the workers that they were being exploited. Growing inequality between the capitalists and the working class and the disruption caused by periodic crises would make the fact and increasing extent of exploitation visible. And, by turning more and more people into wage-workers and concentrating them in towns, capitalism was increasing their capacity for mutual communication, instruction and organization and their effectiveness in struggle. They would also become aware that the economic conflicts which occurred in the workplace were not isolated disputes over limited and local economic issues, but part of a general confrontation between two classes, the ruling capitalist class and the exploited working class, for political control of the whole society.

This is admittedly only a brief condensation of Marx's ideas: we have spoken, for simplicity, as if there were only two classes, capitalists and workers, but Marx himself was well aware there were various middle-class elements too. Likewise, we have spoken as if Marx thought that capitalism would increasingly impoverish the working masses but, again, he was well aware of the other factors determining the living standards of the workers, such as the prosperity of the capitalist economy, or the activities of trade unions, etc, and of how these could vary both in the short and in the long run.

Insofar as Marx did think of the more or less continuing intensification of class struggle as leading to a revolutionary upheaval on the part of the working class, that development has not taken place. The condition of the working class, at least in material terms, has much improved, and the attitudes of the working class towards capitalist society have changed too. Much recent sociology, indeed, has asserted that it is relevant to talk of 'industrial' society rather than capitalist society. Even before the collapse of communism in Eastern Europe and subsequent moves to introduce a market economy, it had long been argued by many that the State socialist societies of Eastern Europe were beginning to 'converge' with capitalism in its Western forms. Marxists, however, have continued to assert that class is no less a reality of capitalist society now than it ever was. Even such seemingly 'socialist' measures as the State ownership of industry are not socialist at all, for the interventions of the State in the economy,

far from being moves toward socialism, are measures for the maintenance of the capitalist system. In like fashion, a Welfare State does
not represent a socialist policy but one designed to eliminate the
possibility of a revolutionary working class.

Max Weber and the Origins of Modern Capitalism

Max Weber is often presented as being in dispute with Marxist
theory, which indeed he is. But he was also in agreement with Marx
on important points. It is especially misleading to present the
disagreement as though Marx believed in the exclusive importance
of material factors – i.e. economic, social and political conditions – in
the development of social life and as if Weber believed that it was
really ideas which were the determining force of history. Weber was
entirely in agreement with Marx that the economic organization of
society was of fundamental importance to an understanding of its
whole structure: his major work has been translated under the title
Economy and Society, which indicates clearly enough the extent to
which Weber recognized the importance of 'material conditions'.

The most basic respect in which Weber differs from Marxists is in
his view of power. For Marxists, social and political power derive
from economic power: they talk of a 'ruling class' because they
assume that the ruling power in society will be in the hands of an
economic group, the class which is economically dominant. Economic
relations are basic, and power relations arise from these. Weber, on
the contrary, thinks that relationships of power are fundamental, and
that economic domination is only one of the sources of power in
society. There is no *necessity* that the economically dominant group
must be the politically and socially dominant one too.

Weber does not deny that an economic group may be the ruling
one. He recognizes that rule by an economic group is one of a range
of historical possibilities. But it cannot be assumed. Whether they
will do so or not will depend on the outcome of a complex power
struggle within society, in which other kinds of groups than classes
and other kinds of interests than economic interests alone are involved, and may be decisive (Gerth and Mills, 1948, ch. 7).

Weber also concurs with Marx in recognizing the importance of
conflict in society. He looks upon society very much as a power
struggle in which groups and individuals attempt to dominate one

another. Whether there is open conflict or not depends upon how effectively one group is able to undermine opposition. Social stratification, for Weber, is a way in which the distribution of power in society becomes institutionalized. Hence, like Marx again, Weber sees class as being rooted in relations of production, and the crucial division as being between those who have property and those who do not. But Weber insists on the need to identify two other kinds of groups which may be formed in the competition for power, in addition to classes. The most important, as we have seen, is the 'status group', a group defined not by property, but by esteem: a group of people who regard each other as equals, and who are regarded either as superiors or as subordinates by other groups. The basis for their mutual regard, however, is not their place in production, but their pattern of consumption, which he called their 'lifestyle'. They regard each other as equals because they live in the same kind of manner, and set themselves off from people who live differently. The second important group, in Weber's view, is the 'party', a group of people which is consciously organized for the purpose of taking power. Such a group may be based upon a social class, drawing its membership from and representing the interests of that class, but it can equally well be made up of people drawn from different classes and pursue interests which are not those of any particular class.

Weber does not want to underestimate the importance of class in history, but he does not want to overemphasize it – as he thinks Marx does. It is perfectly possible for classes to become organized collectivities, pursuing their interests in a coherent way, but it is not very likely, since a class is in the first instance only a collection of people identified by their occupation of like positions in society. There is no necessity that its members will be aware of their common position, however, even less that they will come to see themselves as having common interests and form organizations to advance the cause of their class. But in the kind of groups Weber labels 'status groups' and 'parties' there is. Both require some mutual awareness amongst their members: a status group is a set of people who *look upon each other* as equals, and a party is an organization which is consciously organized for the pursuit of power.

In Weber's sociology, therefore, it is the struggle between status groups which is often crucial in a society's development, and status groups which are often the bearers of innovation and the bringers of change. Status groups, once they impose themselves on the whole society, often strive to prevent further change. Weber thus shows how two status groups had been crucial in the history of Asia: the mandarins, the corps of officials who ran the government of traditional China – who had no part or position in economic life – and the Brahmins, the teachers, priests, and administrators who claimed pre-eminence within the caste-system of India (cf. Bendix, 1960, chs 5 and 6).

Weber accused Marxists of assuming that only economic interests were real and important, whereas he himself thought that there were many other sorts of interests that could be as important, even more important, than economic ones. In particular, Marxists were prone to underestimate the reality and importance of religious interests, and thus to misapprehend the effects of religion on social life and in social change. To a person who believes in an eternal afterlife in which they may be condemned to endless suffering or awarded eternal bliss, the fate of their soul after death may be the most important thing in their life, which is very brief when viewed against the perspective of eternity. Concern over the fate of one's eternal soul may therefore override a person's economic interests. In Weber's view, the sociologist does not make any judgement about whether people are right or wrong in giving that kind of importance to religious interests, or whether such interests are illusory or otherwise: as far as the believers are concerned, their beliefs are real and matter. Any sociologist who does not appreciate this will fail to understand how the actions of those he studies are motivated.

It will not do, then, to contrast Marx and Weber by saying that the former has a theory of social conflict as guided by interests while the latter does not, for Weber too emphasizes the importance of interests in power struggle in society. The difference is in the range of interests which they are prepared to recognize as significant: Marxists tend to acknowledge only class interests, whereas Weber recognizes a wider range.

Weber does regard religion as being historically important in directing social action. Both the status groups mentioned above, the mandarins and the Brahmins, were associated with major religions, Confucianism and Hinduism respectively. Yet it would be quite wrong to imagine that ideas were unimportant for Marx, for he too is very much concerned with the development and role of consciousness. The things that people know and believe are, to him, important in the motivation of their actions. But in Weber's views, Marx underestimates the importance that the *independent* existence of a tradition of ideas may have. In 'vulgar' forms of Marxism, ideas are simply seen to be created in response to the needs of the various classes engaged in the struggle, and religion is nothing but an ideology created to imbue people with the right attitudes and the right social behaviour to make them obedient. Yet Weber does not deny that the economic, social and political conditions affect the development of religion; indeed, he carried out lengthy and detailed scholarly researches to demonstrate precisely this. A religious tradition has, however, what we may call a 'logic' of its own which governs its development. Though religious bodies do have to deal with the world around them, they exert their influence in order to promote their beliefs and their social importance in ways that may or may not coincide with the interests of other groups in society.

The different ways in which Weber and Marx each approached the question of the role of the Protestant Ethic illustrates the wider differences in their approach to religion in general. Both agree that Western capitalism is characterized by the private ownership of productive resources and the use of a formally free labour force in the carrying out of productive activity. Both agree that this takes place in a rational manner, in that it is conducted in a highly calculated way, and involves the persistent, endless pursuit of wealth: the capitalist entrepreneur seeks wealth without limit, to accumulate greater and greater profit; and the industrial worker goes on working in pursuit of an ever-improving standard of living. Both also agree that these attitudes are necessary features of the working of modern capitalism, and both assume that a capitalist society inculcates the appropriate attitudes in its members.

Marx thinks that the capitalist's accumulative disposition is imposed upon him. Capitalists, as individuals, may or may not be greedy, but it is not greed that gives the capitalist his hunger for profit. It is, rather, his position in society: the capitalist is in competition for survival with his fellow capitalists, and if he does not win out in that competition he will cease to be a capitalist and be compelled to join the ranks of wage-labourers. The wage-worker, too, has to be motivated to work in the disciplined, regular and methodical way that capitalist industry requires if he is to keep his job.

To Weber the motivation of the capitalist and the industrial worker respectively raises questions that he thinks Marx has not answered. Granted that a capitalist society has to instil in its members the motivation to carry out acquisitive economic activity; this raises the question of how that motivation arose in the first place. Acquisitiveness is a common enough human motivation, but the *kind* of acquisitiveness found in capitalist society is quite peculiar. It is not undertaken out of greed or similar disreputable motivations, but has a distinctly moral character: hard work and the disciplined pursuit of wealth are regarded as worthy, desirable things, as morally improving. This is a very different attitude to work and to worldly activity, for instance, from that of cultures where work is, at best, a necessary evil, only undertaken insofar as it must be to meet basic material needs. But the 'spirit of capitalism' treats work as something that should be pursued for its own sake, not just because it results in increased wealth. How did such an attitude originate?

Again Weber agrees with Marx on some of the very broad, indispensable economic, social and political preconditions for the rise of capitalism as we know it. But while these may provide the opportunity for capitalist social relations to flourish, people must also be motivated to take advantage of those opportunities.

There were, Weber noted, striking parallels between the spirit of capitalism and the values of Protestantism. The spirit of capitalism looks like a secularized form of the Protestant Ethic. But in the former, hard work and accumulation are worthy for their own sake; in the latter, because of their role in service to God. Weber went on to see if the spirit of capitalism may have developed historically out of Protestant ideas.

To do so, he concentrated on one special form of Protestantism – Calvinism. The teachings of Calvin, he believed, contained a *psychological* contradiction. God, Calvin taught, had predestined the fate of all human souls. Some were saved and some were damned, and God had already decided which were which. What God had decided could not be known to mortals or influenced by them, however: God simply calls upon us all, regardless of our eventual fate, to fulfil his commandments in this world.

This creates an unbearable psychological contradiction in the believer: it is impossible to accept that one's soul's fate is already decided and to accept also that this fate cannot be known. Something has to give, and this was the conviction that the nature of one's fate cannot be known. Calvinists persuaded themselves that signs of salvation could be found in people's behaviour.

Those who lived out God's commandments would be amongst His elect. Thus, by complying with God's will, the believer could create the inner conviction that his soul was saved. However, such a conviction was a fragile one and could easily disintegrate. *Any* backsliding, however trivial, could be taken as a sign of damnation, and there was no possibility of Calvinists returning themselves to a state of grace by 'good works' as Catholics could. This necessitated the most rigorous control of one's behaviour in all departments of life. Thus, a quite *unintended* product of Calvinist teaching was created, motivating people to do the kind of persistent hard work that capitalism calls for. In addition, the accumulation of wealth came to be seen not as something undertaken for its own sake, but as something achieved as a manifestation of God's approval: one's prosperity was a sign of worthiness.

Weber's argument is that the unexpected, even paradoxical logic of Calvinist teaching provided an independent development which affected the believer's attitude towards economic activity, and, occurring in conjunction with favourable conditions for capitalist production, stimulated people to take advantage of these new opportunities. He did not claim to have established a direct causal connection between the Protestant Ethic and the spirit of capitalism, only that the connection was possible. In order to demonstrate this more comparatively, he looked at other societies to see if the economic and other preconditions of capitalism had been present, but without the kind of motivation to exploit them that had emerged in the West. The kind of attitudes to economic activity which other major religions encouraged, he found, were not such as to engender the accumulative energy of a bourgeoisie. Thus, the institutional conditions for the rise of capitalism had existed in traditional China and in India, and yet these societies had not shown comparable economic growth and dynamism. Instead, they had been stable, unchanging. A major difference from the societies of the West, he concluded, was the religious attitudes to economic activity which, in both cases, discouraged involvement in anything like systematic acquisitive, productive activity.

A second respect in which the traditions of East and West differed concerned the central role of 'rationalization'. In the Western world, there was a lengthy tradition, going back to the ancient Greeks, of making everything, even Nature itself, calculable and predictable, embodied particularly in Western science, which was now being increasingly extended to the sphere of human relations, especially in the shape of bureaucratic forms of administration.

Bureaucracy, of course, was by no means unique to the West, as we saw in the case of the mandarin state bureaucracy of traditional China, but the kind of bureaucracy that grew up in the West was quite distinct. A bureaucracy is a hierarchical administrative system made up of specialized functionaries whose activities are regulated by explicit, written rules which govern relations between its members, whose position in the hierarchy is based entirely on expertise and qualifications. Movement from one position to another – promotion – is also based on achievement. The official is also entirely dependent, for his income, on the salary provided by his position, which means that he does not have obligations to any other public or private institution or person. This system is, in Weber's view, the most efficient method of large-scale administration, in its ideal, uncorrupted form at least, for it ensures that decisions will be based on a quite dispassionate consideration of the issues involved by highly trained specialists, rather than as a result of the pressures from powerful figures or personal friends outside the bureaucracy. The bureaucrat therefore works in a wholly impersonal and purely technical fashion.

But though it was an efficient system, Weber did not view its seemingly unstoppable spread with unqualified approval. Bureaucracy had probably originated, he believed, in military and industrial organizations. But it had now become part of modern mass popular democracy and an integral part of the organization of the modern State. Its expansion was beginning to seem inexorable. But the extension of bureaucracy, the attempt to make human behaviour calculable, predictable and therefore controllable, meant the dehumanization of human relations. Modern Western society was rich, comfortable and secure in ways that had not previously been possible, Weber noted. Yet people found life increasingly empty, alienating and constraining – in a famous analogy he likened it to life in an iron cage.

In addition to all of these disagreements with Marx about the origins of capitalism, Weber also disagreed with him about its likely course. Capitalism might possibly give way to socialism, but they had quite different visions of what this would mean. To Marx socialism would mean an awakening from the nightmare of capitalist society; to Weber, the extension and intensification of that nightmare. For bureaucracy tends to spread, and though it may be established as an instrument of administration to be used by politicians in the government of the State, its tendency is to convert all political problems into administrative ones, and to constrict and eliminate the role of the politician. The development of socialism would, in all likelihood, be the triumph of bureaucracy over politics, and therefore the establishment not only of a totally bureaucratized State but of a bureaucratized society too.

Functionalism

Marx and Weber, taken together, can be regarded, despite their disagreements, as the main protagonists of a 'conflict' approach to social relations. Both agree that conflict is endemic, i.e. built into social organization, and hence that the character of institutions is to be understood in relation to their role in group struggles for power. Both Marx and Weber see the organization of society as the product of conflicting social interests. It was against any such conception that Emile Durkheim conducted his polemics, and in opposition to which he developed his own sociological theories.

But it was Herbert Spencer rather than Marx that Durkheim had in mind in developing both his critiques and his own ideas. Spencer thought of society rather as though it were a gigantic market, within which people entered contractual relations with one another. Like a market, society was simply the aggregate of the relationships amongst the separate individuals of which it is composed. In this conception, society is held together through the ties which bind one individual to another, just as economic life is held together through the contractual arrangements which specify the conditions on which goods and services will be supplied and paid for, and the precise entitlements and responsibilities of each partner to the contract. Durkheim thought this was a wholly mistaken conception.

Spencer's approach, he said, led to the erroneous conclusion that many people nonetheless did accept: that society is to be understood through psychology. They think that if we are able to understand the way the individual mind works, we can understand how society works, too, for society is nothing but the sum total of actions and relations of individuals. Durkheim tirelessly polemicized against this view. He argued that there was a need for a distinct science of sociology, because the organization of a society was more than just an aggregation of the activities of the individuals who make it up. Society is a reality in its own right, or, as he put it, a reality *sui generis*.

His basic argument was one that is familiar in science and philosophy: that the combination of elements can create properties which are not present in the elements themselves but which emerge from their combination. There is nothing mysterious or paradoxical in this argument. A commonplace example of emergent properties is provided by the combination of hydrogen and oxygen in the right proportions to make water. Water has the property of liquidity, whereas neither oxygen nor hydrogen, being gases, have: it is a property that is not characteristic of the constituent elements, but a product of their organization. So too, with society: the organization of individuals into relations creates emergent properties, phenomena which are characteristic of society, but not of its individual elements.

Indeed, Durkheim went further, and argued the inverse of his opponents' position. It was not even the case that society was a product of the combination of individuals, for individuals are themselves products of society, are created by society. The individual is a social product, only possible *within* social relations. Arguing against the idea of society as a kind of market writ large, he emphasized the 'non-contractual' elements in a contract. A contract may look like a relationship between two individuals, but they can only establish such a relationship because our society has a practice of making contracts, and because the particular agreement those individuals make is bolstered up by very general understandings that we all have, or which are enshrined in law and enforced by courts, about what the contracting parties can be obliged to do. These things are *not* mentioned explicitly in the specific contracts people make at all; they are presupposed by the contracting parties, because without them there would be no sense in making a contract at all. That is why Durkheim calls them the 'non-contractual elements in contract' (Durkheim, 1984).

To him, then, society is more than relationships between individuals. Individuals themselves are dependent on and produced by society. Durkheim's most famous study, of *Suicide* (Durkheim, 1952), was designed to show that certain kinds of social conditions were necessary even for individuals to want to continue living at all. At first sight, suicide – self-destruction by the individual – might seem to be the most individual of all actions, yet as Durkheim's predecessors had established, *rates* of suicide remain constant for long periods in different societies. What look like isolated and arbitrary individual acts can be seen to display stable patterns. What Durkheim argues is that the extent to which a person is integrated into social relations sets the conditions for survival as an individual. People whose integration into society is either too great *or* too little are more likely to destroy themselves. He goes on to distinguish different types of suicide, based on the extent and kind of integration into society, firstly distinguishing 'egoistic' suicides and 'anomic' suicides, which both result from too little integration into society. 'Altruistic' suicide is a third important type which results from too much integration.

Egoistic suicide is the kind which occurs because a person lacks strong supporting ties (thus, the unmarried can be more prone to commit this type of suicide than the married, or Protestants rather than Catholics or Jews, because family relations and a closely supportive religion can assist a person to carry the burdens and weather the storms of life). Anomic suicide results because society's regulation of the orientation of the individual has broken down. An individual is naturally disposed to have endless and unrealistic desires, but socialization into a group with its own clear standards gives a person more realistic ambitions and preferences. Someone who is brought up in a given social class, for example, is likely to come to accept its way of life as normal and proper. But if there is rapid social and economic change, and the traditions of society and the positions of individuals are dislocated, with people moving rapidly either up or down the social and economic scale, people will find that their accustomed standards are inapplicable and are likely, therefore, to develop quite unrealistic expectations and aspirations. As a result of repeated disappointments and frustrations they take the step of suicide. Thus, anomic suicide will occur in times of economic collapse, when many people's fortunes are lost, but also, and less predictably, in times of economic boom, when people are becoming suddenly much more prosperous. Durkheim's point, however, is not that it is the purely economic loss or gain that precipitates this type of suicide, but the social dislocation and the disruption of controls by traditional standards which is crucial.

Altruistic suicide is found amongst strongly unified social groups such as military units, in which an individual can lose all sense of individual identity and put the interests of the group before his own – as when someone gives his life for his country or to protect his companions, or when a widow throws herself on to her husband's funeral pyre.

Durkheim's objection to the idea that individuals establish social relations in order to pursue their individual interests leads him to the opposite conclusion: that it is only within the setting of social relationships that individual interests are formed and can be pursued at all. Nor can the existence and persistence of society be attributed to the pursuit of interests even by organized *groups* of individuals. The existence of society must be understood in an altogether different way.

The key to the understanding of how society holds together is, in Durkheim's view, the *social* division of labour (Durkheim, 1984). A complex and diversified society, like an industrial society, may seem a promising scene for a great deal of conflict and disorder, for there are so many different ways of life, interests and outlooks that it is perhaps surprising that these societies do not disintegrate into a chaos of sectional struggles.

Durkheim thinks there has been a broad historical shift in the central principle on which society is organized. It has moved away from being based on similarity – away from small, simple, homogeneous societies in which everyone led the same sort of life, had the same sort of experiences and held the same sorts of beliefs and sentiments. He called that kind of society 'mechanical', to remind us that societies like those were rather like gases governed by the laws of mechanics. A gas is made up of a large number of molecules, each one identical to the others. A simple society is similarly made up of a collection of human beings, each identical to the others. In contrast to this kind of society are those large, complex, differentiated societies in which people live different lives, have very different sentiments and hold very different attitudes and outlooks. This kind of society he called 'organic', to draw a biological analogy. A living organism is quite unlike a gas. It is composed of a number of differentiated, specialized organs which are unlike each other, but which have to be interconnected to make up a functioning whole. The parts of an organism are interdependent, so that the organism cannot function properly unless its various parts are playing their respective roles. These parts are held together because they are interdependent; they need each other. The strength of unity in a society governed by mechanical solidarity – the principle of similarity – is weaker than that found in the organic type of society, where the governing principle is that of difference. If a society is made up of identical units, then the loss of some of them makes no difference to the whole, just as the loss of a few molecules makes little difference to a gas. But in an organism, the loss of one part (such as a hand or leg) can have disabling consequences, or (as with damage to the heart or brain) may even be fatal for the organism as a whole.

In arguing about the division of labour, Durkheim is once again stressing the way in which the individual is a creation of society, not the other way about. When we talk of 'the individual', we usually have in mind someone of distinct and unique identity, someone with their own particular ways of behaving, patterns of relationship, preferences, point of view and so on. But the individual, in that sense, cannot exist in a society in which there are no social differences, where everyone is the same, and where all share the same restricted ways of life, opportunities for experience and so forth. All societies are, of course, made up of individual persons. But it is only when societies develop away from mechanical solidarity and towards an organic structure that individuality and individualism, in Durkheim's sense, become possible.

The functional analysis of institutions

The progression from mechanical to organic solidarity involves the increasing specialization of institutions. In many societies, as anthropologists have shown, all social relations – family life; the rearing and educating of children; work; religion; military organization; politics and the administration of law – are conducted through kinship relations. But in more complex societies each of these tasks is carried out by specialized institutions. Thus home and family life become separated from work; religious worship is carried out in churches; State organizations manage politics; the courts and the judiciary administer the law; a police body enforces it; schools take over the education of children from parents, and so on. It is a social division of labour. Just as the economic division of labour involves the specialization of people within the productive process, so a social division of labour involves the separation of the different tasks involved in organizing a society and allocating them to various specialized institutions within the society.

Durkheim's analogy between society and an organism provided a basis for later functionalist theory in both anthropology and sociology.

The most sustained sociological attempt to develop functional analysis in a systematic and generalized way was made by Talcott Parsons during the 1940s and 1950s. Parsons sought to construct a general theory, not just for sociology but for all the social sciences, such as economics and politics, for in his view, the various social sciences were only dealing with the different aspects of one and the same social system. But although economics and political science, for instance, dealt with particular, specialized sub-systems of the social system − those concerned with economic activity and with the distribution of power respectively − these had only been separated out for analytical purposes. Parsons sought to provide a common framework for social science, a 'general theory of action' in which sociology would be only one of the disciplines (Parsons and Shils, 1962, ch. 1).

There were, he thought, four basic requirements in any kind of social system, ranging from small groups to whole societies and even to international relationships.

Firstly, a social system must have some relationship to its outside environment, including other social systems. It must have ways of maintaining its integrity and distinctness from its environment, but it must also transact with the world outside and extract from it the resources it needs to keep itself in operation. This he called the 'adaptive function', a crucial part of which was the economy of a system, that part which generates the material resources for the continuity of society.

Secondly, a social system has to have the capacity to act as a unit, to coordinate the activities of its members in order to achieve various ends. It has, therefore, to have ways of mobilizing its personnel and resources and ways of setting objectives. This function he calls 'goal attainment'. The political sub-system fulfils this function.

A society must also maintain itself as a unified whole. Since there will be stresses and strains in any system, disintegrative forces must be contained if it is to continue in being. This he calls the 'integrative function'. In many societies, religion plays a major role in holding the society together by endowing its agreed values and beliefs with sacredness and, through rituals, impressing them upon society's members and renewing and reinforcing their attachment to them. In addition, agencies of social control, such as the police and the courts, detect and constrain the activities of those who would deviate from the rules institutionalized in the society.

Fourthly, there is 'pattern maintenance and tension management', a function referred to, for brevity, as 'latency'. The efforts, motivation and morale of a system's members have to be kept up if they are to be able to carry out the actions necessary for the achievement of the society's adaptive, goal-attaining and integrative needs. Yet unless they relax and recuperate, the stresses and burdens of their roles may be too much for them, and they may become demoralized and disoriented. So society has to have ways of restoring the energy and enthusiasm of its members. Leisure, then, is important and, according to Parsons, the family plays a crucial part here, providing a haven to which people may withdraw from participation in the life and responsibilities of the wider society.

The pattern of four basic functions, called AGIL (after the initials of the distinct functions) provides a model of both the differentiation of the parts of society (see, e.g., Parsons and Bales, 1955, ch. 2), and of the mechanisms which make for their interdependence, for in addition to fulfilling the four functions, these must be interrelated: there must be 'exchanges' between the various functional sectors of the system. Thus, if political action on behalf of the system is to be carried out, resources have to be raised and placed at its disposal, and this means that the political sector must have access to resources produced by the economy.

The fulfilment of these functional needs, however, often takes place in ways that are not always recognized. Institutions and practices which might seem to be only negative or disruptive can in fact have positive functions, while things which seem pointless can have functions. This kind of analysis has been applied to the study, for instance, of social stratification, political organization and conflict.

In the Introduction, we mentioned how Davis and Moore developed a functionalist analysis of social stratification, not as something negative, which divides society and creates privileges and social tensions, but as a rational means of distributing positions important to the functioning of the society as a whole and for which those filling such positions have to be rewarded for undertaking not only the office but lengthy prior training.

Similarly, political corruption, in the form of the local political 'boss', and his political machine and its place in racketeering and organized crime, is a feature of American society that is usually criticized. Robert Merton (Merton, 1957, ch. 1) has argued, however, that the organization meets needs which would not otherwise be satisfied through legitimate politics. Deprived people who require help with personal problems often avoid applying for help from remote, impersonal officials who pry into their lives. Instead, they get it from the 'machine', in return for what they see as an exchange of personal favours (voting for the machine in return for help), not charity. Disadvantaged groups at the bottom of American society are just as keen on financial and social success as are the more successful. But there are few avenues of mobility available to them, and recruitment into the machine or into the rackets provides one avenue of upward mobility. The machine also provides goods and services, both legitimate and illegitimate. In this analysis, however, Merton points out that what is functionally useful for a sub-group within society may not be so for society as a whole.

Conflict, again, is often thought of as always negative and disruptive, but Lewis Coser (Coser, 1956) has argued that it is not necessarily so. It can serve the function, for example, of clarifying group-boundaries, of reinforcing group loyalties, of venting social strains, etc.

Most conflict theorists, however, are critical of functional analysis. For example, functionalism is often criticized as a species of conservative ideology which seeks to give a rosy portrait of society, implying that all is for the best in the best of all possible worlds. It is said to portray society as a state of natural and generally beneficial harmony, and conflict as an alien, arbitrary and pathological infection. Yet functionalists do recognize the conflictual nature of society: Durkheim was well aware that social classes generated conflicts, and both Parsons and Merton made attempts to show how the structure of society does systematically generate change and conflict. Merton, himself a functionalist, argued against the assumption that every practice or institution must have a function and that this must invariably be positive.

Functionalism has also been criticized for neglecting power. It was not, however, a matter of whether one dealt with power or not, Parsons argued, but of *how* one dealt with it (Parsons, 1960, ch. 6). His critics, he said, all held what he called a 'zero–sum' conception of power: they assumed that the quantity of power available in society was fixed, so that for anyone to increase the power at their disposal they had to do so at someone else's expense. From that point of view, there has to be a struggle to acquire a larger share in a limited stock of power. But, he argued, it need not be so: just as the amount of economic resources available to a society can be increased, so that there can be more for everyone, so too can the amount of power available.

Finally, functional analysis has also been criticized for lacking an historical approach, for being unable to cope with the possibility of social change and – it has sometimes been suggested – for playing an ideological role by conveying the impression that radical social change of the whole social system was impossible. But the analysis of how institutions functioned was not intended to preclude the possibility of historical investigations as to how institutions came into being. Later in his life, indeed, Parsons did produce his own theory of social change, one which surprised many critics because it was evolutionary in character and focused on the progressive differentiation of social institutions (cf. Parsons, 1966).

Interaction and Social Structure

It is commonplace to class together the two approaches we shall be considering in this section – 'symbolic interactionism' and 'ethnomethodology' – as forms of 'interactionism'. It is also often thought that these two approaches, unlike Marxism and functionalism, are concerned with quite different levels of social reality. Thus, it is often assumed that Marxism and functionalism are 'macro-sociologies' and deal with society as a whole, while interactionist approaches are 'micro-sociologies' and deal with face-to-face interaction. It is also often assumed that Marxism and functionalism are concerned with the given social environment of the social actor (and hence with 'objective' aspects of society), while the interactionists are concerned with how things appear to those who inhabit society, and consequently with the 'subjective' character of social reality. Some theorists have therefore concluded that the two kinds of approach, of macro-sociologies on the one hand, and micro-sociologies on the other, are in many respects complementary to one another: that they deal with different aspects of one social reality.

There is, of course, some truth to these assumptions, but much less than is widely imagined. The so-called macro-sociologies do see society as made up of groups and institutions and as forming a system. Hence, they ask the question: how do groups and institutions interrelate so as to constitute a society? The so-called interactionists ask a different question: how are these groups and institutions organized in the first place and how do social relationships become organized so as to form the stable patterns that make up society? The two sets of theorists are not so much concentrating on different *aspects* or levels of society as on different kinds of problems.

The differences between them become visible when we look at a social institution which we have so far not discussed: language. That is not to say that Marxist and functionalist traditions take no notice of language, for that would be untrue, but until recent 'structuralist' and 'semiotic' theories began to influence Marxist thinking, language had not been treated as something of great significance.

Modern linguistic theory holds that language is a system, and that the meaning of a word or any other sign can only be understood within that system. This is so because the system works by contrast: an item, a word or other sign, is not to be understood in terms of what it positively says, but through its relation to other signs with which it contrasts. The most famous exponent of 'structuralism', Claude Lévi-Strauss, devoted his career to the analysis of 'primitive' myths, which, he aims to show, are not primitive at all, but involve complex and sophisticated intellectual operations. In his analysis, Lévi-Strauss looks at the incidents in mythical narratives which depend on contrasts: thus, for example, honey and tobacco figure in many myths across the world because they exemplify a fundamental contrast between that which is natural and that which is cultural, because honey signifies that which is 'raw' whereas tobacco has to be prepared by human activity before it is consumed – a form of 'cooking' (Lévi-Strauss, 1973).

Marxists and functionalists recognize, of course, that human beings are language-using creatures, and that language is a main medium of human communications and therefore of social life. They know, too, that the analysis of social life depends heavily upon the interpretation of documents that people produce and use for their social purposes. On the whole, however, language, for Marxists and functionalists, tends to be just another sociological topic, often quite a long way down the list of topics they think it important to deal with. By contrast, symbolic interactionists and ethnomethodologists both make language a central and fundamental topic of their discussions. For both of these approaches, indeed, the examination of language works is seen to be very much *the same thing* as the examination of social organization.

Symbolic interactionism

The very name of the first school indicates that language is the stuff of social life: society, from this point of view, involves interactions that are mediated by the use of mutually understood symbols. Natural science deals with interactions between forces, fields, bodies and so forth, but all of this is a *mindless* process. It is therefore fundamentally different from the world of social transactions, which take place between creatures with minds, beings capable of communicating with each other. When a billiard ball collides with another, it causes that ball to move. This is a physical effect. When one person tells another to shut the door, the latter does so because he has grasped the meaning of what was said – understands the symbolic significance of the utterance, and interprets it as a command or request.

The symbolic interactionist does not wish to insist that there is a sharp and unbridgeable separation between nature and society: human society is a part of the general and natural process of evolution, and social development itself depends on the organic development of human beings which makes them capable of linguistic activity and the comprehension of symbols. However, since physical and symbolic interactions are quite different in kind, there are inevitably some sharp and unbridgeable differences between the methods of the natural and the social sciences.

Symbolic interactionism often describes itself as a 'social psychology' rather than a sociology in order to emphasize its distinctiveness from other sociologies. They also reject the assumption that either the individual *or* society must have priority. Marxists and functionalists are apt to insist that society is the primary reality, while others, like Max Weber, take an individualist view and insist that society has no reality above and beyond the individuals which comprise it. Symbolic interactionism finds this opposition a false one: one cannot separate the individual from society, or society from the individual. Hence the study of social interaction is also the study of the way the individual mind is developed and formed. One cannot separate psychology and sociology any more than one can separate the individual from society, for there can be no genuine understanding of how the mind works apart from its social setting, nor can one have a sociology which understands social relations without appreciating the mindful character of those engaged in them.

A major strand in symbolic interactionist work has therefore been concerned with the development of the Self. As we saw in the introductory chapter, our actions in society follow very much from, and are responded to by others in terms of conceptions of who we are, and it is through these interactions that we acquire, enact and respond to conceptions of ourselves and others. The growing child develops through communication with others, becoming aware of their points of view and eventually coming to share the same understandings of the meaning of language and the same moral attitudes. As our relations with others change, our Self changes too. Symbolic interactionists use the same approach in studying socialization after childhood, for example, in studies of the professional socialization of medical students and nurses, showing how these people, through transactions with their instructors and their peers, develop conceptions of what a good physician or nurse is and is required to do (Becker *et al.*, 1961; Olesen and Whittaker, 1968). Medical students and trainee nurses are on the way to obtaining desirable positions in society. But others in less desirable positions find that they are deprived of opportunities to better themselves, are even made morally outcast from the society, perhaps because they have been convicted of a crime or diagnosed as suffering from mental illness, and many studies focus on how people cope with this kind of loss. The greatest deprivation of all, normally, is the loss of one's life, and there have even been studies of the way in which the approach of death is managed (Glaser and Strauss, 1966).

The most famous account of the place of the Self in social organization has been given by Erving Goffman in *The Presentation of Self in Everyday Life* (1971). Work like that of Goffman is often thought to exemplify the individualistic bent of symbolic interactionism, but this is to overlook the fact that his concern is not with individuals but with the organization of 'establishments': places like hotels, stores, schools, prison-camps and so on. But he is concerned with the ways in which people communicate to one another, through their speech, their dress, and their demeanour and conceptions of one another; how they project what they think themselves to be; and how they convey their regard, or lack of it, for others. The projection of a particular person's conception of Self in such establishments calls for teamwork; it is a collective effort. His analogy is with the theatre. In a theatre, a performance is given on stage, but it is only possible to give that performance 'out front' because of the preparation and support given by those who work 'backstage'. In the same way, a convincing performance in real life – as, say, a thoroughly competent surgeon who can be completely trusted by his patients – requires active and skilled cooperation on the part of other members of the medical and nursing staff.

The question arises as to how social relationships are coordinated and regularized. It is commonplace in sociology to say that stability in patterns of social relationship is the result of the possession of a 'common culture', of a set of shared understandings about how action is to be organized. But symbolic interaction poses the question as to how a common culture is constructed in the first place.

Equally, many social actions clearly take place within social frameworks which are relatively stable and permanent. To symbolic interactionism, sociologists often seem to be so preoccupied with stable social arrangements that they neglect many kinds of social activity which do not possess that stability – which are transient, short-lived and do not develop into stabilized arrangements. These are the phenomena many of which are often put under the heading of 'collective behaviour' which include such things as riots, panics, movements of fashion, the rise of social movements such as Prohibition in the USA, how rumours circulate and so forth. These are all phenomena in which a pattern of social organization can be seen, whether in the way in which they originate, the way they grow stronger, or in their subsequent disappearance.

In analysing institutions, too, interactionists complain, there is often a tendency to see them as unchanging and long-lasting arrangements even though in some respects they are continually changing, modifying and rearranging themselves. To interactionists, what Marxists and functionalists think of as 'social structures' are better thought of as social processes. The concept of 'structure' invites us to think of a society as a fixed arrangement, which remains unmodified for some time, until it is transformed into another and different structure. Social change, in such a view, is primarily thought of as change from one structure to another. Symbolic interactionism, however, emphasizes the extent to which society is a temporal phenomenon, involving constant change, and that even the most stable structure consists in a wide variety of processes. To draw again on the analogy with organisms, the living creature may for a period of time exhibit a great deal of structural stability – the head, the arms, the eyes remain much the same and play the same roles relative to one another but the whole organism is in fact in constant change as blood flows and energy is circulated through the system, constituent cells develop, die, are replaced, and so on. Society, too, may exhibit stable arrangements, but these also involve constant flows of activity and organization. 'Society as social process' – as the continuous formation and modification of social relations – might well be taken as the symbolic interactionists' slogan.

Symbolic interactionism does not want to deny that there are stable social arrangements. There are of course differences between the short-life phenomena studied as collective behaviour – social panic, sometimes about quite imaginary things, rises rapidly and fades away just as quickly – while such forms of life as the family system can remain virtually unaltered for long periods of time. Both relatively stable and relatively transient social phenomena, however, in their view, result from the same general processes that shape the character and course of any kind of social relationship over time. How stable arrangements emerge out of social processes therefore constitutes one of their fields of special interest.

Anselm Strauss and his colleagues in a study of the organization of a psychiatric hospital developed a notion which does much to crystallize the symbolic interactionists' general conception of social organization. They speak of 'negotiated order' (Strauss *et al.*, 1964, esp. ch. 13).

The hospital, officially, has a hierarchy of authority and a formal division of labour, and in very general terms activities in the hospital follow that outline. But only very loosely because the actual ways in which people develop and use power do not always square with the 'official' formula. The division of labour, for instance, is often re-arranged at the level of the ward, while people who have formal authority over others are not always able to exercise it. Supposed superiors can become so dependent on 'subordinates' that it is they who are in effect under control. Likewise, people officially entitled or required to perform certain kinds of work, will delegate it, farm it out, or exchange it, and undertake someone else's work instead as a favour to them. How the lines of authority and the flow of work are actually arranged is something that is worked out in reality at a local level, in the ward, for example, where medical, nursing, paramedical staff, and the patients are all involved in face-to-face relationships. Those relationships can be in more or less constant flux, and different parties will attempt to rework them or to try and give them greater stability. In the end, a bargain of some kind is often struck and kept to.

The concept of 'negotiated order', then, brings out the extent to which those who are involved in a social setting 'work at' the relationships involved. The structure within which they operate may indeed establish the broad outlines their activity is supposed to follow. But this leaves plenty of room for those who have to carry out the activity to work out amongst themselves just how things are to be done. The concept of negotiated order also emphasizes the extent to which social relations involve 'bargaining' and 'negotiation'. Thus, for example, though most people think of the doctor's authority over the patient as unquestioned, Julius Roth (1963) and Fred Davis (1963) show that treatment and its final outcome is often the result of a process of bargaining between the doctor and the patient: whether and when a person will be released from hospital may formally be in the hands of the doctor, but the patient greatly influences the doctor's decision by pestering him for release, by withholding cooperation in medical treatment and so forth. In the end, the doctor may release someone because it is less trouble than keeping them in treatment.

To symbolic interactionists, the very tendency to look for 'structure' often imposes a clarity, rigidity and stability on to situations which are open, mobile and perpetually developing, whereas social relations, to them, are a constant process of 'becoming'.

Ethnomethodology

We mentioned that a contrast is made between macro-sociologies and micro-sociologies in terms of the former's concern with 'objective' aspects of social structure and the latter's emphasis on 'subjective' aspects. It is frequently suggested that these overplay the emphasis on the subjective side of things, i.e. take undue notice of the way social actors think and feel, neglecting the importance of objective features of social life such as the distribution of wealth and power and the way these control social action. Ethnomethodology is particularly and wrongly criticized for excessive emphasis on subjectivity. Marxists and functionalists, who disagree on so much else, agree on that criticism. The external social world is, to both, an objective reality which exerts a constraining influence on individual action. Though Marxists would not accept much of the rest of Durkheim's ideas, they often share his basic methodological maxim for sociology: treat social facts as things. In other words, do not treat social phenomena as products of the individual mind, for social phenomena are no less real than physical objects, no less capable of resisting and limiting what we can do than a brick wall or a double-decker bus. Many sociologists think that ethnomethodologists reject Durkheim's maxim, but this is quite wrong and is a source of chronic misunderstanding of ethnomethodology.

Ethnomethodology does not *reject* Durkheim's maxim. It does not affirm or deny that social organization is an action-constraining reality. It does, however, interpret Durkheim's maxim in a way that is different from the way most sociologists take him to mean. Ethnomethodology does not dispute the reality of social facts but it does ask about their alleged nature. If social reality *is* an objective reality, then in what does that objectivity consist?

Durkheim himself emphasizes that social reality is 'known from within'. Members of society, that is, encounter the reality of social facts for themselves, they experience them as the conditions which limit what they can and cannot do. Thus, we all know that if we attempt to do things which blatantly violate the law we will be prevented: we will meet with resistance. Other people, the police for example, will take steps – including, perhaps, physically restraining us – to prevent us from performing or continuing in this action. Durkheim appreciated, however, that we do not always experience society as a constraint, because we do *not* usually attempt to go against the institutionalized ways of the society. We fall in with them. Thus, we know what can and cannot practically be done within the constraints that society provides. When we say that society is 'known from within' we mean in part that the member of society knows what the social limits are and acts within them.

Social reality appears to the member of society as 'the world of daily life'. In the world of daily life, whether as members of it or researchers into it, we encounter our society as the everyday round of ordinary activities, a continuing and predictable flow of common-place and quite unsurprising occurrences. As inhabitants of the world of daily life, as participants in it, we are deeply familiar with its operations: we have a huge stock of practical knowledge, of *common sense* knowledge of how the organized events of daily life take place. We speak of this kind of knowledge as 'common sense knowledge', because these are things which we all know *in common* with other members of our society. They are things we not only assume, but *insist* that they know about too. So, if we encounter people who are ordinary adult members of our society, but who claim not to know about the operation of shops – that they open at certain hours, that things can be purchased from them and so forth – we do not believe them. If they seem genuinely sincere in all this, we probably conclude that they are mentally disordered, for *everybody* knows how buying and selling are organized in our society. They are basic facts of life, so obvious that we expect others to support us when we insist that everyone must know about them.

The 'objectivity' of social reality is known, then, in this common sense way. This is hardly likely to be news. Everybody knows that people have common sense knowledge of society. But it is widely thought that part of the purpose of sociology is to improve upon common sense – which can be not only primitive but even erroneous.

Ethnomethodologists, however, neither criticize common sense as mistaken nor defend it as correct. They are interested, rather, in examining how the world of daily life is actually organized; how the regularity and predictability it has for those who know it in a common sense way comes about. For daily life and common sense are socially organized phenomena. How, then, are such forms of ordinary behaviour actually organized, and why do they seem so objective – so outside ourselves – and so unchangeable, and exercise such constraint over us?

Alfred Schutz (Schutz, 1964), an important predecessor of ethnomethodology, undertook the task of describing the structure of the world of daily life, and the character of common sense knowledge, from the point of view of one situated within it. His preliminary and abstract description later inspired Harold Garfinkel to initiate what he called 'ethnomethodology' (Garfinkel, 1967), a programme of investigation into the organization of everyday life and the commonplace activities which make it up.

Ethnomethodology can seem very puzzling to many sociologists. It does not look very much like the sociologies they are more familiar with, but this is to be expected, since it does not set out to resemble them. It starts out in a different place than they do, and pursues very different tasks; attempts to understand ethnomethodology which assume that it has a great deal in common with the kinds of sociologies we have been outlining above miss the point and, consequently, find no real sense in it.

Sociologists may pride themselves upon their capacity to criticize received ways of thinking and upon their independence from our common sense understandings. The latter are frequent targets for disparagement. Ethnomethodology, though, is not so sure that sociologists are or can be as independent of common sense as they assume, and suspects that they are usually and unavoidably 'collusive' with common sense. They do, after all, take the obvious presence of the world of daily life for granted, and in making sociological investigations presuppose that they can make sense of that world on the strength of their own common sense acquaintance with it. Sociology normally *begins* from the fact that the social world is an orderly place, that *anyone* can see that the ordinary affairs of our society have an orderly character to them, that things are predictable and that we can for much of the time premise our own plans on the assumption that other people will behave pretty much as we expect them to. If we just look around us we can see for ourselves what people are doing, that they are – to take random examples – buying newspapers, hailing taxis, making family visits to the zoo, eating business lunches in expensive restaurants. In order to be able to begin making sociological observations, then, we have to be able to recognize the commonplace activities of our society, and we are able to do this not by virtue of any specially acquired sociological expertise, but because we are ourselves members of the society and possessed of the common sense understanding of its ways that *any* adult member of the society has. Sociologists, then, just take it for granted that they can make sense of the life of the society at this level. Ethnomethodology maintains sociologists themselves are inevitably dependent on this common sense knowledge. If they are to be able to say what is definitely happening on an occasion, they have to rely on their common sense knowledge of social structures. So, reliance upon common sense knowledge will be an indispensable feature of their own work.

Ethnomethodology does not take it for granted that the world around us *naturally* makes sense – that the activities that go on around us are self-evidently recognizable and familiar, and carried out by recognizable social types enacting familiar patterns of behaviour. This is why it begins in a very different place from other sociologies, because it asks how it is possible for the world of daily life to make sense in the first place: how do people recognize the familiar scenes of the everyday world for what they are? Consequently, Garfinkel arranged little 'experiments' designed to disrupt the intelligibility of ordinary activities, by creating situations in which someone would behave in 'senseless' ways, to see what happened – how people would respond – and found that people would often make considerable efforts to make sense of these events. Thus, he had his students behave in their own homes as though they were lodgers there (addressing their own mothers not as 'Mom' but as 'Mrs Jones', asking if it was all right if they did things that, as kids in the family, they would not normally ask permission for). These behaviours did seem initially senseless to the rest of the household: they did not understand why they were behaving in this way, but they looked for explanations, such as sickness, the strain of coursework and examinations, etc. They attempted, in other words, to make sense of it and did so by attempting to interpret this seemingly senseless behaviour in terms of a familiar, recognizable pattern of activity: as a practical joke, for example, or as due to the pressures of university education.

Garfinkel thus argued that it is a feature of reasoning in the social sciences that it employs the 'documentary method', which is not a method of research, like the survey or fieldwork, but a method of reasoning, and one which is used in survey work, field research and all other kinds of sociological inquiry. It interprets particular activities by reference to the usual or familiar pattern into which they fall. Thus, if people behave in puzzling ways, we consult our knowledge of the usual, typical, familiar ways of our society to see if the puzzling conduct can be fitted in, identified as an instance of such a familiar pattern. However, the point of these experiments is not confined to bizarre and puzzling activities; it is meant to apply to activities of all sorts. Most activities are not puzzling to us, precisely because they do fit into our understanding of the typical, familiar patterns; they are instances of the general ways of behaving in our society, and we recognize them as such. Thus, if we see somebody standing by the kerbside with an arm outstretched, waving a newspaper, we readily see someone trying to hail a cab, and we can do that because we know that this is how calling a cab is generally done.

The documentary method is somewhat more complicated, though, for although we can identify particular instances of activities in terms of an overall pattern, there is the question of how we come to have familiarity with those general patterns. The general patterns are in fact identified through familiarity with specific instances. Both the pattern and its instances are interrelated such that we work them out *together*. That we are able to identify someone as behaving in the way people in our society usually do is because of our familiarity with the pattern, but our being able to see this person behaving in this way is confirmation of the very pattern itself: that this is how people commonly, usually behave: we see the pattern in the particular activities.

The documentary method is a way of reasoning which is present in society itself – in the reasoning ordinary members of the society use as they make sense of the world around them – and is *inevitably* present in the reasoning of professional sociological researchers and theorists, likewise, since sociological reasoning consists of an attempt to see the underlying pattern in particular activities and of seeing the particular activities as produced by that underlying pattern. The approaches of Marx and Durkheim both aim to show that the activities of individuals in society are governed by underlying patterns of social organization and both seek, therefore, to discover that underlying pattern through the study of the activities of daily life; they then use that underlying pattern to explain why people behave as they do. The reasoning of a Marxist or Durkheimian takes, then, the same form as that which is common throughout society, involving the interplay of general pattern and particular instance. It is for reasons such as this that ethnomethodology maintains that sociology is 'collusive' with common sense, because it begins from and must depend on a possession of a common sense familiarity with the society's affairs and it must use common sense practices of reasoning to describe and interpret social activities.

Ethnomethodology does not claim that it can, by contrast, liberate itself from dependence on common sense. Rather, it sees no reason to regret our dependence on common sense, and hence no need to apologize for its own reliance on it. Instead of worrying about whether we should criticize and correct common sense, why do we not give it a much more central and important place as something that we study? Since common sense understandings are features of social life, why do we not try to see how they figure there and what part they play in organizing the activities of daily life? This is a task ethnomethodology sets itself, through focusing upon the organization of social actions as 'accountable'.

We have said that people in society can easily make sense of the flow of social activity that goes on around them, that even the least thoughtful member of a society can recognize what is going on. From ethnomethodology's point of view, this is a basic and intrinsic fact about the nature of social activities. If, for example, you are driving along a busy road and are approaching a junction and want to turn across the traffic, to do so entails the cooperation of other drivers. You want them to recognize what you are intending to do and to adapt their own responses appropriately. So you give the signal 'I am going to turn right' by using your indicator. The carrying-out of a coordinated action thus involves people being able to recognize and identify each other's actions. Talking about studying social actions as 'accountable' is a matter of studying them from a particular point of view, namely one which looks at the ways they organize themselves to make themselves recognizable, such that other members of society can see and say what is going on. As we have shown with the motoring example, it is essential to the possibility of coordinated human actions that people be able to identify each other's actions if they are to anticipate and respond to them appropriately. Describing what people do to make their actions recognizable as familiar, commonplace, identifiable occurrences is, then, describing something quite fundamental about them.

Looking at actions as accountable involves looking at *all* the ways in which they are organized to make sense to people who can observe them and report on them, at the wide variety of practices people use to make their actions intelligible to others. Something which is very central to the process of making sense of each other's activities is, of course, the exchange of talk: people can tell each other about their activities. Thus, the study of the way in which people organize their activities so that they can be talked about comes to be a very central element in the consideration of the accountable character of actions. This explains our earlier comment that ethnomethodology gives an unprecedented importance to the study of ordinary, everyday language, because the study of how people talk about their activities is something very closely and thoroughly intertwined with the study of how those activities are organized. As far as ethnomethodology is concerned, it is not possible to separate the investigation of how an activity is made into something people can talk about from the examination of how that activity is organized. These are, for it, virtually one and the same thing.

It would be very misleading to think that ethnomethodology wants to study talk *instead* of studying the organization of social action, that it wants to examine what people say about their actions rather than what they actually do. To think this would be to hold to the idea of a relation between talk and activity which ethnomethodology does not accept.

Ethnomethodology emphasizes that accounting is a 'reflexive' feature of social action. It is not something distinct and separate from the actions made accountable, but is part and parcel of the activity which it makes intelligible and recognizable. Thus, the activity of driving is so organized as to make the respective intentions of drivers mutually visible, and learning how to show to other drivers what one is about to do is part of learning to drive, not something done in addition to it. Thus, human social activities invariably and inseparably involve ways of displaying 'what is going on' and the point is to see how the ways of showing this fit into, are organizationally articulated with, other activities. Thus, the point is not to examine talk *instead* of what people 'actually do' but to see that talk is one of the things that people 'actually do', and to see how talking fits in with the other things people do. However, we do not want to maintain the very opposition that the approach is meant to overcome, and must therefore stress that this is not a way of relating talk, on the one hand, to social activities, on the other. It is, instead, an approach designed to allow us to see talk as part and parcel of the activities amongst which it occurs, to see social activities as (very prominently) spoken ones.

This enables understanding of one aspect of ethnomethodology that many find particularly puzzling, namely 'conversational analysis'. Sociologists such as Harvey Sacks (see, e.g., Sudnow, 1972b) have closely examined the details of transcribed recordings of the most ordinary and pointless of conversations, discussing mainly the ways in which people take turns at talking and going to the lengths of noticing and analysing even the ways in which pauses, hesitations, false starts and so on figure in speech. What all this has to do with sociology might seem questionable. But it should be more understandable against the background of what we have been saying. If one is interested in the ways people make sense of each other's actions and the ways they enable one another to understand what they are doing, then one of the places in which such 'making accountable' goes on is in any piece of ordinary conversation, where people say things to each other and where they must make sense of each other's utterances. Each speaker wants to have the sense of what he says recognized by others and has therefore to arrange his activities, to make his remarks in such a way that the sense of them, i.e. their meaning, will be apparent to the others. The ways in which this is done is through the talk itself: he makes himself understood by the way that he says things, by how he relates his remarks to those which others have made, how he relates his own remarks to each other. Conversational analysts, then, examine conversation to see how ordinary talk does make itself understood, how conversation is organized as an accountable system and, in the process, they recognize that the fact that conversation involves taking turns in talking is central to making its constituent utterances intelligible. To take a very simple example, if someone says 'Five' it might seem that we do not know *what* they are saying. They might be saying many different things. But if we knew that just before that person said 'Five' someone else had asked 'What time is it?' we would know what the person saying 'Five' did mean – namely that it was five o'clock. The fact that turns at talk are taken means that the second speaker, in saying 'Five', relied upon the fact that a previous remark had been made in order to have his contribution correctly understood. He does not need to say 'Five o'clock' to make his meaning clear, because others will hear the word 'Five' as an answer to the question just asked. Thus, the fact that the things people say to one another follow in sequence is important to the ways in which they make sense of each other's utterances. It is to describing the complex and varied ways in which this elementary fact of sequential organization figures in organizing the sense of ordinary talk that conversational analysis devotes itself.

We have tried to show that ethnomethodology quite consciously stands outside the usual assumptions about what doing sociology involves. Its root ideas, however, are neither bizarre nor nonsensical, but seek to remind us of commonplace and normally unremarked things which are central to the ways in which people in everyday life interact with each other and make sense of those interactions, and central, therefore, to anyone else – including the social scientist – who is also trying to understand the organization of social life.

The emergence of ethnomethodology is only the latest in an increasingly rapid succession of new theoretical approaches. We have come a long way from the pioneer social surveys of poverty: a rich body of studies of every aspect of social life has now been accumulated. But older schools do not disappear: they simply co-exist alongside the newer ones. One thing will be clear by now: that the study of sociology demands so much hard thinking and careful research that those who dismiss it as a 'soft' science have probably never read any serious modern research monographs, theoretical studies or books like this.

References

Abel-Smith, B. (1960), *A History of the Nursing Profession*, Heinemann.

Acker, S. (1981), 'No woman's land: British sociology of education 1960–1979', *Sociological Review*, Vol. 29, No. 1, pp. 77–101.

Albrow, M. (1970), *Bureaucracy*, Pall Mall.

Alexander, R. (1984), *Primary Teaching*, Holt, Rinehart & Winston.

Allen, S., and Smith, C. (1974), 'Race and ethnicity in class formation: a comparison of Asian and West Indian workers', in *The Social Analysis of Class Structure*, Frank Parkin (ed.), Tavistock, pp. 39–53.

Alpert, H. (1939), *Emile Durkheim and his Sociology*, Columbia University Press.

Althusser, L. (1971), 'Notes on ideology and ideological state apparatuses', in Althusser, L., *Lenin and Philosophy and Other Essays*, New Left Books, pp. 123–73.

Anderson, M. (1988), 'Households, families and individuals: some preliminary results from the national sample from the 1851 census', *Continuity and Change*, 3.

Anderson, M. (1990), 'The social implications of demographic change', in Thompson, F. M. L. (ed.), *Cambridge Social History of Britain*, Vol. II, Cambridge University Press.

Anderson, Perry (1974), *Passages from Antiquity to Feudalism*, New Left Books.

Anyon, J. (1981), 'Social class and school knowledge', *Curriculum Inquiry*, 11(1).

Apple, M. (1983), *Education and Power*, Routledge & Kegan Paul.

Armstrong, D. (1983), *The Political Anatomy of the Body*, Cambridge University Press.

Atkinson, P. (1981), *The Clinical Experience: The Construction and Reconstruction of Medical Reality*, Gower.

Aubert, V., and Messinger, S. (1958), 'The criminal and the sick', *Inquiry*, Vol. 1, No. 1, pp. 137–60.

Auld, J., Dorn, N., and South, N. (1986), 'Irregular work, irregular pleasures', in Matthews, R., and Young, J. (eds), *Confronting Crime*, Sage.

Ausubel, D. P. (1958), *Drug Addiction*, Random House, pp. 166–87.

Avila, M. (1969), *Tradition and Growth*, University of Chicago Press.

Backett, K. C. (1982), *Mothers and Fathers: A Study of the Development and Negotiations of Parental Behaviour*, Macmillan.

Bain, G. S. (1970), *The Growth of White Collar Unionism*, Oxford University Press.

Baldamus, W. (1961), *Efficiency and Effort*, Tavistock.

Balint, M. (1964), *The Doctor, His Patient and the Illness*, Tavistock.

Banks, J. A. (1957), 'The group discussion as an interview technique', *Sociological Review*, Vol. 5, pp. 75–84.

Banks, O. (1956), *Parity and Prestige in English Secondary Education*, Routledge & Kegan Paul.

Banks, O. (1968), *The Sociology of Education*, Batsford.

Banton, M. (1967), *Race Relations*, Tavistock Press.

Banton, M. (1983), *Racial and Ethnic Competition*, Cambridge University Press.

Barker, D., and Allen, S. (eds) (1976), *Dependence and Exploitation in Work and Marriage*, Longman.

Barnes, B. (1982), *T. S. Kuhn and Social Science*, Macmillan.

Barnes, J. A. (1979), *Who Should Know What?*, Penguin.

Barrett, M., and McIntosh, M. (1982), *The Anti-Social Family*, Verso/New Left Books.

Barron, R. D., and Norris, G. M. (1976), 'Sexual divisions and the dual labour market', in Barker, D., and Allen, S. (eds), *Dependence and Exploitation in Work and Marriage*, Longman, pp. 47–69.

Barth, F. (1969), *Ethnic Groups and Boundaries*, Little Brown.

Beauvoir, S. de (1972), *The Second Sex*, Penguin (first published in 1949).

Bechhofer, F. (1967), 'Too many surveys', *New Society*, 245, pp. 838–9.

Bechhofer, F., Elliott, B., and McCrone, D. (1984), 'Safety in numbers: on the use of multiple interviewers', *Sociology*, Vol. 18, pp. 97–100.

Beck, J., *et al.* (eds) (1976), *Worlds Apart: Readings for a Sociology of Education*, Collier-Macmillan.

Becker, H. S. (1952), 'Social class variations in the teacher–pupil relationship', *Journal of Educational Sociology*, Vol. 25, pp. 451–65.

Becker, H. S. (1963), *Outsiders: Studies in the Sociology of Deviance*, Free Press.

Becker, H. S (1967), 'Whose side are we on?', *Social Problems*, No. 14, pp. 239–47.

Becker, H. S., *et al.* (1961), *Boys in White: Student Culture in a Medical School*, University of Chicago Press.

Bell, C. (1968), *Middle Class Families*, Routledge & Kegan Paul.

Bell, C., and Encel, S. (eds) (1978), *Inside the Whale*, Pergamon Press.

Bell, C., and Newby, H. (1971), *Community Studies*, Allen & Unwin.

Bell, C., and Newby, H. (1976), 'Community, communion, class and community action: the social sources of the new urban politics', in Herbert, D. T., and Johnson, R. J. (eds), *Social Areas in Cities*, Vol. 2, Wiley, pp. 189–207.

Bell, C., and Newby, H. (eds) (1977), *Doing Sociological Research*, Allen & Unwin.

Bendix, R. (1960), *Max Weber*, Heinemann.

Bendix, R. (1963), *Work and Authority in Industry*, Harper.

Berg, I. (1973), *Education and Jobs: The Great Training Robbery*, Penguin.

Berger, B. (1969), *Working-Class Suburb*, Cambridge University Press.

Berger, P., and Luckmann, T. (1967), *The Social Construction of Reality*, Allen Lane/Penguin.

Bernstein, B. (1969), 'On the curriculum', in Bernstein, B. (1977), *Class Codes and Control*, Vol. 3, Routledge & Kegan Paul, pp. 79–84.

Bernstein, B. (1971), *Class, Codes and Control*, Vol. 1, Routledge & Kegan Paul.

Bernstein, B. (1977), *Class Codes and Control*, Vol. 3, Routledge & Kegan Paul.

Berreman, G. D. (1979), *Caste and Other Inequalities: Essays on Inequality*, Folklore Institute, Meerut.

Bertaux, D. (ed.) (1981), *Biography and Society: The Life-History Approach in the Social Sciences*, Sage.

Beynon, H. (1984), *Working for Ford* (2nd edn), Penguin.

Beynon, H., and Blackburn, R. M. (1972), *Perceptions of Work*, Cambridge University Press.

Black, Max (1961), *The Social Theories of Talcott Parsons*, Prentice-Hall.

Blackburn, R. (1968), 'A brief guide to bourgeois ideology', in Cockburn, A., and Blackburn, R. (eds) (1968), *Student Power*, Penguin, pp. 24–32.

Blackburn, R. (1988), *The Overthrow of Colonial Slavery, 1776–1848*, Verso.

Blackburn, R. M., and Mann, M. (1979), *The Working Class in the Labour Market*, Macmillan.

Blalock, H. M. (1970), *An Introduction to Social Research*, Prentice-Hall.

Blau, P. M. (1963), *The Dynamics of Bureaucracy*, University of Chicago Press.

Blauner, R. (1964), *Alienation and Freedom*, University of Chicago Press.

Blaxter, M. (1976), *The Meaning of Disability*, Heinemann.

Blaxter, M. (1981), *Health of the Children*, Heinemann.

Blum, R. (ed.) (1965), *Utopians*, Tavistock.

Blum, R., *et al.* (1969), *Society and Drugs*, Jossey-Bass.

Blumer, Herbert (1969), *Symbolic Interactionism*, Prentice-Hall.

Bock, K. (1979), 'Theories of progress, development, evolution', in Bottomore, T., and Nisbet, R. (eds), *A History of Sociological Analysis*, Heinemann, pp. 39–79.

Bonacich, E. (1972), 'A theory of ethnic antagonism – the split labour market', *American Sociological Review*, Vol. 37, pp. 549–59.

Booth, C. (1892–7), *Life and Labour of the People in London*, Vols 1–9; 1902–3, Vols 10–17, Macmillan.

Bordua, D. (1962), 'A critique of sociological interpretations of gang delinquency', in Wolfgang, M., Saintz, L., and Johnson, N. (eds), *The Sociology of Crime and Delinquency*, Wiley, pp. 289–301.

Bottomore, T., and Rubel, M. (1963), *Karl Marx*, Penguin.

Bourdieu, P., and Passeron, J. C. (1977), *Reproduction in Education, Society, and Culture*, Russell Sage.

Bowles, S., and Gintis, H. (1976), *Schooling in Capitalist America*, Routledge & Kegan Paul.

Box, S. (1971), *Deviance, Reality and Society*, Holt, Rinehart & Winston.

Boyd, D. (1973), *Elites and Their Education*, National Foundation for Educational Research.

Braithwaite, J. (1985), 'Corporate crime research: why two interviewers are needed', *Sociology*, Vol. 19, pp. 136–8.

Brannen, P. (1983), *Authority and Participation in Industry*, Batsford.

Braverman, H. (1974), *Labor and Monopoly Capital*, Monthly Review Press.

Brenner, R. (1978), 'The origins of capitalist development – a critique of Neo-Smithian Marxism', *New Left Review*, No. 104, pp. 25–92.

Broadfoot, P. (ed.) (1984), *Selection, Certification and Control*, Falmer Press.

Brotherston, H. J. F. (1976), 'Inequality: is it inevitable?', in Carter, C., and Peel, J. (eds), *Equalities and Inequalities in Health*, Academic Press, pp. 73–104.

Brown, G. W., Bhrolcháin, M., and Harris, T. (1973), 'Social class – psychiatric disturbances among women in an urban population', *Sociology*, Vol. 9, No. 2, pp. 225–54.

Brown, G. W., and Harris, T. (1978), *Social Origins of Depression: A Study of Psychiatric Disorder in Women*, Tavistock.

Brown, R. K. (1976), 'Women as employees: some comments on research in industrial sociology', in Barker, D., and Allen, S. (eds), *Dependence and Exploitation in Work and Marriage*, Longman, pp. 21–46.

Brown, R. K. (1984), 'Work', in Abrams, P., and Brown, R. K. (eds), *U. K. Society: Work, Urbanism and Inequality*, Weidenfeld & Nicolson, pp. 129–97.

Brown, R. K., *et al.* (1972), 'The contours of solidarity: social stratification and industrial relations in shipbuilding', *British Journal of Industrial Relations*, Vol. 10, No. 1, pp. 12–41.

Bruegel, I. (1979), 'Women as a reserve army of labour: a note on recent British experience', *Feminist Review*, No. 3, pp. 12–23.

Bulmer, M. (1979), 'Concepts in the analysis of qualitative data', *Sociological*

Review, Vol. 27, pp. 653–77; reprinted in Bulmer, M. (1984), *Sociological Research Methods* (2nd edn), Macmillan.

Bulmer, M. (ed.) (1982), *Social Research Ethics*, Macmillan.

Bulmer, M. (1984), *Sociological Research Methods* (2nd edn), Macmillan.

Burawoy, M. (1979), *Manufacturing Consent: Changes in the Labour Process under Monopoly Capitalism*, University of Chicago Press.

Burgess, R. G. (ed.) (1982), *Field Research: A Sourcebook and Field Manual*, Allen & Unwin.

Burgess, R. G. (1984), *In the Field: An Introduction to Field Research*, Allen & Unwin.

Burnet, M. (1971), *Genes, Dreams and Realities*, Medical & Technical Publishing Company.

Burns, T. (1967), 'Sociological Explanation', *British Journal of Sociology*, Vol. XVIII; reprinted in Emmett, D., and MacIntyre, A. (eds) (1970), *Sociological Theory and Philosophical Analysis*, Macmillan.

Burns, T. (1969a), 'The revolt of the privileged', *Social Science Information*, Vol. 7, pp. 137–49.

Burns, T. (ed.) (1969b), *Industrial Man*, Penguin.

Burns, T. (1977), *The BBC*, Macmillan.

Burns, T., and Stalker, G. M. (1961), *The Management of Innovation*, Tavistock.

Burroughs, W. (1968), *The Naked Lunch*, Corgi.

Busfield, J. (1983), 'Gender, mental illness and psychiatry', in Evans, M., and Ungerson, C. (eds), *Sexual Divisions: Patterns and Processes*, Tavistock, pp. 106–35.

Byrne, E. (1978), *Women and Education*, Tavistock.

Campbell, D., and Fiske, D. (1959), 'Convergent and discriminant validation by the multi-trait, multi-method matrix', *Psychological Bulletin*, Vol. 56, pp. 81–105.

Campbell, D., and Stanley, J. (1966), *Experimental and Quasi-experimental Designs for Research*, Rand McNally.

Carpenter, M. (1977), 'The new managerialism and professionalism in nursing', in Stacey, M., *et al.* (eds), *Health and the Division of Labour*, Croom Helm, pp. 165–95.

Cartwright, A., and Anderson, R. (1981), *General Practice Revisited: A Second Study of Patients and their Doctors*, Tavistock.

Cartwright, A., and O'Brien, M. (1976), 'Social class variations in health care and in the nature of general practitioner consultations', in Stacey, M., *et al.* (eds), *The Sociology of the National Health Service*, Sociological Review Monograph, No. 22, University of Keele, pp. 77–98.

Carver, T. (1982), *Marx's Social Theory*, Oxford University Press.

Castells, M. (1968), 'Y-a-t-il une sociologie urbaine?' ('Is there an urban sociology?'), *Sociologie du Travail*, Vol. 1, pp. 72–80.

Castells, M. (1976), *The Urban Question*, Arnold.

Caute, David (1969), *Essential Writings of Marx*, Panther.

Cavan, S. (1966), *Liquor License*, Aldine.

Central Statistical Office (1984), *Social Trends No. 14*, HMSO.

Central Statistical Office (1990), *Social Trends No. 20*, HMSO.

Central Statistical Office (1991), *Social Trends No. 21*, HMSO.

Centre for Contemporary Cultural Studies (1981), *Unpopular Education*, Hutchinson.

Centre for Contemporary Cultural Studies (1982), *The Empire Strikes Back*, Hutchinson.

Chadwick, E. (1965), *Report on the Sanitary Conditions of the Labouring Population of Great Britain*, University of Edinburgh Press (first published in 1842).

Chandler, M. (1954), 'An evaluation of the group interview', *Human Organization*, Vol. 13, pp. 26–8.

Chein, I., Gerard, D., Lee, R., and Rosenfeld, E. (1964), *Narcotics, Delinquency and Social Policy*, Tavistock.

Child, J. (1972), 'Organizational structure, environment and performance: the role of strategic choice', *Sociology*, Vol. 6, No. 1, pp. 1–22.

Cicourel, A. V. (1976), *The Social Organization of Juvenile Justice*, Heinemann.

Cicourel, A. V., and Kitsuse, J. I. (1963), *The Educational Decision-Makers*, Bobbs-Merrill.

Clark, A. (1919), *Working Life of Women in the Seventeenth Century*, Cass.

Cochrane, A. L. (1972), *Effectiveness and Efficiency: Random Reflections on Health Services*, Nuffield Provincial Hospitals Trust.

Cockburn, A., and Blackburn, R (eds) (1968), *Student Power*, Penguin.

Cockburn, C. (1978), *The Local State*, Pluto Press.

Cockburn, C. (1983), *Brothers: Male Dominance and Technological Change*, Pluto Press.

Cohen, G. A. (1978), *Karl Marx's Theory of History*, Oxford University Press.

Cohen, P. (1984), 'The new vocationalism', in Bates, I., *et al.*, *Schooling for the Dole*, Macmillan.

Cohen, S. (1972), *Folk Devils and Moral Panics: The Creation of the Mods and the Rockers*, Paladin.

Cohen, S., and Young, J. (eds) (1981), *The Manufacture of News*, Constable.

Collins, E., and Klein, R. (1980), 'Equity and the NHS: self-reported morbidity, access and primary care', *British Medical Journal*, 2, pp. 1113–15.

Collins, R. (1981), 'Some comparative principles of educational stratification', in Dale, R., *et al.* (eds), *Education and the State*, Falmer Press, pp. 277–92.

Corrigan, P. (1980), *Schooling Smash Street Kids*, Macmillan.

Coser, Lewis (1956), *The Functions of Social Conflict*, Routledge & Kegan Paul.

Cowie, C., and Lees, S. (1981), 'Slags or drags?', *Feminist Review*, No. 9, pp. 17–31.

Cowley, J., *et al.* (eds) (1977), *Community or Class Struggle?*, Stage One Books.

Cox, C. B., and Dyson, A. E. (1969), *The Crisis in Education*, Critical Quarterly Society.

Cox, C. B., and Dyson, A. E. (1971), *Black Paper: The Fight for Education*, Davis-Paynter.

Cox, O. C. (1948), *Caste, Class and Race: A Study in Social Dynamics*, Doubleday.

Coxon, A., and Jones, C. (1979), *Class and Hierarchy*, Macmillan.

Coxon, A. P. M. (1982), *The Users' Guide to Multi-Dimensional Scaling*, Heinemann.

Coyle, A. (1984), *Redundant Women*, The Women's Press.

Daniel, W. W. (1968), *Racial Discrimination in England*, Penguin.

Daniel, W. W. (1969), 'Industrial behaviour and orientation to work – a critique', *Journal of Management Studies*, Vol. 6, No. 3, pp. 366–75.

David, M. (1980), *The State, the Family and Education*, Routledge & Kegan Paul.

Davidson, B. R., Slovo, J., and Wilkinson, A. R. (1976), *Southern Africa: The New Politics of Revolution*, Penguin.

Davie, R., Butler, N., and Goldstein, H. (1972), *From Birth to Seven*, Longman.

Davies, J. G. (1972), *The Evangelistic Bureaucrat*, Tavistock.

Davis, F. (1963), *Passage through Crisis*, Bobbs-Merrill.

Davis, J. A. (1971), *Elementary Survey Analysis*, Prentice-Hall.

Davis, K., and Moore, W. E. (1969), 'Some principles of social stratification', in Coser, L., and Rosenberg, B. (eds) *Sociological Theory: A Book of Readings*, Macmillan, pp. 403–15 (originally published in 1945).

Dear, M., and Scott, A. J. (eds) (1981), *Urbanization and Urban Planning in Capitalist Society*, Methuen.

De Kiewiet, C. W. (1941), *A History of South Africa – Social and Economic*, Oxford University Press.

Demerath, N. J., and Petersen, R. A. (1967), *System, Change and Conflict*, Free Press.

Dennis, N. (1970), *People and Planning*, Faber.

Dennis, N. (1972), *Public Participation and Planners' Blight*, Faber.

Dennis, N., Henriques, F., and Slaughter, C. (1956), *Coal is Our Life*, Eyre & Spottiswoode.

Denzin, N. K. (1970), *The Research Act in Sociology*, Butterworth.

Department of Education (1954), *Report of the Central Advisory Council on Early Learning*, HMSO.

Department of Education (1963), *Report of the Committee on Higher Education* (The Robbins Report), HMSO.

Department of Education (1967), *Children and their Primary Schools* (The Plowden Report), HMSO.

Department of Education and Science (1977), *Education in Schools: A Consultative Document*, HMSO.

Department of Employment (1990), *New Earnings Survey 1990*, Part A, HMSO.

Department of Health and Social Security (1983), *Health and Personal Social Services Statistics for England*, 1982, HMSO.

Dexter, L. (1964), 'The sociology and politics of stupidity', in Becker, H. (ed.), *The Other Side: Perspectives on Deviance*, Free Press, pp. 37–50.

Dexter, L. A. (1976), *Elite and Specialized Interviewing*, Northwestern University Press.

Ditton, J. (1977), *Part-Time Crime: An Ethnography of Fiddling and Pilferage*, Macmillan.

Djilas, M. (1957), *The New Class*, Thames & Hudson.

Dobash, R. E., and Dobash, R. P. (1977 8), 'Wives: the "appropriate" victims of marital violence', *Victimology*, 2, pp. 426–42.

Dollard, J. (1935), *Criteria for the Life History*, Yale University Press.

Donald, J. (1981), 'Green paper, noise of crisis', in Dale, R., *et al.* (eds), *Education and the State*, Vol. 1, Falmer Press.

Donald, J., and Grealy, J. (1983), 'The unpleasant fact of unequality: standards, literacy and culture', in Wolpe, A. M., and Donald, J. (eds), *Is There Anyone Here From Education?*, Pluto Press, pp. 88–101.

Donaldson, Peter (1971), *The Economics of the Real World*, Allen Lane/Penguin.

Donnison, D. (1973), 'Micro-politics of the city', in Donnison, D., and Eversley, D. (eds), *London: Urban Patterns, Problems and Policies*, Heinemann, pp. 383–404.

Donzelot, J. (1980), *The Policing of Families*, Hutchinson.

Dore, R. (1973), *British Factory – Japanese Factory*, Allen & Unwin.

Dore, R. (1976), *Diploma Disease*, Allen & Unwin.

Douglas, J. W. B. (1964), *The Home and the School*, MacGibbon & Kee.

Doyal, L. (1979), *The Political Economy of Health*, Pluto Press.

Dubos, R. (1959), *Mirage of Health*, Allen & Unwin.

Dunnell, K., and Cartwright, A. (1972), *Medicine Takers, Prescribers and Hoarders*, Routledge & Kegan Paul.

Durkheim, E. (1952), *Suicide*, Routledge & Kegan Paul (first published in 1897).

Durkheim, E. (1961), *Moral Education*, Free Press (first published in 1925).

Durkheim, E. (1982), *The Rules of Sociological Method*, Macmillan (first published in 1895).

Durkheim, E. (1984), *The Division of Labour in Society*, Macmillan (first published in 1893).

Duster, T. (1970), *The Legislation of Morality: Law, Drugs and Moral Judgement*, Free Press.

Edgerton, R. B. (1967), *The Cloak of Competence: Stigma in the Lives of the Mentally Retarded*, University of California Press.

Edholm, F. (1982), 'The unnatural family', in Whitelegg, E., *et al.* (eds), *The Changing Experience of Women*, Martin Robertson, pp. 166–77.

Edwards, P. K., and Scullion, H. (1982), *The Social Organization of Industrial Conflict*, Blackwell.

Edwards, R. (1979), *Contested Terrain*, Heinemann.

Edwards, R., Reich, M., and Gordon, D. (1975), *Labour Market Segmentation*, D. C. Heath.

Eldridge, J. (1981), 'Images of sociology', *Working Papers in Sociology*, No. 1, University of Glasgow.

Elkins, S. M. (1959), *Slavery, a Problem in American Institutional and Economic Life*, University of Chicago Press.

Elling, R. H. (1979), 'Industrialization and occupational health in under-developed countries', in Navarro, V. (ed.), *Imperialism, Health and Medicine*, Baywood, pp. 207–33.

Elston, M. A. (1977), 'Women in the medical profession: whose problem?' in Stacey, M., *et al.* (eds), *Health and the Division of Labour*, Croom Helm, pp. 115–40.

Elvin, M. (1973), *The Pattern of the Chinese Past*, Eyre-Methuen.

Engels, F. (1884), *The Origin of the Family, Private Property and the State* (Penguin edition 1985).

Engels, F. (1984), 'Health 1844' (extract from Engels, F., *The Condition of the Working-Class in England*), in Black, N., *et al.* (eds), *Health and Disease: A Reader*, Open University Press, pp. 61–5 (first published in 1845).

Equal Opportunities Commission (EOC) (1984), *Eighth Annual Report, 1983*.

Erdos, P. (1970), *Professional Mail Surveys*, McGraw-Hill.

Etzioni, A. (1961), *A Comparative Analysis of Complex Organizations*, Free Press.

Etzioni, A. (1964), *Modern Organizations*, Prentice-Hall.

Evaluation Studies Review Annual (1976–), Sage.

Evans, M. (ed.) (1982), *The Woman Question*, Fontana.

Evans, M., and Ungerson, C. (eds) (1983), *Sexual Divisions: Patterns and Processes*, Tavistock.

Evans-Pritchard, E. (1937), *Witchcraft, Oracles and Miracles among the Azende*, Clarendon Press.

Eysenck, H. (1958), *Sense and Nonsense in Psychology*, Penguin.

Fagin, L., and Little, D. (1984), *The Forsaken Families: The Effects of Unemployment on Family Life*, Penguin.

Fanon, Frantz (1983), *The Wretched of the Earth*, Penguin.

Farris, R., and Dunham, H. (1938), *Mental Disorders in Urban Areas*, University of Chicago Press.

Festinger, L., Riecken, H. W., and Schachter, S. (1956), *When Prophecy Fails*, Harper & Row.

Finer, S. E. (1958), *Anonymous Empire: A Study of the Lobby in Great Britain*, Pall Mall.

Flament, C. (1963), *Application of Graph Theory to Group Structure*, Prentice-Hall.

Fletcher, R. (1966), *The Family and Marriage in Britain*, Penguin.

Flinn, M. W. (1970), *British Population Growth, 1750–1850*, Macmillan.

Floud, J., Halsey, A. H., and Martin, F. (1956), *Social Class and Educational Opportunity*, Heinemann.

Fogelman, K. (ed.) (1976), *Britain's Sixteen Year Olds*, National Children's Bureau.

Fogelman, K. (ed.) (1983), *Growing Up in Great Britain*, Macmillan.

Ford, A. (1985), *Man: A Documentary*, Weidenfeld & Nicolson.

Fothergill, S., and Gudgin, G. (1982), *Unequal Growth*, Heinemann.

Fox, A. (1973), 'Industrial relations: a social critique of pluralist ideology', in Child, J. (ed.), *Man and Organization*, Allen & Unwin, pp. 185–233.

Fox, A. J., and Goldblatt, P. (1982), *OPCS Longitudinal Study: Socio-demographic Mortality Differentials, 1971–5*, HMSO.

Frank, A. G. (1967), *Capitalism and Underdevelopment in Latin America*, Monthly Review Press (Penguin, 1969).

Frank, A. G. (1969), 'The sociology of development and the underdevelopment of sociology', in *Latin America: Underdevelopment or Revolution?*, Monthly Review Press, pp. 21–94.

Frankenberg, R. (1965), *Communities in Britain*, Penguin.

Freidson, E. (1970), *The Profession of Medicine: A Study in the Sociology of Applied Knowledge*, Dodd Mead.

Freire, P. (1971), *Pedagogy of the Oppressed*, Penguin.

Frey, J. H. (1989), *Survey Research by Telephone*, Sage.

Friedl, E. (1975), *Women and Men: An Anthropologist's View*, Holt, Rinehart & Winston.

Friedland, R. (1965), *Power and Crisis in the City*, Macmillan.

Froebel, F., Heinrichs, J., and Kreye, O. (1980), *The New International Division of Labour*, Cambridge University Press.

Furnivall, J. S. (1939), *Netherlands India*, Cambridge University Press.

Furnivall, J. S. (1948), *Colonial Policy and Practice: A Comparative Study of Burma and Netherlands India*, Cambridge University Press.

Gans, H. J. (1962a), *The Urban Village*, Free Press.

Gans, H. J. (1962b), 'Urbanism and suburbanism as ways of life', in Rose, A. (ed.), *Human Behaviour and Social Processes*, Houghton-Mifflin, pp. 625–48.

Gans, H. J. (1967), *The Levittowners*, Allen Lane/Penguin.

Garfinkel, H. (1967), *Studies in Ethnomethodology*, Prentice-Hall.

Garmarnikow, E. (1978), 'Sexual division of labour: the case of nursing', in Kuhn, A. M., and Wolpe, A. M. (eds), *Feminism and Materialism*, Routledge & Kegan Paul, pp. 96–123.

Gay, J., and Cole, M. (1967), *New Mathematics and an Old Culture*, Holt, Rinehart & Winston.

Gerbner, G., Holsti, O. R., Krippendorff, K., Paisley, W. J., and Stone, P. J. (eds) (1969), *The Analysis of Communication Content*, Wiley.

Gershuny, J. I., and Pahl, R. E. (1985), 'Britain in the decade of the three economies', in Littler, C. R. (ed.), *The Experience of Work*, Gower, pp. 247–51 (first published, *New Society*, 3 January 1980).

Gerth, H. H., and Mills, C. W. (eds) (1948), *From Max Weber*, Routledge & Kegan Paul.

Giddens, A. (1972), *Durkheim: Selected Writings*, Cambridge University Press.

Giddens, A. (1978), *Durkheim*, Fontana.

Giddings, F. H. (1898), *The Elements of Sociology*, Macmillan, New York.

Gilbert, G. N. (1981), *Modelling Society: An Introduction to Log-Linear Analysis for Social Researchers*, Allen & Unwin.

Gintis, H. (1972), 'Towards a political economy of education: a radical critique of Ivan Illich's *Deschooling Society*', *Harvard Educational Review*, Vol. 42, pp. 70–96.

Giroux, H. (1983), *Theory and Resistance in Education*, Heinemann.

Gladwin, T. (1970), *East is a Big Bird*, Harvard University Press.

Glaser, B., and Strauss, A. (1964), *The Discovery of Grounded Theory*, Aldine.

Glaser, B., and Strauss, A. (1966), *Awareness of Dying*, Weidenfeld & Nicolson.

Glasgow University Media Group (1976), *Bad News*, Routledge & Kegan Paul.

Glasgow University Media Group (1980), *More Bad News*, Routledge & Kegan Paul.

Glasgow University Media Group Members (1982), *Really Bad News*, Writers & Readers.

Glass, D. (1954), *Social Mobility in Britain*, Routledge & Kegan Paul.

Glass, Ruth (1962), 'Insiders–Outsiders: the position of minorities', *New Left Review*, Vol. 17, pp. 36–45.

Goffman, E. (1961), *Asylums: Essays on the Social Situation of Mental Patients and Other Inmates*, Anchor Books (Penguin, 1968).

Goffman, E. (1968), *Stigma: Notes on the Management of a Spoiled Identity*, Penguin.

Goffman, E. (1971), *The Presentation of Self in Everyday Life*, Penguin.

Gold, R. (1958), 'Roles in sociological field observation', *Social Forces*, Vol. 36, pp. 217–23.

Goldberg, E. M., and Morrison, S. (1963), 'Schizophrenia and social class', *British Journal of Psychiatry*, 109, pp. 785–802.

Goldblatt, P. (1989), 'Mortality by social class, 1971–1985', *Population Trends*, 56, pp. 6–15.

Goldblatt, P., *et al.* (1990), 'Mortality at age 15–59 of women in an occupation by marital status, husband's social class if married and period of death, 1976–1981', in Goldblatt, P. (ed.), *Longitudinal Study: Mortality and Social Organization*, OPCS Series LS 6, HMSO.

Goldthorpe, J. E. (1975), *The Sociology of the Third World*, Cambridge University Press.

Goldthorpe, J. H., *et al.* (1968–9), *The Affluent Worker* (3 vols), Cambridge University Press.

Goldthorpe, J. H., and Hope, K. (1974), *The Social Grading of Occupations*, Clarendon Press.

Goldthorpe, J. H., Llewellyn, C., and Payne, C. (1980), *Social Mobility and Class Structure in Modern Britain*, Clarendon Press.

Goldthorpe, J. H., and Payne, C. (1986), 'On the class mobility of women: results from different approaches to the analysis of recent British data', *Sociology*, Vol. 20, No. 4, pp. 531–5.

Goodman, D., and Redclift, M. (1981), *From Peasant to Proletarian*, Blackwell.

Gorden, R. L. (1980), *Interviewing: Strategy, Techniques and Tactics* (3rd edn), Dorsey Press.

Gordon, D. M. (1972), *Theories of Poverty and Unemployment*, Lexington.

Gottschalk, L., Kluckhohn, C., and Angell, R. (1945), *The Use of Personal Documents in History, Anthropology and Sociology*, Social Science Research Council, New York.

Gouldner, A. W. (1955), *Patterns of Industrial Bureaucracy*, Routledge & Kegan Paul.

Gove, W. R. (1972), 'The relationship between sex roles, marital status and mental illness', *Social Forces*, Vol. 51, pp. 34–44.

Gove, W. R. (1973), 'Sex, marital status and mortality?', *American Journal of Sociology*, Vol. 79, pp. 45–67.

Grace, G. (1978), *Teachers, Ideology and Control*, Routledge & Kegan Paul.

Gramsci, A. (1971), *Selections from the Prison Notebooks*, Lawrence & Wishart.

Gregory, D., and Urry, J. (eds) (1958), *Social Relations and Spatial Structures*, Macmillan.

Gusfield, J. (1967), 'Tradition and modernity: misplaced polarities in the study of social change', *American Journal of Sociology*, Vol. 72, pp. 117–34.

472   References

Habib, I. (1963), *The Agrarian System of Moghul India, 1556–1707*, Asia Publishing House.

Hakim, C. (1979), *Occupational Segregation*, Department of Employment Research Paper No. 9.

Halsey, A. H. (1986), *Change in British Society* (3rd edn), Open University Press.

Halsey, A. H., Heath, A. F., and Ridge, J. M. (1980), *Origins and Destinations: Family, Class and Education in Modern Britain*, Clarendon Press.

Hammersley, M., and Atkinson, P. (1983), *Ethnography: Principles and Practice*, Tavistock.

Hammond, P. E. (ed.) (1964), *Sociologists at Work*, Basic Books.

Haraszti, M. (1977), *A Worker in a Worker's State*, Penguin.

Hargreaves, D. (1968), *Social Relations in a Secondary School*, Routledge & Kegan Paul.

Harris, Nigel (1987), *The End of the Third World: Newly Industrializing Countries and the Decline of an Ideology*, Penguin.

Harrison, P. (1984), *Inside the Inner City*, Penguin.

Hart, C. W. M., and Pilling, A. R. (1960), *The Tiwi of Northern Australia*, Holt, Rinehart & Winston.

Hart, J. H. (1971), 'The inverse care law', *Lancet*, 1, pp. 405–12 (revised version in Cox, C., and Mead, A. (eds) (1975), *A Sociology of Medical Practice*, Collier-Macmillan, pp. 189–206).

Hartmann, H. (1979), 'The unhappy marriage of Marxism and feminism; towards a more progressive union', *Capital and Class*, No. 8, pp. 1–33.

Harvey, D. (1973), *Social Justice and the City*, Arnold.

Heath, A. F. (1981), *Social Mobility*, Fontana.

Hellevik, O. (1984), *Introduction to Causal Analysis: Exploring Survey Data by Crosstabulation*, Allen & Unwin.

Helman, C. G. (1984), 'Feed a cold, starve a fever', in Black, N., *et al.* (eds), *Health and Disease: A Reader*, Open University Press, pp. 10–16.

Helmstadler, G. C. (1970), *Research Concepts in Human Behaviour*, Appleton-Century-Crofts.

Hemingway, J. (1978), *Conflict and Democracy: Studies in Trade Union Government*, Oxford University Press.

Henderson, Jeffrey (1989), *The Globalization of High Technology Production: Society, Space and Semiconductors in the Restructuring of the Modern World*, Routledge.

Heritage, J. (1983), 'Feminisation and unionisation: a case study from banking', in Garmarnikow, E., *et al.* (eds), *Gender, Class and Work*, Heinemann, pp. 131–48.

Heritage, J. (1984), *Garfinkel and Ethnomethodology*, Polity Press.

Herndon, J. (1976), 'The dumb class', reprinted in Beck, J., *et al.* (eds),

Worlds Apart: Readings for a Sociology of Education, Collier-Macmillan, pp. 214–18.

Hiernaux, J. (1965), 'Introduction – the Moscow experts' meeting', *International Social Science Journal*, Vol. XVI, No. 1, UNESCO, Paris, pp. 73–84.

Hillery, G. A. (1955), 'Definitions of community: areas of agreement', *Rural Sociology*, Vol. 80, No. 2, pp. 111–23.

Hilton, R. (ed.) (1976), *The Transition from Feudalism to Capitalism*, New Left Books.

Hindess, B. (1971), *The Decline of Working Class Politics*, MacGibbon & Kee.

Hindess, B. (1983), *Parliamentary Democracy and Socialist Politics*, Routledge & Kegan Paul.

Hinton, J. (1967), *Dying*, Penguin; or 'Coping with terminal illness', in Fitzpatrick, R. M., *et al.* (eds) (1985), *The Experience of Illness*, Tavistock, pp. 227–45.

Hoggart, Richard (1957), *The Uses of Literacy: Aspects of Working Class Life with Special Reference to Publications and Entertainments*, Chatto & Windus.

Hoinville, G., and Jowell, R. (1978), *Survey Research Practice*, Heinemann.

Holsti, O. R. (1969), *Content Analysis for the Social Sciences and Humanities*, Addison-Wesley.

Horton, R. (1967), 'African traditional thought and Western sciences', in Marwick, M. (ed.) (1970), *Witchcraft and Sorcery*, Penguin, pp. 342–68.

Hughes, J., and Benson, D. (1983), *The Perspective of Ethnomethodology*, Longman.

Humphreys, L. (1970), *Tearoom Trade*, Duckworth.

Humphries, S. (1981), *Hooligans or Rebels?*, Blackwell.

Hyman, R. (1984), *Strikes*, Fontana.

Ichiyo, Muto (1984), *Development in Crisis*, Consumers' Association of Penang, Penang.

Illich, I. (1971), *Deschooling Society*, Penguin.

Illich, I. (1977), *Limits to Medicine: Medical Nemesis: The Expropriation of Health*, Penguin.

Illsley, R. (1955), 'Social class selection and class differences in relation to still-births and infant deaths', *British Medical Journal*, 2, pp. 1520–24.

Inglis, B. (1964), *Fringe Medicine*, Faber.

Institute for the Study of Conflict (1977), *The Attack on Higher Education*.

Jackson, P. (1968), *Life in Classrooms*, Holt, Rinehart & Winston.

Jefferys, M., and Sachs, H. (1983), *Rethinking General Practice: Dilemmas in Primary Medical Care*, Tavistock.

Joachimoglu, G. (1965), 'Natural and smoked hashish', in *Hashish: Its*

Chemistry and Pharmacology, Ciba Foundation/J. & A. Churchill, pp. 2–11.

Johnson, R. (1979), 'Really useful knowledge', in Clarke, J., *et al.* (eds), *Working-Class Culture*, Hutchinson, pp. 75–102.

Johnson, T. J. (1972), *Professions and Power*, Macmillan.

Johnstone, F. (1976), *Class, Race and Gold*, Routledge & Kegan Paul.

Kahn, R. L., and Cannell, C. F. (1957), *The Dynamics of Interviewing: Theory, Technique and Cases*, Wiley.

Kaplan, S. (1977), *The Dream Deferred*, Vintage.

Karabel, J., and Halsey, A. H. (eds) (1977), *Power, Ideology and Education*, Oxford University Press.

Keddie, N. (1971), 'Classroom knowledge', in Young, M. (ed.) *Knowledge and Control: New Directions for the Sociology of Education*, Collier-Macmillan, pp. 133–60.

Keddie, N. (ed.) (1973), *Tinker, Tailor – The Myth of Cultural Deprivation*, Penguin.

Keesing, R. M. (1976), *Cultural Anthropology, a Contemporary Perspective*, Holt, Rinehart & Winston.

Kellmer Pringle, M. L., Butler, N. R., and Davie, R. (1966), *11,000 Seven-Year-Olds*, Longman.

Kitsuse, J. I., and Cicourel, A. V. (1963), 'A note on the uses of official statistics', *Social Problems*, Vol. XI, pp. 131–9.

Kolankiewicz, G. (1980), 'The new "awkward class": the peasant worker in Poland', *Sociologia Ruralis*, Vol. 20, No. 1/2, pp. 28–43.

Konrad, G., and Szelenyi, I. (1974), 'Social conflicts of underurbanization', in Brown, A., *et al.* (eds), *Urban and Social Economics in Planned and Market Economies*, Praeger, pp. 206–26.

Konrad, G., and Szelenyi, I. (1977), 'Social conflicts of underurbanization', in Harloe, M. (ed.), *Captive Cities*, Wiley, pp. 157–74.

Kuhn, A. M., and Wolpe, A. M. (eds) (1978), *Feminism and Materialism*, Routledge & Kegan Paul.

Kuhn, T. S. (1962), *The Structure of Scientific Revolutions*, University of Chicago Press, Phoenix Books, p. 159.

Kuhn, T. S. (1970), *The Structure of Scientific Revolutions* (2nd edn), University of Chicago Press.

Lacey, C. (1970), *Hightown Grammar*, Manchester University Press.

Laing, R. D. (1967), *The Politics of Experience*, Pantheon (Penguin, 1967).

Lambert, R. (1963), *Sir John Simon, 1816–1904*, MacGibbon & Kee.

Land, H. (1978), 'Who cares for the family?', *Journal of Social Policy*, Vol. 7, Part 3, pp. 257–84.

Land, H. (1980), *Parity Begins at Home*, Equal Opportunities Commission and Social Science Research Council.

References 475

Larkin, G. V. (1983), *Occupational Monopoly and Modern Medicine*, Tavistock.

Lasch, C. (1977), *Haven in a Heartless World: The Family Besieged*, Basic Books.

Lasch, C. (1980), *The Culture of Narcissism*, Abacus.

Laslett, P. (1971), *The World We Have Lost*, Methuen.

Last, J. (1963), 'The Iceberg: completing the clinical picture in general practice', *Lancet*, 2, pp. 28–31.

Lawton, D. (1980), *The Politics of the School Curriculum*, Routledge & Kegan Paul.

Layton, D. (1973), *Science for the People*, Allen & Unwin.

Layton, D. (1984), *Interpreters of Science*, John Murray.

Lee, R. B. (1979), *The !Kung San: Men, Women and Work in a Foraging Society*, Columbia University Press.

Leftwich, A. (ed.) (1974), *South Africa – Economic Growth and Political Change*, Allison & Busby.

Legassick, M. (ed.) (1976), 'South Africa: capital accumulation and violence', in *Economy and Society*, Vol. 3, No. 3, pp. 253–70.

Leibowitz, A. (1975), 'Women's work in the home', in Lloyd, C. (ed.), *Sex, Discrimination and the Division of Labour*, Columbia University Press.

Lemert, E. (1951), *Social Pathology*, McGraw-Hill.

Leonard, E. (1982), *Women, Crime and Society*, Longman, New York.

Lévi-Strauss, C. (1973), *From Honey to Ashes*, Cape.

Lewis, G. (1979), *Knowledge of Illness in Sepik Society: A Study of the Gnau, New Guinea*, Athlone Press.

Lewis, O. (1951), *Life in a Mexican Village*, Illinois University Press.

Lewis, O. (1961), *The Children of Sánchez*, Random House.

Lewis, O. (1968), *A Study of Slum Culture: Backgrounds for La Vida*, Random House.

Lichtman, R. (1971), 'The political economy of medical care', in Dreitzel, H. P. (ed.), *The Social Organization of Health*, Collier-Macmillan, pp. 265–90.

Lidz, C., and Walker, A. (1980), *Heroin, Deviance and Morality*, Sage.

Lindesmith, A. (1951), *Addiction and Opiates*, Aldine.

Lipset, S. M., Trow, M., and Coleman, J. (1956), *Union Democracy*, Doubleday Anchor.

Little, A., and Westergaard, J. (1964), 'The trend of class differentials in educational opportunity in England and Wales', *British Journal of Sociology*, Vol. 15, No. 4, pp. 301–16.

Littlejohn, J. (1962), *Westrigg*, Routledge & Kegan Paul.

Littler, C. R. (1985), 'Work in traditional and modern societies', in C. R. Littler (ed.), *The Experience of Work*, Gower, pp. 34–49.

Lloyd, C. (ed.) (1975), *Sex, Discrimination and the Division of Labour*, Columbia University Press.

Lockwood, D. (1956), 'Some remarks on the social system', *British Journal of Sociology*, Vol. 7, pp. 134–46.

Lockwood, D. (1958), *The Blackcoated Worker: A Study in Class Consciousness*, Allen & Unwin.

Lockwood, D. (1966), 'Sources of variation in working class images of society', *Sociological Review*, Vol. 14, No. 3, pp. 249–67.

Lofland, J. (1971), *Analysing Social Settings*, Wadsworth.

Lomnitz, L. (1977), *Networks and Marginality: Life in a Mexican Shanty-Town*, Academic Press.

Lonsdale, S. (1985), *Work and Inequality*, Longman.

Lukes, S. (1973), *Emile Durkheim*, Penguin.

Lupton, T. (1963), *On the Shop Floor*, Pergamon.

McCall, G. J., and Simmons, J. L. (eds) (1969), *Issues in Participant Observation: A Text and a Reader*, Addison-Wesley.

MacCormack, C. (1980), 'Nature, culture and gender: a critique', in MacCormack, C., and Strathern, M. (eds), *Nature, Culture and Gender*, Cambridge University Press, pp. 1–24.

MacDonald, M. (1981), 'Schooling and the reproduction of class and gender relations', in Dale, R., *et al.* (eds), *Education and the State*, Vol. 2, Falmer Press, pp. 159–78.

McGee, T. G. (1971), *The Urbanization Process in the Third World*, Bell.

McIntosh, M. (1978), 'The State and the Oppression of Women', in Kuhn, A. M., and Wolpe, A. M. (eds), *Feminism and Materialism*, Routledge & Kegan Paul, pp. 254–89.

MacIntyre, S. (1968), 'The patterning of health by social position in contemporary Britain: directions for sociological work', *Social Science and Medicine*, Vol. 23, No. 4, pp. 393–415.

MacIver, R. M., and Page, C. H. (1950), *Society: An Introductory Analysis*, Macmillan.

Mack, J., and Lansley, S. (1985), *Poor Britain*, Allen & Unwin.

McKeown, T. (1971), 'A social approach to the history of medicine', in MacLachlan, G., and McKeown, T. (eds), *Medical History and Medical Care*, Nuffield Provincial Hospitals Trust and the Joseph Macy Foundation, pp. 1–16.

McKeown, T. (1976), *The Modern Rise of Population*, Edward Arnold.

McKeown, T. (1980), *The Role of Medicine: Dream, Mirage or Nemesis*, Blackwell.

McKinlay, J. B. (ed.) (1975), *Processing People*, Holt, Rinehart & Winston.

McLellan, D. (1978), *Karl Marx: Selected Writings*, Oxford University Press.

McLennan, G. (1984), 'The contours of British politics', in McLennan, G., Held, D., and Hall, S. (eds), *State and Society in Contemporary Britain*, Polity Press, pp. 241–73.

McRobbie, A. (1980), 'Settling accounts with sub-cultures', *Screen Education*, No. 34, pp. 37–50.

McRobbie, A., and Nava, M. (eds) (1984), *Gender and Generation*, Macmillan.

Madge, N. (ed.) (1983), *Families at Risk*, Heinemann.

Malinowski, B. (1922), *Argonauts of the Western Pacific*, Routledge & Kegan Paul.

Malinowski, B. (1944), *A Scientific Theory of Culture*, University of North Carolina Press.

Malinowski, B. (1985), 'The primitive economics of the Trobriand Islanders', in Littler, C. R. (ed.), *The Experience of Work*, Gower, pp. 15–22 (first published in 1921).

Manis, J. G., and Meltzer, B. N. (1967), *Symbolic Interaction*, Allyn & Bacon.

Manson, T. (1977), 'Management, the professions and the unions', in Stacey, M., *et al.* (eds), *Health and the Division of Labour*, Croom Helm, pp. 197–216.

Marglin, S. A. (1974), 'What do bosses do? The origins and functions of hierarchy in capitalist production', *The Review of Radical Political Economics*, Vol. 6, No. 2, pp. 60–112 (reprinted in part in Gorz, A. (ed.) (1978), *The Division of Labour*, Harvester, pp. 13–54).

Marmot, M. G., and McDowall, M. E. (1986), 'Mortality decline and widening social inequalities', *Lancet*, Vol. 2, pp. 274–6.

Marsh, C. (1988), *Exploring Data: An Introduction to Data Analysis for Social Scientists*, Polity Press.

Marshall, G., Rose, D., Newby, H., and Vogler, C. (1989), *Social Class in Modern Britain*, Unwin Hyman.

Marshall, T. H. (1963), *Sociology at the Crossroads*, Heinemann.

Marshall, T. H. (1964), *Class, Citizenship and Social Development*, Greenwood.

Martin, F. M. (1984), *Between the Acts*, Oxford University Press.

Martin, J. (1983), *Miss Manners' Guide to Excruciatingly Correct Behaviour*, Hamish Hamilton.

Martin, J., and Roberts, C. (1984), *Women and Employment: A Lifetime Perspective*, HMSO.

Martin, R. (1968), 'Union democracy: an explanatory framework', *Sociology*, Vol. 2, No. 2, pp. 205–20.

Marwick, M. (ed.) (1970), *Witchcraft and Sorcery*, Penguin.

Marx, K. (1959a), 'Wages, price and profit', in Marx K., and Engels, F., *Selected Works*, Lawrence & Wishart, Vol. 1, pp. 398–447 (first published as 'Value, price and profit' in 1898).

Marx, K. (1959b), 'Wage labour and capital', in Marx, K., and Engels, F., *Selected Works*, Lawrence & Wishart, Vol. 1, pp. 70–105 (first published in 1849).

Marx, K. (1976), *Capital*, Vol. I, Penguin (first published in 1867).

Marx, K., and Engels, F. (1959), *Selected Works*, Lawrence & Wishart.

Marx, K., and Engels, F. (1972), *On Colonialism: Articles from the New York Tribune and Other Writings*, International Publishers.

Marx, K., and Engels, F. (n.d.), *The Communist Manifesto*, Foreign Languages Publishing House, Moscow (first published in 1848).

Massey, D. (1978), 'Regionalism: some current issues', *Capital and Class*, No. 6, pp. 106–25.

Massey, D. (1984), *Spatial Divisions of Labour*, Macmillan.

Masters, W. H., and Johnson, V. E. (1980), *Human Sexual Response*, Bantam.

Matza, D. (1969), *Becoming Deviant*, Prentice-Hall.

Mayer, P. (1962), 'Migrancy and the study of African towns', *American Anthropologist*, Vol. 64, No. 4, pp. 572–92.

Mayhew, H. (1949), *Mayhew's London*, Quennell, P. (ed.), Pilot Press (first published in 1851).

Mead, M. (1935), *Sex and Temperament in Three Primitive Societies*, New American Library.

Mehan, H. (1979), *Learning Lessons: Social Organization in the Classroom*, Harvard University Press.

Merton, R. K. (1957), *Social Theory and Social Structure* (2nd edn), Free Press.

Merton, R. K. (1968), *On Theoretical Sociology*, Free Press.

Merton, R. K., *et al.* (1957), *The Student Physician*, Harvard University Press.

Merton, R. K., Fiske, M., and Kendall, P. (1956), *The Focussed Interview*, Illinois University Press.

Merton, R. K., and Kendall, P. (1946), 'The focussed interview', *American Journal of Sociology*, Vol. 51, pp. 541–57.

Michels, R. (1959), *Political Parties*, Dover (first published in 1915).

Miles, R. (1982), *Racism and Migrant Labour*, Routledge & Kegan Paul.

Miliband, R. (1978), 'A state of de-subordination', *British Journal of Sociology*, Vol. 29, No. 4, pp. 339–409.

Mill, J. S. (1869), *The Subjection of Women*, Longman, Green, Reader & Dyer (republished 1983 by Virago).

Mills, C. W. (1959), *The Sociological Imagination*, Oxford University Press.

Moorhouse, H. F., and Chamberlain, C. W. (1974), 'Lower class attitudes to property', *Sociology*, Vol. 8, No. 3, pp. 387–405.

Moreno, J. (ed.) (1960), *The Sociometry Reader*, Free Press.

Morgan, D. H. J. (1975), *Social Theory and the Family*, Routledge & Kegan Paul.

Morris, R. J. (1983), 'Property titles and the use of British urban pollbooks for social analysis', *Urban History Yearbook*, Leicester University Press, pp. 29–38.

Moser, C. A., and Kalton, G. (1971), *Survey Methods in Social Investigation*, Heinemann.

Moser, K. A., Fox, A. J., and Jones, D. R. (1984), 'Unemployment and mortality', *Lancet*, 2, pp. 324–9.

Moss, P. (1980), 'Parents at work', in Moss, P., and Fonda, N. (eds), *Work and the Family*, Temple Smith.

Mullard, C. (1981), 'The social context and meaning of multicultural education', *Educational Analysis*, 3 January 1981.

Murdock, G. P. (1949), *Social Structure*, Macmillan.

Murgatroyd, L., *et al.* (1984), *Localities, Class and Gender*, Pion.

Musgrave, P. W. (1970), *The Sociology of Education*, Methuen.

Myrdal, G. (1944), *An American Dilemma*, Harper & Row.

Nadel, S. F. (1957), *The Theory of Social Structure*, Cohen & West.

Navarro, V. (1978), *Class Struggle, the State and Medicine: Historical and Contemporary Analysis of the Medical Sector in Great Britain*, Martin Robertson.

Navarro, V. (1979) (ed.), *Imperialism, Health and Medicine*, Baywood.

Newby, H. (1980), 'Rural sociology – a trend report', *Current Sociology*, Vol. 28, No. 1, pp. 1–141.

Nichols, T., and Beynon, H. (1977), *Living with Capitalism*, Routledge & Kegan Paul.

Nisbet, R. (1979), 'Conservatism', in Bottomore, T., and Nisbet, R. (eds), *A History of Sociological Analysis*, Heinemann, pp. 81–117.

Oakley, A. (1974), *The Sociology of Housework*, Martin Robertson

Oakley, A. (1979), *Women Confined: Towards a Sociology of Childbirth*, Martin Robertson.

Office of Population Censuses & Surveys (1978), *Occupational Mortality, England & Wales, 1970–72*, Decennial Supplement, HMSO.

Office of Population Censuses & Surveys (1988), *General Household Survey 1987*, HMSO.

Office of Population Censuses & Surveys (1990), *General Household Survey 1988*, HMSO.

Olesen, V., and Whittaker, E. (1968), *The Silent Dialogue*, Jossey-Bass.

Onselen, C. van (1976), *Chibaro: African Mine Labour in Southern Rhodesia, 1900–1933*, Pluto Press.

Oppenheim, A. N. (1966), *Questionnaire Design and Attitude Measurement*, Heinemann.

Oral History Society (1985–), *Life Histories/récits de vie*.

Ortner, S. B. (1972), 'Is female to male as nature is to culture?' *Feminist Studies*, Vol. 1, pp. 5–31.

Ortner, S. B., and Whitehead, H. (eds) (1981), *Sexual Meanings: The*

Cultural Construction of Gender and Sexuality, Cambridge University Press.

Pahl, J. (1980), 'Patterns of money management within households,' *Journal of Social Policy*, Vol. 9, No. 3, pp. 313–35.

Pahl, R. E. (1965), *Urbs in Rure*, Weidenfeld & Nicolson.

Pahl, R. E. (1966), 'The rural–urban continuum', *Sociologica Ruralis*, Vol. 6, No. 3/4, pp. 299–329.

Pahl, R. E. (1970), *Whose City?*, Longman.

Pahl, R. E. (1984), *Divisions of Labour*, Blackwell.

Panikkar, K. M. (1959), *Asia and Western Dominance: A Survey of the Vasco da Gama Epoch of Asian History*, Allen & Unwin.

Parkes, C. M. (1972), *Bereavement: Studies of Grief in Adult Life*, Tavistock.

Parkin, F. (1972), *Class Inequality and Political Order*, Paladin.

Parkin, F. (1974), 'Strategies of social closure in class formation', in Parkin, F. (ed.), *The Social Analysis of Class Structure*, Tavistock, pp. 1–18.

Parkin, F. (1979), *Marxism and Class Theory: A Bourgeois Critique*, Tavistock.

Parkin, F. (1982), *Max Weber*, Ellis Horwood.

Parsons, T. (1937), *The Structure of Social Action*, Free Press.

Parsons, T. (1943), 'The kinship system of the contemporary United States', *American Anthropologist*, Vol. 45, pp. 22–38; reprinted in Parsons, T. (1964), *Essays in Sociological Theory*, Free Press.

Parsons, T. (1951), *The Social System*, Routledge & Kegan Paul.

Parsons, T. (1960), *Structure and Process in Modern Societies*, Free Press.

Parsons, T. (1964), *Essays in Sociological Theory*, Free Press.

Parsons, T. (1966), *Societies, Evolution and Comparative Perspectives*, Prentice-Hall.

Parsons, T., and Bales, R. F. (1955), *Family, Socialization and Interaction Process*, Free Press.

Parsons T., and Shils, E. (eds) (1962), *Toward a General Theory of Action*, Harper & Row (first published in 1957).

Pateman, T. (ed.) (1972), *Counter-Course*, Penguin.

Paton, K. (1970), *The Great Training Robbery*, privately published, Keele.

Payne, S. L. (1980), *The Art of Asking Questions*, Princeton University Press (first published in 1951).

Pickvance, C. (ed.) (1976), *Urban Sociology: Critical Essays*, Methuen.

Platt, J. (1976), *Realities of Social Research*, Sussex University Press.

Platt, J. (1981a), 'Evidence and proof in documentary research: some specific problems of documentary research', *Sociological Review*, Vol. 29, pp. 31–52.

Platt, J. (1981b), 'Evidence and proof in documentary research: some shared problems of documentary research', *Sociological Review*, Vol. 29, pp. 53–66.

Platt, J. (1986), 'Functionalism and the survey; the relation of theory and methods', *Sociological Review*, Vol. 34, pp. 501–36.

Plummer, K. (1983), *Documents of Life: An Introduction to the Problems and Literature of a Humanistic Method*, Allen & Unwin.

Policy Studies Institute (1984), *Black and White in Britain*, Heinemann.

Pond, C. (1989), 'The changing distribution of income, wealth and poverty', in Hamnett, C., McDowell, L., and Sarre, P. (eds), *The Changing Social Structure*, Sage, Open University Press, pp. 43–77.

Pöntinen, S. (1983), *Social Mobility and Social Structure: A Comparison of Scandinavian Countries*, Commentationes Scientiarium Socialium, 20, Finnish Society of Sciences & Letters, Helsinki.

Popper, K. (1947), *The Open Society and its Enemies*, Routledge & Kegan Paul.

Powles, J. (1973), 'On the limitations of modern medicine', *Science, Medicine & Man*, Vol. 1, No. 1, pp. 1–30.

Pugh, D. S., and Hickson, D. J. (eds) (1976), *Organizational Structure in its Context*, Saxon House.

Purcell, K. (1979), 'Militancy and acquiescence among women workers', in Burman, S. (ed.), *Fit Work for Women*, Croom Helm, pp. 112–33.

Psathas, George (1979), *Everyday Language*, Irvington.

Rasor, R. (1968), 'Narcotic addition in young people in the USA', in Wilson, C. (ed.), *Adolescent Drug Dependence*, Seabury, pp. 37–44.

Razzell, P. E. (1965), 'Population change in eighteenth-century England: a reinterpretation', *Economic History Review*, Vol. 18, pp. 312–32.

Redfield, R. (1930), *Tepoztlán: A Mexican Village*, University of Chicago Press.

Redfield, R. (1947), 'The folk society', *American Journal of Sociology*, Vol. 52, No. 3, pp. 293–308.

Rees, G. (1985), 'Introduction: class, reality and ideology', in Rees, G., *et al.* (eds), *Political Action and Social Identity*, Macmillan.

Reid, I. (1989), *Social Class Differences in Britain* (3rd edn), Fontana.

Reimer, E. (1971), *School is Dead*, Penguin.

Reiss, A. J. (1961), *Occupations and Social Status*, Free Press.

Rex, J. (1974), 'The compound, the reserve and the location – the essential institutions of South African labour exploitation', *South African Labour Bulletin*, Vol. 1, No. 4, pp. 5–17.

Rex, J. (1983), *Race Relations in Sociological Theory* (revised edn), Routledge & Kegan Paul.

Rex, J., and Moore, R. (1967), *Race, Community and Conflict*, Oxford University Press.

Rex, J., and Tomlinson, S. (1979), *Colonial Immigrants in a British City – A Class Analysis*, Routledge & Kegan Paul.

Rice, A. K. (1958), *Productivity and Social Organization*, Tavistock.

Richards, C. E. (1972), *Man in Perspective: An Introduction to Anthropology*, Random House.

Richardson, S. A., Dohrenwend, B. S., and Klein, D. (1965), *Interviewing: Its Forms and Functions*, Basic Books.

Rimmer, L. (1981), *Families in Focus: Marriage, Divorce and Family Patterns*, Occasional Paper No. 6, Study Commission on the Family.

Ringer, B. (1984), *We, the People – and Some Others*, Tavistock.

Roberts, B. (1978), *Cities of Peasants*, Arnold.

Roberts, K., Noble, M., and Duggan, J. (1984), 'Youth unemployment: an old problem or a new lifestyle?', in Thompson, K. (ed.), *Work, Employment and Unemployment*, Open University Press, pp. 238–46.

Robinson, D. (1976), *From Drinking to Alcoholism: A Sociological Commentary*, Wiley.

Robinson, D., and Henry, S. (1977), *Self-Help and Health: Mutual Aid for Modern Problems*, Martin Robertson.

Robinson, P. (1981), *Perspectives on the Sociology of Education*, Routledge & Kegan Paul.

Rodney, W. (1972), *How Europe Underdeveloped Africa*, Tanzania Publishing House.

Rosaldo, M. Z. (1974), 'Woman, culture and society: a theoretical overview', in Rosaldo, M. Z., and Lamphere, L. (eds), *Woman, Culture and Society*, Stanford University Press, pp. 17–42.

Rosaldo, M. Z. (1980), 'The use and abuse of anthropology: reflections on feminism and cross-cultural understanding', *Signs*, Vol. 5, No. 3, pp. 389–417.

Rose, A. (ed.) (1962), *Human Behaviour and Social Processes*, Routledge & Kegan Paul.

Rose, E. J. B., *et al.* (1969), *Colour and Citizenship: A Report on British Race Relations*, Oxford University Press.

Rose, G. (1982), *Deciphering Social Research*, Macmillan.

Rose, M. (1975), *Industrial Behaviour: Theoretical Development since Taylor*, Allen Lane/Penguin.

Rose, S. J. (1983), *Social Stratification in the U.S.: An Analytic Guidebook*, Social Graphics, Baltimore, Maryland.

Rostow, W. W. (1960), *The Stages of Economic Growth: A Non-Communist Manifesto*, Cambridge University Press.

Roszak, T. (1969), *The Dissenting Academy*, Penguin.

Roth, J. A. (1963), *Timetables*, Bobbs-Merrill.

Rowntree, B. S. (1901), *Poverty: A Study of Town Life*, Macmillan.

Roy, D. F. (1952), 'Quota restriction and goldbricking in a machine shop', *American Journal of Sociology*, Vol. 57, pp. 427–42.

Roy, D. F. (1953), 'Work satisfaction and social reward in quota achievement:

an analysis of piecework incentives', *American Sociological Review*, Vol. 18, pp. 507–14.

Roy, D. F. (1955), 'Making-out: a counter-system of workers' control of work situation and relationship', *American Journal of Sociology*, Vol. 60, pp. 255–66; reprinted in Burns, T. (ed.) (1969), *Industrial Man*, Penguin.

Roy, D. F. (1960), 'Banana time: job satisfaction and informal interaction', *Human Organization*, Vol. 18, pp. 156–88 (published in part in Salaman, G., and Thompson, K. (eds) (1973), *People and Organizations*, Longman, pp. 205–22).

Royal College of Physicians (1977), *Smoking or Health*, Third Report, Pitman Medical.

Rubery, J. (1978), 'Structural labour markets, worker organization, and low pay', *Cambridge Journal of Economics*, Vol. 2, No. 1, pp. 17–36.

Runciman, W. G. (1963), *Social Science and Political Theory*, Cambridge University Press.

Runciman, W. G. (1966), *Relative Deprivation and Social Justice*, Routledge & Kegan Paul.

Runciman, W. G. (1978), *Weber: Selections in Translation*, Cambridge University Press.

Rutter, M., and Madge, N. (1976), *Cycles of Disadvantage: A Review of Research*, Heinemann.

Sahlins, M. (1972), *Stone Age Economics*, Aldine-Atherton.

Sampson, A. (1982), *The Changing Anatomy of Britain*, Hodder & Stoughton.

Saunders, P. (1978), *Urban Politics: A Sociological Interpretation*, Penguin.

Saunders, P. (1983), *Social Theory and the Urban Question*, Hutchinson.

Saunders, P. (1990), *Social Class and Stratification*, Routledge.

Sayers, J. (1982), *Biological Politics: Feminist and Anti-Feminist Perspectives*, Tavistock.

Sayles, L. R. (1958), *Behaviour of Industrial Work Groups*, Wiley.

Scambler, G. (1985), 'Perceiving and coping with stigmatizing illness', in Fitzpatrick, R. M., *et al.* (eds), *The Experience of Illness*, Tavistock, pp. 203–26.

Schatzman, L., and Strauss, A. L. (1973), *Field Research: Strategies for a Natural Sociology*, Prentice-Hall.

Scheff, T. (1966), *Being Mentally Ill*, Aldine.

Scheff, T. (1968), 'Negotiating reality', *Social Problems*, No. 16, pp. 27–53.

Schur, E. (1973), *Radical Non-Intervention*, Prentice-Hall.

Schutz, A. (1964), *Collected Papers*, Vol. I, Nijhoff.

Scott, C. (1961), 'Research on mail surveys', *Journal of the Royal Statistical Society*, Series A, 124.

Scott, W. H., *et al.* (1963), *Coal and Conflict: A Study of Industrial Relations at Collieries*, Liverpool University Press.

Segalen, M. (1983), *Love and Power in the Peasant Family*, Blackwell.

Segalen, M. (1985), 'The household at work', in Littler, C. R. (ed.), *The Experience of Work*, Gower, pp. 50–71.

Seldon, A., and Pappworth, J. (1983), *By Word of Mouth: Elite Oral History*, Methuen.

Sennett, R. (1977), *The Fall of Public Man*, Cambridge University Press.

Sharp, R., and Green, A. G. (1975), *Education and Social Control*, Routledge & Kegan Paul.

Sharpe, S. (1976), *Just Like a Girl: How Girls Learn to be Women*, Penguin.

Sharrock, W. W., and Anderson, R. J. (1985), *The Ethnomethodologists*, Horwood.

Shaw, M. (1974), *Marxism versus Sociology: A Guide to Reading*, Pluto Press.

Sheth, N. R. (1968), *The Social Framework of an Indian Factory*, Manchester University Press.

Shils, E. (1972), *The Intellectuals and the Powers*, Vol. I, Selected Papers, University of Chicago Press.

Silverberg, J. (1978), 'Social categories v. organizations: class conflict in a caste-ordered system', in Raj Gupta, G. (ed.), *Main Currents in Indian Sociology*, Vol. III: *Cohesion and Conflict in Modern India*, Vikas Publishing House, New Delhi/Carolina Academic Press, Durham, North Carolina, pp. 1–32.

Silverman, D. (1968), 'Formal organizations or industrial sociology: towards a social action analysis of organizations', *Sociology*, Vol. 2, No. 2, pp. 221–38.

Silverman, D. (1970), *The Theory of Organizations*, Heinemann.

Simmel, G. (1950), 'The metropolis and mental life', in Wolff, K. H. (ed.), *The Sociology of Georg Simmel*, Free Press, pp. 409–24 (first published in 1903); 'The stranger', pp. 402–8 (first published in 1900).

Simpson, M. A. (1972), *Medical Education: A Critical Approach*, Butterworth.

Singer, P. (1980), *Marx*, Oxford University Press.

Singer, P. (1983), *Hegel*, Oxford University Press.

Sivanandan, A. (1976), *Race, Class and the State*, Race and Class Pamphlet, No. 1, Institute of Race Relations.

Sklair, Leslie (1991), *Sociology of the Global System*, Harvester Wheatsheaf.

Skultans, V. (1975), *Madness and Morals: Ideas on Insanity in the Nineteenth Century*, Routledge & Kegan Paul.

Smelser, N. (1959), *Social Change in the Industrial Revolution*, Routledge & Kegan Paul.

Smith, D. J. (1977), *Racial Disadvantage in Britain*, Penguin.

Smith, M. G. (1965), *The Plural Society in the British West Indies*, University of California Press.

Smith, M. G. (1974), *Corporations and Society*, Duckworth.

Sorokin, P. A., and Zimmerman, C. C. (1929), *Principles of Rural–Urban Sociology*, Holt.

Spradley, J. P. (1979), *The Ethnographic Interview*, Holt, Rinehart & Winston.

Spradley, J. P. (1980), *Participant Observation*, Holt, Rinehart & Winston.

Srinivas, M. N. (1952), *Religion and Society among the Coorgs of South India*, Clarendon Press.

Stacey, M. (1969), 'The myth of community studies', *British Journal of Sociology*, Vol. 20, No. 2, pp. 134–47.

Stacey, M. (1988), *The Sociology of Health and Healing: A Textbook*, Unwin Hyman.

Stanworth, M. (1984), 'Women and class analysis: a reply to Goldthorpe', *Sociology*, Vol. 18, No. 2, pp. 159–70.

Stavrianos, L. S. (1981), *Global Rift: The Third World Comes of Age*, Morrow.

Stein, M (1984), *The Eclipse of Community*, Harper & Row.

Stimson, G. V. (1974), 'Obeying doctor's orders: a view from the other side', *Social Science and Medicine*, Vol. 8, No. 2, pp. 97–104.

Stimson, G. V., and Webb, B. (1975), *Going to See the Doctor: The Consultation Process in General Practice*, Routledge & Kegan Paul.

Stinchcombe, A. L. (1978), *Theoretical Methods in Social History*, Academic Press.

Stoller, R. (1968), *Sex and Gender*, Science House.

Stone, G. P., and Farberman, H A (1970), *Social Psychology through Symbolic Interaction*, Xerox College Press.

Strathern, M. (1981), 'Self-interest and the social good: some implications of Hagen gender imagery', in Ortner, S. B., and Whitehead, H. (eds) *Sexual Meanings: The Cultural Construction of Gender and Sexuality*, Cambridge University Press, pp. 166–91.

Strauss, A. (ed.) (1964), *George Herbert Mead on Social Psychology*, University of Chicago Press.

Strauss, A., *et al.* (1964), *Psychiatric Ideologies and Institutions*, Free Press.

Strauss, A., *et al.* (1971), 'The hospital and its negotiated order', in Castles, F. G., Murray, D. J., and Potter, D. C. (eds), *Decisions, Organizations and Society*, Penguin, pp. 103–23 (originally published in Freidson, E. (ed.), *The Hospital in Modern Society* (1963), Macmillan, pp. 147–69).

Sudman, S., and Bradburn, N. M. (1982), *Asking Questions: A Practical Guide to Questionnaire Design*, Jossey-Bass.

Sudnow, D. (1972a), *Passing On: The Social Organization of Dying*, Prentice-Hall.

Sudnow, D. (ed.) (1972b), *Studies in Social Interaction*, Free Press.

Szasz, T., and Hollender, M. H. (1956), 'A contribution to the philosophy of medicine: the basic models of the doctor–patient relationship', *Archives of Internal Medicine*, Vol. 97, pp. 585–92.

Szelenyi, I. (1984), *Urban Inequalities under State Socialism*, Oxford University Press.

Taylor, C. (1975), *Hegel*, Cambridge University Press.

Taylor, H. (1983), 'The hospice movement: its role and its future', *Centre for Policy on Ageing*, CPA Reports 2.

Thompson, E. P. (1967), 'Time, work-discipline and industrial capitalism', *Past and Present*, 38, pp. 56–97.

Thompson, E. P. (1968), *The Making of the English Working Class*, Penguin.

Thompson, E. P. (1970), *Warwick University Ltd*, Penguin.

Thompson, P. (1978), *The Voice of the Past*, Oxford University Press.

Thompson, P. (1989), *The Nature of Work*, Macmillan.

Tilly, C. (1981), *As Sociology Meets History*, Academic Press.

Tönnies, F. (1957), *Community and Society*, Harper (first published in 1887).

Townsend, P. (1979), *Poverty in the United Kingdom*, Penguin.

Townsend, P., and Davidson, N. (1982), *Inequalities in Health: The Black Report*, Penguin.

Trevor-Roper, H. (1966), *The Rise of Christian Europe*, Thames & Hudson.

Trist, E. L., *et al.* (1963), *Organizational Choice*, Tavistock.

Tumin, M. (1969), 'Some principles of stratification: a critical analysis', in Coser, L., and Rosenberg, B. (eds), *Sociological Theory: A Book of Readings*, Macmillan, pp. 415–27.

Turner, H. A., Clack, G., and Roberts, G. (1967), *Labour Relations in the Motor Industry*, Allen & Unwin.

Turner, R. (1974), *Ethnomethodology*, Penguin.

Urry, J. (1984), 'Capitalist restructuring, recomposition and the regions', in Bradley, T., and Lowe, P. (eds), *Locality and Rurality*, Geo Books, Norwich, pp. 45–64.

Van den Berghe, P. (1967), *Race and Racism – A Comparative Perspective*, Wiley.

Van den Berghe, P. (1983), *The Ethnic Phenomenon*, Elsevier.

Vidich, A., and Bensman, J. (1958), *Small Town in Mass Society*, Princeton University Press.

Vidich, A., Bensman, J., and Stein, M. (1964), *Reflections on Community Studies*, Wiley.

Voysey, M. (1975), *A Constant Burden: The Reconstitution of Family Life*, Routledge & Kegan Paul.

Wadsworth, J., *et al.* (1983), 'Family type and accidents in pre-school children', *Journal of Epidemiology & Community Health*, Vol. 37, No. 2, pp. 100–104.

Wadsworth, M., *et al.* (1971), *Health and Sickness: The Choice of Treatment*, Tavistock.

Wainwright, H. (1978), 'Woman and the division of labour', in Abrams, P. (ed.), *Work, Urbanism and Inequality: UK Society Today*, Weidenfeld & Nicolson, pp. 160–205.

Wall, W. D., and Williams, H. L. (1970), *Longitudinal Studies and the Social Sciences*, Heinemann.

Waller, W. (1932), *The Sociology of Teaching*, Wiley.

Wallerstein, I. (1974), *The Modern World System: Capitalist Agriculture and the Origins of the European World Economy in the Sixteenth Century*, Academic Press.

Wallerstein, I. (1979), *The Capitalist World Economy*, Cambridge University Press.

Wallis, R. (1976), *The Road to Total Freedom: A Sociological Analysis of Scientology*, Heinemann.

Warner, W. L. (1936), 'American class and caste', *American Journal of Sociology*, Vol. XLII, Sept. 1936, pp. 234–7.

Warner, W. L., and Lunt, P. (1941), *The Social Life of a Modern Community*, Yale University Press.

Warner, W. L., Meeker, M., and Eells, K. (1960), *Social Class in America*, Harper (first published in 1949).

Warren, B. (1980), *Imperialism: Pioneer of Capitalism*, New Left Books.

Warren, R. (1963), *The Community in America*, Rand McNally.

Warwick, D. P., and Lininger, C. (1975), *The Sample Survey: Theory and Practice*, McGraw-Hill.

Watts, A. G. (1983), *Education, Unemployment and the Future of Work*, Open University Press.

Webb, E. J., *et al.* (1966), *Unobtrusive Measures: Non-reactive Research in the Social Sciences*, Rand McNally.

Weber, M. (1961), *General Economic History*, Collier (first published in 1923).

Weber, M. (1968), *Economy and Society*, Bedminster Press.

Weber, M. (1976), *The Protestant Ethic and the Spirit of Capitalism*, Scribner (first published in 1904/5; Allen & Unwin edition 1930).

Wedderburn, D. (ed.) (1974), *Poverty, Inequality and Class Structure*, Cambridge University Press.

Weiss, C. H. (1972), *Evaluation Research: Methods for Assessing Program Effectiveness*, Prentice-Hall.

Werthman, C. (1963), 'Delinquents in schools', in Beck, J., *et al.* (eds) (1976), *Worlds Apart: Readings for a Sociology of Education*, Collier-Macmillan, pp. 258–78.

Weselowski, W., and Krauze, T. (1981), 'Socialist and meritocratic principles of remuneration', in Berreman, G. (ed.), *Social Inequality: Comparative and Developmental Approaches*, Academic Press, pp. 337–49.

Westergaard, J. (1972), 'Sociology: the myth of classlessness', in Blackburn, R. (ed.), *Ideology in Social Science*, Fontana, pp. 119–63.

Westergaard, J., and Resler, H. (1976), *Class in a Capitalist Society: A Study of Contemporary Britain*, Penguin.

Wexler, P. (1976), *Beyond Inequality: The Sociology of Education*, Bobbs-Merrill.

Whitelegg, E., *et al.* (eds) (1982), *The Changing Experience of Women*, Martin Robertson.

Whitty, G. (1985), *Sociology and School Knowledge*, Methuen.

Whitty, G., and Young, M. (1976), *Explorations in the Politics of School Knowledge*, Nafferton Books, Driffield.

Whyte, W. F. (1955), *Street Corner Society* (2nd edn), University of Chicago Press.

Whyte, W. H. (1957), *The Organization Man*, Penguin.

Wilkins, L. (1965), 'Some sociological factors in drug addiction control', in Rosenberg, B., Bernard, I., and Howton, F. (eds), *Mass Society in Crisis*, Free Press, pp. 645–62.

Wilkinson, R. G. (1986), *Class and Health*, Tavistock.

Williams, R. (1961), *The Long Revolution*, Chatto & Windus.

Williams, W. M. (1964), *A West Country Village: Ashworthy*, Routledge & Kegan Paul.

Willis, P. (1977), *Learning to Labour: How Working Class Kids Get Working Class Jobs*, Gower.

Willmott, P., and Young, M. (1960), *Family and Class in a London Suburb*, Routledge & Kegan Paul.

Wilson, E. (1977), *Women and the Welfare State*, Tavistock.

Wilson, E. O. (1975), *Sociobiology: The New Synthesis*, Harvard University Press.

Wilson, W. (1978), *The Declining Significance of Race: Blacks and Changing American Institutions*, Chicago University Press.

Winch, P. (1958), *The Idea of a Social Science*, Routledge & Kegan Paul.

Winick, C. (1965), 'Marihuana use by young people', in Harms, E. (ed.), *Drug Addiction in Youth*, Pergamon Press.

Wirth, L. (1938), 'Urbanism as a way of life', *American Journal of Sociology*, Vol. 44, No. 1, pp. 1–24.

Wolf, E. R. (1982), *Europe and the People without History*, University of California Press.

Wolpe, H. (1970), 'Industrialization and race in South Africa', in Zubaida, S. (ed.), *Race and Racialism*, Tavistock Press.

Wolpe, H. (1976), 'The white working class in South Africa', *Economy and Society*, Vol. 5, No. 2, pp. 197–240.

Wong, Siu-lun (1988), *Emigrant Entrepreneurs: Shanghai Industrialists in Hong Kong*, Oxford University Press, Hong Kong.

Wood, J. (1984), 'Groping towards sexism: boys' sex talk', in McRobbie, A., and Nava, M. (eds), *Gender and Generation*, Macmillan, pp. 54–84.

Wood, S. (ed.) (1989), *The Transformation of Work?*, Unwin Hyman.

Woodward, J. (1958), *Management and Technology*, HMSO.

World Bank (1985), *World Development Report 1985*, Oxford University Press.

Worsley, P. (1968), *The Trumpet Shall Sound*, Shocken.

Worsley, P. (1982), *Marx and Marxism*, Horwood.

Worsley, P. (1984), *The Three Worlds: Culture and World Development*, Weidenfeld & Nicolson.

Wright, H. M. (1977), *The Burden of the Present Liberal–Radical Controversy over South African History*, Collins.

Young, J. (1981), 'Thinking seriously about crime', in Fitzgerald, M., McLennan, G., and Pawson, J. (eds), *Crime and Society: Readings in History and Theory*, Routledge & Kegan Paul, pp. 248–309.

Young, K., and Harris, O. (1976), 'The subordination of women in cross cultural perspective', in Evans, M. (ed.) (1982), *The Woman Question*, Fontana, pp. 543–72.

Young, M. (ed.) (1971), *Knowledge and Control: New Directions for the Sociology of Education*, Collier-Macmillan.

Young, M., and Willmott, P. (1957a), *Family and Kinship in East London*, Penguin.

Young, M., and Willmott, P. (1957b), 'Social grading by manual workers', *British Journal of Sociology*, Vol. 7, No. 4, pp. 337–45.

Young, M., and Willmott, P. (1973), *The Symmetrical Family*, Routledge & Kegan Paul.

Zborowski, M. (1969), *People in Pain*, Jossey-Bass.

Zola, I. (1973), 'Pathways to the doctor: from person to patient', *Social Science and Medicine*, Vol. 2, pp. 677–89.

Zola, I. (1975), 'Medicine as an institution of social control', in Cox, C., and Mead, A. (eds), *A Sociology of Medical Practice*, Collier-Macmillan, pp. 23–48.

Zubaida, Sami (1989), *Islam, the People and the State: Essays on Political Ideas and Movements in the Middle East*, Routledge.

Further Reading

Chapter 1: Introduction

For those new to sociology, there is a lively eighteen-minute video, *So What's Sociology Anyway?*, made by Life's Rich Tapestry Ltd for the Scottish Branch of the British Sociological Association, and obtainable from Paul Littlewood, Department of Sociology, University of Glasgow, Glasgow G12 8RT. The most comprehensive source of concise and expert information on sociologists and their ideas is the nineteen-volume (plus index) *International Encyclopaedia of the Social Sciences*, ed. David L. Sills (Macmillan/ Free Press, 1968).

By contrast, the handiest reference book is the *Dictionary of Sociology* by Nicholas Abercrombie, Stephen Hill and Bryan S. Turner (Penguin, 1984), which eclipses previous and larger dictionaries in its selection of entries – which range from 'abstracted empiricism' to 'zones of transition' – that are central to modern sociological debate. *The Founding Fathers of Social Science* (T. Raison (ed.), Penguin, 1969) is an excellent collection of brief introductory sketches. *A History of Sociological Analysis*, edited by Tom Bottomore and Robert Nisbet (Heinemann, 1978), is a more advanced, more historically oriented, less portable and more expensive, but invaluable survey of theoretical schools and major topics.

The best 'reader' in sociological theory is still that edited by Lewis A. Coser and Bernard Rosenberg: *Sociological Theory: A Book of Readings* (Collier-Macmillan, 1976); while C. Wright Mills's *The Sociological Imagination* (Oxford University Press, 1959) is still the liveliest discussion of what doing sociology is all about. Peter Berger's *Invitation to Sociology* (Penguin, 1967) is an equally readable and stimulating starting-point, written from a very different, more phenomenological position.

For an introduction to the principal theoretical schools of contemporary sociology, see E. C. Cuff and G. Payne (eds), *Perspectives in Sociology* (second edition, Allen & Unwin, 1984).

Finally, *The State of the Nation*, by Stephen and Jill Vincent (Pan, 1985), uses visual presentation rather than words to provide a provocative set of social maps of one country, Britain.

Chapter 2: Development

A. Foster-Carter's *The Sociology of Development* (Causeway, 1985) is a lucid introduction to the various aspects of this wide field, some of which have been only briefly discussed in our chapter.

For basic data on economic development, using social indicators such as population size, growth, levels of education, urbanization, etc, the *World Development Report 1990* is the standard source (Oxford University Press, 1990). *The Third World Atlas* produced for the Third World Studies course (U 204) of the Open University (1981) is outstanding. The *New State of the World Atlas*, by Michael Kidron and Ronald Segal (Pan, 1986), is a provocative and sardonic way of looking at development and underdevelopment in vivid, graphic form. The best history of the Third World is L. S. Stavrianos's *Global Rift* (Morrow, 1981). Eric Wolf's *Europe and the People without History* (University of California Press, 1982) is a valuable complement by an anthropologist.

A. G. Frank's 'The sociology of underdevelopment and the underdevelopment of sociology', in his *Latin America: Underdevelopment or Revolution?* (Monthly Review Press, 1969) is essential reading, as is Immanuel Wallerstein's *The Capitalist World Economy* (Cambridge University Press, 1979). Ian Roxborough's *Theories of Underdevelopment* (Macmillan, 1979) is a concise and clear guide, while Peter Worsley's *The Three Worlds* (Weidenfeld & Nicolson, 1984) examines the cultural as well as the political and economic characteristics of the Third World.

On nationalism, Benedict Anderson's *Imagined Communities* (New Left Books, 1983) and Ernest Gellner's *Nations and Nationalism* (Blackwell, 1984) are both excellent.

Of the older literature, W. W. Rostow's *The Stages of Economic Growth* (Cambridge University Press, 1960) and Frantz Fanon's *The Wretched of the Earth* (MacGibbon & Kee, 1965), though offering widely contrasting approaches, are still obligatory reading. For an iconoclastic view of underdevelopment from the Left, see Bill Warren's *Imperialism: Pioneer of Capitalism* (New Left Books, 1980).

Chapter 3: The Research Process

Professional sociologists engaged in research have to get to grips with problems of method. But few people have an intrinsic interest in methodology itself, and in this respect it is unlike other branches of sociology. The best way to become engaged with the study of methodology, then, is to put oneself as far as possible in the position of the professional researcher, by looking at the way particular studies were carried out. Accounts which sociologists have given of their own work are therefore a helpful starting-point, and several are listed in the text on p. 80. M. Shipman's *The Limitations of Social Research* (Longman, 1981) discusses various pieces of research critically, while R. G. Burgess's *The Research Process in Educational Settings* (Falmer Press, 1984) is useful for those interested in educational research.

Learning *how* to evaluate a particular piece of empirical research itself requires forethought, and an invaluable book here is G. Rose's *Deciphering Social Research* (Macmillan, 1982). The many references it contains can be followed up according to your own particular interests and needs.

Concentrating on one kind of research approach to the exclusion of others which may be less congenial or more difficult is a temptation to be resisted. A wide range of empirical techniques can be encountered relatively quickly by browsing in journals. You will find a few articles on each of the main branches of sociology in the issues produced by any major journal over a couple of years, and these provide an opportunity to practise evaluating the various methods employed and to focus on one technique or another.

For a mixture of approaches, sample three major British journals: *Sociology*; the *British Journal of Sociology*; and the *Sociological Review* (the last-named has a more qualitative flavour). The balance is more towards the quantitative in the *American Journal of Sociology*, the *American Sociological Review*, and the *European Sociological Review*. The American journal *Social Forces* favours relatively brief articles using a wide range of techniques.

There are a great many general textbooks, with more appearing every year, and the choice of one over another is largely a matter of taste. They should be used selectively to gain a preliminary grasp of a particular topic, not read from end to end, which is bound to produce both boredom and intellectual indigestion. H. M. Blalock discusses a wide range of approaches in *An Introduction to Social Research* (Prentice-Hall, 1970), as do M. Bulmer in *Sociological Research Methods* (Macmillan, 1984), N. K. Denzin in *The Research Act in Sociology* (Butterworth, 1970), D. and C. Nachmias in *Research Methods in the Social Sciences* (Arnold, 1976) and B. Phillips in *Sociological Research Methods: An Introduction* (Dorsey Press, 1985).

The literature on specific topics can be followed up using the many references given in the chapter itself. Certainly, no one should neglect the study of the ethics of research and J. A. Barnes's *Who Should Know What?* (Penguin, 1982), which, together with Martin Bulmer's *Social Research Ethics* (Macmillan, 1982), provides an excellent introduction to these issues. B. Barnes's *T. S. Kuhn and Social Science* Macmillan, 1982) contains an outstanding introduction to the much-quoted work of Thomas Kuhn. C. Marsh's *The Survey Method* (Allen & Unwin, 1982) aims at convincing the reader of the *value* of survey research rather than explaining how to do it.

For useful 'handbooks', see C. A. Moser and G. Kalton, *Survey Methods in Social Investigation* (Heinemann, 1971), and G. Hoinville and R. Jowell, *Survey Research Practice* (Heinemann, 1978).

On survey analysis, M. Rosenberg's *The Logic of Survey Analysis* (Basic Books, 1968) is still as good an introduction as any. One of the best accounts of cross-tabular analysis is O. Hellevik's *Introduction to Causal Analysis* (Allen & Unwin, 1984).

There are many statistics 'cook-books', and the choice is again very much a matter of taste. H. M. Blalock's *Social Statistics* (McGraw-Hill, 1979) is the latest edition of a book which has long been popular with sociologists. B. H. Erickson and T. A. Nosanchuk, in *Understanding Data* (Open University Press, 1979), take a rather different line and can also be recommended highly; so, too, can Catherine Marsh, *Exploring Data* (Polity Press, 1988).

It is extremely difficult to learn about fieldwork from a book, but Robert Burgess, *In the Field* (Allen & Unwin, 1984), is well worth reading, as are the other books mentioned in the text.

Sage Publications have published a very large number of short handbooks on specific aspects of qualitative and quantitative methodology in their Applied Social Research Series, Qualitative Research Series and Quantitative Applications in the Social Science Series. These are often a useful point of reference although many are fairly advanced.

Chapter 4: Sex, Gender and the Family

Some useful books on gender are: Ann Oakley, *Subject Women* (Martin Robertson, 1981); Elizabeth Whitelegg *et al.* (eds), *The Changing Experience of Women* (Martin Robertson, 1982); Mary Evans (ed.), *The Woman Question* (Fontana, 1982); Michèle Barrett, *Women's Oppression Today* (Verso/New Left Books, 1980). On the family: D. H. J. Morgan, *Social Theory and the Family* (Routledge & Kegan Paul, 1975); and C. C. Harris, *Family and Industrial Society* (Allen & Unwin, 1983).

For further discussion of cross-cultural material, see Ann Oakley, *Sex, Gender and Society* (Temple Smith, 1972), which also has an introduction to questions of biological and psychological sex differences and socialization; and Ernestine Friedl, *Men and Women: An Anthropological View* (Holt, Rinehart & Winston, 1975).

On gender and employment, in addition to the items discussed in the chapter, see Lindsay Mackie and Polly Pattullo, *Women at Work* (Tavistock, 1977); Jackie West (ed.), *Work, Women and the Labour Market* (Routledge & Kegan Paul, 1982); Ann Game and Rosemary Pringle, *Gender at Work* (Allen & Unwin, 1983); Feminist Review (ed.), *Waged Work: A Reader* (Virago, 1986).

On the family and gender: Ann Oakley, *The Sociology of Housework* (Martin Robertson, 1974), which also includes a hard-hitting critique of sexism in sociology; and Pauline Hunt, *Gender and Class Consciousness* (Macmillan, 1980).

Finally, Joni Seager and Ann Olson, in *Women of the World: An International Atlas* (Pan Books, 1986), provide a stimulating visual survey of women's lives today.

Chapter 5: Education

By far the most comprehensive textbook is Philip Robinson's *Perspectives in the Sociology of Education* (Routledge & Kegan Paul, 1981), though it is now a little out of date. Roland Meighan's *A Sociology of Educating* (Holt, Rinehart & Winston, 1981) has a lively and accessible approach and so is a good starting-point. The best overview of American work is Philip Wexler's *Beyond Inequality* (Bobbs-Merrill, 1976), though it, too, is somewhat dated and not too easy to get hold of. The most original and influential books tend to be the result of sociologists bringing together their own past work: e.g., M. Apple's *Education and Power* (Routledge & Kegan Paul, 1983); B. Bernstein's *Class, Codes and Control* (Routledge & Kegan Paul, 1977); H. Giroux, *Theory and Resistance in Education* (Heinemann, 1984); and G. Whitty, *Sociology and School Knowledge* (Methuen, 1985).

Another valuable resource is collections of readings. Many of the best have been produced in association with the Open University. They include: B. Cosin *et al.* (eds), *School and Society* (Routledge & Kegan Paul, 1971); M. Hammersley and P. Woods (eds), *The Process of Schooling* (Routledge & Kegan Paul, 1976); B. Cosin *et al.* (eds), *Schooling and Capitalism* (Routledge & Kegan Paul, 1976); R. Dale *et al.* (eds), *Education and the State* (two vols) (Falmer Press, 1981); and J. Karabel and A. H. Halsey (eds), *Power, Ideology and Education* (Oxford University Press, 1977).

For examples of empirical research, there are a number of monographs, often based on case-studies of particular schools. For example: A. Cicourel and J. Kitsuse, *The Educational Decision-Makers* (Bobbs-Merrill, 1963); D. Hargreaves, *Social Relations in the Secondary School* (Routledge & Kegan Paul, 1968); C. Lacey, *Hightown Grammar* (Manchester University Press, 1970); R. Sharp and A. Green, *Education and Social Control* (Routledge & Kegan Paul, 1975); and P. Willis, *Learning to Labour* (Saxon House, 1977).

An excellent and readable account of teaching is available in R. Connell's *Teachers' Work* (Allen & Unwin, 1986).

Examples of larger-scale studies based on survey data are J. Floud, A. H. Halsey and F. Martin, *Social Class and Educational Opportunity* (Heinemann, 1956); A. H. Halsey, A. F. Heath and J. M. Ridge, *Origins and Destinations* (Clarendon Press, 1980); and M. Rutter and N. Madge, *15000 Hours: Secondary Schools and Their Effects on Children* (Open Books, 1979).

Collections of papers are often focused on the analysis of a particular topic. The following deal with the analysis of the curriculum and are accessibly written: G. Whitty and M. Young, *Explorations in the Politics of School Knowledge* (Nafferton Books, 1976); M. Hammersley and A. Hargreaves, *Curriculum Analysis: Sociological Case Studies* (Falmer Press, 1984); and P. Broadfoot's *Selection, Certification and Control* (Falmer Press, 1984) is another interesting and accessible collection of papers which focuses on the theme of assessment and examinations.

Two collections which bring together the issues of race and gender in education are M. Arnot's *Race and Gender* (Blackwell, 1986) and R. Deem's *Schooling for Women's Work* (Routledge & Kegan Paul, 1980).

Finally, there are a number of books by radical critics of schooling which, though not strictly sociological, do explore some of the issues raised in this chapter, particularly Ivan Illich's *Pedagogy of the Oppressed* (Penguin, 1971) and his *Deschooling Society* (Penguin, 1971).

There are two English-language journals specifically concerned with the field – in the USA, *Sociology of Education* and, in the UK, the *British Journal of Sociology of Education*. All the general introductory texts in sociology have chapters on education. M. O'Donnell's *A New Introductory Sociology* (Nelson Harrap, 1981) is one of the fullest and best. You may also find, in libraries, course-units on the sociology of education written by staff of the Open University. These are usually very clearly presented and give good expositions.

Chapter 6: Health, Illness and Medicine

Highly recommended for those interested in how sociology contributes, along with other biological and social sciences, to a better understanding of health issues are the publications of the Open University Press for their second-level course *Health and Disease* (U 205). The Reader (1984) with this title contains useful articles from a variety of standpoints. Eight paperbacks support the course. Four of special interest to sociologists are *The Health of Nations; Birth to Old Age: Health in Transition; Experiencing and Explaining Disease;* and *Caring for Health: History and Diversity*; all were published in 1985.

Other well-constructed textbooks are D. L. Patrick and G. Scambler (eds), *Sociology as Applied to Medicine* (Bailliere Tindall, second edition, 1986); D. Robinson, *Patients, Practitioners and Medical Care: Aspects of Medical Care* (second edition, Heinemann, 1978); and M. Morgan *et al.* (eds), *Sociological Approaches to Health and Medicine* (Croom Helm, 1985). C. Cox and A. Mead (eds), in *A Sociology of Medical Practice* (Macmillan, 1975), have assembled some important papers showing the early development and range of the subject-matter. A more critical statement is contained in

R. Illsley, *Professional or Public Health: Sociology in Health and Medicine* (Nuffield Provincial Hospitals Trust, 1980).

Important source-books for specific topics include P. Townsend and N. Davidson, *Inequalities in Health: The Black Report* (Penguin, 1982), which summarizes much of the available evidence relating to the social distribution of health, illness and health care. H. Graham, *Women, Health and the Family* (Wheatsheaf Press, 1984), deals with gender inequalities. So, among other things, does J. Mitchell, *What is to be Done about Illness and Health?* (Penguin, 1984). G. W. Brown and T. Harris, in their *Social Origins of Depression* (Tavistock, 1978), broke new ground by showing that it was certain social and psychological aspects of the lives of working-class women which made them more vulnerable to depressive illness than their middle-class sisters. L. Doyal takes a Marxist feminist approach in her broad-ranging study, *The Political Economy of Health* (Pluto Press, 1979).

Chapter 7: Community and Urban Life

The demise of community studies during the 1970s discussed in this chapter has resulted in a dearth of texts. *Community Studies*, by Colin Bell and Howard Newby (Allen & Unwin, 1971), thus remains rather more up to date than ought to be the case and offers a general overview of the field. Urban sociology has, however, thrived over the last decade, and an excellent review is Peter Saunders's *Social Theory and the Urban Question* (second edition, Hutchinson, 1986). Recent discussion has, not surprisingly, been dominated by the problems associated with inner city areas. Paul Harrison's *Inside the Inner City* (Penguin, 1984) offers an accessible account; a useful comparative collection is M. Dear and A. Scott (eds), *Urbanization and Urban Planning in Capitalist Society* (Methuen, 1983). More analytical accounts are Gareth Rees and John Lambert, *Cities in Crisis* (Arnold, 1985), and Roger Friedland's *Power and Crisis in the City* (Macmillan, 1983). An Eastern European perspective is provided by Ivan Szelenyi's *Urban Inequalities under State Socialism* (Oxford University Press, 1984). Some of the *gemeinschaftlich* themes alluded to in this chapter have been further explored in a recent study of Elmdon, Essex, by Marilyn Strathern, *Kinship at the Core* (Cambridge University Press, 1983), and in a collection edited by Anthony Cohen, *Belonging* (Manchester University Press, 1983). R. E. Pahl has recently used the community study as a method with great success in *Divisions of Labour* (Blackwell, 1984), based on the Isle of Sheppey in Kent. Finally, a useful collection, whose title is self explanatory, is Richard Sennett (ed.), *Classic Essays on the Culture of Cities* (Prentice-Hall, 1969).

Chapter 8: Work, Industry and Organizations

K. Thompson (ed.), *Work, Employment and Unemployment* (Open University Press, 1984), is a stimulating collection of readings about work of all sorts;

T. Burns (ed.), *Industrial Man* (Penguin, 1969), remains an equally useful collection concerned more narrowly with employment in industry; and C. R. Littler (ed.), *The Experience of Work* (Gower, 1985), contains mostly descriptive accounts of work in a wide variety of societies and settings. R. K. Brown's chapter on 'Work' in P. Abrams and R. K. Brown (eds), *U.K. Society* (Weidenfeld & Nicolson, 1984), and S. Lonsdale, *Work and Inequality* (Longman, 1985), both outline the variations in conditions of employment in Britain and their relations with other social factors. D. Gallie (ed.), *Employment in Britain* (Blackwell, 1988), provides a comprehensive discussion of all aspects of employment.

R. E. Pahl, *Divisions of Labour* (Blackwell, 1984), introduces research on household work-strategies by tracing the historical development of work in Britain. His important arguments would be contested by some, and this applies also to the work of H. Braverman, *Labor and Monopoly Capital* (Monthly Review Press, 1974), which provides a powerful Marxist interpretation of the development of work and production in modern capitalist societies; it should be read together with some of the secondary critical literature such as P. Thompson, *The Nature of Work* (Macmillan, 1989), C. R. Littler, *The Development of the Labour Process in Capitalist Societies* (Heinemann, 1982) or S. Wood (ed.), *The Transformation of Work?* (Unwin Hyman, 1989).

A useful starting-point for the consideration of employer–employee relations is A. Fox, 'Industrial relations: a social critique of pluralist ideology', in J. Child (ed.), *Man and Organization* (Allen & Unwin, 1973) – arguments which are further developed in Fox's *Beyond Contract: Work, Power and Trust Relations* (Faber, 1974). R. Bendix, *Work and Authority in Industry* (Harper, 1963), provides a fascinating and important comparative account of how employers and managers established the legitimacy of their authority in four different societies during industrialization, and also discusses the growth of industrial bureaucracy. R. Hyman, *Strikes* (Fontana, 1984), is a useful introduction to industrial conflict. H. Beynon, *Working for Ford* (Penguin, 1984), and T. Nichols and H. Beynon, *Living with Capitalism* (Routledge & Kegan Paul, 1977), describe management–worker relations, in vivid detail, in a car plant and a chemical works respectively, whilst P. Edwards and H. Scullion, *The Social Organization of Industrial Conflict* (Blackwell, 1982), analyses industrial conflict in the light of comparative data from seven factories.

A. Etzioni, *A Comparative Analysis of Complex Organizations* (Free Press, 1961), develops an illuminating typology of organizations, though one which is not without problems. T. Burns and G. M. Stalker, *The Management of Innovation* (Tavistock, 1961), and J. Woodward, *Industrial Organization: Theory and Practice* (Oxford University Press, 1965), are concerned more specifically with the comparative analysis of industrial organizations.

D. Silverman, *The Theory of Organizations* (Heinemann, 1970), critically reviews these and many other studies, and develops an alternative 'action approach' to organizational analysis, one which is similar to that advocated by J. H. Goldthorpe *et al.*, *The Affluent Worker: Industrial Attitudes and Behaviour* (Cambridge University Press, 1968). S. Clegg and D. Dunkerley, *Organization, Class and Control* (Routledge & Kegan Paul, 1980), provides a somewhat uneven coverage of an encyclopaedic range of research on and approaches to organizations. P. Brannen, *Authority and Participation in Industry* (Batsford, 1983), and J. Hemingway, *Conflict and Democracy* (Oxford University Press, 1978), discuss the problems of the democratic control of industrial organizations and of trade unions respectively, whilst E. Goffman, *Asylums* (Anchor, 1961), illuminates aspects of some 'people-processing' organizations, such as mental hospitals.

In addition to their own investigation of a local labour-market R. M. Blackburn and M. Mann, *The Working Class in the Labour Market* (Macmillan, 1979), provide a useful introduction to the ways in which labour-markets work more generally, at least so far as manual workers are concerned. J. Martin and C. Roberts, *Women and Employment: A Lifetime Perspective* (HMSO, 1984), use the findings of a national survey to discuss the overall patterns of women's labour-market participation. S. Walby, *Patriarchy at Work* (Polity Press, 1986), and H. Bradley, *Men's Work, Women's Work* (Polity Press, 1989), both describe the changing gender division of labour in a number of different industries and discuss how this can best be explained theoretically, a task which is also undertaken by V. Beechey, 'Women's employment in contemporary Britain', in V. Beechey and E. Whitelegg (eds), *Women in Britain Today* (Open University Press, 1986). A. G. Watts, *Education, Unemployment and the Future of Work* (Open University Press, 1983), includes an extensive discussion of possible alternatives for work and employment over the next few decades. The journal *Work, Employment and Society* monitors the latest theory and research in these fields.

Chapter 9: Ethnicity and Race

A good starting-point is Richard Schermerhorn's *Comparative Ethnic Relations* (Random House, 1970). Schermerhorn approaches the study of race and ethnic relations systematically by placing them within a framework of functionalist, conflict and pluralist theory. Other general introductions based on comparative material are provided by P. van den Berghe, *Race and Racism: A Comparative Perspective* (Wiley, 1967); Michael Banton, *Race Relations* (Tavistock, 1967) and *Racial and Ethnic Competition* (Cambridge University Press, 1983); and Philip Mason, *Patterns of Dominance* (Oxford University Press, 1970). None of these works, however, place their central emphasis on class analysis or on pluralist theory. For an approach using a Weberian form of class analysis, see J. Rex's *Race Relations in Sociological Theory* (Routledge & Kegan Paul, 1983); his *Ethnicity and Race* (Open University Press, 1986); and J. Rex and S. Tomlinson, *Colonial Immigrants in a British City* (Routledge & Kegan Paul, 1979). For pluralist theory, see J. S. Furnivall's *Netherlands India* (Cambridge University Press, 1939); his *Colonial Policy and Practice* (Cambridge University Press, 1945); M. G. Smith, *The Plural Society in the West Indies* (University of California Press, 1965), and his *Corporations and Society* (Duckworth, 1974). These works are important in that they draw attention to the political as distinct from the economic differentiation between ethnic groups. A Marxist text which claims that Rex's approach is based on 'race relations' rather than on class is R. Miles, *Racism and Migrant Labour* (Routledge & Kegan Paul, 1982.) A symposium bringing together some of the above-mentioned approaches is provided in David Mason and John Rex (eds), *Theories of Race and Ethnic Relations* (Cambridge University Press, 1986).

For the study of race relations in the United States, Gunnar Myrdal's *An American Dilemma* (Harper, 1964) is still an essential introduction, not merely to the study of race in America but to race relations in general, particularly its appendix on 'Facts and Valuations', which is central to all policy-oriented sociology. There are numerous later texts, but W. J. Wilson's *The Declining Significance of Race* (Chicago University Press, 1978) is an especially interesting study of the effects of Civil Rights and Affirmative Action programmes on race relations. B. Ringer's *We, The People* (Tavistock, 1984) emphasizes the necessity of a dual approach to the United States, including both its origins in the slave plantations and its later development as a settler society.

On South Africa, a Marxist approach is emphasized in B. R. Davidson, J. Slovo and A. R. Wilkinson, *Southern Africa: The New Politics of Revolution* (Penguin, 1976), and H. Wolpe's essays on 'Industrialization and race in South Africa', in S. Zubaida (ed.), *Race and Racialism*, (Tavistock, 1970), and 'The White working class in South Africa', in *Economy and Society*, Vol. 5, No. 2 (1976). An alternative view of South Africa is provided in the chapter on 'The plural society – the South African case', in J. Rex's *Race, Colonialism and the City* (Routledge & Kegan Paul, 1977). A good recent attempt at a sociology of race relations in South Africa is Stanley Greenberg's *Race and State in Capitalist Development* (Yale University Press, 1980).

There are numerous studies of race in various localities of Great Britain. Some of the essentials of the race relations debate in Britain are provided by E. J. B. Rose *et al.*, *Colour and Citizenship* (Oxford University Press, 1969). More recent studies of discrimination, based on national samples, are provided by W. W. Daniel, *Racial Discrimination in Britain* (Penguin, 1968), and D. J. Smith, *Racial Disadvantage in Britain* (Penguin, 1977). J. Rex and S. Tomlinson raise many of the issues involved in local studies in their *Colonial Immigrants in a British City* (Routledge & Kegan Paul, 1979).

Chapter 10: Class

C. W. M. Hart and A. R. Pilling's *The Tiwi* (Prentice-Hall, 1960) gives a clear and economical account of inequalities in a classless society, while M. N. Srinivas's *Religion and Society among the Coorgs of South India* (Oxford University Press, 1952) is a classic study of caste society.

The diagrams in this chapter are taken from a much larger, colour-coded wall-chart, *Social Stratification in the United States*, designed by Kathryn Shagas, Dennis Livingston and Stephen J. Rose, which, together with the accompanying 'analytic guidebook' of the same title by Stephen Rose, ought to be in every sociology department (third edition, 1983, Social Graphics Company, 1120 Riverside Avenue, Baltimore, Maryland 21230).

The Grand Parade of wealth and illth originally came from Jan Pen's *Income Distribution* (Allen Lane/Penguin Press, 1971), and is described in more detail in Peter Donaldson's *The Economics of the Real World* (Allen Lane/Penguin Press, 1971).

P. Saunders provides a lucid introduction to theorizing about *Social Class and Stratification* (Routledge, 1990), while A. H. Halsey's expanded version of his Reith Lectures, *Change in British Society* (third edition, Open University Press, 1986), condenses a vast amount of knowledge into a small space. The literature cited is an invaluable resource for anyone wishing to go further into this field.

The definitive studies of social mobility in the UK are the Oxford Social Mobility Survey of 1972 – Chapters 1, 2, and 9 of John H. Goldthorpe, Catriona Llewellyn and Clive Payne, *Social Mobility and Class Structure in Modern Britain* (Clarendon Press, 1980), contain the key overall evidence and conclusions – and the 1983–5 Essex University study of *Social Class in Modern Britain* by G. Marshall *et al.* (Unwin Hyman, 1989).

Peter Worsley's *Marx and Marxism* (Ellis Horwood/Tavistock, 1982) provides a succinct account of the main ideas of Marx, including the place of class in his general theoretical schema. Frank Parkin's *Class Inequality and Political Order* (Paladin, 1972); his article on 'social closure' in F. Parkin (ed.), *The Social Analysis of Class Structure* (Tavistock, 1974), plus the other contributions to that volume; and Parkin's polemical and witty *Marxism and Class Theory* (Tavistock, 1979) are all clear and thought-provoking.

The *Affluent Worker* studies of 1968–9 (Cambridge University Press) by Goldthorpe and his colleagues were a landmark in post-war research, since much debated. Joanna Mack and Stewart Lansley have documented the subsequent shift from affluence to poverty in *Poor Britain*, based on a MORI survey carried out for a London Weekend TV series (Allen & Unwin, 1985). The collection of essays edited by Dorothy Wedderburn, *Poverty, Inequality and Class Structure* (Cambridge University Press, 1974), is of high quality. Inequalities in health were definitively examined in a book

Further Reading 501

of that title, based on a government report known as the 'Black Report', edited by Peter Townsend and Nick Davidson (Penguin, 1982).

A massive amount of data on all aspects of class in Britain is marshalled by John Westergaard and Henrietta Resler in a trenchant Marxist analysis of *Class in a Capitalist Society* (Penguin, 1976). W. G. Runciman's *Relative Deprivation and Social Justice* (Routledge & Kegan Paul, 1966) is a classic exploration of variations in perceptions of and attitudes towards class, while David Lockwood's 1958 study of white-collar workers, *The Blackcoated Worker* (Allen & Unwin), is still the most illuminating study of this growing segment of the labour force.

For an informative, brief survey of the middle classes, see Frank Bechhofer, Brian Elliott and David McCrone, 'Structure, consciousness and action: a sociological profile of the British middle class', in Angus Stewart (ed.), *Contemporary Britain* (1983, pp. 74–128).

By contrast, studies of the upper classes are thin both in quality and in quantity. G. Walford's edited collection, *British Public Schools* (Falmer Press, 1984), contains a useful article on 'The political arithmetic of public schools' by Halsey, A. F. Heath and J. M. Ridge (pp. 9–44). Ceri Thomas's 'Family and kinship in Eaton Square', in Frank Field (ed.), *The Wealth Report* (Routledge & Kegan Paul, 1979, pp. 129–59), shows what might be done more intensively, while a skilled journalist like Anthony Sampson provides interesting information on the powerful in his *The Changing Anatomy of Britain* (Hodder & Stoughton, 1982).

Finally, Ivan Reid's *Social Class Differences in Britain* (third edition, Fontana, 1989) is a marvellous mine of information about everything from religion to sex. It is even, as one reviewer wrote, 'good bedtime reading', too.

Chapter 11: Deviance

The best introduction to new deviancy theory is Howard Becker's classic text *Outsiders* (Free Press, 1963). In contrast, a clear, easily available exposition of the positivistic approach is Hans Eysenck's *Crime and Personality* (Paladin, 1977). The article by Jock Young, 'Thinking seriously about crime', attempts to contrast the six major theoretical approaches to crime and deviancy: classicism, positivism, conservatism, strain theory, new deviancy theory, and Marxism, and will take you beyond the comparison of just two theories in this book. It is in the Open University textbook *Crime and Society*, by M. Fitzgerald, G. McLennan and J. Pawson (eds) (Routledge & Kegan Paul, 1981), which also contains a series of excellent articles on crime and deviance in an historical perspective.

Geoff Pearson's *Hooligan* (Macmillan, 1983) is a witty and incisive book on the constant moral panic about youthful misbehaviour over the last hundred years. As far as moral panics and the mass media are concerned, the collection of readings in *The Manufacture of News*, by S. Cohen and J. Young (eds) (Constable, 1981), details both the portrayal of deviance in the media and the effects on both the public and on the deviants themselves.

Up until recently there has been little work focusing on two important topics: women as offenders, and crimes committed by the powerful. Eileen Leonard's *Women, Crime and Society* (Longman, New York, 1982) is both the most comprehensive book to date on women and crime and also a good introduction to deviancy theory in general. Steve Box's *Power, Crime and Mystification* (Tavistock, 1983) is a well-written text which covers three examples of crimes of the powerful: corporate crime, police crime and crimes of men against women.

In terms of specific topics, by far the best book on classroom deviance is Paul Willis's *Learning to Labour* (Saxon House, 1977). This should be read also as an excellent example of the ethnographic method in deviancy research whose theoretical approach goes beyond both positivism and the new deviancy theory. On juvenile delinquency, a pivotal text is R. Cloward and L. Ohlins, *Delinquency and Opportunity* (Free Press, 1960); in terms of adult crime read Stuart Henry's *The Hidden Economy* (Martin Robertson, 1978), and on professional crime Wally Probyn's *Angelface* (Allen & Unwin, 1974). The best introduction to the sociology of the prison is *The British Prison*, by Mike Fitzgerald and Joe Sim (Blackwell, 1981). A powerful radical critique is Jeffrey Reiman's *The Rich Get Richer and the Poor Get Prison* (Wiley, 1979). The most useful summary and analysis of the extensive literature on policing is Rob Reiner's *The Politics of the Police* (Wheatsheaf, 1985) and a critique of the failure of the police to control crime is *Losing the Fight Against Crime*, by R. Kinsey (Blackwell, 1986).

An imaginative overview of trends in social control is *Visions of Social Control* by Stan Cohen (Polity Press, 1985). Two important conservative books are *Punishing Criminals*, by Ernest van den Haag (Basic Books, New York, 1975), and *Thinking About Crime* (Basic Books, 1983), by J. Q. Wilson, who was President Reagan's adviser on crime. For recent debates in radical criminology, you should read *What is to be Done about Law and Order?* by John Lea and Jock Young (Penguin, 1984) and R. Matthews (ed.), *Confronting Crime* (Sage, 1986).

By far the liveliest journal in the field is *Crime and Social Justice*, but you should also read *Social Problems* and the *British Journal of Criminology*.

Chapter 12: Theoretical Schools

There is an enormous and fast-expanding literature on Marx. From amongst that vast number, the following books provide brief and accessible sources. Marx's own words make up the *Communist Manifesto* (written with Friedrich

Engels and published in several cheap versions) as well as the selections edited by T. B. Bottomore and M. Rubel, *Karl Marx: Selected Writings in Sociology and Social Philosophy* (Penguin, 1963); David Caute, *Essential Writings of Marx* (Panther, 1969); and David McLellan, *Karl Marx: Selected Writings* (Oxford University Press, 1978). Short commentaries are provided by Peter Worsley, *Marx and Marxism* (Horwood, 1982); Terrell Carver, *Marx's Social Theory* (Oxford University Press, 1982); and Peter Singer, *Marx* (Oxford University Press, 1978). Marx's own major finished work is *Capital*, Volume I (Penguin, 1976).

Weber's writings are selected in H. H. Gerth and C. W. Mills (eds), *From Max Weber: Essays in Sociology* (Routledge & Kegan Paul, 1948), and W. G. Runciman, *Weber: Selections in Translation* (Cambridge University Press, 1978). His *The Protestant Ethic and the Spirit of Capitalism* (Allen & Unwin edition, 1930) states the thesis about the origins of capitalism. Commentaries include Frank Parkin, *Max Weber* (Horwood, 1982), and Reinhard Bendix, *Max Weber* (Heinemann, 1960). A good but difficult interpretation is given in T. Parsons, *The Structure of Social Action* (Free Press, 1937, Part 3). Weber's own major comprehensive statement is *Economy and Society* (Bedminster Press, 1968).

On Durkheim, there is a *Selected Writings*, edited by A. Giddens (Cambridge University Press, 1972), who has also written a brief guide, *Durkheim* (Fontana, 1978). Two of Durkheim's major works, *The Rules of Sociological Method* (in which the notion that we should treat social facts as things is expounded in Chapter 1) and *The Division of Labour in Society* (in which the attack on Spencer and the argument about non-contractual elements in contract are made – see Book I, Chapter 7), have recently been retranslated and published by Macmillan (1982 and 1984 respectively). Commentaries include H. Alpert, *Emile Durkheim and his Sociology* (Columbia University Press, 1939), and S. Lukes, *Emile Durkheim* (Penguin, 1973). Again useful but rather difficult is Parsons's discussion in *The Structure of Social Action*, Part 2, Chapters 8–12.

On functionalism, a clear statement of Robert Merton's position can be found in 'Manifest and latent functions', in his *Social Theory and Social Structure* (second edition, Free Press, 1957). Talcott Parsons's *The Social System* (Routledge & Kegan Paul, 1951) is an important source for his thinking, but this too is a demanding work; a short and clear account of 'Parsons's Sociological Theory' is given by Edward C. Devereux, Jr, in Max Black (ed.), *The Social Theories of Talcott Parsons* (Prentice-Hall, 1961). A comprehensive selection of articles debating functionalism is collected in N. J. Demerath and R. A. Petersen, *System, Change and Conflict* (Free Press, 1967).

Symbolic interactionist views are well represented in the collection edited by Arnold Rose, *Human Behaviour and Social Processes* (Routledge & Kegan

504   **Further Reading**

Paul, 1962); G. P. Stone and H. A. Farberman, *Social Psychology through Symbolic Interaction* (Xerox College Press, 1970); and J. G. Manis and B. N. Meltzer, *Symbolic Interactionism* (Allyn & Bacon, 1967). Herbert Blumer's *Symbolic Interactionism* (Prentice-Hall, 1969) contains his most important papers.

The ideas of Alfred Schutz, the precursor of ethnomethodology, are well expressed in the papers included in his *Collected Papers*, especially Volumes 1 and 2 (Nijhoff, 1962). The key work in ethnomethodology is Harold Garfinkel's *Studies in Ethnomethodology* (Prentice-Hall, 1967), but this is very difficult going. Accounts of Garfinkel's work are given in J. Heritage, *Garfinkel and Ethnomethodology* (Polity Press, 1984); J. Hughes and D. Benson, *The Perspective of Ethnomethodology* (Longman, 1983); and W. W. Sharrock and R. J. Anderson, *The Ethnomethodologists* (Horwood, 1985). A selection of writings is included in *Ethnomethodology*, edited by Roy Turner (Penguin, 1974). The work of Harvey Sacks remains largely unpublished and it is difficult to obtain any accessible account of his work. Some idea of what it is about and of the kind of research it has spawned can be found in David Sudnow (ed.), *Studies in Social Interaction* (Free Press, 1972), and in G. Psathas, *Everyday Language* (Irvington Press, 1979).

Index

Discover more about our forthcoming books through Penguin's FREE newspaper...

Penguin
Quarterly

It's packed with:

- exciting features
- author interviews
- previews & reviews
- books from your favourite films & TV series
- exclusive competitions & much, much more...

Write off for your free copy today to:
Dept JC
Penguin Books Ltd
FREEPOST
West Drayton
Middlesex
UB7 0BR
NO STAMP REQUIRED

READ MORE IN PENGUIN

In every corner of the world, on every subject under the sun, Penguin represents quality and variety – the very best in publishing today.

For complete information about books available from Penguin – including Puffins, Penguin Classics and Arkana – and how to order them, write to us at the appropriate address below. Please note that for copyright reasons the selection of books varies from country to country.

In the United Kingdom: Please write to *Dept. JC, Penguin Books Ltd, FREEPOST, West Drayton, Middlesex UB7 OBR*

If you have any difficulty in obtaining a title, please send your order with the correct money, plus ten per cent for postage and packaging, to *PO Box No. 11, West Drayton, Middlesex UB7 OBR*

In the United States: Please write to *Penguin USA Inc., 375 Hudson Street, New York, NY 10014*

In Canada. Please write to *Penguin Books Canada Ltd, 10 Alcorn Avenue, Suite 300, Toronto, Ontario M4V 3B2*

In Australia: Please write to *Penguin Books Australia Ltd, 487 Maroondah Highway, Ringwood, Victoria 3134*

In New Zealand: Please write to *Penguin Books (NZ) Ltd, 182–190 Wairau Road, Private Bag, Takapuna, Auckland 9*

In India: Please write to *Penguin Books India Pvt Ltd, 706 Eros Apartments, 56 Nehru Place, New Delhi 110 019*

In the Netherlands: Please write to *Penguin Books Netherlands B.V., Keizersgracht 231 NL–1016 DV Amsterdam*

In Germany: Please write to *Penguin Books Deutschland GmbH, Friedrichstrasse 10–12, W–6000 Frankfurt/Main 1*

In Spain: Please write to *Penguin Books S. A., C. San Bernardo 117–6° E–28015 Madrid*

In Italy: Please write to *Penguin Italia s.r.l., Via Felice Casati 20, 1–20124 Milano*

In France: Please write to *Penguin France S. A., 17 rue Lejeune, F–31000 Toulouse*

In Japan: Please write to *Penguin Books Japan, Ishikiribashi Building, 2–5–4, Suido, Tokyo 112*

In Greece: Please write to *Penguin Hellas Ltd, Dimocritou 3, GR–106 71 Athens*

In South Africa: Please write to *Longman Penguin Southern Africa (Pty) Ltd, Private Bag X08, Bertsham 2013*

READ MORE IN PENGUIN

POLITICS AND SOCIAL SCIENCES

National Identity   Anthony D. Smith

In this stimulating new book, Anthony D. Smith asks why the first modern nation states developed in the West. He considers how ethnic origins, religion, language and shared symbols can provide a sense of nation and illuminates his argument with a wealth of detailed examples.

The Feminine Mystique   Betty Friedan

'A brilliantly researched, passionately argued book – a time-bomb flung into the Mom-and-Apple-Pie image ... Out of the debris of that shattered ideal, the Women's Liberation Movement was born' – Ann Leslie

Peacemaking Among Primates   Frans de Waal

'A vitally fresh analysis of the biology of aggression which deserves the serious attention of all those concerned with the nature of conflict, whether in humans or non-human animals ... De Waal delivers forcibly and clearly his interpretation of the significance of his findings ... Lucidly written' – *The Times Higher Educational Supplement*

Political Ideas   David Thomson (ed.)

From Machiavelli to Marx – a stimulating and informative introduction to the last 500 years of European political thinkers and political thought.

The Raw and the Cooked   Claude Lévi-Strauss

Deliberately, brilliantly and inimitably challenging, Lévi-Strauss's seminal work of structural anthropology cuts wide and deep into the mind of mankind, as he finds in the myths of the South American Indians a comprehensible psychological pattern.

The Social Construction of Reality
Peter Berger and Thomas Luckmann

The Social Construction of Reality is concerned with the sociology of 'everything that passes for knowledge in society', and particularly with that 'common-sense knowledge' that constitutes the reality of everyday life for the ordinary member of society.

READ MORE IN PENGUIN

POLITICS AND SOCIAL SCIENCES

Conservatism Ted Honderich

'It offers a powerful critique of the major beliefs of modern conservatism, and shows how much a rigorous philosopher can contribute to understanding the fashionable but deeply ruinous absurdities of his times' – *New Statesman & Society*

Karl Marx: Selected Writings in Sociology and Social Philosophy Bottomore and Rubel (eds.)

'It makes available, in coherent form and lucid English, some of Marx's most important ideas. As an introduction to Marx's thought, it has very few rivals indeed' – *British Journal of Sociology*

Post-War Britain A Political History Alan Sked and Chris Cook

Major political figures from Attlee to Thatcher, the aims and achievements of governments and the changing fortunes of Britain in the period since 1945 are thoroughly scrutinized in this stimulating history.

Inside the Third World Paul Harrison

This comprehensive book brings home a wealth of facts and analysis on the often tragic realities of life for the poor people and communities of Asia, Africa and Latin America.

Medicine, Patients and the Law Margaret Brazier

'An absorbing book which, in addition to being accessible to the general reader, should prove illuminating for practitioners – both medical and legal – and an ideal accompaniment to student courses on law and medicine' – *New Law Journal*

Bread and Circuses Paul Veyne

'Warming oneself at the fire of M. Veyne's intelligence is such a joy that any irritation at one's prejudice and ignorance being revealed and exposed vanishes with his winning ways ... *Bread and Circuses* is M. Veyne's way of explaining the philosophy of the Roman Empire, which was the most successful form of government known to mankind' – *Literary Review*

READ MORE IN PENGUIN

PSYCHOLOGY

Introduction to Jung's Psychology   Frieda Fordham

'She has delivered a fair and simple account of the main aspects of my psychological work. I am indebted to her for this admirable piece of work' – C. G. Jung in the *Foreword*

Child Care and the Growth of Love   John Bowlby

His classic 'summary of evidence of the effects upon children of lack of personal attention … it presents to administrators, social workers, teachers and doctors a reminder of the significance of the family' – *The Times*

Recollections and Reflections   Bruno Bettelheim

'A powerful thread runs through Bettelheim's message: his profound belief in the dignity of man, and the importance of seeing and judging other people from their own point of view' – William Harston in the *Independent*. 'These memoirs of a wise old child, candid, evocative, heart-warming, suggest there is hope yet for humanity' – Ray Porter in the *Evening Standard*

Sanity, Madness and the Family   R. D. Laing and A. Esterson

Schizophrenia: fact or fiction? Certainly not fact, according to the authors of this controversial book. Suggesting that some forms of madness may be largely social creations, *Sanity, Madness and the Family* demands to be taken very seriously indeed.

I Am Right You Are Wrong   Edward de Bono

In this book Dr Edward de Bono puts forward a direct challenge to what he calls the rock logic of Western thinking. Drawing on our understanding of the brain as a self-organizing information system, Dr de Bono shows that perception is the key to more constructive thinking and the serious creativity of design.

READ MORE IN PENGUIN

also edited by Peter Worsley:

The New Modern Sociology Readings

The New Modern Sociology Readings, a companion volume to the best-selling *New Introducing Sociology*, is an entirely new collection of excerpts from outstanding articles and books selected by sociologists who are themselves leading authorities in their fields.

The main emphasis is on recent research into modern industrial society: its emergence and spread across the globe; the growth of urbanism and the development of classes; and the position of women and of ethnic minorities. The links between the social order and the educational system, and the ways in which social relations affect health are examined, together with the tensions of contemporary society that result in criminal and deviant behaviour.

Spanning the breadth of current sociological research, this stimulating collection gives vital insights into the industrial societies of today,

READ MORE IN PENGUIN

PSYCHOLOGY

Psychoanalysis and Feminism Juliet Mitchell

'Juliet Mitchell has risked accusations of apostasy from her fellow feminists. Her book not only challenges orthodox feminism, however; it defies the conventions of social thought in the English-speaking countries ... a brave and important book' – *New York Review of Books*

The Divided Self R. D. Laing

'A study that makes all other works I have read on schizophrenia seem fragmentary ... The author brings, through his vision and perception, that particular touch of genius which causes one to say "Yes, I have always known that, why have I never thought of it before?"' – *Journal of Analytical Psychology*

Po: Beyond Yes and No Edward de Bono

No is the basic tool of the logic system. *Yes* is the basic tool of the belief system. Edward de Bono offers *Po* as a device for changing our ways of thinking: a method for approaching problems in a new and more creative way.

The Informed Heart Bruno Bettelheim

Bettelheim draws on his experience in concentration camps to illuminate the dangers inherent in all mass societies in this profound and moving masterpiece.

The Care of the Self Michel Foucault
The History of Sexuality Vol 3

Foucault examines the transformation of sexual discourse from the Hellenistic to the Roman world in an inquiry which 'bristles with provocative insights into the tangled liaison of sex and self' – *The Times Higher Education Supplement*

Mothering Psychoanalysis Janet Sayers

'An important book ... records the immense contribution to psychoanalysis made by its founding mothers' – Julia Neuberger in the *Sunday Times*